A Concise Encyclopaedia of the Italian Renaissance

Edited by J. R. Hale

A Concise Encyclopaedia of the Italian Renaissance

with 237 illustrations

NEW YORK AND TORONTO
OXFORD UNIVERSITY PRESS
1981

Library of Congress Catalog Card Number 81-81905

Filmset in Great Britain by Keyspools Ltd
Printed and bound in Spain
DLTO-513-81

A reader's guide to the use of this book

In political and social development, in intellectual and creative achievement, no other country rivals the variety of what happened in Italy between *c.*1320 and *c.*1600. So many political units; so much accomplished by artists, writers, musicians, businessmen, political and scientific thinkers, churchmen, soldiers and statesmen; so many wars; so wide a spectrum over which ideas changed: all this is a heavy burden for the memory to bear without assistance. In addition, the seductiveness of the period is such that new discoveries, new interpretations never cease.

This concise encyclopaedia aims to supplement memory and suggest the current state of thinking about, as well as knowing about, Renaissance Italy. *Aide-mémoire*, vade-mecum, interpreter: it tries to fulfil all these roles. It has the scholar, the student, the traveller – and, too, the enquiring general reader – in mind; anyone, that is, whose interest strays habitually or merely congenially to this country at that time. It is designed to answer questions about what went on but also to suggest what it might have been like to have lived then.

Though a reference book, it is not conceived as an inert body of facts. The **subject index** following this introduction, as well as indicating the book's range and nature, is intended to draw attention to thematic entries that might not suggest themselves alphabetically and to suggest other entries that can supplement the interest of single ones: it will perhaps be particularly useful to readers seeking an introduction to an aspect of the period with which they are unfamiliar. **Cross-references** have been kept to a minimum in order to make the entries as readable as possible. The majority of frequently occurring names of places and states, and most proper names (especially those with no Christian name or birth and death dates attached), may be assumed to have entries of their own. Cross-references, indicated by SMALL CAPITALS, are given when the reader might not expect them, when the information in one entry is notably extended in another, or in entries, like WARS OF ITALY, designed to offer a synopsis of information about a topic. Figures in **square brackets** indicate pages in other parts of the book on which illustrations relating to the subject of the entry will be found.

A list of principal Italian **reference works** is provided on p. 360, where also are indicated abbreviations employed in the bibliographies within entries. There is a brief **glossary** of Italian words and phrases on pp. 358–59. There are **maps** on pp. 350–51 and comparative **tables of succession** on pp. 352–57. The attribution of entries to their authors is by initials according to the key given in the **list of contributors** on p. 14.

The range of entries, necessarily selective, reflects the search for a balance between current scholarly activity and what readers might want to check, extend their knowledge of, or discover. I have sought to achieve an even-handed coverage of names, events and themes within a period chosen to offer fairly generous houseroom to the variety of chronological expectations awakened by the word Renaissance, and a few, such as Dante, Aquinas and classical authors, because of their influence throughout the period. In the end, despite the valuable guidance and corrective advice I have received from friends, books, and especially my fellow contributors, the selection remains a personal one.

An austere house rule of the publishers does not, alas, allow me to name the individual who has done so much to correct and sustain an editor with so many indecisions and second thoughts. But I may record my gratitude to my colleague Laura Lepschy, who read the proofs with a buoyancy and care that will give those errors that remain my responsibility an especially bitter taste.

JOHN HALE
University College London

Subject index

Topics, places and people covered in this book, listed according to fields of interest

PAINTING, SCULPTURE AND ARCHITECTURE

THEMES AND TOPICS

BIOGRAPHIES

Painting

Peruzzi, Baldassare
Piero della Francesca
Piero di Cosimo
Pinturicchio, Bernardo, il
Pisanello, Antonio Pisano, il
Polidoro Caldara da Caravaggio
Pollaiuolo, Antonio di Jacopi Benci
Pontormo, Jacopo Carucci, il
Pordenone, Giovanni Antonio, il
Primaticcio, Francesco
Raimondi, Marcantonio
Raphael
Roberti, Ercole de'
Romanino, Girolamo
Rosso Fiorentino, Giovanni Battista di Jacopo, il
Salviati, Francesco
Salviati, Leonardo
Santi di Tito
Sassetta, Stefano di Giovanni, il
Savoldo, Gian Girolamo
Sebastiano del Piombo
Signorelli, Luca
Sodoma, Giovanni Antonio Bazzi, il
Squarcione, Francesco
Tintoretto
Titian
Tura, Cosmè
Uccello, Paolo
Vasari, Giorgio
Veronese
Verrocchio, Andrea del
Vivarini family
Zoppo, Marco
Zuccaro, Federico
Zuccaro, Taddeo

Sculpture

Amadeo, Giovanni Antonio
Ammannati, Bartolomeo
Bandinelli, Baccio
Benedetto da Maiano
Bertoldo di Giovanni
Buon (or Bon), Bartolomeo
Cellini, Benvenuto
Danti, Vincenzo
Della Porta, Guglielmo
Della Robbia, Luca
Desiderio da Settignano
Donatello
Ghiberti, Lorenzo
Giambologna (Giovanni Bologna)
Laurana, Francesco
Leoni, Leone
Lombardo family
Michelangelo Buonarroti
Mino da Fiesole
Nanni di Banco
Orcagna, Andrea
Pisanello, Antonio Pisano, il
Pisano, Andrea
Quercia, Jacopo della
Riccio, Andrea Briosco, il
Rossellino, Bernardo and Antonio
Sansovino, Andrea
Sansovino, Jacopo
Torrigiano, Pietro
Verrocchio, Andrea del
Vittoria, Alessandro

Architecture

Alberti, Leon Battista
Alessi, Galeazzo
Bramante, Donato
Brunelleschi, Filippo
Buontalenti, Bernardo
Codussi (or Coducci), Mauro
Cronaca, Simone del Pollaiuolo, il
Della Porta, Giacomo
Falconetto, Giovanni Maria
Filarete
Fontana, Domenico
Francesco di Giorgio Martini
Giocondo, Fra (Giovanni da Verona)
Laurana, Luciano
Ligorio, Pirro
Michelangelo Buonarroti
Michelozzo di Bartolomeo
Paciotto, Francesco
Palladio, Andrea
Peruzzi, Baldassare
Pontelli, Baccio
Rossetti, Biagio
Sangallo family
Sanmicheli, Michele
Scamozzi, Vincenzo
Serlio, Sebastiano
Tibaldi, Pellegrino
Vignola, Giacomo Barozzi da
Vitruvius

HISTORIC CENTRES

Ancona
Bologna
Corsica
Ferrara
Florence (*see also* Livorno)
Genoa
Lucca
Mantua
Milan (*see also* Cremona)
Naples, kingdom of
Padua
Parma
Perugia
Pisa
Rimini
Rome (*see also* Pienza)
Sardinia
Savoy-Piedmont
Sicily
Siena
Urbino
Venice (*see also* Brescia, Ragusa)
Verona

HISTORY AND POLITICS

THEMES AND TOPICS

Balance of power
Byzantine Empire
Condottieri
Constitutions
Council of Ten
Crusade
Despots
Diplomacy
Empire, Holy Roman
Factions
Fortification
Galley
Guelfs and Ghibellines
Mercenaries
Myth of Venice
Otranto
Ottoman empire
Piracy
Renaissance
Sack of Rome
Stradiots
Swiss, the
Tyrannicide
Uscoks (or Uskoks)
Warfare

WARS, BATTLES, TREATIES

Agnadello, battle of
Ambrosian Republic
Anghiari, battle of
Arbedo, battle of
Bicocca, battle of
Blois, Treaty of
Cambrai, League of
Caravaggio, battle of
Cascina, battle of
Cateau-Cambrésis, Peace (or Treaty) of
Cerignola, battle of
Chioggia, War of
Cognac, League of
Eight Saints, War of the
Ferrara, War of
Fornovo, battle of
Garigliano, battle of
Holy League
Lepanto, battle of
Lodi, Peace of
Maclodio, battle of
Marignano, battle of
Montemurlo, battle of
Novara, battle of
Pavia, battle of
Salt War, the
S. Romano, battle of
Volterra, War of
Wars of Italy
Zonchio, battle of

FAMILIES

Acciaiuoli family
Albizzi family
Anjou, house of
Appiano family
Aragon, house of
Baglioni family
Barbarigo family
Bardi family
Bentivoglio family
Borgia family
Caetani (or Gaetani) family
Capponi family
Caracciolo family
Carrara family
Colonna family
Della Rovere family
Della Scala family
Doria (or D'Oria) family
Durazzo, house of
Este family
Farnese family
Fregoso family
Gonzaga family
Habsburg, house of
Loredan family
Malatesta family
Manfredi family
Martinengo family
Medici family
Montefeltro family
Orléans, house of
Orsini family
Pazzi family
Petrucci family
Pitti family
Riario family
Rucellai family
Sanseverino family
Savorgnan family
Savoy, house of
Sforza family
Strozzi family
Trivulzio family
Valois, house of
Venier family
Visconti family

BIOGRAPHIES

Heads of state and consorts

Alfonso I
Alfonso II
Boccanegra, Simone
Borgia, Lucrezia
Carlo Emanuele I
Charles V
Charles VIII
Cornaro, Caterina
Cosimo I de' Medici
Doria, Andrea
Doria, Gian Andrea
Emanuel Philibert
Este, Alfonso I d'
Este, Alfonso II d'
Este, Beatrice d'
Este, Ercole I d'
Este, Isabella d'
Falier, Marino
Federico II da Montefeltro
Ferdinand II of Aragon
Ferrante (or Ferdinand) I (of Naples)
Foscari, Francesco
Francis I
Giovanna I of Anjou
Gonzaga, Federico II
Gonzaga, Francesco I
Gonzaga, Gianfrancesco II
Gonzaga, Lodovico
Gritti, Andrea
Ladislas of Durazzo
Louis I of Anjou
Louis II of Anjou
Louis XII
Malatesta, Carlo I
Malatesta, Sigismondo
Maximilian I
Medici, Cosimo de'
Medici, Lorenzo de'
Philip II
René of Anjou
Robert of Anjou
Sforza, Caterina
Sforza, Francesco
Sforza, Lodovico
Soderini, Piero di Tommaso
Visconti, Bernarbò
Visconti, Filippo Maria
Visconti, Giangaleazzo

Administration

Borgia, Cesare
Cardona, Raymond de
Lannoy, Charles de
Vasto, Alfonso d'Avalos del

War

Alberghetti family
Alberico da Barbiano
Alviano, Bartolomeo d'
Attendolo, Micheletto
Barbarossa
Bragadin, Marcantonio
Canale, Cristoforo da
Cane, Facino
Carmagnola, Francesco Bussone
Castracani degli Antelminelli, Castruccio
Colleoni, Bartolomeo
Cordoba, Gonzalo de
Dal Verme, Jacopo
Fortebraccio, Braccio
Gattamelata, Erasmo da Narni, il
Hawkwood, John
Missaglia family
Niccolò da Tolentino
Pescara, Ferdinando Francesco d'Avalos
Piccinino, Niccolò
Valturio, Roberto

Conspiracy

Boscoli, Pietro Paolo
Burlamacchi, Francesco
Cola di Rienzo
Morone, Girolamo
Porcari, Stefano

Scandal

Accoramboni, Vittoria
Borgia, Lucrezia
Cappello, Bianca
Cenci, Beatrice

Historical and political writing

Ammirato, Scipione
Botero, Giovanni
Contarini, Cardinal Gasparo
Corio, Bernardino
Giannotti, Donato
Giovio, Paolo
Guicciardini, Francesco
Machiavelli, Niccolò
Nardi, Jacopo
Paruta, Paolo
Priuli, Girolamo
Sanuto, Marin the younger
Varchi, Benedetto
Villani, Giovanni
Villani, Matteo

SOCIAL HISTORY

Active v. contemplative life
Age
Campanilismo
Carnival
Children
Chivalry
Ciompi
Class, social
Clientage
Costume
Courtesans and prostitutes
Crime
Cuisine
Education
Family structure
Festivals
Foundlings
Glory
Homosexuality
Humour
Impresa
Jews
Mirrors
National feeling
Plague
Poison
Population
Poverty, relief of
Professions
Recreations, games
S. Stefano, order of Knights of
Slaves
Spectacles (glasses)
Sumptuary laws
Time reckoning
Tullia d'Aragona
Witches
Women, status of

ECONOMIC HISTORY

Agriculture
Alum
Arsenal
Banking
Business methods
Chigi, Agostino
Comacchio
Communications
Datini, Francesco
Economy, the
Galley
Guilds
Industry
Taxation

RELIGION

THEMES AND TOPICS

Anti-clericalism
Aquileia
Avignon
Bologna, Concordat of
Censorship
Clergy, secular
College of Cardinals
Confraternities
Councils of the Church
Counter-Reformation
Crusade
Evangelism
Heresy, pre-Reformation
Inquisition
Nepotism
Papacy
Preachers
Reformation
Religious orders and congregations
Schism, the Great
Trent, Council of

BIOGRAPHIES

Adrian VI
Albornoz, Egidio de
Alexander VI
Antonino, S.
Aquinas, St Thomas
Augustine, St
Bellarmine, Cardinal Robert (Roberto Bellarmino)
Benedict XIII
Bernardino, S., of Siena
Boniface IX
Borromeo, Cardinal Carlo
Calixtus III
Carnesecchi, Pietro
Catherine, St, of Siena
Clement VI
Clement VII
Clement VIII
Contarini, Cardinal Gasparo
Eugenius IV
Giberti, Gian Matteo
Giustiniani, Paolo
Gregory XII
Grimani, Cardinal Domenico
Innocent VI
Jerome, St
John XXII
John XXIII
Julius II
Leo X

Martin V
Neri, S. Filippo
Nicholas V
Ochino, Bernardino
Paul II
Paul III
Pico della Mirandola, Gianfrancesco
Pius II
Pole, Cardinal Reginald
Ricci, Matteo
Sarpi, Fra Paolo
Savonarola, Girolamo
Sixtus IV
Sixtus V
Vermigli, Peter Martyr (Pietro Martire)
Zabarella, Giacomo

LITERATURE

(broadly conceived to include themes and authors outside the mainstream of 'pure' literature)

THEMES AND TOPICS

Academies
Arms and letters
Autobiography
Censorship
Commedia dell'arte
Commedia erudita
Critical theory of literature
Drama
Fortuna
History and chronicle
Humanism
Humour
Hypnerotomachia Polifili
Italian language
Liberal arts
Literature
Mythology
Nature
Occasio
Pastoral play
Printing
Renaissance
Rhetoric
Sacra rappresentazione
Tragedy
Triumph
Virtù

BIOGRAPHIES

Alberti, Leon Battista
Aretino, Pietro
Ariosto, Lodovico
Bandello, Matteo
Beccadelli, Antonio
Bembo, Pietro
Benivieni, Girolamo
Beolco, Angelo
Berni, Francesco
Bisticci, Vespasiano da
Boccaccio, Giovanni
Boiardo, Matteo Maria
Bruno, Giordano
Burchiello
Caro, Annibale
Casa, Giovanni della
Castelveltro, Lodovico
Castiglione, Baldassare
Cavalcanti, Guido
Cellini, Benvenuto
Cicero, Marcus Tullius
Claudian
Colocci, Angelo
Colonna, Vittoria
Contarini, Cardinal Gasparo
Dante, reputation of
Della Porta, Giambattista
Doni, Anton Francesco
Dovizi, Bernardo (il Bibbiena)
Firenzuola, Agnolo
Folengo, Teofilo
Fracastoro, Girolamo
Franco, Veronica
Galilei, Galileo
Gambara, Veronica
Gelli, Giambattista
Giannotti, Donato
Giraldi, Giambattista Cinzio
Giovio, Paolo
Grazzini, Anton Francesco
Groto, Luigi
Guarini, Battista
Guicciardini, Francesco
Horace
Livy
Machiavelli, Niccolò
Masuccio Salernitano
Nardi, Jacopo
Ovid
Palmieri, Matteo
Paruta, Paolo
Petrarch
Pius II
Plautus, Titus Maccius
Poliziano
Porto, Luigi da
Pulci, Luigi
Quintilian
Sacchetti, Franco
Salviati, Leonardo
Sannazaro, Jacopo
Seneca, Lucius Anneus
Serafino Aquilano
Stampa, Gaspara
Straparola, Gianfrancesco
Tansillo, Luigi
Tasso, Torquato
Terence
Trissino, Gian Giorgio
Varchi, Benedetto
Vergil, Polydore
Vida, Marco Girolamo
Virgil

LEARNING AND PHILOSOPHY

THEMES AND TOPICS

Academies
Active v. contemplative life
Cabbala
Cyclical concept
Education
Epicurus
Hermeticism
Humanism
Magic
Plato and neo-Platonism
Printing
Renaissance
Scepticism
Scholasticism
Stoicism
Subiaco

BIOGRAPHIES

Alciato, Andrea
Aldus
Argyropoulos, Janos
Aristotle
Averroes
Barbaro, Daniele
Barbaro, Ermolao, the younger
Bartolus of Sassoferrato
Bessarion, Cardinal
Biondo, Flavio
Bracciolini, Poggio
Bruni, Leonardo
Chrysoloras, Manuel
Cicero, Marcus Tullius
Ciriaco d'Ancona
Epicurus
Ficino, Marsilio
Filelfo, Francesco
Gaza, Theodore
Gemistus Pletho (George Gemistos Plethon)
Giolito, house of
Giunti, house of
Giustiniani, Bernardo
Guarino da Verona
Landino, Cristoforo
Leone Ebreo
Leto, Pomponio
Lucretius
Maggi, Girolamo
Marsuppini, Carlo
Niccoli, Niccolò
Patrizi, Francesco
Pico della Mirandola, Giovanni
Platina
Plotinus
Plutarch
Polybius
Pomponazzi, Pietro
Pontano, Giovanni (or Gioviano)
Sadoleto, Cardinal Jacopo
Salutati, Coluccio
Scala, Bartolomeo
Tacitus, Cornelius
Traversari, Ambrogio
Valla, Lorenzo
Vergerio, Pietro Paolo
Vittorino da Feltre

TRAVEL AND EXPLORATION

BIOGRAPHIES

Anghiera, Pietro Martire d'
Cabot, John
Cadamosto (or Ca' da Mosto), Alvise
Casola, Pietro
Columbus
Conti, Niccolò dei
Marco Polo
Mauro, Fra
Pegolotti, Francesco Balducci
Pigafetta, Antonio
Pliny the Elder
Ptolemy
Ramusio, Giovanni Battista
Strabo
Varthema, Lodovico de
Verrazzano, Giovanni
Vespucci, Amerigo

MUSIC

Brumel, Anton (or Antoine)
Caccini, Giulio
Cara, Marchetto
Ciconia, Johannes
Corteccia, Francesco
Croce, Giovanni
Dufay, Guillaume
Festa, Costanzo
Frottola
Gabrieli, Andrea
Gabrieli, Giovanni
Gaffurio, Franchino
Galilei, Vincenzo
Gesualdo, Carlo
Hothby, John
Isaac, Heinrich (Henricus)
Josquin des Prez
Landini, Francesco
Landino, Cristoforo
Luzzaschi, Luzzasco
Marenzio, Luca
Merulo, Claudio
Music
Obrecht, Jacob
Opera
Palestrina, Giovanni Pierluigi da
Peri, Jacopo
Petrucci, Ottaviano
Ramos, Bartolomé de Pareja
Rore, Ciprien de
Squarcialupi, Antonio
Striggio, Alessandro senior
Tinctoris, Johannes de
Tromboncino, Bartolomeo
Vecchi, Orazio
Vicentino, Nicola
Wert, Giaches de
Willaert, Adrian
Zarlino, Gioseffo

SCIENCE

THEMES AND TOPICS

Astrology
Magic
Mathematics
Medicine
Science
Technology

BIOGRAPHIES

Aldrovandi, Ulisse
Archimedes
Berengario da Carpi, Jacopo
Biringuccio, Vannoccio
Bombelli, Raffaele
Cardano, Girolamo
Cesalpino, Andrea
Columbus, Realdus
Commandino, Federico
Della Porta, Giambattista
Euclid
Eustachio
Fabricius of Aquapendente
Falloppio, Gabriele
Fausto, Vettor (or Vittore)
Fontana, Giovanni
Fracastoro, Girolamo
Frontinus, Julius
Galen
Galilei, Galileo
Hippocrates
Mattioli, Pierandrea
Maurolico, Francesco
Monte, Guidobaldo, Marchese del
Pacioli, Luca
Pliny the Elder
Ptolemy
Pythagoras
Ramelli, Agostino
Taccola, Mariano di Jacopo
Tartaglia, Niccolò
Toscanelli, Paolo dal Pozzo
Vegetius
Vesalius
Vigo, Giovanni da

List of contributors

RA Richard Andrews, Senior Lecturer in Italian, University of Kent at Canterbury

DA Denis Arnold, The Heather Professor of Music, University of Oxford

CA Charles Avery, Director, European Sculpture, Christie's, London

AB Allan Braham, Keeper and Deputy Director, The National Gallery, London

PB Peter Burke, Fellow of Emmanuel College, Cambridge

MC Michael Caesar, Lecturer in Italian, University of Kent at Canterbury

JC-S John Cassayd-Smith

DC D. S. Chambers, Reader in Renaissance Studies, The Warburg Institute, University of London

LGC Louise George Clubb, Professor of Italian and Comparative Literature, University of California, Berkeley

CE Caroline Elam, Lecturer in the History of Art, Westfield College, University of London

LDE L. D. Ettlinger, Professor Emeritus of History of Art, University of California, Berkeley

PG Paul Grendler, Professor of History, University of Toronto

WG Werner Gundersheimer, Professor, Director of Center for Italian Studies, University of Pennsylvania

PH Peter Hainsworth, Lecturer in Italian, University of Oxford

JRH J. R. Hale, Professor, Head of Department of Italian, University College London

MH Marcia B. Hall, Associate Professor, Tyler School of Art, Temple University, Philadelphia

MBH Marie Boas Hall, Imperial College, University of London (retired)

GH George Holmes, Fellow of St Catherine's College, Oxford

JH Judith Hook, Senior Lecturer in History, University of Aberdeen

JKH J. K. Hyde, Professor of Medieval History, University of Manchester

SJ Susan Johnson

JL John Larner, Titular Professor of History, University of Glasgow

LL Laura Lepschy, Senior Lecturer in Italian, University College London

RL Ralph Lieberman, Assistant Professor of Art History, Hamilton College, Clinton, New York

OL O. M. T. Logan, Lecturer in the School of Modern Languages and European History, University of East Anglia

MM Michael Mallett, Professor of History, University of Warwick

JM John D. Moores, Lecturer in Italian, University College London

LP Loren Partridge, Professor, Chairman of Department of History of Art, University of California, Berkeley

BP Brian Pullan, Professor of Modern History, University of Manchester

CS Charles Schmitt, The Warburg Institute, University of London

JW John White, Durning Lawrence Professor in the History of Art, University College London

JHW J. H. Whitfield, Serena Professor Emeritus, University of Birmingham

Abbate, Niccolò dell' (*c.*1509–71) followed Primaticcio in bringing high *maniera* painting from northern Italy to France. Early works in his native Modena (such as the *Aeneid* illustrations, *c.*1540; Modena, Galleria Estense) reflect the influence of Parmigianino as well as that of the more conservative Correggio and Dosso Dossi. Engaging narrative frescoes of scenes from ancient history and Ariosto's *Orlando furioso* (1547–52; Bologna, Palazzo Torfanini and Palazzo Poggi respectively) demonstrate his predilection for romantic secular themes that were fully developed in his career at the French court of Henry II in Fontainebleau after 1552. LP

S. Beguin *Mostra di Niccolò dell'Abbate* (Bologna 1969)

A Renaissance impression of an **academic** discussion in the 2c. AD, from a manuscript of Aulus Gelius' *Noctes Atticae* (Milan, Ambrosiana Library).

Academies in the Renaissance world originated in imitations of the Academy which PLATO founded as a learned and religious society and school at Athens. The first revival of the idea in the West was an offshoot of the enthusiasm of Cosimo de' Medici and Ficino for Plato's dialogues. From the 1460s there was a loose association which held meetings at the Medici villa at Careggi in imitation of the gathering in Plato's *Symposium*. They were patronized by Lorenzo de' Medici and attended by Ficino, Poliziano, Landino and others. The Academy did not survive long after the death of Lorenzo (1492) but there was a brief revival in the early 16c. when meetings were held in the Rucellai Gardens (Orti Oricellari). The Academy started in Rome by Pomponio Leto in the mid-15c. was more directed to Roman studies. After a chequered early history dependent on papal approval and disapproval, during which its membership also included Platina, it entered a flourishing period under the patronage of Julius II and Leo X, both of whom were enthusiastic classicists. Bembo and Castiglione belonged to it at this time. It was ended by the Sack of Rome in 1527. At Naples the Academy originated in the humanist patronage of Alfonso V, under the leadership of Beccadelli. Its leading figure in the later 15c. was Pontano. At Venice Aldus founded an Academy in 1500 with a strongly Hellenist orientation: Greek was to be spoken and Greek literature promoted. These early Academies were essentially informal associations of humanists, professional or dilettante.

The 16c. produced a new wave of academies, many of them little more than literary mutual admiration societies, but a few with more defined scholarly or scientific aims from which the modern notion of the academy really descends. An academy of natural sciences existed at Naples from the 1560s. The Accademia della Crusca, founded at Florence in the 1580s, devoted itself at the end of the century to the publication of a dictionary of the Italian language – the first of many academies to assume such an undertaking. The Accademia dei Lincei of Rome, founded under the leadership of Federico Cesi in 1603, was oriented towards research in the natural sciences, particularly biological and medical. The earliest groups regarded as academies of fine arts date from the late 15c. They are the 'school' directed by Bertoldo in the Medici Gardens, attended by Michelangelo, and the circle around Leonardo da Vinci at Milan. They are really too loose to deserve the name. Organized academies of artists with a teaching purpose are to be found in Florence under Cosimo I (1563) and at Rome (the Accademia di S. Luca) in the 1590s. GH

A. della Torre *Storia dell' Accademia Platonica di Firenze* (1902); M. Maylender *Storia delle accademie d'Italia* (5 vols 1926–30); N. Pevsner *Academies of art* (1940)

Acciaiuoli family Coming from Bergamo to Florence in the 12c., the Acciaiuoli prospered as businessmen and by the 14c. were in the same league of international bankers as the Bardi and Peruzzi, with especially prosperous branches in Rome and Naples; by 1345, however, they were forced into liquidation by the failure of Edward III of England to repay his loans from them and by heavy war taxation at home. They continued to play a major role in domestic politics, coming to support the Medici against the Albizzi régime. This began an association that brought members of the family to positions of responsibility in Church and state up to 1494, and again under the Medici dukes of the 16c. JRH

C. Urgugieri della Berardenga *Gli Acciaiuoli di Firenze* (1961)

Accoramboni, Vittoria (1557–85) Webster's play *The white devil* of 1612, based on her story, reflects the interest taken first in Italy and thence elsewhere in scandal and crime in high places. Vittoria was married at 16 to Francesco Peretti, a nephew of the cardinal who was to become pope as Sixtus V. She soon started a liaison with the Duke of Bracciano, Paolo Orsini, already notorious for having killed his wife, Isabella de' Medici, for *her* infidelity. In 1581 Paolo had Francesco assassinated and married her. Though proof of Paolo's guilt was unclear, the then pope, Gregory XIII, declared the marriage void, and when Vittoria refused, as he ordered, to seclude herself in her parents' house, she was first imprisoned in Castel S. Angelo and then confined to her birthplace, Gubbio. In 1583, however, she married Orsini again in his castle at Bracciano. A short period of calm was broken when the election of Sixtus V renewed his relatives' desire to avenge Francesco. The couple sought safety in Venetian territory but in 1585 Paolo died. Jealousy of the fortune he left Vittoria in his will led to her murder at the hands of assassins hired by Paolo's cousin Lodovico Orsini. Without importance save to the protagonists, the story was one of those which confirmed the decadence of Catholic Italy in Protestant eyes. JRH

Active v. contemplative life Save for the root-eating, cave-dwelling hermit, the meditative few ride on the backs of the actively employed many; the cloister, the study, the university and the scriptorium are supported and guarded by those who administer, negotiate and fight. The medieval Christian emphasis on the renunciation of this world in order to achieve salvation in the next had led to the theoretical division of society into those who worked and fought and those who prayed. It was a formula that seemed increasingly inappropriate in the busy, socially complex and politically demanding context of Italian civic life in the 14c. Specifically, it put individuals who meditated primarily on the significance of classical, rather than Christian, moral and ethical works into a position of precarious respectability. The dilemma was movingly expressed by Petrarch in his *Secretum* (1342–43), a nervous dialogue in which the author allows his inclination to love women, achieve fame and study pagan literature to be rebuked by St Augustine, who had first yielded to and then triumphed over the same temptations.

Of all pagan authors, Petrarch was most drawn to Cicero, the courageous moralizer on such themes as the supportive but transient nature of human affections, or death. When in 1345 he discovered Cicero's letters to T. Pomponius Atticus, a friend who was so close as to be a second self, and realized the depth of Cicero's immersion in affairs of state, he expressed – in a letter to the shade of Cicero – his shocked dismay. This was at a time when increasing knowledge of the ancient world was revealing how freely philosophers like Aristotle and Plato had put their wisdom at the service of princes, and how far moral philosophy had been designed to bridge the gap between the individual's urge towards self-perfection and his role in society.

It was probably the employment of philosophically inclined humanists like Salutati and Bruni in Florence as chancery officials, and therefore quasi-politicians, that helped the idea that the pursuit of wisdom and, indeed, of salvation, was not necessarily at odds with participation in public affairs. By the mid-15c., supported by such thinkers as Palmieri and Alberti, the notion had lost most of its apologetic tone, especially with the development of theories of education, based on both classical and Christian ideals, that were designed to fit men for a responsible participation in secular life. Though jolts of conscience could perturb the merchant as he made his will because of the Church's disapproval of usurious (i.e. large) profit, by the end of the 15c. the active *v.* contemplative issue was no longer lively save for those conscious of a dawning religious vocation. So demanding were the standards of conduct imposed on the individual by classically influenced moral philosophy that no conflict with Christian, otherworldly ethics was apparent. Certain virtues, indeed, such as justice and magnanimity, were seen to be fully operative only in those with power to exercise them. In works like Castiglione's *The courtier* the issue became transposed into the less strenuous atmosphere of debate about the relative merit of a life devoted to the public profession of arms or the private one of letters. *See* ARMS AND LETTERS; HUMANISM; PALMIERI; PARUTA. JRH

H. Baron *The crisis of the early Italian Renaissance* (revised ed. 1966); E. Rice *The Renaissance idea of wisdom* (1958)

Adrian VI Pope 1522–23 (b.1495) Adrian Dedal, born at Utrecht and educated at Deventer and Louvain, became tutor to the future Charles V. Created cardinal in 1517, he was elected pope as a compromise candidate, but successfully alienated both the Curia and the Roman populace. He valued the learning of Vives and Erasmus but had no further sympathy with Renaissance culture. Making a virtue of parsimony, he campaigned against simony and nepotism, and refused to uphold the temporal rights of the Papacy. The Romans celebrated his death by hailing his physician as their liberator. JH

Age Average expectation of life at birth was below 30. Consequently contemporaries did not look at the lifecycle in the same way as we do. They did not think in terms of 'middle age'; what we call the 'mid-life crisis' was for them a sign of approaching senility. Michelangelo called himself 'old' at 42, Aretino at 45. The young formed the majority of the population; in Tuscany in 1427, 44 per cent of the total population were 19 or less. Hence it is scarcely surprising to find children beginning work as apprentices or servants at 7, while nuns tended to take their vows at 12 and other girls to marry at 18. An unmarried 20-year-old was often regarded as an old maid. In Florence, boys came of age politically at 14 (when they became eligible for a summons to a *parlamento*), while at 18 they became liable for taxes and military service. In Venice, nobles generally took their seats in the Great Council at 25 and could not become senators till 30, but it was well known that Venice was ruled by old men. Of the 23 doges 1400–1570, the age at election averaged 72. Popes, by contrast, were elected at an average age of about 54. In this period it was normal for people to be imprecise about their date of birth (like Titian, for example). They were somewhat more precise in Tuscany than elsewhere, thanks to pressures from governments concerned with eligibility for public office. This precision was not the least of the modernities of Renaissance Florence. PB

The qualities of the three **ages** of man depicted in Titian's *Allegory of Prudence* (London, National Gallery).

C. Gilbert 'When did a man in the Renaissance grow old?' *Studies in the Renaissance* (1967); R. Finlay 'The Venetian Republic as a gerontocracy: age and politics in the Renaissance' *Journal of Medieval and Renaissance Studies* (1978)

Agnadello, battle of (14 May 1509) Also known as the battle of Ghiaradadda. It was here, NW of Crema, that the French struck the first blow in the League of Cambrai's onslaught against Venice. The Venetian army, under the Count of Pitigliano, was broken and scattered, and its second-in-command, Bartolomeo d'Alviano, was taken prisoner. It was the most crushing and traumatic defeat in the whole of Venice's history. *See* WARS OF ITALY. JRH

Agriculture Despite the multiplicity of local variations, it may be useful to distinguish 3 main zones of Italian agriculture; Lombardy, Tuscany and the south. Agriculture was most prosperous on the plains of Lombardy and the Veneto. The heavy plough was used, many fields were irrigated, a high proportion of the land was under cultivation (some 85 per cent of the land between Pavia and Cremona by 1500), and agriculture was increasingly diversified and oriented towards the market. Crops included mulberries (for silk), woad (for dyeing), rice and, in the later 16c., maize. Dairy farming was important, and Parma already exported its famous cheese in the 14c. In the 14c. and 15c. there was an 'agricultural revolution' in which land passed from the Church to lay landlords with a greater interest in development, and cultivation was therefore intensified.

South of the river Po agriculture tended to follow the classic Mediterranean pattern. The terrain was hilly and the soil light, worked with a light plough. Sunshine and a low rainfall encouraged the cultivation of vines and olives. Cattle were few. Sheep were numerous in some areas such as the Tuscan Maremma and the Roman Campagna, but wool tended to be of low quality. In other respects, Tuscany and the south need to be distinguished. Tuscany was essentially a region of peasant proprietors living on isolated farms (*poderi*), practising polyculture for subsistence. In the neighbourhood of Florence, sharecropping (*mezzadria*) was spreading as townsmen bought up farms, but holdings remained small. At 6 to 1, yield ratios were relatively good for Europe in the period. Three-course rotation was practised, and beans were planted on the fallow, but the famines of the early 14c. may have been due to the exhaustion of the land.

Of the 3 zones, agricultural performance was worst in the south. With the exception of an area around Naples, the soil was not fertile. Crop rotation was generally 2-course, with yield ratios of 4 or 5 to 1. The dominant form of holding was the large estate (*latifondo*). Labourers tended to live in towns and walk to work: Europe's first commuters. As in the Roman Campagna in the 16c., southern landowners found it increasingly profitable to use their land for grazing rather than arable farming, and villages were deserted. Crops included oranges, lemons and sugar (grown on plantations in Sicily).

Although the extent and intensity of the cultivation of the soil naturally varied with the pressure of population, there were significant long-term trends towards monoculture (at the level of the individual holding), the diversification of crops (at the regional level), disafforestation (for the sake of fuel and shipbuilding), and the dispossession of peasant proprietors as urban élites turned increasingly to investment in land. Peasant proprietors tended to survive only in the less fertile areas such as the highlands. In short, the growth of cities such as Naples, Venice and Florence led to the commercialization of agriculture.

Some changes on the land are reflected in the art and literature of the Renaissance. The rise of terraced agriculture on the hills is faithfully recorded in the backgrounds of 15c. paintings, while a literature of advice to farmers developed for the sake of townsmen who had acquired villas. Among the more famous treatises are Pietro Crescentio's *Liber ruralium commodorum (The advantages of the country)* of *c.*1305, and Agostino Gallo's *Le dieci giornate della vera agricoltura (Ten chapters on true agriculture)*, first published in 1550. PB

P. Jones 'Italy' *Cambridge economic history of Europe* I (2nd ed. 1966); E. Sereni *Storia del paesaggio agrario italiano* (1961)

Alberghetti family First employed by Venice late in the 15c., members of this family served as gunfounders in the ARSENAL, generation by generation into the 18c. Chiefly concerned with the making of the Republic's bronze artillery, they also made bells and cast 'art' objects like the well-head in the courtyard of the Ducal Palace, signed as by Alfonso Alberghetti and dated 1556 – which may be compared with his decorated culverin in the Armoury of the COUNCIL OF TEN. JRH

Alberico da Barbiano (1348–1409) A Romagnol who commenced his career as a professional soldier under HAWKWOOD. Wars between Milan and Verona, Florence and its exiles, pope and anti-pope, the Durazzo and Angevin contenders for Naples, kept him fully employed. The sources do not permit a clear judgment of his generalship and he is best known for his direction of the first all-Italian mercenary company, that of St George. 'Patriotic' motives may have joined practical considerations in its formation. On his defeating at Marino in 1379 the Breton army of the anti-pope Clement VII, Urban VI gave him a banner inscribed with the slogan 'Italy freed from the barbarians'; but nothing about his career suggests any policy deeper than that of keeping Italian pickings for Italian hands. JRH

E. Solieri *Alberico da Barbiano* (1908)

Alberti, Leon Battista (1404–72) 'Where shall I put Battista Alberti: in what category of learned men shall I place him?' As his contemporary Landino saw, Alberti evades any pigeonholing: humanist scholar, natural scientist, mathematician, architect, cryptographer, pioneer of the Italian vernacular and author of Latin pastiches, he also transformed the theory and practice of the visual arts with his treatises on painting and architecture.

The illegitimate offspring of an exiled Florentine family, Alberti was born in Genoa and educated at Padua and Bologna in the classics, mathematics, and canon law. In the 1430s a papal secretary's job in Rome brought the financial security necessary for a literary life, and, the ban on his family now lifted (1428), he could accompany Eugenius IV to Florence, where the works of Brunelleschi, Masaccio and Donatello reassured him – as he says in the preface to *Della pittura* (1436) – that the arts could be revived. First written in Latin (1435), this treatise lent intellectual respectability to painting by grounding it in the rational laws of mathematical perspective, giving to pictorial composition a dignified structure derived from rhetoric, and recommending mythological subjects for the narratives (*historiae*) which are taken to be the painter's proper aim. Though literary in form, the *De pictura* is also a practitioner's guide, and shows a painter's sensitivity to questions of light and colour, expression and movement. Enormously influential on patrons and painters, Alberti's ideas were the starting point for Leonardo's *Trattato*, and the basis of subsequent academic art theory.

From the later 1430s Alberti combined papal service with protracted visits to Florence and peripatetic artistic advice to the Italian courts (Ferrara, Mantua, Urbino, Rimini). These were the years of the *Della famiglia*, in which members of his own family are made the mouthpieces for discussions of domestic morality. Works of satire (*Intercenales*; *Momus*) and moral philosophy (*Teogenio*; *Della tranquillità dell'animo*) gradually yielded to an increasing preoccupation with the physical remains of antiquity, seen in the brief treatise *De statua* and the outline for a survey of Rome. Study of Vitruvius's obscurities led to Alberti's own architectural treatise *De re aedificatoria* (completed 1452, published 1485), and to the practice of architecture which dominated his later life. Alberti used the Ciceronian division between utility and ornament as the framework for his view of architecture, where beauty is identified with harmony (*concinnitas*), and derived partly from fixed numerical proportions based on the intervals of music.

Façade of **Alberti**'s basilica of S. Andrea, Mantua.

Equally fundamental is the firm socio-political basis Alberti gives to architecture, seen as responsive to the nature of different societies and their inhabitants: within a hierarchy of building types, culminating in churches, the emphasis is on appropriateness and variety of solution.

Despite his praise for Brunelleschi in the *Della pittura*, Alberti's own architecture was based on unified hierarchies, not modular repetitions, and on a more specific use of ancient models: his first building, an outer shell for the church of S. Francesco in Rimini, already draws on the nearby Arch of Augustus. In his Mantuan churches Alberti had a freer hand: he gave S. Sebastiano (1460f.) a Greek cross form, and turned S. Andrea (1470f.) into his own interpretation of Vitruvius's *templum Etruscum*, a single barrel-vaulted nave buttressed by thick-walled side chapels, and fronted by a portico which combined temple façade and triumphal arch. Alberti's buildings can be seen as a series of experimental reinventions of *all'antica* types for modern use, incorporating the Vitruvian language of the orders. At the Palazzo Rucellai in Florence, the façade is unified by a delicate grid of superimposed pilasters.

Alberti's treatise is packed with technical guidance, and he should not be seen as an architectural dilettante: when forced to design by correspondence, he nevertheless controlled the smallest details of design and construction. His ideas influenced Pius II's Pienza, and the Ducal Palace at Urbino, while his treatise was closely studied by patrons like Lorenzo de' Medici and Ercole d'Este. Printed in 1485, and translated into many languages, it continued to be essential reading for architects well into the 18c. *See* ARTIST, STATUS OF THE; CRITICAL THEORY OF ART.[174, 284] CE

C. Grayson in *DBI*; F. Borsi *Alberti* (1975); — *Leon Battista Alberti: the complete work* (1977)

Albizzi family Moving to Florence (from Arezzo) in the 12c., the Albizzi soon came to play a consistently weighty part in communal government until their exile after the CIOMPI revolt. From their return to the city in 1382, under the headship first of Maso, then from his death in 1417 of Rinaldo (1370–1442), the Albizzi became the leaders of an oligarchical régime that in many ways anticipated that of the Medici. Rinaldo was chiefly responsible for Cosimo de' Medici's exile in 1433 and was himself exiled with the rest of his family on Cosimo's return in 1434. JRH

Albornoz, Egidio de (1310–67) Archbishop of Toledo (1338), cardinal (1350), Chancellor of Castile, exiled by King Pedro the Cruel to Avignon, Albornoz was appointed by Innocent VI as his legate in Italy to restore the fortunes of the Papal State (1353–57, then 1358–64), and after a long series of wars achieved there some measure of stability and formal recognition of papal authority. But his achievement largely came to nothing after his death, and his appointment of local tyrants as legitimate papal vicars did much to ensure the powers enjoyed by their families up to the 16c. His true fame rests less on any claim that he was 'the second founder of the Papal State' than on his codification of its laws in his *Constitutions* and his foundation of the Spanish College at Bologna. JL

P. Colliva *Il Cardinale Albornoz, lo stato della Chiesa, le Constitutiones Aegidianae* (1977)

Alciato, Andrea (1492–1550) The outstanding Italian jurist of the Renaissance period. Born in Milan, in 1518 he was called to the legal chair at Avignon. After moving to Bourges (1529–33), he returned to Italy to teach at Bologna, Ferrara and Pavia, where he died. Civil law then depended heavily on the compilation of Roman statutes issued in AD529 by the Emperor Justinian, and known as the *Corpus iuris civilis*: or rather, it depended on successive layers of interpretation that had accreted over it. These were in the main concerned with demonstrating the statutes' congruence with Natural Law (laws which followed inevitably and timelessly upon the problems inherent in the human, social, condition), or with striving to update them to fit contemporary circumstances.

Alciato turned on the *Corpus* a formidable knowledge of late ancient history and literature which, allied to philological gifts of a high order, enabled him to sort out the chronological layers within the *Corpus* and to show to what issues they had been addressed. Thus the *Corpus* lost much of its Natural Law status and became the historical record of laws being made or varied in response to particular needs in the past. Alciato achieved this as a scholar applying humanistic techniques to an important text. But as a lawyer he was aware of the practical value of much of the previous glossators' work; by a discriminating retention of this in his lectures and published work he was able to stimulate an interest in humanistic, historical jurisprudence without alienating the traditionalists; to represent law as a means of retaining principles while updating applications. Among his many books, however, the most startling success was his *Emblemata* of 1531; it went through over 170 editions, was widely translated, and pioneered the study and diffusion of emblems in their Renaissance, classicizingly moralistic, form. JRH

DBI; P.-É. Viard *André Alciat* (1926); E. Garin 'Leggi, diritto e storia nelle discussioni dei secoli XV & XVI' *Storia del diritto nel quadro delle scienze storiche* (Florence 1966)

Aldrovandi, Ulisse (1522–1605) Naturalist and zoologist. After a scientific and humanistic training at Bologna and Padua he settled in his native Bologna, teaching and botanizing, becoming a professor and curator of the botanic garden, and forming a botanical and zoological museum which he bequeathed to the city and university. His manuscripts and many specimens survive in the university library. He was an immensely influential teacher, whose work established botany, entomology and zoology as

Engraved illustration of a parrot from **Aldrovandi**'s *Ornithologiae*, 1559.

disciplines separate from medicine. He himself published on ornithology (1600) and insects (1602); his manuscripts on quadrupeds, reptiles and fishes, edited by pupils, were published posthumously. His work made Bologna a zoological centre, and his books were widely read. MBH

Aldus (?1450–1515) Aldus did more than any other man to make the classics, the foundation of Renaissance humanism, available to the educated reading public. Aldo Manuzio was born at Bassiano, near Rome. He was a humanist and tutor before he became a printer and publisher. He eloquently argued that only an upright teacher could foster learning and virtue in youth, in the preface of his first publication, his own Latin grammar printed in 1493. Two years later, with the financial support of a successful publisher, Andrea Torresani, and a doge's nephew, Pierfrancesco Barbarigo, Aldus began his Venetian publishing house at the sign of the dolphin and anchor.

Aldus published about 130 editions between 1495 and 1515. His first love was Greek, and his printings of Greek classical and post-classical authors comprised the largest and most important part of his list. He issued around 30 first Greek editions of literary and philosophical texts, sometimes rescuing the text from obscurity or possible permanent loss. Many of his Greek printings were of great significance, such as, for example, his monumental 5-volume Greek Aristotle of 1495–98. He also published a number of introductory dictionaries, grammars and texts to help improve the reader's Greek. The books were printed in Greek cursive type that he commissioned. He published Latin classics in a handsome cursive type designed by Francesco Griffo. These usually appeared in small octavo format in press runs of about 1000 copies, intended for the busy reader who lacked the space for folio volumes. He also put out a small number of vernacular titles, including the beautifully illustrated vernacular 'novel' *Hypnerotomachia Polifili* (1499) of Francesco Colonna, as well as works by Dante, Petrarch, Sannazaro and Bembo.

Aldus had a remarkable commitment to classical learning and the ability to inspire others to join him in his enterprises. The Aldine

μένῳ τἀντίγραφον τῶνδε
τῶν τύπων ἀνηκέ-
στοις ἕλκεσι
πολλα-
χῆ
διεφθο-
ρός,
ἀλλ' ἐμῷ
πολλὰς μὲν μυ-
ριάδας διορθώσαντι
σφαλμάτων πολλοὺς δὲ στί-
χους τῶν παρεισαγομένων κατα-
λογάδην πρότερον ἀναγινωσκομένους
καὶ χύδην, εἰς τὴν προσήκουσαν τῆς ἐμμέτρου
τάξεως συνέχειαν ἀποκαταστήσαντι, χάριν εἰδείη.

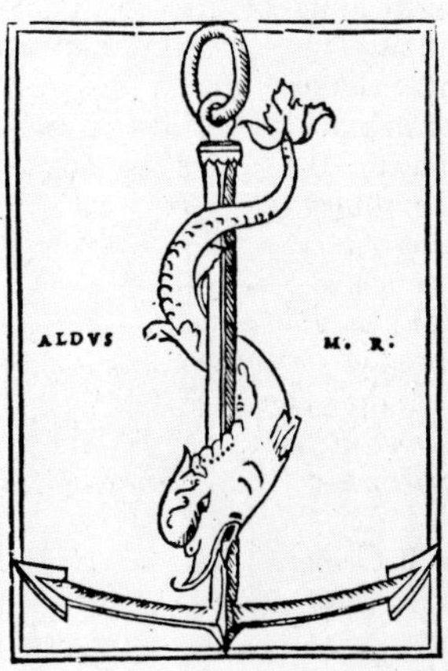

Fine Greek typography, with the **Aldus** anchor and dolphin *impresa*, in the *editio princeps* of the Greek grammarian Athenaeus, 1514.

circle, the associates and friends who helped him edit and publish, included some of the ablest scholars of the day. Erasmus joined Aldus in 1508, and Aldus, in turn, published the expanded version of Erasmus' *Adages* that year. It became a best seller. The Aldine press was the busiest in Venice, which was the most important publishing centre in Europe by the end of the incunable period. In addition, Aldus' distinctive and well-designed books established a standard for beautiful printing. His furious publishing came to a temporary halt in 1505 because of over-expansion; after several years of reduced activity, the press again became very busy in 1512. He married Maria, daughter of his partner Andrea Torresani, in 1505. They had several children, including Paolo, who continued the press after Aldus' death. PG

A. A. Renouard *Annales de l'imprimerie des Alde, ou histoire des trois Manuce et de leurs éditions* (3rd ed. 1834; reprinted 1953); Martin Lowry *The world of Aldus Manutius: business and scholarship in Renaissance Venice* (1979)

Alessi, Galeazzo (1512–72) Perugian architect who founded an individual school of villa and palace design, widely known through Rubens's *Palazzi di Genova* (1622). A stay in Rome (*c.*1536–42) brought curial contacts which furthered Alessi's career, first in Perugia, then in Genoa, where Cardinal Sauli commissioned S. Maria di Carignano (1549f.), a somewhat rigid adaptation of Bramante's Greek cross plan for St Peter's. Alessi probably designed the Strada Nuova, a kind of patrician housing estate on a new street, where the palace courtyards exploit the sloping site. His Genoese villas (e.g. Villa Cambiaso, *c.*1550f.) and palaces (e.g. Palazzo Pallavicino, *c.*1550f.) form compact blocks, with tripartite façades around recessed centres, superimposed orders, and rich detail. The Palazzo Marino in Milan (*c.*1557f.), with its statuary orders and Michelangelesque windows, complies with the patron's Lombard *horror vacui*, while the modest church of S. Barnaba (*c.*1561f.) has the clearly differentiated longitudinal plan associated with monastic reform. Alessi's architectural loyalties reveal a characteristically mid-16c. division between orthodoxy and licence. CE

Alessi's courtyard in the Palazzo Marino in Milan.

Galeazzo Alessi e l'architettura del suo tempo (Genoa 1975)

Alexander VI Pope 1492–1503 (b.*c.*1431) Rodrigo Borgia was first promoted by his uncle Pope Calixtus III, having been a canon law student at Bologna. He rapidly became a cardinal (1456), Archbishop of Valencia (1458) and Vice-Chancellor of the Church (1457), the highest office in papal administration, which he retained, together with numerous lucrative benefices, until his election as pope. Sensual pleasure and dynastic ambition were not unusual in the Curia, but the degree of both displayed by this Catalan noble earned him a disrepute which still outweighs the positive qualities urged by modern apologists: administrative skills and energy, doctrinal and devotional propriety, private frugality and some promotion of learning (e.g. his support for the university of Rome).

It is argued that, even if his election, a genuine majority verdict, was secured by bribes and promises (Cardinal Ascanio Sforza, who received the vice-chancellorship, ensured it, to exclude Giuliano della Rovere – later Julius II), so was that of many other popes. Moreover, a strong personality was needed to cope with disorder in the Papal State and the threat of foreign invasion; there were, again, many papal precedents for using his own family to meet the first problem. On account of his enmity to Ferrante of Naples Alexander did not at first discourage Charles VIII in his invasion of Italy, but he refrained from formally investing him with Naples and in 1495 promoted the League against him. On the other hand he was a

Portrait of **Alexander VI** in Pinturicchio's fresco of *The Resurrection*, in the Borgia Apartments of the Vatican.

protagonist of Louis XII's invasion (1499), anticipating dynastic and political advantage.

Alexander did perform one act effectively as the supreme authority of Christendom – fixing the line of demarcation between the Spanish and the Portuguese in the New World (1493); but his consuming earthly interest was his family. This is clear from his promotion of his children's careers (four were born of the same mistress, Vanozza Catanei, 1474–81) and those of nephews and other relatives. Most got on in the Church, but his eldest son Juan, Duke of Gandia (d.1497), was intended for military and political leadership, and subsequently Cesare, who renounced his cardinalate in 1498, assumed this role, assisted by a French marriage and military backing. Alexander's daughter Lucrezia was relieved of her first husband Giovanni Sforza of Pesaro by papal annulment, and of her second, Alfonso, Duke of Bisceglie, by murder (May 1500), probably instigated by Cesare.

By this time (and perhaps owing to Cesare) Alexander was coming to inspire little but fear and revulsion; as late as 1497, however, his more human qualities were evident in his grief at the assassination of the Duke of Gandia, which for some months zealously inspired him to seek reform proposals which would have reduced corruption and luxury in the Curia. Cesare's ruthless military initiatives (1499–1503), deceptions and assassinations depended upon papal authority if not on direct control (Cesare was much more decisive than his father and sometimes disregarded him). Even so, Cesare's advent (1498) cannot altogether have determined Alexander's ill reputation; nervous cardinals had fled from Rome before then, and there had been a punitive, if not very successful, war against the Orsini barons (1496–97).

If neither incestuous nor murderous, Alexander certainly remained lascivious; several children were born after he became pope. He was not discriminating as a patron or collector, though he promoted some minor street improvements in Rome and had rooms in the Vatican decorated by Pinturicchio with subjects which illustrate not only his devotional attachments (particularly to the Virgin Mary) but also his interest in astrology and the mythology of the bull, his family emblem. His death was followed by a funeral and burial hasty and ignominious by any normal papal standards, although it was hot weather; it is striking how many contemporary sources (not only hostile ambassadors) refer to him discreditably, even if a xenophobic element of prejudice against Spaniards must also be taken into account. DC

M. Mallett *The Borgias* (1969); *DBI*

Alfonso I of Aragon King of Naples 1443–58 (b.1395) Known as 'The Magnanimous' because of his generous, if ostentatious, patronage of art and learning, Alfonso inherited the Aragonese empire (as Alfonso V) in 1416; and at an early date he seems to have become convinced that continued Aragonese domination of the western Mediterranean, and his hold on Sicily and Sardinia, would be dependent on acquiring a foothold in mainland Italy. His opportunity occurred in 1420, the year in which he first reduced the kingdom of Sicily to his obedience. Giovanna II, who wanted Alfonso's aid against Louis III of Anjou, adopted him as her heir in the kingdom of Naples. Three years later she disowned Alfonso and, on her death in 1435, left her kingdom to René of Anjou. There followed a long and costly war of succession from which Alfonso emerged the victor, entering Naples as king in February 1443. Thereafter Alfonso made Naples the brilliant centre of his empire.

Alfonso's policies were thus always expansionist and in pursuit of his imperial ambitions he played a prominent, if largely

Alfonso I and his court, in a relief by Francesco Laurana on the triumphal arch at Castel Nuovo in Naples.

unsuccessful, part in the war for the succession of Milan between 1447 and 1450, and in the war against Sforza between 1450 and 1453; he refused to adhere to the Peace of LODI until 1455. Such adventures placed an intolerable strain even on the resources of an empire as large as his and he was forced to impose heavy taxes. He also earned unpopularity among the Neapolitans from the distinctly Spanish flavour of his court.

Yet Neapolitan historiography has, on the whole, dealt kindly with Alfonso, who succeeded in keeping the unruly barons of the kingdom under some kind of control. His popularity was further enhanced by his public acts of piety, for he was a conscientious churchgoer and a connoisseur of sermons. Equally, Alfonso is commended for his success in making Naples one of the great centres of Renaissance culture. He made many provisions which favoured public instruction, and strengthened the university of Naples. In Sicily he showed the same concern for learning, instituted a school of Greek at Messina, and founded a new university at Catania. Recognizing the value of humanists as propagandists, Alfonso proved a generous patron of such men as Valla, Filelfo and Beccadelli. In one year alone he was reputed to have distributed 20,000 ducats to literary men, and he paid Bartolomeo Fazio an annual pension of 500 ducats while he wrote the *Historia Alfonsi*. With a clear understanding of Neapolitan needs and aspirations he left his empire divided on his death: his son was designated heir to Naples, his brother, Giovanni, to the rest of the Aragonese empire. JH

A. Ryder *The kingdom of Naples under Alfonso the Magnanimous* (1976)

Alfonso II of Aragon King of Naples 1494–95 (b.1448) Educated by humanists, Alfonso became a discriminating patron of the arts, particularly architecture, but is chiefly remembered as a soldier and, in particular, for the campaign of 1480–81 when (as Duke of Calabria) he forced the Turks to withdraw from Otranto. Throughout his life Alfonso argued in favour of a repressive policy towards the Neapolitan barons. This made him so unpopular once he became king that, on the advance of Charles VIII in 1494, he was forced to abdicate. He took refuge in Messina, where he died in 1495. JH

Allori, Alessandro (1535–1607) Florentine late Mannerist painter, the nephew, pupil and principal follower of Bronzino. During his sojourn in Rome (1554–56) he came in contact with Roman 'Counter-Maniera'; the influence of Michelangelo's *Last Judgment* is reflected in his frescoes in SS. Annunziata (early 1560s). He contributed an altarpiece to the S. Maria Novella cycle (1575) and two panels to the Studiolo of Francesco de' Medici (1570–72), whose favourite painter he became. He purged and simplified Bronzino's *maniera* of ambiguity and complexity; as he grew older he retreated into a dream-like, visionary style. MH

Alum A mineral used in glassmaking, tanning and especially to fix dyes. It was imported by the Genoese from the Gulf of Smyrna till *c.*1450. When Turkish conquests interrupted this supply, alum was discovered at Tolfa (a small town inland from Civitavecchia) in the Papal State in 1462, and at Volterra (*c.*1470; mine abandoned 1483). The Tolfa mine, which employed some 700 workers in 1550, made an important contribution to the finances of the Pope and his bankers, including the Medici, Agostino CHIGI and, after 1531, a series of Genoese financiers. PB

J. Delumeau *L'Alun de Rome* (1962)

Alviano, Bartolomeo d' (1435–1515) Born into a noble Umbrian clan, the Liviani, and related to other such militant clans as the Orsini, Bartolomeo almost automatically adopted a military career. His conduct of it gives the lie to any hazy dismissal of mercenary commanders as disloyal to their employers and concerned mainly to avoid more than the necessary minimum of bloodshed.

His boldness was widely recognized as being a crucial factor in the Spanish victory over the French at the GARIGLIANO in 1503. From 1507 he served Venice, brilliantly conducting the Republic's successful mountain campaign against Maximilian I's armies in the following year. In 1509 his impetuous attack, made against the advice of his senior colleague the Count of Pitigliano, was held responsible for the Venetian defeat at AGNADELLO. However, on his return in 1513 after being taken and held prisoner, the Republic at once recontracted him as commander-in-chief. He reconquered Friuli and, though unsuccessful in other actions on the terraferma, his contingent contributed notably to the allied victory at MARIGNANO in 1515, a victory he outlived only by a month. Very much a soldier's soldier, his relations with civilian military commissioners and with government were close and harmonious, and he was one of the first commanders to show an interest in learning from the military practice of the ancients. JRH

L. Leonij *La vita di Bartolomeo d'Alviano* (1858)

Amadeo, Giovanni Antonio (1447–1522), Lombard sculptor, spent most of his career from 1466 working on sculptural decorations for the Certosa (Carthusian monastery) outside his native town of Pavia. In 1474 he took responsibility jointly with the Mantegazza brothers for its façade, carving reliefs on Biblical themes. He was employed on the construction of the Colleoni Chapel and the monument of Medea Colleoni in Bergamo (1470–76). After 1490 he also worked on Milan cathedral, where his portrait appeared on a medallion. CA

J. Pope-Hennessy *Italian Renaissance sculpture* (1958)

Ambrosian Republic Born of hostility to the possible accession of an alien ruler, of ambition among wealthy families and of dislike of signorial rule, the *Aurea Respubblica Ambrosiana* of Milan was constituted (14 August 1447) on the day following the death of Filippo Maria Visconti. Its leaders could draw upon no republican tradition or popular support, were themselves divided by clan factions, and worked in an atmosphere of disorder and suspicion. Above all, unwilling either to concede freedom to the cities which had formed part of the Visconti *signoria* or to allow them to pass under the control of rival powers, they were forced to assign military authority to a powerful condottiere. Their choice of Francesco Sforza, who had his own ambitions towards the Visconti inheritance, argues a certain desperation. Sforza's military and diplomatic successes soon forced the republicans to face the inevitable; on 11 March 1450 he was assigned ducal powers in the Assembly of the People. JL

Ammannati, Bartolomeo (1511–92) Tuscan sculptor and architect trained in the workshop of Pisa cathedral. He later worked with Giovanni Angelo Montorsoli, through whom he absorbed the influence of Michelangelo, and subsequently in Urbino, Venice and Padua. In 1550 he moved to Rome and executed the sculpture on the Del Monte tombs in S. Pietro in Montorio, under the supervision of Michelangelo. In 1555 he went to Florence to serve the Medici dukes, producing a spectacular *Fountain of Juno* (Florence, Bargello) and the celebrated *Fountain of Neptune* in Piazza della Signoria, Florence (*c.*1560–75). His most important architectural projects were the redevelopment of the Pitti Palace with its capricious rustication in the courtyard (1558–70) and the graceful bridge of S. Trinita (1567–70). By 1582 he was

Ammannati's *Fountain of Neptune* in the Piazza della Signoria, Florence.

so strongly influenced by the Counter-Reformation as formally to renounce the public display of nudity in his statues. In sculpture and architecture Ammannati was a prime exponent of Mannerism: while his style was derived from Michelangelo, he concentrated on grace of form at the expense of realism and emotion. CA
C. Avery *Florentine Renaissance sculpture* (1970); J. Pope-Hennessy *Italian High Renaissance and Baroque sculpture* (1970)

Ammirato, Scipione (1531–1600) Before settling in Florence in 1560 this versatile and antiquarian-minded man of letters passed most of his life in his native kingdom of Naples. In 1570 he was commissioned by Cosimo I to write a history of Florence from its origins. The portion reaching 1434 was published in 1600, that taking the story up to 1574 posthumously. Benefiting from access to the recently opened public archives, his history is chiefly remarkable for its uneasy but admirably copious use of original sources. JRH
DBI; E. Cochrane *Florence in the forgotten centuries* (1973)

Ancona One of the major cities of the Papal State, in the Middle Ages Ancona was a trading port with its own consuls in Constantinople and Acre. It was ruled by a citizen council and executive, but communal rule was being superseded by papal rule. Captured by the Malatesta (1348), it was retaken by Albornoz. Subsequently Ancona reasserted its independence and withstood sieges by Francesco Sforza and Alfonso I of Aragon, but the city was weakened by the fall of Constantinople and, although able to withstand an attack by Innocent VIII (1477), and to revolt against the Papacy (1488), its days of independence were numbered. Clement VII sold Ancona to Cardinal Accolti and ordered his legate to seize the city (1532). Almost the first action of the régime was the destruction of the communal archive. Any opponents of papal rule were exiled and, after 1532, the history of Ancona followed that of the Papal State. JH

Andrea del Castagno (active *c.*1442, d.1457) demonstrates, in a particularly dramatic way, the fusion of the sculptural and pictorial vision which is characteristic of a very high proportion of Florentine, and indeed of central Italian, painting throughout the Renaissance and the period leading up to it. His debt to Donatello and to the sculpture of the early part of the century is clear. So is the linear accent within his sculptural vision which links him to so many of the sculptors and painters active in the mid-century.

His masterpiece, the *Last Supper*, and the associated frescoes in the refectory of S. Apollonia, Florence, reveal him as a most exciting and dramatic colourist. The *sinopie* or underdrawings for these frescoes are of especial interest, since they range from a virtually fully finished design in monochrome to mere poster-like silhouettes of the main forms. His painted equestrian monument for Niccolò da Tolentino (1456; Florence cathedral), with its lively line and its emphasis on anatomy and movement, epitomizes the changes in artistic outlook which had supervened in the 20 years since his fellow perspectivist, Paolo Uccello, completed the grave and geometrically abstract monument to Sir John HAWKWOOD (1436), for which it acts as both a pendant and a critical commentary.[144] JW
A. M. Fortuna *Andrea del Castagno* (1957)

Andrea del Sarto (1486–1531) is, alongside Fra Bartolommeo, the supreme exponent of Florentine early High Renaissance style and the counterpart of Michelangelo in Rome. His gentle, classical paintings of the Virgin and

Andrea del Sarto, *Madonna delle Arpie* (Florence, Uffizi).

Child, such as the *Madonna delle Arpie* (1517; Florence, Uffizi), are notable for their softly atmospheric qualities and the richness of their colour, in contrast to the linear definition and clear, bright hues of artists like Botticelli and Ghirlandaio. Whilst never himself becoming a Mannerist, he is important also as the master of such leading exponents of the new style as Rosso, Pontormo and Vasari. JW

S. J. Freedberg *Andrea del Sarto* (1963); J. Shearman *Andrea del Sarto* (1965)

Angelico, Fra Giovanni de Fiesole (active *c.*1418–55) entered the Observant Dominican convent of Fiesole in the period 1418–21 and not, as was once thought, in 1407. Elected prior in 1449, Angelico was early associated with S. Antonino and Lorenzo of Ripafratta, and later knew Popes Eugenius IV and Nicholas V, under whom he frescoed a chapel in the Vatican. He is one of those rarities among artists, monastic or otherwise, of whom we can be reasonably sure that the apparent spirituality of their art reflects intense personal devotion. The quintessential purity of his style is seen in the 45 frescoes in the cells and corridors of the convent of S. Marco, Florence, handed over to the order in 1436 on the initiative of Cosimo de' Medici. The *Annunciation* at the head of the stairs and that in one of the cells, designed for a lifetime of meditation and quiet contemplation, are two of the most memorable images in the history of religious art. They are a reminder that increasing secularization, however significant, is only one aspect of Renaissance artistic production.

Confusion of Angelico's style with those of collaborators such as Zanobi Strozzi, endlessly copied and photographically reproduced for pious purposes, have given his work an undeserved reputation for mere prettiness. His early *Linaiuoli Triptych* (commissioned 1433; Florence, Museo di S. Marco), with its marble frame by Lorenzo Ghiberti (1432), reveals the monumental, sculptural aspects of his art. Clear light, often brilliant colour, simply conceived figure volumes, meticulous attention to detail, incomparable technique, and a spatial clarity dependent on a subtle but unslavish use of the new Artificial PERSPECTIVE, are characteristic of a whole series of major altarpieces from the *Deposition* and the *Virgin Enthroned with Saints* in the S. Marco to the *Coronation of the Virgin* in the Louvre.[277] JW

J. Pope-Hennessy *Fra Angelico* (1974)

Fra **Angelico**'s *The Annunciation* in the convent of S. Marco, Florence.

A study by Leonardo for his fresco of the battle of **Anghiari** (Windsor, Royal Library).

Anghiari, battle of (29 June 1440) A Florentine and papal army defeated a Milanese force under PICCININO outside this town near Arezzo. Machiavelli, in his *History of Florence*, used it shamelessly as an example of the reluctance of mercenaries to risk death in battle: he put the casualties as 'one man killed, and he fell off his horse and was trampled to death', whereas sources available to him put the joint fatalities at some 300. It was the subject of a fresco painted by Leonardo da Vinci in the Palazzo Vecchio in Florence (chosen because it was primarily a cavalry engagement and he could show horses in combat). The fresco rapidly decayed and its composition is best known from the sketch Rubens made of its central part. JRH

G. Neufeld 'Leonardo da Vinci's Battle of Anghiari' *Art Bulletin* (1949)

First house of Anjou

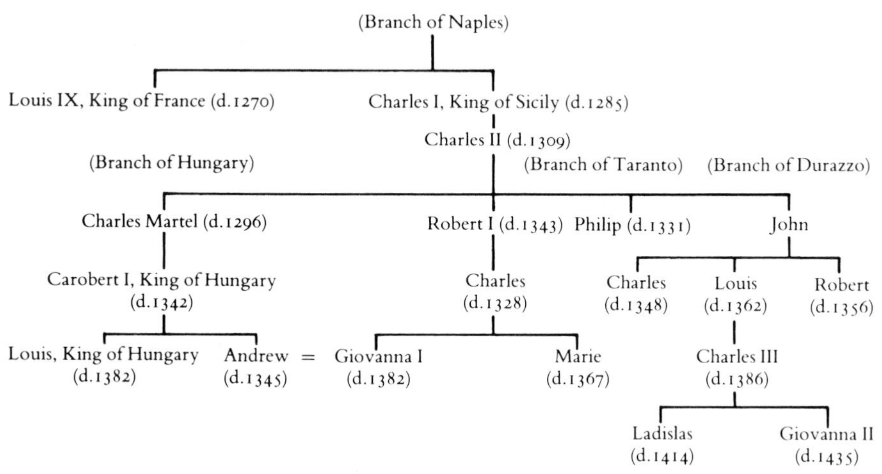

Anghiera, Pietro Martire d' (1459–1526) The name comes from Angera, on Lago Maggiore, the home of his family. After a sound humanistic education he occupied various secretaryships in Rome before being taken to Spain in 1487 with the returning Castilian ambassador. He fought in the campaigns that led to the conquest of Granada in 1492. He was then employed by Isabella, first as head of a school through which she hoped to reduce the ignorance of young nobles at the court, and later (also under Ferdinand) increasingly in connection with the administration of the growing Spanish empire in the New World. From Columbus's first voyage he had taken a close interest in the voyages of discovery and settlement alike, and with his *De orbe novo* was their first and fullest published chronicler. The work was printed in 3 instalments: in 1511, 1516 and 1530. He was well informed about Columbus; he knew Vasco da Gama, Vespucci, Cortes and Magellan. He only revisited Italy once, though many of the 'decades' or sections comprising his work were dedicated to Italians, among them Popes Leo X, Adrian VI and Clement VII and Duke Francesco Sforza. JRH

J. H. Mariéjol *Un lettré italien à la cour d'Espagne: 1488–1526* (1887)

Anjou, house of The first house of Anjou was founded by Charles of Anjou (brother of King Louis IX of France), who ruled the kingdom of

Second house of Anjou
(and claim of French monarchy to Naples)

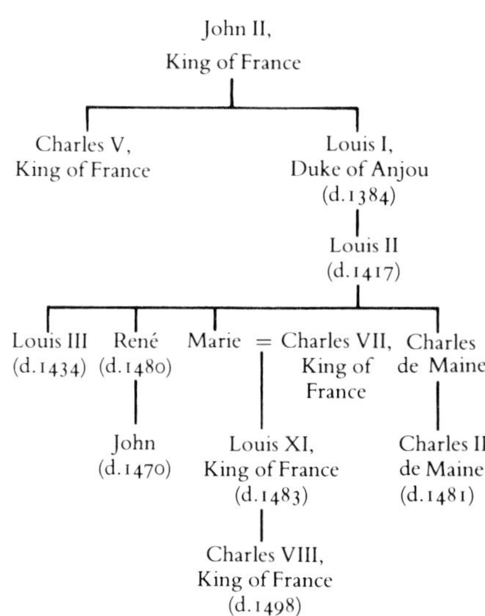

Sicily 1266–85. His descendants ruled the kingdom of NAPLES to 1435 (line of Naples to 1382, line of Durazzo to 1435) and the kingdom of Hungary 1308–82. The second house of Anjou was founded by the brother of King Charles V of France, Louis I (d.1384). In 1379 Queen Giovanna I of Naples promised him the inheritance of the kingdom in return for support against her domestic enemies. He and his successors (Louis II, d.1417; Louis III, d.1434; René, d.1480) struggled intermittently thereafter to make good their claim, though without success. On the extinction of the male line in 1481 the rights claimed by the second house passed to the French crown and provided the pretext for Charles VIII's invasion of Naples in 1494. JL

E. G. Léonard *Les Angevins de Naples* (Paris 1954)

Anti-clericalism exists in any society with an entrenched and familiar church; but perhaps the anti-clericalism of Renaissance Italy was sharper and more frequently expressed than elsewhere. Vernacular literature contained some of the strongest and most enduring criticism of churchmen. Boccaccio's *Decameron* describes enough double-dealing, lecherous or stupid monks to fill many a monastery. Castiglione's *The courtier* narrates the tale of a monk who impregnated several nuns but escaped punishment from his bishop because of his adroit use of Scripture. In Machiavelli's comedy *Mandragola* (*The mandrake*), a depraved friar helps a young man to possess the virtuous wife of a ridiculous and pompous old man. And in the conclusion of Aretino's witty, scabrous *I ragionamenti* (*The dialogues*), relating the loves of nuns, wives, and prostitutes, the last are judged the most honest because they act without hypocrisy. It is no exaggeration to note that there is hardly an honest religious in the entire vernacular novella tradition of the Renaissance. The Church suffered literary anti-clericalism in silence until the Counter-Reformation; then Index and Inquisition banned or expurgated many anti-clerical books.

Humanists undermined the status of the Church on philosophical grounds and directly attacked clergymen on moral grounds. Petrarch, Salutati and Valla argued that the lay, active life was just as worthy as the religious and contemplative life. Other humanists condemned the worldliness and ignorance of the clergy, and the temporal pretensions of the Papacy. In the 16c., writers flayed prelates for the abuses common in the Renaissance: nepotism, non-residence, avarice, etc. Guicciardini in a memorable maxim confessed a preference for Luther, not because he approved of Luther's teaching, but in the angry desire that papal rascals might get their due.

The Papacy's political role generated anti-clericalism on political grounds. Savonarola scourged it from the dual perspectives of a moral reformer and a civic patriot who saw it opposing Florentine interests. Machiavelli condemned it as the cause of Italian disunity, the reason why Italian states could not summon the political strength and will to repel the northern European barbarians.

Jurisdictional disputes sparked anti-clericalism. Both Church and state claimed the right to regulate the moral, religious and social lives of clerics and laymen. The key issue was whether lay or ecclesiastical authority should judge and punish sinners who were simultaneously criminals in the eyes of civil law. Frustrated in attempts to shave the Church's legal powers, laymen expressed their anger through anti-clericalism. Economic conflicts produced additional anti-clericalism. The Venetians, for example, deeply resented the refusal of church institutions to pay taxes. The Venetian republic developed a public policy favouring the secular acquisition of ecclesiastical land, because of the failure of the Church to pay taxes on it, and because laymen wanted church lands.

Anti-clericalism existed because Church and society were so tightly interwoven. Since the sins of Church and clergy were the same as those of states and laymen, anti-clericalism never stopped, but only very rarely did mockery of the clergy lead to mockery of the roles they should ideally play, let alone to disbelief in the faith they professed. PG

Antique, drawings after the Just as humanists beginning with Petrarch collected the writings of classical authors, so artists from the early 15c. showed growing interest in the remains of ancient art and architecture. These were drawn and often collected in sketchbooks, which could serve as pattern books, or simply as antiquarian studies. Gentile da Fabriano and Pisanello were among the first to make such records. The latter incorporated them with other studies in a volume (Codex

Vallardi; Paris, Louvre) which must have been used in his workshop. On the other hand the learned amateur Ciriaco d'Ancona made such drawings on his business trips to Greece and Asia Minor: unfortunately only copies of these survive.

As far as drawings after architecture go, we do not know what those Brunelleschi is supposed to have done in Rome looked like, but we have two volumes of drawings by Giuliano da Sangallo. They were compiled over a period of years and contain not only entire monuments – either in their ruined state, or rather fancifully reconstructed – but also details such as capitals, bases and columns. Perhaps the most interesting collection of varied drawings after the antique – statues, reliefs, architectural details, and also a few picturesque views – is found in a sketchbook now in the Escorial. It may be from Ghirlandaio's workshop and can only have been a pattern book for the use of painters. From the 16c. a number of similar sketchbooks survives, e.g. by Amico Aspertini and Ligorio. Unfortunately nothing is known about the appearance of Raphael's never-completed record – text and drawings – of ancient Rome, commissioned by Leo X in 1519. *See* CARPI, GIROLAMO DA. LDE

E. Mandowsky and C. Mitchell *Pirro Ligorio's Roman Antiquities* (1963)

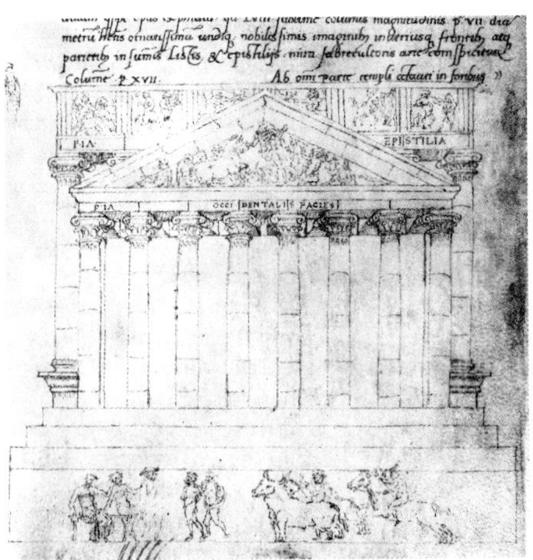

One of Giuliano da Sangallo's drawings of **antique** architecture: the Parthenon, based on a sketch by Ciriaco d'Ancona, showing the Elgin Marbles in place (Rome, Vatican Library).

Antonello da Messina (active *c.*1445–79), Sicilian painter, was possibly a pupil of Colantonio in Naples under Alfonso of Naples who, in the years immediately following his accession, acquired at least 3 paintings by Van Eyck, as well as works by Rogier van der Weyden and other Flemish artists. The idea that oil painting was suddenly introduced into Italy at one particular moment by one particular artist is a persistent fiction: experiments with many mixed media involving oil were certainly being carried out by various artists from the 1430s onwards. Nevertheless, Antonello seems to have learned his specifically Netherlandish technique with a thoroughness which suggests that he did indeed go to Flanders, possibly on one of the vessels going constantly back and forth from Naples.

Certainly his works are a superb combination of Northern oil technique, a Northern interest in light and in cast shadows, as well as in the meticulous portrayal of natural detail, and a totally Italian delight in volumetric simplification of form. The result is a uniquely compelling style and it is no surprise that, when he went north to Venice, such works as his monumental but now fragmentary S. Cassiano altarpiece (1475–76) and his remarkable portraits had a profound influence on Giovanni Bellini and on the whole course of Venetian art, as well as upon artists such as Piero della Francesca. JW

G. Vigni *Tutta la pittura di Antonello da Messina* (1952)

Antonino, S. (1389–1459) Antonio Pierozzi, born in Florence, entered the Dominican order at the age of 15. Adhering to the party of the Strict Observants within the order, he became Superior of the reformed Tuscan and Neapolitan congregations, prior of Fiesole (1425) and of San Marco in Florence (1439). A friend of Cosimo de' Medici and of Pope Eugenius IV, he was named Archbishop of Florence in 1446. For the age he showed an untypical attention to his pastoral duties which, combined with simplicity of life and care for the poor, brought him fame as a worker of miracles. Of limited culture, tending to regard all non-religious learning as 'idle curiosity', he wrote several works of a moralizing cast, among which a *Summa moralis* and a *Chronicle of universal history* are notable. He was canonized in 1523. JL

G. Calzolai *Fra Antonio, Arcivescovo di Firenze* (1961)

S. **Antonino**: posthumous portrait drawing by Fra Bartolommeo in the Museo S. Marco, Florence.

Appiano family The Appiano prospered in Pisa from the late 13c. to such good effect that by 1392 Jacopo had become signore of Pisa – a position his son could not sustain against Visconti ambitions to control the city and its port and hinterland. They then withdrew to one of the other zones of power they had acquired, the small but strategic port of Piombino, and thence governed a miniature empire which included the adjacent islands of Pianosa, Montecristo and, above all, Elba. Though occasionally ousted for short periods during the power struggles that convulsed Italy and the Tyrrenean Sea 1494–1559, the family showed remarkable resilience, continuing their rule and at least a quasi-independence from Tuscany until 1634. JRH

Aquileia Near the coast some 20 miles W of Trieste, Aquileia, whose patriarchs had played an important political as well as ecclesiastical role in NE Italy, had become by the 14c. a place of only token importance. Following the Venetian conquest of Friuli, the feudal rights granted to the patriarchs by successive Emperors were sharply curtailed in 1420. In 1451 Venice, which had always supported the far less powerful rival patriarchate at Grado, persuaded Pope Nicholas II to reconstitute this as the Patriarchate of Venice, thus leaving the patriarchs of Aquileia a status hardly higher than their title of bishops of Udine, whither they moved after the earthquake of 1438 which ruined a city already cut off by silt from access to the lagoon of Grado and dying economically. JRH

Aquinas, St Thomas (?1225–74) Dominican theologian and philosopher, whose system of thought, called 'Thomism', remained influential throughout the Renaissance. He was born of a baronial family in Campania, and taught at Paris and in Italy. His great works are the *Summa contra gentiles* (*A compendium to confute the pagans*) and the *Summa theologica*. He was outstanding among theologians of his age for his receptivity to profane philosophy, for his high valuation of reason and for his vindication of 'nature', being thereby one of the most liberal influences in medieval Latin Christian thought.

He was deeply indebted to Aristotle and to Latin neo-STOICISM. His metaphysical concepts were essentially Aristotelian, *vide* his concepts of 'form' and 'matter', corresponding respectively to essence and existence, and his teleology. He followed Aristotle in defining the rational soul as the 'form' of man although, as Pomponazzi was to assert in the 16c., his belief that the soul could survive separation from the body was probably incompatible with Aristotle's concept of entelechy (actualizing form). Following the Stoics he regarded 'nature' as normative, i.e. the good of a being was to follow its own nature.

In his theological system the sphere of nature was a substratum to the sphere of 'grace'. 'Grace', he asserted, 'does not annul nature but perfects it.' His theory of Natural Law (i.e. universal moral law knowable by reason) derived from Latin neo-Stoicism and Roman jurisprudence. His influence was mainly within the Dominican order up until the 16c., when the Jesuits as well officially adopted him as their master, but he was also much respected by certain eclectic philosophers of the Renaissance, including Marsilio Ficino and Giovanni Pico della Mirandola. *See* SCHOLASTICISM. OL

E. Gilson *Le Thomisme* (1944); G. di Napoli *Studi sul Rinascimento* (1973)

Aragonese house of Naples

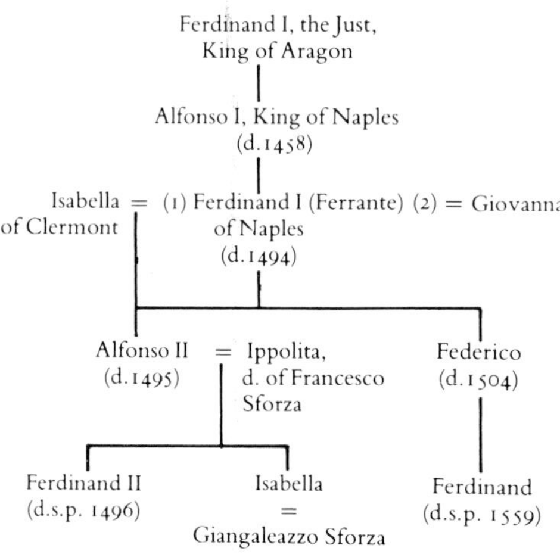

Aragon, house of Ruled over Aragon, Catalonia, Majorca, Sicily, Sardinia, Naples, Athens and other territories, tracing descent from Ramiro I of Aragon (1035–63), illegitimate son of Sancho III. The intervention of the house of Aragon in Italy resulted partly from the dynastic ambitions of the family but also from the commercial aspirations of Catalonia in the Mediterranean. Its involvement in Sicily dates from the Sicilian Vespers, when King Peter of Aragon was proclaimed King of Sicily by the rebels in 1282. He was succeeded by his younger son James. In 1296 the throne was usurped by James's brother Frederick, and the royal lines of Aragon and Sicily consequently diverged until 1380, when the heiress to the Sicilian throne, Maria, married the only child of Martin I of Aragon. Sicily was officially annexed to the crown of Aragon in 1409.

The connection with Naples began with the conquest of the kingdom by Alfonso V of Aragon in 1442. On Alfonso's death in 1458 his possessions were divided between his brother and his illegitimate son Ferdinand, who became King of Naples. In 1494 Ferdinand was succeeded by his son Alfonso II of Naples. Alfonso inherited little of the organizing ability or political genius of his antecedents and was widely hated by the Neapolitan barons. Confronted by the invasion of Charles VIII of France in 1495, he abdicated in favour of his son Ferdinand, and took refuge in Sicily. Although Ferdinand was defeated by the French, he was restored briefly to the throne after their departure. He died in 1496 and was succeeded by his uncle, Federico. Peace-loving but ineffectual, Federico proved unable to repel the joint Franco-Spanish invasion of his country in 1501 and fled to France. He was succeeded as King of Naples by Ferdinand of Aragon, who thus reunited Naples with the crown of Aragon. *See* NAPLES; WARS OF ITALY. JH

Arbedo, battle of (June 1422) Here, just N of Bellinzona, an army under the Milanese general the Count of CARMAGNOLA defeated an invading Swiss army so convincingly as to remove the Swiss threat to Milan's and Venice's northern frontiers for the rest of the century. Arbedo is chiefly remembered as showing that a mercenary force was capable of breaking a skilled and disciplined national one. JRH

Archimedes (*c.*287–212BC) Mathematician and mathematical physicist of Syracuse, whose feats of military engineering at the siege of Syracuse are described by Plutarch. One of the greatest mathematicians of all time, he made remarkable contributions to pure mathematics, and established a characteristic form of mathematical physics in his treatises on statics (the concept of centres of gravity), hydrostatics (*On floating bodies*) and the law of the lever. These profoundly influenced Renaissance physicists, who had previously known only the dynamic

Portrait from a late 15c. manuscript of **Archimedes** from the workshop of Jacomo da Fabriano (Rome, Vatican Library).

approach to mechanics expounded in the pseudo-Aristotelian *Mechanical problems*. His *Sand reckoner* (edited by Commandino), which deals with very large numbers, contains important information on Greek astronomy. He was long (rightly) regarded as epitomizing the Greek geometrical tradition with its elegance and rigour. MBH

Marshall Clagett in *Dictionary of scientific biography* (1970–80)

Arcimboldi, Giuseppe (1527–93) was a Milanese painter especially renowned for his fantastic heads, made up of flowers, vegetables, domestic objects and even landscapes. He became a Habsburg court painter in Prague (1562–87) and, under Rudolf II, a Count Palatine. His paintings anticipate present-day assemblages of *objets trouvés*. He was seen as a forerunner by modern Surrealists and does often achieve a thoroughly surreal effect. In his own day he fitted naturally into the stylistic world of Mannerist art which, with its emphasis on style and paradox, on wit and fantasy and illusion, was often at its most intense in the hothouse climate of court circles, large and small, all over Europe. JW

Aretino, Pietro (1492–1556) Perhaps the most vigorous and versatile vernacular writer of the 16c. Aretino rejected the family name of his wastrel cobbler father and preferred to be known as Pietro 'of Arezzo' (his birthplace). It is doubtful whether he received any formal education. However, thanks to contacts derived from an aristocratic 'protector' of his attractive bourgeoise mother, he was much in the company of cultivated men, especially during a formative period of his life spent in Perugia (before 1510–17). There he showed an interest in painting and wrote his first poems. In 1517 he was passed on to the Roman household of Agostino CHIGI, the wealthy banker and patron of artists (including Raphael), and thence moved into the outer circle of *letterati* surrounding Pope Leo X.

Here on the raffish fringe of an elegant society he developed a lively interest in political and clerical gossip, expressing this in pasquinades and lampoons that earned him the shrewd, if perhaps grudging, patronage of Cardinal Giulio de' Medici, especially when, after Leo's death in 1521, Giulio wished to see the reputation of his rivals for the succession blackened. When the conclave elected instead the puritanical Adrian VI, Aretino thought it wise to withdraw, attaching himself to new patrons, the Marquis Federico Gonzaga of Mantua and – the beginning of a true friendship between equally frank and impetuous temperaments – the condottiere Giovanni de' Medici 'dalle Bande Nere'. Returning to Rome when, on Adrian's early death in 1523, Giulio became pope as Clement VII, Aretino had to flee briefly in 1524 after publishing some sonnets to go with a series of banned engravings by Giulio Romano showing positions adopted in love-making; and once more, this time permanently, in 1525, when the chief target of his pen, Bishop Giovanni Giberti – a man Clement could not afford to offend publicly – nearly succeeded in having him assassinated. After a renewal of his contacts with Giovanni de' Medici and Federico Gonzaga, Aretino moved in 1527 to Venice, where he spent the rest of his life.

By then, aged 35, he had not only become a master of the pasquinade but had transformed the crude Prognostications and *Avisi*, or news broadsheets, of the day into satirical and alarmingly well-informed sources of political and personal comment. He had also widened his repertory to include circulated copies of the letters he wrote praising or scolding the great political figures, Italian and foreign, whose actions were of wide public interest. Alternately goaded and flattered, a number of those they were addressed to placated him with gifts. These remained the chief source of his income, at a time when publication was unlikely to provide even the most prolific author with a living.

It is on his letters, launched from the congenial security of Venice, which he collected and published at intervals (1537, 1542, 1544, 1550 and – emerging posthumously – 1557), that his reputation as a writer rests most firmly. Though he was explicit in his condemnation of linguistic pedantry, the vigour, colour and inventiveness of his prose is the result of great care, usually well concealed beneath a surface of apparent spontaneity. They reveal him as a nimble if shallow thinker, a writer capable of expressing a wide range of feeling, a gifted and – for the time – uniquely sympathetic appreciator of the works of his artist friends, among whom Titian was prominent. Thanks to his early correspondence, in 1532 he was given by Ariosto in the final revision of *Orlando furioso* the soubriquet that has stuck to him: the

Scourge of Princes. In further evidence of its success, in 1533 King Francis I sent him a placatory golden chain.

The running commentary on his times which made the basis of his career was, however, accompanied by more orthodox literary activity. In 1534 alone, for instance, he published the first part of his *Ragionamenti*, dialogues about brothel affairs that deliberately punctured the vogue for high-minded discussions on Platonic themes; the revised version of his defiantly anti-'erudite' comedy *La cortigiana* (first version 1525); and two effortlessly devotional works, one on the Passion, the other an extended paraphrase of the penitential psalms. Of his other works, those that have best stood the test of time are plays: *Il Marescalco* (1526–27, published 1533) and *La Talanta* (1542). Until the last decades Aretino's reputation, because of his unshifty interest in sex, was either academic or clandestine. While not yet the subject of a full reappraisal, he can at last be openly judged and enjoyed. JRH

Lettere (Books I and II), ed. F. Flora (1960); *Selected letters* tr. George Bull (1976); *Sei giornate* (the *Ragionamenti*) ed. G. Aquilecchia (1975); *The stablemaster* (*Il Marescalco*) tr. George Bull in B. Penman ed. *Five Italian Renaissance comedies* (1978); *DBI*

Argyropoulos, Janos (1415–87) Byzantine scholar who played a prominent part in the revived study of Greek philosophy in Italy. He came to the West temporarily at the time of the Council of Florence (1439), permanently (1456) soon after the fall of Constantinople. Until 1471 he held a chair at the university of Florence, where he lectured chiefly on Aristotle, basing his comments on the Greek text. He also introduced his listeners to the doctrines of Plato and earned both admiration and enmity by his contempt for the principally Latin scholarship of the older school of Florentine humanists. His influence, as a guide to the exciting world of Platonism, on the new generation of Lorenzo de' Medici, Ficino and Poliziano was therefore considerable. When he moved to Rome, where there were other Greeks and a less enthusiastic audience, he was unsuccessful. *See* PLATO AND NEO-PLATONISM. GH

G. Cammelli *I dotti Bizantini e le origini dell'humanesimo: II, Giovanni Argiropulo* (1941)

Ariosto, Lodovico (1474–1533) Ferrarese poet and dramatist. His masterpiece *Orlando*

ORLANDO FVRIOSO DI MESSER
LVDOVICO ARIOSTO ALLO ILLVSTRIS-
simo, e Reuerendissimo Cardinale donno Hippo-
lito da Este suo Signore.

IN QVESTO PRIMO CANTO SI COMPRENDE L'INGRATI-
tudine delle Donne, sotto la fuga d'Angelica, laquale essendo amata da quattro valorosissimi Ca-
ualieri, & ella niuno amandone, mossa solamente a beneficio di semedesima si
dimostra cortese a Sacripante. PER il souragiunger di Bradamante,
& poi di Rinaldo si conosce quanto gli amorosi piaceri
siano breui: & come le piu volte ci sono
tolti prima, che si gustino.

CANTO PRIMO.

Illustrated title page from an edition of **Ariosto**'s *Orlando furioso* published in 1542.

furioso (published in 3 versions, 1516, 1521 and 1532) continued Boiardo's *ottava rima* poem *Orlando innamorato*, using the 'matter of France', the medieval accumulation of legend around the figure of Charlemagne and his paladins, and some elements of the Arthurian 'matter of Britain' as foundation for a dynastic celebration of the Este family. He augmented the romance tradition with humanistic echoes of Virgil, Ovid and Horace, evocations of Petrarch, Boccaccio and Dante, and references to contemporary events: all unified by Ariosto's ironic narrative stance and stylistic control into a vision of the ideal, the irrational and the real in human life.

Forced to study law at the university of Ferrara and inheriting responsibility for his large family in 1500, Ariosto could not devote himself exclusively to literature. He entered Este service before 1501 and, although stimulated by the cultural ferment of the Ferrarese court and the visits of such mentors as Bembo, was kept busy on military and diplomatic missions, as retainer first to Cardinal Ippolito and later to his brother, Duke Alfonso I, both of whom are addressed in the *Furioso*. Ariosto's youthful Latin odes, elegies and epigrams testify to his study of Propertius, Catullus and Horace. In the *terza rima Satire* (1517–25) his themes offer a small panorama of court life, with calculated glimpses of his personal existence. A pioneer in Renaissance drama and in his last years director of Ferrarese court spectacles, Ariosto composed 2 prose comedies, *La cassaria* (1508) and *I suppositi* (1509), both later revised in verse, completed 2 other verse comedies, *Il negromante* and *La Lena*, in the 1520s, and left another to be finished by his heirs. Unpublished in his lifetime were the *Cinque canti* (1518–19 or 1521–28), probably intended as an addition to the first version of the *Furioso* in 40 cantos, and continuing the account of events leading to, but breaking off before, Orlando's death at Roncevaux through Gano's treachery. The disillusioned tone and stiffer style of the *Canti* were apparently recognized by Ariosto himself as unsuitable for mixing with the *Furioso*: he in fact lengthened it by 6 other cantos in its 'definitive' version of 1532. The language of the third version is significantly Tuscanized and stylistically smoothed, sacrificing some variety of tone while gaining in metrical regularity and rhetorical control, as well as in the integration of vastly diverse materials.

The *Furioso* is the funniest and saddest of poems, personal and detached, simple and artful. Into 2 major story lines inherited from Boiardo – Orlando's fall into unrequited pathological love for the irresistible Cathayan princess Angelica, with the subsequent loss and recovery of his reason, and the education and conversion to Christianity of the pagan prince Ruggiero, destined to wed the warrior maiden Bradamante and to found the Este line – Ariosto's technique of arbitrary suspense weaves a multitude of characters and motifs from medieval and classical sources, with historical addenda, apostrophes and continuous comment by an omnipotent, capricious and self-mocking narrative persona. Ariosto's own love (Alessandra Benucci, not called by name in the poem) is insistently blamed for the madness that the poet of the *Furioso* claims to share with his obsessed hero Orlando and with the greater portion of mankind.

An instant classic, despite Cardinal Ippolito's reported belittling of it, the *Furioso* became an issue in the late 16c. literary debate about the epic genre, and was pitted against Tasso's *Gerusalemme liberata* in a contest between the defenders of multiplicity and the exponents of classical unity. The idea of the *Furioso* as a poem detached from reality, perpetuated by Benedetto Croce's essay on its cosmic harmony, is challenged by modern critics who emphasize Ariosto's historical topicality and the seriousness of the themes and ethical concerns expressed in his well-modulated octaves. LGC

M. Catalano *Vita di Ludovico Ariosto* (2 vols 1930–31); C. Segre *Esperienze ariostesche* (1966); R. M. Durling *The figure of the poet in Renaissance epic* (1965)

Aristotle (384–322BC), born at Stageira in Thrace, was first a student of Plato (428–348BC). He founded the peripatetic school of science and philosophy which remained dominant in Western culture until the end of the 17c. His voluminous writings, which survive only in part, include the *Organon* (logic), the *Physics*, *On the soul*, *On the heavens*, *On animals*, the *Metaphysics*, the *Poetics*, *Rhetoric*, the *Politics*, and the *Nicomachean ethics*. He was as much a scientist as a philosopher, and some of his best works are in the field of detailed biological investigation. In contrast to Plato, he emphasized the role of experience and empirical investigation in knowledge, though abstract reasoning also had its place. He was the first to treat logic in a systematic and comprehensive way, formulating in his *Organon* (literally, 'tool') a method for clear thinking which could be applied to many fields of study. In moral philosophy, e.g. politics and ethics, he

Aristotle, from Raphael's fresco of *The School of Athens* (Rome, Vatican).

was equally original in providing useful guides for the practical aspects of life. The *Poetics*, which became the basis of Renaissance literary criticism, shows his sensitivity to man's aesthetic possibilities.

Peripatetic philosophy continued to be influential in antiquity down to 529, when the pagan schools of Athens were closed by Imperial decree. From there the main lines of the tradition passed through Christian Syrians and the Muslim culture finally to the Latin West. From the 12c. onward Aristotelian thought dominated western European intellectual life, playing a central role in the university arts curriculum, principally in the new translations of William of Moerbeke (*c.*1230–86). Renaissance Aristotelianism is complex and has frequently been misunderstood and undervalued. In general, it can be said to have followed 2 separate lines: the continuing tradition of university-based scholasticism, and the new direction of 'humanistic Aristotelianism'.

While to some extent modified by Italian humanism, scholastic Aristotelianism still dominated university education throughout the Renaissance in all parts of Europe as well as in the Spanish dependencies of the New World. In 15c. Italy, even while humanism was in full flower, traditional Aristotelian philosophy, influenced in no small measure by the 14c. developments in logic and natural philosophy especially coming from Paris and Oxford, was a fundamental component of university medical education. The writings of men such as Paul of Venice (*c.*1372–1429) and Gaetano of Thiene (d.1465) reflect such an interest and were themselves, in turn, influential.

In post-Reformation Europe the works of Aristotle still dominated advanced education in both Catholic and Protestant countries. In Italy, figures such as Pomponazzi, famous above all for *De immortalitate animae* (1516), which rekindled the controversy on man's nature, and Jacopo Zabarella (1533–89), perhaps the best logician of the period, showed the continuing vigour of the tradition. After the founding of the Society of Jesus, Aristotle was adopted as the major philosophical authority in Jesuit educational institutions, resulting in high-level works such as the commentaries produced at the university of Coimbra (1592–98). Protestant education, under the influence of figures such as Philip Melanchthon (1497–1560) and Johannes Sturm (1507–89), also accepted Aristotle as the major philosophical and scientific authority for a reformed educational system. In Germany, Holland and England many new philosophical textbooks, compiled on peripatetic principles, were used to instruct the young. Consequently, in spite of a vast polemical literature separating Protestant from Catholic on many issues, both camps agreed that Aristotle provided the best basis for a coherent philosophical and scientific education.

'Humanistic Aristotelianism' followed a parallel but different tradition during the 15c. and 16c., though it did interact with and influence the scholastic variety to some degree. The Italian humanists, beginning with Bruni, rejected many aspects of scholastic Aristotelianism as 'barbarous'. They retranslated many works in what they considered to be a more accurate and more elegant style, while also emphasizing the practical and useful nature of Aristotle's works on moral philosophy and playing down those on logic and natural philosophy. By about 1500 the new (and generally better) Latin translations of the humanists began partially replacing the medieval ones in many printed editions. Humanists were also involved with the publication of Aristotle in Greek. After the first edition at the hands of Aldus Manutius in Venice, many further Greek Aristotle texts issued from the presses of Italy, Switzerland, France and Germany. A limited range of works was also printed in vernacular versions, especially in French and Italian.

Aristotle without a doubt was the most widely read classical author of the Renaissance. From the beginning of printing until 1600 there were more than 1500 printed editions containing 1 or more works of Aristotle and an equal or greater number of interpretative works based on Aristotle. Not until about 1675 did he cease to be the major authority in university education. Though progressively rejected in physical science, Aristotle was still a major source of inspiration for William Harvey (1578–1657), and in fields as diverse as logic and literary theory his works remained standard until long after the Renaissance had passed. *See* AQUINAS; SCHOLASTICISM; CRITICAL THEORY OF LITERATURE. CS

P. O. Kristeller *Renaissance thought* (1961); C. B. Schmitt *A critical survey ... on Renaissance Aristotelianism* (1971); — 'Towards a reassessment of Renaissance Aristotelianism' *History of Science* (1973)

Arms and letters: portrait of Federico, Duke of Urbino, attributed to Justus of Ghent, showing him studying a manuscript while dressed in armour (Urbino, Palazzo Ducale).

Arms and letters The comparative worthiness of careers dedicated to war or to study and writing became a topic much debated from the 15c. It derived some pointedness from the split between the patrician republics, which paid others to fight, and the states where rulers and courtiers were themselves fighters. The ideal was a combination of the two: thus the condottiere Federico, Duke of Urbino, had a picture painted of himself in 1476 studying a manuscript while in armour. Would the glorious deeds achieved by Caesar's sword be remembered if he had not also wielded the pen? Discussion on the topic usually (as in Castiglione's *The courtier*) moved towards such an equilibrium, reflecting the groundswell of an educational theory that sought to produce cultivated warriors more than militant civilians. JRH

Arsenal This walled, state-controlled dock and ship construction zone in Venice was the largest single industrial plant in Europe, at times

A schematic drawing by Antonio di Natale of the Venetian **arsenal** in the 16c. (Venice, Museo Correr).

employing up to 4000 men. Famous for its assembly-line methods, it was also the site where the Republic's bronze artillery was cast, and it contained armouries capable (in theory, at least) of equipping 10,000 men. Its workers, the *Arsenalotti*, provided the doge's personal guard and acted as the city's fire-fighters. JRH

F. C. Lane *Navires et constructeurs à Venise pendant la Renaissance* (1965)

Artist, status of the Throughout the Renaissance the majority of artists were of fairly humble origin; among the exceptions were Brunelleschi (son of a notary), Alberti (a patrician), Leonardo (bastard son of a notary), Titian (the Vecellio were a family of some standing in the Veneto), and Michelangelo (whose father thought his choice of career a scandal to the Buonarroti's aristocratic pretensions). In a sample of 136 painters, sculptors and architects in the years 1420–1540, 96 were the sons of artisans or shopkeepers. They were also pegged low in the social structure by their compulsory membership of a trades guild, a requirement not waived until 1571, and then only in Florence. Yet from Dante's praise of Giotto (*Purgatorio* XI, 95) onwards individual artists could acquire widespread fame; from as early as the list of painters in Giovanni Villani's chronicle (*c.*1340) it was clear that societies felt a pride in their artists that was different in kind from their estimate of the skills of their smiths or carpenters.

Moreover, during the Quattrocento a number of factors combined to raise public interest in art and its practitioners: the humanistic rediscovery of Pliny's account of the respect accorded to artists in antiquity; the recognition (largely prompted by Alberti's treatises) that intelligence and a grasp of theoretical principles were as much a component of good art as craft training and manual competence; the emergence of the notion of individual genius, the artist's God-like ability to create as well as record, that led to Michelangelo's being dubbed 'divino'. In *The courtier* Castiglione produces a discussion of the comparative dignity of sculpture and painting as a subject of natural interest in aristocratic society, stresses his personal friendship with Raphael and recommends that his courtier should be able to draw (hitherto only musicianship had been thought suitable for the well-born), though only for the strictly utilitarian purpose of producing sketches useful in a military campaign.

A further stage was reached with Vasari, whose *Lives* (1550 and 1568) sedulously advertised the enhanced respect accorded to artists by great men: Francis I holding the dying Leonardo in his arms, Charles V lavishing honours on Titian. By then Titian had acquired his own propagandist in Pietro Aretino and art its first full-scale discussion in the *Aretino* of Lodovico Dolce (1557). In 1531 Bandinelli dubbed his modest art school an 'Academy'. Then followed the founding in Florence of Europe's first true ACADEMY of art (the Accademia del Disegno, 1563) and the Council of Trent's acknowledgment in its decree of the same year of the power of art to influence the mind.

The **artist** takes himself seriously: Baccio Bandinelli's engraving *The Painter's Studio* (London, Witt Print Collection, Courtauld Institute of Art).

For all this, the artist's social position remained equivocal, depending mainly, as in the past, on personality and success. He was still a craftsman, waiting upon orders, still (if to a lesser extent than heretofore) expected to turn his hand to whatever decorative objects his patron required. His chances of being accepted in the higher reaches of society were not so different from those of the actor or the cricketer or, indeed, the artist of today. JRH

P. Burke *Culture and society in Renaissance Italy 1420–1540* (1972); R. and M. Wittkower *Born under Saturn* ... (1963)

Asolo *See* CORNARO, CATERINA

Astrology, the art of predicting the influence of the stars on terrestrial events, played an important part in Renaissance thought and was a generally accepted branch of learning. The objections to it, of course, were religious – the limitation of free will – rather than scientific. The mystical tendencies of neo-Platonism rather encouraged it. Ficino was uneasily conscious of the need to guard against astrological determinism, but in fact attributed considerable potency to the stars and recommended to his readers, in his treatise *De vita coelitus comparanda* (*On the life to be obtained from the heavens*), that they should make use of astrology in planning their lives. His younger contemporary Giovanni Pico della Mirandola, however, wrote in the *Disputationes adversus astrologiam* (*Disputations against astrology*) a many-sided attack on astrology, denying both the possibility of making the precise time calculations needed by the science and the general influence of the stars on human destinies. Savonarola adopted Pico's views. The prevalence of astrological beliefs is shown by the hostile reception of Pico's book.

Interest in astrology was not only theoretical. Predictions were frequently offered to princes and popes and sometimes used by them. An astrologer wrote an *Anulus astronomicus* for Alexander VI, for example, and Leo X's physician also published on astrology. In the early 16c. the Paduan philosopher Agostino Nifo defended astrology and attributed the crimes of Cesare Borgia to celestial influences. One of the most influential astrological writers of the early 15c., Luca Gaurico, impressed Paul

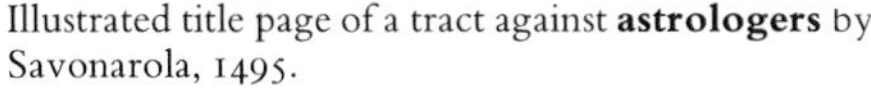
Illustrated title page of a tract against **astrologers** by Savonarola, 1495.

St **Augustine** by Botticelli (Florence, Ognissanti).

III by his predictions and became a bishop. During the later 16c., while popular belief remained equally strong, attempts were made to strengthen the scientific basis of astrology, but the main enemy was probably the hostile attitude of the reformed Papacy, especially in the bull of Sixtus V (1586), rather than scientific scepticism. GH

Lynn Thorndike *History of magic and experimental sciences* (8 vols 1923–58); D. C. Allen *The star-crossed Renaissance* (1941)

Attendolo, Micheletto (*c.*1390–1451) A member of a Romagnol family of professional soldiers. He served Naples and the Papacy, becoming the outstanding condottiere in the south, before entering the service of the Florentines, for whom he gained the Casentino region by the battle of ANGHIARI, and then the Venetians, who offered him the command previously held by Gattamelata. His victory over the Milanese, led by Piccinino, at Casalmaggiore in 1446 was rewarded by his being knighted and given a Venetian fief. He had previously been knighted by the Emperor Sigismund at the prompting of his then (1433) employer Pope Eugenius IV. JRH

Augustine, St (354–430) Latin Church Father. Born at Thagaste in Numidia, he taught rhetoric at Rome and Milan, was converted from Manichaeanism to Catholic Christianity and became bishop of Hippo (Bône) in Numidia. Himself educated in classical rhetoric and Platonist philosophy, he asserted the justification of 'despoiling the Egyptians', i.e. using the best elements of classical culture in the service of Christianity, a position that was taken up by Renaissance humanists.

Augustine's thought was constantly evolving and several distinct theological systems can be analyzed within it, hence the ambiguity of the word 'Augustinianism'. His suggestions regarding the soul's ascent through a hierarchy of contemplative levels and his concept of mental illumination were influential in the high Middle Ages and again in the 15c. and 16c., these being aspects of his thought that especially recommended him to Platonists, not least to Ficino. In a 16c. context, however, 'Augustinianism' most often refers to a range of theological positions on grace and justification. Augustine in his *Confessions* had explored the psychology of conversion and expressed the conviction that God had transformed his soul from a level of nullity to a state of true being. Further, in his relatively late anti-Pelagian writings, he had urged that man could never gain merit by his own unaided powers. The Augustinian theology of all-efficient divine grace inspired the Protestant theologians and many anxious searchers who remained within the Catholic Church. Augustine's psychology was also highly authoritative in the Renaissance; this, instead of positing a reason-passion dichotomy, centred on the concept of will. Connected with this psychology was Augustine's valorization of emotion. This latter was to be a significant influence in Counter-Reformation spirituality. *See* EVANGELISM. OL

P. O. Kristeller 'St Augustine and the early Renaissance' *Studies in Renaissance thought and letters* (1956, 1969); E. V. Teselle *Augustine the theologian* (1970)

Autobiography as a distinct literary genre was one of the more original products of the Renaissance; there had been relatively little of it in antiquity and even less in the Middle Ages. The *Confessions* of St Augustine provided the example of an inward autobiography – the story of the author's search for God – but no imitator was able to approach its level of introspection until Petrarch's *Letter to posterity* and *Secretum*. Dante's *Vita nuova* – and the *Comedy* – are intensely autobiographical but are not autobiographies.

The roots of the secular autobiography are to be found in the books of *ricordanze* (memoranda) kept by Italian professional and business men from the late 13c. From bare accounts of land purchases and marriage settlements, these personal notebooks could develop into family histories which might also contain soul-searching and self-examinations, like those of the early 15c. Florentine merchants Goro Dati and Giovanni Morelli, or the *Zibaldone quaresimale* of Giovanni Rucellai (1457–85). Records of business ventures and public offices were the starting point for autobiographies of external action: while the *Cronica* of Jacopo Salviati is a fairly wooden account of captaincies and embassies 1398–1411, that of Buonaccorso Pitti is a lively narrative of fortunes won and lost through trading and gambling (written 1412–22). The *Commentaries* of Enea Silvio Piccolomini (Pius II) similarly concentrate on events, leaving the character of the author to be deduced from his actions. The supreme example of the (apparently) unconsciously revealing autobiography is the famous *Life* of Cellini: of the deliberately revealing one, that of CARDANO. JKH

Il libro segreto di Goro Dati ed. C. Gargiolli (1869; repr. 1968); *Ricordi di Giovanni di Pagolo Morelli* ed. V. Branca (1969); *Zibaldone quaresimale di Giovanni Rucellai* ed. A. Perosa (1960); Jacopo Salviati *Cronica o memorie* ed. Ildefonso di S. Luigi *Delizie degli eruditi Toscani* XVIII; *Cronica di Buonaccorso Pitti*, ed. A. Bacchi della Lega (1905); *Two memoirs of Renaissance Florence* ed. G. Brucker (New York 1967) is a partial translation of Dati and Pitti.

Averroes The latinized version of the name of Ibn-Rushd (1126–98), an Arabic philosopher who wrote among other things a number of commentaries on the works of Aristotle. These were translated into Latin in the 13c. and widely used as keys to the understanding of Aristotle's thought; hence Averroes was commonly known as 'The Commentator'. His importance in Western thought sprang from the fact that he interpreted Aristotle at crucial points in a sense which was incompatible with Christian dogma: for example, in the question of the immortality of the soul. 'Averroism' therefore came to be connected with suspect philosophical tenets and in the late 13c. Aquinas reacted strongly against it, insisting on an interpretation of Aristotle which was acceptable to Christian theologians. Though nobody actually maintained a 'double truth' theory of the incompatibility of revelation with conclusions based on rational argument, Averroes was connected with heretical opinions.

Averroism in the sense in which Aquinas attacked it died out in northern Europe in the early 14c. But Averroes continued to be widely used, especially in Italian universities, notably Padua, down to the early 17c. A superb edition of Aristotle with his commentaries was printed in Venice in the 1550s. There was nothing that could be called an Averroist school, but Averroes did influence philosophers in the direction of accepting the existence of a consistent body of Aristotelian thought, or in favour of the idea of a universal intellect into which the rational faculties of individuals were absorbed after death. Averroes influenced the thought of such important Paduan philosophers as Agostino Nifo (1473–1538) and Zabarella. GH

E. Gilson *History of Christian philosophy in the*

Middle Ages (Eng. tr. 1955); Bruno Nardi *Saggi sull'aristotelismo padovano dal secolo XIV al XVI* (1958)

Avignon The decision to move the Papacy here was made in August 1308 by Pope Clement V, who had been residing in France since 1305. The actual move was made in 1309. Six pontificates later, in 1377, the Papacy was brought back to Rome by Gregory XI. All the popes elected at Avignon were French, as were 113 of the 134 cardinals appointed during this time. Yet though the period has been called one of 'captivity' to France, the Avignonese residence was not one of uninterrupted truckling to French kings. The city was not on French territory: it belonged to the Angevin princes of Naples. 'Captivity', like Petrarch's 'unholy Babylon', which he likened to the harlot of the Apocalypse 'full of abominations and the filth of her fornication', was mainly a term of abuse directed at a Papacy that had acquired security enough to revive its legal and financial pretensions and to build lavishly and live well. Between 1100 and 1309 the popes had only spent 82 years in Rome. Avignon gave them a long breathing space to assemble the machinery and the values which characterized the Renaissance Papacy after its final resettlement in Rome. JRH

G. Mollat *The popes at Avignon* (1963); B. Guillemain *La cour pontificale d'Avignon, 1309–1376* (1964)

Baglioni family The Baglioni were a magnate family prominent in the political life of Perugia from the 13c. With wealth derived from employment as condottieri they came from the 1420s to constitute the most powerful family in the commune. They are principally famed for their crimes: Braccio di Malatesta's murder of his cousin Pandolfo and nephew Niccolò (1460); massacres of the rival Oddi family (1482, 1484); the killing by lesser members of the family of Carlo, Filippo di Braccio, Guido, Rodolfo and Astorre (1500). For this reason, perhaps, Machiavelli was to lament the failure of Giampolo Baglioni to win eternal renown by murdering Pope Julius II on his entry into Perugia (1506). Malatesta IV commanded the army of the Florentine Republic and offered its surrender to the Medici in 1530. JL

B. Astur *I Baglioni* (1964)

Balance of power The notion that the aim of peaceful statecraft is, by means of shifting alliances, to keep opposing power blocks at roughly the same strength depends upon 3 factors: a clear geopolitical grasp of the problem; the existence of a threat identified as such by more than one state; and a system of information-gathering and diplomacy that can form, and evaluate the effectiveness of, alliances.

All these factors first came to be present in the small and fairly closed arena of Italian interstate politics in the course of the 15c., and it was at the beginning of the 16c., when the equilibrium that had been attained by the Peace of LODI in 1454 was smashed by foreign invasions, that the nostalgically used term 'balance' was launched on its long career. Bernardo Rucellai used it in his appraisal of Lorenzo the Magnificent in *De bello italico*, and it was given international currency in Guicciardini's *History of Italy* (pub. 1561), where he said of Lorenzo that 'he diligently sought to maintain the affairs of Italy in such a balance that they might not favour one side more than another.' In the rest of western Europe the phrase became applicable to the efforts expended to prevent either a Habsburg or a Valois hegemony from the 1520s. This is not to say that in earlier periods rulers had not acted instinctively in ways which anticipated the workings of 'balance of power' politics. JRH

See DIPLOMACY.

E. W. Nelson 'The origins of modern balance-of-power diplomacy' *Medievalia et Humanistica* (1942); E. Pontieri *L'età dell'equilibrio politico in Italia* (Naples n.d.).

Bandello, Matteo (1485–1561), writer of novellas, Dominican friar, secretary in great houses of his native Lombardy, became bishop of Agen in France from 1550. Rich experience, travel, and Terentian kinship with everything human make his 214 *Novelle* (1554, 1573) a useful social document. Whatever the source or mode, Bandello was not inclined to idealize or edify (his Lucretia confesses to pleasure in spite of herself during Tarquin's rape), although he sometimes takes a sombre moral tone. Lacking Boccaccio's art and vision, Bandello aimed to report facts accurately, observe nature, atmospheres and settings closely, comprehend motives and feelings justly. His tales, especially the more sensational ones, were used by dramatists like Della Porta, Groto, Shakespeare, and Massinger, who drew upon them either directly or in translations by Belleforest, Painter, or Fenton. LGC

Tutte le opere ed. F. Flora (1934–45)

Bandinelli, Baccio (1488–1560) Florentine sculptor. Trained under his father, a Medicean goldsmith, and later under Rustici, he was deeply influenced by, and spent his career vainly attempting to emulate, Michelangelo (e.g. *Hercules and Cacus,* 1534; Florence, Piazza della Signoria). His family connections brought a stream of commissions from Medici cardinals, popes and dukes. Bandinelli excelled in carving variations on classical statues, either in the round (e.g. *Orpheus and Cerebus,* 1519 (Florence, Medici Palace); *Laocoön,* 1525 (Florence, Uffizi)) or when working in low relief (e.g. the *Prophets* in the choir of Florence cathedral, *c.*1555). He was court sculptor to Cosimo I, and unchallenged until the return from France in 1545 of Cellini, when they became fierce rivals. Bandinelli also produced drawings, engravings and paintings, as well as bronze sculpture. [38] CA

C. Avery *Florentine Renaissance sculpture* (1970); J. Pope-Hennessy *Italian High Renaissance and Baroque sculpture* (1970)

Banking From the 14c. to the early 16c. Italian, above all Florentine, bankers were the busiest and richest in Europe: making loans, collecting money due to others (e.g. the Papacy), cashing or underwriting bills of exchange, changing currencies, arranging insurance. In addition most diversified the use of their capital, buying wool or silk manufactories and engaging directly in commerce with the help of their branch offices. Of the great banks of the early 14c., Frescobaldi, Peruzzi, Acciaiuoli, Bardi, the last had branches in Ancona, Aquila, Bari, Barletta, Genoa, Naples, Orvieto, Palermo, Pisa and Venice and, abroad, in Seville, Majorca, Barcelona, Marseilles, Nice, Avignon, Paris, London, Bruges, Rhodes, Cyprus, Constantinople and Jerusalem.

Though the over-extension of credit to rulers (especially Edward III of England) brought the Bardi and Peruzzi to bankruptcy in the 1340s, others survived and Florentine supremacy in banking was confirmed by the rise of the Medici bank which, established in 1397, at the mid-15c. had branches in Milan, Pisa, Venice and Rome, abroad in Geneva, Bruges, London, Avignon. From the early 16c. Italian banks, already hit by a decline in the demand for their services, ceased to be prominent abroad save in the case of Genoa, where bankers like the Pallavicini, Spinola and Sauli became richer than ever through the increasing dependence on them of the Spanish economy, strained by the challenge of dealing with trade to, and income from the gold and silver of, the New World. In Europe leadership passed to the great German banks: Fugger, Welser, Höchstetter.

All these banks were known as *banchi grossi*, 'great banks'. They did not serve the mass of the community: that was the province of the pawnbrokers and their socially superior relatives the *banchi a minuto*, small banks which changed money and advanced loans against pledges, usually jewels. The great banks also engaged in these last functions, adding to them dealing on an international scale, especially in bills of exchange which merchants or other travellers, or the paymasters of troops, could cash in the knowledge that the firm's capital base was adequate. Profit came chiefly from the turnover of day-to-day transactions. Large loans to princes came to be avoided after the 1440s, unless they were essential to obtain trading or even residence privileges.

Another precaution, dating from the same period, was to add, to the existing practice of keeping a company in being through steadily renewed short-term contracts between the partners, the system of distinguishing legally between branches through having them set up as individual corporations linked to the parent company only by the head of the firm's signature and capital investment. The Medici branch at Bruges could not, thus, be sued to make good any default by the London branch. These individual (and still temporary, commonly for 3 or 4 years) contracts also recognized that the slowness of communications made it essential for a branch manager to be encouraged to make decisions on his own. This system of semi-independent branches, each linked separately to a parent company (which resembled the modern holding company), required both steady surveillance and the employment of trusted men. Lorenzo the

Woodcut showing the interior of a **bank**, from a commercial treatise by Giorgio Chiarini, Florence 1490.

Magnificent's comparative indifference to both was a major influence in the decline of the Medici bank.

Bankers got round the Church's condemnation of usury (interest charges on loans) by disguising loans as temporary gifts (repayable with a voluntary thank-you present) or disguising them among what looked like exchange transactions: to cash a bill in a foreign currency or from a foreign source legitimated a charge to cover risk; bankers' account books (using double entry increasingly from 1340), instead of the heading 'interest', had 'profit and loss on exchange'. Respectability was bought at the cost of time-consuming ingenuity. *See* BUSINESS METHODS. JRH

A. Sapori *La crisi delle compagnie mercantili dei Bardi e dei Peruzzi* (1926); Y. Renouard *Les hommes d'affaires italiens du moyen age* (1949); R. de Roover *The rise and decline of the Medici bank* (1963); C. Bec *Les marchands écrivains. Affaires et humanisme à Florence 1375–1434* (1967)

Barbarigo family The Barbarigo are chiefly famous among Venetian patrician families for providing two successive doges: Marco (Doge 1485–86) and Agostino (Doge 1486–1501). The survival of the account books of a member of a secondary branch of the family, Andrea (1399–1449), gives an understanding of the government-sponsored trading and business life of the Venetian patriciate as a whole. JRH

F. C. Lane *Andrea Barbarigo, merchant of Venice* (1944)

Barbaro, Daniele (1513–70) Polymath and generous patron of the arts. He came of a Venetian noble family with large landed properties in the Trevigiano. Up to the mid-1540s his milieu was Padua, where he pursued philosophy, mathematics, science and *belles-lettres*. His first public office in 1545 was as superintendent of the Orto dei Semplici or botanical garden in Padua, probably the finest of its age, of which he was also the founder. He was ambassador to England 1548–50 and in 1550 became Patriarch Elect of Aquileia; he never exercised pastoral functions but he did attend the Council of Trent. He and his brother Marcantonio commissioned the Villa Barbaro at Maser, designed by Palladio; the iconography of the great mural cycle by Veronese represents Daniele's intellectual interests. His major works were an edition of Vitruvius's *De architectura* in translation (1556), with highly philosophical commentaries, and the *Pratica della prospettiva* (1569), significant for its description of the camera obscura. OL

DBI; O.M.T. Logan *Culture and society in Venice 1470–1790* (1972)

Barbaro, Ermolao, the Younger (1453–93) Almoro di Zaccaria was a major pioneer of *cultura filosofica*, i.e. the application of humanist philological techniques to the study of ancient philosophical texts. A Venetian noble, he passed his life between teaching and state office. In 1491, while ambassador in Rome, he was nominated Patriarch of Aquileia by Innocent VIII, but the Venetian government would not permit him to accept and he died in exile. He was a man of encyclopaedic interests, scientifically erudite, a practising botanist and aesthetically sensitive. As an Aristotelian scholar he sought to explain the philosopher's meaning in terms of the vocabulary available to him, and emphasized the need to study the Aristotelian corpus as a whole, not merely the portions taught in university faculties. His most ambitious work was *Castigationes Pliniae* (*Emendations of Pliny*; 1492), where he elucidated many previously obscure passages of the *Natural history* with the aid of his deep knowledge of Greek and Latin etymology. OL

V. Branca 'Ermolao Barbaro and late Quattrocento Venetian humanism' in J. R. Hale ed. *Renaissance Venice* (1973)

Barbarossa (*c.*1465–1546) So called by the Spaniards and Italians on whose shipping he

Barbarossa in an imaginative engraving of 1577 by T. Mueller.

preyed as a corsair in peace and an admiral in war, Khair ed-Din was the outstanding Turkish naval commander of the 1530s and 40s. Having begun, along with his brothers, in piracy as a private business in the eastern Mediterranean, he was led, as its scope and success expanded, to establish bases further west on the Tunisian and Algerian coasts.

His relations with the local rulers became close and Barbarossa thus acquired a political importance at a time when Constantinople was seeking to extend its influence in North Africa. To harness his knowledge, contacts and skill to this endeavour the Sultan Selim encouraged him, and in 1533 Selim's successor Suleiman formally appointed Barbarossa admiral of the fleet. In this capacity he was the chief antagonist by sea of Charles V and Venice, feared equally for his prowess as a naval tactician and for the havoc he caused as he raided, burned and slaughtered his way from one strategic rendezvous to another. JRH

Bardi family The firm run by this Florentine family is a notable example of the hazards attending the great fortunes that could be built up through international trade and banking in the late 13c. and early 14c. Working through branches in Italy, England, France and Flanders, by 1310 the Bardi had become the wealthiest family in Florence. Much of their capital, however, was deployed in loans to rulers extended in exchange for monopolistic export licences for commodities varying from dairy products (Naples) to wool (England). In spite of large landholdings their fortunes were overdependent on those of their chief debtors and the bankruptcy of Edward III of England was followed by their own in 1345–46. *See* BANKING. JRH

A. Sapori *La crisi delle compagnie mercantili dei Bardi e dei Peruzzi* (1926)

Barocci, Federico (*c.*1535–1612) linked Correggio's art to that of the 17c. Born in Urbino and educated in the Mannerist tradition, he studied and worked in Rome (e.g. Casino of Pius IV, 1560–63) before an allegation of poisoning laid against him interrupted his career. Beginning about 1567 with works like the *Madonna of St Simon* (Urbino, Gallery), Barocci developed a Correggesque fusion of Venetian and Mannerist principles in a series of monumental altarpieces, culminating with the *Martyrdom of S. Vitalis* (1580–83; Milan, Brera). In later work, Barocci's formal complexity is sometimes moderated (see the *Calling of St Andrew*, Brussels, Musée des Beaux-Arts), but his emotional intensity remains unabated. Wide dispersal of his works spread Barocci's influence outside his native Marche, especially into Tuscany. LP

H. Olsen *Federico Barocci* (1966); A. Emiliani ed. *Mostra di Federico Barocci* (1975)

Bartolommeo, Fra (active *c.*1484–1517) Fra Bartolommeo della Porta was in the Florentine convent of S. Marco in 1498 when it was stormed and Savonarola was captured. He became a monk in 1500, a year after painting the now ruined *Last Judgment* (Museo di S. Marco) which profoundly influenced Raphael's *Disputa* (Rome, Vatican). His soft, broad, deeply folded drapery style and balanced compositions, his clarity of pose, gesture, and expression, reduction of detail, and concentration on ideal forms convincingly presented, together with his knowledge of Venetian (1508) and of Roman art (1514–15), give him a pivotal position in the formation of the Florentine High Renaissance style. [31] JW

Bartolus of Sassoferrato (1314–57), commonly regarded as the greatest Italian civil lawyer of the 14c. for his commentaries on the texts of Roman law, which he taught at Perugia, also wrote important works of political thought. In *De regimine civitatum* (*On the government of cities*) he discussed political authority and the types of constitution. Though he favoured monarchy as an ideal, he was an early advocate of the suitability of the republican commune for Italian cities and in *De tyrannis* (*On tyrants*) he allowed that they might be deposed. GH

C. N. S. Woolf *Bartolus of Sassoferrato* (1913)

Bassano, Jacopo da Ponte (*c.*1510–92) The leading artist of a family of painters working principally in Bassano in the Veneto. Jacopo's style developed in a surprising manner, his earlier paintings including masterpieces that show a deep awareness of Roman and central Italian art (*The Procession to Calvary*, Bradford Collection), while the later paintings are more distinctly Venetian, though with a regional emphasis on rustic genre. Assisted by his sons, of whom the eldest, Francesco, was the most talented, Jacopo Bassano created an industry in the production of night scenes of religious subjects in which a stress on genre details predominates. AB

C. Arslan *I Bassano* (1960)

Beccadelli, Antonio (1394–1471) Born at Palermo (whence his 'literary' name, Il Panormita, from the Latin for Palermo, 'Panormus'), Beccadelli was in a number of north Italian university cities 1420–34, combining study of the law with an avid reading of classical poetry. The latter is reflected in the Latin poem that in 1425 made him both famous and notorious at a blow: his sexually explicit and morally equivocal *Hermaphroditus*. All the more scandalous for the pioneering nonchalance with which it clothed brothel activities in classical elegancies previously reserved for more respectable themes, its skill, and his maturing scholarship, brought him security as court poet and teacher at Pavia before he returned to Naples, where he spent the rest of his life as a respected civil servant of the Aragonese monarchs Alfonso the Magnanimous and Ferrante. JRH

Hermaphroditus ed. F. Wolf Unterreichen (1908); It. tr. P. Massimo (1922)

Beccafumi, Domenico (*c.*1486–1551) practised during the early 16c. an archaizing style characteristic of late Quattrocento Siena, yet slightly inflected by Florentine models, as in the *Trinity and Saints* (Siena, Pinacoteca). After 1520, a re-exposure to Roman classicism produced a rapid evolution in Beccafumi's style, culminating in a developed Mannerism strongly tied to central Italian tradition, as in the *Nativity* (Siena, S. Martino). During the 1530s, this complex style became more disciplined, e.g. *Christ in Limbo* (Siena, Pinacoteca), then somewhat looser, finally relaxing into a restrained, inward mode. LP

G. Briganti and E. Baccheschi *L'opera completa del Beccafumi* (1977)

Bellarmine, Cardinal Robert (Roberto Bellarmino) (1542–1621) Jesuit controversialist and political theorist. Born in Montepulciano, a nephew of Pope Marcellus II through his mother, he was one of a group of Jesuit political thinkers who based themselves on St Thomas AQUINAS and were particularly noted for their doctrines of popular institution of government and of indirect papal power. In *De potestate summi pontificis* (*The power of the Pope*; 1586) he asserted that, while rulers were essentially autonomous in their own sphere, the Pope had the right to intervene and to depose them when they manifestly abused their trust. This traditional and moderate approach got him into trouble in Rome in 1590. In the propaganda war between the Papacy and Venice of 1606–07, in which he was the leading papalist pamphleteer, his position was that, although God had established secular power as such, it was the people who decided who should exercise it. OL

J. Brodrick *The life and work of Blessed Robert Cardinal Bellarmine S.J. 1542–1621* (2 vols 1928)

Bellini, Gentile (active *c.*1460, d.1507), brother of Giovanni, was ennobled by the Emperor in 1469 and in 1479–81 was in Constantinople, where he painted Sultan Mahomet II (London, National Gallery). Major histories painted for the Doges' Palace are lost and his fame now rests on his large paintings of Venetian ceremonial occasions, such as the *Procession of the Relic of the True Cross* (1496; Venice, Accademia) with its meticulous view of the Piazza S. Marco and portrait record of Venetian personalities

Gentile Bellini, detail from the *Procession of the Relic of the True Cross* (Venice, Accademia).

and costumes. He, with Carpaccio, is the Venetian counterpart of Ghirlandaio in Florence. [50] JW

Bellini, Giovanni (active *c.*1460, d.1516) changed the course of Venetian painting and laid the foundations for a revolution in the history of European art. He did this not only through his own work and his overwhelming effect on contemporaries such as Cima, Marco Basaiti, Bartolomeo Montagna and Vincenzo Catena, but above all through his formative influence on his pupils Palma Vecchio, Giorgione – whose brief career was over 6 years before Bellini's own death – and finally Titian. His working life begins in the early 1460s in an artistic world dominated by the linear description and sculptural definition of form characteristic of Donatello and of Giovanni's brother-in-law Mantegna. When Titian died some 110 years later (1576), the single most important step in the transition to the modern world in the history of Western art had been taken. The individual coloured mark, the brush stroke in its full physical embodiment, had taken on a clearly identifiable, independent existence and compositional meaning over and above its representational function.

Bellini's debt to Mantegna and the direction of his future travel are most easily seen by comparing their two versions of the *Agony in the Garden* (London, National Gallery). Although it is no longer at its peak, the Mantegnesque influence is still clear in the foreground figures, but the sense of unifying light and atmosphere is wholly new. The subsequent stages of Bellini's development are punctuated by a series of major altarpieces, the Pesaro (early 1470s), the Frari (1488), the S. Giobbe, the S. Zaccaria (1505) and the *St Jerome* (1513; Venice, S. Giovanni Crisostomo). In them he explores Antonellesque volumes and painterly techniques, moves on to include the spectator in the pictorial world and finally produces his own rich, colouristic version of Leonardo's largely monochrome sfumato. In his S. Zaccaria altarpiece even the foreground figures are dissolved in atmosphere. His late works spread the forms, defined in terms of light and colour of unprecedented richness, over the whole pictorial surface. They provide the starting point for Giorgione and Titian and reflect his own personal response to the challenge of these two young geniuses of Italian High Renaissance art.

Having revolutionized almost every aspect of devotional painting from the grandest altarpiece to the smallest and most personal private panel; having absorbed the lessons of the Netherlandish school and taken the Italian bust and half-length portrait to new heights of sensitivity; having poured out paintings decade after decade in an unending torrent, he was still

Giovanni Bellini, *Lady at her Toilet* (Vienna, Kunsthistorisches Museum).

producing masterpieces in his 80s and still innovating in technique, in composition, and in iconography. *The Drunkenness of Noah*, the *Feast of the Gods* (1514), completed and transformed by Titian, and the *Lady at her Toilet* (1515; Vienna) are among the works produced a decade after Dürer had, in 1506, remarked that he was 'very old, but still the best in painting'. It is no surprise that when he died he was still chief painter to the state of Venice. [191] JW

G. Robertson *Giovanni Bellini* (1969)

Bellini, Jacopo (active *c.*1424, d.1470/1) is notable as the father of Gentile and Giovanni and father-in-law of Mantegna and, artistically, as the author of a silverpoint sketchbook divided between the British Museum and the Louvre. Exquisite in its own right and remarkable for the compositional range of its designs, it is the source for many ideas reflected in the work of his sons and son-in-law. JW

Portrait medal of Pietro **Bembo**, *c.*1540 (London, Victoria and Albert Museum).

Bembo, Pietro (1470–1547), poet, literary theorist and cardinal, won lasting recognition for his enunciation of the principle of imitation, that is, of classical, especially Ciceronian, models, and for his championing of Trecento Tuscan as the basis of the literary vernacular debated in the '*questione della lingua*'. Proposing, in *De imitatione* (1512), Boccaccio as a guide for prose and Petrarch for verse, Bembo adds that, in the case of the latter, imitation of the man as well as of his art is necessary to restore poetry to classical excellence, as Petrarch himself had done.

Son of a noble Venetian envoy to various courts, Bembo received a thoroughly humanistic and cosmopolitan education and grew up unencumbered by linguistic chauvinism. At 20 he wrote fluent Latin, used correct Florentine and would soon acquire some Greek in Messina. The *Asolani* (1505), Bembo's dialogue on the nature of love, set within a narrative and containing many lyrics, reflects his imitation of Petrarch, his neo-Platonic love for Maria Savorgnan and a similarly conventional passion for Lucrezia Borgia, to whom the work is dedicated, although most of it had been written before he met her at the Este court (1502–03). The equipoise of *gravità* (serious decorum) and *piacevolezza* (pleasing gracefulness) in this work and in his *Rime* (both circulated long before their publication in 1530) brought Bembo an invitation to the Montefeltro court in Urbino. There he began the *Prose della volgar lingua* (1525), which gives the fullest formal expression to his linguistic doctrines.

Great personal distinction accounts in part for his influence on the development of Italian literature in his century. Bembo was an ideal courtly poet-savant, if there is any truth in Castiglione's portrait of him in Book IV of *The courtier*. He became cardinal in 1539. Like his great predecessor himself, Bembo has been a victim of 'Petrarchism'. In contrast with his usual vein, the *Stanze* written at Urbino in 1507 at carnival time are melodiously instinct with that form of love usually classified as inferior in his dialogues. He loved some women other than *de more platonico*: one of them bore him 3 children. *See* ITALIAN LANGUAGE. LGC

Prose e rime ed. C. Dionisotti (1960); G. Santangelo *Il Bembo critico e il principio d'imitazione* (1950)

Benedetto da Maiano (1442–97) Florentine sculptor. He trained as a woodcarver, like his brother Giuliano, and matriculated in the Florentine sculptors' guild in 1473. He was associated with Antonio Rossellino and continued his tradition of fine marble carving for chapels, tombs, pulpits and portrait busts. Narrative reliefs were Benedetto's forte (e.g. those on the pulpit of S. Croce, Florence) and he produced many charming compositions of the Virgin and Child. He influenced High

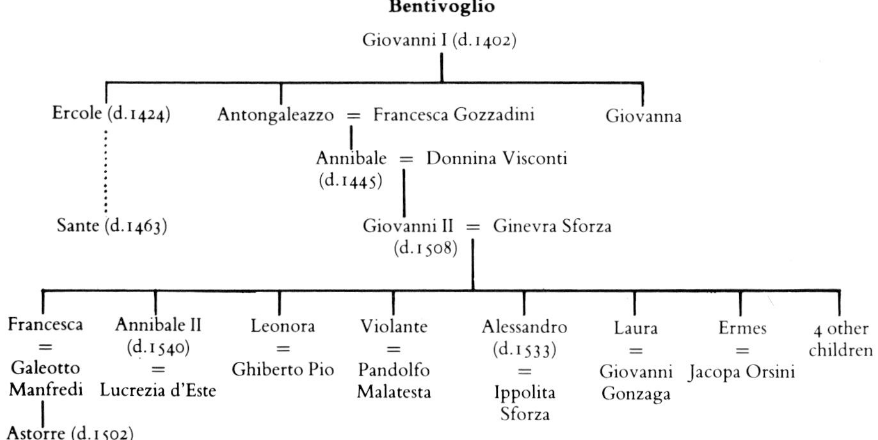

Renaissance marble sculptors such as Andrea Sansovino and Michelangelo. CA

C. Avery *Florentine Renaissance sculpture* (1970); J. Pope-Hennessy *Italian Renaissance sculpture* (1971)

Benedict XIII anti-Pope (d.1423) Pedro de Luna, a Spanish jurist, was elected pope by the Avignon cardinals (1394) on the understanding that he would end the SCHISM by resigning his office in conjunction with the Roman pope. 'This,' he declared before election, 'would be as easy as taking off my hat.' In the event it proved more difficult. Declared a heretic by the Council of Constance (1417), he ended his days at Peñiscola, in Aragon, daily excommunicating the princes of Europe who had deserted his cause. JL

Benivieni, Girolamo (1453–1542) A native of Florence and a member of the circle of writers who enjoyed the patronage of Lorenzo de' Medici, he composed a quantity of lyric, narrative and theoretical verse. A *canzone* of his, *De lo amore celeste*, in which he sought to embody Ficino's interpretation of Platonic love, achieved a fame somewhat disproportionate to its value by virtue of the attention it received in a commentary by Giovanni Pico della Mirandola. Benivieni rejected such attitudes when in later life he became a devotee of Savonarola. JM

Opere (1522); G. Pico della Mirandola *A platonick discourse upon love*, tr. Thomas Stanley (1914); C. Re *Girolamo Benivieni fiorentino* (1906)

Bentivoglio family The foundations of their power in Bologna were established by Giovanni I who, amid the faction-conflicts of the commune, declared himself signore in March 1401 – but was murdered by the city mob 15 months later. His son, Anton Galeazzo, a lecturer in law, made a brief *coup d'état* (1420), was rapidly dispossessed, became a condottiere, and was killed by papal officials. Annibale, his putative son (his mother was said to be uncertain of the boy's paternity and the matter was decided by dice), was pre-eminent in Bologna's revolt against the Papacy in 1438, but was assassinated in 1445. His place as party leader was taken by Sante, an apprentice of the wool guild of Florence and putative bastard of the family (though again whether in reality a Bentivoglio is uncertain). Sponsored by Cosimo de' Medici, Sante dominated the government of Bologna to his death (1463). He was succeeded by Annibale's son Giovanni II, who controlled the commune for the following 43 years. With no formal position as signore, but holding power as 'first citizen', Giovanni resisted the designs of Cesare Borgia but fled before the attack of Julius II (1506) and died in exile. His son, Annibale II, made a brief return to Bologna in the rebellion against Julius (1511–12). JL

Cecilia M. Ady *The Bentivoglio of Bologna* (1937)

Beolco, Angelo (*c*.1496–1542) Paduan actor and dramatist. The illegitimate son of a peasant girl and a well-to-do landowner, Beolco divided his time between managing family property and organizing theatrical entertainments in the Veneto, especially for the intellectual circle of his patron Alvise Cornaro. He invented and played the role of Ruzante, who is both a butt of satire and an embodiment of the peasant and of his condition in a time of war and social collapse. He and other dialect-speaking characters figure in works ranging from dialogues (*Parlamento de Ruzante*) to 5-act comedies drawing on *commedia erudita* (*La vaccària: The comedy of the cows*) or foreshadowing the *commedia dell'arte* (*L'anconitana: The woman from Ancona*). LGC

N. Dersofi *Arcadia and the stage: an introduction to the dramatic art of Angelo Beolco called Ruzante* (1978)

Berengario da Carpi, Jacopo (*c.*1460–?1530), anatomist, received his doctorate at Bologna in 1489, practised successfully as physician and surgeon in that city, and was appointed lecturer in surgery in 1502. His books deal with surgery (for which he was well known) and anatomy (upon which he lectured). His *Isagogae breves* (Bologna 1522) is an early example of Italian independence and practical experience in anatomy, and contains realistic though crude illustrations. MBH

A short introduction to anatomy tr. L. R. Lind (1959)

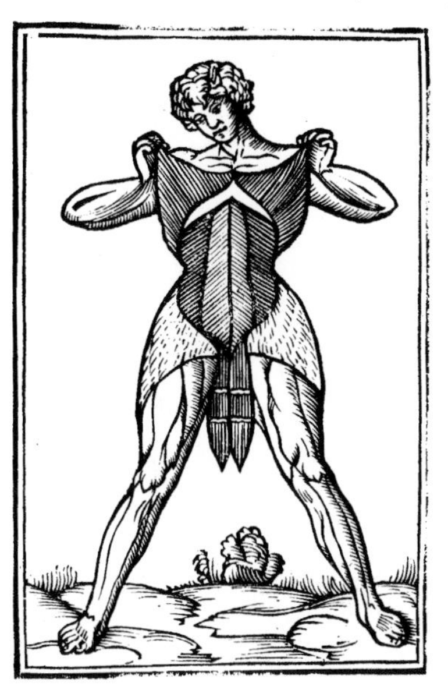

Anatomical illustration from **Berengario da Carpi**'s *Isagogae breves*.

Bernardino, S., of Siena (1380–1444) Bernardino degli Albizzeschi joined the Franciscan order in 1402, and from 1417 emerged as the greatest preacher of his day. His surviving sermons display a remarkable vivacity, gaiety, and colloquial rhetorical force. Their principal themes were the condition of the poor ('the purple shade of the blood of the poor'), the sanctity of poverty, the reconciliation of factions, devotion to 'the Holy Name of Jesus', and the supposed wickedness of the Jews. In 1438 he was elected Vicar General of the (new and reformed) Observant branch of the Franciscan order and was the most influential figure in the remarkable growth of 'the Observance' in 15c. Italy. He was canonized in 1450. JL

I. Origo *The world of San Bernardino* (1963)

A standardized portrait of S. **Bernardino** of Siena by Sano di Pietro, in Siena cathedral.

Berni, Francesco (?1497–1535) Florentine canon, whose type of lyric burlesque bears his name ('*bernesco*'). He 'lived cheerfully' in the service of church notables until he was poisoned by one for refusing a request to poison another, a fate symbolic of the corruption he portrayed.

In his satire, whether literary or popular in theme, purity and elegance of style contrast with artful nonchalance and seeming spontaneity. His tailed sonnets, *capitoli* (humorous poems) in *terza rima*, and letters treat both universal and occasional topics: eels, needles (with obscene double meanings), the Mugello flood, Pietro Aretino, etc. Berni is known also for a Tuscan rewriting of *Orlando innamorato*, today discarded in favour of Boiardo's own 'Ferrarese' verse. LGC
A. Momigliano *Il Berni e i berneschi* (1945)

Berruguete, Pedro (d.1503) was a Spanish painter of broadly Italo-Flemish stylistic affinity, who first appeared in Spain working at Toledo cathedral (1483–1500). Prior to this, he seems to have worked in Italy: stylistic and indirect documentary evidence connects him to the decoration, under Federico da Montefeltro, of the Ducal Palace at Urbino. Berruguete worked also at Ávila, at the cathedral and S. Tomás, and seems to have been associated with the court of Ferdinand and Isabella. LP
R. Láinez Alcalá *Pedro Berruguete* (1943)

Bertoldo di Giovanni (*c.*1420–91), Florentine bronze sculptor, is documented as having helped Donatello to work up the bronze narrative reliefs for the pulpits in S. Lorenzo (*c.*1460–70). His career is linked with the Medici family, of which he may perhaps have been a member. He produced statuettes (e.g. *Bellerophon and Pegasus*, Vienna, Kunsthistorisches Museum; *Orpheus*, Florence, Bargello), reliefs (e.g. the *Battle of Horsemen*, Florence, Bargello, once over a mantlepiece in the Medici Palace), plaquettes and medals (e.g. the *Pazzi Conspiracy* of 1478, recording the assassination of Giuliano and survival of Lorenzo de' Medici). He was in charge of Lorenzo's collections of sculpture and thus played a role in training the young artists recruited to study there, e.g. Michelangelo, Andrea Sansovino, Torrigiano. CA
C. Avery *Florentine Renaissance sculpture* (1970); J. Pope-Hennessy *Italian Renaissance sculpture* (1971)

Bessarion, Cardinal (?1403–72) was a learned churchman, humanist, and collector of manuscripts. Born in Trebizond (Greece), he went to the Council of Ferrara and Florence (1438–39) to promote union between Eastern and Western churches. Named cardinal in 1439,

Bertoldo di Giovanni's bronze of *Bellerophon and Pegasus* (Vienna, Kunsthistorisches Museum).

Cardinal **Bessarion** praying before a reliquary: painting by Gentile Bellini on the door of a tabernacle (Vienna, Kunsthistorisches Museum).

Bessarion then lived in Italy, serving the Papacy in numerous diplomatic and administrative charges. He was also patron and friend to most of the major Italian and Greek *émigré* humanists of his time. His own writings were works of Platonic philosophy and translations from Greek into Latin. Bessarion bequeathed his collection of Greek manuscripts to the Republic of Venice in 1468; this gift became the nucleus of the Library of St Mark, the Marciana. He died in Ravenna. *See* BYZANTINE EMPIRE. PG

H. Vast *Le cardinal Bessarion 1403–1472* (1878)

Bibbiena *See* DOVIZI.

Bicocca, battle of (27 April 1522) Named from an estate outside Milan where a German-Spanish force, defending Milan on behalf of the Emperor Charles V's protégé Francesco Sforza, defeated a French army heavily supported by Swiss pikemen. Bicocca was technically significant as showing the efficacy of hand-held firearms. *See* WARS OF ITALY. JRH

Biondo, Flavio (1392–1463), one of the founders of Renaissance historiography, joined the papal court as a mature humanist in 1433 and remained there for the rest of his life. Though he did important business as papal diplomat, he was chiefly a scholar. On the basis of his *Decades* (1437–42), a survey of European history from the 5c. to the 15c. which departed from the commoner humanist concern with ancient history, he has been described as 'the first medieval historian'. In *De verbis Romanae locutionis* (*Concerning the words of the Roman speech*; 1435) he attacked the not uncommon view of Bruni and others that Latin and Italian had always been two parallel coexisting languages. He also made large contributions to the current humanist interest in Roman archaeology and topography, publishing the first substantial survey of the subject in *Roma instaurata* (*Rome restored*; 1444–46). GH

Denys Hay 'The Decades of Flavio Biondo' *Proceedings of the British Academy* (1959); B. Nogara *Scritti inediti e rari di Biondo Flavio* (1927)

Biringuccio, Vannoccio (1480–1538/9) Engineer and industrial chemist. He travelled widely in Italy and Germany, acquiring practical experience in mining and metallurgy before being appointed to a number of posts at the arsenal, mint and cathedral in his native

LIBRO SESTO

per poterla come a vn torno girare,& tanto piu quanto ſopra la doue ha da eſſer la bocca che vi poſsiate adattare vna matarozza per ſopra a gitto, & queſto douete lauorare o far lauorare a tondo, o a faccie,o a volto,o a mezze faccie,come piu vi piace,& con ogni diligẽtia & obſeruãtia dele ſue miſure iuſtisſimamẽte partito, & appreſſo ſi deue mettere ſopra a dui bilighi fermi in terra vn da capo & vn da piei,come far ſi coſtuma agli ſpedoni de gli aroſti come qui diſegnato vedete.

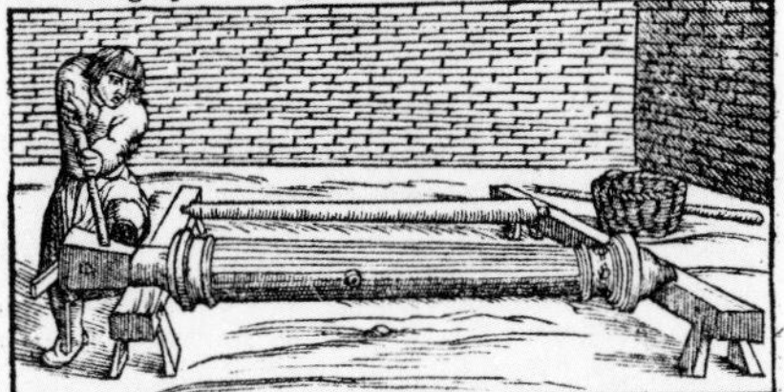

Et fatto queſto doue volete che ſia la boccha,& da piei doue ſi da el fuocho metterete eſſendo a faccie le cornici di pezzi che ſconfitte quando voi tirarete tal ſtile fuor dela forma ſi lasſino & reſtino nela forma fatta

Preparation of a wooden model for casting a cannon: an illustration from **Biringuccio**'s *Pirotechnia*.

Siena between absences coinciding with the periods of exile of his patrons, the Petrucci. He died shortly after becoming head of the papal foundry and director of munitions. His one work, *Pirotechnia* (1540), reflects his practical experience of chemical industries, with mostly original technical descriptions of mineralogy, metallurgy, glassmaking, guncasting, bell-founding, goldsmithery, typecasting (the earliest printed account) and gunpowder technology, which went well beyond his predecessors technically. The work was highly influential, often reprinted, quoted from and copied in the 16c. *See* TECHNOLOGY. MBH

Pirotechnia tr. C. S. Smith and M. T. Gnudi (1942, 1959)

Bisticci, Vespasiano da (1421–98) ran a manuscript copying business in Florence capable of working on a large scale at a calligraphic standard high enough to make collectors at the level of Duke Federico of Urbino and Cosimo de' Medici dependent on him. Unsympathetic to the reproductions of texts through printing, he retired in 1482 and produced in his *Vite* lively sketches of the careers and characters of contemporaries and clients that add much to our knowledge of and feeling for the Quattrocento. JRH

Vite tr. by W. G. and E. Waters as *The Vespasiano memoirs* (1926 and frequent later eds)

Blois, Treaty of The attraction of this charming town for the kings of France led to the signature there of a confusing number of international agreements. Of greatest significance for Italy were that of September 1504, which sealed a *rapprochement* between Louis XII and Maximilian I, preparing the ground for the aggressive League of Cambrai against Venice; and the treaty of May 1513, which made Venice an ally of France against Maximilian. *See* WARS OF ITALY. JRH

Boccaccio, Giovanni (1313–75) Born in Certaldo or Florence (not Paris as was once believed), Boccaccio spent his youth in Naples, studying commerce and law and living on the fringes of the court: his youthful love 'Fiammetta' may have been the natural daughter of King Robert. His literary and scholarly interests began in Naples, and continued after 1340 when his family called him back to Florence. It was this double experience, of courtly Naples with its French feudal traditions and of mercantile bourgeois Florence, that enabled him to present in the *Decameron* such a remarkably complex synthesis of 14c. life and attitudes.

Boccaccio's early writings are uneven but consistently innovatory, providing among other things the first attempts at sustained narrative in artistic Italian prose, and (probably) the first verse narratives in *ottava rima*. (The dates of composition are very approximate.) The *Filocolo* (1336–38) tells in prose the story of Florio and Biancofiore; while the *Filostrato* (*c.*1335) and the *Teseida* (1339–41) are the verse antecedents respectively of Chaucer's Troilus poem and of his *Knight's tale*. The *Caccia di Diana* (*c.*1334) mythologizes some ladies of his Neapolitan circle, and he continued in this vein after the move to Florence with the more complex *Ameto* (or *Commedia delle ninfe fiorentine*, 1342). This work mythologizes the history of Florence, Boccaccio's own life, and a new circle of female companions, and at the same time attempts to make pagan sensuality symbolize Christian charity – all in a pastoral setting which is itself a new revival of a classical literary mode. The *Fiammetta* (1343–44), on the other hand, is a psychological novel with autobiographical overtones, analyzing the torments of a woman abandoned by her lover. Other Florentine works are the *Amorosa visione* (1342–43) and the *Ninfale fiesolano* (1344–46).

In the celebrated *Decameron* (*c.*1350), 10 young aristocrats flee from the Florentine plague of 1348, set up an idyllic court of pleasure, and entertain each other with a total of

Scenes from a tale in the *Decameron* of **Boccaccio** painted on a marriage chest, attributed to Rossello di Jacopo Franchi (Edinburgh, National Gallery of Scotland).

100 stories which cover an immense range of tone from the most idealistic to the most scurrilous. The majority are tales of trickery, enterprise, survival and self-reliance which have led Vittore Branca to speak of a 'merchant epic'; and the numerous zestfully triumphant adulteries have variously condemned the book and exalted Boccaccio as a champion of 'natural' behaviour against social and religious prohibitions. The truth is probably more complex. Alongside the examples of self-seeking mercantile opportunism there are others of selfless gentlemanly 'courtesy', and the collection ends with an account of the inhumanly chaste and patient Griselda. Whether the subversive sexual behaviour should be seen as prescriptive, as well as entertaining, may depend on one's view of how fiction works, remembering that these fictitious stories are told by fictitious narrators who themselves behave with impeccable propriety. Nevertheless, the book seems to shatter medieval literary moulds with its unprejudiced and detailed realism, the flexibility of its imagination and style, and its presentation of human behaviour with small reference to any supernatural context. Immensely successful and rapidly diffused, the *Decameron* was influential on a European scale. In 16c. Italy it was proposed by Bembo as a canonical model for vernacular prose language.

By the time of the misogynist outburst of the *Corbaccio* (*c.*1365), Boccaccio had already turned to humanist compilations in Latin under the influence of his new friendship with

Petrarch. His compendia of classical mythology and history were used as reference works in the later Renaissance: particularly influential was the *Genealogia deorum gentilium* (composed and revised from *c.*1350), which involved a systematically allegorical approach to mythology and to poetry in general. He also wrote a eulogistic biography of Dante (*c.*1355, revised *c.*1364), and a series of commentaries, first delivered as lectures (from 1373), on early cantos of the *Divine comedy*. His newly acquired humanist gravity led him to regret and disown the *Decameron*; but posterity has tended to take a different view. RA

Opere (selections, 2 vols, 1952 and 1965); *Opere* ed. V. Branca (12 vols incomplete, 1964–); C. G. Osgood *Boccaccio on poetry* (Chapter XIV of *Genealogia*) (1956); V. Branca *Boccaccio: the man and his works* (1976); C. Muscetta *Boccaccio* (1972)

Boccanegra, Simone (*c.*1301–63) Born into a celebrated Genoese family – his grandfather's brother had enjoyed great fame as Captain of the People (1257–62) – he was appointed perpetual doge in the crisis of 1339, when Genoa was menaced by severe internal GUELF-GHIBELLINE conflict. His acquisitiveness, together with the heavy taxation necessary to maintain it, provoked a reaction which resulted in his exile to Pisa in 1344. But he returned to take part in the city's revolt against the Visconti and was again proclaimed perpetual doge in 1356, 7 years before his sudden death. He is the grandly sympathetic protagonist of Verdi's opera of the same name. JL

Boiardo, Matteo Maria (1441–94) Count of Scandiano, functionary and courtier of the Este dukes of Ferrara, Boiardo was one of the best lyricists of the Quattrocento, but is remembered chiefly for the chivalric epic *Orlando innamorato*, of which he wrote two books (pub. 1483) and began a third (pub. 1495). The first book has Orlando and the paladins wandering lovelorn in the legendary East like Arthurian knights-errant; the second introduces a dynastic theme in praise of Boiardo's Este lords. In both cases he was imposing courtly tastes and functions upon a popular genre, and unwittingly preparing the ground for Ariosto, who continued the same story in his *Orlando furioso*. The *Innamorato* has all the energy, irony and fantasy of its more famous successor, and lacks only Ariosto's intangible sense of a higher significance underlying the entertainment. It was rewritten in less provincial language by Francesco BERNI (pub. 1541), and was read in this academically respectable version until the 19c. RA

Opere ed. A. Scaglione (1951); G. Ponte *La personalità e l'opera del Boiardo* (1972)

Bologna With access to the trade of the river Po, set where the highway across the Apennines to Florence meets the Via Emilia, Bologna was an important strategic centre and, thanks to its university, one of the most influential intellectual focuses of Europe. It had a population in the city, of, perhaps, 50,000 in 1500, 62,000 in 1570, and an extensive contado. Seat of an important mint, the city engaged in some working of wool textiles, hemp, and – its more valuable industry in the Renaissance – silk. But the notables of its commune were mainly landowners or connected with the university. From 1278 it formed part of the Papal State.

Amid the troubles which shook the Papal State during the 14c., it experienced a multifarious variety of governments – a free commune, direct rule by papal legate (Bertrand du Poujet; 1325–34), government by signore (Taddeo Pepoli; 1337–47), a Visconti régime (Archbishop Giovanni; 1350–55) succeeded by the rule of a rebellious cadet of the Visconti family (Giovanni da Oleggio; 1355–60), direct rule by papal legate again (1360–76), and from 1376 a free commune once more. At the end of the 14c. authority in government was concentrated in the hands of a narrow oligarchy, acknowledging papal suzerainty and ruling through the committee known as 'the Sixteen Reformers of the State of Liberty'. It was against a background of continual conflict between the leading families that in the 15c. the BENTIVOGLIO, utilizing the committee of 'the Sixteen' and still acting as 'principal citizens' rather than princes, came to dominate the commune (1443–1506). Returning to the direct rule of the Church with Julius II's restoration of the Papal State, Bologna was notable in the 16c. only as the site of the coronation of Charles V (1530), for the severe rule of Francesco Guicciardini as papal governor (1531–34), and for the temporary transfer of the Council of Trent to the city (March–September 1547).

Apart from the circle of Vitale (mid-14c.) and Francesco Francia (d.1515), no native artists gained fame before the great flowering of the Carracci and their followers in the second half of the 16c. But many fine palaces and churches – among them S. Petronio (begun 1380) – were constructed in the 14c. and 15c. and were allowed to survive the splendid architectural reconstruction of the city in the second half of the 16c. and 17c. The true glory of Bologna, however, rests with its university, seat of the 12c. legal renaissance, still in the 15c. 'mother of the laws', and remarkable in the 16c. for a variety of other studies. JL

Storia di Bologna ed. A. Ferri and G. Roversi (1978)

Bologna, Concordat of (1516) Traditionally seen as a victory for the French crown because it was signed by Francis I and Leo X at the height of French power in Italy. Francis did gain substantially from the Concordat, in particular from those clauses which gave him the right to nominate his own higher clergy and thus the ability to control the French church, but Leo also won concessions. The Concordat repealed the Pragmatic Sanction of Bourges (1438) which had asserted that the authority of a General Council was superior to that of a pope. JH

Bombelli, Raffaele (1526–72) Bolognese mathematician. He worked under the patronage of the Roman Alessandro Rufini as engineer and architect, but his chief interest was in pure mathematics. His *Algebra* (Bologna 1572) was influenced both by the work of the recently rediscovered Greek mathematician Diophantos and by the controversy between Cardano and Tartaglia over the solving of cubic equations. He intended merely to display the best methods for solving equations but went mathematically far beyond this towards true analysis. His *Algebra* was widely influential for a hundred years. MBH

Dictionary of scientific biography (1970–80)

Bon *See* BUON

Boniface IX Pope 1389–1404 (b.1356) Pietro Tomacelli's rule as pope of the Roman party was beset by the problems of the SCHISM. His defects arose perhaps rather from inexperience than malice. But financial difficulties drove him to widescale simony. Above all, his reluctance to end the Schism by agreeing to resign his office were the rival pope of the French party to do the same exposed him to accusations of placing his own ambitions before the welfare of Christendom. JL

Borgia family A Spanish-Italian noble family of Aragonese extraction, the Borgias were always regarded as foreigners in Italy and this partially explains their unenviable reputation. The first prominent member of the family and creator of its fortunes was Pope Calixtus III (1455–58). When he became pope several relatives joined him in Rome, along with numerous Catalan fortune-hunters. Calixtus's nephew Rodrigo became Pope Alexander VI and Rodrigo's children included Lucrezia and Cesare. It was the career of Cesare that subsequently made the family name synonymous with greed and treachery. JH

M. Mallett *The Borgias* (1969)

Borgia, Cesare (*c.*1475–1507) Son of Rodrigo Borgia and Vanozza Catanei, Cesare Borgia grew up to be a man of great charm and political skill, a soldier of ability, but also, while not the monster anti-Spanish propaganda made him out to be, capable of great cruelty. Originally destined for an ecclesiastical career, he studied at the universities of Perugia and Pisa and there acquired an acquaintance with the new learning. In addition, he developed an abiding interest in architecture, particularly military architecture. Meanwhile Cesare's father had been elevated to the papacy as Alexander VI, and Cesare was created Archbishop of Valencia (1492) and cardinal (1493). He began to play a vital role in Vatican politics, becoming his father's closest adviser. After the death of his brother, the Duke of Gandia, in 1498, Cesare renounced his ecclesiastical dignities and embarked upon that secular career which earned him the admiration of Machiavelli.

French support for Alexander's policy of subjecting all the Papal State to obedience was essential and, accordingly, in 1499 Cesare married Charlotte d'Albret, sister of the King of Navarre, having first been created Duke of Valentinois and Dios. Alexander's intention was to use Cesare in the reconquest of the Papal State, but it remains a matter of debate among historians whether Alexander made more use of Cesare than the latter did of his father. Certainly, in a series of brilliant campaigns Cesare established his own authority over most of the Papal State, removing the local signori and attacking the power of the Roman barons. He captured Imola, Forlì and Cesena (1499–1500) and, with the assistance of the Orsini, defeated the Colonna (1501). He captured Rimini, Pesaro and Faenza and took Urbino, Camerino, Piombino and Elba (1500–02). In 1501 Alexander created him Duke of Romagna, whereupon he set about the creation of that new state which many contemporaries praised as a model of good government. The administration of the duchy displayed 2 novel features, an emphasis on centralization and an insistence on the equitable treatment of all subjects before the law.

Open opposition to Cesare's career of conquest was delayed until 1502, although by that date Louis XII had already turned against him. In the summer of 1502 several of Cesare's leading condottieri conspired against him in the revolt of Magione. The ease with which he subsequently tricked the conspirators and lured them to their deaths earned him the admiration rather than the disapproval of his contemporaries. Cesare's brilliant career was terminated by his father's premature death in 1503. At the time Cesare was also ill and so unable to influence the outcome of the conclave. The new pope, Pius III, did confirm Cesare as Gonfaloniere of the Church and papal vicar of the Romagna but, even during this brief pontificate, Cesare lost all his conquests with the exceptions of Cesena, Forlì, Faenza and Imola. The sudden death of Pius III and the election of Julius II, a sworn enemy of the Borgias, spelt ruin for Cesare.

In Chapter VII of *The prince*, Machiavelli was to argue that Cesare's failure to prevent this election by throwing the weight of his influence behind an alternative candidate was the sole political error of his life. Certainly, it was one that cost him dear. Although Julius at first showed himself conciliatory and used Cesare to prevent an outbreak of chaos in the Romagna, this proved but a temporary respite. Cesare was forced to resign his strongholds in the Papal State and it was soon clear that his life was in danger. He fled from Rome to Naples and thence to Spain. There he was imprisoned by Ferdinand of Aragon. Louis XII, meanwhile, deprived him of his French fiefs. The only refuge left was the court of the King of Navarre, whither Cesare escaped on 25 October 1506. He was killed, fighting for Navarre against rebel troops, on 12 March 1507. JH

M. Mallett *The Borgias* (1969)

Portrait medal of **Lucrezia Borgia** as Duchess of Ferrara (London, British Museum).

Borgia, Lucrezia (1480–1519) Much-loved and beautiful daughter of Alexander VI by Vanozza Catanei. Her adolescence was dominated by the intrigues of her father and her brother Cesare, to whom she was very close. There is, however, no foundation to stories which suggest that Lucrezia was involved in Borgia poison schemes and guilty of incest with her father or brother. To further their aims she was married to Giovanni Sforza of Pesaro (1492) and for the same aims that marriage was annulled (1497). In order to bring about a *rapprochement* between Alexander and Naples she was married to Alfonso, Duke of Bisceglie, illegitimate son of Alfonso II (1498). Her father made her regent of Spoleto (1499), a post she filled well, but in 1500 Bisceglie was murdered at Rome, probably by agents of Cesare Borgia.

In 1501 Lucrezia was betrothed to Alfonso d'Este, whom she married the following year. She bore her husband 7 children, of whom 4 survived infancy. As wife of the heir to the Duke of Ferrara, and after 1505 as duchess, Lucrezia presided over a glittering court and won much admiration for her kindness and generosity as a patroness. She was responsible for attracting many writers and artists of distinction to Ferrara and numbered among her closest friends Ercole Strozzi and Bembo. Her impassioned correspondence with the latter (1503–05) has tempted historians, unfamiliar with the conventions of neo-Platonism, to assume the two were lovers. In Europe, Lucrezia was famous as a leader of fashion but she was equally well known to the people of Ferrara for her acts of charity. She died, like so many married women of her age, of an infection following childbirth, surrounded by an aura of piety. JH

M. Bellonci *Lucrezia Borgia* (1960)

Borromeo, Cardinal Carlo (1538–84) Pastoral reformer, born in Arona (Milanese) of a baronial family. He was called to Rome in 1560 by Pius IV, his maternal uncle, being made Cardinal Nephew and Archbishop of Milan. He dominated the Roman court and was the animator of an academy of learned churchmen, whose proceedings were published as the *Noctes Vaticanae* (*Vatican nights*). He went into residence in his diocese on his uncle's death in 1565 and has been constantly cited as the great example of the post-Tridentine pastor. His diocesan legislation, collected in the *Acta ecclesiae Mediolanensis* (*Documents of the Milanese church*), was certainly the model for that of other bishops in Italy and France. The hallmarks of the Borromean pastoral approach are regarded as having been method and detailed regulation; here indeed he was imitated by other bishops. What was really distinctive about Borromeo, however, was his sensitivity to symbolism, which emerges even in his pastoral letters. Certainly he was a moral rigorist in his campaign to discipline the laity and a martinet where his clergy were involved, while his uncompromising assertion of ecclesiastical jurisdiction led to conflict with the Milanese senate. OL

Storia di Milano X Fondazione Treccani degli Alfieri (1962)

Boscoli, Pietro Paolo (*c*.1478–1513) was a bungling idealist, executed after the discovery of his plot to assassinate the newly returned Medici. Having been motivated by a humanist education to act as a Brutus for the sake of Florentine liberty, he spent his last night trying to recapture his faith as a Christian in order that he should die having recognized the sinfulness of his intent and repented. The friar Luca della Robbia, who spent these last hours with him, left a moving *recitazione* or account of the conflict of values in Boscoli's mind. JRH

'Recitazione del caso di Pietro Paolo Boscoli' *Archivio Storico Italiano* (1842)

Botero, Giovanni (1544–1617) was born in Savoy and educated in a Jesuit seminary in Palermo. A sharp mind and a fluent literary Latin were held by his superiors to compensate for a restless and rebellious temperament, and he was sent to continue his education and to serve the order as propagandist and priest-of-letters in Rome, Paris, Milan, Padua and elsewhere. Leaving the order in 1580 he entered the reformist circle of Cardinal Carlo Borromeo, becoming his secretary and, after his death, the young Cardinal Federico Borromeo's. From 1599 he was tutor and increasingly a trusted adviser at the court in Turin of Duke Charles Emanuel of Savoy.

By then he had acquired a European reputation as a secular writer. Most notable were his *On the causes of the greatness of cities* (1588), a pioneering scientific attempt to establish what features promote and limit the growth of urban populations, and his *The reason of state* (1589). Though devised as a Christian polemic against the Machiavellian dissociation of ethics from politics, the work as it developed came to treat politics largely as the art of the possible, and the exercise of power as being justified by right conduct at the moment rather than by the subordination of all political action to defined ethical goals. The work's wide appeal lay, in any case, less in its moralizing than in the mass of information and comment about how states were actually governed. In his discussion of administration, commerce and industry, fiscal policy, population, military organization, legal institutions and other aspects of the increasingly bureaucratized and centralized state, he was not only describing to contemporaries changes in their political world never before so revealingly stated, but also anticipated something of the much later approach of the social scientist. JRH

DBI; The reason of state tr. P. J. and D. P. Waley (1956) includes a tr. of *The greatness of cities*

Botticelli, Sandro (1445–1510), born Alessandro di Moriano Filipepi, is one of the outstanding geniuses in the history of Western art. He began his training under Filippo Lippi, alongside Filippino, and seemingly worked for a time with Leonardo in Verrocchio's workshop. His understanding of perspective and foreshortening, of architectural design and, indeed, of anatomy, were all that might have been expected of a man with such a background, but it is to the pure visual poetry of the outcome that he owes his fame. His manipulations of the visual facts for artistic purposes

Religious intensity in a late work of **Botticelli**: detail from the *Pietà* (Munich, Alte Pinakothek).

should no more be put down to ignorance or inability in these respects than in the case of Picasso in the 20c. Although he was a superb colourist, delicate at times, strong at others, and capable, in his last years, of harsh and powerful effects, the essence of his art lies in the unsurpassed, singing quality of his line. This can be seen at its purest in the drawings with which he illustrated Dante's *Divine comedy* (Berlin, Dahlem museum; E. Berlin, Staatliche Museen; Rome, Vatican).

A series of Adorations of the Magi painted in the 1470s and early 80s, notably those in the National Galleries in London and Washington and the Uffizi, Florence, show Botticelli experimenting with the new pyramidal, centralized form which was taken up by Leonardo. They also show the ability as a portraitist which he demonstrated in a number of full-scale works, for they contain, particularly in the case of the Uffizi panel, a whole gallery of Medici portraits. As with the technical aspects of his art, so in terms of the ideas which underlie it Botticelli moved in the highest circles: much of his work is imbued with the ideas of the Florentine neo-Platonists surrounding Lorenzo de' Medici, and particularly of Marsilio Ficino. But just as he was neither a 'perspectivist' nor an 'anatomist', so he was clearly not a neo-Platonist in the sense that his work could be taken as a straightforward transfer into visual terms of particular philosophical precepts.

His great series of mythologies, also of the 1470s and 80s, the *Mars and Venus* (London, National Gallery), the *Primavera*, the *Birth of Venus*, the *Pallas and the Centaur* (Florence, Uffizi), have been the subject of innumerable essays in interpretation without ever losing that essential, multi-faceted ambiguity which is characteristic of his approach to visual description. The central figure in the *Primavera* is as much a Christian Virgin as a figure from antiquity. The classic group of the Three Graces owes as much to gothic as to antique linear sensitivity. Indeed, however deeply he may have been involved in the particular attempt at Christian-classical synthesis which was characteristic of the humanist Medici circle, he was later intimately involved with Savonarola, and the intense religious feeling characteristic of such late works as the *Mystic Nativity* in London (inscribed, 1500) or the *Pietà* in Munich owes its power to this conversion. [39] JW

R. Lightbown *Sandro Botticelli* (1978); R. Salvini *Tutta la pittura del Botticelli* (1958)

Bracciolini, Poggio (1380–1459) was one of the most typical and outstanding figures of early Florentine humanism. His career was based on his great skill as a Latinist, acquired in the circle of Salutati at Florence around 1400. In this ambience he developed his passion for the recovery of manuscripts of the Latin authors. From 1403 he was employed as a scriptor, or secretary, at the papal court. In this position he

Illuminated initial with portrait of Poggio **Bracciolini**, from the first page of a manuscript of the *De varietate fortunae*, mid-15c. (Rome, Vatican Library).

travelled with the court to the Council of Constance (1414–18) from which he made his famous journeys to the abbeys of Cluny and St Gallen to discover in these and other ecclesiastical libraries manuscripts of unknown speeches of Cicero and parts of the text of Quintilian. He was also one of the earliest scholars to collect classical inscriptions.

After a period of exile in England he was again employed continuously at the papal court 1423–52. In this agreeably privileged environment, enjoying ecclesiastical favours but remaining a layman, he wrote most of his famous Latin works, mostly couched in dialogue form, often unedifying and irreligious, sometimes obscene. Dialogues such as *De avaritia* (*On avarice*; 1428), *De infelicitate principum* (*On the unhappiness of princes*; 1440), *De varietate fortunae* (*On the vicissitudes of fortune*; *c.*1448), and *Contra hypocritas* (*Against hypocrites*; 1449) contain much entertaining comment on the society of the time and unite the literary classicism of Petrarch with the story-telling of Boccaccio. Ecclesiastical corruption and religious enthusiasm were both frequent butts. His *Facetiae* was a popular book of indecent stories throughout the Renaissance.

His last work was a *History of Florence*, written when he had retired to the city, which he had never left in spirit, to occupy the honoured position of Chancellor in the line of Bruni and Machiavelli. He had little sympathy with the enthusiasm for Greek, which he never mastered, then beginning to dominate humanist circles. GH

E. Walser *Poggius Florentinus* (1914); *Opera omnia* (2 vols 1964–66)

Bragadin, Marcantonio (1523–71) The heroic Venetian defender of Famagosta against a vastly greater Turkish army. When eventually forced to capitulate he was flayed alive and his skin, stuffed with straw, was hung from a mast and taken in triumph to Constantinople. JRH

Bramante, Donato (*c.*1444–1514) Undisputed founder of Roman High Renaissance architecture. Born near Urbino, Bramante trained as a painter, becoming an expert in Mantegnesque illusionism (Palazzo del Podestà, Bergamo, 1477). He turned to architecture at the Milanese court of Lodovico il Moro, where Leonardo's knowledge of Brunelleschi's buildings and experiments in centrally-planned church design may have influenced his development. Also crucial were his memories of Urbino, and some knowledge of Alberti's Mantuan churches. At S. Maria presso S. Satiro (1482–86) Bramante compressed Albertian monumentality into a tiny barrel-vaulted space with an illusionistic choir, while the tribune of S. Maria delle Grazie (1493f.) is a colossal reworking of Brunelleschi's Old Sacristy.

The tempietto at S. Pietro in Montorio, Rome, by **Bramante**.

Increasing interest in the language of the orders, evident in the cloisters (1497–98) and *canonica* (1492) of S. Ambrogio, was intensified by Bramante's move to Rome and direct experience of antiquity. The round tempietto at S. Pietro in Montorio (1502), the first building to reuse the full Doric order, assumed for the 16c. the exemplary status of an ancient building, while the Palazzo Caprini ('House of Raphael', 1501–02), with its rusticated ground floor shops and applied orders on the *piano nobile*, established a new palace type that was influential for centuries. Julius II's papacy brought the large-scale reshaping of Rome which earned the architect his nickname 'Ruinante'. New streets (Via Giulia, Lungara, Via de' Banchi) were built; the Vatican Palace was connected to the Villa Belvedere with a series of ascending courtyards forming a perspectival vista flanked by covered loggias; and in 1506 the foundation stone was laid for new St Peter's. Of Bramante's first Greek cross plan only the crossing was built, but his ideas were the starting point for all later work at the basilica, and for many churches elsewhere in Italy. Some idea of the now destroyed choir which, as part of his reduced scheme, Bramante built on 15c. foundations can be inferred from the tribune of S. Maria del Popolo (*c.*1507–09), with its coffered barrel vault, shell niche, and 'Serliana' windows.

Bramante devised an architecture based on a clear set of principles synthesized from antiquity, and invented cheap materials and techniques (stucco, cast vaults) appropriate to the speed required by Julius's megalomaniac programme. In a contemporary satirical dialogue Bramante's shade outlines to St Peter as his conditions for entering heaven a full-scale redevelopment of paradise, including the replacement of the strait and narrow path with a Belvedere-like 'spacious spiral ramp staircase by which the souls of the old and weak could ascend on horseback' (A. Guarna, *Simia*). [232]

CE

A. Bruschi *Bramante* (London, 1977)

Part of the 15c. fortifications of **Brescia**.

Brescia was taken from the Visconti in 1426 by Venice, primarily for strategic reasons but also because it was an armaments centre drawing on the unusually pure iron deposits in the valleys to its north. It was with the increasing use of firearms that the city became of crucial importance to Venice (as its still-surviving fortifications attest). While Milan remained the chief Italian producer of fine armour and weapons (used especially in tourneys and the chase), Brescia was Italy's chief 16c. centre for the assembly and finishing of straightforward military hand-held firearms. As such it was the subject of strict legislation against the emigration of labour, and of artifacts as well in times of crisis when the Republic had to equip weaponless men. Though the home of Moretto, Romanino and Moroni, Brescia was primarily known then as now (the Biretta factory) for its guns.

JRH

Storia di Brescia Fondazione Treccani degli Alfieri (4 vols 1961)

Bronzino, *Venus, Cupid, Folly, Time* (London, National Gallery).

Bronzino, Agnolo (1503–72), the pupil of Pontormo and his lifelong friend, was the principal practitioner of Florentine Mannerism. He is best known for his portraits of

Cosimo de' Medici's family and his courtiers, which reveal beneath their glacial exteriors the sitters' anxieties. His frescoes reflect his admiration for Michelangelo. His secular paintings evince the extreme sophistication of court taste: the so-called *Venus, Cupid, Folly, Time* is an allegory purporting to revile vice while making it irresistibly alluring. His altarpieces show similar multiplicities of intended and suggested meanings. The absence of grief in the *Pietà* (Besançon) is explained only when (if ever) the viewer discovers the allusions to the Eucharist. The impact of the Counter-Reformation began to disrupt the exquisite balance of his style; his later altarpieces reveal unresolved agitation. [309] MH

S. J. Freedberg 'Observations on the painting of the Maniera' *Art Bulletin* (1965); M. B. Hall *Renovation and Counter-Reformation* (1979)

Brumel, Anton (or Antoine) (*c.*1460–before 1520) Composer of both church music and French chansons. He was probably born in Flanders and later worked in Florence, at Chartres cathedral, at Notre-Dame in Paris, and in Lyons. He was invited about 1505 to become a musician at the Este court in Ferrara, but it is not certain whether he ever went. His style is close to that of Josquin des Prez, showing a trend towards simplicity and careful setting of words, probably as the result of humanistic thinking about music. DA

Brunelleschi, Filippo (1377–1446) Florentine architect who was considered in the Renaissance to have 'restored the ancient Roman manner of building' (Manetti). Trained as a goldsmith, Brunelleschi turned to architecture some time after losing to Ghiberti the competition for the Baptistery Doors. His 15c. biographer Antonio Manetti's circumstantial account of his early visit to Rome with Donatello to study the ancient ruins is still disputed, but it is now thought that the constructional technique of his most famous achievement, the cupola of Florence cathedral (1420f.), was derived less from ancient Rome than from Byzantine or Ravennate dome types. The pointed profile and 8 faces of the dome had been foreseen in the Trecento design, and Brunelleschi's contribution in devising a continuously self-supporting masonry system without centring was above all a feat of structural engineering.

Brunelleschi's cupola of Florence cathedral.

Brunelleschi's architectural system was immediately apparent in his first complete buildings, the Innocenti Hospital (1419f.) and the Old Sacristy at S. Lorenzo (1421f.). It is based on pure geometrical proportions, the use of sail vaults and saucer domes on pendentives, and a simple *all'antica* vocabulary of grey sandstone columns and pilasters articulating white plaster walls. His proportional systems are refinements of those used in medieval Florence, his orders and ornamentation are almost entirely based on Romanesque models like the Florentine Baptistery (then thought to be an ancient Temple of Mars), and specific Trecento models have been adduced for his buildings (e.g. the Baptistery at Padua for the Old Sacristy). Nonetheless, his synthesis is an entirely personal one, which far exceeds its component sources in intellectual rigour and control of design; the bichromatic combination of sandstone and plaster was certainly his own invention.

We do not know the exact date of the lost paintings of the Baptistery and the Palazzo Vecchio in which Brunelleschi demonstrated the application of geometrical principles to the perspectival representation of 3-dimensional space on a plane surface. Immediately adopted by his friends Donatello and Masaccio, and diffused by Alberti in his treatise on painting, linear PERSPECTIVE became a dominant preoccupation of Italian Renaissance painting and relief sculpture, as well as conditioning ways of looking at architectural and urban space. Brunelleschi's own tendency to see buildings in terms of a perspectival *point de vue* can be inferred from his unfulfilled project to reorientate S. Spirito on to an open piazza facing the river, and from the way his buildings exploit an axial approach (Pazzi Chapel) or articulate the space around them (Innocenti Loggia).

The differences between Brunelleschi's two great basilical churches, S. Lorenzo and S. Spirito, show the maturing of his architectural ideas. The crossing area of S. Lorenzo, designed for a parishioners' building committee which included the father of Cosimo de' Medici, who took over patronage of the building in 1442, is similar in ground plan to Florentine gothic churches like S. Trinita, despite its characteristically Brunelleschian articulation. (Most of the nave, the side chapels, and the cupola were constructed after Brunelleschi's death, contradicting his intentions.) The plan of S. Spirito (1436f.), which, according to Manetti, gave Brunelleschi particular satisfaction, has side aisles and semicircular side chapels which continue right round the nave and the 3 arms of the crossing, giving a unity based on the repetition of identical elements. The concave chapels flanked by applied half-columns convey a richer spatial rhythm than the flat pilaster articulation of S. Lorenzo. A similar exploitation of the wall mass can also be found in Brunelleschi's unfinished octagonal church of S. Maria degli Angeli (1434f.), while the Pazzi Chapel, in some ways his most satisfying interior, further develops the forms of the Old Sacristy. Although he scarcely worked outside Florence except as a fortifications expert, Brunelleschi's fame was enormous, and his influence reached important centres like Urbino and Milan, thus conditioning the early experiences of Bramante. [141] CE

A. Manetti *The life of Brunelleschi* ed. H. Saalman (1970); E. Battisti *Brunelleschi* (1981)

Bruni, Leonardo (1370–1444), born in Arezzo and hence often called 'Aretino', was the central figure in Florentine humanism during the first half of the 15c. Under the influence of Salutati and Chrysoloras he became outstandingly expert in both Latin and Greek. About 1401 he composed a *Laudatio Florentinae urbis* (*Panegyric of the city of Florence*) in praise of Florentine republicanism and literary culture: this has an important part in Hans Baron's recent theory about the development of Florentine political humanism in reaction to the oppression of despotic Milan. How far Bruni wrote with political conviction, how far as a practitioner of the art of rhetoric, is disputable. In any case the work is important as the beginning of Bruni's massive contribution to Florentine political thought.

After a spell as a secretary at the papal court he returned to Florence in 1415 and never left it. From 1427 he was Chancellor, like Salutati before him, holding a unique central position in political and literary life and, in spite of humble origins, becoming both affluent and influential. From 1415 he was intermittently composing a Latin *History of the Florentine people* (from classical to recent times) which is the first major work of Renaissance historical writing: imitating the continuous prose and literary grace of classical historians, conscious of cultural evolution, also based on the critical use of original sources. At the beginning of it he developed the ideologically important link between the foundation of Florence and republican, rather than imperial, Rome, and emphasized the

Part of the tomb of Leonardo **Bruni** by Bernardo Rossellino, in S. Croce, Florence.

association of republicanism, classicism and social well-being. Among other works related to Florentine politics Bruni composed in 1421 a treatise *De militia* which argues in favour of a citizen army to replace the contemporary dependence on hiring unreliable condottieri. One of his last works, the *Commentary on the history of his own times*, contains an original treatment of contemporary history in humanist style extending down to 1440.

Bruni was one of the leading Greek scholars and an early contributor to the Renaissance programme of translation from Greek into Latin. He translated Aristotle's *Ethics* and *Politics* explicitly to replace the medieval translations with better scholarship and greater elegance. With more originality he translated several of Plato's works, hitherto totally inaccessible to Latin readers. He seems however to have been unaffected, or even repelled, by Plato's ideas. He remained wedded to philosophical impressions taken from Aristotle and Cicero, and to Cicero's ideal of the philosopher-statesman, without seriously considering their relationship to Christianity. In this too he was typical of the age of Florentine humanism over which he presided. GH

Hans Baron *The crisis of the early Italian Renaissance* (1955); E. Santini 'L.B. Aretino e i suoi "Historiarum Florentini populi libri XXII"' *Annali d.R. Scuola Normale Superiore di Pisa* (1910)

Bruno, Giordano (1548–1600) was brought by his critical and fierily speculative temperament into conflict with one form of Counter-Reformation establishment after another. He was born near Nola. Having entered the Dominican order he became a priest in 1572. The heterodoxy of his reading and his spoken opinions led to his quitting the order and leaving Italy to avoid trial for heresy. In Geneva he became a Calvinist. Again, heterodox opinions led to his excommunication. After a stay in France he visited England (1583–85), where irritation with a third form of rigid orthodoxy, that represented by the philosophers of Oxford, goaded him into putting down his views in a series of Italian dialogues. Further wanderings followed in France and Germany (where he was again excommunicated, this time from the Lutheran church). In 1591 he felt it safe to return to Italy but was again accused of heresy and after a long trial was burned at the stake in Rome.

Bruno's interests included natural MAGIC and the cultivation of memory systems as means of storing the mind with knowledge and thus giving it a quasi-magical power, but his chief concern was cosmology. Influenced alike by LUCRETIUS and by Nicolas Copernicus (1473–1543), he believed that the universe was infinite and that it contained a number of 'worlds', Copernican sun-centred systems each with an inhabited 'earth', our own 'world' not necessarily being at or anywhere near the centre of the universe. He believed that all matter and form represented a single unity, coterminous with God, whose World Soul admitted little particularity for the individual souls of men. Religion he saw as a way of policing the ignorant: for the few, it was philosophy that revealed the true nature of God and universe alike and urged men to aspire to knowledge of and conscious union with them. While men's behaviour should be selfless, this did not call for asceticism. Differences between their beliefs should be accepted in a spirit of toleration. Among his works was a single but most impressive vernacular comedy, *Il candelaio* (*The candlemaker*; 1582). JRH

Dialoghi italiani ed. G. Aquilecchia (1958); G. Aquilecchia *Giordano Bruno* (1971); P. H. Michel *The cosmology of Giordano Bruno* (1973); Frances Yates *Giordano Bruno and the hermetic tradition* (1964); *Il candelaio* tr. J. R. Hale in E. Bentley ed. *The genius of the Italian theatre* (1964)

Buon (or Bon), Bartolomeo (*c.*1374–?1467) The greatest Venetian architectural sculptor of the early 15c. He was trained in the workshop of his father Giovanni. They worked together on the façade of S. Maria dell' Orto (1392) and on the Ca d'Oro, where Bartolomeo is documented as having carved an elaborate well-head (1427). He carved tympanum reliefs for the Scuola di S. Marco and the Scuola Vecchia di S. Maria della Misericordia, later working on the Porta della Carta of the Ducal Palace. CA

J. Pope-Hennessy *Catalogue of Italian sculpture in the Victoria and Albert Museum* (1964); W. Wolters *La scultura gotica veneziana* (1976)

Buontalenti, Bernardo (1531–1608) Versatile and inventive Florentine architect, whose career at the grand ducal court embraced theatre design, hydraulic entertainments and rediscovering techniques for porcelain and rock crystal, as well as the gamut of civil and military

Buontalenti's Porta delle Suppliche, Uffizi, Florence.

architecture. Taken early into the service of Cosimo I, Buontalenti trained as a miniaturist, and amused Prince Francesco with the mobile toys which earned his soubriquet '*delle Girandole*'. He began his career in military architecture in the Papal State, but after a visit to Spain in 1563–64 never again left Tuscany. A steady lifetime salary came from his job as river engineer (1567f.), conscientiously documented in hundreds of surviving reports. Among his many works of military engineering are the bastioned port of Livorno (1576f.) and the fortifications of the Belvedere, the Medici villa which overlooks Florence from the south.

Buontalenti's villas were notable as much for their spectacular waterworks and automata – especially at Pratolino (*c.*1569f.), where little but Giambologna's mountainous *Appenino* survives – as for their frugal semi-fortified architecture (Artimino, 1594f.), ultimately derived from Sangallo's Poggio a Caiano. Buontalenti's urban palaces concentrate on bizarre door and window details, best exemplified by the Porta delle Suppliche (1580), where the two volutes of a Michelangelesque broken pediment are reversed, mocking their structural function. Similarly perverse is the staircase for S. Trinita (now in S. Stefano al Ponte), which both invites and repels ascent, while on the church façade floats capricious, proto-Baroque ornament. Buontalenti's architectural drawings – impressionistic sketches with reckless shading – betray his painterly origins, also evident in his splendid costume designs. [227] CE

I. M. Botto *Proporzioni* (1963); F. Borsi *Firenze del Cinquecento* (1974)

Burchiello (1404–49) Domenico di Giovanni, known always by his unexplained nickname which means literally 'little boat', was a Florentine barber, whose sideline as a writer of satirical verse with an anti-Medicean political stance succeeded in procuring him poverty, exile and early death. Topical, lively and idiosyncratically colloquial, but rendered obscure by frequent political and personal allusions, his style constitutes a recognized manner of composition *alla burchia*. JM

Sonetti del Burchiello, del Bellincioni e di altri poeti fiorentini alla burchiellesca (1757); R. Watkins 'Il Burchiello' *Italian Quarterly* (1970)

Burlamacchi, Francesco (1498–1548) was born into one of the richest and most politically influential families of Lucca. Active in commerce as a young man, he came to prefer to support his family's position by playing a prominent role in a variety of government offices. He became gonfalonier, or temporary head of state, in 1533. Apart from a slightly suspect (in thoroughly mercantile Lucca) devotion to classical literature, his standing as a sturdy representative of the oligarchy and its interests was high. He was elected gonfalonier again in 1546.

That he obtained rather more than the average number of commissions to inspect the militia of the contado, and successfully advocated the raising of additional numbers, appeared merely patriotic in a city uneasy about Cosimo's attitude to its continuing independence. It was, then, to universal amazement that, thanks to a treacherous accomplice, Burlamacchi was revealed in 1546 as the inventor of a plot to use the militia, on his own initiative, to enter Pisa. There he had planned to exhort the citizens to throw off their Medicean chains in a movement that was (by means not very clear) to lead Pistoia and Florence to follow suit, eventually producing a free and independent Tuscan federation of self-governing towns, of which Lucca would be one. This political vision was capped by a still vaguer religious one: purification of the Church and a reinvigoration of personal faith.

While there is no doubt that Burlamacchi was a sane and experienced politician, the discrepancy between the means he commanded – even assuming the help he was expecting from the heads of the exiled Strozzi family had been forthcoming – and the ends he aimed at were so great as to leave an air of mystery lingering about this episode. He revealed nothing under prolonged bouts of torture before being executed for treason in 1548. Was this personal ambition, sparked by reading in Plutarch's *Lives* about the careers of men who did wonders with the smallest means? Was it hatred of tyranny of the kind that had produced such anti-Medicean plots as that of Pietro Paolo Boscoli in 1513? Burlamacchi was disowned by his contemporaries but in the Risorgimento was seen as one of the great prophets of Italian independence and unity, if only on a Tuscan scale. JRH

M. Berengo *Nobili e mercanti nella Lucca del Cinquecento* (1965)

Business methods Italian business methods were the most sophisticated in Renaissance Europe. Italian businessmen kept relatively elaborate records, believing that 'it befits a merchant always to have ink-stained hands' (Alberti). They were pioneers in the use of double-entry book-keeping ('the Italian method'), maritime insurance, trading companies, banks, and the public debt.

The Genoese and Venetians developed the *commenda*, or *colleganza*, a short-term association between a sleeping partner (who supplied the capital) and a working one. The Florentines developed the *compagnia*, a partnership in which both sides supplied capital and both worked. Banking was an Italian speciality, with Florence as its 14c. and 15c. centre, and the banks of Barcelona, Bruges, London, Lyons, etc. were in Italian hands. These banks changed money and dealt in letters of credit for travellers and in bills of exchange, in which the deliverer paid the taker a sum in one currency so that a third party, the payer, would hand over to a fourth, the beneficiary, an equivalent sum in another currency in a different city some months later. Exchange transactions sometimes disguised loans at interest, to avoid the Church's condemnation of 'usury'. Foreign princes from Edward III of England to Philip II of Spain were dependent on loans from Italian bankers.

The public debt developed early in Italy, being funded in Venice in 1262 and in Florence in 1345 (the creation of the *Monte*). At a more humble level, credit was extended by pawnshops, often run by Jews, or by their public rivals, the Monti di Pietà. Even in Italy, economic modernity must not be exaggerated. Family firms were predominant, many merchants kept their accounts in their heads, and although cheques (*polizze*) existed, oral orders of transfer (which were then recorded) were preferred. *See* BANKING. PB

I. Origo *The merchant of Prato* (1957); R. de Roover *The rise and decline of the Medici bank* (2nd enlarged ed. 1963)

Byzantine Empire Historians will never agree when the eastern half of the Roman Empire, which had been given a new capital by Constantine in 330, became the Greek Byzantine Empire of the Middle Ages, for in the East continuity was not broken until 1453, and just as Emperors continued to look back to Augustus and Constantine, men of letters went on trying to maintain the standards of Homer and Thucydides. Up to the mid-14c., westerners had been interested in Greek works, whether of logic, theology or mysticism, solely for their factual content; Petrarch and Boccaccio seem to have been the first Latins for many centuries to wish to learn Greek in order to appreciate the aesthetic qualities of Greek literature. Their difficulty in finding adequate teachers is surprising; the Calabrian monk Barlaam who gave lessons to Petrarch in Avignon in 1342 was a skilled mathematician and logician, who was able later in Naples to assist Paolo di Perugia (d.1348) in his work on pagan mythology. However, Greek studies were not effectively taken up among the humanists until Salutati invited Chrysoloras to lecture in Florence in 1397. Chrysoloras had literary interests similar to those of the humanists and was therefore able to interpret the Greek world to the Italians; his pupils, notably Bruni and Vergerio, became the leading humanists of the next generation. The main subject of communications between the Latins and the Greeks in the Middle Ages was the ecclesiastical differences which gradually hardened into a state of schism between the Catholic and Orthodox churches. Reunion was seriously discussed on no less than 30 occasions between 1054 and 1439. Most of these negotiations proved as sterile intellectually as they were politically, but as the situation of the Empire became desperate, contacts with the West became more intense; John V spent 1369–71 in Italy and died a Catholic, and Manuel II toured Europe in search of help, visiting Milan, Paris and London 1399–1403.

The last century of the Empire witnessed a remarkable artistic flowering whose common features with early Renaissance art have not yet been satisfactorily explained; the Greeks discovered Western thought from *c.*1360, when Demetrius Cydones translated Thomas Aquinas. Thus the meeting of the Greeks and Italians at the Council of Ferrara-Florence 1438–39 generated a much more cordial atmosphere than had previous encounters; the humanists welcomed Greeks like the Platonist Gemistos Pletho as living representatives of ancient culture, while artists like Ghiberti and Gozzoli incorporated reminiscences of the exotic Eastern visitors into their works. The reunion proclaimed in Florence cathedral 6 July 1439 proved stillborn even before the fall of Constantinople in 1453, but the cultural impetus of the Council was felt for a generation. Platonism took root in Florence. Bessarion settled in the West and left his library to Venice, where a group of Cretan expatriates helped to keep Greek studies in a flourishing state; a chair of Greek was established at Padua in 1463 and Marcos Musuros (d.1517) edited the first printed Greek texts for Aldus. Because antiquity never really died in Constantinople, there could be no Byzantine renaissance to compare with that of the West; the role of the Byzantines was that of librarians to the world. JKH

K. M. Setton 'The Byzantine background to the Italian Renaissance' *Proceedings of the American Philosophical Society* (1956); A. A. Vasiliev *History of the Byzantine Empire* (1952); D. M. Nicol *The last centuries of Byzantium* (1972).

Cabbala A term derived from the Hebrew *kabbalah*, literally meaning 'something handed down by tradition'. It refers primarily to the esoteric teachings of Judaism and Jewish mysticism from the 12c. onward. The cabbala incorporated many magical and occult elements, including much numerological speculation based on the Hebrew alphabet. During the Renaissance, besides the continuing role it played in Jewish thought, the cabbala was popular with certain Christians of a mystical and theosophical persuasion, beginning with Giovanni Pico della Mirandola, who transmitted his interest to Johannes Reuchlin (1455–1522), the author of *De verbo mirifico* (*The wondrous word*; 1494) and *De arte cabbalistica* (1517). These works were widely read and were absorbed into the mystical works of Francesco Zorzi (Giorgi) (1460–1541), Guillaume Postel (1510–81) and many other writers. CS

G. Scholem *Kabbalah* (1974)

Cabot, John (*c.*1450–?1498), born Giovanni Caboto in Genoa, had lived long enough in Venice to be admitted to citizenship in 1476 after trading in the eastern Mediterranean. Unlike most of his commercial rivals he made the dangerous overland journey to the staging centre for eastern luxury goods at Mecca, whence they were transported to the outlet normally used by the Venetians at Alexandria. It was probably this wish to get nearer the source of eastern products that took him to England – for like Columbus he thought Asia was much nearer to Europe than it really was.

He settled in Bristol, where there was a Venetian community, and whence, in addition to regular voyages to Iceland for fish, attempts had been made to reach Greenland and beyond. In 1496 Henry VII granted a licence to explore westwards into the Atlantic to 'our well beloved John Cabot, citizen of Venice'. Sailing in the *Matthew* in 1497, he reached Nova Scotia and Newfoundland. A second voyage in 1498 took him back to Newfoundland and possibly as far south as Chesapeake Bay and, though the circumstances are uncertain, to his death. He has a claim to be the first non-Scandinavian to make contact with parts of Canada and the northern USA, and it was the ventures of this Venetian that focused English attention on the search for a north-west passage to Asia. JRH

T. J. Oleson *Early voyages and northern approaches* (1963)

Caccini, Giulio (*c.*1550–1618) One of the earliest composers of opera, also known as Giulio Romano. Born in Rome, where he studied with a famous singing teacher, Scipione della Palla, he entered the service of the Florentine court as a singer in the 1560s and remained there for the rest of his life. He was much involved in the performances of *intermedii* given in Florence in 1579 and 1589, which helped to originate the idea of OPERA, and after being involved in the discussions of Count Bardi's famous Camerata he wrote his setting of Rinuccini's *L'Euridice*, performed with indifferent success in 1602. In that year he published a book of songs, *Le nuove musiche*, which created the vogue for so-called monody and became known throughout Europe. His second wife was a singer and one of his daughters, Francesca, became a very competent composer. *See* PERI. DA

Cadamosto (or Ca' da Mosto), Alvise (*c.*1426–83) Venetian nobleman who wrote the first eyewitness account of sub-Saharan Africa. He sailed with the Portuguese to Senegal in 1454, and returned with the Genoese Usodimare, discovering the Cape Verde Islands, in 1456. He gives a lively description of the exotic peoples of the Canaries and the kingdom of Senegal, distinguishing the black peoples of the forest from the brown peoples of the desert; he liked the blacks and tried to imagine their difficulties in facing Europeans and their advanced technology. JKH
G. R. Crone *The voyages of Cadamosto* Hakluyt Society (1937)

Caetani (or Gaetani) family Hereditary enemies of the Colonna, the Caetani rose to prominence at the time of Boniface VIII (Benedetto Caetani; Pope 1294–1303) who gave a solid legal basis to the family's effective hegemony in the Campania. The Caetani were weakened and their estates confiscated by Alexander VI, but the family was reinstated by Julius II and enjoyed a period of relative distinction in the later 16c. JH

Calixtus III Pope 1455–58 (b.1378) Born Alfonso Borgia, a canon lawyer by training, and a favoured servant of the house of Aragon, Calixtus was the founder of his family's fortunes. His pontificate was dominated by his enthusiasm for a crusade, but marred by his nepotism and xenophobia, which caused him to surround himself with relatives and other fellow Catalans. *See* BORGIA FAMILY. JH

Inventive draughtsmanship in a study of figures by Luca **Cambiaso** (Florence, Uffizi).

Cambiaso, Luca (1527–85) Founder and principal painter of the Genoese school. He received his early training from his father, but was decisively influenced by the Mannerist painters imported into Genoa: Perino del Vaga, Pordenone, Giulio Romano. He probably also visited Rome. He established the Genoese style of monumental fresco decoration and was a draughtsman of great inventiveness and individuality. By 1570 his religious paintings reflected the Counter-Reformation in content and style. In 1583 he accepted the invitation of Philip II of Spain to become court painter at the Escorial. He died there. MH

Cambrai, League of In NE France, lying near the border of the Burgundian Netherlands, Cambrai was the setting for several international agreements between Valois and Habsburgs and their allies. None was as important to Italy as the League contracted there on 10 December 1508. Ostensibly for the purpose of a crusade against the Turks, its secret provisions made it a treaty of aggression designed by its signatories (or those who subsequently joined

Palma Giovane's allegory of the Venetian response to the League of **Cambrai**: Doge Leonardo Loredan unleashes the lion of Venice (Venice, Doges' Palace).

it) to turn back the clock by cancelling a century of Venetian expansion on the mainland. France, by virtue of Louis XII's 'right' to Milan (which had led him to invade Italy in 1499), was to gain Cremona, Crema and the Ghiaradadda, Brescia and Bergamo. Maximilian, on behalf of the Empire, was to receive Verona, Vicenza, Padua, Treviso and the Friuli. The Marquis of Mantua wanted cities ceded to Venice in 1441: Peschiera, Asola, Lonigo; the Duke of Ferrara wanted Rovigo, which he had surrendered in 1484. Pope Julius II claimed towns in the Romagna such as Faenza, Rimini and Ravenna; Ferdinand of Aragon was promised the Venetian-held ports from Trani to Otranto in 'his' kingdom of Naples.

The initial success of the League armies at Agnadello on 14 May 1509 began the stripping from Venice of practically all her possessions except Treviso, and, though the allies began to fall out among themselves from 1510, it was not until January 1517 that Venice was once again master of its whole land empire, ceding only Cremona in the west and Gradisca and Gorizia in the east. The events of the intervening years were the most testing and psychologically shocking in Venice's history before 1797, and formed a major theme within the WARS OF ITALY. JRH

Campanilismo A term, derived from *campanile* ('bell tower'), signifying an intensely local patriotism. Machiavelli, in his play *Mandragola*, reveals another nuance of the term when one character reproaches the unadventurousness of another by accusing him of feeling uneasy whenever he cannot see the cupola of the Florentine cathedral. Both politically and emotionally *campanalismo* has to be taken into account when reflecting on the absence of NATIONAL FEELING in the peninsula – or on the nature of a people who produced so many men of migrant practical energy and unparochial imaginativeness. JRH

Canale, Cristoforo da (1510–62) Born into a poor branch of a patrician Venetian family, he adopted a naval career, obtaining his first command in 1536 and serving with distinction in the Turkish War of 1537–40. It was largely on his urging that the Senate in 1545 accepted the principle of employing convicts as GALLEY oarsmen. Though there was a need to supplement the dwindling supply of free oarsmen, there was some doubt whether convicts could be properly controlled without losing the advantage of their armed support in combat, but Canale showed that these fears were in practice unfounded, and Venice came to rely increasingly on convict crews. His career continued to advance through naval commands of increasing responsibility, and his advice on naval organization, manning and strategic deployment was valued above that of any other naval commander.

Although he was apparently without formal education, it is all the same clear from his dialogue treatise *Della milizia marittima* that he had acquired not only a certain acquaintance with classical history and with the works of such authors as Machiavelli, but the ambition to write a work that had literary as well as practical value. A mine, *the* mine, of information about Venetian naval affairs at the time of its composition in the 1540s or early 50s, it is also remarkable as the first full-scale treatment of naval warfare that has survived, long anticipating the first to be printed, Pantero Pantera's *L'armata navale* (Rome 1612). The *Della milizia* did not appear in print until 1930. JRH

Della milizia marittima ed. M. Nani Mocenigo (1930); A. Tenenti *Cristoforo da Canal, la marine vénitienne avant Lepante* (1962)

Cane, Facino (*c.*1350–1412) A professional soldier from his youth, he quickly acquired a reputation for ferocity and speed of movement, and for keeping the loyalty of his troops by permitting every sort of pillage and rapine. After fighting chiefly in Savoy and his native Piedmont he received his first major command in 1394, for Genoa, over 1000 horse and 100 foot. After a year he was on the move again, and it was not until 1397 that he established the steady connection with the Visconti that was to make him, on the death of Giangaleazzo in 1402, the chief arbiter in the succession crisis that followed. For some years the functioning of the government depended on his presence and that of his troops. When Giovanni Maria's rule was firmly established in 1404 it became clear that he was still dependent on Cane, who remained in practice the most powerful figure in the Milanese. The idea that only an early death prevented him from deposing Giovanni Maria (aided by strong anti-Viscontean support within the city) has led to his being compared with Francesco Sforza, and he has become a type of the politically too powerful condottiere. JRH

N. Valeri *La vita di Facino Cane* (1940); *DBI*

Cappello, Bianca (1548–87), born into one of the leading patrician families of Venice, eloped at 15 with a young Florentine merchant. They married, protected from Venetian demands for their extradition by Cosimo I's son Francesco, and she became, increasingly obviously, the prince's mistress. Gossip was exacerbated when Francesco married without casting her off, when her husband was mysteriously assassinated, and above all when, on the death of Francesco's wife Joanna of Austria, he married Bianca, making her Grand Duchess of Tuscany. Her life has been a rich source for romantic authors and remains an interesting one for students of life and manners; before her second marriage she had a curious and entertaining court of her own, based on a house Francesco commissioned Buontalenti to design for her on that site once symbolic of republicanism, the RUCELLAI Gardens. JRH

R. Cantagalli 'Bianca Cappello e una leggenda da sfatare' *Nuova Rivista Storica* (1965)

Capponi family 'In the annals of Florentine history, from the beginning to the end, probably no family appears as frequently – almost on every page – as the Capponi' (Goldthwaite). Resident from 1210, the family was among the richest in Florence by the end of the century, and in Gino (1350–1421) and Neri (1388–1475) it produced two of the outstanding office-holders and ambassadors of the period, the former supporting the Albizzi, the latter the Medici. It was Piero (1446–96) whose fiery reply to Charles VIII in 1494 – 'if you sound your trumpets we shall peal our bells' – reflected pride of lineage as well as of his city. In 1527 Niccolò di Piero (1437–1529) was elected gonfalonier and, at the height of the popular Savonarolan revival, proclaimed Christ as King of Florence. From 1530 its anti-Medicean stance cost the family its prominence and a number of them, exiled, had to seek their fortunes elsewhere. JRH

R. A. Goldthwaite *Private wealth in Renaissance Florence* (1968)

Cara, Marchetto (d. after 1525) A prolific composer of FROTTOLAS. Born in Verona in the latter half of the 15c., he seems to have been in the service of Isabella d'Este during the 1480s and 90s, probably as a singer and lutanist. He also worked for Massimiliano Sforza at Milan *c.*1512. His frottolas show some of the serious attention to setting verse that was to produce the madrigal. Many were published by Petrucci. DA

J. Haar ed. *Chanson and madrigal 1480–1530* (1964); A. Einstein *The Italian madrigal* (1949)

Caracciolo family Reputedly of Byzantine origin and certainly one of the more ancient of Neapolitan noble families. Of its many branches the most important was that of Avellino. The Caracciolo of Avellino became counts of Gallerate (1539) and Torella (1560), Dukes of Atripalda (1572) and Avellino (1589), and were hereditary Grand Chancellors of Naples after 1609. Another branch of the family, that of Melfi, was distinguished by Giovanni Caracciolo (1480–1539), the general who fought for the Last Florentine Republic and subsequently became Governor of Marseilles and Piedmont for Francis I. JH

Caravaggio, battle of (29 July 1448) The defeat of a Venetian by a Milanese army near this town just S of Bergamo checked Venice from taking over the weak AMBROSIAN REPUBLIC in Milan, while enabling the Milanese general Francesco Sforza to do so two years later. JRH

Caravaggio, Michelangelo Merisi (1573–1610) was born at Caravaggio in Lombardy.

He was the most influential, in European terms, of all 17c. Italian painters. The Italians Carlo Saraceni, Orazio and Artemisia Gentileschi and Bartolomeo Manfredi, and a host of copyists, were profoundly influenced by him, and the Spaniard José de Ribera ensured the continuation of his influence on subsequent Neapolitan art. The Frenchman Simon Vouet and that singular genius Georges de la Tour were inspired by him. In Antwerp, Theodor Rombouts and Gerard Seghers spread his influence, and major figures such as Gerrit van Honthorst, Dirck van Baburen and, above all, Hendrick Terbruggen ensured that his effect on Dutch art, and through it upon the young Rembrandt himself, was as profound as his direct impact upon Rubens during the latter's Italian sojourn.

During his short and murderous life – he killed a man in a quarrel over tennis in 1606 and, after trouble in Valletta and subsequent serious wounding in Naples, died on a beach at Port' Ercole – he had a revolutionary part to play in the transition from the Mannerist experiments of the 16c. to the developed Roman Baroque art of the 17c. Despite its almost total contrast with the academic eclecticism of the Carracci, and the sustained opposition of fashionable late Mannerist painters such as Taddeo and Federico Zuccaro, his alliance of intense realism with a masterly simplification of form was irresistible.

Focusing attention by dramatic lighting, excluding all but the essential, telling detail; overwhelming the onlooker by bringing the figures right into the foreground; concentrating attention and increasing the feeling of dramatic nearness and involvement on the part of the spectator by close cropping with the frame; the instantaneous, momentary quality of movement and the violent unexpected poses and foreshortenings of the figures, concentrating time into mere fractions of an unexpected second caught upon the wing; transforming familiar iconography by means of a literal, realistic approach to sacred themes, as in the rustic, peasant figure of St Matthew or the thoroughly dead Virgin caught, ungainly, on her rumpled bed (*Death of the Virgin*; Paris, Louvre), he opened the way towards the dramatic naturalism and dynamic, focused unity which were to be prime characteristics of developed Roman Baroque art.

Undoubtedly Caravaggio is the only artist in the history of post-antique Italian art who could give, not merely visual impact, but true

Caravaggio's use of dramatic foreshortening and lighting in *The Supper at Emmaus*, *c.*1598 (London, National Gallery).

drama, even to a *Bowl of Fruit* (Milan, Pinacoteca Ambrosiana). Even after the better part of 4 centuries of artistic shocks and revolutions, to see for the first time such paintings as his *Narcissus* (Rome, Galleria Nazionale), his *Crucifixion of St Peter* and *Conversion of St Paul* (Rome, S. Maria del Popolo), is to be overwhelmed. JW

M. Kitson *The complete paintings of Caravaggio* (1968); A. Moir *The Italian followers of Caravaggio* (1967)

Cardano, Girolamo (1501–76) Milanese physician, mathematician (*Ars magna*, 1545), inventor (e.g. gimbal-mountings for use at sea) and an influential writer (*De subtilitate*, 1551) on natural MAGIC. The last was the search for explanations of phenomena that could not be accounted for experimentally: magnetism, climate, the functioning and psychological effect of the senses, the properties of herbs, and so forth. Natural magic veered between true science and mere superstition, and Cardano's temperament, which led him to practise astrology and the divination of dreams and omens, held the extremes in an uneasy but fascinating balance.

This temperament is known through his autobiography *De vita propria* (*The book of my life*), written in old age and published posthumously in 1643. It is a work unique in the age for its clinical self-scrutiny, dwelling more closely on his body, features, habits and states of mind than on the progress of a successful career. A characteristic observation: 'I have discovered, by experience, that I cannot be long without bodily pain, for if once that circum-

stance arises, a certain mental anguish overcomes me, so grievous that nothing could be more distressing. Bodily pain, or the cause of bodily distress – in which there is no disgrace – is but a minor evil. Accordingly I have hit on a plan of biting my lips, of twisting my fingers, of pinching the skin of the tender muscles of my left arm until the tears come. Under the protection of this self-chastisement I live without disgracing myself.' *See* MATHEMATICS. JRH
The book of my life tr. J. Stoner (1931); *DBI*

Cardona, Raymond de (d.1522) Of Spanish birth, Raymond Folch served as a soldier in Italy under Gonzalo de Cordoba and was created Duke of Cardona in 1491. During the War of the Holy League (1511–13) Cardona, who had been appointed Viceroy of Naples, assumed command of Spanish and papal troops, besieged Bologna unsuccessfully, and was defeated by the French at Ravenna (1512). He subsequently conquered Milan and led the League against Florence. He was thus responsible for the sack of Prato (1512) and the Medici restoration. As Viceroy of Naples, Cardona proved to be a first-class administrator. JH

Carlo Emanuele I Duke of Savoy 1580–1630 (b.1562) From any realistic point of view Carlo Emanuele's life must be accounted a failure, but he was known to contemporaries as *Il Grande*, 'the Great'. Trying to steer a middle course between the conflicting demands of France and Spain while pursuing a largely personal vendetta with Geneva, Carlo Emanuele ended up in a state of constant warfare. He thus weakened the economy of Savoy and virtually destroyed its fine administration. Yet, despite the marked development of absolutist forms of government during his reign, his subjects remained devoted to a prince who consistently favoured learning and the arts, did his best to promote commerce and industry, made Turin a centre of culture and had a clear vision of Savoy's future greatness. The people of Savoy took pride in his role as the main upholder between 1610 and 1630 of Italian independence against Spanish imperialism, and in his successful expansion of Savoy's boundaries at Spanish expense. JH
R. Bergadani *Carlo Emanuele I* (1926)

Carmagnola, Francesco Bussone (*c.*1385–1432) served with Facino Cane until the latter's death in 1412, and then rapidly became the most trusted of Filippo Maria Visconti's condottieri, reconquering the territories and towns that had split away from the duchy during the confusion that followed the death of Giangaleazzo. Monza, Lodi, Alessandria, Bergamo, Cremona, Brescia: a remarkable series of successful siege campaigns was crowned in 1422 by his defeat of a Swiss army at ARBEDO. Though he was wary of accepting battle, preferring lightning raids or methodical sieges, this action confirmed his reputation as the outstanding soldier in northern Italy.

A rift at this point with Filippo Maria (possibly uneasy at Carmagnola's political following and territorial ambition) led him to enter Venetian service in 1425, and in the following year he was given the chief command of the army sent against his former employer. An initial success, the storming of Brescia in 1426, was followed in 1427 by victory over the Milanese at MACLODIO. Thereafter Venice sensed that their general's zeal was waning. He was in touch with Filippo Maria and apparently abusing his position to play the diplomatist, appearing to be chiefly concerned to see which side would offer him the larger amount of territory for him to rule as a state of his own. In 1432 he was recalled to Venice, tried for treason and executed between the columns on the Piazzetta. JRH
A. Battistella *Il conte di Carmagnola* (1889)

Carnesecchi, Pietro (1508–67) was a victim of the Inquisition. A Florentine noble, he made a brilliant curial career under Clement VII but disengaged himself after the accession of Paul III. He was always exceptionally well connected. Linked to the leading proponents of EVANGELISM and a personal disciple of Juan de Valdes, he held a doctrine of justification by faith. He was tried by the Roman Inquisition in 1546 and 1566. The inquisitors in 1566 were primarily interested in finding out about his friends, particularly Cardinal Morone. Failing to make him an informer, they got him to confess and he was executed. The transcripts of his trial are a key source on the evangelical group. OL

Carnival lasted from 26 December to Shrove Tuesday. The most spectacular celebrations took place in the centres of great cities, along the Corso in Rome and on Piazza S. Marco in Venice. The more formally structured events, often organized by festive societies, included

Masked singers in the woodcut title page of a Florentine book of **carnival** songs (1493–97).

processions of richly-decorated floats (Florence), the ritual killing of animals (Venice, Rome), races (Rome, Florence) and mock-battles. Plays, weddings, banquets and tournaments tended to occur at this season. The less formally structured events included eating and drinking on a heroic scale; wearing masks or complete fancy dress (it was conventional for men to dress as women and women as men); singing songs with double meanings, composed by Lorenzo de' Medici and Machiavelli among others; and throwing water, eggs, oranges, lemons, stones, etc. Brawls were common and deaths not unusual. In short, Carnival was the opportunity for acting out oral (gluttonous), anal, genital and aggressive fantasies which were inhibited for the rest of the year.

Many of the clergy participated in Carnival. A few, notably Savonarola and Cardinal Borromeo, violently disapproved of these licentious and 'pagan' customs. By 1600 the reformers had managed to bowdlerize the proceedings to a limited extent. *See* FESTIVALS. PB

F. Clementi *Il carnevale romano* (1899)

Caro, Annibale (1507–66) pursued the literary interests of a respected man of vernacular letters and lived the life of a typical courtier of the 16c. Born at Civitanova Marche, he studied in Florence and then became secretary to Pierluigi Farnese until the latter's murder in 1547. He next served Cardinal Alessandro Farnese and others until in 1563 he obtained enough benefices to devote all his time to literature. Caro wrote Petrarchan poetry and satirical sonnets, and engaged in contemporary literary debates and quarrels. His prose comedy *Gli straccioni* (*The ragamuffins*; 1554) showed classical influence and mirrored his times. Over 1000 of his letters were collected and published in 1573 and 1575; written in a rhetorical style praised in his time, they were full of notices of artistic and cultural life. His vernacular blank verse translation of Virgil's *Aeneid* (published 1581) was highly rated. PG

Carpaccio, Vittore (active *c.*1488–1525/6) took the ideas nascent in the somewhat dry work of his probable master, Gentile Bellini, and raised them to new heights of artistry. Like Gentile, he worked principally for the Venetian *scuole* or confraternities, and his major surviving achievement is the series of large paintings of the *Legend of St Ursula* (begun 1490; Venice, Accademia). Throughout these, as in all his other works, the quality of mellow, cool, yet glowing light is one of the chief glories. Another is the fact that the religious subject is used as an opportunity for a meticulously controlled, and yet untrammelled, description of every facet of Venetian life, customs, costumes, day-to-day activities and working methods; of shipping, docks, and ports and architecture; of every aspect of the Adriatic world, its landscapes, its townscapes, and its canal-scapes as they were at the turn of the 16c. An untold wealth of documentary information is transmuted into art, constituting a landmark on the path that leads eventually to Canaletto and Guardi. JW

J. Lauts *Carpaccio* (1962)

Carpi, Girolamo da (1501–56) exemplified the spreading influence of Roman Mannerist painting in Ferrara and Bologna. His early exposure to Raphaelesque classicism through Garofalo and Dosso Dossi was followed by a complete absorption of Giulio Romano's dynamic Mannerist style demonstrated in the *Marriage of St Catherine* (1532–34; Bologna, S.

Salvatore), while his portraiture shows the direct influence of Parmigianino. Girolamo's Roman sketchbook, probably used as a pattern book of decorative motifs, and consisting primarily of copies of drawings by other artists, represents the largest extant Renaissance compilation of antiquities. LP

N. Canedy *The Roman sketchbook of Girolamo da Carpi* (1976); A. Mezzetti *Girolamo da Ferrara detto da Carpi* (1977)

Carracci, Annibale (1560–1609) One of a Bolognese family of painters, the oldest of whom, Lodovico (1555–1619), founded a school in Bologna. His cousins Agostino (1557–1602) and Annibale worked in their early years with Lodovico, but left Bologna, working first in north Italy and later in Rome. After 1595 Annibale was employed by Cardinal Odoardo Farnese, charged with decorating two rooms in the family palace. Of these the famous gallery, a vast and splendid room, was frescoed with an elaborately arranged system of erotic and sensuous mythological pictures – love stories of the classical deities: surely a strange choice for a cardinal – painted in emulation of Michelangelo's Sistine ceiling and Raphael's story of Amor and Psyche in Agostino Chigi's villa (now the Farnesina). Agostino Carracci worked with his brother in the Palazzo Farnese, as did Domenichino. These frescoes, as well as Annibale's many religious pictures in Rome, show the profound influence of 16c. painting, in particular of Titian and Correggio. In his turn Annibale became a decisive influence on Baroque painters and on academic art. Through his sensitive use of landscape he also became the forerunner of Poussin and other 17c. masters. LDE

D. Posner *Annibale Carracci* (1971); R. Wittkower *Art and architecture in Italy 1600–1750* (1958)

Diana and Endymion in the frescoes by Annibale **Carracci** in the Farnese Palace in Rome.

Carrara family Landowners of military character whose domination of Padua developed during the war against della Scala Verona (Giacomo elected *dominus generalis* 1318; Marsilio signore 1328) but reached its peak after the city regained its independence (1337) with Francesco il Vecchio (1350–88, b.1325), who curtailed civic liberties (1362) and exploited Paduan resources mainly for expansionist wars against Venice (1372–73, 1378–81). His illusions of princely greatness found expression on coins and frescoes (1367–79) commemorating famous men, following suggestions by Petrarch, who bequeathed to him most of his books. He was exiled when Giangaleazzo Visconti occupied Padua (1388–90) and his son Francesco Novello (1390–1405) was deposed and murdered after the Venetian annexation. DC

B. Kohl 'Government and society in Renaissance Padua' *Journal of Medieval and Renaissance Studies* (1972); *DBI*; T. E. Mommsen 'Petrarch and the decoration of the Sala Virorum Illustrium in Padua' *Art Bulletin* (1952)

Casa, Giovanni della (1503–56), Archbishop of Benevento and a prominent Counter-Reformation clerical administrator, wrote, among other secular works in verse and prose, *Il Galateo* in the early 1550s: it was published posthumously in 1558 and translated before the end of the century into French, English, Latin, Spanish and German. Still read today, it was, after Castiglione's *The courtier*, which it trivializes, the most influential of Italian books on behaviour. It is more attractive in style than in tone, of which a fair sample is: 'We must subscribe not necessarily to the best customs but to those which prevail in our day'. JRH

Il Galateo tr. R. S. Pine-Coffin (1958); ed. C. Cordié (1960); A. Santosuosso *Vita di Giovanni della Casa* (1979)

Cascina, battle of The Florentines defeated a Pisan force here on 28 July 1364, taking some of them by surprise while they bathed in the Arno. The engagement is best known as the subject of a fresco commissioned for the Palazzo Vecchio from Michelangelo. Worked

Bastiano da Sangallo's copy of part of Michelangelo's cartoon for his fresco of the battle of **Cascina** (detail) (Holkham Hall).

on at intervals 1504–06, this remained unfinished and is known (in part) only from a somewhat later copy of the cartoon, and from the contemporary fame the cartoon acquired for its treatment of the abruptly alerted bathers. JRH
C. Gould *Michelangelo's Battle of Cascina* (1966)

Casola, Pietro (1427–1507) Milanese cleric who wrote an unusually personal and alert account of a pilgrimage to the Holy Land in 1494. It contains a richly detailed account of Venice, whence he – in common with nearly all pilgrims similarly bound – embarked. JRH
M. Newett *Canon Pietro Casola's pilgrimage to Jerusalem* (1907); *DBI*

Castagno *See* ANDREA DEL CASTAGNO

Castelvetro, Lodovico (1505–71) Born in Modena, he was one of the leading critics and linguists of his age, and a vigorous polemicist. Condemned *in absentia* for doctrinal error by the Inquisition (1560), he escaped to Switzerland and France. His main works are commentaries to Aristotle's *Poetics* (1570), which gave him an important position in the history of Renaissance rhetoric, to Petrarch's *Rime* (1582), to the first 29 canti of the *Inferno*, a *Giunta* to Bembo's *Prose* (1563), which concentrates on the historical development of Italian, and corrections to Varchi's *Ercolano* (1572). He stands out not so much for his poetic sensibility as for his exceptional knowledge of ancient and modern languages and for his rigorous philological approach. He died, still in self-exile, at Chiavenna. LL
Opere varie critiche with a *Vita* by L. A. Muratori (1727); B. Weinberg, 'Castelvetro's theory of poetics' in R. S. Crane ed. *Critics and criticism ancient and modern* (1952); C. R. Melzi *Castelvetro's annotations to the Inferno: a new perspective in sixteenth century criticism* (1966)

Castiglione, Baldassare (1478–1529) Diplomat and author of *Il cortegiano* (*The courtier*). Born at Casàtico to a minor landowning family of soldiers and administrators in the service of successive rulers of nearby Mantua, Castiglione was sent to Milan to have his education 'finished' on the fringe of Lodovico Sforza's court, then renowned above all others for its chivalric tone and its protection of men of learning. Though the details of this period are scarce, it is clear that it was in Milan that he acquired the military knowledge and sense for public affairs that led to his engagement successively by the rulers of Mantua (1500–04), Urbino (1504–16) and Mantua again (1516–24), and also to his lifelong, if amateur,

Castiglione: the portrait by Raphael (Paris, Louvre).

interest in the literature of classical antiquity. Though he occupied minor military commands, his status was that of an equerry rather than of a combat soldier, and the address he brought to the arrangement of truces and liaison with allies led to his being employed increasingly as a diplomat. It was while he was residing as Mantuan ambassador in Rome that Pope Clement VII obtained leave from Duke Federico II Gonzaga to send him in 1524 as papal nuncio to Spain. Here, in Toledo, he died in 1529, mourned by Charles V as 'one of the world's finest gentlemen'.

His Latin and Italian poems appeared in print but he is remembered for his dialogue-treatise *Il cortegiano* (redrafted from 1508 in ever more extensive and thoughtful forms until its publication in Venice in 1528.) In it he had 2 aims: to give 'a portrait' of the court of Urbino at a moment (1506) he came to regard with deepening nostalgia, and to describe the formation of a courtier so widely and gracefully accomplished that his advice could, by being acceptable to a prince, contribute to the security and welfare of a badly governed Italy. Writing in an eclectic and widely accessible Italian, Castiglione employed change of pace and touches of characterization and description to bring to life people and place and to exemplify his moral imperative: never be tedious. This principle underlies his teaching that none of the courtier's attainments in arms, letters, art, sport, music or conversation should lack 'sprezzatura', an unforced ease of accomplishment, the flavour of effortless superiority which was to be looked on for centuries as the trade mark of the gentleman. Not untainted by self-grooming for effect or snobbish scorn for overt professionalism, the notion of 'sprezzatura' nevertheless arose directly from the strain in Aristotle's and Cicero's moral philosophy which dealt with the social behaviour of the balanced and responsible citizen. Here, as in its treatment of the Platonic notion that human love can be transmuted into an apprehension of the divine, *The courtier* provided a skilful popularization of the ideas of humanist philosophers. Both form and content led to the book's lasting influence, first through translation (English, French, Spanish, Latin) and plagiarism, and then through absorption into the enormous literature of etiquette which it did much to stimulate. JRH

J. Cartwright *Baldassare Castiglione* (2 vols 1908); J. R. Woodhouse *Baldesar Castiglione: a reassessment of 'The courtier'* (1978); *Il cortegiano* ed. V. Cian (4th ed. 1947); tr. G. Bull (1967)

Castracani degli Antelminelli, Castruccio (1281–1328) Prominent among the Ghibelline faction in Lucca, the Castracani were banished after a Guelf *Putsch* in 1300. Castruccio turned briefly to a mercantile career (which brought him to England) then to one of arms, at first in Flanders and then in Italy, where he served first the della Scala of Verona and then Venice, while awaiting a change in the political situation in Tuscany. The challenge to the Florence-dominated Guelf hegemony there came with the arrival in Italy of the Emperor Henry VII in 1310, but it was not until 1314 that Castruccio (by then, as was so common with restless exiles, both soldier and schemer) re-entered Lucca in reluctant association with the conqueror, the signore of Pisa, Uguccione della Faggiuola.

In the following year Castruccio turned on him, defeated his troops and got the Lucchesi to entrust him with the leading voice in the city's government as its liberator from subjection to Pisa. His authority was enhanced when he obtained the title of Imperial vicar in Lunigiana, and still further extended by his victory over Florence at Altopascio in 1325. For his recovery of much of Tuscany for the Ghibelline cause the Emperor Lewis made him Duke of Lucca in 1327, and extended his vicariate to include Pisa. In 1328 he recaptured Pistoia, which had revolted after he had taken it for Lucca before Altopascio. Before he was able to consolidate and further extend his self-made empire, however, he contracted malaria and died of it. Lewis refused to recognize his son as either duke or vicar, and the whole structure of Castruccio's rule collapsed into its several parts. As a story of ambition vaulting too far above a properly organized political base, his career fascinated Machiavelli, who in 1520 wrote a short *Vita di Castruccio*. JRH

Cateau-Cambrésis, Peace (or Treaty) of (3 April 1559) Signed in a dilapidated castle (*château*) near Cambrai in NE France, this international settlement was one of the very few agreements of the Renaissance that all parties were prepared to consider enduringly binding. Like all successful treaties it was the product of mutual exhaustion. England, with a girl monarch, Elizabeth I, and yet another religious realignment in view, accepted the

An allegory of the Peace of **Cateau-Cambrésis** by Stradanus. Philip II presides over the reconciliation of Germany and Italy (left), France and Spain (right) (Oxford, Ashmolean Museum).

St **Catherine** of Siena's vision of Christ: detail from a panel by Giovanni di Paolo (New York, Metropolitan Museum).

French reconquest of Calais of the previous year. The French returned Piedmont-Savoy, which they had occupied since 1536, to its duke, Emanuel Philibert, and accepted – after two generations of costly interventions – Spanish control over Milan, Naples, Sicily and Sardinia. Florence was permitted to embrace Siena and its territories – recently another source of draining Habsburg-Valois rivalry. Though threatened 1562–64 by a renewal of English claims on Calais, the Peace set enduring guidelines for Henry II of France and Philip II of Spain and their successors, and confirmed the Habsburg occupation or orientation of much of Italy – with Venice, pertinaciously neutral and independent, the most conspicuous exception. JRH

J. E. A. de Ruble *Le traité de Cateau-Cambrésis* (1889)

Catherine, St, of Siena (1347–80) Caterina Benincasa, 24th child of a prosperous dyer, saw visions and cultivated piety from the age of 6, joined the Dominican Third Order in 1363, and passed her days in self-flagellation, ecstasies and service in hospitals and leper-houses. In 1367 she claimed that Jesus, in company with the Madonna and other saints, appeared to her and placed a wedding ring upon her finger; in 1375 she received the stigmata. Her fame as a thaumaturge drew her, at the suggestion of her spiritual directors, to play a public role. She was sent by Florence as ambassador to Gregory XI, by Gregory XII to Florence. Together with mystical writings, 350 letters dictated by her, before her early death aged 33, survive. She was canonized in 1460, and is now revered as one of the two 'primary patron saints' of Italy. JL

Bibliotheca sanctorum ed. F. Caraffa and G. Morelli III (1963)

Cavalcanti, Guido (?1259–1300) The best of the Florentine *Dolce Stil Novo* school of poets before Dante, who was befriended and encouraged by Cavalcanti in his youth. Guinizelli, the Bolognese founder of the school, had offered an implicit paradox between the near-heavenly qualities of an adored lady and the pain and confusion which she provoked in the poet. Cavalcanti made this opposition more explicit, and interiorized it (using Averroist psychology) into an unresolvable incompatibility between intellectual perception and emotional desire. The impasse was to be broken by Dante in the *Vita nuova*. Cavalcanti meanwhile expressed it in poetry of great force and tension, by personifying the lover's inner faculties and depicting them in disarray. His obscure manifesto-poem *Donna mi prega* was glossed in the Quattrocento as a neo-Platonist tract, a misreading which may have helped to maintain the interest of Renaissance readers and scholars. RA

Rime ed. G. Favati (1957); M. Corti 'Dualismo e immaginazione visiva di Guido Cavalcanti' *Convivium* (1951)

Cellini, Benvenuto (1500–71) No Renaissance artist can be better known, in temperament or career, than Cellini, thanks to his *Autobiography*. It is all the more irritating, then, to read of a life of such furious activity as goldsmith, medallist and sculptor from which so few authenticated works survive: 2 seals, 3 medals, 7 coins, 1 piece of goldsmith's work (the great saltcellar of Francis I); 7 sculptures – though the base of the *Perseus* contains 4 additional figures: these have now been replaced by replicas and are in the Bargello, where almost the whole range of his sculptural work can be seen. There also remain a wax and a bronze model for the *Perseus*. Regret that greed and time have destroyed so much (Cellini himself melted down objects from the treasury of St Peter's when Clement VII was preparing to flee after the Sack of Rome) is all the greater in that Cellini's intense feeling for and knowledge of his craft is so obvious in his *Treatises on goldsmithing and sculpture*.

His father, a mason, hoped that his son would take up as a trade what was to him only a part-time occupation and become a woodwind player, and only grudgingly allowed him to follow a career prompted by his love of drawing. From 1519 to 1540 he worked in Rome, with short spells in Florence, Venice and France. From 1540 to 1545 he resided in France, mostly working for Francis I (to whom he took the uncompleted saltcellar, now in the Kunsthistorisches Museum, Vienna), and here he made his first large sculpture, the *Nymph of*

Benvenuto **Cellini**'s bronze *Perseus*, in the Loggia dei Lanzi, Florence.

Fontainebleau (Paris, Louvre). In 1545 he received the commission for the *Perseus* from Cosimo I, which he relished as an invitation to put the other sculptors working in Florence (especially Bandinelli) in their place. Here he remained until his death, broadening his repertory with two portrait busts, of Cosimo and of Bindo Altoviti, and a marble figure of Christ on the Cross (Madrid, Escorial).

Composed between 1558 and 1562, largely through dictation, the *Autobiography* was doubtless produced under the spur of the first edition of Vasari's *Lives* (1550); Cellini, both victim and protagonist of backbiting, was not one to let others record his achievements. It gushes, welcomely, from a tap of self-regard. It is not artless. No one, however under-educated, could cater for the classical or in other ways arcane taste of patrons demanding table-sculpture or medals without acquiring a gloss of fashionable culture. It is special pleading, but it does not seek to lie or conceal. From the strongly picaresque flavour emerges a character fiercely, at times viciously, independent, an artist-condottiere apt to brawl, ambisexually promiscuous, but above all passionately concerned with being an artist, as eager to learn from as to denigrate his fellows. He saw life as an alternation of battles and banquets, each involving risk and, at the same time, some possible advantage to his craft, gained by force or cajolement. The book has a tone strikingly – and cautionarily – at odds with the style of his work: ruminatively elegant, calculatedly finicking, an art both buoyed up and restricted by a sense of responsibility to Art. [143] JRH

E. Camesasca *Tutta l'opera del Cellini* (1955); *Vita* ed. E. Carrara (1944); E. Carrara *Cellini* (1938); *Autobiography* tr. G. Bull (1956)

Cenci, Beatrice (1577–99) Shelley's tragedy *The Cenci*, of 1819, is one of many literary treatments of a story whose chief importance lies in what it reveals about the desire to see the late Italian Renaissance in terms of decadence and lurid scandal. Daughter of a father who was violent, avaricious and morbidly jealous of his children, Beatrice was imprisoned by him in such misery that she planned, with the aid of her brother, stepmother and lover, to murder him. The crime, soon detected, was prosecuted with a vehemence that reflected the personal feelings of Pope Clement VIII. Late in the trial Beatrice's advocate produced his best argument: murder was the only weapon she had against being raped by her father. The reactions of the Romans after she, with the other accused, was executed, were divided: to some she was 'the Roman virgin', hounded by a Pope who was after her family's lands; to others she was a whore, a liar and a parricide. It was this rich mixture of contemporary debate that got stirred into the imagination of romantic authors. JRH

Cennino d'Andrea Cennini of Colle di Val d'Elsa, a pupil of Agnolo Gaddi, owes his fame entirely to his *Libro dell'arte* or *Craftsman's handbook*, probably written in the 1390s. It constitutes a unique source book for almost every aspect of the technique and materials of late medieval Italian painting. Its intense conservatism is reflected in the fact that, in matters such as perspective, Cennini's prescription is well to the rear of Giotto's practice more than 75 years earlier. JW

The craftsman's handbook tr. D. V. Thompson (1960)

Censorship, in the vague sense of attempts by the authorities in Church and State to suppress books of which they disapproved and punish their authors, existed in the Renaissance as in the Middle Ages. What was new in the 16c. was the institutionalization of censorship. In Italy, as elsewhere, this was primarily a response to the spread of printed Protestant propaganda. The first Italian Index of Prohibited Books, issued in 1538 by the Senate of Milan, was primarily concerned with the works of the reformers. Similar indexes were issued in Siena, Venice and elsewhere in the 1540s. The Roman Index of 1554 was more sweeping than its predecessors, and Paul IV's 1559 Index, which was concerned with morals as well as faith, more sweeping still. It included Poggio's *Facetiae* (*Jokes*) and the works of Machiavelli and Aretino, and was accompanied by public book-burning in Rome and elsewhere. The Index of the Council of Trent (published 1564) was somewhat milder, and prohibited some books merely 'until they are corrected', but Pius V (Pope 1566–72) was a former Grand Inquisitor, and censorship continued to tighten.

This tightening may be illustrated by the fortunes of Boccaccio's *Decameron*. Attacked by S. Bernardino of Siena in sermons of the 1420s, and burned in Savonarola's bonfire of 'vanities' in 1497, the *Decameron* was ordered to be expurgated in 1559. Cosimo de' Medici sent an ambassador to the Council of Trent to plead for the book, which was reprieved till corrected. A version censored by Vincenzo Borghini appeared in 1573, and another, censored more severely by Salviati, in 1582. Anti-clerical stories and remarks suffered in particular from the blue pencil. Similarly, Castiglione's *The courtier* was expurgated in 1584 because some criticisms of the clergy had given offence. In the short term, the Index involved considerable loss for booksellers and publishers, who were caught with unsaleable stock on their hands. In the long term, it encouraged them to concentrate on orthodox religious books, though some booksellers, notably in Venice in the 1570s and 80s, were prepared to run the risk of supplying customers with 'underground' copies of Luther and Machiavelli.

Not only books were censored. Paintings too could cause offence. Veronese was summoned before the Inquisition at Venice in 1573 and ordered to correct his *Last Supper* by removing irrelevant halberdiers and buffoons (in fact he simply changed the title to *Feast in the House of*

Censorship: drapery (by Daniele da Volterra) clothes the immodesty of Michelangelo's figure of St Bartholomew in *The Last Judgment* in the Sistine Chapel, Rome.

Levi). Draperies were painted over some naked figures in Michelangelo's *Last Judgment*. Cardinal Borromeo and Gregory XIII were among the clerics who attempted to censor or prohibit plays. The effectiveness of the policy of censorship cannot be measured by indexes and penalties alone. Tasso, who insisted on being examined by the Inquisition, and himself revised his *Jerusalem delivered* to make it more orthodox, is a dramatic instance of a general trend; the censor was internalized. PB

A. Rotondo 'La Censura' *SI* V (1973); P. Grendler *The Roman Inquisition and the Venetian press, 1540–1605* (1977)

Cerignola, battle of (28 April 1503) At this village SE by E of Foggia in Apulia, the defeat by a Spanish force under Gonzalo de Cordoba of a large part of the French army occupying Naples opened the way for the complete control of the kingdom of Naples by Aragon (later, Spain) and the cancellation of the terms of the Treaty of Granada of 1500, whereby the Kingdom had been divided between Aragon and France. JRH

Cesalpino, Andrea (1519–1603) Botanist and physiologist. After receiving his doctorate at Pisa in 1551 he became professor of MEDICINE and director of the botanic garden there; in 1592 he migrated to Rome to become papal physician and professor at the Sapienza. He published on botany, medicine and metallurgy. His two most important works are *Questionum peripateticum libri V* (5 books of Aristotelian questions; Venice 1571), a strongly Aristotelian work in which he threw doubt on the Galenic functioning of the heart; and *De plantis libri XVI* (Florence 1583), which dealt for almost the first time with the physiology of plants – that is with the structure and function of their parts, departing from the traditional interest in botany as a mere adjunct to medicine. MBH

Charles V Emperor 1519–56 (b.1500) On the death of his father Philip the Handsome of Burgundy, the son of the Habsburg Emperor Maximilian I, in 1506 Charles began to accumulate the hereditary lands that were to make him a European ruler on a scale only to be surpassed by Napoleon. In 1506 came Franche-Comté, much of the Netherlands and a claim to Burgundy, though the duchy was, by agreement, in French hands. In 1515 he was made regent of Castile because of the insanity of his mother, Queen Joanna. In 1516 Ferdinand of Aragon died and he became ruler of the whole of Spain and its American dominions. With Maximilian's death in 1519 he inherited the Habsburg domains in Germany and Austria: the marriages of his brother Ferdinand and his sister Mary extended the connection to Bohemia and Hungary. Moreover, also in 1519, Charles, against the optimistic but half-hearted rival candidatures of Henry VIII of England and Francis I, bribed his way to succeeding to Maximilian's elective Imperial title. The significance of this assemblage of powers in the hands of a 19-year-old was pointed out with relish by Charles's Italian (he was born at Vercelli) chief minister Mercurino Gattinara: 'God has set you on the path towards world monarchy'.

Charles's empire touched not only the Mediterranean but the Atlantic and the North Sea. In any account of his career his problems in Spain (to which he came as an unpopular foreigner), in the Netherlands (an uneasy mosaic of economically self-sufficent and politically restless regions), in Germany (where as a Catholic-universalist he faced Protestant heresy as well as the inherent fissiparousness of that cluster of 'free' cities and jealous princes), in eastern Europe and in Africa (the Turks besieged Vienna in 1529 and his reign was the hey-day of the Barbary pirate emirates): these problems bulk more largely than his concern with Italy. All the same, from the narrower perspective of the peninsula his power and policies were of crucial importance.

Least controversial was his connection with the south. In 1516 he simply took over a Spanish link with Sicily that had existed since the Sicilian Vespers of 1282 had substituted Aragonese for Angevin rule. His viceroys accepted, as had Ferdinand's, that their job was to inject occasional jolts of regal control into a country largely self-governing, riven by family and regional feuds and rife with banditry as well as the discreeter forms of corruption; in spite of the island's potential agricultural wealth, the building of anti-Turkish coastal defences and the maintenance of a galley patrol in the 1530s and 40s required an injection of Spanish money. In the kingdom of Naples, too, he stepped into his predecessor's shoes. Here, however, a shorter term of Aragonese government, the confusions of the Franco-Aragonese contestation of 1501–04, and the renewal of French claims in the Neapolitan war of 1528–29 had left a less traditionally structured form of local government and had so riven political loyalties that Charles's viceroys could drive their demands for financial support through the gaps. Even so, they had to step cautiously over native susceptibilities. From the 1530s Spain put more money into Naples (again, for anti-Turkish strategic purposes) than it extracted. In the 1540s Charles had to stomach the withdrawal of the Spanish Inquisition, his most favoured export to his dependencies.

His position in Milan was quite different. This was not an inherited area but one that had to be fought for. It was the Italian Gattinara who convinced Charles that, as long as France controlled the Milanese, contact between his Spanish and German dominions would be imperilled by the power geography had appointed his chief adversary. By committing an army to its conquest in 1521 Charles became for the first time immersed in the intricacies of Italian affairs and with allies, like the Papacy and Venice, that his northern upbringing and Spanish tyroship had given him no comprehension of. It was only after the French defeat at Pavia in 1525, the consequent treachery of his Milanese supporter, Girolamo Morone, and of his ally Pope Clement VII, and Francis I's breach of the 1526 Treaty of Madrid and the renewed fighting for Milan that broke out, that Charles learned of the true volatility of peninsular power struggles.

After Francis's capitulation in 1529 Charles restored the Sforza to Milan, made his relationship to Clement clear by forcing him to give him the Imperial crown not in Rome (which would have been an act of apology for the Imperial Sack of 1527) but in Bologna, and, after leaving an army to restore the Medici to Florence in 1530, insisted on an Imperial garrison presence there and in other strategic Tuscan cities. Only on the death of Francesco II Sforza did he exert direct rather than veiled power over Milan. Thereafter it was ruled by governors responsible at first directly, and, from 1540, when he made his son Philip Duke of Milan, indirectly, to him. Charles did not fully share his ministers' insistence on the strategic importance of Milan. Twice (in 1535 and 1544) he considered giving it to Francis in return for support for his non-Italian objectives: the crushing of Protestantism and the

Bronze bust of **Charles V** by Leone Leoni (Vienna, Kunsthistorisches Museum).

launching of a crusade against the Turks. But throughout he treated it financially as a conquest; hence the Italian saying 'in Sicily the Spaniards nibble, in Naples they eat, and in Milan they devour'. All the same, though Milan was taxed at will and became a Spanish *place d'armes*, the forms of local government were preserved, from the mid-1530s Spain put in more cash than it extracted, and the standard of living at least of those engaged in commerce and industry was not seriously impaired.

Charles, unlike his successor Philip II, came to Italy in person: to Bologna twice, to be crowned in 1529 and to confer with the Pope in the winter of 1532–33; to Sicily and Naples in 1535–36 (after his attack on Tunis); to Genoa in 1543. It was on the second of these visits that he met Titian. Thanks to the artist's appointment in 1533 as his court painter it is primarily through Italian eyes that we see the two most salient aspects of Charles's character: the horsed and armoured victor over his rebel German subjects (the portrait commemorating the battle of Muhlberg in 1547), and the over-travelled paterfamilias of an uncooperative brood of political offspring (the portrait in the Alte Pinakothek, Munich). It was in the latter mood that he abdicated in 1556 and retired to a modest villa next to the remote Castilian monastery of Yuste, where he died in 1558. *See* WARS OF ITALY. JRH

K. Brandi *The Emperor Charles V* (1939); H. Koenigsberger 'The empire of Charles V in Europe' *New Cambridge modern history* II (1958)

Charles VIII King of France 1483–98 (b.1470) For a man whose invasion of Italy in 1494 was to be seen by Italians within a generation as a turning point in their history (as it was for Europe as a whole by historians until recently), Charles was curiously unimpressive in both mind and body. Son of the remarkably business-like, if eccentric, 'Spider King', Louis XI, he inherited the throne at the age of 13, but was overshadowed by the personalities of his imperious sister Anne and her ambitious husband Pierre de Beaujeu until 1492.

He had, meanwhile, cultivated a genealogical and chivalric dream of what he would do when he had the chance: reactivate the shaky Angevin claim he had inherited to the throne of Naples and use that kingdom as base for a crusade against the Holy Land. In this he was supported by councillors aware that this scheme was not without possible advantage to

Terracotta bust of **Charles VIII** by an unknown Florentine master (Florence, Bargello).

France. Though possessing a Mediterranean frontier, France lacked the stepping stones that would facilitate trade with the Near East – the most lucrative available at that time. 'Crusade' remained a word calculated to still the opposition of powers guiltily conscious of their determination to make no Quixotic move of their own. Such an expedition may have been against the true interests of France which, in a later perspective, could be seen to have pointed north-east, not south, but its apparent common sense at the time was confirmed by Italian exiles and dissidents who emphasized the welcome a French intervention would receive. These representations reached the status of a guarantee of success when Lodovico Sforza of Milan, who had come to feel hazardously isolated from the other Italian powers, promised support in 1493.

This determined Charles – who had already guarded his flanks by agreements (costly in cash or territory) with his neighbour states – to move. Having assembled an army large enough to overawe or brush aside any opposition, he found himself, after entering Italy in September 1494, master of Naples by February 1495. On 12 May he was crowned King of Naples, and added the titles King of Sicily and Jerusalem. His return home was blocked by a hastily assembled league of Italian states, but his army fought through their forces at FORNOVO on 6 July and by October he was back in France. He was preparing a force to return to the support of the garrisons he had left in Naples when he died in 1498 at the age of 28.

Though it was scorned, understandably, by Italians as misshapen and naïve, there had been both political and economic logic behind his plan and military expertise of a high order in its execution. In the history of France his reign is an embarrassing interlude. In that of Italy, however, he is a portent, administering a shock to a system that could not survive the repetition of his invasion by his successors Louis XII and Francis I. *See* WARS OF ITALY. JRH

F. Delaborde *L'expédition de Charles VIII en Italie* (1885); A. Denis *Charles VIII et les Italiens: histoire et mythe* (1979)

Charles Emanuel *See* CARLO EMANUELE I

Chigi, Agostino (1465–1520) Sienese banker and entrepreneur, with a vast fortune in shipping and real estate, a principal financier of popes from Alexander VI to Leo X and a prominent social figure in Rome. He was granted a lease (1500) to exploit the papal ALUM mines at Tolfa and given a nominal office (1507) as an apostolic secretary. The luxurious style of Chigi's domestic life was notorious; after the deaths of his first wife and of the Roman courtesan Imperia, he lived for 7 years with a young mistress who bore him 5 children and whom he married only in 1519. His suburban villa (later known as the Farnesina), planned by Peruzzi, contains paintings of classical inspiration: Sodoma's erotic scene of the marriage of Alexander and Roxana, based on Lucian; an Amor and Psyche cycle painted by Raphael's pupils; and Raphael's famous Galatea in the Loggia. Chigi's horoscope, painted by Peruzzi, also appears here. His serious literary patronage included the setting up of a Greek printing press (it produced an edition of Pindar's works, 1515). His fame (he was dubbed 'Il Magnifico') was to be commemorated in two monumental chapels, at S. Maria della Pace and S. Maria del Popolo, but neither was completed during his lifetime. DC

G. Cugnoni 'Agostino Chigi il Magnifico' *Archivio della Società Romana di Storia Patria* (1879–83); O. Montenovesi 'A. Chigi, banchiere e appaltatore dell' allume a Tolfa' *ibid.* (1937); F. Saxl *Lectures* I (1957) (on the Farnesina); M. Hirst and J. Shearman in *Journal of the Warburg and Courtauld Institutes* (1961) (on the chapels); F. Gilbert *The pope, his banker, and Venice* (1980)

Children About a quarter of all babies died before they were one. Infanticide and the abandonment of infants were not uncommon. Children were supposed to be brought up strictly and to be deferential to their parents, calling them *Messer Padre* and *Madonna Madre*. Childhood ended early. It was not unusual for 7-year-olds to be apprenticed, placed in convents or employed as servants (of the servant population in Florence in 1427, 42 per cent of the males and 34 per cent of the females were aged 8–17).

Yet there is evidence that awareness and enjoyment of the distinctive characteristics of childhood did exist in some circles, and probably earlier in Italy than elsewhere. The Florentine merchant Giovanni Morelli confided to his journal *c.*1400 his love for his 'sweet son', his pleasure in little Alberto's 'childish speech', and his 'incalculable sorrow' when the boy died. In 1478 Clarice wrote to her husband Lorenzo de' Medici that their 3-year-old (later Leo X) 'keeps asking, when will Loencio come?' (note the child's use of the father's first name and the mother's attempt to reproduce childish speech). Machiavelli records that Lorenzo 'was often seen taking part in the games of his sons and daughters', although he remarks that such behaviour is inappropriate for a head of state. *See* AGE. PB

J. B. Ross 'The middle-class child in urban Italy' in L. de Mause ed. *The history of childhood* (1974); D. Herlihy and C. Klapisch *Les Toscans et leurs familles* (1978)

Chioggia, War of (1378–81) The fourth and last episode in Genoa's series of challenges to Venice for commercial leadership in the eastern Mediterranean. The Venetians emerged victorious, but not without suffering the most serious threat to the city itself before the wars of the League of Cambrai, for while the war was fought partly at sea, a larger Genoese fleet broke through the Republic's vessels patrolling the Adriatic, landed at Chioggia in August 1379, and, with assistance from the Carrara ruler of Padua, Francesco I, occupied the town. Even with the return in January 1380 of the Venetian offensive fleet, which had been successfully devastating Genoese shipping between

Doge Andrea Contarini returns victorious from the War of **Chioggia**: detail from a painting by Veronese in the Doges' Palace.

Image of **chivalry**: the tomb of Tiberto VI Brandolini (d.1397) in the church of S. Francesco, Bagnacavallo.

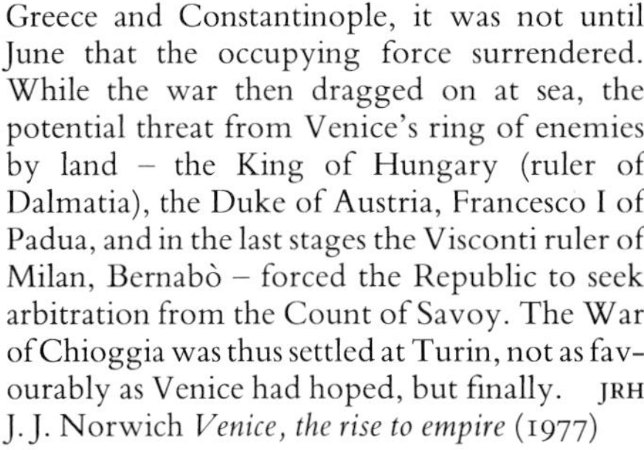

Greece and Constantinople, it was not until June that the occupying force surrendered. While the war then dragged on at sea, the potential threat from Venice's ring of enemies by land – the King of Hungary (ruler of Dalmatia), the Duke of Austria, Francesco I of Padua, and in the last stages the Visconti ruler of Milan, Bernabò – forced the Republic to seek arbitration from the Count of Savoy. The War of Chioggia was thus settled at Turin, not as favourably as Venice had hoped, but finally. JRH

J. J. Norwich *Venice, the rise to empire* (1977)

Chivalry The place of chivalry in the imagination and life of Renaissance Italy has yet to be assessed. For long it seemed out of key either with a rational, commercial, humanistically biased society in the republican cities or with the ethos of princely states which fostered bureaucracy and saw military prowess as something to hire or sell. It was recognized that a popular taste for chivalrous romances (chiefly taken from the Carolingian cycles) existed, and that these were exploited for a more sophisticated audience by such authors as Boccaccio, Pulci, Boiardo, Ariosto and Tasso. Increased attention to the dating of manuscripts, especially those written in the Franco–Veneto idiom of Lombardy, and to the products of the printing press, has led to an enhanced sense of the continuity of interest in such romances, whether in prose or verse, throughout the 15c. and 16c. Such an interest, however, whether expressed in jousts and tournaments, praise of hunting and country life, or the adoption of 'knight-errant' mottoes and IMPRESE by men (often members of literary societies) who normally used horses only for transport, is seen primarily as an escape, hardly to be differentiated from other secular escapes from the steady realities of life: processions, pageants, CARNIVAL.

The recent discovery of a series of frescoes (*c.*1453) by Pisanello in the Ducal Palace of Mantua illustrating – uniquely – an episode from the Arthurian cycle of romances is a warning that conclusions must remain tentative. But two 15c. tendencies suggest that chivalry should be seen as more than a form of spare-time play. Republicanism in the 15c. was using French-Burgundian formalities to establish its 'aristocratic' distance from the pell-mell disorderliness of communal days. And the teaching of humanist educators, with its emphasis on combining physical hardihood with intellectual training, its selection from ancient historical and biographical literature of episodes emphasizing military prowess, and its stress on moral qualities like magnificence, justice and magnanimity that could only be exemplified by those with wealth or power, was by no means at odds with chivalric values. An indigenous form of chivalry, as the snobbish, martial companion of humanism, may have had a positive as well as an escapist influence both on personality and on fashionable social rituals. But from the 1520s the problem is confused by the growing and largely external hispanization of manners in the peninsula. JRH

R. M. Ruggieri *L'umanesimo cavalleresco italiano da Dante al Pulci* (1963)

Chrysoloras, Manuel (1350–1415), the legendary founder of Greek studies in Italy, was perhaps an even more important influence than the traditional legend suggests. He first came to the West in 1394 as an emissary of the Byzantine Emperor Manuel II, seeking help against the Turks. As a result of contacts made then, Salutati secured for him an invitation from the commune of Florence to accept a salaried professorship of Greek. After 3 years of decisive importance in Florence, 1397–1400, he left the city, and, though he returned later to the West, the rest of his life was largely taken up with diplomatic business. His pupils included Bruni, Vergerio, Palla Strozzi, Niccoli and others, to whom he imparted not only the Greek language but, perhaps more important, a boundless enthusiasm for classical literature, thought and art. GH

G. Cammelli *I dotti Bizantini e le origini dell'humanesimo; I Manuele Crisolora* (1941)

Manuel **Chrysoloras**: a sketch made in Florence at the beginning of the 15c. (Paris, Louvre).

Church architecture and liturgy Liturgical reform was only finally codified at the Council of Trent. Practice until then had remained essentially unchanged since the Middle Ages. The symbolic division of the layman and the religious was effected generally in monastic churches by the rood screen (*tramezzo*), behind which was located the choir and, at the back of it, the high altar. This arrangement provided warmth and privacy for the monks while they were saying their offices; permitted simultaneous celebration of Mass at numerous side altars; protected *clausura* (separateness from the laity) because the monks were provided access from the cloister to their choir without passing through the layman's church. It seems likely that women were not permitted through the gates of the *tramezzo*, as remains true of the related structure in the Eastern Orthodox Church, the iconostasis.

In the course of the Renaissance there was a gradual movement to consolidate the *tramezzo* and choir (cf. Michelozzo's S. Marco) in order to reduce the barrier between laymen and the celebrant at the high altar. The earliest plan we know of, so far, that placed the altar in front of the choir in a monastic church is Michelozzo's SS. Annunziata, where the old *tramezzo* was demolished and the choir planned for the rotunda behind (1444). When construction was about to begin, a barrage of criticisms on liturgical grounds was launched by Florentine laymen. In cathedrals, and wherever else there were canons who were not cloistered, there were only enclosed choirs, the walls of which were kept low to permit a better view of the high altar. Brunelleschi even placed the canons' choir behind the altar in S. Lorenzo. Medieval-style *tramezzi* continued to be used in the Renaissance as the stage for morality plays and feast-day celebrations, as well as for the reading of the Gospel, because its second storey was the only place where the speaker could be heard by both lay and religious. The organ was typically located there. The high altarpiece, if large enough and sufficiently raised, might be glimpsed by the congregation through the central gate in the *tramezzo*.

Numerous side chapels patronized by private families provided them with a burial place. Masses for the deceased were normally exchanged for an annual stipend to the monastery. Most of the decorations in churches were commissioned by patrons for their chapels. The religious had very little direct control over the fabric of the church. A committee of patrons (*Opera*) exercised the decisive authority. Experiments with the central-plan church in the 15c. proved unsatisfactory for liturgical needs and were abandoned in the 16c. They violated the symbolism of the priest acting as intercessor on behalf of the congregation, standing behind him as he consecrated the elements, and they disrupted the processional character of the worship.

Following the close of the Council of Trent (1563) there began a wave of renovations of monastic churches, demolishing *tramezzi* and transferring monks' choirs behind the high altar. In accordance with Counter-Reformation ideals, newly constructed and renovated churches were intended to bring the worshipper into closer contact with the celebrant and to increase lay participation in the Mass. Side chapels were treated as a series, sometimes even with the subjects of the altarpieces forming a cycle. Although private families and confraternities patronized these chapels, their control over the decorations had been gradually diminishing. An overall plan increasingly assured coherence of the whole. MH

B. Brown 'The building history and patronage of the Tribuna of SS. Annunziata in Florence . . .', *Mitteilungen des Kunsthistorischen Instituts in Florenz* (1981); M. B. Hall, *Renovation and Counter-Reformation* (1979); S. Sinding-Larsen 'Some functional and iconographic aspects of the centralized church in the Italian Renaissance' *Acta ad Archaeologiam et Atrium Historiam Pertinentia* (1965)

Cicero, Marcus Tullius (106–43 BC) For Dante it was one of the miracles of God's intervention in the history of Rome that Cicero defended its liberties against Catiline; but Cicero is not an important author for Dante; and for the Middle Ages generally his presence had dwindled, and his nature had been masked. St Ambrose had adapted the *De officiis (On public duties)* for the benefit of clerics *(De officiis ministrorum)*, and St Jerome, in his fight for the monastic ideal, had misattributed to Cicero a remark that one could not serve both philosophy and a wife. In the absence of a continuing knowledge of Cicero's career he became a symbol of misogyny and the contemplative ideal.

In 1238 one voice asserted the civic spirit of *De officiis* as an equal choice with the contemplative ideal, but it is in the 14c. that Cicero returns to life: 'If Petrarch is the father of humanism, Cicero is its grandfather.' Even before he grasped his sense, Cicero was Petrarch's author. True, Petrarch found the *Letters to Atticus* in 1345, and, in his hesitation before the old contemplative ideal, was dismayed at the spectacle of Cicero's political involvement, and his death. Petrarch sadly contrasted the vain and restless activity of Cicero with the fruitful solitude of his old age, which produced his philosophical works. But even more important than this lingering medieval attitude in Petrarch is his acceptance, in the *De ignorantia* (1366), of the positive message of Cicero on the providence that rules the world, for the good of man. It remained for the heirs of Petrarch, who propagated his humanism in the civic environment of Florence, to overlap the one corner of Petrarch's resistance. Coluccio Salutati found the *Epistolae familiares* in 1394, and responded to Petrarch's disappointment over Cicero's career with admiration for the part he had played in political life. In the same year Coluccio's pupil Vergerio answered Petrarch's letter to Cicero (which had accused Cicero of betraying the scholar's ideal), asserting 'that has always seemed to me the best philosophy, which dwells in cities and flees solitude'. And in 1415 Bruni wrote a biography, the *Cicero novus*, which sets out his admiration for the ideal union of political action and literary creation in Cicero. Palmieri borrowed much from Cicero for his *Della vita civile* (1430), and his conclusion recalls the celebrated remark in the *Somnium Scipionis*: 'For there is indeed nothing more acceptable on earth to that great God who rules all the world, than those assemblies and gatherings of men in social bond, which we call cities.'

Cicero, for Petrarch and the early 15c. humanists, is *magister vitae*, a master of life. It was the Middle Ages that lived by rhetorical guidebooks, and Petrarch's recapture of a purer latinity is based on the great authors of Rome, not on sets of rules. But already Bracciolini, in one of his letters, confesses 'whatever is in me, this I owe all to Cicero whom I have chosen as my guide to eloquence.' And as the civic lesson of Cicero fades, so does the formal authority of Cicero as Latin writer *par excellence* grow. Valla in the *Elegantiae* (1444) notes how all the Fathers of the Church drew on Cicero, and praises him and eloquence together. Here Cicero is still a vital part of an essential bloodstream; but when in the second half of the century Paolo Cortese reproaches Poliziano with using words that cannot be found in Cicero, and draws that swift retort – that Poliziano expressed himself, and would be no man's ape – the path was opening up. On the one side it led the way to an eclectic latinity, with lots of rancid words from late sources, and on the other to an exclusive Ciceronianism. When Bembo published his *Prose della volgar lingua* (1525) he offered models for verse and prose, Petrarch and Boccaccio, Virgil and Cicero. There were those who by then carried a Ciceronian affectation to excess, and against these (or at least against one of them, Christophe de Longueil, not an Italian) Erasmus produced a few years later his heavy satire *Ciceronianus* (1528). This was an overprescription for what was not really a general disease, but it symbolizes the fact that the role of Cicero as a vital constituent of Renaissance culture was limited to the period from Petrarch to Poliziano. But we should not forget that Cicero was also the master of the prevalent dialogue form, down at least to *The courtier* of Castiglione (1528). JHW

P. de Nolhac *Petrarch and the ancient world* (1907); H. Baron 'Cicero and Roman civic spirit' *Bulletin of the John Rylands Library* (1938)

Ciconia, Johannes (d.1414) One of the earliest Netherlands composers to settle in Italy, working in Padua for at least the last 9 years of his life. A Walloon from Liège, he became a fluent composer of Italian songs, but his most significant achievement lies in his motets, which show a distinct flair for sonority, especially those written for some ceremonial occasion. DA

Cigoli, Lodovico (1559–1613) Painter, architect and author of treatises on colour (lost) and perspective, he began as a pupil of Allori. With frank eclecticism he drew upon Barocci and his stylistic ancestor, Correggio; upon Titian and Veronese; and upon Lodovico Carracci, in order to free his style from Florentine Mannerism. Called to Rome by Pope Clement VIII, he spent most of his later years there and became a progressive and respected member of that school. MH

Cima da Conegliano, Giovanni Battista (1459/60–1517/18) was a Venetian painter who combined the volumetric simplifications of Antonello with a sense of light and colour derived from Giovanni Bellini, to whose images of the Virgin and Child many of his own are intimately related. JW

Ciompi was the name given to the most numerous class of day-labourers (dismissible without notice) in Florence's chief industry: those employed in the manufacture of woollen cloth as weavers, beaters, combers, etc. They were forbidden to form a trade association, as also were those in the associated, but self-employed, craft of dyeing. Without being members of a guild, none could seek redress save from the Arte della Lana, the manufacturers' corporation which employed them, or achieve political representation. Their armed revolt in July 1378, supported by some of their betters who were out of sympathy with the leaders of the régime at the time, forced the government to grant them guild status and to make other changes that would improve their standard of living. After only a few weeks, however, the petty employers in other industries and crafts closed ranks with the members of the Arte della Lana in a common fear of worker dictation, and after a purge of ringleaders all legislation passed during the crisis was cancelled. Though shortlived (hence Ciompi 'revolt' or 'rebellion' rather than 'revolution'), the episode was traumatic, further consolidating the oligarchical tendency in Florentine society that led to the dominance first of the Albizzi and then of the Medici. JRH

G. Brucker 'The Ciompi revolution' in N. Rubinstein ed. *Florentine studies* (1968)

Ciriaco d'Ancona (*c*.1390–1455) Ciriaco Pizzicolli was a passionate collector of antiquities and instrumental in introducing them into Italy. He made his first trip to Constantinople as a merchant in 1418: extended visits to Greece, the Aegean islands and Egypt followed. He searched for and collected gems, medallions, manuscripts, and especially epigraphs, these last published posthumously in his *Commentaria*. Since much of the material he collected was later destroyed in a fire, his sketches are sometimes the only information avalable on particular classical antiquities. [30] PG

R. Weiss *The Renaissance discovery of classical antiquity* (1969)

Class, social Italy did not follow the classification of 3 'estates' – those who prayed, fought and worked – that was normal in the rest of Europe. In the towns, it was most common to distinguish 2 groups, the rich and the poor, or 3, adding the 'middling' (*mezzani*). In practice, as contemporaries knew, social stratification was more complex. The nobles (*magnati, grandi*) were distinguished by their lifestyle from the rest of the rich. The middle group, or *popolo* – often divided, especially in Florence, into upper-middle and lower-middle (*popolo grasso, popolo minuto*) – was arranged in a complex hierarchy, from goldsmiths to tanners, and, within each workshop, from master to apprentice. Below the guildsmen the unskilled and the poor had their own hierarchy. The countryside had its own social system. Below the great and middling landowners, nobles or townsmen, came the *contadini* or peasants, divided into the rural entrepreneurs (*fittaioli*), the leaseholders who in effect owned their land (*livellari*), the sharecroppers (*mezzadri*), and a rural proletariat of landless labourers, often hired by the day (*pigionali*). There were also some serfs, though serfdom was declining and *villano* changing from 'villein' to a contemptuous term for 'peasant'.

Some historians have described Italian society in this period in Marxian class terms. The great bankers and wool merchants of Florence and elsewhere certainly look like a 'bourgeoisie'; in 1427, 27 per cent of the wealth of Florence was owned by the hundred richest households. Similarly, the unskilled workers excluded from the guild system (the CIOMPI, for example) look like a 'proletariat'. It is harder to fit the small masters, at once employers and workers, into the Marxian framework, and there is little evidence in this period of class consciousness in the strict sense of cross-craft solidarity (class consciousness in the vague sense of the hostility of the poor to the rich, or vice versa, exists in plenty). A more useful working model of the social structure might distinguish 6 major groups on the basis of their lifestyles; the clergy, the nobility, merchants and professional men, craftsmen and shopkeepers, the peasants, and the poor.

The place of any individual in the social hierarchy depended on several factors besides his occupation, notably descent, marriage, wealth and (especially in Florence) public office. It is impossible to measure the rate of social mobility in Renaissance Italy, but there are signs that for a preindustrial society it was relatively high. Migration to a town was the common way for a family to begin its ascent of the social ladder. Trade, the Church and the law were all major avenues of social mobility. It is likely that opportunities for social mobility were greatest in the 13c. and 14c. In Florence, for example, the 'new men' (*gente nuova*) so disliked by Dante were able to marry into old noble families, and the lesser guildsmen were admitted into the *signoria*. It even became a political disadvantage to be noble, and families such as the Pazzi and the Tornabuoni (formerly Tornaquinci) had themselves officially declared 'commoners' (*popolani*). In the 15c. and 16c., however, the social structure became more rigid. As it became harder to enter the ruling class of the Italian cities, so its members behaved more and more like a traditional nobility, despising trade, investing heavily in land, fighting in the occasional tournament, and cultivating their family trees. Thanks to this process of 'refeudalization', the Italian social structure was more like that of France or Spain and less 'modern' in 1600 than it had been in 1400. *See* CHIVALRY; PROFESSIONS. PB

L. Martines *The social world of the Florentine humanists* (1963); P. Burke *Culture and society in Renaissance Italy* (1972)

Claudian (working AD 395–404) Claudius Claudianus came from Egypt, and his first language was Greek but, since he learnt his Latin from books, he wrote, despite the fact that he lived in the 4c., the purest and most correct poetry since the Silver Age. Because of a dedication to a Florentinus, the Middle Ages, as well as making him out a Christian, thought him a Florentine, and Boccaccio, in pressing Dante on Petrarch, referred to Claudian as his compatriot and predecessor. Petrarch had little use for Claudian, and among the innumerable echoes in his *Rime* from all the poets of Rome there are only three from Claudian. The 15c. saw a new interest in him (there are 6

manuscripts dating from the Quattrocento), and when Poliziano began his teaching with courses on Statius and Quintilian he specifically recommended the minor writers like Claudian to the young, as being easier to grasp and imitate. Moreover, in the *Stanze per la giostra* Poliziano looks to Claudian for the rich description of Venus's palace, and Claudian becomes an essential ingredient in the transformation of the *ottava rima* from the rough narrative medium invented by Boccaccio to the meditative and colourful style which Ariosto would inherit for the *Orlando furioso*. The basis of Claudian's poetry lies in the luxuriance of the descriptive passages, which stem from the preoccupation of the Imperial age with *ekphrasis* (the description of pictures, real or imaginary), and here the narrative tends to be forgotten. Apart from the pictorial qualities of his poetic style, Claudian had what Addison called a love for 'pretty contradictions': these also came to be imitated, especially by Tasso and Guarini. JHW
A. Cameron *Claudian* (1970)

Clement VI Pope 1342–52 (b.1291) Pierre Roger cultivated a princely style of life ('my predecessors did not know how to be popes'), completed the Palace of AVIGNON, and dispensed largesse to all applicants, among whom were artists and writers. To maintain his generosity he further extended the financial bureaucracy of the Church, thus provoking hostility throughout Europe. His extravagance ensured that he would be unable to regain those areas of the Papal State which resisted his authority and at his death the Curia was on the point of bankruptcy. His passing was celebrated by Petrarch in a series of vituperative and defamatory letters. JL

The coronation of Pope **Clement VI** illustrated in a manuscript of Villani's chronicle in the Vatican Library.

Clement VII Pope 1523–34 (b.1478) Giulio de' Medici, illegitimate son of Giuliano di Pietro de' Medici, was one of the most handsome men ever elected pope. Fortunately he inherited more than the good looks of his father, growing up to be a fine humanist and one of the best musicians in Europe. He had a good head for figures and a wide experience of life, for, during the Medici exile (1494–1512), he travelled throughout Europe.

On the restoration of the Medici, Giulio was created Archbishop of Florence and cardinal by his cousin, Leo X. In 1517 he became papal vice-chancellor and was largely responsible for determining policy during the rest of Leo's pontificate, directing his efforts towards freeing Italy from foreign domination. He tried to restore the faltering papal finances and it was largely owing to his exertions that the papal see avoided bankruptcy in these years. From 1519 onwards, Giulio de' Medici was responsible for governing Florence, where he gained a reputation for ready accessibility. He loved the city and was genuinely anxious to broaden his family's power base, seeking advice about how Florence should be run from a variety of sources. He was elected pope after one of the most bitterly fought of all conclaves and took the name of Clement to signify reconciliation with his enemies.

Historians have condemned Clement as a weak and vacillating pope. It is true that he was a highly sophisticated intellectual, able to see both sides of any question, and thus in difficulties when it came to decision-making, but critics rarely take account of the serious problems he faced: the Papacy was virtually bankrupt, in Germany the Protestants continued to make headway and there was a growing desire for church reform; in England Henry VIII was demanding annulment of his marriage; the Ottomans were advancing in Hungary, while in Italy the Papacy was drawn into the Habsburg-Valois conflict. In addition, Clement's pontificate was bedevilled by the hostility of the Colonna.

Although he had been elected as an Imperial candidate, Clement's political aim continued to be to prevent any foreign domination of Italy. Thus while France appeared the greater danger Clement supported Charles V, but the battle of

Sebastiano del Piombo's portrait of Pope **Clement VII** (Naples, Capodimonte).

Pavia convinced him that Spain rather than France was now the threat and in the following year he joined the anti-Imperial League of Cognac (1526). This decision in fact led to the humiliation of the Sack of Rome (1527) and the Pope's incarceration in Castel S. Angelo, but at the time it was applauded by many intelligent observers, including Guicciardini. After his release from Castel S. Angelo Clement fled to Viterbo, and did not return to Rome until October 1528. He made peace with Charles by the Treaty of Barcelona, and crowned him at Bologna (1530).

It is easy to forget the positive aspects of Clement's pontificate, but at Rome he did much to revive the arts and had proved himself a discriminating patron of Raphael, Cellini, Sebastiano del Piombo and Michelangelo. Although he did not initiate thoroughgoing church reform, Clement's personal devotion and piety are beyond question. He always lived simply and even his worst enemies were unable to suggest that his was anything other than a blameless moral life. His greatest virtue was charity and he was renowned as a liberal almsgiver. It was, in addition, his careful patronage that ensured the election to the papacy of Cardinal Farnese who, as Paul III, became one of the great reforming popes. *See* WARS OF ITALY. JH

J. Hale *Florence and the Medici* (1977)

Clement VIII Pope 1592–1605 (b.1563) Ippolito Aldobrandini was born in Florence and became a cardinal in 1585. Brought up in the strictest principles of the Counter-Reformation, which did nothing to soften his authoritarian character, Clement VIII is remembered chiefly because his unbending rectitude led to the execution of Beatrice Cenci and Giordano Bruno. In addition, he devoted much energy to curbing banditry and suppressing crime and immorality in the Papal State. In politics he proved more flexible. He was opposed to any extension of Spanish power, which he considered already excessive, recognized Henry IV as King of France, and was chiefly responsible for the Treaty of Vervins (1598) in a valiant attempt to normalize Franco–Spanish relations. In Italy, on the death of the last Este duke in 1597, he absorbed Ferrara into the Papal State. JH

Clergy, secular Legally speaking, a cleric was a man who had been tonsured and was therefore immune from secular jurisdiction. Before 1563, the boundary between clergy and laity was not so sharp as it became after the Council of Trent, and some Italians who were legally clerics lived in the manner of laymen. The secular (i.e. non-monastic) clergy, in Italy as elsewhere, may be divided into 2 groups, one small and rich and the other large and poor. There was a small episcopal élite. In 1500 Italy possessed over 250 sees. Although the Church did offer opportunities for social mobility, most of the secular clergy who became bishops were of noble origin (70 per cent of the 56 at the Council of Trent in 1545–47). The system of resignations in someone's favour allowed some noble families to gain a virtual monopoly of certain sees, passing them from uncle to nephew. A little below the bishops came the cathedral canons, often nobles and usually well off.

Far below the bishops, economically and socially, came the parish priests who formed the majority of the secular clergy. We do not know how many there were, but a reasonable estimate might be 10,000 at a given time, or one priest to every 1000 people. Some villages had no priest at all. Some parish priests earned less than unskilled labourers, and it was not uncommon for them to work in the fields or even trade in horses. Until seminaries were founded at the end of the 16c., most priests were trained informally by an 'apprenticeship' system. Some did not learn very much; an early 15c. visitation of the diocese of Bologna revealed priests unable to name the 7 deadly sins. Yet the priest played a central part in parish life, settling disputes and administering poor relief as well as watching over the morals of his flock. In some places, notably Venice, the parish priest was elected by his parishioners.

There is little evidence of lay hostility to the secular clergy; monks and friars were another matter. The social and cultural importance of the clergy did not remain constant between 1300 and 1600. Roughly speaking, they lost wealth, status and power in the first half of the period but regained it in the second. Catholic reformers such as Giberti and Borromeo were concerned to make the clergy more respected. Italian intellectuals were increasingly tempted by careers in the Church. Symbolic of the change is Baldassare Castiglione, who took the tonsure in 1521 and became a papal nuncio in 1524. PB

D. Hay *The Church in Italy in the 15th century* (1977)

Clientage The term is increasingly used to describe the non-contractual ties between men of standing and those they were in a position to help: with protection, loans, advice over lawsuits, advancement in a career, political preferment and so forth. The practice, universal in Renaissance Italy, is broadly that described by social anthropologists as patronage, a word too connected with cultural patronage to be useful in a Renaissance context. Clientage well describes the nature of political parties or followings in Florence – those of the 15c. Albizzi or Medici families, for instance. The followers gained favours, the man deferred to gained information, useful or potentially useful contacts, political, social or economic leverage, and prestige.

The operation of clientage is particularly clear in oligarchical republics: not only Florence but Lucca, Genoa, Siena. Venice's closed aristocracy reflected conventions of deference and authority that operated within a more exclusively family-and-clan structure. In Milan and Naples, and generally in rural areas dominated by noble landlords, clientage blurs into a more (at times a positively) feudal form of protection in exchange for service. And in general it becomes less useful as a term in the 16c., when deference relationships became more formalized through the conventions of court life and more rule-bound bureaucracies. As a loosely hierarchized practice of 'I'll scratch your back if you'll scratch mine', however, 'clientage' has earned its place among the conceptual guides to an understanding of Renaissance society. JRH

P. Kent *Family and lineage in Renaissance Florence* (1977); J. Heers *Parties and political life in the medieval West* tr. D. Nicholas (1977)

Codussi (or Coducci), Mauro (*c.*1440–1504) Architect, born near Bergamo, active mostly in Venice. Nothing is known of his training or work before his appearance in Venice in 1469 as architect of the church of S. Michele in Isola. His Venetian work is remarkably synthetic in style. In the S. Michele façade (*c.*1475) he fused local gothic traditions (the tri-lobed façade) with an Albertian classical vocabulary. At S. Zaccaria, where he took over as architect in 1483, he changed the ambulatory rib vaults to a ring of elliptical cupolas, creating one of the most interesting spatial sequences in Venetian architecture. At S. Maria Formosa (1492–1504) he began to integrate vaulting types and

Façade of **Codussi**'s S. Michele in Isola, Venice.

ground plan in a new way, placing barrel vaults, groin vaults and domes in careful relationships to the axes of the plan. From 1490 to 1495 he worked at the Scuola Grande di S. Marco, completing the façade begun by Pietro Lombardo and building an innovatory double-ramp staircase, now lost. In the façade of the Palazzo Corner-Spinelli (c.1490) he introduced new patterns of masonry and window tracery to Venetian domestic architecture. Codussi's last three works are his greatest achievements. At the church of S. Giovanni Crisostomo (1497–1504) he developed ideas from S. Maria Formosa, creating a tightly controlled sequence of barrel vaults, pendentive domes, and a dome on pendentives over a Greek cross plan. In the double-ramp staircase at the Scuola Grande di S. Giovanni Evangelista (1498) his earlier researches with staircases and vaulting sequences are combined in a brilliant design in which changes of axis are marked by domes and the straight staircase ramps covered by barrel vaults. The façade of the Palazzo Vendramin-Calergi (*c.*1502) carries ideas from the Palazzo Corner-Spinelli into more complex rhythmical sequences, richer sculptural detail, and the first use in Venice of free-standing classical orders and paired columns on a palace façade. Characteristically, this last work preserves Venetian palace tradition in the window placement and shows the same determination to fuse tradition and new ideas as is found in his first work. RL

L. O. and L. Puppi *Mauro Codussi* (1977) and review by R. Lieberman in *Journal of the Society of Architectural Historians* (1979)

Cognac, League of (22 May 1526) Captured at the battle of PAVIA, Francis I was released from captivity in Spain after signing the Treaty of Madrid (14 January 1526), whereby he renounced his interest in Italy and agreed to support Charles V. At Cognac this was reversed. Released by Pope Clement VII from an agreement made under duress, Francis allied against Charles with the Pope, Venice, the Duke of Milan and Florence. Part of Charles's response was the mobilization of the army which marched to the Sack of Rome in the following year. *See* WARS OF ITALY. JRH

Cola di Rienzo (?1313–54) Roman notary and son of an innkeeper who held power in Rome, taking the title of tribune, 20 May to 15 December 1347 and 1 August to 8 October 1354, on which last date he was hacked to death by the mob. Cola's régimes were part of a series of fruitless attempts to assert the interests of the Roman citizens against the nobility and the absentee papal government; his ideas, on the other hand, were unique and of lasting interest.

Inspired by his readings of Roman history, the ruins of antiquity and their inscriptions, Cola sought, through a programme of political action and education, to restore the glories of the Roman republic: in extending Roman citizenship to the citizens of the free cities of Italy he seems to have envisaged some kind of Italian federation under an Emperor to be elected in Rome. For Cola, antiquity provided political but not aesthetic models; his letters are full-blown examples of medieval rhetoric and the ceremonies at which his programme was unveiled were indelibly medieval. The full force of his message reached only a few, notably Petrarch, who encouraged and then deserted him, and the anonymous Roman chronicler whose life of Cola would long ago have been recognized as a masterpiece had it not been written in a barbarous-looking dialect. However, it provided most of the material for a French life by De Cerceau (1733), a copy of which was found in Napoleon's baggage after Waterloo. Lord Lytton's novel *Rienzi* (1842) was the basis for the libretto of Wagner's first successful opera; Cola has also been the subject of a play by Engels and a short life by Gabriele d'Annunzio. JKH

P. Piur *Cola di Rienzo* (1931); I. Origo *Tribune of Rome* (1938); *Life of Cola di Rienzo* tr. J. Wright (1975); Anonimo romano *Cronica* ed. G. Porta (1979)

College of Cardinals The corporate identity of this body, comprising the highest dignitaries of the Roman Curia (cardinals who might be bishops, priests or deacons), dates from the 11c. As well as electing popes and holding high offices, they advanced claims to be able to depose popes and call General Councils of the Church. In 1378 a majority of cardinals declared their own election of Urban VI invalid and precipitated the Great Schism by electing the anti-Pope Clement VII. As late as 1511 rebel cardinals were attempting to replace Julius II. Increases in the size of the College may have helped to reduce this danger; according to one theory its maximum membership was 24, but by the later 15c. this was disregarded. Sixtus IV created 34 cardinals; Alexander VI and Leo X

The **College of Cardinals** in an early 14c. manuscript of the Decretals of Boniface VIII in the British Museum.

created 43; in the single year 1517, after a conspiracy scare, Leo X appointed 33; in 1586 the maximum was fixed at 70. Although the Council of Constance debated proportional representation from all parts of Christendom, and 'cardinal protectors', pledged to advance the interests of individual nations and rulers, appear to date from then, after 1417 protégés of the various Italian powers made up the majority, together with a varying number of papal relatives: loyalty to himself and security in Italy were essential for any pope.

From the Avignon period or earlier most cardinals lived expensively, dispensing lavish patronage, with households of several hundreds, appropriate to notions of their dignity; many collected libraries and antiquities (e.g. Prospero Colonna, Francesco Gonzaga, Giuliano della Rovere); they built or rented palaces in Rome, often spending much on decoration, and by the early 16c. were having suburban villas built on an ornate scale (e.g. Cardinal Giulio de' Medici's Villa Madama). Incomes varied enormously, but the hyper-rich with many accumulated benefices were in a minority – as were libertines like Pietro Riario (1472–74). An appreciable number of cardinals were learned and rigorous (e.g. Nicholas Cusanus, Bessarion, Oliviero Caraffa or Giles of Viterbo), even if when Paolo Cortese's comprehensive *De cardinalatu* was published (1510) the office seemed one most appropriate for cultivated young aristocrats with few pastoral or doctrinal concerns (e.g. Alessandro Farnese, Domenico Grimani). Only a minority of cardinals, usually political figures (e.g. Georges D'Amboise, Wolsey), never or seldom resided in Rome, as all were supposed to do. The Counter-Reformation seems to have brought about few essential changes in the College's character, though it made differences in its administrative functions. *See* PAPACY. DC

D. S. Chambers 'The economic predicament of Renaissance cardinals' *Studies in Medieval and Renaissance History* (1966); A. Antonovics 'Counter-Reformation cardinals, 1534–90' *European Studies Review* (1972); D. Hay *The church in Italy in the fifteenth century* (1977)

Colleoni, Bartolomeo (1400–76), born into a militant aristocratic family near Bergamo, began his career as a condottiere in 1419 in southern Italy, first under Braccio da Montone and then under Muzio Attendolo Sforza. His first major engagement was the battle of Aquila in 1424. His first Venetian contract came in 1431 and he took part, under the command of Gattamelata, in the anti-Visconti campaign around Cremona. After returning to the south once more he followed Gattamelata back into Venetian service in 1438–41 for the fourth phase of the Republic's war against Milan. Such success as came to Venice was acknowledged as in no small measure due to his courage and shrewdness, and when Gattamelata died in

An equestrian portrait of Bartolomeo **Colleoni** from a 15c. manuscript *Life* (Bergamo, Biblioteca Civica).

1443, and Piccinino in 1444, only Francesco Sforza stood in such high esteem among Italian condottieri.

Colleoni fought under Sforza for Venice in 1448, but it was not until the Peace of Lodi in 1454 settled the interminable wars between the Republic and Milan that he was offered the command-in-chief; it was thereafter Venice's chief concern to prevent his going off in search of wars elsewhere. From contracts, booty and the gifts Venice made to keep him faithful he became rich in money and properties. During the last years of enforced idleness his favourite residence, the castle of Malpaga, became the centre of a lavish court where painters and men of letters were welcomed among Colleoni's comrades-in-arms; in scale and fame Malpaga was a less refined anticipation of Caterina Cornaro's Asolo. It was after his death that Colleoni came to be most closely associated with the arts. In part this was through the completion of the superb Cappella Colleoni (Bergamo), designed by Giovanni Antonio Amadeo (it had been begun in 1472), and the erection in it of his elaborate tomb, topped in 1500 by his life-size effigy on horseback in gilded wood.

But chiefly he is remembered for Verrocchio's bronze equestrian statue alongside the church of SS. Giovanni e Paolo in Venice. Colleoni, in his will, had left 100,000 ducats to the Republic to spend on war against the Turk. He did this, he said, as a sign of his gratitude for the favours he had received, and he coupled with the gift a request that to keep his name alive a statue of him on horseback might be erected in Piazza S. Marco. There is no doubt that Colleoni wished to be viewed by posterity with no less respect than was accorded other condottieri who had been remembered in this way, such as Hawkwood or, most notably, Gattamelata. Whether or not the words '*super platea S. Marco*' were deliberately read as meaning 'on the piazza of the *scuola* of S. Marco', it is inconceivable that Venice, habitually suspicious of its military commanders, would have allowed a monument to one so near to the Doge's Palace and his church, S. Marco. Colleoni had fought and lived on a grand scale (and had enjoyed the display of his emblem: a set of *coglioni* – testicles), but if he was the state's benefactor, he was also its servant. JRH

B. Belotti *La vita di Bartolomeo Colleoni* (Bergamo n.d.)

Colocci, Angelo (1474–1549) Humanist and philologist, secretary to Leo X and Clement VII and bishop of Nocera Umbra from 1537. He was an expert in Old Portuguese, Provençal and early Italian poetry and was in favour of the *lingua cortigiana* in the debates on language, in which he also appeared as an interlocutor in Pierio Valeriano's *Dialogo della volgar lingua*. Important as an antiquarian, he had a rich collection of statues, coins and medals; those of his manuscripts that were not destroyed in the Sack of Rome are now in the Vatican Library. *See* ITALIAN LANGUAGE. LL

S. Debenedetti *Gli studi provenzali in Italia nel Cinquecento* (1911); *Atti del convegno di studi su A. Colocci 1969* (1972)

Colonna family Ghibelline Roman baronial family, possessed of vast estates in the southern Papal State and in the kingdom of Naples. The Colonna's power and wealth were considerably increased after the election of Cardinal Oddone Colonna as Pope Martin V in 1407. Martin made wide grants of property in the Papal State to the Colonna, and also persuaded Giovanna of Naples to give his brothers large fiefs in her kingdom. Eugenius IV ordered the restoration of this territory but had little success in enforcing the order; hence, despite the attacks of the Borgias on their estates, until the mid-16c. the Colonna remained the most dangerous of all baronial opponents of the Papacy. It was not until the time of Paul IV that the Papacy succeeded in reducing the Colonna to a position of political and economic dependency which ensured their loyalty as subjects. JH

J. Hook 'Clement VII, the Colonna and Charles V' *European Studies Review* (1972)

Colonna, Vittoria (1490–1547), daughter of Fabrizio Colonna, was for contemporaries the paragon of woman poets. The first hundred sonnets of her *Rime* she said she sang 'only to relieve the inner pain', grief for the death of her young husband, the Marquis of Pescara. The rest are on religious and neo-Platonic themes. In all her poetry an austerely logical mind and style – though contemporaries like Michelangelo, a friend of her old age, admired them – seemed to preclude the free play of lyrical impulse. Her world of sonnets is narrow, bleak, Calvinistic. Drawn into reformist circles, she was kept from breaking openly with Rome by her spiritual adviser, Cardinal Pole. LGC

A. Reumont *Vittoria Colonna* (1892)

The King of Spain watches **Columbus** landing in the Indies: woodcut from a book about the Spanish discoveries published in Florence in 1493.

Columbus (1451–1506) In spite of considerable past controversy, it is now accepted that Cristoforo Colombo was, as he proudly claimed to be, a Genoese. But his career lies outside the scope of this book (save for the impression that news of his discoveries made in Italy), and his culture was non-Italian too. Everything he wrote was in a Spanish heavily influenced, especially in its spelling, by Portuguese. This is as true of his private jottings as of his formal letters. He owed something to the portolan makers of Genoa in his youth and, later, much to the cartographical theories of the Florentine mathematician Paolo Toscanelli and his circle. But he belongs not to Italy, nor, save for 2 or 3 apprentice voyages, to the Mediterranean, but to Iberia and the Atlantic. JRH
S. E. Morison *Admiral of the ocean sea: a life of Christopher Columbus* (1946)

Columbus, Realdus (*c.*1510–69) Anatomist. Educated as a pharmacist and surgeon, he was a student at Padua in 1538. He was appointed as a temporary replacement for Vesalius (1543), and made a professor in 1544, subsequently migrating to Pisa and Rome. *De re anatomica* (1559), published posthumously, contains the substance of his lectures. He was an original anatomist and an excellent teacher. He was the first to describe publicly the pulmonary or lesser circulation (whereby *all* the blood goes

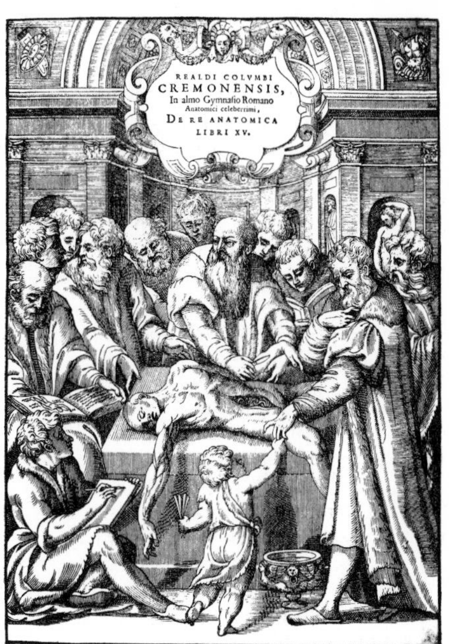

Title page of **Realdus Columbus'** *De re anatomica.*

from the right to the left side of the heart through the lungs, and none through the septum). This was apparently an independent discovery and it certainly was from him that others (including Harvey) learned of it. MBH

Comacchio The shallows and islets around this small town at the mouth of the Po allowed the extraction (by evaporation) of salt on a greater and cheaper scale than elsewhere in northern Italy. Given the universal human need for salt and the facility with which its sale could be controlled and taxed, this gave Comacchio an importance out of all proportion to its size. Formally belonging to Ferrara, its occupation was hotly contested by Ravenna, Genoa (before the decline of its seapower following the 1379–81 wars with Venice) and Venice. Venetian campaigns against Ferrara in 1482–84 and 1509–10 failed to secure the area and it remained in Este hands, contributing to the tax income with which the dukes embellished their capital. JRH

Commandino, Federico (1509–75) Urbino humanist and mathematician. Educated in languages, philosophy and medicine at Padua, and gaining a doctorate at Ferrara, he settled in Urbino as mathematical tutor and medical adviser to the Duke while editing, translating and commenting upon Greek texts. He later went first to Rome and then to Bologna as physician to the Duke's brother-in-law, Cardinal Ranuccio Farnese. His Latin editions of Archimedes (1558 and 1565), Euclid (1572), Aristarchus (1572), Hero's *Pneumatica* (1575) and Ptolemy's minor works were all of great influence; as a contemporary mathematician put it, he restored a lost mathematical heritage. His own contributions are contained in commentaries and in his *De centro gravitatis* (Bologna 1565). *See* MATHEMATICS. MBH

Commedia dell' arte Comedy of a technique practised in the acting profession (*arte* connoting both *tecnica* – craftsmanship – and *mestiere* – guild), characterized by improvisation on a 3-act scenario, with fixed roles assumed by players specializing in them: lovers speaking Tuscan; old men, the Venetian Pantalone and the Bolognese Doctor Graziano; various *zanni* or zanies, Bergamask Arlecchino or Harlequin, Neapolitan Pulcinella or Punch and their fellows; braggart soldiers with names such as Capitan Spavento or Matamoros; bawdy maidservants, Franceschina and others. The first documented actors' troupe was formed in 1545; by 1560 there were companies that included women. Among the most famous companies were the Gelosi, the Confidenti, the Desiosi, led by acting families such as the Andreini.

The professional troupes and their improvising style strongly influenced the development of Italian drama and established a symbiosis with literary drama: the *comici* also memorized and performed *commedie erudite*, tragedies and pastoral plays, and borrowed from them for scenarios on which to improvise, while many literary dramatists learned from the theatricality, movement, stage business and visual and verbal gags (*lazzi*) of the professionals. The most successful players gained high standing in Italian artistic and court circles. Various companies travelled to France, Spain and England in the late Cinquecento and for the next two centuries the *commedia dell'arte* was a powerful theatrical force throughout Europe. LGC

P. L. Duchartre *The Italian comedy* tr. R. T. Weaver (1929)

Characters of the **commedia dell'arte** in an anonymous painting of *c.*1580 (Stockholm, Drottningholms Theatre Museum).

Commedia erudita Vernacular stage comedy, called erudite because it was a literary imitation of the structure, types and situations of PLAUTUS and TERENCE; called also *osservata* or regular because it observed the 'rules' derived from a classical genre. The action was limited by unity of time and place to one day in one street scene representing, according to principles of generalized realism, middle-class society in a contemporary Italian city. Lovers and elders in conflict over love and money are helped by servants and engage in deceits, disguises and encounters with procurers, courtesans, friars, soldiers, pedants and charlatans. Construction is based on the combination of two or more plots, mixing Latin comedy with novellas and anecdotes, and on complication, producing intrigues ruled by fortune and concluded by weddings.

Ariosto's *La cassaria* (1508) and the subsequent examples of Bibbiena and Machiavelli gave the models of high comedy to Agnolo Firenzuola (1493–1543), Francesco d'Ambra (writing 1544–65), Alessandro Piccolomini (writing 1536–43), the Sienese Intronati academicians, Grazzini, Giovanni Maria Cecchi (1518–87), Aretino, Caro, Sforza Oddi (writing 1572–90), Giambattista della Porta and many others. In time the intrigue form grew more challengingly labyrinthine, while the plots often drew on serious and romantic sources and included moral and abstract themes, as well as more theatrically effective action and exchanges owed to increased contact with the professional players of the COMMEDIA DELL'ARTE. LGC

M. T. Herrick *Italian comedy in the Renaissance* (1960); I. Sanesi *La commedia* (2nd ed. 1954)

Communications In the early 16c. the normal number of days letters took to reach Venice was, from Florence, 3; Genoa, 6; Milan, 3; Rome, 4; Naples, 8; London, 24; Antwerp, 16; Nuremberg, 21; Barcelona, 19; Constantinople, 34; Lisbon, 43; Vienna, 13. These times could be bettered by professional couriers going hard over routes well supplied with 'posts' for replacement horses: Brussels–Rome in 10 days, Venice–Rome in 1. Using such a service, which developed after the more settled conditions which followed the Peace of Lodi in 1454, couriers could keep going at something like 90 miles a day; the ordinary traveller, keeping his own horse from the beginning of a journey to its end, averaged 20–25 miles. Courier service was so expensive as only to be used by governments and wealthy merchant companies; both ran their own services (Venice used the multi-generational services of a family called Gobbo – a touch of verisimilitude in Shakespeare's *Merchant of Venice*?) and only one major private postal service operated, that of the Tassis family of Bergamo who gained a monopoly of the Habsburg Netherlands-Germany-France-Italy postal service.

In Italy travellers and couriers on horseback could calculate times fairly closely, even though the state of the roads was generally poor. Most of the old Roman roads had decayed and medieval substitute surfaces (and new local roads) suffered from the extreme reluctance of local peasants to keep them up – a much resented labour service. Few Roman bridges remained, and their wooden replacements were narrow. Bad roads and narrow bridges restricted the use of carriages (rare before the 16c.) to towns and of carts to local traffic between farm and market. The horse was the chief means of personal travel, the mule of goods transport. Dredging costs and variations in water level meant that water transport, theoretically cheaper because of the lower expenditure of energy required, carried a far lesser volume of traffic than roads along the same route. And the convenience of river transport was mitigated by its slowness and the difficulty boatmen had in getting a balance of trade upstream and downstream: using the river-systems of Lombardy goods could travel with the current from Milan to Venice in 18 days; it took a month for the less popular return journey. Canals, the ideal form of water transport, were hardly used for this purpose (as opposed to irrigation) before the mid-16c., so great were the costs of maintaining them. The distributive genius of Italian Renaissance trade was not the carter or the bargee but the muleteer, whether the route lay over Alpine or Apennine passes or through the peninsular plains.

All the same, overland times between governments, between trade distribution points and international fairs or other markets could be calculated within limits that made forward planning not too difficult. It was different when letters or goods had to take to sea. The use of the compass and of sea-charts (portolans) on a fairly regular basis from the early 14c. meant fewer delays due to coast-hugging or foul weather in the Mediterranean, and made voyages from that sea to Atlantic ports in France, England and the Low Countries practicable. But even with the increasing use of oared galleys for merchandise, and with improvement in the rigging and steering of 'round' vessels, wind and weather made voyage times difficult to calculate, and the build-up of piracy in the late 15c. and 16c. made insurance rates soar. By the late 16c. land transport had been substituted for much Italian coastal traffic (between Naples and Rome, for instance), and the Venetians were discussing with the Turks a

Communications: horses and mules on the road in Ambrogio Lorenzetti's fresco in the Palazzo Comunale, Siena.

Balkan land route to Constantinople. Trade in 1600 was even more dependent on the mule than it had been 3 centuries before. JRH

P. Sardella *Nouvelles et spéculations à Venise au début du XVIe siècle* (1948); J. Day 'Strade e vie di comunicazione' *SI* V

Condottieri The condottiere was the holder of a military *condotta*, or contract, for the raising and leadership of troops. While *condotte* were being issued by Italian cities and states as early as the second half of the 13c. as a means of recruiting a part of their armies, it was only in the later years of the 14c. that such contracts became the main method of raising armies in Italy. The companies, often made up largely of foreigners, which dominated Italian warfare for much of the 14c. were normally employed under contract, but they were surprisingly democratic in their organization, and the contracts with employing states were signed by representative groups of leaders. By about 1370 individual military commanders had largely gained control of the companies and had become the sole contractors for their services. From this moment onwards the vast majority of condottieri were Italians and they dominated the military scene in Italy throughout the 15c.

The nuclei of the companies which condottieri contracted to provide were normally kept permanently in being and augmented for specific contracts and campaigns by recruitment of additional rank and file. The condottiere, therefore, was invariably a man of substance possessing estates and permanent income which enabled him to maintain his principal followers between contracts and recruit rapidly from amongst his own tenants and dependants. These socio-economic conditions were of more importance than military reputation in dictating the size of the contract which a condottiere could obtain, and hence his prestige and reputation. Many of the leading condottieri were either independent princes like the Gonzaga lords of Mantua or the Este lords of Ferrara, or were members of extensive landowning families like the Orsini or Dal Verme.

The main strength of the condottiere company lay in its 'lances', a term which describes not only the main weapon of heavily armed cavalrymen but also the group of attendants who supported them. However, during the 15c. condottieri began to take an increasing interest in infantry as an essential support to their cavalry, and a number of leading captains also possessed some artillery. While it would be wrong to see a willingness to experiment and innovate as an outstanding characteristic of the condottieri, there were among them some major military personalities. Men like Francesco Sforza, Bartolomeo Colleoni and Federico da Montefeltro had European reputations in the mid-15c., and in the Wars of Italy many of the most successful leaders of the French and Spanish armies in Italy were Italian condottieri.

Undoubtedly the contract system of service tended to breed a sort of military individualism which weakened the cohesion of a large army, but in fact by the 15c. the system did not mean that condottieri changed their employment with every contract. The Italian states were among the first in Europe to develop permanent armies, and most Italian condottieri settled into a pattern of routine renewals of increasingly long-term contracts with one or other of the states. There remained the exceptional figures whose reputations, and whose control of what amounted to large private armies, prompted political ambitions and made them targets of increasingly tempting offers from potential employers. But at this level the *condotta* took on some of the characteristics of a diplomatic alliance, and a switch of allegiance has to be seen in terms of international politics rather than individual infidelity. In formal terms the *condotta* system and the role of the condottiere as a leader of cavalry survived throughout the 16c. But the declining importance of cavalry in war and the growing political domination of France and Spain in Italy meant an end to their political role and a decline in social prestige. MM

E. Ricotti *La storia delle compagnie di ventura in Italia* (2nd ed. 1893); P. Pieri *Il Rinascimento e la crisi militare italiana* (1952); M. E. Mallett *Mercenaries and their masters: warfare in Renaissance Italy* (1974); M. del Treppo 'Gli aspetti organizzativi economici e sociali di una compagnia di ventura italiana' *Rivista Storica Italiana* (1973)

Confraternities, often called *compagnie* or, in Venice, *scuole*, were religious associations of lay persons devoted to specific pious practices or works of charity, often under the direction of, or with the spiritual assistance of, clergy. Guilds *qua* religious associations had the character of confraternities.

Several major historic waves of foundations can be distinguished. (1) *Compagnie dei disciplinati* or *dei laudesi*, i.e. flagellant confraternities, which were conformist offshoots of the partly heterodox flagellant movement of 1260. The Venetian *scuole grandi* were especially prestigious examples. By the 16c., although flagellant practices were retained in some cases, these functioned more as mutual aid societies and as administrators of charitable funds. (2) *Confraternite del Rosario*, which spread in the 15c., being primarily promoted by the Dominicans. (3) A group of confraternities which spread from the mid-15c., commonly called either *Compagnia di S. Girolamo* or *Compagnia del Divino Amore* ('Company of Divine Love'; perhaps the first example was the Florentine Buonuomini di S. Martino), associated with certain specialized charitable enterprises, in the first place relief of the *poveri vergognosi* or 'shamefaced poor', i.e. respectable people who had to be aided discreetly. In the 16c. they also promoted hospitals of the *incurabili*, primarily for syphilitics, convents of *convertite*, i.e. reformed prostitutes, and refuges for maidens. To this movement belonged the famous Roman Company or Oratory of Divine Love, founded *c.*1514 in S. Dorotea in Trastevere. This recruited some leading churchmen and papal officials (as a confraternity it was unusual in its heavy clerical membership), but many ascriptions of leading church reformers to it are without sound foundation and there is no basis for its reputation as a seminal body in the Catholic reform movement. The new congregation of the Clerks Regular called Theatines was, however, an offshoot and these took the lead in propagating *Compagnie del Divino Amore* in Italy. Other types of confraternity were those of the *buona morte*, which accompanied condemned prisoners, and those which aided imprisoned debtors, e.g. the Florentine *Neri*.

Confraternities commonly had chapels in parish churches or in the churches of religious orders, but sometimes had their own premises, e.g. the splendid ones of the Venetian *scuole grandi*; in Florence, the hall of Orsanmichele housed a devotional and almsgiving confraternity as well as being a grain dispensary. Great confraternities might exercise public functions: certain Florentine ones concerned with welfare became effectively state magistracies, while the Venetian government, in addition to giving them a ceremonial role, relied upon the *scuole grandi* to distribute funds. Confraternities, notwithstanding their location, tended to be manifestations of lay piety independent of ecclesiastical institutions, or at least outside the framework of the parish and the diocese. OL

Procession of the **confraternity** or *scuola* of S. Giovanni Evangelista with the Relic of the True Cross at a funeral in Venice: detail from a painting by Giovanni Mansueti (Venice, Accademia).

P. Paschini *Tre ricerche sulla storia della chiesa nel Cinquecento* (1945); B. Pullan *Rich and poor in Renaissance Venice* (1972)

Constitutions The states of Renaissance Italy lived under constitutions which were inherited from the Middle Ages; whatever may have happened north of the Alps, in Italy the Renaissance at most changed the style of government and ways of thinking about the state, not the fundamental characteristics of political administration. Over much of Italy – the mountainous areas of the north and everywhere south of Rome – states did not differ very much from those in the rest of Europe; Naples and Sicily were kingdoms and

Savoy and Montferrat hereditary principalities whose government was based on the household of the ruling dynasty. Only in the economically advanced regions of the north and centre did the communes, which were found throughout western Europe, evolve into characteristically Italian city states.

The commune was essentially a group of local men of wealth and power who, united by an oath, took on the rudiments of government on the breakdown of the Imperial administration of counts and bishops *c.*1075–1140. The majority of these men were landowners, with a significant leaven of lawyers; only in Genoa and Venice did the merchant element predominate. Membership of the early communes was restricted to 200 or 300 individuals at the most; between 1198 and 1250 the communes underwent a series of revolutions through which middling landowners, local merchants and shopkeepers and members of the craft guilds obtained a share of political rights, increasing the governing class in major cities to between 2000 and 4000. By the late 13c. the major communes had subjugated the surrounding territory (contado) and evolved elaborate constitutions based on detailed, codified statutes. There were salaried officials (podestà, capitano del popolo, bargello and numerous judges); citizens sat in rapid rotation on executive committees (as *anziani* in Lombardy, priors in Florence) and on larger legislative councils; for better or worse, the notarial bureaucracy was much in evidence in town and country, reaching its maximum extension around 1300.

From the mid-13c. the communes began to fall one by one under the domination of a single individual or family. These men were party leaders, often drawn from among the landowning magnates, and they secured their lordship (*signoria*) sometimes by 'election' in a citizen assembly (*parlamentum*) or legislative council, sometimes by recognition as papal or Imperial vicars. In 1395, Giangaleazzo Visconti of Milan opened a new chapter by buying the title of duke from the Emperor Wenceslas. Nevertheless the division of power within the signorial family often remained ill-defined, leading to family feuds and murders. The signori generally ruled through a small circle of officials and partisans – often magnates like themselves – but the communal councils were retained with membership reduced to reliable supporters of the régime. Although by the 15c. the major Italian states – Milan, Venice, Florence, the Papal State – had swallowed up many lesser cities, their citizens continued to think of themselves as members of the local commune, whose laws and officials continued to impinge most frequently upon their daily lives.

By 1340 there were only a handful of cities without a signore. Selfconscious republicanism began in Florence with the expulsion of the elected signore Walter of Brienne in 1343. The 9 priors, the 12 *bonihomines* or Good Men, and the 16 standard-bearers of the companies, making up the main executive committees, were selected by lot from lists of citizens prepared by periodic scrutinies. These elaborate procedures could not check a drift towards oligarchy but prevented the concentration of power until 1434, when Cosimo de' Medici established a tentative despotism, party-supported, which was gradually consolidated by his descendants. With the expulsion of Piero in 1494, the Florentines turned to the example of Venice, whose uniquely stable government was thought to embody the virtues of the Aristotelian 'mixed constitution'. A Consiglio Maggiore of 3000 with a smaller Senate were set up on the Venetian model, and in 1502 a gonfalonier was elected for life in imitation of the doge. With the final fall of Florence to the Medici in 1530, Venice remained the outstanding republic in Italy, and as such attracted wonderment, study and sometimes imitation throughout the Renaissance period and beyond. *See* MYTH OF VENICE; VENICE. JKH

J. K. Hyde *Society and politics in medieval Italy* (1973); N. Rubinstein *The government of Florence under the Medici* (1966); F. Gilbert 'The Venetian constitution in Florentine political thought' in N. Rubinstein ed. *Florentine studies* (1968); L. Martines *Power and imagination: city-states in Renaissance Italy* (1980)

Contarini, Cardinal Gasparo (1483–1542) Venetian philosopher, statesman, theologian and religious reformer. He studied philosophy at Padua and remained primarily a Thomist in his philosophy and theology. In 1511 he underwent a spiritual crisis comparable to Luther's. Around 1516 he composed a famous treatise on the office of the bishop, *De officio viri boni ac probi episcopi*. Between 1520 and 1534 he held major Venetian state offices, primarily diplomatic ones. In 1534 he was appointed cardinal and moved to Rome, being made bishop of Belluno in 1536. In Rome, he was an accomplished string-puller in the interests of church reform. His role as an eirenic theologian had been foreshadowed by a courteously framed confutation of Luther written prior to 1534. In 1541–42, as papal legate at Ratisbon, he presided over the last serious attempt to reach agreement between Catholics and Lutherans in Germany, and here was responsible for putting forward the 'double justification' theory as a mediatory formula.

He is also, and perhaps better, known as an author for his ardent defence of the Venetian system of government, the *De magistratibus et republica Venetorum libri quinque*. Written in 1523–24 and revised in 1531, this was published in 1543. It became widely influential in later European debates about the 'best' form of constitution. Lewis Lewkenor's English translation of 1599 had a prefatory sonnet by Spenser and it was one of the books Ben Jonson represents Sir Politick Would-be in *Volpone* as reading in Venice. OL

F. Dittrich *Gasparo Contarini (1483–1542)* (1885); G. Fragnito 'Cultura umanistica e riforma religiosa' *Studi Veneziani* (1969); W. J. Bouwsma *Venice and the defence of republican liberty* (1968)

Conti, Niccolò dei (*c.*1395–1469) One of the most intrepid and observant of the Quattrocento successors of Marco Polo. A Venetian (actually from Chioggia), he spent some 25 years travelling and trading across Persia, down the Red Sea to India and Bengal. Having next reached as far east as Java, he returned via India, Ethiopia and Egypt. The account of his travels was published by Bracciolini in 1447 as one of the parts of his *De varietate fortunae*, and had a wide circulation in manuscript before it was printed in 1492. JRH

R. H. Major *India in the fifteenth century* Hakluyt Society (1858)

Cordoba, Gonzalo de (1453–1515) Gonzalo (or Gonsalvo) emerged from the campaigns of 1482–91 waged by Ferdinand of Aragon and Isabella of Castile against the Moors of Granada with the nickname 'the Great Captain'. This had been earned not only by his daring but also by his outstanding capacity as an organizer and military reformer. In 1495 he was appointed commander of the Spanish army sent to assist King Ferdinand of Naples in recovering his kingdom from the French garrisons left after Charles VIII's successful invasion in January-February of that year. On Ferdinand's death in 1496 he stayed on at the request of his successor, Federico, until the reimposition of law and order was complete. Back in Spain in 1498 he was put in charge of the punitive campaign that followed the Moorish rebellion in the Alpujarras mountains south of Granada. In 1500 he was sent to assist the Venetians in their war against the Turks, successfully expelling them from the island of Cephalonia.

But it was with the second Spanish Neapolitan war, this time in association with France (under the terms of the Treaty of Granada of 1500) and against Federico, that Gonzalo's fame became international, earning him 50 years later (1551) the most admiring of Paolo Giovio's biographies of military heroes, *The life of Consalvo Ferrando of Cordova the Great Captain*. In the first phase of this war he occupied Calabria. In its second (1502–03), when France turned against its ally, he defeated the French first at Cerignola (April 1503) and then at the battle of the Garigliano (December 1503). One of the most decisive engagements of the WARS OF ITALY, this placed the kingdom of Naples in foreign hands until the Risorgimento. Gonzalo was subsequently made Viceroy of Naples until 1507, but his last years, back in Spain, were clouded by the suspicion in which Ferdinand held his all-too-successful subject, and he was given no part in Spain's subsequent interventions in Italy.

As Giovio, expanding on earlier Italian admirers of Gonzalo (such as Castiglione), pointed out, his success owed much to a strategic flexibility and an interest in military techniques that was strikingly unusual at the time. He emphasized the role of infantry and light horse at the expense of the traditional aristocratic heavy cavalry. This was a lesson of guerrilla warfare in Spain. In Naples he adopted the long German-Swiss pike as his own hitting weapon and trained swordsmen with shields to slide under those of their opponents. He increased the number of arquebusiers to above the Italian norm and was (with the advice of his chief artillerist, Pedro of Navarre) a pioneer of gunpowder mining techniques in siegecraft. But having improved the military machine, he guarded it from being used until he was confident of victory, at the risk of accusations of cowardice. Even allowing for the excessive praise of those Italians dissatisfied with their own military traditions, he emerges as the outstanding soldier of his age. JRH

A. Rodriguez Villa *Cronicas del Gran Capitan* (1908); L. M. de Lojendio *Gonzalo de Cordoba* (1942); G. de Gaury *The Grand Captain: Gonzalo de Cordoba* (1955)

Corio, Bernardino (1459–before 1512) A member of the household of Lodovico Sforza, who commissioned him to write the history of Milan from its origins. His lengthy book, published in 1503, goes up to 1499 and is remarkable both as the first serious historical work to be written in the vernacular and for its dependence (in the 15c. part) on archival material – put specifically at his disposal by Lodovico. JRH

Patria historia ed. A. Morosi Guerra as *Storia di Milano* (2 vols 1978)

Cornaro, Caterina (1454–1510) This Queen of Cyprus exiled by Venice to the small hill town of Asolo has enjoyed an inflated posthumous reputation as a great beauty and patroness. She was the daughter of the Venetian patrician Marco Cornaro, who had extensive properties in Cyprus; married by proxy (1468) to James II of Lusignan, she arrived in Cyprus in 1472, ruling it herself in widowhood from 1474. Her brother Giorgio was sent to demand her resignation (1489); compensation included an income to maintain a household of 80. The reputation of Asolo (near Treviso) as a court of literary and artistic distinction is mainly the result of its having been chosen as the fictitious setting for Pietro Bembo's Platonic dialogues on love *Gli asolani* (written *c.*1497, published 1505). Caterina also spent much time in Murano and Venice, where portraits of her were painted by Gentile Bellini and (possibly) Giorgione, but there is little to suggest that she was in education and tastes exceptional among rich Venetian women of her class. DC

'Loredana' *Caterina Cornaro* (1938); A. Chastel 'Le mirage d'Asolo' *Arte Veneta* (1978)

Correggio, Antonio Allegri (1494–1534) of Parma, influenced by Leonardo's sfumato technique and, through Raimondi's engravings, by Raphael's work in Rome, evolved a personal style of astonishing subtlety, whether in oil or fresco. His female nudes are amongst the most ravishing creations of the High Renaissance. The bold foreshortenings and dynamic freedom of movement of his *Vision of St John* in the relatively small dome of S. Giovanni Evangelista, Parma (1520), and of his even more astonishing *Assumption of the Virgin* (1526–30) in the vast octagonal dome of the cathedral, transcend all architectural limitations in a way that demands comparison with Roman Baroque designs of over a century later. JW

C. Gould *The paintings of Correggio* (1976)

Correggio, *Mercury Instructing Cupid before Venus* (London, National Gallery).

Corsica Although nominally a Genoese dependency, the mountainous island of Corsica was normally abandoned to the misrule of the local baronage, until a threatened Aragonese invasion (1453) led to its being placed under the control of the Genoese Casa di S. Giorgio. However, even the bank failed to curb the lawlessness of Corsica, which was abandoned to Milan (1464), sold to the Fregosi (1478), and only restored to the Casa di S. Giorgio in 1485. In the following half-century the bank had some success in breaking the power of the Corsican barons but in 1553 Corsica was invaded by the French and Ottomans. Genoese rule, restored in 1559, was confirmed by the suppresssion of the revolt (1564–69) of Sampiero. The following 150 years of Genoese rule are known as 'the Iron Century', but historians now look favourably on a government which brought prosperity for the first time in Corsica's history. *See* GENOA. JH

P. Antonetti *Histoire de la Corse* (1973)

Corteccia, Francesco (1502–71) Principal composer of music for several royal entertainments given in Florence. Born into a humble Florentine family, he was first a choirboy, then took Holy orders before becoming organist of S. Lorenzo in 1531. Thereafter he was the chief musician to the Medici, for whom he wrote music for the celebrations after the wedding of Cosimo I de' Medici and Eleonora di Toledo in 1539. In the later part of his life he was a canon of S. Lorenzo. DA

A. Minor and B. Mitchell ed. *A Renaissance entertainment: festivities for the marriage of Cosimo I, Duke of Florence in 1539* (1968)

Cortese, Paolo (1465–1510) entered the papal bureaucracy and in 1481 became head of the department in the chancery responsible for drafting correspondence and briefs, a position reserved for scholarly latinists (he succeeded Platina, Sixtus IV's librarian). In 1489 he composed a pioneering critical account of Latin writing from the time of Dante to his own, *De hominis doctis*, which led to an exchange of letters with Poliziano on the theme of imitation (especially of Cicero) versus a more eclectic form of self-expression. His *De cardinalatu*, published shortly after his death, is an important contribution to the literature delineating ideal types. Written by an insider, it gives a portrait of the perfect cardinal which, with its emphasis on a refined but lavish and many-sided style of life, is not too dissimilar to the perfect courtier described by Castiglione. JRH

Cosimo I de' Medici Duke of Florence 1537–69, Grand Duke of Tuscany 1569–74 (b.1519). Until quite recently Quattrocento Florence has diverted interest from the most thoroughly competent and effective member of the Medici family and the impress of his patronage on the city. When the last republican régime (1527–30) of Florence was besieged into surrender by a papal and Imperial army, nominal control of the city was vested in Alessandro, a direct, if illegitimate, descendant of Cosimo de' Medici *il Vecchio*. He was the last male in this line, and when he was assassinated in 1537 the conservative elements, Charles V's representative Cardinal Cybo and the old guard of patricians (Guicciardini prominent among them), reached for a Medici who, though not of the main line, could – under careful tutelage – check yet further aspiration to see Florence governed as an independent republic. They chose Cosimo, a fourth-generation descendant of the older Cosimo's brother Lorenzo. The son of a notable professional soldier, Giovanni dalle Bande Nere ('of the black bands'), who had been killed fighting in 1526, Cosimo was an inexperienced 18. Having been brought up in the country by Giovanni's widow, Maria Salviati, he was also something of an outsider. Thus doubly removed from enmeshment in the city's factional traditions, he was free to see his role as analogous to that of the majority of other Italian rulers, who were princes backed by a core of professional bureaucrats. The energy and acumen with which he grew into this role were remarkable.

Almost at the outset he was aided by fortune: his army defeated a gathering of patrician exiles at MONTEMURLO. This was seen as an earnest of firm and stable government by a city anxious at last to put prosperity above politics, and enabled Cosimo to devote himself to the 4 themes of his reign: the easing of the duchy away from Imperial control, the detachment of the governing process from the class historically responsible for it, the closer integration of Florence with its possessions in Tuscany, and the open glorification of the house of Medici.

Cosimo I de' Medici as a patron of architecture: ceiling-painting by Vasari in the Palazzo Vecchio, Florence.

Taking advantage of Charles V's embarrassments elsewhere, he quickly bargained and paid his way free from the Emperor's leading strings: Cybo, and the Spanish garrisons Charles had left in Tuscany to patrol its loyalty to him. Thereafter he played the Valois *v.* Habsburg power game with such address that, after conducting a war against Florence's old rival, Siena, nominally as the Emperor's henchman, he was left in 1557 in undisputed possession of that city and the greater part of its subject territories: the largest single accession of land ever achieved by Florence.

At home, his appetite for desk-work and relish for detail had its own wearing-down effect on others who wanted to share in the making of decisions. Backed first by officials he had inherited from Alessandro, then increasingly by patricians who were prepared to serve him rather than protect their traditional family interests, he changed, definitively, the position of the leader of Florence from chief-among-equals to unchallenged chief of state. Within Tuscany (and it is significant that he chose the title Grand Duke of Tuscany, not of Florence) he built border fortifications and carried out public works programmes, roads and land reclamation, in a manner that made it clear that he thought of his possessions as a whole, as a state of a recognizably modern sort rather than as the exploitative 'city state' that he had inherited; so also did his annual progresses and his relaxation of legal and fiscal legislation that had subordinated Tuscan towns to Florence.

This was all done – before he fell ill and passed much of his responsibility to his son Francesco in 1564 – doggedly, thoroughly and somewhat charmlessly; and always to the greater glory of the Medici. His embellishments of Florence – Ammannati's Ponte S. Trinita and Neptune fountain in Piazza della Signoria, the Lungarni Corsini and Acciaiuoli, the Uffizi, the extension of the Pitti Palace – were calculated to impress, as were the coolly commanding portraits he commissioned or the propagandistic cycles of paintings he ordered for the Palazzo della Signoria. That he should have been commemorated by a triumphal equestrian statue (in Piazza della Signoria) is a fitting comment on the new attitude to state and status that characterized the Cinquecento, as opposed to the Quattrocento Medici. JRH

E. Cochrane *Florence in the forgotten centuries, 1527–1800* (1973); G. Spini *Cosimo I de' Medici: lettere* (with linking commentary) (1945)

Cossa, Francesco del (active *c.*1456, d.1477) was, with Cosmè Tura and Ercole de' Roberti, one of the 3 key figures in the late 15c. Ferrarese school of painting. His major work, the frescoes of the months for Borso d'Este in the Palazzo Schifanoia, Ferrara, are, in the complexity of their iconography and the variety of the sources upon which they draw, prime examples of the taste and thought processes to be found in a leading North Italian court. In their pristine decorative splendour they were Renaissance counterparts of the teeming late gothic tapestries of northern Europe. JW

Costume As in other parts of Europe 1300–1600, costume in Italy was one of the main indicators of social position and one of the chief objects of conspicuous consumption. Jewels, cloth of gold and furs revealed the status as well as the wealth of the wearers, and their use was regulated by SUMPTUARY LAWS. Cardinals, Venetian senators and other dignitaries were instantly recognizable by their magnificent robes. Hence Carnival fancy dress was a potent symbol of social subversion. Well-to-do non-employed women displayed their status by wearing anti-functional clothes such as long trains, high heels and elaborate head-dresses (which S. Bernardino of Siena compared to 'fortifications'). A veil, or the lack of one, declared a woman to be unmarried, married, or widowed, as a red cap or a bell declared her to be a prostitute. Genoese women were as conspicuous by their lack of veils as

Social standing reflected in **costume** among the spectators at a courtly entertainment: detail from a mid-15c. Florentine panel (Oxford, Ashmolean Museum).

ordinary Venetian patricians by the simplicity of their black gowns. It is impossible to summarize changes in fashion over 300 years, but the evolution of sumptuary laws, which began by prohibiting luxury and ended by restricting it, reveals a progressively less egalitarian social structure. PB

R. L. Pisetzky 'Moda e Costume' *SI* V

Council of Ten Set up (at first on a temporary basis) in 1310 to investigate the conspiracy of Baiamonte Tiepolo, this became perhaps the most famous of all Renaissance organs of state. It was never literally a council of ten. The doge and his 6 councillors could join its meetings. It was afforced by a *zonta* of 20 (15 from 1529) non-voting members. Membership was for one year, with a year's disqualification before reappointment was permitted. The Council's responsibility was to protect the state from treason, whether at home or abroad: in addition to receiving security reports on individuals from rectors and other officials in the Venetian territories it employed spies and, on occasion, assassins. In time of war it was the Ten that licensed the use (never successful) of poison in water supplies used by enemies. In addition, it became, because of its small number, the body that conducted diplomacy considered too secret to be entrusted for the time being to the Senate. Finally, until 1582 (when this function passed to the Senate), it supervised the production and disposal of artillery, ball and gunpowder.

Except in the case of assassinations, which were usually abortive, its judicial procedures were strictly controlled and, given the size of the body, reasonably open. The Council's interpretation of its powers in the interest of political security led – especially in 1582, when its area of competence was redefined – to occasional conflict with the Senate, which elected its members. But its malign reputation is chiefly derived from its offshoot, the 3 Inquisitors of State, who from 1539 were empowered by the Ten to investigate and punish crimes against the state in which an enhanced degree of secrecy was considered necessary. JRH

G. Maranini *La constituzione di Venezia* ... (1931); M. Lowry 'The reform of the Council of Ten' *Studi veneziani* (1971)

Councils of the Church When the Great Schism broke out in 1378, theologians and canon lawyers were well aware that many fundamental points of the faith had been settled by General Councils of prelates called by Roman and Byzantine Emperors, notably at Nicaea (325) and Chalcedon (451). The stages in the growth of the papally centralized medieval Church had been marked by the four Lateran Councils of 1123, 1139, 1179 and 1215, followed by the first and second Councils of Lyons (1245 and 1274) and the Council of Vienne in 1311. It was recognized that the decisions of a General Council, once they were ratified by the pope, were the supreme authority in faith and discipline, but the western tradition did not allow a Council to be summoned by anyone except the pope; since there were now two popes it was impossible to hold a Council which would be recognized by both sides. This deadlock lasted for 30 years, during which time a body of 'conciliar' thought built up which argued the legality of action by a Council representing the body of the Church to reform the head in an emergency. Thus, when a group of dissident cardinals drawn from both the Roman and the AVIGNON 'obediences' called a Council to meet at Pisa in March 1409, the assembly was well attended and the 'conciliar' pope Alexander V, who was elected there, obtained widespread but not universal recognition.

The Council of Constance (1414–18), called by the Emperor Sigismund and the second 'conciliar' pope, John XXIII, was a massive gathering not only of prelates but of numerous doctors and lower clergy as well; representatives of secular powers, who had attended the Councils of the 13c., were present in strength so that the meeting resembled a European congress. The Council healed the SCHISM and burned the Bohemian heretic John Huss, while a notable exchange of ideas took place; Bracciolini, for example, searched the Alpine monasteries for classical manuscripts. The conciliarists hoped that Constance would be followed by regular General Councils which would carry through a thorough reform of the Church's administration. The Council of Basle, unwillingly called by Eugenius IV in 1431, was dominated by the radical voices of the lower clergy. When they refused to transfer to Ferrara to meet the Greeks in 1437, Eugenius withdrew his recognition and the Council retaliated by electing the last anti-pope, Felix V (1439–49). Support for the Council drained away because princes – including the Greek Emperor –

preferred to do business with the pope rather than with a leaderless assembly. Thus with the conciliar movement collapsed the last chance to reform the Church before Luther; the Fifth Lateran Council (1512–17) was almost exclusively Italian and firmly under papal control, and fought shy of radical changes. *See* PAPACY; TRENT, COUNCIL OF; EUGENIUS IV. JKH

B. Tierney *The foundations of conciliar theory* (1955); H. Jedin *Ecumenical councils of the Catholic Church* (1960)

Counter-Reformation The term covers both the ideological offensive against Protestantism and movements of reform and reorganization in the Catholic Church from the mid-16c. In the latter sense it is largely interchangeable with 'Catholic Reformation'. However, this term has broader period connotations and some historians have distinguished between 'Catholic Reform' and 'Counter-Reformation' in Italy in order to highlight a hardening of attitudes and a split among leading reformers between intransigent zealots and moderate 'evangelicals' in the early 1540s (*see* EVANGELISM). The question arises as to how far the reform movement was itself a response to the Protestant challenge; certainly it was this threat that induced Paul III to bring leading reformers to positions of power in Rome in the 1530s and to summon the Council of Trent; however, the roots of the movement antedate Protestantism. Further, the Church in the long run set its house in order less to defend pre-existing positions than to extend its control over and to discipline a laity over which it had hitherto had limited influence, especially in rural areas.

Aspects of the ideological offensive were the organization of the INQUISITION and book CENSORSHIP; catechisms were introduced and programmes of evangelization (*see* PREACHERS) and propaganda were conducted by religious orders, most notably the Jesuits. Major elements of the reform movement were: (1) developments in the sphere of religious CONFRATERNITIES, especially with the Companies of Divine Love, which sought through their welfare work to save souls as well as aid bodies; (2) the rise of new RELIGIOUS ORDERS and zealant movements within old orders; (3) the pastoral reform. Historians now emphasize the last. Here the stress was upon episcopal action. An ideology of the bishop as pastor was being forcefully expressed in Italy before the Council of TRENT and at the Council itself (1545–63). The attempt on a large scale to strengthen pastoral organization at diocesan level began only after the Council. This was primarily an assembly of bishops. It fulfilled 2 functions, definition of doctrine and legislation on church discipline and organization. The latter only came in the final sessions in 1563. Basically, the disciplinary decrees restated traditional canon law but a new element was the educational decree on clerical seminaries.

Reforming bishops after Trent tried to mould the CLERGY as a priestly caste, marked out from the laity by dress and comportment, abstaining from vulgar amusements and having sufficient training to be able to preach and administer the sacraments. Again, they sought to ensure the religious conformity of the laity and for purposes of control of the laity parish priests must keep a register of the 'state of souls' with the vital statistics of their flocks and details of miscreants. Together with evangelists from the religious orders, they often made war on 'profane' popular festivities such as CARNIVAL, on the 'licence' of clowns and players, on *décolletage* and on other feminine 'vanities' such as cosmetics. Legalism, rigorism and hierocratic ideology are regarded as being among the hallmarks of *controriformismo*. *See* CHURCH ARCHITECTURE AND LITURGY. OL

H. O. Evennett *The spirit of the Counter Reformation* ed. J. Bossy (1968); A. G. Dickens *The Counter Reformation* (1968); M. Rosa *Religione e società nel Mezzogiorno tra Cinque e Seicento* (Naples 1976)

Courtesans and prostitutes The term 'courtesan' (*cortigiana*) was a euphemism for a high-class prostitute first used in the late 15c. Their less successful professional colleagues were known as *meretrici* or *puttane*. The aristocrats of the profession were generally to be found in Rome or Venice, perhaps because of the high proportion of bachelors in the population of those cities. These courtesans were distinguished not only by their beauty and their high price but also by their graceful manners, splendid clothes and jewels, and sumptuous surroundings. Some of them had intellectual pretensions, like the girl nicknamed 'Matrema non vole' ('Mama doesn't want me to'), whose views on U and non-U Italian have been immortalized in a dialogue by Aretino. At least two courtesans made contributions of their own to Renaissance literature: TULLIA

A Blonde Woman, assumed to be a **courtesan**, by Palma Vecchio (London, National Gallery).

D'ARAGONA of Rome, who kept a salon, published her poems (1547), and was nicknamed 'courtesan of the academicians' (her clients including Sperone Speroni and Varchi); and Veronica FRANCO of Venice, who published both poems (1575) and letters (1580). The great age of the courtesans, paralleled only in classical Athens and Tokugawa Japan, seems to have ended in Rome in the 1560s and in Venice *c.*1600.

Life was less glamorous for the rank and file, who were also concentrated in Rome and Venice, where the numerous visitors increased the demand (though Florence, which pioneered civic brothels in the 14c. and 15c., had 200 prostitutes in 1560 – one to every 300 people). Prostitutes were generally expected to live in particular quarters, to wear distinctive clothes (bells on their heads in some places), and to keep out of the more respectable churches. Their troubles with their protectors and with the officers of the law were no different in kind from those of their modern descendants. They could look forward to a working life of only 15-odd years, followed by begging or the *convertite* (workhouse for the 'repentant'). The hazards of the job increased dramatically with the spread of syphilis from the late 15c. onwards, though the cautionary publicity attending the disease had scant effect either on supply or demand. PB

G. Masson *Courtesans of the Italian Renaissance* (1975)

Cremona In 1344 Visconti conquest brought the history of Cremona as an independent city-state (most recently under the Cavalcabò family) to an end. Apart from a 10-year occupation by Venice, 1499–1509, resulting from the Republic's early alliance with Louis XII, Cremona continued to be subject to the rulers (from 1525, Spanish) of Milan. By the end of the 16c. Cremona was beginning, with Antonio (1550–1638) and Girolamo (1556–1630) Amati, to establish its reputation for the making of fine string instruments. JRH

Crime People – or, in particular, governments – define crime. They have many guidelines in so doing: religious traditions; inherited social and economic practices and values; and a general awareness of the kinds of behaviour a given population is likely to agree to condemn and punish. The cities of Renaissance Italy, in other respects so varied and individualistic, tend to reveal strong similarities in their definition of, and their response to, criminality. This reflects their evolution through comparable stages of political and juridical development.

Historians study crime in the Renaissance by means of three distinct kinds of sources: (1) urban law codes, which provide detailed evidence of the content of public law, and of the sanctions available; (2) trial records, which help us to determine precisely how the laws were (or were not) enforced; (3) ancillary sources, such as the evidence of contemporary chronicles on criminal behaviour and law enforcement, diaries and memoirs that reflect such concerns, and moral and philosophical treatises addressing such issues as part of the problem of evil. In general, the sources make us see crime from the viewpoint of an offended society, rather than giving us the perspective of an idealistic revolutionary, a starving burglar, a crazed artisan about to have his tongue severed for blasphemy, or a senile woman facing a slow death by fire for witchcraft. Yet such voices as these do occasionally appear in the records, enabling us to witness the seething variety of a complex and tormented social world, ill-housed, ill-clothed, ill-fed, and above all, illiterate. The perpetrators of Renaissance

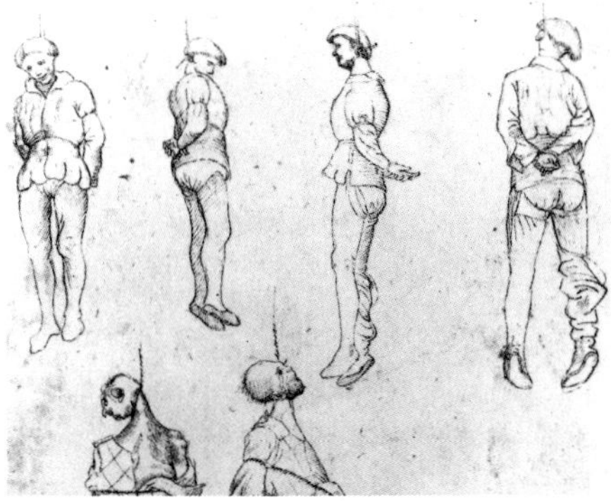

The price of **crime**: studies of hanged men by Pisanello (London, British Museum).

crimes were often themselves the victims of a savagely neglectful society.

Renaissance legal codes reflect an obsessive concern for political and social order. Those who threatened such order, conspirators in particular, faced death or at least exile. Lese-majesty, even mild criticism of some princeling, could bring down the most awesome reprisals; and the death penalty was available for crimes ranging from murder and arson to burglary, counterfeiting, and a wide range of sexual offences. The severity of criminal sanctions was commonly justified not only by the *lex talionis* (an eye for an eye), but also by a theory of deterrence. Thus many sentences (especially for political and moral offences) were carried out in public. The mentality behind such practices is revealed in the decisions of several 15c. municipalities to paint on the walls of public buildings images of men sentenced to death, in cases where the intended victims had managed to escape. These *pitture infamanti* ('defamatory pictures') were the most ephemeral paintings of the period: not a single one is known to have survived.

Family wealth and social position certainly made it easier to avoid the full force of the law, especially in sexual offences. In these society also viewed the same offences committed by men and by women in very different terms. It is perhaps most surprising that, given the often shaky authority of city governments, their judicial systems worked quite effectively to safeguard public order, in the general absence of extensive facilities for incarcerating, let alone rehabilitating, offenders. Perhaps the most successful criminals of the Renaissance were the bandits, living in the interstices of civilization, enjoying advantages of mobility and knowledge of terrain, and exploiting the land and a helpless and terrified peasantry. WG

L. Martines ed. *Violence and civil disorder in Italian cities, 1200–1500* (1972); G. Brucker *The social world of Renaissance Florence* (1971); A. Solmi *Storia del diritto italiano* (1930)

Critical theory of art A critical vocabulary suited to the appraisal of works of art developed well in the rear of demand for, and admiration of, works in the novel manner of Cimabue, Giotto and their successors. In the 14c. there was a clear awareness of the change that was taking place. Dante noted that Giotto's reputation had overtaken Cimabue's. Giovanni Villani saw Florence's painters as a recent source of civic pride and developed the notion of a progressive master-pupil relationship. But there was no sense that words could describe the quality of a work of art or might be used to communicate the nature of a personal reaction to it. Appraisal of a painter was expressed in terms merely of manual skill, talent suited to the job and, increasingly, the lifelikeness of his painting.

There was a model available for a more complex critical approach: the narrative and evaluative account of ancient art in Pliny's *Natural history*. But humanistic scholars were more concerned with shaping a critical approach to their own primary activity; it was entirely characteristic that in the margin of the passage in PLINY where Apelles is described as chiding the painter Protogenes for not knowing when to stop 'improving' his work, Petrarch noted 'Watch out for this, Francesco, when you are writing.' The chief contribution of 14c. humanism to art criticism was the classical rhetorical device of *ekphrasis*, or a detailed description essayed as a sort of prose-poem; this at least helped to focus attention on the work described.

In the 15c. even an artist as intellectually sophisticated as Ghiberti, in his *Commentaries*, is more or less tongue-tied. Speaking of his admired Giotto he praises him because 'he brought in natural art, and grace with it,' but when evaluating his works he limits himself to saying that they had been painted 'excellently' or 'learnedly' or 'perfectly' or 'finely'. It was only with Alberti's *De pictura* (1435) that a critical stance developed, and then not because this was his aim, but because he called attention to the intellectual importance of the artist's *métier* and isolated certain of his aims that later critics could use as standards of judgment: the geometrical organization of space through rational perspective; modelling by light and shade; the 'freezing' of natural movement (of hair, drapery, foliage, etc.); accurate observation, based on the use of models, of the human body and facial expression; narrative eloquence; the attainment of a beauty suited to art by a fusion of examples of the not-quite-perfect beauties produced by nature (as in the case, cited by Pliny, of Zeuxis' selection of 5 pretty girls to produce a single image of ideal beauty).

It was from Alberti's formulation – supported by his writing on sculpture and architecture – of what 'art' was, and from an awareness of the increasing status accorded to individual artists like Leonardo and Raphael, that in the 16c. a theory-buttressed critical approach was able to develop further, and with it the ability to express reactions to the experience of confronting works of art. Both were retarded, however, by a reluctance to see a work of art in its own terms: it was good if it was like nature, or like a work described by

LXXVIII LIB. II.

ARS DOCTA NATVRAM ÆMVLATVR
VT POTEST
QVIN VINCIT: VSVS DVM ADSIT
ET DVRVS LABOR.
Symb. XXXVI.

Critical theory of art: an allegory of the exact imitation of nature in sculpture, from Achille Bocchi's *Symbolicarum quaestionum*, 1574.

Pliny, or like a poem. Castiglione expressed a discriminating pleasure; Aretino a fervent one and a new sensitiveness to the link between the transitoriness of natural phenomena and art's ability to capture them. Significantly, though, both men were the close friends of artists, the former of Raphael, the latter of Titian. But with VASARI, himself a painter, a deliberate and methodical critical approach finally emerged: how expert is the technical preparation (drawing, colouring, composition, anatomy, perspective) and how successful is its transmutation, in terms of an individual or shared 'manner', into a graceful, emotionally satisfying effect? How effective is the relationship between observation, ability and interpretation? With these criteria applied with fair consistency to a vast number of works, art criticism reached its maturity at a moment when, in Vasari's view, the maturity of art itself was already over. *See* ARTIST, STATUS OF; ALBERTI. JRH

M. Baxendall *Giotto and the orators* (1971); C. E. Gilbert ed. *Italian art 1400–1500* (1980) (for Alberti); T. S. R. Boase *Giorgio Vasari: the man and the book* (1979)

Critical theory of literature Renaissance critical theory inherited from humanist debates a Platonic and Ficinian notion of ideal beauty, and developed the principle of imitation and rules of literary composition drawn from classical rhetoric. Different positions coexisted concerning the relationship between poetics and grammar, rhetoric, history and moral philosophy. During the first half of the 16c. the imitation of a model was a central feature of literary theory: of Virgil for poetry and Cicero for prose in Latin, and of Petrarch for poetry and Boccaccio for prose in the vernacular. These were the ideals of Bembo, for whom the problem of language (grammar and rhetoric) was paramount. The ideal of imitation is illustrated for Latin, in practice as well as in theory, by the work of Vida, who considered (1527) epic the loftiest genre and Virgil the finest model. What Virgil was for Vida, Petrarch was for Bembo's follower Bernardino Daniello (1536) who, alongside his Horatian belief that the dual role of poetry is to delight and instruct, develops the notion of verisimilitude, which distinguishes poet from historian.

Aristotle's *Poetics*, known in the Middle Ages only from the commentary by Averroes, became very influential after the appearance of Latin translations by Giorgio Valla (1498) and Alessandro Pazzi (1536) and the Italian translation by Bernardo Segni (1549). It is important for Trissino's *Poetica* (1529, 1563), among the earliest vernacular poetics, in which problems of language and rhetoric relating to Italian poetry are accompanied by an exposition of Aristotle, who was now gradually to supplant HORACE as the critical authority; and for Fracastoro's *Naugerius* (1555), which concentrates on the universality of the poet. The *Poetics* was the object of detailed commentaries which established the European classicist tradition. Particularly noteworthy are those by Francesco Robortello (1548), for whom imitation is considered an intermediate aim leading to pleasure and ethical utility; by Bartolomeo Lombardi and Vincenzo Maggi (1550), for whom poetry, representing human actions, is seen as a kind of moral philosophy; and by Castelvetro (1570), who claims that the sole aim of poetry is to delight, interpreting the Aristotelian concept of catharsis as another means to this end. In the context of tragedy Castelvetro extends Aristotle's unity of action to time and place; he adapts to comedy Aristotle's analysis of tragic drama, establishing in comic theory the categories of plot, character, thought, diction, spectacle, music etc. Giraldi Cinthio's discourse on comedy and tragedy (1554) is also indebted to Aristotle, but while accepting the fictitious quality of comedy it claims that the plot of tragedy need not be historical. There was also an attempt in the Renaissance to apply Aristotelian principles to the new genres of tragicomedy and pastoral (Guarini, 1588, 1593).

Classicism was strengthened by further elaboration of the empirical rather than speculative elements in Aristotle. Minturno (Antonio Sebastiani) examines literary genres (1559, 1563), adding lyric to the two traditional ones of narrative and dramatic poetry; Giulio Cesare Scaligero (1561) stresses the superiority of art over nature, and thus the excellence of Virgil, representing the essential virtue of decorum, compared to Homer, with all his indecorous spontaneity. Against prevailing Aristotelianism (and in the context of discussions on rhetoric by Sperone Speroni (1542) and Bernardino Tomitano (1545), Patrizi (1562, 1586) claims that the poet is a creator rather than an imitator, and emphasizes the importance of 'enthusiasm' rather than rules, whilst the synthesis of Aristotelian and Platonic motifs in Tasso's theoretical works (1587, 1594) is rendered more powerful by his experience as a poet. LL

B. Weinberg *A history of literary criticism in the Italian Renaissance* (1961); E. Bonora 'Dalla critica umanistica all'aristotelismo' *SLI* IV

Crivelli, Carlo (active *c.*1457, d.1495) was a Venetian painter who worked largely outside his native city. His emphasis on wiry line and almost metallic finish owe much to Donatello and Mantegna. He is a skilled perspectivist and, unlike the Florentine masters of dramatic narrative, delights in space and illusion for its own sake. His love of gold and bright colour reflects the continuation of the medieval emphasis on precious materials. His illustrative details are often so compelling that from a few feet it is impossible to tell which parts of a painting are embossed, often in quite high relief, and which are purely 2-dimensional. In his own day his achievements must have seemed quite breathtaking. JW

A. Bovera *L'opera completa del Crivelli* (1975)

Croce, Giovanni (*c.*1557–1609) Composer of madrigals. Born in Chioggia, he was discovered by Zarlino, then *maestro di cappella* at St Mark's in Venice, and employed there as a singer. He subsequently became *vice-maestro* there, finally taking charge of the *cappella* in 1603. His madrigals, mainly in lighter vein, were popular in Italy and England, but he also wrote a large quantity of church music for small churches and for ceremonial occasions. DA

A. Einstein *The Italian madrigal* (1949)

Cronaca, Simone del Pollaiuolo, il (1457–1508) Florentine architect and stonemason who collaborated with Giuliano da Sangallo on a number of projects including the Sacristy of S. Spirito, the Casa Horne and the Palazzo Strozzi, for which he provided the designs of the elegant courtyard and imposing cornice. The aisleless church of S. Francesco (S. Salvatore) al Monte, with its simple *pietra serena* articulation, shows his understanding of classical architecture, which he studied in Rome (1475–85), and is also related to the drawings and measurements he took from early Romanesque buildings in Florence, such as the Baptistery, which were thought in the Renaissance to be antique structures. Il Cronaca was also involved in the construction of the

Salone dei Cinquecento (Palazzo Vecchio), built between July 1495 and February 1496 to house the Grand Council instituted by Savonarola. [306] SJ

Crusade With the fall of Acre in 1291 and the end of Christian rule in the Levant (Jerusalem had been reconquered by the Muslims in 1244), the era of the 'true' crusades, of the international hordes of pious brigands and armed pilgrims who had recaptured the Holy Places and governed them, came to a close. In the 14c. crusades, international in scope, sponsored by popes and promising spiritual credits to participants, continued to be planned and, on occasion, launched, but the mood had changed: the infidel was more clearly seen as a permanent geopolitical presence to be reckoned with in European inter-state terms, as a commercial threat as well as a spiritual affront, as a foe to be dealt with through a wily strategy rather than through a direct assault in a heady spirit of derring-do.

Though the chief sponsors of crusading propaganda were the rulers of France and Burgundy, a notable expression of the new approach was the weighty tract *Secreta fidelium crucis* (1309) by Marin Sanuto (1274–*c.*1343), called the Elder to distinguish him from the Venetian diarist of the same name. He advised a complete maritime blockade of Egyptian trade until the country was so weak that conquest, prior to an advance into Palestine, would be easy. A more dramatic flank attack was projected when successive popes encouraged the Christianization of the Tartars and Mongols, who would then apply pressure on the Muslims from the east. Notable among such missions were those of the Italians Giovanni da Montecorvino (d.1328) and Fra Oderic of Pordenone (d.1331) in China.

The actual campaigns of the second half of the 14c. were political counter-attacks rather than all-out crusades; the capture in 1344 of Smyrna from the Turks (held until 1402) by the so-called Aegean Crusade (Venice, Cyprus and the Order of St John, with the backing of Pope Clement IV); the sacking of Alexandria in 1365 by a fleet of heterogeneous origin led by the Lusignan King of Cyprus, Peter I; the Genoese-French campaign of 1390 against Tunis which at least secured a temporary cessation of piratical activity on the part of the Muslim emirates of the Barbary Coast. The century ended, however, with the raising of an army as large as any assembled for a medieval crusade. With volunteers from practically every Christian state, and with transport provided by Venice and Genoa, the aim was to repel the latest Turkish menace: pressure on Hungary. The campaign was a fiasco: at the Bulgarian town of Nicopol (or Nicopolis) on the Danube, a crushing Turkish victory in 1396 put paid to any visions of expelling the Muslims from the Balkans, let alone from the Holy Land. To the notion of counter-attack had now to be added the more sobering one of defence.

In the 15c. a further series of campaigns, with little Italian participation, regained territory from the Turks in Albania, Bosnia and Bulgaria, but came to another disastrous conclusion in 1448 at Kossovo in Serbia. Constantinople fell 5 years later. The maritime Italian states had by now settled for coexistence. Pilgrims found that they were increasingly well catered for by the Mamluk authorities in the Holy Land and Sinai. Hampered by schism and wrangles with General Councils, the leadership of the popes had been hamstrung, and when they became free agents again the western powers found their hands too full with domestic and dynastic affairs to heed calls to save the Holy Sepulchre. Eugenius IV had contributed to the movement that foundered at Kossovo. Pius II died in 1464 awaiting an international crusading fleet at Ancona. But crusade had become a foreign policy, the concern of the Muslims' neighbours and trading contacts.

In the 16c. the word was almost meaningless save to individual propagandists (of which there were many) and imaginative writers in idealizingly nostalgic mood, like Tasso. Reading the old chivalrous literature was more appealing than seeing current power politics in terms of a crusade. Castiglione could see crusade as the sole legitimate outlet for the natural aggressiveness of Christian princes, but Machiavelli saw the Turks as providing not a scandal to Christians but a model of sound organization and devotion to the public cause. Francis I signed an alliance with them in 1536 to bolster his position in the Mediterranean. The anti-Turkish wars, like those waged by Venice with its allies Spain, Genoa and the Papacy in 1537–40 and 1570–73, were, simply, wars fought with political and economic aims in mind. JRH

A. S. Atiya *The crusade in the later Middle Ages* (1938); —*Crusade, commerce and culture* (1962)

Cuisine The subject still invites its historian. There are plenty of books about food, from the anonymous *Libro della cocina* (*c.*1400) to the *Opera divisa in sei libri* (Venice 1570) of Bartolomeo Scappi. They reflect first the influence of medieval herbal and bestiary lore; then, from the mid-15c., the dietary aspects of classical medical and agricultural works (constituting what may be called the humanistic approach to food); lastly, from the 1520s and 30s, the 'display' cuisine of northern Europe. But the emphasis throughout is on health, domestic economy and the place of cooking within the more general art of hospitality; there is a shortage of detailed recipes.

Certain general tendencies emerge: the reliance on animal fats rather than olive oil in the north; the preference for pre-cooked (e.g. boiled before roast) meats; a preference for spices over sauces; an emphasis on the freshness of produce; an acceptance that distribution problems as well as local traditions meant that there was no 'Italian' cuisine. All today's farinacious foods are mentioned, such as pasta (*maccheroni, tortellini, lasagna*), *gnocchi, polenta*, rice and, in the kingdom of Naples, pizza, as are the meats (including veal), with a strong emphasis on game; cheeses (as far as their contemporary names are translatable); sausages (from Florence and Bologna northward); fish; and vegetables, apart from tomatoes and fennel. But between the lists of essentials issued to garrisons and ship's crews (beans, flour, vinegar, oil, salt fish and meat, wine) and the description of menus suitable for distinguished guests, there is little – apart from some general culinary procedures – to enable us to know what the ordinary household ate, to guess how their meals tasted, or to estimate the influence of the cuisines of Italy on other countries. JRH

Libro della cucina ed. F. Zambrini (1963); E. Faccioli *Arte della cucina ... dal XIV al XIX secolo* (2 vols n.d.); 'La cucina italiana nel Rinascimento' *SI* V

Cyclical concept The notion that human affairs were in a constant state of flux, developing, reaching a peak and then decaying, was a commonplace by *c.*1500. Behind it lay the medieval image of the Wheel of Destiny, which showed men bound to its rim as it turned, bearing them up, then dashing their hopes. It was nourished by awareness of the growth and decline of ancient civilization, of classical emphasis on the slide from monarchy to tyranny, aristocracy to oligarchy, and by an observation of contemporary events that led to formulations on the lines: peace breeds wealth, wealth breeds indolence, indolence breeds quarrelsomeness, quarrels breed war – and so on. Vasari applied it to the fine arts, borne up to the peak of Michelangelo, then inevitably declining. Unchecked by any idea of straight-line secular progress, the concept prompted optimism or pessimism depending on where an individual placed himself or his society within the cycle. JRH

Dal Verme, Jacopo (1350–?1409) Descended from a Veronese family who had been professional soldiers for generations, Jacopo trained under Alberico da Barbiano. He passed most of his life in the service of the Visconti, combining the role of commander-in-chief with that of a trusted minister of state. His most famous action was the victory near Alessandria over a French army under Jean d'Armagnac that was coming to assist Florence in its campaign of 1391 against Giangaleazzo Visconti. As an early example of an Italian defeat of a 'barbarian' army, it was celebrated by Ariosto in his *Orlando furioso* (XXXIII, 5). JRH

Dante, reputation of The *Divine comedy* (called simply '*il Dante*') remained a central point of cultural reference in Italy until the end of the 16c. For most of this time it was a controversial text, one of the 5 or 6 by which, or against which, an autonomous literary culture sought to define itself. The material presence of the poem was considerable. Some 600 manuscripts survive from the century-and-a-half between Dante's death in 1321 and the *editio princeps* (Foligno 1472). Nearly 50 printed editions follow in the course of the next 130 years (but only 3 in the 17c.). The early stages of Dante's fortunes were entrusted not only to a mass of allusions, anecdotes, compendia and imitations, but to substantial commentaries, in both Latin and the vernacular, on all or part of the poem: 12 by the first centenary of Dante's death. The public *lecturae Dantis*, initiated by Boccaccio at Florence in 1373, were adopted by other cities in rapid succession.

The first generation of readers were broadly in agreement with each other, and with Dante (if he is indeed the author of the 'Epistle to Cangrande', ?1317), as to the allegorical method to be employed in the reading of a poem whose theme is moral. But Boccaccio's work on Dante, stretching over 25 years and including an influential biography (1357–62) as well as the lectures delivered at the end of his life, at the same time as it contained the highest exaltation of his predecessor in the 14c., registers the first signs of the anxiety which was repeatedly to attach itself to Dante during the Renaissance. The exaltation is directed, not to the encyclopaedic learning and doctrinal authority of the *poeta Theologus* celebrated earlier in the century, but to the rhetorical skill and devotion of a *poeta philologus* whose achievement is to have restored dead poetry to life. The anxieties have to do with the class or caste implications of a poetry that appears to operate a double betrayal: by using a language which not only makes superior philosophical, scientific and doctrinal knowledge improperly available to a wide, non-specialist, audience, but is also inadequate to the dignity and nobility of the subject-matter.

Reservations about Dante's use of the vernacular rather than Latin had already been expressed directly to the poet by Giovanni del Virgilio in 1319, were argued strongly by Petrarch in a letter to Boccaccio of 1359, and had become a commonplace of pre-humanist culture at the turn of the century. One should not make too much of the social and linguistic hostility to Dante ('a poet fit for cobblers') recorded indirectly around 1400; nevertheless, the pre-eminence of Latin in 15c. humanism allowed Dante's admirers to celebrate his learning and morality, but left them little ground on which to advance his claims as a literary model.

In one respect, however, humanism, at least in Florence, generated a 'new' Dante: the citizen-patriot (see Bruni's *Vita*, 1436), worthy son of a Florence whose political and cultural hegemony was beginning to be asserted in the peninsula. The myth of Florence as a 'new Athens' or a 'new Rome' entailed also a positive revaluation of Dante's part in civilizing the rough speech of earlier times and laying the foundations of a vigorous and elegant modern language. This atmosphere of cultural revival contributed to a renewal of interest in Dante's lyric poetry and in the *Vita nuova*, which featured as the first item in Lorenzo de' Medici's 1477 anthology of Tuscan verse, the *Raccolta aragonese*. (It was not, however, to be printed in its entirety until 1576, over 80 years after the first edition of the *Convivio* (Florence 1490)). But interest in the 'stilnovistic' dimension of Dante's poetic experience was also stimulated by the neo-Platonism of the Florentine academy with its emphasis on love and beauty, rather than intellect, as the way to truth. Neo-Platonism provided the conceptual basis for the only new, but often reprinted, commentary of the 15c., that of Landino (Florence 1481), an edition graced not only with 19 illustrations by Botticelli, but also with a Latin letter written by the leading neo-Platonist, Ficino, solemnly welcoming the exiled Dante back to Florence, where triumph at last awaited him.

This triumph, however, was shortlived. With the decline of Florentine power and the opening up of the *questione della lingua*, Dante once again found himself on the wrong side of a linguistic divide, this time representing not the vernacular against Latin, but forms of the vernacular whose propriety was called into question. In the view of Bembo (*Prose della volgar lingua*, 1525), Dante's language is too often base and lacking in decorum: Petrarch is the preferred model in Italian poetry. Bembo's judgment was important not only because it fixed a canon of taste inside and outside Italy for several generations (it was of course strongly disputed, though the translation of Dante's own *De vulgari eloquentia*, Vicenza 1529, confused rather than clarified matters; 1st ed. of Latin text Paris 1577). It was important above all because it was the first to ignore the power of the moral and intellectual world of the *Comedy* in passing a purely aesthetic/rhetorical judgment.

This same delimitation underlay almost all subsequent discussion of the poem in the Cinquecento. Drawing on the norms and categories distilled from Aristotelian poetics, specialist rhetoricians turned their attention particularly to questions of the genre, structure and verisimilitude of the poem. These discussions were highly technical, necessarily enclosed and excluding. Too often dismissed as pure pedantry, they nevertheless signal an appropriation of Dante by the learned which is perhaps also reflected in the relative absence of Dante's work from the ideological battles of the Reformation and Counter-Reformation. Certainly, the anti-papal passages of the

Comedy and the theses of the ever-controversial *Monarchia* (first printed in Basle by Johannes Oporinus, 1559) are cited by Protestants, and these citations refuted by Catholic apologists. But both sides limit themselves to a few selected and obvious passages. As a result of changes in both taste and social structures, Dante was about to enter upon over a century of relative eclipse. *See* ITALIAN LANGUAGE; CRITICAL THEORY OF LITERATURE. MC

C. Grayson 'Dante and the Renaissance' in C. P. Brand *et al.* ed. *Italian studies presented to E. R. Vincent* (1962); L. Martinelli *Dante* (1966); 'The quarrel over Dante' B. Weinberg *A history of literary criticism in the Italian Renaissance* II (1961).

Danti, Vincenzo (1530–76) Perugian goldsmith who turned to bronze and marble sculpture. Having made his name with a colossal bronze statue of *Pope Julius III Enthroned* outside Perugia cathedral (1553–56), he moved to Florence to serve the Medici (1557–73). His masterpiece is an over life-size group in bronze on the Baptistery, the *Execution of St John the Baptist* (1571): like all his figures these are gracefully elongated and elaborately coiffed, and arranged in balletic poses characteristic of Mannerist sculpture. In 1567 he published a treatise on proportion and in 1573 he returned to Perugia as a founder member of its academy, probably ousted from Florence by the success of Giambologna. CA

C. Avery *Florentine Renaissance sculpture* (1970); J. Pope-Hennessy *Italian High Renaissance and Baroque sculpture* (1970)

Datini, Francesco (*c.*1335–1410) was the founder of an international trading company, based on his home city of Prato, which had branches in Pisa, Florence, Genoa, Avignon, Barcelona, Valencia and Majorca, and subsidiary agencies which covered much of north-west Europe. For the scale of his trade, the variety of goods dealt with, and the wealth of documentation relating to his ventures and methods, his career has become more richly explained than that of any other Renaissance Italian businessman. Some idea of his wealth is conveyed in his bequest of 70,000 florins to found an institution for the deserving poor of Prato. JRH

I. Origo *The merchant of Prato* (1957); E. Bensa *Francesco di Marco da Prato* (1928); F. Melis *Aspetti della vita economica medievale* I (1962)

Della Porta, Giacomo (*c.*1537–1602) synthesized Michelangelo's Mannerist architectural style and Vignola's classicism to become the leading Roman architect of the late 16c. His monumental style was characterized by a pronounced vertical emphasis and strong surface tensions, produced by structural contrasts (e.g. Palazzo della Sapienza, begun 1579; S. Andrea della Valle, begun 1591). His façade design for the Gesù, mother church of the Jesuit order (begun 1571), was imitated throughout the world. LP

V. Tiberia *Giacomo della Porta* (1974); K. Schwager 'Giacomo della Porta's Herkunft und Anfänge in Rom' *Römisches Jahrbuch für Kunstgeschichte* (1975)

Della Porta, Giambattista (*c.*1535–1615) Neapolitan dramatist and writer on natural magic. Della Porta interested himself all his life in natural MAGIC, the study of the inexplicable forces of nature, so popular in the Renaissance, which lay on the borders between true magic and experimental science. Besides writing extensively on all its branches (including physiognomy, cryptography, the art of memory, the doctrine of signatures and optics), he tried to form groups of like-minded men to effect systematic investigations. His foundation of the Accademia dei Segreti led the Inquisition to investigate his activities in 1580. Although he became a Jesuit lay brother, in the years 1592–98 he was forbidden to publish. In 1610 he became a member of Prince Cesi's Accademia dei Lincei, of which Galileo was proud to be a member also.

His most important book is *Magia naturalis* (Naples 1558), which was much reprinted, with Italian, French and Dutch editions. A revised, enlarged edition appeared in 1589 and was again reprinted and retranslated. It deals with practical methods of making things appear other than they are, from housekeeping and beauty culture to magnetism, optics (including magnifying lenses and the camera obscura), hydraulics, statics and pneumatics. Della Porta believed that by observing the sympathies and antipathies of objects one could understand their nature and hence control their operation for useful ends.

He may have written his first comedies in adolescence, but he published none until 1589, when *L'Olimpia* was printed in Naples, followed by 13 others and by 3 verse plays; a tragicomedy, *La Penelope*; a tragedy, *L'Ulisse*;

and a sacred drama, *Il Giorgio*. Some of the prose *commedie erudite* are close to tragicomedy – *La sorella* (*The sister*), *Gli duoi fratelli rivali* (*The two rival brothers*), *Il moro* (*The moor*). Others are more farcical – *La fantesca* (*The servant girl*), *La Trappolaria* (*The comedy of Trappola*), *La Chiappinaria* (*The comedy of Chiappino*). Several were translated in France and England. Constructed of combinations of typical elements from the Cinquecento theatrical repertory, they are stageworthy and contain speeches and actions characteristic of the *commedia dell'arte*, which in turn borrowed plots from della Porta. MBH/LGC

Natural magick (1658; repr. 1957); L. G. Clubb *Giambattista della Porta, dramatist* (1965); R. Sirri *L'attività teatrale di G. B. della Porta* (1968)

Della Porta, Guglielmo (*c.*1490–1577) Lombard sculptor, trained in his family workshop in Milan and was active first in Genoa (*c.*1534) and later in Rome (*c.*1540). Employed at the Vatican, he succeeded Sebastiano del Piombo in the sinecure office of *piombatore* in 1547 and began work on his major commission, the monument of Pope Paul III, over the design of which he came into conflict with Michelangelo. Guglielmo was an excellent craftsman in bronze and precious metals and his figure style was indebted to Michelangelo. CA

J. Pope-Hennessy *Italian High Renaissance and Baroque sculpture* (1970)

Della Robbia, Luca (1400–82) A major Florentine Renaissance sculptor, trained in the workshop of Florence cathedral, for which he carved a marble *Singing Gallery* in 1431, famed for its charming rendering of child musicians. He is best known for a technical invention, the use of vitreous glazes to colour sculpture modelled in terracotta, which rendered the polychromy impervious to damp and thus durable in architectural settings out of doors. Reliefs of the Virgin and Child and coats of arms in this material abound on Tuscan exteriors, as well as in museums internationally. Luca sometimes combined his colourful glazed terracotta with carved marble in architectural projects such as tabernacles and tombs. His nephew Andrea (1434–1525) inherited the workshop and the secret of the technique, and introduced virtual mass-production, with a corresponding diminution of artistic originality and quality. Luca was an exponent of the 'sweet style' in Florentine sculpture, like

Glazed terracotta roundel by Luca **della Robbia** at Orsanmichele, incorporating the device of the Florentine republic.

Ghiberti and the Rossellino, avoiding the dramatic extremes of Donatello and introducing a quiet, religious charm to his compositions, which evidently suited his patrons. [122] CA

J. Pope-Hennessy *Luca della Robbia* (1980)

Della Rovere family From an obscure status in Savona (Liguria) the della Rovere acquired fame and wealth when Francesco became pope in 1471 as Sixtus IV. Instantly supplied with a genealogy and a coat of arms (an oak tree – *rovere* in Italian), the family soon further enhanced its position when Francesco's nephew Giuliano was elected pope, with the title Julius II, in 1503. Meanwhile, the secular fortunes of the family began when Sixtus invested his nephew Giovanni (1457–1501) with the lordship of Senigallia, thus giving him a rank which made possible his marriage to Duke Federico of Urbino's daughter. Giovanni, on his death, entrusted his son Francesco Maria to Federico's successor Guidobaldo (Duke 1482–1508) who, without an heir, devised the duchy on the boy. Thus from 1508 to 1631, when their line expired, Urbino came to be ruled by successive della Rovere dukes. JRH

Della Scala family The della Scala dominated Verona and its territory from 1262 (election of

Mastino I as capitano) until 1387 (conquest by Giangaleazzo Visconti). Their authority was further sanctioned by the grant of the Imperial vicariate in 1311. Cangrande (signore 1311–29; b.1291), and initially his nephews Alberto II (d.1352) and Mastino II (d.1351), seized opportunities to expand their dominion widely in north-east Italy, but by 1337–39 all their acquisitions except Vicenza (obtained 1312) had been lost. Cangrande's reputation for courtly qualities and generosity rests on the respect accorded him by Dante, Boccaccio and other writers, though it was probably Bartolomeo (d.1304) who first gave Dante hospitality. Benzo da Alessandria (Chancellor 1325–33) was a significant proto-humanist, and according to Vasari Cangrande employed Giotto, but the régime's chief monuments were the equestrian tombs initiated by Mastino II, the castle in Verona built for Cangrande II (1352–59) and the works carried out for his brother and murderer Cansignorio (1359–75): the Ponte delle Navi and the fountain in Piazza Erbe. In exile the della Scala never surrendered their claims to Verona; Guglielmo was briefly restored in 1404 but died suddenly; after Venice acquired Verona (1405), Brunoro (d.1437) retained Imperial protection, though without success. DC

C. Cipolla *Compendio della storia politica di Verona* (1899; repr. 1976); Istituto per gli Studi Storici Veronesi *Verona e il suo territorio* III i (1975) and ii (1969); A.M. Allen *A history of Verona* (1910)

Detail of the carving on **Desiderio da Settignano**'s tomb of Carlo Marsuppini in S. Croce, Florence.

Desiderio da Settignano (*c.*1430–64) Marble and stone sculptor of great virtuosity who matriculated in Florence in 1453. He was strongly influenced if not trained by Donatello. His precocious and brief career was chiefly occupied by 2 commissions: the tomb of Carlo Marsuppini (d.1453) in S. Croce; and the Altar of the Sacrament in S. Lorenzo (completed by 1461). Desiderio specialized in low reliefs, which he learned from Donatello, and in charming portrait renderings of young ladies and children in a happy mood. CA

C. Avery *Florentine Renaissance sculpture* (1970); J. Pope-Hennessy *Italian Renaissance sculpture* (1958)

Despots Implying unfettered tyranny, this is a term to avoid when describing the nature of the authority wielded by the signori who emerged from the factional disturbances that had brought communal government to a standstill in many medieval (12c. to 14c.) cities. After a vogue consolidated by John Addington Symonds's picturesque and emotionally convincing *Age of the despots* (1875), it has been outmoded by an understanding of how far 'despotic' rule was both sought and shared. JRH

L. Martines *Power and imagination: city-states in Renaissance Italy* (1979)

Diplomacy Italy invented diplomacy in the sense in which it is understood today: permanent embassies in capitals where political relations and commercial links need continual monitoring. In the 14c. alliances and trade agreements were arranged by ambassadors, or sometimes by princes and monarchs themselves, on an *ad hoc* basis: travelling to reach agreement, then returning home. It was in the 15c., and in Italy, that the close-packed major city-states found that maintaining alliances – or anticipating shifts in them – called for continuous mutual observation.

The usefulness of having representatives *en poste* abroad had been demonstrated by the trade consuls Florence, Genoa and Venice had placed in the Levant to assist their merchants and alert government to changes in attitude towards Christian traders. It had also been anticipated by the reliance of the Papacy on key churchmen to keep it informed, and by the custom whereby monarchs made payments to men at the courts of their rivals in return for support for their own policy or for useful information regarding the prospects. But –

though there had been in the 14c. a few scattered examples of a more formal and full-time diplomatic information service (as when in 1375 Milan and Mantua exchanged ambassadors to further their cooperation against the della Scala of Verona) – the maintenance of a steady succession of diplomatic representatives was a phenomenon of the 15c., and especially of its second half, when the Italian states established such contacts not only with one another but also with the non-Italian powers who showed such a threatening interest in peninsular affairs. With the beginning of the Wars of Italy in 1494, and the increasingly competitive stance of the European powers concerned with them, the practice of 'permanent' diplomacy was adopted north of the Alps and in Spain. There remained some uncertainty about the legal status of resident diplomats abroad: were they – whatever their letters of accreditation said – representatives of their governments, or spies? Fosterers of alliances or *agents provocateurs*? But in spite of these uncertainties, and although there was an occasional need to supplant resident agents, who were often, like Machiavelli, men of modest background and humiliatingly underpaid, with the old pompous trains of grandees, the Italianate system became part of European political life.

Italian diplomats were expected to write home frequently and, at the end of their terms of duty, to submit a full report. These *relazioni* were treated with especial seriousness in Venice, and their formal reading to the Senate, before being carefully filed, played a notable part in keeping the governing class constantly informed about current events and about the chief personalities, the economic and military strength and the political aims of other states. They remain an essential source for historians of Europe. *See* BALANCE OF POWER. JRH

G. Mattingly *Renaissance diplomacy* (1955); G. Zeller, *Histoire des relations internationales: les temps modernes, de Christophe Colomb à Cromwell* (1953); H. Lapeyre *Les monarchies européennes du XVIe siècle et les relations internationales* (1967); F. Gaeta 'Origini e sviluppo della rappresentanza stabile ...' *Annuario dell' Istituto Storico Italiano* IX and X (1958)

Domenico Veneziano (active *c.*1438–61) is an artist whose importance is as great as his surviving works are rare. His assistant in the substantially destroyed frescoes of S. Egidio, his first major work in Florence, was Piero della Francesca, and his surviving masterpiece, the *St Lucy Altarpiece* (Florence, Uffizi; Cambridge, Fitzwilliam; etc.), shows him to be a master of the new Artificial PERSPECTIVE in terms of proportional and compositional control, as well as of spatial description. Above all, however, his genius lies in the subtle handling of light as it bathes the delicate pinks and greens and blues of his designs and penetrates the diaphanous veils of the shadows, hardly shadows but transmuted light, that float across them. JW

M. Salmi *Paolo Uccello, Andrea del Castagno, Domenico Veneziano* (Rome 1936)

Donatello (1386–1466) Donato di Niccolò di Betto Bardi was the greatest sculptor of the early Renaissance in Italy and one of the most versatile of all time, unmatched in his technical and expressive range. Born in Florence, he is first documented between 1404 and 1407 as an assistant of Ghiberti on the bronze doors for the Baptistery. Shortly afterwards he is recorded as carving marble statuary, beginning with modest commissions, but proceeding rapidly to important ones for the façade of the cathedral – *St John the Evangelist* (1408) – and of Orsanmichele – *St Mark* (1411–13) and *St George* (*c.*1415). Between 1415 and 1436 he delivered 4 statues of prophets for the campanile. He also produced a number of major bronzes including *St Louis of Toulouse* (for Orsanmichele, now in the refectory of S. Croce), and the effigy for the tomb of the anti-Pope John XXIII (Baptistery), as well as a relief and several gilt bronze statuettes for the font of Siena cathedral, where he collaborated with Jacopo della Quercia and Ghiberti (1423–34). Donatello was one of the pioneers of scientific perspective, along with Masaccio and Brunelleschi, as can be seen in his shallow reliefs in marble: e.g. *St George and the Dragon* (*c.*1415), the *Feast of Herod* (Lille Museum) and the *Ascension of Christ and Giving of the Keys to St Peter* (London, Victoria and Albert Museum). For his private patrons, the Medici family, he made his bronze statue of *David* (now Florence, Bargello) to stand on a pedestal in the centre of the courtyard of their newly-constructed palace: it is justly celebrated as being the first life-size nude statue of the Renaissance, recalling Graeco-Roman statues of athletes.

Leaving Florence for Padua in 1443, Donatello began to concentrate on sculpture in

Donatello's bronze *David* (detail) (Florence, Bargello).

bronze, producing the great equestrian monument to the condottiere Gattamelata – the first since antiquity, a Crucifix, and a Madonna, Saints and reliefs of *The Miracles of St Anthony* for the high altar of the basilica of St Anthony in Padua. This was a tableau of nearly life-size bronze figures standing free under an architectural canopy, in a scheme which became popular in painting, the 'Sacra Conversazione'. This project took him a whole decade, largely owing to the technical problems involved, and ended in disagreements with his patrons. Returning to Tuscany, he divided the rest of his career between Florence and Siena. His principal statues were highly dramatic – and possibly unpopular: *St Mary Magdalene*, carved out of a tree trunk, gessoed, painted and partly gilded, and *St John the Baptist* (for Siena cathedral) and *Judith and Holofernes* (Piazza della Signoria), cast in bronze. In the same intensely dramatic vein were his last sculptures, a series of religious narrative reliefs in bronze for the twin pulpits of S. Lorenzo, commissioned by his devoted patron Cosimo de' Medici *il Vecchio* for his parish church, in order that Donatello should not be out of work in his old age. This implies that the sculptor's late, deliberately disquieting style, so popular in the 20c., was out of touch with contemporary taste in Florence, which probably preferred the gilded elegance of Ghiberti's *Gates of Paradise*, unveiled in 1452. It should not be forgotten, however, that Donatello also produced many works in a sweeter vein, particularly reliefs showing the Virgin and Child, which influenced the best sculptors in the middle of the century, such as Desiderio da Settignano. [179] CA

J. Pope-Hennessy *Italian Renaissance sculpture* (1958); H. W. Janson *The sculpture of Donatello* (1957)

Doni, Anton Francesco (1513–74) chronicled the discouragement and disillusionment at the end of the Renaissance when Italy was racked by war, petty tyranny, loss of independence and a failure of nerve. Born in Florence, the son of a scissors-maker, he entered the Servite order as a youth, but left in 1540 to follow the wandering life of a popular writer, living by his pen and his wits, usually in close proximity to the vernacular presses of Venice. He wrote about 17 original works in a lively but often undisciplined style. He boasted that he sat at a desk in the printer's shop furiously writing while the presses rolled; as he finished each sheet, a copy boy at his elbow snatched it and dashed to the typesetters. His best-known works were *La zucca* (*The gourd*; 1551), *I marmi* (i.e. things overheard on the marble steps of the *Duomo* of Florence; 1552–53) and *I mondi* (*The worlds*) with its companion piece *Gl'inferni* (*The infernos*; 1552–53). They were often reprinted.

In his books Doni criticized most of the authorities and values of the Renaissance. He attacked the unjust social structure and the maldistribution of wealth in Italy. He denied that Renaissance princes could be educated by humanist maxims to govern wisely and for the benefit of their subjects. If the world was beyond reform and not amenable to reason, then the humanistic education for the active life offered by 15c. humanists was irrelevant. Savage and often funny anti-clerical passages pointed out the failures of the Church. Nor could Doni resist the temptation to mock learned authorities. In a dialogue loosely based on Dante in *Gl'inferni*, grammarians were condemned to carrying their own moaning heads in an endless circle, while serpents bit authors, just as their books had 'bitten' readers. Doni half seriously proposed a utopian alternative, a 'New World' where property and women were held in common, and everyone lived in peace and perfect equality without distinctions of birth or wealth. He died quite alienated from his time. PG

P. F. Grendler *Critics of the Italian world 1530–1560: Anton Francesco Doni, Niccolò Franco, and Ortensio Lando* (1969)

Doria (or **D'Oria) family** Leading Genoese noble family of Ghibelline sympathies. The power of the Doria was based on extensive landholdings, particularly in Sardinia, on banking, and on naval and military prowess. From at least 1125, when Martino Doria founded the family church of S. Matteo, until the 14c. the Doria shared power uneasily with the other great Genoese feudal families. After 1339 the family lost its political predominance, being rigorously excluded from all positions of authority in Genoa. The Doria tried several times to raise the contado in rebellion against the city, but were conspicuously unsuccessful. They did, however, continue to play a prominent part in the naval and military history of Genoa, and produced in Pagano Doria the most famous of Genoa's 14c. admirals. Under Andrea Doria's leadership the family emerged once more in the early 16c. to play the fullest possible role in Genoa's civic and political life. JH

C. Fusero *I Doria* (1973)

Doria, Andrea (1466/8–1560) Most famous admiral of his age and Genoese statesman. In his youth Doria was a member of the papal guard of Innocent VIII and, as a mercenary, served several other Italian rulers. In the long conflict between Charles V and Francis I, Doria was at first employed by France but, when the French gave commercial privileges to Savona at the expense of Genoa, Doria allied himself with Charles V. He drove the French from GENOA in 1528 and established a new republican constitution under Spanish protection. His position made him an effective dictator in Genoa and he proved ruthless in suppressing conspiracies by the Fieschi in 1547 and the Cibo in 1548–49. He continued his naval career, serving Charles V in the Mediterranean until well into old age, and leading the expedition which recovered Corsica for Genoa in 1559. Within Genoa, his generous patronage of the arts helped to create a new and flourishing Genoese civilization. JH

A. L. Fiorita *Andrea Doria* (1950); E. Petit *Andrea Doria: un amiral condottiere au XVIe siècle* (1887)

Anonymous 16c. portrait of **Andrea Doria** with his cat (Genoa, Palazzo del Principe).

Doria, Gian Andrea (1539–1606) Great-nephew of Andrea Doria, who made him his heir, Gian Andrea was indulged by his uncle from his earliest youth. He grew up with a character that was proud, harsh and intolerant, but lacking neither in ability nor in courage. After Andrea Doria's death, Gian Andrea abandoned the position of detached neutrality affected by his uncle in relation to the factional disputes of Genoa. He threw himself enthusiastically into the struggle between the old and new nobility, lending his support to the former and even going so far as to invite Spanish intervention on their behalf. This has made him a somewhat controversial figure in Genoese history. Controversy similarly surrounds his career as a naval commander, in particular his failure to capture Jerba in 1560, and his mediocre performance at the battle of LEPANTO in 1571, when he commanded a squadron under Don John of Austria. JH

R. Bracco *Il principe Gian Andrea Doria* (1960)

Dossi, Dosso (active 1512, d.1542) The popular name of Giovanni Luteri, the principal painter at the court of Alfonso d'Este in Ferrara. With his brother Battista, Dosso provided for the court mainly mythologies, portraits and decorative frescoes. The style of Giorgione, especially of his landscapes, is developed, even intensified, in Dosso's most evocative paintings, like the *Circe* (Rome, Borghese Gallery) and the *Adoration of the Magi* (London, National Gallery), though in others a contrary influence is apparent, that of Raphael, in whose studio Battista was apparently working in 1520. AB

F. Gibbons *Dosso and Battista Dossi* (1968)

Dovizi, Bernardo (Il Bibbiena) (1470–1520), a Medici protégé, followed Cardinal Giovanni in exile from 1494. Castiglione depicts his elegant person and wit in *The courtier*. He contributed to Giovanni's rise to the Papacy as Leo X, for which he was rewarded with important diplomatic missions and the cardinalate. He died of natural causes in Rome, not poisoned, as once was thought. He is known for his *Lettere* and a famous COMMEDIA ERUDITA, *La Calandria*, first performed in Urbino (1513), in which the figure of girl-in-boy's-clothes is introduced to the stage and contemporary manners are mixed with Boccaccian tricks and prose in a brilliant imbroglio. It was repeatedly performed and imitated in the Renaissance. LGC

G. L. Moncallero *Il cardinale Bernardo Dovizi da Bibbiena umanista e diplomatico* (1953)

Drama Out of the social, intellectual and religious life of the Middle Ages came mime, seasonal celebrations, rural festival and urban spectacle, recitations and dialogues, that contributed in various regions to vernacular drama. Religious drama appeared first in Latin liturgical tropes, but by the Trecento its most vital manifestation was the *lauda drammatica*, a vernacular, lyrical and ritual enactment of moments from Scripture, developed in Umbria and the Abruzzi by lay companies of penitents, the *Disciplinati*. In the Quattrocento the dramatic laud was overshadowed, especially in Florence, by the capacious SACRA RAPPRESENTAZIONE, more festival than ritual, more dramatic and secular than lyrical and devotional.

Of several kinds of neo-Latin drama written in the early Renaissance, some reflected the entertainments of university student life, like the Goliardic farce *Janus sacerdos* (1427). The proto-humanist Albertino Mussato fashioned the history of the tyrant Ezzelino into a Christian Senecan cautionary tragedy, *Ecerinis* (?1314). Quattrocento experiments with classical genres and metres produced rhetorical tragedies of Senecan stamp on contemporary historical or mythical subjects, as in Correr's *Progne* (*c.*1429). Latin comedies by Bruni, Alberti, Tito Livio Frulovisi and Piccolomini were among the literary reconstructions of a dormant dramatic genre, into which matter from novellas and contemporary life, sometimes with allegory, were mixed. Together with vernacular texts such as those accompanying spectacles of the Ferrarese and Mantuan courts – the *favola mitologica*, represented by Niccolò da Correggio's *Cefalo* (1487) and by Poliziano's *Orfeo* (1480), for example – and undecided combinations of narrative and dialogue like Accolti's *ottava rima* 'comedy' *Virginia* (1494), they illustrate both the vigour and the tentativeness of a growing Renaissance appetite for secular drama.

Early in the Cinquecento true Italian drama was established in COMMEDIA ERUDITA, which set the pattern for neo-classical comedy, and in TRAGEDY which adapted Senecan and Greek structures to Renaissance taste. Almost as soon as 'pure' genres were defined there appeared a tendency to mix the new discoveries, avoiding regression into medieval formlessness but blending genres in ways justifiable by the emerging rules of unity, decorum and verisimilitude. The Cinquecento search for mixed genres produced a variety of hybrids, crowned by the PASTORAL PLAY that matured in the second half of the century. The *intermezzi* which joined music and spectacle with poetry between the acts of regular plays grew into a substantial sub-genre. The compact but elastic *farsa*, often realistic and dialectal, sometimes allegorical, was cultivated by Alione in Piedmont, Sannazaro in Naples, and later in such diverse environments as the Amalfitan village of Cava de' Tirreni, the artisan Congrega dei Rozzi of Siena and the Florence of Grazzini and Giovanni Maria Cecchi (1518–87). Some of the unique Paduan plays that Beolco wrote as vehicles for his role of the disquieting peasant Ruzante have a core of farce. The most long-lived product of Cinquecento theatre was the COMMEDIA DELL'ARTE, depending upon the improvisation of the professional *comici*, who absorbed whatever suited the stage and transmitted techniques, characters and plots to the rest of Europe. *See* SENECA. LGC

E. Faccioli ed. *Il teatro italiano: dalle origini al Quattrocento* (1975); Accademia dei Lincei *Il teatro classico italiano nel '500* (1971); L. G. Clubb *Italian plays (1500–1700) in the Folger Library* (1968)

Duccio di Buoninsegna (documented from 1278, d.1318/19) revolutionized the Sienese school of painting. His influence on Simone Martini, the Lorenzetti brothers and numerous lesser followers was such that his art dominated Siena for much of the 14c. He also had considerable, though often underrated, in-

Christ washing the feet of the disciples: panel from **Duccio**'s *Maestà*

fluence in Florence, where it was he, and not his great Florentine contemporary Cimabue, who was commissioned to paint the *Rucellai Madonna*, his major early work (commissioned 1285). This panel, 4.50 m (nearly 15 ft) high, was, in its naturalism as well as in its line and colour and intense spirituality, the most advanced altarpiece of its day. Partly because the early writers, from Dante, his contemporary, to Vasari and beyond, were largely Florentine, and because his later masterpiece, the double-sided *Maestà* for the cathedral in Siena (1308–11), has been dismembered (1771), his position in relation to Giotto has often been misunderstood.

Duccio was undoubtedly the greatest panel painter of his day both in technical and in artistic terms. The richness and complexity of his *Maestà*, with its more than 50 separate compartments, was never subsequently rivalled. His work was the major single Italian influence on the evolution of the International Gothic style, and he was one of the founders of the new Tuscan visual language which underlies Renaissance art. JW

J. H. Stubblebine *Duccio di Buoninsegna and his school* (1979); J. White *Duccio* (1979)

Dufay, Guillaume (*c.*1400–74) Composer. A choirboy at Cambrai cathedral before settling in Italy as a young man, he had dealings with the Malatesta family of Rimini in the 1420s, then became a member of the papal choir in Rome. He wrote a motet for the dedication of Brunelleschi's new cathedral cupola in Florence in 1436. Shortly after this he returned to Cambrai, where he was a member of the cathedral chapter. He remained there until his death, making only brief visits abroad. His significance is as a composer representative of the change from essentially medieval to typically Renaissance attitudes to music. His great motets and Mass settings use the late medieval constructional techniques such as *cantus firmus* and isorhythm, but the sonorousness of his music, probably learned from the English school led by Dunstable, and the melodiousness of his chansons, represent a more humanistic approach than that displayed by the previous Ars Nova composers. DA

H. M. Brown *Music in the Renaissance* (1976)

Durazzo, house of The line of the dukes of Durazzo, a branch of the first house of Anjou, was founded by John, brother of Robert I of Naples. John's grandson Charles deposed Giovanna I at the instigation of Pope Urban VI and became Charles III of Naples in 1382. He left Naples in an attempt to win the crown of Hungary from Louis I's daughter Mary, but was assassinated at Buda (27 February 1386). He was succeeded in Naples by his son Ladislas (1386–1414), then by his daughter Giovanna II (1414–35), with whom the line expired. JL

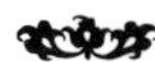

Economy, the In the Renaissance there was no such thing as an 'Italian economy'. Rather, there were many economies, some of regional and some of international scope, sited within the geographical unity of the peninsula. Some were mutually dependent, others periodically locked in a savage rivalry. Certain dense concentrations of people arose, great cities serving as magnets for prosperous immigrants from lowland villages or casual labourers from the mountains, as havens for traders, moneylenders and seekers of fortunes. Drawing to themselves grain, salt, fuel, timber, industrial raw materials and building supplies, they created a demand that could stimulate development far beyond the boundaries of the regions in which they stood. Lombardy,

Tuscany, Liguria, Venice and its hinterland bred aggressive, inventive entrepreneurs, adventurers and colonists whose influence thrust outwards into northern and western Europe, into the east Mediterranean and beyond. In Venice and Florence at least, they created expanding states, resting on guilds or ruled by merchant patricians, whose purpose was at least in part to muster the physical force which protected, promoted and disciplined enterprise. Other cities – Rome, Palermo, Naples, Messina – were essentially centres of consumption, where revenues from country estates or benefices or taxation were spent by barons, courtiers, officials or cardinals. But they could still, by demanding the services of merchants and financiers more skilled and productive than their own native inhabitants, stimulate the inventiveness of other Italians and help to distribute wealth.

When economic historians speak of the rise or decline of Italy, they are usually discussing the success or failure of the great innovating regions, within the quadrilateral formed by Genoa, Milan, Venice and Florence, in maintaining the leadership in transport, industry, finance and business practice which they had established by the early 14c., and in defending their impressive share in world trade. Some of the prosperity so generated might seep through to other parts of Italy. These things depended partly on geography: on the ability of northern and central Italy to exploit the positions on the routes which led, by land or sea, from the Levant to the Low Countries and England. They depended, furthermore, on those routes being the principal axes of trade between Europe and the world outside, and on Italians being able to control and transport – in, say, the armed and disciplined galley fleets of Venice and Genoa, or in those of 15c. Florence – distinctive and prized oriental goods, such as pepper, other spices, and silks. More prosaically, prosperity could rest in part on the shipment, in such great vessels as the Genoese cogs, of goods essential to the textile industries of Europe, including the cotton of Egypt or the ALUM of Phocaea. The leadership of Italians was closely linked to their capacity for offering financial services to rulers and obtaining concessions, such as licences to export wool free of duty, which would further their own manufacturing. In the industrial sphere they staked much on producing for export goods, especially textiles, of such quality and reputation that they could take the place of money, and stem the drainage of specie from Europe to the East.

Like all developed economies, those in Italy faced the danger that their clients might learn to perform these services for themselves. Should they find substitutes for Italian bankers, repudiate their debts, weave their own cloth instead of exporting their wool, or launch upon the market cheap imitations of Italian goods, then much would depend on the adaptability of the entrepreneur and on the energy with which he moved on into new lands or spheres of opportunity until all possibilities had been exhausted. Constraint was always imposed on the economy of Italian cities by the state of agriculture, not only in Italy itself but in the countries to which Italians exported goods and services. It had to be capable of supporting both a population of consumers and one fully employed in trade or manufacturing. Naturally, the expansion of markets depended in part on the size of the population, and if the cultivators and the grain merchants could not meet its demands there was a danger that the high and unstable price of bread might reduce people's capacity for purchasing manufactured goods, and also that the labour force producing them might be decimated by famine or disease. Save in one or two favoured regions, such as Lombardy, Italian agriculture made few spectacular advances, and farmers were seldom able to save enough to improve their land. Among the discouragements were the extraction of rent and dues by feudal landlords and churchmen, the operation of tax systems biased in favour of townsmen and against peasants, and the use of sharecropping contracts.

The Black Death – the worst of many outbreaks of pestilence – ushered in a general crisis in the economies of the mid-14c. One might think the plague a remedy, if a savage one, for the evils of overpopulation. In fact, however, patchy evidence suggests that in the Florentine woollen industry production fell faster than the numbers of the people, and that food prices rose. Demographic stagnation in Tuscany, till well into the 15c., probably bore witness, not only to epidemic disease, but also to a low birth rate responding to grim conditions. Population had not merely been adjusted; it had swung to another extreme, and was unable for the time being (perhaps not until the demographic recovery of the 16c.) to stimulate economic development.

In the 15c. and 16c., each of the major economies was at intervals faced with difficulties caused partly by foreign competition, partly by non-economic forces such as war, weather and disease, and partly by the widening of the economic world through the discoveries of the 15c. and the opening of oceanic routes. To some extent all the economies proved able, at least until the early 17c., to compensate for losses in traditional spheres of action by exploring new ones. In the absence of all-embracing statistics it is impossible to tell any straightforward stories either of long-term economic decline or of prosperity sustained. It seems likely that these crises helped to redistribute prosperity, e.g. by altering the relative positions of Tuscany and Lombardy, although recessions in the woollen industry of Florence were offset by the manufacture of silks. If the Genoese lost the Black Sea to Turkish conquest, they compensated themselves – perhaps amply – by involvement in Spain and in financing voyages to the New World, and by offering services, sometimes as naval contractors, to the Spanish crown. Their loans to the King, however, were in the end to make them and their creditors sadly vulnerable to the bankruptcies of Philip II. More conservative and more tenacious in the Levant, the Venetians were faced by the Portuguese threat to undersell them in the spice markets. But Portuguese control over spices was not firm enough to prevent seepage through to Egypt and Syria, the intrinsic advantages of the oceanic routes were not great enough to secure their instant triumph, and much Venetian capital was successfully transferred in the 16c. into industry and agriculture (involving some reclamation of swampy land). Spanish dominion over north and south did not only imply the extraction of wealth from the Viceroyalties of Milan and Naples to further the dynastic ambitions of the Habsburgs, for certain subsidies were sent, at least to Lombardy. After the outbreak of war in the Low Countries in 1572, troops and treasure *en route* for the Netherlands passed across northern Italy and some Spanish silver was injected into the Italian economies.

In the 16c., the Italian economies probably claimed a smaller share of world trade, but since the volume of world trade had increased through the expansion of population and the exploitation of markets in other continents it is unlikely that they were in absolute decline. Their prosperity sustained a massive, and perhaps more final, blow from the actions of the English and Dutch in both by-passing and invading the Mediterranean and the Levantine markets at the start of the 17c.; and it suffered, too, from the prolonged depression which coincided with the Thirty Years War, and from renewed outbreaks of the terrible plague. Even then, the decline of the cities was probably much steeper than that of the countryside, where much industry came to be newly located, where lower wages could more easily be paid, and where the rigidity of town guilds or state supervision could be escaped. *See* AGRICULTURE; BANKING; BUSINESS METHODS; COMMUNICATIONS; GUILDS; INDUSTRY; POPULATION. BP

Gino Luzzatto *An economic history of Italy from the fall of the Roman Empire to the beginning of the 16th century* (1961); R. S. Lopez, H. A. Miskimin and C. M. Cipolla 'The economic depression of the Renaissance' *Economic History Review* (1961–62 and 1963–64); C. M. Cipolla 'The economic decline of Italy' in B. Pullan ed. *Crisis and change in the Venetian economy in the 16th and 17th centuries* (1968) or in C. M. Cipolla ed. *The economic decline of empires* (1970)

Education In pre-industrial Europe education did not serve the modern function of prolonging adolescence and keeping the young out of the labour force. In medieval and Renaissance Italian cities it served much more immediate social, vocational and professional needs. Historians of Renaissance education have concentrated so exclusively on a handful of relatively innovatory humanist teachers like GUARINO DA VERONA and VITTORINO DA FELTRE that this elementary fact has not been sufficiently appreciated. Villani's *Chronicle* provides some interesting figures, largely accepted by modern scholars as only slightly exaggerated. In the 1340s approximately 10,000 boys – roughly 10 per cent of the urban population – were enrolled in Florentine private schools. Here they learned the rudiments of the literacy they would need to work in a complex social world. Instruction was in the vernacular, and basic reading and writing seems to have been the goal. Only about 1000 of these boys went on to learn the quantitative skills needed in the mercantile life, skills like arithmetic, bookkeeping and the use of the abacus. Perhaps as many as 500 went on to study the ancient disciplines needed in law and the other

Education: stone relief by Luca della Robbia showing boys being taught grammar (1437–39) (Florence, Museo dell'Opera del Duomo).

professions – Latin, rhetoric and logic. These were the boys destined for university.

Florence appears to have placed higher stress on literacy and education than other Italian towns, which suggests that the merchants and guildsmen held learning in high esteem. Elsewhere, and especially in the dynastic states of Lombardy and Emilia, monastic and conventual schools provided much of the early tutelage, and understandably emphasized devotional Latin, together with moral instruction in a very traditional context. The fact that the most innovatory schools of the 15c. were attached to the northern courts of Ferrara and Mantua may reflect the failure of these and similar centres to develop a system of elementary schooling comparable in scope and quality with that of Florence. It also appears consistent with a centralized system of patronage, in which cultural initiatives of all kinds are taken only in response to a specific demand from a ruling élite. Just as this élite is smaller and more concentrated in the dynastic towns than in Florence, so the educational system it demands and supports is geared to its particular interests and values.

In the humanistic schools of Guarino and Vittorino boys received instruction in a variety of skills, disciplines and graces. These learned pedagogues, far from merely catering for an aristocracy, sought to train the young according to a system of values derived from their own intense responses to classical literature, history, and moral philosophy. Instruction in Greek and Roman texts was, in their view, fully compatible with the ethical and spiritual teachings of Christianity, and their students were to be familiar with both traditions. Training of the body and appreciation of music and the visual arts had important places in their schemes, so that it is fair to regard them as pioneers in humanistic or, for want of a better term, liberal education. While Guarino, Vittorino and their successors extended the range and content of education, their methods remained traditional. Until well into the 16c., when the impact of printing began to be felt in the classroom, school learning stressed repetition and memorization. Much teaching consisted simply of reading to the students from a book. Independent thought was strictly subordinated to rote learning, so that knowledge of the classics often appears to have been an end, rather than a means to the further intellectual growth of the student. But if the system sometimes inclined toward pedantry and dullness, it did often serve also to stimulate and inspire boys who grew up to be scholars or the cultivated princes, prelates, and patrons who supported them.

The education of girls in the Renaissance posed special difficulties. The small minority of women who received a classical education found little or nothing to do with their learning. Most girls, however, did not have any formal schooling at all, while those who did were normally instructed only in basic literacy, sufficient to administer a household. They also acquired the skills that were believed to be specifically appropriate to women – sewing, spinning, weaving, dancing, sometimes playing an instrument. Of course many girls who were accepted into the religious life learned some Latin, but that was purely for devotional purposes. Even noblewomen who acquired personal libraries owned mainly breviaries, Books of Hours, saints' lives and the like. No women of the period went on to university; the first woman to earn a doctorate from an Italian university was Elena Cornaro Piscopia, a Venetian noblewoman, in 1678. In its approach to the education of women humanism followed the cultural values of the ancient civilizations it admired and sought to imitate. WG

W. Boyd *History of Western education* (6th ed. 1961); E. Garin *L'educazione in Europa* (1957); W. H. Woodward *Vittorino da Feltre and other humanist educators* (1905; repr. 1963); F. Battaglia *Il pensiero pedagogico del Rinascimento* (1960)

Eight Saints, War of the War between Florence and the Papacy, August 1375 to 18 July 1378, misnamed through confusion of the Eight of War who directed operations for the republic with the 8 'Saints' who raised war taxes from the clergy. The conflict marked the eruption of a latent rivalry for hegemony in central Italy which shattered the traditional Guelf alliance. The division between the protagonists of the war, whose spokesmen included Salutati and Luigi Marsili (d.1394), and its conservative opponents grouped around the Parte Guelfa was deepened by Pope Gregory XI's excommunications and interdict, and the economic distress caused by high taxation and disrupted trade precipitated the revolt of the CIOMPI. Florence was compelled to buy peace with a high indemnity; nevertheless, the war represented a decisive stage in weaning the Florentines from their political dependence on the Papacy. JKH

R. C. Trexler *The spiritual power: republican Florence under interdict* (1974)

Emanuel Philibert Duke of Savoy 1553–80 (b.1528) Trained as a soldier, he became Lieutenant-General of the Imperial army in Flanders (1553) and Governor of the Netherlands (1556). The victory of St Quentin (1557) made his fortune, the ransoms of French prisoners subsequently paying for the creation of an embryonic Savoyard navy. Restored to his duchy and married to Marguerite of Valois (1559), he began the reconstruction of his ravaged state. He induced France and Spain to evacuate the fortresses they held in Piedmont, made a sensible exchange of territory with Berne, and extended Piedmont's coastline. A convinced absolutist, he asserted his authority over all other feudal, civic and ecclesiastical powers, and encouraged the revival of agriculture, trade, and commerce and the spread of education. Although personally a pious Catholic and a supporter of the Jesuits, he made peace with his Waldensian subjects and allowed them freedom of worship within their valleys. JH

Empire, Holy Roman The phrase was first used in 1254, though from Charlemagne's coronation in Rome by Pope Leo III in 800 (and still more from the coronation by Pope John XXII of Otto I in 962 – an event which brought Italy within the orbit of rulers based not in France but nearer in Germany) the Imperial title had carried overtones of an authority that was superior to others because it belonged to the Papacy's secular counterpart and echoed that of ancient Rome. Otto and his 11c. successors had established a legal claim to Italy north and west of the Papal State (that is, to Tuscany and northern Italy from Piedmont to Friuli) by military expeditions that took advantage of the political weakness of the peninsula. From 1194 marriage brought Sicily and southern Italy within the Empire.

By the early 14c. Imperial control of Italy had virtually disappeared. Quarrels between Popes and Emperors, the emergence of wealthy city communes determined to assert their independence, sometimes with papal backing, the commitment of Emperors to the non-Italian parts of their always ramshackle power structures: these factors had in northern Italy and Tuscany led to an almost purely indigenous political life. Of the grand territorial and ideological struggles between Popes and Emperors (as between Gegory VII and Henry IV in the 11c. and between Innocent IV and Frederick II in the 13c.) little remained but the Guelf and Ghibelline slogans under which cities and feudal magnates fought for their own local advantage. Only Venice, not yet a land empire, denied owing allegiance to either. In the south, from Frederick II's death in 1250 the direct link with Germany and thus with the Empire was snapped; from 1266 Naples was ruled by the Angevin, from 1442 by the Aragonese, dynasties; Sicily was ruled from Aragon after the anti-Angevin Sicilian Vespers of 1282.

Italian-Imperial relations during the Renaissance centuries may be divided into 3 phases. The first runs from 1310 to 1519. In the former year the Emperor Henry VII, determined to reassert the Imperial presence in Tuscany and Lombardy, entered Italy with an army. His first purpose was to reassure and assist those who had been fighting for themselves but under the Ghibelline flag, and to cajole from them at least some semblance of unity in the Imperialist cause. His second was to have himself crowned in Rome: without this ceremony a claimant could not entitle himself Holy Roman Emperor, but only add the title of King of the Romans to his local, German rank. Clement V sent cardinals from Avignon for this purpose, but Henry died near Pisa in 1313, having confirmed the titles of his supporters in Lombardy (e.g. the Visconti in Milan, the della Scala in Verona, the Bonacolsi in Mantua) but not yet having rallied in Tuscany the Ghibelline opponents of Guelf Florence. The most abiding legacy of this anachronistic Imperial progress was the hope it gave the Florentine exile Dante, expressed in his *De monarchia* (*c.*1308–14), that a restoration of Imperial authority, so universal that its holder would be beyond personal ambition, would bring back that Augustan peace into which God chose to manifest Himself as Christ.

The first phase closes with the death of the Holy Roman (self-styled, because uncrowned by the Pope) Emperor Maximilian, who, on his own in 1508 and in conjunction with the allies of the League of Cambrai in 1509–10, tried unsuccessfully to regain the Venetian territories from Verona to Friuli which had once acknowledged Ghibelline overlordship. Between Henry and Maximilian there were a few Imperial descents into Italy: those of Lewis IV in 1327–29 (during which he endorsed Castruccio Castracani's challenge to Florence by making him Imperial vicar and standard-bearer in Tuscany); Charles IV in 1354–55 and again in 1368–69; Sigismund in 1413 and 1431–33; Frederick III in 1452 and again in 1468–69. Though these led to the conferment of titles – a marquis here, there a duke – and created minor eddies of political ambition or alarm, they were recognized for what they now were: leaks from an august but closed tradition. When Florence (of all states!) flirted with the idea of an Imperial rather than a French alliance in 1507, and sent Machiavelli to sound Maximilian, it was in a historically unresonant spirit: simply an attempt to deal with a potential nuisance.

The second phase spans the period from Charles V's election to the Imperial title in 1519 to his resignation in 1556. With hereditary dominions stretching from Spain to Hungary and a conscious desire to recreate the universalist associations of the Holy Roman Empire (he had himself crowned King of Lombardy – one of the oldest Imperial titles – and Emperor in 1530 by a reluctant Pope Clement VII), his inheriting Aragonese Naples and his conquest of Milan in 1525 from France made him the dominant figure in the peninsula, territorially the long-delayed successor to Frederick II. During this phase 'Empire' and 'Imperialist' once more become part of the Italian political vocabulary, but only in terms of current events and with a strongly hispanist, not German, flavour, since Charles's garrisons and viceroys in Milan and Naples were predominantly Spanish. The third phase begins when Charles relinquished the Imperial title to his brother Ferdinand and his successor rulers of the Habsburg interests in Germany, Austria, Bohemia and Hungary: Maximilian II (ruled 1564–76) and Rudolph II (ruled 1576–1612). In this phase the Emperors, none of whom sought papal coronation, were of little concern to any Italian power save Venice, whose frontiers they intermittently challenged in their subsidiary capacity as archdukes of Austria. *See* MAXIMILIAN I; CHARLES V. JRH

G. Barraclough *The medieval Empire: idea and reality* (1950); W. M. Bowsky *Henry VII in Italy* (repr. 1974)

Epicurus (342/1–271 BC) Greek philosopher born at Samos, founder of Epicureanism. Though most of his writings are lost, his teachings are known through fragmentary remains and the testimony of other ancient writers. Epicurus developed the physical atomism of Leucippus (5c. BC) and Democritus (*c.*460–*c.*362 BC), and in particular promoted an ethical system based upon the principle of greatest pleasure. Owing to its materialistic, hedonistic and rather untheological basis, Epicureanism was generally held in abhorrence by later Christians, often being equated with atheism. Interest in the philosophy was revived in the 15c. by Valla and others. CS

Este family Although the earliest evidence concerning this ancient noble house dates from Carolingian times in Tuscany, it is best known for its leading role in the politics and culture of northern Italy from 1250 to the Napoleonic era. Expanding its terrains from an Imperial land-grant at Este, near Padua, the family gradually came to dominate the eastern half of the Po valley in the late Middle Ages. From 1267 the Este controlled Ferrara and its hinterland, ultimately extending their rule to Modena and Reggio in the west and the flatlands of Rovigo to the north. For a dynastic house of the time, the Este enjoyed a remarkably long and uninterrupted régime. Recent attempts to explain their success have cited their administrative abilities, attention to social and economic problems, and swift suppression of internal dissent. The family includes a number

The Este rulers of Ferrara

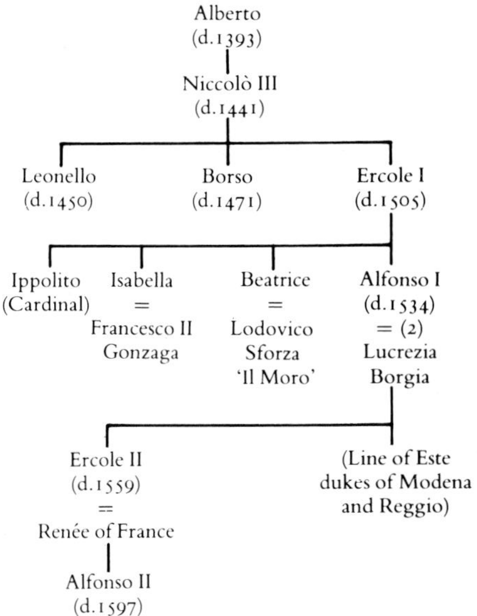

of celebrated rulers, prelates, and patrons of the visual, literary and performing arts. The adroit use of dynastic marriages assured close relationships, especially in the 16c., with such noble families as the Sforza, the Gonzaga and the Montefeltro in Italy; and the Habsburgs, the Valois and the Hanoverians in northern Europe. WG

L. Chiappini *Gli Estensi* (1967); W. L. Gundersheimer *Ferrara: the style of a Renaissance despotism* (1973)

Este, Alfonso I d' Duke of Ferrara 1505–34 (b.1476) was the son of Ercole I. At 15 he had been married to Anna Sforza, daughter of the Duke of Milan. She died in childbirth in 1497, and Alfonso later (1501) married Lucrezia Borgia, daughter of Pope Alexander VI. Leaving much of the cultural and social life of his brilliant court to Lucrezia, he devoted his considerable energies to statecraft and war. The new technology of firearms fascinated him, and he established a celebrated foundry for casting huge cannons. He enjoyed tinkering with artillery and painting maiolica, but his reputation for intellectual triviality is unjustified. His intelligence, applied to military and diplomatic problems, preserved his state at a time of intense danger. In him great reserves of keenness lay beneath an inarticulate, even stolid appearance. WG

M. Catalano *Vita di L. Ariosto* (2 vols 1930–31); E. G. Gardner *The king of court poets: Ariosto* (1906); P. Giovio *La vita di Alfonso d'Este, Duca di Ferrara* tr. G. B. Gelli (1597)

Este, Alfonso II d' Duke of Ferrara 1559–97 (b.1533), the elder son of Ercole II of Ferrara and Renée de France (daughter of King Louis XI and Anne of Brittany), was the fifth, and last, Duke of Ferrara. He was one of the gentlest and most cultivated princes of the late Renaissance. Proficient in Latin and French as well as Italian, he preferred courtly entertainments to diplomacy and war, and took special pleasure in the hunt and in the balls and tournaments that filled the social calendar of the Ferrarese nobility. Perhaps he had had his fill of the military life as a young man in the service of King Henry II of France, fighting against the Habsburgs. In any event, as Duke of Ferrara he tended to avoid conflict, for instance allowing himself to be persuaded by the pope to send his mother away for her Calvinist sympathies. Aside from a recurrent, but sterile, controversy with the Medici over matters of diplomatic protocol, his long reign was exceptionally tranquil.

But it was also in many ways unproductive. In particular, notwithstanding attempts with 3 wives (Lucrezia de' Medici, Barbara of Austria, Margherita Gonzaga), he produced no successor, and the last years of his reign brought recurrent anxiety on this score. Finally, near the end of his life, Alfonso designated Cesare d'Este, the illegitimate son of his father's brother, as his successor, but this choice was unacceptable to the Papacy, under whose grant the Este ruled as vicars in Ferrara. Upon Alfonso's death, the family was obliged to leave the city it had ruled for over 300 years, and the government was turned over to a cardinal legate. This change might have been forestalled. But the extravagant splendour of Alfonso's court had for 38 years been sustained by fiscal oppression which did little to win popular support for the dynasty. Although under Cesare and his successors the Este state enjoyed new and vigorous life in Modena, in Ferrara it had come to an inglorious end. WG

A. Solerti *Ferrara e la Corte Estense nella seconda metà del sec.XVI* (1891); L. Chiappini *Gli Estensi* (1967)

Este, Beatrice d' (1475–97), the most lovable of Renaissance princesses, was the second child of Ercole I d'Este and Eleonora of Aragon. Raised at the court of Ferrara and educated by its leading humanists, Beatrice was married at 15 to Lodovico Sforza, *Il Moro*, to whom she had been betrothed at the age of 5. For the 6 years following her wedding until her death in childbirth, Beatrice helped to make the Milanese court a showplace of literary and artistic creativity. She was sunnier and less imperious than her older sister Isabella: but her influence was, like her life, ephemeral. WG

J. Cartwright *Beatrice d'Este, Duchess of Milan* (1902)

Este, Ercole I d' Duke of Ferrara 1471–1505 (b.1431) continued most of the programmes and policies of his half-brothers Leonello and Borso during his generally prosperous reign. His long and fruitful marriage to Eleonora of Aragon put an end to dynastic problems, and after the failure of an attempted coup by his nephew Niccolò an era of stability in the Este domains ensued. This period of demographic and urban growth – interrupted and almost destroyed by the War of Venice-Ferrara (1482–84) – produced a major enlargement of Ferrara, designed by Rossetti. Known after its patron as the Herculean Addition, it trebled the area within the city walls and stimulated much new construction, especially of palaces and religious establishments. Apart from his vigorously pro-French foreign policy after 1494, Ercole is known chiefly for his generous patronage of religion and the arts and sciences, especially vocal music and the theatre. As the result of a wound suffered in 1467, he was obliged to restrain his passion for soldiering. Recently discovered evidence reveals his serious cultural interests. Though not a learned man (he knew little or no Latin) he worked closely with Rossetti and with court painters such as Roberti, and assembled a great library. Several of his children, notably Isabella, Beatrice, and Cardinal Ippolito, carried this tradition into the 16c. WG

E. G. Gardner *Dukes and poets in Ferrara* (1904); W. L. Gundersheimer ed. *Art and life at the court of Ercole I d'Este: the 'De Triumphis Religionis' of Giovanni Sabadino degli Arienti* (1972)

Este, Isabella d' (1474–1539), daughter of Ercole I d'Este and Eleonora of Aragon, enjoyed the benefits of a classical education in

Leonardo's portrait drawing of **Isabella d'Este** (Paris, Louvre).

one of Italy's most distinguished courts, despite the disruptions occasioned by the War of Venice-Ferrara (1482–84). Among her teachers was Battista Guarini, Guarino da Verona's son and his successor in the chair of rhetoric at Ferrara. Her later concerns for classical learning and astrology also suggest the influence of the ducal librarian, Pellegrino Prisciano, and other humanists in the ducal circle.

At the time of her marriage at the age of 16 to Francesco Gonzaga (15 February 1490), Isabella was already recognized as an exceptionally astute and cultivated woman, clearly the equal of her husband both intellectually and socially. Francesco's predilections for military life, combined with Isabella's manifest skills and interests in diplomacy, meant that they spent little time together.

She brought energy, intelligence and judgment to her patronage of literature, music and the visual arts, as to her pursuit of statecraft. Her wealth and taste, and her imperious manner, enabled her to compete – not always successfully – for the services of some of the most eminent artists of the age. Leonardo, Francia and Titian, among others, painted portraits of her. Her contracts and her instructions to artists reveal a discriminating and somewhat arbitrary purchaser who clearly knew her own mind. In 1503 she went so far as to send Perugino a sketch for an allegory she wanted from him. Her artistic patronage reveals the guidance of humanist advisers, arising from her literary interests. Paride da Ceresara helped her formulate the 'inventions' for decorating her study; men of letters such as Bembo and Mario Equicola contributed other decorative schemes. Her circle included Battista Spagnoli, Castiglione and Bandello, and a coterie of other, less well known Mantuan humanists. One of these, Floriano Dolfo, sought to regale her with a series of pornographic letters. Ariosto, Bernardo da Bibbiena and G. G. Trissino numbered her among their benefactors.

She saw nothing inconsistent about combining a devout Christianity with her classical and even pagan interests. She supported convents and monasteries, and took a keen interest in recruiting singers for the ducal chapel. Some of these, however, may have doubled in service as performers of the secular songs (*frottole*) composed at Mantua by Cara and Tromboncino. Any more than it stood in the way of her festive life at Mantua, her piety did not interfere with her anti-papal policy, designed to prevent threats to the autonomy of Mantua and Ferrara. When in 1519 her dull and unfaithful husband died, Isabella continued to function as a trusted adviser to her eldest son, Federico II, and succeeded in helping her second, Ercole, to obtain a cardinalate. The years before her death were divided between Rome and Mantua. WG

G. Coniglio *I Gonzaga* (1967); A. Luzio and R. Renier *Mantova e Urbino* (1893)

Euclid (*fl.c.*300 BC) Geometer. Nothing is known of his life save that he lived in Alexandria. He is said to have taught geometry to Ptolemy I. The Renaissance knew 2 of his works: the *Elements* [*of Geometry*] and *Optics*. The *Elements* is the oldest surviving geometrical textbook, so well conceived that it was used virtually intact into the present century. Medieval university students studied the first 6 books (plane geometry and theory of proportion); by the 15c. mathematicians were exploring Books VII-IX (number theory) and X-XIII (solid geometry). Euclid established both the content of geometry and its methods of presentation and proof. There were 2 Latin editions of the *Elements* printed before 1500; there were numerous Latin and vernacular

Page from an early edition of **Euclid**'s *Elements*, printed in Venice in 1482.

editions in the 16c. The *Optics* is an elementary treatise on perspective in which Euclid established the basic laws of optics on a strictly geometrical basis. MBH

Dictionary of Scientific Biography (1970–80)

Eugenius IV Pope 1431–47 (b.*c.*1383) Gabriele Condulmer, born in Venice, was eased when still a youth into an ecclesiastical career by the influence of an uncle who was Latin Patriarch of Constantinople and who, as Pope Gregory XII, made Gabriele a cardinal in 1408. From the beginning of his own pontificate Eugenius was embroiled in conflict with the Council of Basle, whose challenge to his authority culminated in its declaring him deposed from his office in 1439 and electing Felix V in his place in the following year: the last of the anti-popes. Eugenius died with the question of papal authority unresolved.

At least he died in Rome. In 1434 his secular authority there had been challenged by the Romans in riots from which he barely escaped with his life. Thereafter, until 1443, he, and with him the Papacy, was based on Florence. There was celebrated in 1439 the most memorable event of his pontificate, the decree of union between the Latin and Greek churches.

Detail of bronze door by Filarete in St Peter's showing the coronation of the Emperor Sigismund by Pope **Eugenius IV** in 1433.

Though the decree was greeted with scorn in Constantinople, the long residence in Florence of Greek scholars and theologians had a permanent influence on the development of humanistic studies in Italy. By temperament a monk, by circumstance an embattled administrator and politician, Eugenius was not indifferent to the arts or learning, inviting Donatello and Fra Angelico to Rome and employing Bracciolini and Biondo in his chancery. JRH

J. Gill *Eugenius IV* (1961); — *The Council of Florence* (1959)

Eustachio (1500/10–74) Anatomist. In early life a humanist, learned in Greek and Arabic, Bartolomeo Eustachi later turned to medicine. He was physician to the Duke of Urbino and to his brother Cardinal Giulio della Rovere, and lectured on anatomy in Rome. His first writings were pro-Galenic and anti-Vesalian, but he soon turned to anatomical research. *Opuscula anatomica* (1564) deals more accurately than Vesalius with the kidney, ear (the Eustachian tube is named in his honour), venous system and teeth. His handsome *Tabulae anatomicae* were published (without his text) in 1714. MBH

Evangelism The term is used in an Italian context to designate spiritual currents manifest around 1540 which might be said to have occupied the confessional middle ground between Catholicism and Protestantism; hence it does not relate at all to the term 'Evangelical' as used in German or English contexts. It has been applied particularly to the so-called *spirituali* of the Viterbo circle, notably Cardinal Pole, Vittoria Colonna, Marcantonio Flaminio, Carnesecchi and Ochino, and also to Giulia Gonzaga, Contarini, Giovanni Morone, Gregorio Cortese and Vermigli. Such persons combined a zeal for personal religious renewal with spiritual anxieties akin to those of Luther, to which they sought an answer in the study of St Paul and St Augustine; convinced of the inefficacy of human works, they stressed the role of faith and the all-efficacy of divine grace in justification. Few of them broke with the Catholic Church. *See* REFORMATION, COUNTER-REFORMATION. OL

E. G. Gleason 'On the nature of sixteenth-century Italian Evangelism: scholarship 1953–1978' *Sixteenth-Century Journal* (1978)

Fabricius of Aquapendente, Girolamo (*c.*1533–1619) Anatomist and embryologist. A lifelong member of Padua university, lecturer on surgery and anatomy in succession to Falloppio (William Harvey was his most famous pupil), he was also a highly successful physician and anatomist and a voluminous writer on medical subjects. His most important discovery was that all the veins in the body contained membranes which controlled the flow of blood: he saw them as controlling the *amount* of flow ('floodgates'), while actually, as Harvey saw, they are valves to control the *direction* of flow. In embryology he was the first since Aristotle to attempt a systematic study of the developing foetus in animals and man. MBH

De venarum ostiolis (1603) ed. K. J. Franklin (1933); *The embryological treatises* ed. H. B. Adelmann (1942; 1967)

Factions (*fazioni*, *parti*) were essentially political groupings in competition for the control of a city or region. Each was composed of one or more leading families and their followers ('friends', 'adherents' or 'partisans'). The relation of leader to follower was that of patron to client; deference and loyal support against the other side was rewarded (by the Medici, for example) with jobs, offices, marriage alliances and other favours. Among the best-known opposing factions of the period were the Orsini and the Colonna in Rome and the Oddi and the

Baglioni in Perugia; Pistoia was another proverbially factious city.

The most famous factions of all, GUELF and GHIBELLINE, were not limited to particular families or cities, but these general labels often masked local conflicts. Since Florence was Guelf, Siena and Pisa had to be Ghibelline; and in Friuli, to be Guelf meant little more than to support the Savorgnan family. Moralists such as S. Bernardino of Siena attacked faction as divisive, and its cost in lives lost in street-fighting and in disturbances fomented by exiles was sometimes high. Yet, in a Renaissance city-state, a balance of power between factions may have been the most reliable way of keeping the peace and of allowing the ruled to exert a little pressure on their rulers. *See* CLIENTAGE. PB

D. Kent *The rise of the Medici: faction in Florence, 1426–1434* (1978)

Falconetto, Giovanni Maria (1468–1534) Veronese painter and architect who introduced High Renaissance architectural forms to Padua. The antiquarianism of his paintings and drawings is echoed in the city gates for Padua (Porta S. Giovanni, 1528; Porta Savonarola, 1530), modelled on Roman triumphal arches. For Alvise Cornaro, himself an architectural amateur and theorist, Falconetto designed the Loggia (1528) and Odeon Cornaro, delicate essays in Bramantesque applied orders, the latter exquisitely decorated inside with stuccoes. Like the Villa dei Vescovi at Luvigliano, which, with its loggias and complex staircase ramps exploits a hill-top site, these buildings impressed the young Palladio, who also owned architectural drawings by Falconetto. CE

G. Fiocco *Alvise Cornaro* (1964)

Falier, Marino (1274–1355) In the long line of portraits of doges in the Sala del Maggior Consiglio in the Ducal Palace in Venice appears, instead of Falier's face, the inscription: 'Hic est locus Marini Falieri decapitati pro criminibus' ('This is the place of Marino Falier, beheaded for his crimes'). Elected in 1354 after a long and distinguished public career as naval commander and ambassador, Falier, with the connivance of a few influential commoners, plotted unsuccessfully to destroy the restrictive patrician hold over government and establish himself as the effective wielder of (presumably) a hereditary monarchical power. Of all attempts to explain the freakish behaviour of this distinguished septuagenarian, only one seems acceptable. Dissatisfaction with the running of the recent long war (1370–74) with Genoa had prompted a fairly wide resentment against the patricians as a class, and against the limitations on speedy and sustained action in times of crisis that were inherent in a republican constitution. Falier hoped to satisfy personal ambitions while bringing Venice into line with the constitutional practice of the majority of other states. The psychological motives drawn on by Byron in his verse tragedy *Marino Faliero* derive from later inventions. JRH

V. Lazzarini *Marino Faliero* (1963)

Falloppio, Gabriele (?1523–62) Anatomist. After an early humanist education he studied medicine at Modena and perhaps at Padua under Realdus Columbus. He lectured on pharmacy at Ferrara and on anatomy at Pisa (1549–51) before teaching anatomy at Padua. His *Observationes anatomicae* (1561), ostensibly a commentary on Vesalius' *Fabrica*, contains many original observations on the bones, muscles, nerves and kidneys, as well as the discovery of the 'Fallopian tubes'. MBH

Family structure was generally of the patriarchal type characteristic of the Mediterranean region. Wives tended to be considerably younger than husbands. Women and children were kept firmly under control. Wives and daughters were expected to stay at home. Sons often remained under paternal control until their father died. In other respects, family structure varied with social groups, regions and centuries. The majority of the population lived in small households (mean household size in Tuscany in 1427 was 4.4); the nuclear family was the most common residential unit.

But the better-off, especially the nobility, lived in much larger groups. Eleven per cent of the Tuscans surveyed in 1427 lived in households of 11 to 25 people, including not only parents and their legitimate children but also grandparents, brothers of the husband, bastards, and of course servants. It was to all these people that the contemporary term *famiglia* referred. Noble households belonging to the same lineage or 'clan' often lived in the same quarter (in separate palaces), met regularly in a particular piazza or loggia, made business partnerships with members of other branches and helped them to obtain political offices. There were, of course, regional variations. In

Genoa, where the state was particularly weak, the noble clan (locally known as the *albergo*) was particularly strong; it recruited members by adoption as well as descent and it had its own officials or 'governors'. In Venice, the links between noble brothers, who often lived with their families in the same palace, seem to have been unusually close.

Changes over time are particularly visible in the family structure of the Florentine patriciate. In the 14c. the *consorteria*, the Tuscan equivalent of the *albergo*, disintegrated. The clan gradually ceased to hold property in common. Its members did not lose all sense of economic, political and social solidarity with one another, and they continued to be concerned with the honour and glory of their whole 'house'. However, in Florence brothers did not necessarily live under the same roof. There is some evidence (though the question is controversial) of an increasing sense of privacy and of the solidarity of the nuclear family against outsiders. More generally, the increasing numbers of manuscript genealogies, advice to children, and family portraits suggest an increasingly acute sense of lineage among the Italian upper classes of the 16c. So does the rise of the entail (*fedecommesso*), a legal arrangement for the inheritance of property designed to protect the family against the prodigality of individual members. PB

R. Goldthwaite *Private wealth in Renaissance Florence* (1968); J. Heers *Family clans in the Middle Ages* (Eng. tr. 1977); D. Herlihy and C. Klapisch *Les Toscans et leurs familles* (1978)

Farnese family Rulers of Parma and Piacenza, 1545–1731. First mentioned as a noble family in the 12c., when they held several fiefs in Latium, the Farnese were consistent supporters of the Papacy and enjoyed considerable prestige in the time of Alexander VI because of the Pope's supposed liaison with Giulia Farnese. Their history as an Italian ruling family dates from 1534, when Alessandro Farnese became Pope Paul III. In 1545 Paul created his son Pierluigi (1503–47) Duke of Parma and Piacenza. Pierluigi's attempt to subject all the inhabitants of his duchy to the rule of law earned him the hatred of the nobility and he was assassinated. His son Ottavio further strengthened the family's position by marrying Margaret, illegitimate daughter of Charles V. Ottavio's brother Cardinal Alessandro (1520–89), patron of Bembo and Vasari, was responsible for completing the Farnese Palace in Rome. Ottavio's son Alessandro (1545–92) was one of the greatest generals of his age. JH

E. N. Rocca *I Farnese* (1969); G. Drei *I Farnese* (1954)

Fausto, Vettor (or **Vittore**) (*c.*1490–*c.*1540) offers a striking example of the fitness of a classical education as a preparation for life at its most practical. Fausto, a largely self-educated Venetian, was appointed public lecturer in Greek in 1519. In 1526 he persuaded the Senate to give him dock space in the Arsenal to build a quinquereme (5 men to a bench, each with an oar) on the ancient Greek model. In its trial in 1529 – a race against a light galley – the quinquereme won: others were not built only because of the adverse effects of overcrowding on the crew in cold and wet conditions. Fausto continued to work in the Arsenal on prototypes and new construction methods – all in the name of Archimedes and the revival of Greek technology. JRH

F. C. Lane *Venetian ships and shipbuilders* (1934)

Federico II da Montefeltro Signore of Urbino 1444–74, Duke 1474–82 (b.1422) was a bastard, and succeeded on the assassination of his half-brother. He has deservedly become the paradigm of the man as adept in letters as in arms. The point was made in the *Life* by his contemporary, Vespasiano da Bisticci, who said that 'he was the first of the Signori who took up philosophy and had knowledge of the same'. The same point is made in the portrait by Justus of Ghent of *c.*1475, which shows him studying a manuscript while in armour. His grounding in letters was provided at the Mantuan school of Vittorino da Feltre, that in arms in the even more famous 'school' of the condottiere Niccolò Piccinino. His military career was indeed an impressive one, at first followed as a conventional employment for a younger brother, then pursued as a means of enlarging his duchy (to 3 times its size when he succeeded) and of obtaining the money for his expensive tastes as a builder and a collector of manuscripts. With warlike peasant subjects to follow him, his services were in steady demand. Though a prince, he fought simply for cash and on short-term contract, never as an ally. Thus he served Venice, the Papacy, the Aragonese in Naples; now Florence against the Papacy (1469), now the Papacy against Florence (1479). Similarly, from fighting with Piccinino he could find himself on the other side. For a while he was a comrade in arms of Francesco Sforza. Among his rivals he had had to face Colleoni.

This immersion in the confused world of condottiere values, together with the forceful illegality with which at times he extended his territory (especially at the expense of his bitter rival Sigismondo Malatesta), makes all the more remarkable the use to which he turned periods of peace, and perhaps more understandable his pious dependence on astrological forecasts when returning to the hazards of war. He was an effective, paternalistic ruler. His interest in the full range of the humanist curriculum never faltered. Latin was a delight to him. His library of manuscripts (he deplored the printing of books) was probably larger than that of any European university. Above all it was judgment, not just a lucky use of available talent, that made of the proportions, the spaces and the decorations of his palace the purest and most harmonious expression of Quattrocento aesthetic ideals, and as a result of which he is remembered as the patron of Luciano Laurana, Francesco di Giorgio, Pontelli, Melozzo da Forlì, and his portraitist, Piero della Francesca. [37] JRH

W. Tommasoli *La vita di Federico da Montefeltro* (1978); P. Rotondi *The ducal palace of Urbino* (1969); J. Dennistoun *Memoirs of the dukes of Urbino* I (1851)

Ferdinand II of Aragon King of Aragon 1479–1516 (b.1452), known as Ferdinand the Catholic, was recognized, even by Machiavelli, as one of the best and strongest rulers of his age and one particularly favoured by fortune. On the death of his mother, Ferdinand was nominated King of Sicily and co-regent of Aragon and Sardinia (1468); he became King of Aragon in his own right in 1479. Since Aragon had enjoyed an indirect influence in Naples from the time of Alfonso V, it was inevitable that Ferdinand should become involved in Italian politics. This was already apparent by 1486, when he acted as guarantor of the peace between Naples and Innocent VIII, but the confused state both of Aragon and of Castile (the kingdom of his wife, Isabella), together with their campaigns against the Moorish kingdom of Granada, initially kept Ferdinand occupied in Spain. It was not until after the fall of Granada in 1492 that he was able to exploit Aragon's Mediterranean interests to the full.

In Italy Ferdinand was widely regarded as a useful ally against the French and from 1494, therefore, his influence in Italian politics was very marked. Ferdinand's interest in Italy was also constantly encouraged by his great captain, Gonzalo de Cordoba. Ferdinand was a major partner in the Italian League of 1495 which restored Ferdinand II of Naples to the Neapolitan throne, but in 1500 he signed the secret treaty of Granada with Louis XII by which they agreed to invade, conquer and divide the kingdom of Naples between them. Subsequently, Ferdinand broke with his erstwhile ally and drove the French from Naples by 1504. Naples was annexed to the Spanish crown, and thereafter, apart from his participation in the League of Cambrai, Ferdinand pursued an anti-French policy in Italy. The famous duplicity of his diplomacy, which modern historians often find morally distasteful, was widely admired by his contemporaries. *See* ARAGON, HOUSE OF. JH

Ferrante (or **Ferdinand**) **I** King of Naples 1458–94 (b.1423) Illegitimate son of Alfonso V, Ferrante was educated by Valla and became a generous patron of the arts and learning. He believed in the value of just administration and tried to reform the tax structure of Naples. However, even after his marriage to the niece of the Prince of Taranto, Ferrante was always faced by baronial opposition. A rebellion in 1458 developed into a civil war in which the king was victorious, but the vengeance he then took led to another rebellion in 1485. JH

Ferrara The most easterly of the major cities of the Po valley. Until late in the 17c. a navigable branch of the Po flowed by the city walls. The economy of the city and its hinterland in early times derived from riverine commerce, with its attendant tolls and duties, as well as from the agricultural produce of the rich alluvial soil of the delta. During the late Middle Ages a hereditary nobility established firm control over the labour-intensive agrarian economy of Ferrara. This nobility was in turn dominated from 1332 by an hereditary dynasty, the ESTE, whose tenure as marquises and, from 1471, dukes of Ferrara spanned 300 years. It was under their rule that Ferrara, from being a squalid backwater, developed into an elegant and prosperous regional capital with a distinctive architectural and cultural style. Their success was based on a prosperous rural economy, revenues from foreign military campaigns, the administrative skill of a loyal

The Torre dei Leoni (Tower of the Lions) of the Este Castle, principal residence of the Este family in **Ferrara**.

group of office-holders, and a series of judicious marriages. The Este managed to weather not only the War of Ferrara but also the Wars of Italy.

Given the weakness of the bourgeois patron class, Ferrara's court-centred art maintained a remarkable homogeneity. Though during its hey-day in the late 15c. the city probably never numbered more than 30,000 inhabitants, it preserves the aspect of a larger city. The most monumental of its secular buildings is the Este Castle, exactly in the centre of the town, the work of Benvenuto da Imola (1385). Built in the aftermath of an abortive plot against Niccolò II d'Este, its looming presence symbolizes the virtually unshakeable power of the régime. Attached to it by an elevated and covered bridge (*c.*1475) was the official residence of the Este family, whose façade faces the Romanesque cathedral of St George across a small square.

In addition to these central buildings, and others destroyed in World War II, Ferrara has many palaces and churches dating from the 15c. and 16c.

The principal surviving palace from the 15c. is the Schifanoia ('*sans-souci*'), an Estean residence and guest house. Its grand hall, the Sala dei Mesi ('room of the months'), preserves part of a major fresco cycle (1471) illustrating scenes from the court of Borso d'Este (1450–71; b.1413), zodiacal symbols and mythical and allegorical illustrations of the months, perhaps inspired by Petrarch's *Triumphs*. This cycle has taken on new importance as recent research has shown that several other Ferrarese palaces, long since destroyed, were extensively decorated by court artists working in the same illustrative tradition. Among the larger buildings erected in the 16c., the Palazzo dei Diamanti provides the best example of noble domestic architecture. Faced on two sides with 12,600 stones cut in diamond-like facets, it was designed by Rossetti to function as the centrepiece of his large, formally planned addition to the city.

Rossetti's extension of the walls, called the Herculean Addition after his patron, Ercole I d'Este, trebled Ferrara's urban space. In the new part private palaces, churches and convents sprang up. But the design was too ambitious, and large portions of the city within the walls remained undeveloped until the 20c. Montaigne, who passed through Ferrara in 1580 and was amiably received by Alfonso II, noted the depopulation and reported that grass grew in the broad streets. By then a complacent, increasingly provincial aristocracy had run the economy virtually into the ground. It remained for the Papacy, exercising an ancient legal claim to Ferrara in 1598, to complete through its legate-governors the fiscal and cultural eclipse of a vital Renaissance city, the home of Boiardo, Ariosto, Tasso; of Tura, Cossa, Roberti and the brothers Dossi; and, for shorter periods, of Guarino, Titian, Copernicus and Calvin. *See* FERRARA, WAR OF; COMACCHIO. WG

L. Chiappini *Gli Estensi* (1967); W. L. Gundersheimer *Ferrara: the style of a Renaissance despotism* (1973); A. Frizzi *Memorie per la storia di Ferrara* (5 vols 1791 and later eds)

Ferrara, War of Fought largely by diplomats, this conflict, which opened on 2 May 1482 and was concluded with the Peace of Bagnolo on 4 August 1484, anticipated the escalation of local conflicts which was to bring foreign powers into Italy from 1494, and the frequent changing of sides which characterized the WARS OF ITALY. Invited by Pope Sixtus to give aid by sea to his campaign against Naples in return for territories belonging to Ferrara (in theory the duchy was a papal fief), Venice responded by occupying the Polesine. But when Spain declared for the Aragonese King of Naples and Milan and Florence armed in defence of Ferrara and the *status quo* in northern Italy, the Pope broke with Venice. The Republic countered by appealing to France to invade Naples in support of the old Angevin claim to the kingdom, and Milan in support of the claim of the family of Orléans. The Peace was signed hurriedly, with all parties aware of the menacing spectres they had invoked. JRH

E. Piva *La guerra di Ferrara* (1893)

Ferrari, Gaudenzio (*c.*1475/80–1546) Piedmontese painter. He began his career in a gothicizing vein, the effect of which he moderated by an appeal to Leonardesque Milanese models, as in the Arona altar (1511). Following the decoration of the Sacro Monte (Varallo; after 1517) – a vehemently non-classical combination of painting and sculpture produced in a militantly Catholic ideological context – Milanese classicism reasserted itself in Gaudenzio's style (e.g. *Madonna degli Aranci*, Vercelli, 1529). Although his most original conception is certainly the Saronno *Assumption* (1534–*c.*1537), his style became progressively rigid after a move to Milan, 1535–39. LP

V. Viale *Gaudenzio Ferrari* (1969); L. Malle *Incontri con Gaudenzio* (1969)

Festa, Costanzo (*c.*1490–1545) One of the earliest composers of madrigals. Apparently of Piedmontese origin, he was a member of the Cappella Sistina in Rome from 1517, but also had strong Florentine connections, writing both popular madrigals in a simple frottola-esque style and more sonorous ones for ceremonial occasions in Florence. DA

A. Einstein *The Italian madrigal* (1949)

Festivals As in most pre-industrial societies, leisure and play were not associated with weekends or evenings so much as with public holidays and festivals. All over Italy the 12 days of Christmas and Carnival were major festivals; the others varied in importance according to the city. The feast of St John the Baptist was a major event in Florence; the Ascension in Venice; the Assumption in Siena; and so on, these events having a civic as well as a religious significance – occasions for the community to reaffirm its identity and its basic values. The festivals centred on civic rituals. On Ascension Day in Venice, the doge was rowed out in the state barge, the *bucintoro*, to throw a ring into the Adriatic. There were also feasting, pageants, processions, plays (mysteries for Corpus Christi, comedies for CARNIVAL), ball games, bull-baiting, races, mock-battles and displays of skill like sword dancing and tightrope-walking. In the 16c., fireworks became an increasingly important item.

In the course of the period the religious, popular and civic elements in all these festivals tended to be submerged by the secular, aristocratic and princely elements. Festivals were becoming spectacles in which ordinary people were relegated to an increasingly passive role. With this aristocratic 'annexation' of popular festivals went the development of more and more splendid and expensive happenings at court, especially for the weddings of princes and the formal 'entry' of rulers into cities. Alfonso of Aragon's entry into his newly-conquered capital of Naples in 1443 was modelled on an ancient Roman triumph, as was Louis XII's entry into Milan (designed by Leonardo da Vinci) in 1509. Among the most splendid wedding festivals in 16c. Italy were those of the Medici, notably the marriage of Grand Duke Francesco to Joanna of Austria (1566), for which Vasari created his masquerade *The genealogy of the pagan gods*, and the marriage of Grand Duke Ferdinand to Christine of Lorraine (1589), which involved not only plays, jousts and musical *intermezzi* but also a mock sea battle in the courtyard of the Pitti Palace. On occasions like this painters, poets,

Cassone panel showing the procession approaching the Baptistery for the feast of St John the Baptist, one of the most important **festivals** in Florence (detail) (Florence, Bargello).

architects and musicians worked together to produce magnificent if ephemeral works of art, like the triumphal arch created by Palladio, Veronese and Tintoretto for the entry into Venice of Henry III of France in 1574. The celebration of the community had been displaced by the celebration of the prince. PB

J. Jacquot ed. *Fêtes de la Renaissance* (3 vols 1956–76)

Ficino, Marsilio (1433–99), the most important of the founders of Renaissance neo-Platonism, took up the study of Greek in the 1450s after a humanistic and medical education. From 1462 he was lavishly patronized by Cosimo de' Medici to satisfy the latter's craving for Latin translations of Plato. In 1463–69 he produced translations of all Plato's dialogues, thus making his thought genuinely available to the West for the first time (so many having paid lip service to it for so long) and providing the essential tool for Renaissance Platonism. He followed this by composing a substantial philosophical work of his own, the *Theologia Platonica de immortalitate animae* (*Platonic theology concerning the immortality of the soul*; 1469–74), which, besides stating a general metaphysic, argued for the independence of the soul from the body, and its immortality on the grounds of its participation in the divine characteristics of unity, self-sufficiency and reason.

Though intensely devoted to pagan philosophy, Ficino became a priest in 1473 and was supported in a modest ecclesiastical career by the patronage of Lorenzo de' Medici. He remained the leading spirit of the Medicean circle of the Platonic Academy until the overthrow of the Medici in 1494. His attitude to Savonarola after that was ambiguous. A second major effort of translation, of PLOTINUS, an author of whom the West previously had had no direct knowledge, occupied him 1484–92. By this and his translations of Proclus and other writers he transmitted to his followers the basic texts of the neo-Platonism of late antiquity: a second achievement comparable with his translation of Plato.

Apart from the *Platonic theology*, Ficino's ideas are contained mainly in commentaries on books of Plato and Plotinus and in 2 other original works: *Concerning the Christian religion* (1474) and *De triplici vita* (*On the threefold life*; 1489). His philosophy, though loosely constructed, was a highly influential revival of the neo-Platonic tradition. He sees the universe as a hierarchy of being, ascending from the grossest and most diversified matter to the purest unity and indivisibility of the Godhead. Creation is spread out at various points on this scale. The human soul, with its capacity for pure thought, is at a mid-point on the scale, and the purpose of life is to free it as far as possible from matter and ascend as near as possible to God. Ficino propagated the image of the soul supported in its ascent towards God by the two wings of will and reason, and thought that the supreme human activity was contemplation, by which gifted men could free themselves from matter.

Marble portrait bust of the neo-Platonist Marsilio **Ficino** by Andrea Ferrucci da Fiesole, in Florence cathedral.

Ficino was responsible for various paradoxical conflations of pagan and Christian ideas which were to be important in Renaissance thought. In his early commentary on Plato's *Symposium* he expounded his theory of love. 'Platonic love', the affection of human beings, could approximate to and prepare for a truly spiritual love. Ficino was much concerned with the relationship between Christianity and earlier religions. He believed that the writings of the pre-Christian ancients, Greek, Egyptian and others, embodied a primitive theology (*prisca gentilium theologia*) which contained intimations of Christian truth. While upholding the uniqueness of Christianity, he was one of the pioneers of the attempt to place it within a general world of religions. He also attributed great importance to the Hermetic writings of late antiquity, some of which he translated, erroneously believing them to be much earlier, and repositories of primitive wisdom. These writings stimulated his interest in MAGIC, connected also with his earlier medical training, and led him to advocate magical practices, particularly in *De triplici vita*. He was also interested in ASTROLOGY. These tendencies led to understandable ecclesiastical suspicion at Rome near the end of his life, from which he freed himself with some difficulty. *See* PLATO AND NEO-PLATONISM; HERMETICISM. GH

P. O. Kristeller *The philosophy of Marsilio Ficino* (Eng. tr. 1943); Raymond Marcel *Marsile Ficin* (1958); *Opera omnia* (2 vols; repr. 1959)

Filarete (*c.*1400–69) Antonio Averlino, Florentine goldsmith and architect, author of a proto-Utopian architectural treatise, assumed this hellenizing nickname. His bronze doors for St Peter's (1445) mix childish figure style with pioneering antiquarianism. In Milan from *c.*1451 he combined Brunelleschian forms with Lombard brickwork at the Ospedale Maggiore (1456–65), the first hospital with symmetrical cross-shaped wards. Fantasy and practicality coexist in his illustrated treatise (*c.*1460–64), described as 'mostly ridiculous' by Vasari. A star-shaped city, Sforzinda, is conceived by patron (father) and architect (mother), and filled with every building type from cathedral to brothel. Circulating in manuscript, the treatise was widely read (e.g. by Bramante, Leonardo, Scamozzi). [128] CE

J. R. Spencer *Filarete's treatise on architecture* (1965)

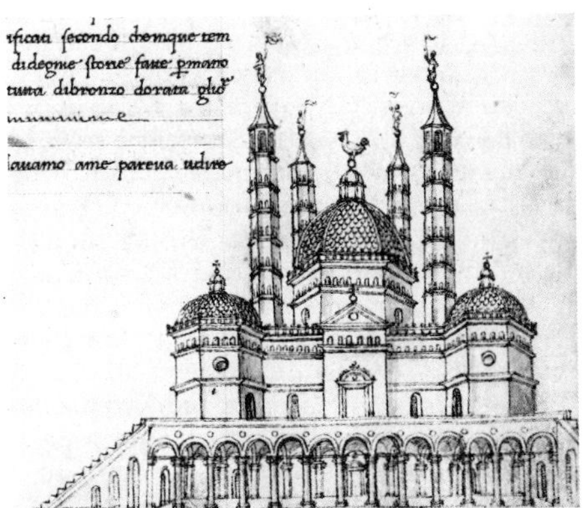

Drawing of a temple in an ideal city, from **Filarete**'s architectural treatise (Florence, Biblioteca Nazionale).

Filelfo, Francesco (1398–1481), a skilful scholar and inveterate controversialist who sold his literary talents to many patrons, acquired his knowledge of Greek during a stay at the Byzantine court in the 1420s. He was appointed to a chair at Florence in 1429, then quarrelled with the native humanists and had to flee when Cosimo de' Medici came to power in 1434. Eventually finding refuge at Milan, he was patronized both by the Visconti and later by the Sforza while he pursued a scurrilous literary war with his Florentine enemies. GH

Firenzuola, Agnolo (1493–1543) Florentine writer. His works, noted for their linguistic and stylistic refinement, were mostly published posthumously, although they had a wide circulation in manuscript during his lifetime. More memorable than his 2 plays *La trinutia* (*The triple marriage*) and *Lucidi* (1549) is his unfinished collection of novellas: *Ragionamenti d'amore* (*Discourses on love*), influenced by the *Decameron* and by Bembo's *Asolani*. His *Asino d'oro* (1550) is a version of Apuleius' *Golden ass* and his *Prima veste dei discorsi degli animali* (*First version of the animals' discourses*; 1548) is an adaptation of the Spanish rendering of the stories from the Indian *Panchatantra*. He also wrote dialogues *De la bellezza delle donne* (*On women's beauty*) and the *Discacciamento de le nuove lettere* (*Driving out the new letters*; 1524), a pamphlet against Trissino's *Epistola*. LL

Opere ed. A. Seroni (1958); G. Fatini *Agnolo Firenzuola e la borghesia letterata del Rinascimento* (1907)

Florence In 1338 Giovanni Villani reckoned the population of Florence at 90,000, reflecting the peak of a steady immigration which took advantage of the most flourishing economy in Italy. Recent building projects included the third, expanded circle of walls, the Palazzo Vecchio, the Ponte Vecchio, the cathedral and its campanile, the vast churches of S. Maria Novella and S. Croce, built respectively for the Dominicans and the Franciscans. From the 12c. the independent commune had steadily extended its control over the magnate and clerical landlords of the countryside; now rich merchants were beginning to buy up farms and build villas there themselves. From 1282 the magnate element within the city itself had been politically gelded; only members of the guilds – bankers, merchants, manufacturers and the like – could qualify for civic office. Strengthened by further anti-magnate legislation in 1293 (the Ordinances of Justice), the city's government was run by the creators of its wealth.

Yet, however rational its constitution, so nicely calculated to prevent the formation of parties or the pursuit of individual ambition, the city's society in Villani's day was violent and divided. The landed wealth and militant character of the magnates enabled them to exert considerable indirect power through the clients they cajoled or bullied into supporting them. The law was not theirs but they could intimidate it. Their feuds could make civic life seem more like civil war. Dante was exiled in 1301 for being on the wrong side in a victory of the Black (more hawkish in their support of the Papacy) GUELFS over the more dove-like Whites. And as a Guelf city Florence was exposed to the external crises that arose when Emperors either brought armies into Italy or encouraged their supporters to prey on their Guelf neighbours. Thus in 1315 Florence's army was defeated by Ghibelline Pisa at Montecatini, in 1325 by the Ghibelline Castruccio CASTRACANI at Altopascio. The social antipathies which hamstrung the city's ability to reply to this challenge led to the desperate remedy of temporarily suspending the constitution and granting executive authority to a foreigner, Charles, Duke of Calabria, son of King Robert of Naples. This was the remedy that had led to so many communes' being converted into *signorie*. And though it was short-lived, the government was forced to the same expedient again in 1342–43.

This time the government's helplessness arose from its inability to deal with an economic crisis worsened by the bankruptcy of the Bardi and Peruzzi companies. So overbearing, however, was the new saviour, Walter of Brienne, Duke of Athens, that within a year he was expelled by a coalition of all social groups. It was in a period marked by a sober determination to keep social tensions from immobilizing government that in 1348 the Black Death struck, killing something under half the population. Economic recovery, though slow, was remarkable, partly because the plague hit the poorest and least productive inhabitants hardest. But it was followed by war with an expansionist Milan, and, in 1375, by an unpopular war, that of the EIGHT SAINTS, against the Avignonese agents of the Papacy, thought by the then dominant faction in government to be threatening Florence's trade routes across the Papal State to the Adriatic. War taxation of foodstuffs produced a new mood of desperation among the poor, especially among the in any case badly paid CIOMPI – the day-workers in the city's largest industry, the fabrication of wool. In 1378 they revolted, forcing the government, but only for a few frightened weeks, to extend representation to them.

Internally, this is a key date: from now until 1494 government took on an increasingly oligarchic tone, with rich mercantile families and magnates (using the loophole permitting them to hold office by joining a guild) cooperating to protect themselves from the plebs, the *popolo minuto*. Externally it is lost amid a series of new wars against Milan. In 1402 the city was saved at a moment of almost complete encirclement in VISCONTI conquests by the death of Duke Giangaleazzo. A few years later there were two Neapolitan thrusts to ward off. In 1425 Florence only broke a new threat from Visconti expansion by allying with Italy's new land power, Venice. Yet at the same time, by conquest or purchase, the city's control within Tuscany was expanding: Arezzo (1384), Montepulciano (1390), Cortona (1411), Pisa (1406), Livorno (1421). The momentum of this imperialism carried the republic, once peace had been made with Milan in 1428, into an attempt to conquer the stubbornly independent Lucca. It was expensive, it failed, and it drew odium on the oligarchical group responsible for it, especially on the faction-leader Rinaldo degli ALBIZZI. His response was to exile the leader of the chief opposition faction, Cosimo de' MEDICI, in 1433. But his support dwindled. In the next year he himself was exiled and Cosimo invited to return.

As after the crises of 1343 and 1378, there was in 1434 an impulse to close ranks, this time about a figure discreetly equipped with a loyal clientage and representing the values most Florentines with a regard for their lives and fortunes respected, whether old aristocracy or new rich. That Cosimo manipulated the constitution, was a 'father' in the Mafia sense long before he was posthumously voted the title 'Father of the Patria' in 1464, was accepted. It was done decorously. It had been done before. And it worked. Social rivalries had never been so calm, Florence's external relations never so stable – even when Cosimo linked Florence to the old enemy Milan, now ruled by Francesco Sforza, his client and friend. For his banker's wealth, even when somewhat perilously displayed in the largest palace that had yet been seen in Florence, was a crucial ingredient in his success in ensuring that in most matters his views prevailed. And they were, after all, largely the views of a class. It was therefore agreed by those who had supported or refrained from ostentatiously opposing him that, on his death, his son Piero should take over as helmsman of the still republican ship of state. He lacked his father's authoritative approachability. In 1466 there came a challenge from within the régime. But, as in 1434, the instinct for self-protection prevailed over ideology, and when Piero died in 1469 the succession passed without friction to his 20-year-old son Lorenzo.

But with the third generation of a single family's predominance in civic affairs a natural reaction was to come. It was expressed in its most violent aspect in the plot of the PAZZI to assassinate him in 1478, and in the war which followed, in which Florence's enemies, Pope Sixtus IV and King Ferrante of Naples, both claimed that they were attacking Lorenzo, not the city he illegitimately ruled. In the end it led, 2 years after Lorenzo's death, to the expulsion of his son Piero and to a widely representative form of government supported by Savonarola and designed, once and for all, to prevent the concentration of power in oligarchical, let alone individual, hands.

This 'democratization' of the constitution, however, which enfranchised some 3000 citizens, coincided with the opening stages of the WARS OF ITALY. Inevitably, the delays and indecisiveness that resulted when men without experience held office for short periods led many to yearn for less egalitarian but more effective leadership. A formal step in this direction was taken in 1502 when the gonfalonierate was made a life office, and Piero SODERINI was elected to this doge-like position. Informally, key positions came to be held (with the apathetic connivance of the newly enfranchised) by members of the old régime. In 1512, when Pope Julius II was determined to make Florence toe the line of his anti-French

The major monuments of **Florence** clearly discernible in a woodcut of *c.*1500.

policy (which Soderini resisted), there was sufficient pro-Medici feeling to bow to the pressure exerted by the Pope's Spanish army; Soderini fled and the Medici, chiefly represented by Lorenzo's son Cardinal Giovanni, were reinstated as, at first, no more than prominent citizens.

It was Giovanni's promotion to the Papacy in the following year, as LEO X, and the succession, after the pontificate of Adrian VI, of yet another Medici pope, CLEMENT VII, that helped habituate the Florentines to the idea of princely rule, though it was not until after a final veering away in the Last Republic of 1527–30 that this ceased to be exercised through deputies. With the rule of Alessandro de' Medici the city at last joined the ranks of those communes who had, centuries before, accepted signorial rule. Even the opportunity for change offered by the assassination of Alessandro in 1537 was not taken. With COSIMO I a long line of dukes (from 1569 grand dukes) ruled by unchallenged hereditary succession. Not the least tribute to this long-delayed conformity is the reluctance of scholars, until quite recently, to turn their attention to the history of Florence (and to that of an increasingly integrated Tuscany) in the 16c., instead of in the 14c. and 15c., the republican centuries. *See* CONSTITUTIONS. JRH

F. Schevill *History of Florence* (1936); J. R. Hale *Florence and the Medici* (1977); R. Caggese *Firenze dalla decadenza di Roma al Risorgimento d'Italia* (3 vols 1912–21); G. Brucker *Renaissance Florence* (1969); A. Tenenti *Firenze dal comune a Lorenzo il Magnifico* (1970)

Folengo, Teofilo (1491–1544) Benedictine monk, author of *Baldus*, a mock epic in macaronic Latin hexameters. Comic contamination of Latin grammar by vernacular forms and semantics was not new, but Folengo's was distinctive for witty merging of multiple sources in single phrases and for the variety of styles and effects employed. Commandeering elements from Erasmus, Pulci and Boiardo, and itself a source for Rabelais, *Baldus* is the burlesque, parodic, realistic, picaresque, satirical tale of a noble youth raised as a rustic among grotesque companions and led into fantastic adventures. Folengo augmented and polished his text from the first edition (1517) to the fourth, published posthumously (1552). LGC
G. Billanovich *Tra don Teofilo Folengo e Merlino Cocaio* (1948)

Fontana, Domenico (1543–1607) Architect and engineer, famous less for his standardized and derivative architectural style (e.g. Lateran Palace, 1586) than for his execution of Sixtus V's new plans for Rome (1585–90). Sixtus's vast network of new roads and fountains fed by a rebuilt ancient aqueduct was aimed at linking the major pilgrimage churches, repopulating the hills, and purging the antiquities of their pagan associations. Fontana's most celebrated achievement was the re-erection of the Vatican obelisk in St Peter's Square, recorded in his *Della trasportatione dell'obelisco Vaticano* (1590). CE
A. Muñoz, *Domenico Fontana, architetto* (1944)

Fontana, Giovanni (*c.*1393–*c.*1455) Engineer and natural philosopher. In 1418 he was studying medicine at Padua and thereafter (1420–32) was physician with the Venetian armies in Brescia. His *Bellicorum instrumentum liber* (*Book of war machines*) describes, in spite of its name, mainly hydraulic devices, including syphons and automata; the legends on the one surviving manuscript are in cipher, although the pictures are clear. His *Liber de omnibus rebus naturalibus quae continentur in mundo* (*Book on all natural things in the world*) was published pseudonymously in 1544; it is a typically medieval encyclopaedic work, except for its interest in geography and pride in contemporary knowledge. It refers to his own writings and those of contemporaries. He also wrote a treatise on perspective addressed to Jacopo BELLINI. MBH
Marshall Clagett 'The life and works of Giovanni Fontana' *Annali dell' Istituto e Museo di Storia della Scienza di Firenze* (1976)

Foppa, Vincenzo (*c.*1428–*c.*1515) played a key role in the early Lombard Renaissance: his earliest known work, a *Crucifixion* (1456; Bergamo, Accademia Carrara), already displayed a distinctive grey tonality and a coherent atmospheric perspective. Attracted to a monumental idiom, Foppa refined his vision in numerous fresco cycles, especially that for the Portinari Chapel of S. Eustorgio, Milan (*c.*1467–68). His long career is marked by a continuing monumental breadth, and experiments with both format and perspective. LP
F. Wittgens *Vincenzo Foppa* (1948)

Fornovo, battle of (6 July 1495) Here, 13 miles SW of Parma, Charles VIII's army, returning from Naples, was challenged by the much larger forces of the anti-French Holy League headed by Venice, with some Milanese troops in support. The battle, fought on the banks of the river Taro (after which it is sometimes named), was short and confused. Both sides claimed to be the victor, but the superior morale and coordination of the French was clearly demonstrated and, above all they were able to resume their march homeward. JRH

Fortebraccio, Braccio (1368–1424) Born into a powerful noble family of Perugia who lost their lands – and therefore their tenants – in one of the city's frequent inter-family feuds, Braccio began his military career as a freelance, and it was a long time before he had acquired sufficient capital, from prisoners' ransoms and loot, to receive the higher commands reserved for condottieri with a following of their own. Even when, from 1414, he was Captain General of the Church he put a feud of his own above his employer's interest, using the Pope's army in 1414 to conquer Perugia and thereafter to widen the boundaries of his personal rule, which came to extend throughout Umbria and into the Marche. He died of wounds after being defeated near Aquila (Abruzzi) by a Neapolitan force under his greatest rival as a soldier, Francesco Sforza, and an ex-colleague, Jacopo Caldora. Braccio's fame sprang from his tactics – the use of small units in constant (and constantly refreshed) support of one another – as well as from his personal bravery. Used by Caldora with a larger army, Braccio's tactics secured his own defeat. Bands of his followers, known and feared as the *Bracceschi*, played a prominent part in Italian wars for the next three generations. JRH

Fortification While there were regional differences, town walls and castles were constructed on similar defensive principles all over western Europe. The wall was high and thin, with a narrow walkway on top sheltered by crenellations. This defence, pierced to allow the defenders to see and fire at an approaching enemy, was frequently bracketed outwards as a machicolation, with gaps through which the defenders could drop missiles or incendiary materials downwards on troops who reached the foot of the wall. To take them in flank, towers projected forward at intervals with firing slits in their sides. These towers rose to a greater height than the walls could be made without weakening them; they thus served as lookout positions and to give an extra range of fire. The same dependence on high wall and tower was reflected in castle design, with many variations depending on the accommodation required, the open space allotted to shelter local inhabitants and their animals, and the desire to have fall-back defences of especial strength within the others. While vulnerable in the last resort to storming by siege ladders, to the blows of battering rams or to mining under the foundations, fortifications constructed on these principles only became inadequate with the use of effective gunpowder artillery in the first half of the 15c. and the use of gunpowder in mining at the end of the second.

It was in response to this new challenge that Italy produced a solution, the bastioned trace, that was to be worked out in the peninsula from the 1450s, adopted (again with regional variations) by the rest of Europe at home and overseas from the 1530s, and retained in its essentials until the 19c. To reduce the vulnerability of defences to the impact of cannon balls, walls were built with a slight inward slope from base to top and massively backed with earth, forming a rampart wide enough to permit the handling of guns on its top; crenellations were replaced by thick parapets pierced by gun embrasures. The towers were first cut down to wall level, then replaced by solid bastions projecting further from their neighbouring walls and forming platforms for heavy guns. From *c.*1510 preference was given to the pointed, rather than the rounded, form of bastion: the former did not leave an area of dead ground at its front – an area which could not be reached by flanking fire and was therefore a boon to mining parties; and it was easier to construct protected casemates for guns in its flanks. It was the need to provide enfilading or covering fire between every part of a fortification and its adjacent parts that decided the relationship between walls and bastions, a relationship that came to be determined with geometrical precision.

Fortification: Giuliano da Sangallo's Poggio Imperiale, 1487f.: an intermediate stage in the evolution of the angle-bastioned trace.

Between the forward-looking but still timid solution proposed at Brolio in Chianti (*c.*1484) and the mature angle-bastioned trace of the Florentine Fortezza da Basso (1534) there was a transitional phase during which nostalgia for the soaring and varied outline of pre-gunpowder fortifications was allied to the massiveness now required (Giuliano da Sangallo's Poggio Imperiale, 1487f.; Baccio Pontelli's Ostia, 1483–86). It was partly as a result of the realization that such buildings, in which the aesthetic impulse was as strong as the practical, were out of step with the findings of soldiers and gunners as to what actually worked in time of siege that fortification came (but not until the mid-16c.) to be left to the specialist military engineer. Even then, the tradition that had turned artists or 'art' architects to an interest in fortifications, from Giotto and Brunelleschi to Leonardo (designs for Piombino, 1503–04),

Bramante (*rocca* at Civitavecchia, 1508f.) and Michelangelo (supervisor of fortifications at Florence, 1529) remained in Buontalenti's work at Livorno and his design of the Belvedere Fortress in Florence (1590–95). Of the 33 books published in the 16c. dealing with fortification with any originality, only 6 were not by Italians. *See* TOWN PLANNING. JRH

J. R. Hale 'The early development of the bastion' in J. R. Hale, R. Highfield and B. Smalley ed. *Europe in the late Middle Ages* (1965); —*Renaissance fortification: art or engineering?* (1977)

Fortuna Chance, fate, ill-luck, adversity, accident, destiny: aspects of all these diversions or blockages of man's aspirations had been expressed in the ancient world through the whimsically powerful goddess *Fortuna*. Resurrected by humanistic interest in classical mythology, this personification of the forces that baffle human endeavours was used sometimes as a modish subterfuge to avoid invoking God's will to explain phenomena which seemed rationally inexplicable, whether it were a reverse in love or battle. She (for both the noun, fortune, and the personification, *Fortuna*, were feminine, echoing the opinion of men and the law alike that women were to be identified with irrationality) was invoked more commonly in a political context during Italy's inability to deal with the waves of foreign invasion after 1494.

It was because Machiavelli realized that any positive advice for dealing with political problems was likely to be countered by a pessimistic allusion to fortune that he devoted the penultimate chapter of *The prince* to this theme. Even he accepted that *Fortuna* was the arbiter of half of men's actions, but he stressed that this should not lead to defeatism. In two memorable images he likened fortune to a river whose floodwaters could be harmlessly diverted by precautionary dykes and ditches, and to a woman who, being a woman, could be subdued by ardour and violence. The increasing sensitiveness of the Counter-Reformation Church to the invocation of a pagan goddess in place of deference to the will of God led the Censorship to expunge references to *Fortuna* from a work as innocent of heretical intent as Castiglione's *The courtier*. *See* OCCASIO. JRH

M. Santoro *Fortuna, ragione e prudenza* ... (1967)

Title page of Sigismondo Fanti's *Triompho di* **fortuna**, published in 1526.

Foscari, Francesco (1373–1457) His career strikingly illustrates the control a Venetian doge could have over policy in spite of the constitutional and procedural devices for keeping him powerless. When in 1423 Doge Tommaso Mocenigo lay dying, Venice had already won the greater part of its terraferma empire, from the Veronese to Friuli. In a fervent speech Mocenigo pleaded that he should be succeeded by a man of peace. Of Foscari, one of the likely candidates, he warned 'if you make him doge, which God forbid, you will shortly be at war; and whoever has 10,000 ducats, will find himself with only 1000.' Though at 49 he was almost uniquely young to be considered, Foscari was elected.

War in 1425–28 gave Venice Bergamo and Brescia, but further wars resulted against the Visconti (1431–33 and 1435–41) which cost so much that the Republic's defences were neglected at a time of increasing Turkish expansion. When the Turks defeated a Hungarian army at Varna in 1444 Venice, having alienated the Italian states through the persistence of its aggressive policy in Italy, was disturbingly vulnerable throughout the whole length of its sea empire. This realization, plus the heavy cost of war taxation, at last slowed

Posthumous portrait of Francesco **Foscari** as doge of Venice, by Lazzaro Bastiani (Venice, Museo Correr).

the momentum of Foscari's militarism. His last years were harried by outspoken criticism and darkened by the repeatedly criminous actions of his son Jacopo (the chief theme in Byron's tragedy of 1820, *The two Foscari*). Such was the extent of his physical and mental decline that he was formally deposed. His death followed shortly after this unprecedented action. During the period of gloom that followed the loss of the terraferma 50 years later in 1509, the cause of the disaster was seen as the man who, neglecting the sage advice of Mocenigo, had forced his countrymen to exalt the land above the sea: Foscari. JRH

W. C. Hazlitt *The Venetian Republic* I (1915)

Foundlings We do not have figures for the percentage of babies abandoned by their parents, but we do know that some contemporaries thought abandonment was a serious problem, and tried to do something about it. Major cities like Florence and Venice had their homes or 'hospitals' for foundlings, like the Hospital of the Innocents founded in 1419 and designed by Brunelleschi, a civic institution to supplement its ecclesiastical predecessors. Notes left with the infants of the *Innocenti* tell us

Foundlings in swaddling clothes, from the façade of Brunelleschi's Innocenti Hospital, Florence.

something of the motives of the parents; 'fear of scandal' in the case of bastards, economic necessity in that of the rest. The mother who wrote that 'she had no bread to give her by reason of the war and the costs' probably spoke for the majority. PB

R. C. Trexler 'The foundlings of Florence, 1395–1455' *History of Childhood Quarterly* (1973–74)

Fracastoro, Girolamo (1478–1553), a physician of Verona, published in 1530 a Latin poem, *Syphilis sive morbus gallicus* (*Syphilis, or the French pox*), which gave a name to the new strain of venereal disease which, from its appearance in Naples in 1495, was called *mal francese* by Italians because of the presence there of French troops. Dedicated to Bembo and written in Latin hexameters that reveal a sensitive admiration for Virgil and Lucretius, the story of the shepherd Sifilo's punishment by Apollo and subsequent cure (a nymph prescribes mercury) sums up Fracastoro's remarkable combination of humanistic, literary and scientific interests. From his *Dialogue on poetry* to his writings on botany, geography, cosmology and medicine, the width of his interests, which included classical metaphysics as well as Christian theology (he was official doctor to the Council of Trent from 1545), makes him a most notable example of Renaissance intellectual omnivorousness. Yet he remains a neglected figure. JRH

E. Barbarani *Girolamo Fracastoro e le sue opere* (1897); *Sifilide* It. tr. F. Winspeare (1955)

Francesco di Giorgio Martini (1439–1502) Sienese painter, sculptor, architect and military engineer, whose buildings and manuscript treatises were formative for High Renaissance architecture. Francesco was trained in the artist Vecchietta's (1412–80) studio, but we may agree with Vasari that his paintings are 'not comparable to his sculptures', which demonstrate a Donatellesque mastery of movement and emotion in bronze low relief.

In 1477 Francesco succeeded Laurana as architect to Federico da Montefeltro, continuing construction at the Ducal Palace of Urbino and designing by his own account over 70 fortresses in the Marches, of which several splendid examples survive (e.g. S. Leo, Sassocorvaro). His treatises, begun in Urbino, show him to have been a pioneer in the theory of the triangular bastion, and his designs for machines were copied throughout the 16c. Francesco must be the architect of S. Bernardino at Urbino, which conforms with his written views on architecture and shares many characteristics with his documented church, S. Maria di Calcinaio at Cortona (1484f.). Both are Latin cross churches with centralized east ends, their vaults supported by massive exterior walls. Francesco believed in structural logic, expressed in the vertical and horizontal continuity of elements, and these ideas inform his studies of ancient buildings, where apparent inaccuracies can be partially interpreted as critical reconstructions.

After a stay at Alfonso's court at Naples (1491–97) Francesco spent his last years in Siena, with which he had always maintained professional links. The second versions of his treatises show that, although he owned a translation of VITRUVIUS, he never grasped the morphological differences between the classical orders, while his adoption of Vitruvian anthropomorphism goes to eccentric lengths. He took from Alberti his emphasis on TOWN PLANNING and his insistence on a variety of solutions but, unlike Alberti, he made prolific use of marginal diagrams. Peruzzi, Serlio, and even Palladio were influenced by his approach to design and illustration. *See* FORTIFICATION. CE

R. Papini *Francesco di Giorgio architetto* (3 vols 1946); H. Burns 'Progetti di Francesco di Giorgio per i conventi di S. Bernardino e S. Chiara di Urbino' *Studi Bramanteschi* (1974)

Francia, Francesco Raibolini, il (1450–1517) Bolognese goldsmith and painter whom Vasari called the 'rarest Master of his day' for medals. He was equally famous as a jeweller and for work in niello, but much of this work was destroyed when the Bentivoglio were defeated. He began to paint only in the 1490s and appears to have been largely self-taught, but he shows the influence of Cossa, Lorenzo Costa (with whom he painted on occasion) and Perugino. Julius II had him strike the medal commemorating the conquest of Bologna in 1506 and made him director of the mint there. Although it is frequently thought that he was a follower of Raphael, the two in fact never met. Vasari describes their relationship as that of correspondents put in touch by mutual friends, and claims Raphael sent his S. Cecilia altarpiece to Bologna in the care of Francia, who died shortly after its arrival. LDE

Francis I King of France 1515–47 (b.1494) was closely connected with both the politics and the culture of Italy. Brought up as heir presumptive to Louis XII, his education stressed modern languages (Italian and Spanish) and arms. Having succeeded in January, in August 1515 he was in Italy with an army whose victory at MARIGNANO left him in occupation of Milan and Genoa and (by a separate treaty with Pope Leo X) Parma and Piacenza. This was the highest point of French power in Italy; and in the following year, by the terms of the ecclesiastical concordat negotiated with Leo, Francis increased his control over the personnel of the church in France.

The election of Charles of Habsburg to the Empire in 1519 – to which Francis had aspired himself – weakened the French position in Italy. With the support of Charles and encouraged by the Milanese exile Morone, Leo raised an army in 1521 which retook Parma and Piacenza and, in the Milanese, left the French a toe-hold only in the castle of Milan itself; and this was yielded in 1523. In 1524 Francis sent an army which made some progress in recapturing territories in the Milanese. Joining it himself in October, he prepared the siege of PAVIA which continued throughout the winter. In February 1525, however, an Imperial relief army forced an engagement on the French and at the battle of Pavia Francis himself, fighting with great gallantry, was taken prisoner and then shipped off to Spain. To free himself, he signed in 1526 the Treaty of Madrid, leaving Charles a free hand in Italy. And though he later disclaimed this agreement, on the grounds that he had

A cast of the seal of **Francis I**, designed by Cellini (London, Public Record Office).

signed under duress, he was unable to muster sufficient support to re-establish France as an occupying power in Italy. In partial compensation, however, he conquered the quasi-Italian duchy of Savoy, together with much of Piedmont, in 1536.

The tentative cultural imports from Italy that had occurred in previous reigns became under Francis a deliberate policy which pronouncedly influenced, though never dominated, the native arts. He invited Leonardo to France in 1515 (he died there in 1519 – according to an attractive legend, in the King's arms). Other royal invitations brought Cellini, Serlio, Primaticcio and Rosso Fiorentino. Italian military engineers brought their new bastioned system. This Italianate flavour was given a social dimension through the marriage Francis arranged in 1531 between his son Henry (later king, 1547–59) and Caterina de' Medici, the great-granddaughter of Lorenzo the Magnificent, a match which brought to France a succession of Italians who acquired considerable influence in commerce and in military commands. (Another legend has it that the cooks in her train were responsible for making France the centre of gastronomic excellence, but travellers had long commented on the superior subtlety of the French cuisine).

How far Francis's generally repressive policy towards the Protestant minorities in France was responsible for the religious wars that so preoccupied his successors as to prevent further intervention in Italian affairs is uncertain. But his is the last French reign to which the student of Renaissance Italy is forced to give serious attention. JRH

C. Terasse *François 1er, le roi et le règne* (2 vols 1945–48)

Franco, Veronica (1546–91) Celebrated Venetian courtesan and poet; although married, she adopted her mother's trade by taste. 'Protected' by princes, polygraphs and painters, she was admitted to the circle of Domenico Venier, who, it has been said, helped polish her compositions (*Terze rime*, 1575). Encouraged by the Inquisition to amend a mode of existence notorious even abroad, she retired (1580) to found an asylum for those like herself but less fortunate. Her style is vigorous, candid and, while faultlessly decorous, realistic without falling into anti-Petrarchism. Frequently grouped with Vittoria Colonna and Gaspara Stampa, she is more narrative and satiric than they, less a poet. LGC

Le rime di Gaspara Stampa e Veronica Franco ed. A. Salza (1913)

Veronica **Franco**: an engraving based on an anonymous 16c. drawing (Venice, Museo Correr).

Fregoso family One of the more famous Genoese *popolano* families. In origin the Fregoso were merchants who first became active in civic life in the 13c. They gave to Genoa 13 doges, including the Domenico Fregoso whose deposition of Gabriele Adorno in 1370 initiated a bitter struggle between the Fregoso and Adorno families which was to dominate Genoese history for 2 centuries. After 1528, the Fregoso family disappeared into the Albergo (branch) de Fornari and the Albergo de Ferrari, until the family name was reassumed in 1576. JH

Fresco Save in Venice, where the atmosphere was too damp, fresco painting was the habitual way of decorating wall surfaces in Italy, both in churches and in private and public palaces. During the 16c. a liking for the more brilliant effect of large canvases painted in oils, and to a lesser extent for tapestries, diminished the use of frescoes save for covering upper walls, covings and ceilings. The technique of *buon fresco*, or true fresco, involved covering the area with a medium-fine plaster, the *intonaco*, just rough enough to provide a bond (sometimes enhanced by scoring) for the final layer of fine plaster. Either a freehand sketch of the whole composition (*sinopia*) was drawn on the wall, or a full-scale cartoon was prepared and its outlines transferred to the *intonaco* by pressing them through with a knife or by pouncing – blowing charcoal dust through prickholes in the paper. Then over the *intonaco* enough of the final thin layer was applied to contain a day's work. That portion of the design was repeated on it either by the same methods or freehand, and the artist set to work with water-based pigments while the plaster was still damp; this allowed them to sink in before becoming dry and fixed. (Thus 'pulls' or slices of frescoes could be taken by later art thieves without actually destroying the colour or drawing of the work.) It is usually possible to estimate the time taken to produce a fresco by examining the joins between the plastered areas representing a day's work. Final details, or effects impossible to obtain in true fresco pigments, could be added at the end in 'dry' paints, or *fresco secco*, a technique in which pigment was laid on an unabsorbent plaster; the best known example of an entire composition in *fresco secco* is Leonardo's *Last Supper*. JRH

U. Procacci *Sinopie e affreschi* (1961)

The *sinopia* on the first layer of plaster of Andrea del Castagno's **fresco** of *The Resurrection*, and the finished fresco, painted between 1445 and 1450 (Florence, Refectory of S. Apollonia).

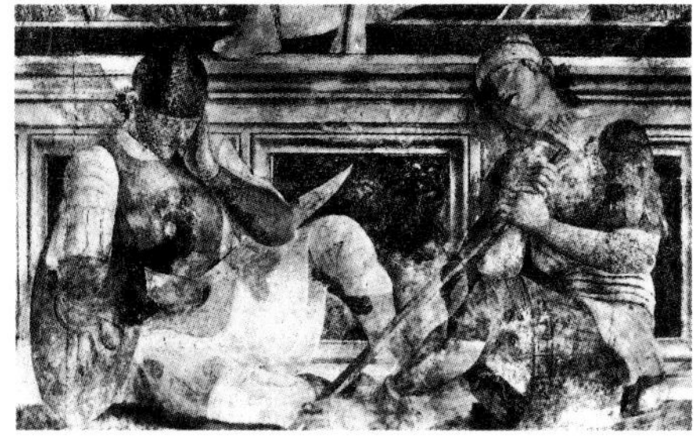

Frontinus, Julius (*c.*35–103) Roman consul and water commissioner; his writings reveal him as an able administrator who enjoyed understanding technical problems. He wrote on the art of war (now lost), surveying (only fragments survive), *Stratagema* (*Stratagems*) and *De aquis urbis Romae* (*The aqueducts of Rome*). The *Stratagems*, consisting of historical examples, is full of good and often familiar stories; it was much read by military practitioners, including Leonardo, and often printed after 1487. The *Aqueducts*, which survived in one manuscript discovered by Bracciolini in 1429, was equally widely read by hydraulic engineers and architects. It names the aqueducts, their sources, capacities, construction and maintenance, describes the uses of their waters and even the fraudulent practices of the watermen. MBH

Loeb Classical Library (1925; 1950; 1961)

Frottola A genre of secular song which flourished from about 1490 to 1530. It is an offshoot of the custom of improvised singing to stock verse forms common in the 15c. Patterns were invented so that such genres as sonnets, odes and *strambotti*, each of which have predictable syllable stresses in various lines, could be set to the same music. Similarly fixed rhythmic schemes encouraged the repetition of various musical phrases. Thus any sonnet could be sung to the same music, regardless of verbal content or mood. The poetry was not always elegant, although it tended to become so around 1520. The singer sang syllabically-set tunes of a narrow range, to accompanying parts which were sometimes more flowing. The use of movable type in music printing by Ottaviano dei Petrucci (d.1539) gave considerable encouragement to the genre, and the frottolas of several minor composers, notably Tromboncino, Cara and M. Pesenti, were given wide circulation. The frottola eventually gave way to the madrigal. DA

A. Einstein *The Italian madrigal* (1949); J. Haar ed. *Chanson and madrigal 1480–1530* (1964)

Gabrieli, Andrea (*c.*1520–86) A famous composer of the Venetian school. He appears to have been born in the Venetian *sestiere* of Cannaregio, where he became organist of S. Geremia in the 1550s. In the following decade he went to Munich to work in the Bavarian court chapel under Orlando di Lasso, returning to Venice to be appointed one of the organists of St Mark's in 1566. He remained there for the rest of his life. He soon became one of the most sought-after composers of madrigals, contributing to many anthologies, presumably because he acquired a singularly pleasant style, setting fashionable pastoral verse to music which was expressive of the words and yet easily performable. He was equally at home in the lighter forms such as the *villanella* and *mascherata*. But his most significant achievement lies in his grand music for St Mark's, in which he developed the use of several choirs in combination as well as exploiting the sonorities allowed by the use of instruments. He was also a notable teacher, his most famous pupil being his nephew Giovanni. DA

D. Arnold *Giovanni Gabrieli and the music of the Venetian High Renaissance* (1979)

Gabrieli, Giovanni (*c.*1555–1612) Nephew of Andrea Gabrieli and the greatest composer of the Venetian school. Like him he went to Munich for some years, becoming one of the court organists there *c.*1575, and returned to Venice in the 1580s. He was made temporary organist in St Mark's in 1584, being confirmed in the post from 1 January 1585: thus uncle and nephew were colleagues for over a year. He held this and a similar post at the Scuola Grande di S. Rocco until the end of his life.

He edited his uncle's larger-scale music for a posthumous publication called *Concerti* which came out in 1587. This included some works of his own which show that he was following the same path of using several choirs and an instrumental ensemble to gain grand effects suitable for ceremonial music. Even at this early stage he appears to have been a more introverted composer than his uncle, tending to set devotional rather than brilliant texts, and exploiting the lower sonorities rather than the more obvious effects of higher instruments. Although he was quite popular with the madrigal anthologists, his secular music also tends to be more serious than his uncle's, and by middle age he had given up composing madrigals. The retrospective collection of his own church music, the *Sacrae symphoniae*, also of 1587, contains much of his ceremonial music for St Mark's, showing increasing sophistication in the use of instruments: Giovanni was principally responsible for the development of the basilica's instrumental ensemble to the famous virtuoso group it became around 1600. As well as motets and a setting of the mass, the collection included a number of purely instrumental works which show considerable flair for creating original abstract forms, including the *Sonata pian e forte*, which is one of the earliest pieces to use expression marks.

In later years he suffered from a kidney stone. He seems to have composed less, though he became an even more famous teacher than his uncle. One of his pupils was Schütz, to whom he gave his signet ring on his death-bed. His surviving music from this period was all published posthumously and it is impossible to date accurately, but it is clear that he was interested in Monteverdi's developments in harmony, and some of his late motets put the new dissonance to expressive use, especially in setting penitential texts. He also wrote grand pieces in which solo voices are extensively employed and the structure becomes sectional, prefiguring the Baroque church cantata. His late instrumental music is some of the best of the period, not only refining the formal patterns but also developing specific instrumental idioms. He had little influence in Italy, but German composers throughout the 17c. knew and admired his music. DA

D. Arnold *Giovanni Gabrieli* (1974); — *Giovanni Gabrieli and the music of the Venetian High Renaissance* (1979)

Gaddi, Agnolo (active *c.*1370, d.1396) son of Taddeo, possibly designed some of the windows, and certainly painted the frescoes in the choir of S. Croce, Florence, which, with its 14c. altarpiece and hanging crucifix, provides an unrivalled opportunity to savour a virtually unaltered late medieval architectural and decorative complex. He is notable for the range and brilliance of his light-toned colour harmonies. JW

B. Cole *Agnolo Gaddi* (1977)

Gaddi, Taddeo (active *c.*1325, d.1366) was the first and most important of the painters who developed and modified the new artistic language of Giotto, with whom he probably worked for many years. His frescoes in the Baroncelli Chapel, S. Croce, Florence (1332–38) can be directly compared with Giotto's nearby Bardi and Peruzzi Chapels. JW

Gaffurio, Franchino (1451–1522) Musical theorist. Born near Lodi, he lived much of his earlier life in Mantua, Genoa and Naples, meeting Tinctoris and several other Netherlanders there. A codifier of current practice rather than a humanistic theorist, he was a great collector of Netherlandish music for the *cappella* of the cathedral at Milan, of which he was director for the last 38 years of his life. DA

Woodcut showing Franchino **Gaffurio** lecturing on music, from the title page of his *Practica musice*, 1512.

Galen (*c.*AD 130–*c.*200) Medical writer. Born in Pergamon, educated in Alexandria, he first served as physician to the gladiators at Pergamon, and then moved to Rome, where he was to establish an extensive medical practice and become physician to Marcus Aurelius. He wrote innumerable treatises on medical practice which were to become textbooks in medieval university medical schools. He is now remembered for his works on anatomy and physiology. His *On the use of the parts* was translated into Latin by Niccolò da Reggio in 1322 (published 1528). The *Natural faculties* was translated by Thomas Linacre and published in 1523. The *Anatomical procedures*, translated by Guinther of Andernach (teacher of Vesalius), was published in 1531. From about 1500 Galen's correlation of form and function and his emphasis upon the importance of a thorough knowledge of anatomy produced a 'new Galenism' which, although it could be stultifying, at its best fired a generation of medical men to pursue anatomical and physiological research in a quest for new knowledge. *See* MEDICINE. MBH

O. Temkin *Galenism: rise and decline of a medical philosophy* (1973)

Galilei, Galileo (1564–1642) Born into a slightly decayed Florentine patrician family, Galileo entered the university of Pisa in 1581 to study medicine. However, he became so attracted to mathematics (traditionally against his father's wishes) that in 1585 he returned to Florence to study mathematics, and taught it there and at Siena. He was much influenced in this by Guidobaldo del Monte and, through him, by Archimedes. Thanks to Guidobaldo's patronage he obtained the chairs of mathematics at Pisa in 1589 and at Padua in 1592. While at Pisa he wrote *De motu* (*On motion*), an anti-Aristotelian, Archimedean work of physics which does not yet show a complete understanding of the law of falling bodies which he was to discover only in 1604. If he had ever dropped weights from the Leaning Tower of Pisa (probably he did not), it would have been as a test of the theory he then held, that only bodies of the same material fall at the same speed, whatever their weight. At Padua he lectured on mathematics, astronomy and mechanics and gave private instruction in military engineering. He was not then much interested in astronomy, although he privately claimed to be a Copernican in 1597.

In the summer of 1609 his life and work were drastically altered by reports from Holland about a new optical instrument. From the description of its properties he was quickly able to put together an effective combination of lenses (a plano-convex objective with plano-concave eyepiece); with improvements it became the best telescope in existence. With it he saw those celestial phenomena which he described in *Sidereus nuncius* (*Starry messenger*; 1610): myriads of stars invisible to the naked eye; the planets differing from the stars in having disks; the configuration of the Moon (clearly like the Earth); the four satellites or moons of Jupiter. Arguing from analogy he emerged as a Copernican, a conviction soon strengthened when he detected the phases of Venus and the shape of Saturn (actually its rings). All this secured for him fame and the post of mathematician and philosopher to the Grand Duke of Tuscany in Florence. In 1611 he visited Rome, was elected to the Lincean Academy and convinced many Jesuit astronomers of the reality of his discoveries. After returning to Florence he involved himself in many controversies: on floating bodies, on sunspots, on the relation of scientific and theological proof, and (later) on comets. By 1615 many theologians publicly opposed Copernicanism which was, for the first time, officially condemned. When Galileo went again to Rome (with his newly invented microscope) he failed to convince the Pope and cardinals that Copernicanism was really consonant with Biblical authority, and in 1616 he was told to cease holding or teaching Copernican cosmology.

Only temporarily discouraged, Galileo returned to Rome in 1624, seeking permission from the new pope, Urban VIII, to discuss Copernicanism in print. The Pope agreed, provided that Galileo fairly set out the Ptolemaic point of view, reminding him that God was not constrained by human logic, so that human arguments from physical evidence (which Galileo thought he had) were fallible. In 1632 there appeared *Dialogo sopra i due massimi sistemi del mondo* (*Dialogue concerning the two chief world systems*), a convincing exposition of the Copernican system, with an account of

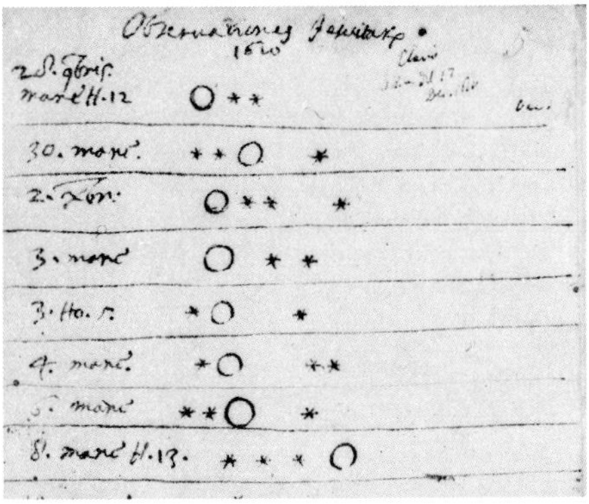

Galileo's observations on the movements of Jupiter and its satellites, made through a telescope in 1610 (Florence, Biblioteca Nazionale).

Galileo's discoveries about falling bodies. It is written in Italian (Latin tr. 1635) as a Platonic dialogue between Salviati (a Copernican), Sagredo (an educated amateur) and Simplicio (a diehard but intelligent Aristotelian). Galileo was a witty and effective writer and the *Dialogo* presents a realistic defeat for Simplicio by the new Galilean science, the arguments used being mathematical, logical and empirical in turn. Salviati abolishes the traditional world-view step by step until, when Copernicanism is clearly triumphant, Simplicio takes refuge in the Pope's argument, to which the others calmly assent. The book aroused an immediate storm in clerical circles: it clearly went against the spirit if not the letter of the Pope's concessions towards Copernicanism, and there was the interdiction of 1616. The result was a dramatic trial, after which the *Dialogo* was put on the Index. Galileo was made to abjure Copernicanism and was sentenced to life imprisonment – commuted to house arrest first in Siena, later (1634) in his villa at Arcetri, outside Florence. Here he completed his other great work, *Discorsi e dimostrazioni matematiche intorno a due nuove scienze* (known in English as *The two new sciences*; London 1638), the two new sciences being the strength of materials and the study of moving bodies, already partly discussed in the *Dialogo*.

Galileo's youth was passed in the atmosphere of late Renaissance Tuscany and Venice, but by his new discoveries in astronomy and physics (all made after the age of 40) he became one of the creators of 'the new philosophy' which is recognizably a part of modern science. Both his discoveries and his scientific method greatly influenced the development of the scientific revolution. Many of the problems then solved had first been posed by Galileo. His trial made him a hero of science in the struggle against authority. *See* SCIENCE. MBH

S. Drake *Galileo at work* (1978); *Dialogue concerning the two chief world systems* tr. S. Drake (2nd ed. 1967)

Galilei, Vincenzo (*c*.1520–91) Influential musical theorist of the later 16c. He spent most of his youth in Tuscany, learning to play the lute in Florence, then studied in Venice with Zarlino and went to Rome to learn about Greek music from Girolamo Mei. He also studied Turkish and Moorish music in Messina and Marseilles. He returned to Pisa to marry a daughter of a noble family, their eldest son becoming the famous scientist. In his treatise *Dialogo della musica antica et della moderna* (Florence 1581) and subsequent writings he diverges significantly from Zarlino's theories, advocating a monodic style in which the words would be enunciated clearly, a theory which had great influence on various Florentine amateurs who later took part in the creation of opera. DA

C. V. Palisca *Baroque music* (1968)

Galley By the 14c. the galley, a long, thin vessel of shallow draft and low-lying enough to be propelled efficiently by oars, was the characteristic warship of the Mediterranean. The type was also used, especially by Florence, Genoa and Venice, for merchantmen conveying 'luxury' goods as opposed to 'bulk' cargoes (wine, grain, sugar), which were carried in slower, and therefore more vulnerable, craft which relied – far more cheaply in terms of crew wages – on sail as their sole means of propulsion. Merchant galleys did ply between the Mediterranean and the English channel ports (mainly Southampton) and the North Sea (chiefly to Antwerp); a few even crossed the Atlantic. Naval galleys were experimented with by Henry VIII and were once brought by the French from Marseilles into the Channel. But essentially the galley was too vulnerable to oceanic weather conditions to be relied on, in spite of its advantages. These were: a means of propulsion when the wind dropped or was adverse; manoeuvrability when in combat or while entering or leaving port; the ease with

Galleys attending the ceremonial arrival of Henry III of France at Venice in 1574: an engraving dated 1592.

which they could be beached; bursts of speed (they could be rowed for stretches of up to 20 minutes at some 7 knots).

Whenever possible, galleys used sail. Thus they needed a complement of mariners as well as oarsmen, and their large crew and slight bulk meant that they had to take in food and water every 2 to 3 weeks – less if they were also carrying marines in wartime or when in pirate-infested waters. Thus there was a need for strings of fortified harbour bases, as for Spain on the North African coast or in Venice's sea empire. As they were slim, the recoil of heavy artillery could only be absorbed safely down the length of the vessel: so instead of broadside fire, galleys relied on guns firing fore and aft; this determined the tactics of naval battle in the Mediterranean throughout the period. While some oarsmen were 'slaves' in the sense of being captured from a hostile power, most were men serving sentences for crimes, though it was only in 1545 that Venice supplemented volunteers in this way. Though accompanied by stouter vessels capable of broadside fire from the mid-16c., Mediterranean war fleets, whether Turkish or Christian, remained light galley fleets. With the slackening traffic in luxury goods, however, and the difficulty of assembling crews of oarsmen, more merchantmen were built on the lines of the 'round' ships used in other waters. JRH

F. C. Lane *Navires et constructeurs à Venise pendant la Renaissance* (1965); M. E. Mallett *Florentine galleys in the fifteenth century* (1967); J. F. Guilmartin *Gunpowder and galleys* (1974);

J. R. Hale 'Men and weapons: the fighting potential of Venetian galleys' *War and Society* (1975)

Gambara, Veronica (1485–1550) Her husband's death (1518) left her two sons and Correggio to govern. Unusually well-educated, she became a poet and a patron of poets. Her slender work (37 sonnets, several other short pieces), faithful to Petrarch and Bembo, sings elegantly of homeland, husband, and *lacrimae rerum*; exhorts Emperors and generals; meditates on currently fashionable evangelical doctrines; celebrates the loves or nuptials of friends. Modern readers find in her letters the more lively reflection of the intelligence that left Correggians no cause to regret a woman's rule. LGC

Rime e lettere di V. Gambara ed. P. Mestica Chiapetti (1879)

Garigliano, battle of (29 December 1503) At a point on the river of the same name, 9 miles ENE of Gaeta, the Spanish commander Gonzalo de Cordoba defeated a French army that had arrived to reassert control over the kingdom of Naples. The exiled Piero de' Medici, son of Lorenzo the Magnificent, was drowned while serving with the French. JRH

Gattamelata, Erasmo da Narni, il (1370–1443) It is not clear how this distinguished condottiere, son of a baker and graduate of the military 'schools' of Braccio da Montone and Piccinino, got his nickname, which means 'honeyed cat'. By all accounts he was one of the sturdiest and least devious of the men who rose to supreme command. He came from Padua and, after service with Florence and the Papacy, first served Venice in a minor command in 1434. During the Republic's wars against the Visconti he acquired a high reputation for his coolness and resourcefulness, on one occasion having 5 galleys and 25 other vessels dragged overland from Mori on the Adige to Lake Garda in order to launch a surprise attack (which, in fact, failed) on the Milanese transports there. When he died he was Venice's captain general; the Republic gave him a state funeral and paid for the equestrian statue by Donatello which stands outside the church of the Santo in Padua. JRH

Tomb by Bartolomeo Bellano of the condottiere **Gattamelata** in S. Antonio, Padua.

G. Eroli *Erasmo Gattamelata da Narni* (1879)

Gaza, Theodore (1400–75), one of the leading Greek scholars active in Italy in the mid-15c., came to the West at the time of the Council of Florence (1538–39), and was employed as a teacher and translator in various places, notably Ferrara. He was one of the team of Greek translators attracted by Nicholas V to Rome, where he produced some new Latin versions of Aristotle. He was later patronized by Alfonso of Naples and befriended by Bessarion. He compiled a popular Greek grammar. GH

Gelli, Giambattista (1498–1563), a Florentine shoemaker, believed that the learning stored in Latin should be communicated in the vernacular. Of humble birth and self-taught, Gelli nevertheless had a strong foundation in philosophy. He wrote comedies, translated philosophical works, lectured on Dante and Petrarch and argued for contemporary Florentine as the preferred vernacular; he viewed it as a living language unbound by rules derived from the great 14c. authors.

Gelli is chiefly remembered for two vernacular dialogues, *I capricci del bottaio* (*The caprices of the cooper*; 1546) and *La Circe* (1549). The former treated satirically moral and religious issues in order to argue that wisdom does not guarantee virtue. Its failure to stress the importance of works for salvation, and its seemingly Lutheran emphasis on sin and Scripture, earned it ecclesiastical condemnation. *La Circe* discussed man's condition: a group of men turned into animals refused the opportunity to return to human form because they preferred the happy animal state to the troubles of man. Despite much moral and social criticism of contemporary Italy, Gelli in the end affirmed the Renaissance theme of the dignity of man. Man was superior to the animals because of his intellect and free will. PG

A. L. de Gaetano *Giambattista Gelli and the Florentine Academy: the rebellion against Latin* (1976)

Gemistus Pletho (George Gemistos Plethon) (1355–1452), the leading thinker of the last age of Byzantium, was probably a crucial influence on the Italian Renaissance. He spent most of his life at the intellectual centre at Mistra in the Peloponnese. There he evolved a surprising Platonic philosophy, expounded in *The laws*, and appears to have advocated a return to classical polytheism. He attended the Council of Florence 1438–39 in the train of the Emperor John VIII. There he seems to have made a profound impression on the native humanists: this may well have been the source of Cosimo de' Medici's passionate desire to promote translations of Plato and perhaps explains Italian knowledge of the *Geography* of STRABO. His *On the differences between the Platonic and Aristotelian philosophies* (1439) helped to stimulate that study of Plato's writings at Florence and Rome which produced Renaissance Platonism. GH

F. Masai *Pléthon et le platonisme de Mistra* (1956)

Genoa presents the paradox of a politically weak city-state with a resilient economy. Despite the gloomy picture painted by some historians, Genoa's economy recovered without too much difficulty from such blows as the loss of its overseas empire in the 14c., and the advances of the Ottomans and the discovery of the sea route to India in the 15c. By 1500 its population was about 85,000. In fact, in the 16c. Genoa emerged as one of the most important money markets in Europe and a centre of silk production. Much of this success can be attributed to the strength of the Casa di S. Giorgio, which functioned both as a state treasury and as a private bank.

The political life of Genoa, on the other hand, is a sorry and confused record. From the time of the exclusion of the nobility from government and the creation of the popular dogeship (1339), the story is one of unending civic strife between noble and non-noble, between *popolani* and artisans, and between contending families who, with their private prisons and miniature armies, more or less controlled the areas of the city where their clans were concentrated. Of all the doges, only 4 died while still in office, only 1 ruled for more than 8 years, and several were forced to resign on the day they were elected. The Genoese resorted to the device of surrendering power to foreign governments: Savoy, 1382–83 and 1390–92; France, 1396 and 1499; Monferrat, 1409; Milan, 1463.

Genoa played a full if largely involuntary part in the upheavals of the WARS OF ITALY. suffering in May 1522 all the horrors of a sack by Spanish troops. The city was retaken for the French by Cesare Fregoso (1527), but in 1528 Andrea DORIA, with Spanish support, finally drove them from Genoa. Doria established a new constitution, based on power-sharing among the commercial oligarchy of Genoa, who were grouped into 28 *alberghi*. With only minor adjustments the new régime, consisting of a senate, council and biennially-elected doge, lasted until 1797. Doria's success in ending the relentless Genoese power struggle is partially explained by the fact that he was backed by Spain, but it also owes something to a belated recognition by the Genoese themselves that their state was now so weak that it could not survive unless the old divisions were abandoned. The new stability may also be explained as a closing of ranks between the aristocrats and *popolani*, who realized that frequently the only true beneficiaries of their squabbles had been the poorer classes of the city.

Despite the success of Doria's new constitution, dependence on Spain proved expensive, and Genoa's public treasury was seriously depleted. Heavy taxation destroyed the wealth of several families and trade was

Genoa in the 15c.: a woodcut from a chronicle printed in Venice in 1486.

brought almost to a standstill by the operations of the French and Ottoman fleets. In consequence, despite the opposition of Spain, the Genoese tried (1557) to reopen negotiations with Constantinople but were thwarted by the French. They sent an ambassador with condolences to the French court on the death of Henry II, but were again rebuffed and consequently thrown back upon dependence on Spain. In addition, the mid-16c. brought renewed civic strife. Under Doria's reforms civic offices had been equally divided between the old and the new nobility, although there were far more of the latter. Fighting broke out between the two groups (1573), the artisans of Genoa supporting the new nobility, the hill-dwellers and farmers of the *contado* the old, and the latter were forced to leave the city. Peace was brought about by a combined papal-Spanish intervention (1576), when all distinctions between the nobility were abolished along with the *alberghi*, and each family reverted to its original name.

Before the time of Andrea Doria Genoa played little part in the cultural developments of the Renaissance. Although good humanists were to be found in Genoa, they had little impact on political life, and virtually none on the development of the visual arts. Genoa's trading links made her more open to artistic influences from Flanders and Lombardy than from Tuscany, and as late as the period 1515–30 the most successful artist in Genoa was a Fleming, Joos van Cleve. The only art form where Genoa seems to have been receptive to Tuscan ideas in the 15c. was sculpture and, although the practitioners of that art were normally Lombard in origin, their work was considered Genoese and enjoyed a considerable reputation in both France and Spain. The real turning point in the history of Genoa's contribution to the Renaissance came when Andrea Doria entrusted Perino del Vaga with the decoration of his new palace and villa, thus exposing the Genoese to all the triumphs of the Roman High Renaissance. Thereafter, for the rest of the 16c., supported by the high resale value of silver bought in Spain, Genoa became one of the major artistic centres of Italy, with the palaces of the Strada Nova designed by Galeazzo Alessi and his assistants in the 1550s as its chief monument. JH

C. Constantini *La repubblica di Genova nell'età moderna* (1978); J. Heers *Gênes au XVe siècle* (1961)

Detail of one of the small scenes below the main panel of **Gentile da Fabriano**'s altarpiece of the *Adoration of the Magi* (Florence, Uffizi).

Gentile da Fabriano (active *c.*1390, d.1427) First recorded in Venice in 1408, he erupted on to the Florentine scene in 1423 with his altarpiece of the *Adoration of the Magi* (Florence, Uffizi), arguably the greatest single masterpiece associated with the International Gothic style. It represents the mainstream of European, and not least of Italian, art, flowing on in a late medieval world, as yet largely undeflected by the achievements of the tiny group of Renaissance pioneers. Gorgeous in colour, teeming with detailed natural observation, gilded and embossed, it is a splendid decorative apparition to set beside the sober investigations of human form and spatial definition of Donatello and Masaccio. But it is more than a gay cavalcade of incomparable detail, for the small scenes below the main panel contain the first Italian observation of distinctive shadows cast at night by three separate light sources, of raking morning sunlight, and of morning mists rising into low clouds below the towers of a hilltop town. JW

E. Micheletti *L'opera completa di Gentile da Fabriano* (1976)

Gesualdo, Carlo Prince of Venosa (*c.*1560–1613) Composer of madrigals. His estates, inherited in 1585, were in the Campagna about 50 miles from Naples, where he also had a palace. He became notorious by ordering the murder of his first wife and her lover, taken *in flagrante delicto*. His arranged marriage with Leonora d'Este resulted in a prolonged stay in Ferrara, where he studied music with Luzzaschi, who deepened his studies of chromaticism. Already a considerable lutanist and composer, he now produced several books of extraordinary madrigals, using extremely unusual (though not particularly

Title page of a book of madrigals by **Gesualdo**, published in Ferrara in 1594.

dissonant) harmony, setting Mannerist verse in a vivid style which matched the poems in the greatest detail and brought out the erotic elements with great intensity. In his later years he suffered from a pathological condition of masochistic melancholia. He turned to church music, composing motets (surviving only in an incomplete form, one of them being completed, unstylistically, by Stravinsky) and music for Holy Week in a style not noticeably dissimilar from that of his madrigals. His music is the counterpart of the Mannerist painters, extravagant yet perfectly logical within the limits of its novel style. DA

C. Gray and P. Heseltine *Carlo Gesualdo, musician and murderer* (1926); G. Watkins *Gesualdo, the man and his music* (1973)

Ghiberti, Lorenzo (1378–1455), the most successful bronze sculptor of the early Renaissance in Florence, spent most of his career working on two successive pairs of bronze doors for the Bapistery, those now in the north and east portals. The commission for the earlier set was awarded after the celebrated competition of 1401 in which 7 sculptors submitted designs, and Ghiberti finally beat

Ghiberti, *The Baptism of Christ*, from the font in the Baptistery at Siena.

Brunelleschi only by a narrow margin. Their trial panels of the Sacrifice of Isaac (Florence, Bargello) epitomize their different interpretations and mark the beginning of Renaissance art. Ghiberti managed to amalgamate the swinging, linear patterns of Gothic drapery with figures and groups based closely on the Antique. The north doors (1403–24) occupied the first half of his career and assured his contemporary fame, leading to the commission for the yet more famous pair (1425–52), called by Michelangelo the 'gates of paradise'. They are the epitome of the Renaissance reinterpretation of antiquity – in this case subsuming the Old Testament – as a golden age. Ghiberti also created 3 great bronze statues for Orsanmichele, increasingly less gothic and more classical in character: *St John the Baptist* (1412), *St Matthew* (1419) and *St Stephen* (1426–28). He also produced some bronze casket shrines, statuettes and precious metalwork and wrote some commentaries on art. [167] CA

J. Pope-Hennessy *Italian gothic sculpture* (1970); R. Krautheimer *Lorenzo Ghiberti* (1956; 1971)

Ghirlandaio, Domenico (1449–94) worked with his brother Davide and was master of a large workshop which, in the late 1480s, included the young Michelangelo among its many apprentices. Michelangelo, through his pupil and ghost-writer Condivi, made a deliberate attempt, ably countered by Vasari, to

Detail from **Ghirlandaio**'s fresco of the *Confirmation of the Rule of St Francis* in S. Trinita, Florence.

play down his debt to Ghirlandaio. Nevertheless, it was almost certainly from him that Michelangelo learnt the cross-hatching which is characteristic of his early drawings and remained throughout his life the foundation of his handling of the claw chisel.

Ghirlandaio painted alongside Botticelli, Perugino, Signorelli and others in the Sistine Chapel (1481–82), but his chief source of patronage was the Florentine business and banking community surrounding the Medici, who themselves preferred the more adventurous and intellectually demanding work of Pollaiuolo, Verrocchio and Botticelli. In terms of light and colour and the calm coordination of pictorial space with its real architectural surroundings, his frescoed *Last Supper* (1480) in the Refectory of Ognissanti, Florence, represents the peak of his quiet, essentially non-dramatic art. His most famous works are, however, his frescoes in the family chapel in S. Trinita of Francesco Sassetti, a banker in the Medici circle, and those in the choir of S. Maria Novella for Giovanni Tornabuoni, who was related to the Medici by marriage. Sassetti's will reflects his open contempt for the friars of S. Maria Novella, who had removed the family arms from the high altar, whilst Tornabuoni's commission witnesses his own determination to control every aspect of the decorative scheme for which he was paying. In either case the religious themes are virtually submerged beneath a dazzling portrait gallery in which every member of the family concerned, together with a high proportion of the entire Medici circle, are shown. The position of the Medici as *primi inter pares*, their governmental style, the changing attitudes to religion, the values of the ruling oligarchy and its own view of itself, are caught and held as if in amber. Whether on panel or in fresco, Ghirlandaio had no rivals as a portraitist of individuals and of a social system at what was to prove a climactic moment in its history. [260] JW

J. Lauts *Domenico Ghirlandajo* (1943)

Giambologna (Giovanni Bologna) (1529–1608), a Fleming by birth, whose real name was Jean Boulogne, trained as a sculptor in Belgium before travelling to Italy in 1550 to complete his artistic education. After spending 2 years in Rome studying classical sculpture, and meeting Michelangelo there, he went to Florence and in 1561 entered the service of the Medici, becoming their court sculptor – and the most famous practitioner of his art in the whole of Europe – for almost half a century.

He worked in every medium, producing models in wax or clay for transformation into bronze statuettes or monumental marble

Giambologna's spiralling *Rape of a Sabine*, displayed in the Loggia dei Lanzi, Florence.

groups, in which he was assisted by a corps of skilled craftsmen and apprentices. Giambologna's style developed out of his appreciation of the technical brilliance of antique sculpture and the compositional genius of Michelangelo. A typical Mannerist artist however, he was not interested in the emotional depth of Michelangelo's work and confined himself to the production of virtuoso compositions. He forms a vital stylistic link between Michelangelo and Bernini (1598–1680). His growing technical prowess is apparent in the 3 main marble groups which span his career: *Samson and a Philistine* (*c*.1560–62; · London, Victoria and Albert Museum); *Florence Triumphant over Pisa* (*c*.1565; Florence, Bargello); and the *Rape of a Sabine* (1579–83; Florence, Loggia dei Lanzi). He carved many other single figures and complexes and produced a wide range of models for small bronzes, whose casting was delegated to Antonio Susini. Such statuettes served to disseminate his style throughout the courts of Europe, as too did his many pupils when they returned home after their training in Florence. [224] CA

C. Avery and A. Radcliffe *Giambologna, sculptor to the Medici* Arts Council of Great Britain exhibition catalogue (1978); C. Avery *Giambologna* Open University, A.352, Unit 15 (1979)

Giannotti, Donato (1492–1573) Educated as a lawyer, Giannotti served as a secretary in the chancery during the Last Florentine Republic (1527–39), was then banished by the returning Medici, and spent the rest of his life in exile. An ardent republican, he at once wrote a treatise defending a republican constitution for Florence. Among other political writings and plays (one of which, the Plautine comedy *Il vecchio amoroso*, is still just worth reading), his work in dialogue describing and, in the main, lauding the republican constitution of Venice is best remembered. The *Libro della repubblica de' Viniziani*, written 1526–7 and subsequently revised, was published in 1540. Reprinted 5 times before 1600 and translated into German, the book was only one step behind Contarini's in nourishing the MYTH OF VENICE. JRH

R. Ridolfi 'Sommario della vita di Donato Giannotti' *Opuscoli* (1942)

Giberti, Gian Matteo (1495–1543) Curialist and diocesan reformer. He was born in Genoa, his illegitimate birth perhaps explaining why he was never made a cardinal. As datary to Clement VII he was effectively master of the papal Curia, and furthermore was the major anti-Imperial influence on Clement VII's diplomacy. After the SACK OF ROME in 1527 he moved to his diocese in Verona, where he undertook a thoroughgoing pastoral reform with the main aims of raising the standard of the clergy and making them more responsive to episcopal direction. What distinguished his reform and accounts for its success was his care in obtaining the full support of the Papacy and in placating the Venetian government, faced as he was by recalcitrant clergy. After his death Borromeo, the reforming archbishop of Milan, showed great interest in his methods. OL

A. Prosperi *Tra evangelismo e Controriforma: G. M. Giberti (1495–1543)* (1969)

Giocondo, Fra (Giovanni da Verona) (1433–1515) was a scholarly student of architecture whose designs had a wide influence on what others actually built. Little is known of his life (even the name of the order of friars to which he belonged is in doubt) before he was employed as architectural consultant in the kingdom of Naples, 1489–93. Here he designed both gardens and fortifications. This versatility, backed up by his large repertory of drawings of details of the classical ruins of Rome, and rendered all the more attractive to patrons by his competence as a humanist (culminating in 1511 with his edition of VITRUVIUS), led to his being called to France in *c*.1495. Here his repertory was extended to the planning of an irrigation system for the gardens at Blois and the design of the bridge of Notre-Dame in Paris.

From 1506 he worked for Venice, first on hydraulic projects connected with the river Brenta, then in 1509–11 on new fortified circuits for Padua, Treviso, Legnano and Cremona (at the first 2 his innovatory large, low round bastions can still be seen), and on a project for a new Rialto Bridge, after damage by fire in 1512. Nothing came of this, but in 1514 he was called to Rome to assist Raphael in the design of the new St Peter's – a tribute to the union of technical knowledge and classicizing taste in a man whose influence on architectural thinking (even including town planning) can, alas, be more readily sensed than seen. JRH

G. Fiocco 'Giovanni Giocondo Veronese' *Atti e Memorie dell'Accademia d'Agricoltura ... di Verona* (1916)

Giolito, house of The Giolito press of Venice was the most important vernacular press in Italy. Giovanni Giolito founded it in 1536, but his son Gabriele (d.1578), who began publishing alone in 1541, really built the firm that published about 1050 editions up to 1599, by which date it had practically ceased operations. He was a man of acumen and vision who played a role in the dissemination of vernacular literature comparable to that of ALDUS in the dissemination of the classics. Possessed of excellent literary judgment and adequate financial resources, he led public taste by financing works of lesser-known authors until their popularity rewarded him with demand for reprints.

From 1541 to 1560 he published all manner of vernacular literature: dialogues, plays, collections of letters, *novelle*, history, poetry and devotional matter, by such authors as Aretino, Ariosto, Castiglione, Lodovico Dolce, Doni and Tullia d'Aragona. He commissioned a series of popular vernacular histories based on the ancients. On the other hand, he practically ignored Dante, and refused works of law, philosophy, science, mathematics, and Latin titles generally. Secular vernacular literature dominated his list until 1560. He then took advantage of the religious revival of the Counter-Reformation, and the prohibition of such authors as Aretino and Machiavelli, by publishing a great quantity of popular vernacular religious literature, works of piety and devotion by such authors as the Spaniard Luis de Granada and Cornelio Musso. He never published theological works. As he grew older, the press became less active. After his death his heirs continued, but they lacked the energy to revitalize the firm, although it published the first edition of Botero's *Ragion di stato* (1589). Clear italic type, attractive layout and judicious use of illustrations distinguished Giolito books, published under the sign of the phoenix rising from the fire. PG

S. Bongi *Annali di Gabriel Giolito de' Ferrari da Trino di Monferrato, stampatore in Venezia* (2 vols 1890–97; repr. n.d.)

RIME DELLA
SIGNORA TVLLIA
DI ARAGONA; ET
DI DIVERSI
A LEI.

CON PRIVILEGIO.

IN VINEGIA APPRESSO GABRIEL
GIOLITO DE FERRARI.
MDXLVII.

Title page of the *Rime* of Tullia d'Aragona, published in 1547 by the house of **Giolito**, displaying the phoenix *impresa*.

Giorgione (?1478–1510) Giorgio da Castelfranco (in the Veneto), who 'from his stature and the greatness of his mind was afterwards known as Giorgione [great George]' (Vasari). Giorgione's achievement in transforming the character of Venetian painting has always seemed the more remarkable in a life, terminated by the plague of 1510, that was even shorter than Raphael's. Our knowledge of his career is confined to a few contemporary references, from the years 1506–10, and only a handful of paintings are undisputedly attributed to him, including the Castelfranco altarpiece (in the church of S. Liberale in the town of his birth), the portrait of *Laura* and *The Three Philosophers* (Vienna), and the *Tempesta* (Venice, Accademia).

Probably trained in the workshop of Giovanni Bellini, at the same time as Lotto and Palma Vecchio, Giorgione began his career, according to Vasari, as a specialist of small devotional Madonnas. The Castelfranco altarpiece shows him to have been equally alive to central Italian art (Costa and Perugino), while the more experimental outlook of Leonardo, who visited Venice in 1500, is mentioned by Vasari as a major influence. In such later works as the *Tempesta*, landscape itself is the main subject of the painting, and the technical potentialities of oil paint are used to suggest an atmospheric unification, with light and shade falling softly across the figures and their setting. The *Laura* of 1506 (her name identifiable from the laurel branch behind the sitter) is comparable in technique and colouring, and shows the new idealism of the early

Giorgione, portrait of *Laura* (Vienna, Kunsthistorisches Museum).

16c. in the formulation of the composition and in the psychological remoteness of the image. Giorgione worked for private collectors, then beginning to emerge as a new class of patron, as well as for the Church, and he was also employed by the state in 1507–08 on a large canvas (since lost without trace) for the presence chamber of the Council of Ten. At the same time, together with Titian, he decorated with frescoes the façade of the Fondaco de' Tedeschi, near the Rialto (finished in November 1508): damaged fragments of the decorations, which were engraved in the 18c., survive in the Accademia, Venice.

The extraordinary confusion that has always beset the attribution of a group of major works related to Giorgione's later style is itself an indication of his pivotal position in Venetian art and his importance in the formation of Titian and Sebastiano del Piombo. The *Concert Champêtre* (Paris, Louvre) is now usually attributed to Titian, and *The Judgment of Solomon* (Bankes Collection) to Sebastiano del Piombo, while the *Sleeping Venus* (Dresden) is known from a near-contemporary source to have been left partly unfinished, and completed by Titian, who later adapted the figure for his own *Venus of Urbino* (Florence, Uffizi) of 1538. AB

T. Pignatti *Giorgione* (1969); J. Wilde *Venetian art from Bellini to Titian* (1974)

Giotto di Bondone (b.1267 or 1277, d. 1337) was already recognized by Dante as the leading artist of his day. His significance to the Renaissance can be gauged from the fact that not only the leaders in the early 15c. transformation of the arts, such as Masaccio, but the key figures of the High Renaissance, such as Raphael and Michelangelo – one of whose early studies of Giotto's frescoes in the Peruzzi Chapel, S. Croce, has survived – were still learning from him and partly founding their style on his example. The reasons for this are twofold. Firstly, his art is notable for its clear, grave, simple solutions to the basic problems of the representation of space and of the volume, structure, and solidity of 3-dimensional forms, and above all of the human figure. Secondly, he was a genius at getting to the heart of whatever episode from sacred history he was representing, at cutting it down to its essential, dramatic core, and at finding the compositional means to express its innermost spiritual meaning and its psychological effects in terms of simple areas of paint. His solutions to many of the problems of dramatic narrative were fundamental. They have subsequently been elaborated on in many ways, but they have never been surpassed.

Part of the secret of Giotto's success in the representation of the fundamentals of human form and human spiritual and psychological reaction to events was his close attention to, and deep understanding of, the achievements of the sculptors Nicola Pisano, Arnolfo di Cambio and, above all, Giovanni Pisano, who were tackling the same basic representational problems in a naturally 3-dimensional medium. The essential unity of the arts in Giotto's day is even more dramatically illustrated by the fact that in the last years of his life he was assigned the major architectural commission in Florence, namely the building of the campanile of the cathedral (1344). The fact that it would almost certainly have fallen down if his successor, Andrea Pisano, had not immediately doubled the thickness of the walls is, in its way, no less informative of the nature of late medieval attitudes and of the triumphs and disasters that attended them.

There can be no doubt whatsoever about Giotto's artistic stature and historical importance. Indeed, he so dominated the Florentine Trecento through his collaborators and followers, from Taddeo Gaddi onwards, that there was until relatively recently a thoroughly misleading tendency to lump together almost every artist in sight under the somewhat derogatory title of 'Giotteschi'. On the other hand, almost everything else about Giotto's career is problematic. His cut down mosaic of the *Navicella* (?*c*.1300) in Rome, which was for his contemporaries by far his most important work, is now a ghostly echo of its former self. His 3 signed altarpieces, the *Stigmatization of St Francis* (Paris, Louvre), the Baroncelli Altarpiece (Florence, S. Croce) and the polyptych of the *Madonna and Saints* (Bologna, Pinacoteca Nazionale), seem to be very largely shop work protected by his signature. The frescoes in the Arena Chapel, Padua (*c*.1304–13), the masterpiece on which the whole modern concept of his style is based, are unsigned and undocumented, as are those in the Bardi and Peruzzi Chapels in S. Croce, which are generally accepted as the only reasonable foundation for an idea of his stylistic evolution during his maturity.

All this, however, is as nothing to the endless controversy which surrounds his date of birth and the attribution to him of the frescoes of the *Life of St Francis*, painted, probably in the mid-1290s, on the lower walls of the Upper Church of S. Francesco at Assisi. For virtually all Italian scholars they constitute the early work of Giotto. For the majority of non-Italian specialists on the subject they do not, and a daunting proportion of the almost 2000 major items in the ever more rapidly accumulating Giotto bibliography is largely devoted to fanning the flames. Fortunately, perhaps, for the sanity of the earnest and discriminating inquirer only a handful of these outpourings can be said to clarify the issue in any substantial way. What should at least be obvious by now is that the frescoes at Assisi are, in detail and as an entire, coherent, carefully planned scheme, like the Arena Chapel frescoes, amongst the seminal achievements in the history of Italian late medieval painting. They stand at the dawning of a new age and their appeal as works of art is not one whit diminished if, as may well be the case, they are not in fact by Giotto. JW

The Naming of John the Baptist from the fresco cycle by **Giotto** in the Peruzzi Chapel in S. Croce, Florence.

A. Martindale *The complete paintings of Giotto* (1969); G. Gnudi *Giotto* (1959); A. Smart *The Assisi problem and the art of Giotto* (1971); R. Salvini *Giotto bibliografia* (2 vols 1938; 1973)

Giovanna I of Anjou Queen of Naples 1343–82 (b.1327) On her accession to the throne of Naples at the age of 16, royal authority swiftly fell apart. Rumour asserted that she took lovers among leaders of the court factions. Her husband, Andrew, was murdered in obscure circumstances (1345), and his brother, King Louis I of Hungary, seized the opportunity to attempt the conquest of the kingdom. Giovanna survived this assault (1347–52) and, under the guidance of her Florentine grand seneschal, Niccolò Acciaiuoli (1352–65), recovered some measure of control. With the Great Schism, however, her support of the anti-Pope Clement VII gave a pretext for Charles, Duke of Durazzo, to usurp the kingdom. Giovanna was imprisoned and her death announced shortly after (1382). JL

E. G. Léonard *Histoire de Jeanne Ire* (1932–37)

Giovanni di Paolo (active *c*.1425, d. 1483) is chiefly notable for carrying the brilliantly colourful vision of Sienese 14c. paintings on into the Renaissance. His landscapes and his figures still reverberate with echoes of Duccio's work. His art most beautifully reflects the 15c. artistic conservatism of a commercially declining city. [75] JW

J. Pope-Hennessy *Giovanni di Paolo* (1937)

The ermine of King Ferrante of Naples from **Giovio**'s *Dialogo dell' Imprese*.

Giovio, Paolo (1483–1552) Starting life as a doctor in his birthplace, Como, Giovio then served successive popes from *c.*1513 to 1551, when he moved to Florence. By then, though he had become a bishop (of Nocera), he had been present at a remarkable number of those battles or key diplomatic congresses in which the Papacy had an interest, and had become a passionate chronicler of military and political events and their protagonists. As a biographer he was stimulated by the portraits he accumulated for his palace in Como. In accord with the idea behind his own collections of lives of warriors and men of letters, he urged VASARI towards recording the lives of artists.

He is best known, however, as a somewhat facile but well-informed historian, first for his *Commentari delle cose de' Turchi* (*Commentary on Turkish affairs*; 1531) and then for his history of his own time (1550–52). Far from limiting itself to Italy, this was a pioneer attempt to write a universal chronicle in the modern manner. It covered the period 1494–1547 with a detail that still renders it useful – along with the best of his *Lives* (e.g. those of Leo X, Gonzalo de CORDOBA and Ferdinando d'Avalos, Marquis of PESCARA). Indeed, the fact that he was a professional courtier and catered to court interests, for instance with books on chivalric devices, has caused his historical writings to be undervalued. His audience at the time was very large, thanks to the almost instantaneous translation (by others) of his Latin works into the vernacular, and vice versa: a pioneer example of satisfying the market for works in both languages. There is still no satisfactory study of his life and work. JRH

Giraldi, Giambattista Cinzio (1504–73) Born in Ferrara, where he taught rhetoric from 1541 to 1562, he is notable for a collection of *novelle* entitled *Ecatommiti* (*The hundred stories*, among which are those of Shakespeare's *Othello* and *Measure for measure*), a number of tragedies (the most celebrated of which is the gruesome and horrific *Orbecche* of 1541) and a theory of TRAGEDY which, basing itself on Aristotle, relates the power of focusing attention on calamity to man's capacity for compassion. To Giraldi falls the distinction of being the first Renaissance tragedian to stage atrocities in full view of the audience. In Elizabethan England he was often known as 'Cynthio', from the name Cinzio (or Cinthio) by which he refers to himself in his poetry. JM

Tragedie (1581–83); *Ecatommiti* (1879); P. R. Horne *The tragedies of G. B. Giraldi* (1962)

Giulio Romano (1492–1546) Giulio Pippi, Raphael's chief assistant from 1515 to his death in 1520, formed his pictorial style whilst working with the master in the Stanza dell'Incendio in the Vatican. Like Michelangelo, who also influenced him profoundly, he is no less important as an architect, and the two professions are spectacularly united in the Palazzo del Tè, which he built and decorated for the Gonzaga in Mantua (1527–34).

The architecture, at once intensely witty and intensely serious, is based on a profound knowledge of antique precedent and High Renaissance practice. It questions all the basic assumptions of architecture in a manner comparable to, but even more extreme than, the design of Michelangelo's Biblioteca Laurenziana in Florence. Double functions and ambiguity in the disposition of supports accompany the use of members built as if already in a state of collapse. Everywhere, mass and solemnity in one aspect are counterbalanced by light-heartedness and grace in another, and the same is true of the pictorial decoration. In rooms of boldly varied plan, the reality of the wall and of the actual architectural container, the meaning and reality of pictorial space and its relation to the spectator, are constantly called in question. Realistically painted horses stand indoors, high up on painted ledges. Decorations *all' antica*, of Pompeian grace and gravity, follow painted rocks and painted giants falling in on the spectator. The demands made on the know-

Tumbling giants and rocks in **Giulio Romano**'s Sala dei Giganti (Mantua, Palazzo del Tè).

ledge and understanding of the onlooker are unprecedented in the history of European art, and only subsequently matched in the 20c. by artists such as Picasso. [183] JW

F. Hartt *Giulio Romano* (1958)

Giunti, house of With the presses of Aldus and Giolito, Giunti made up the trio of the largest and most influential Italian publishers of the Renaissance. The Giunti were a Florentine merchant family, but Luca-Antonio (1457–1538) moved to Venice in 1477 and founded the Venetian branch, the largest of the 3 Giunti publishing firms, with the printing of a vernacular version of the *Imitation of Christ* by Thomas à Kempis on 26 November 1489. Fifty-two other incunables followed. In 1493 he published his first liturgical work; by 1500 breviaries, missals and other liturgical works comprised the major part of his list. In the 16c. the Venetian Giunti press was the most active publisher and exporter of liturgical works in Catholic Europe. Luca-Antonio Giunti the Younger (1542–1602) later headed the house and became very wealthy, although his income came from many other commercial enterprises in addition to publishing. By 1600 the Venetian Giunti press had published about 1050 editions; it added another 400 before the firm came to an end in 1657.

Filippo (1450–1517) founded the Florentine house in 1497. The Florentine Giunti published a greater variety of titles in Latin, Italian and Greek than the Venetian branch. In a limited way it competed with the Aldine press. By 1600 it had published less than half as many editions as the Venetian branch. It was still a large firm: its expansion may have been hampered by Cosimo I de' Medici, who suspected the Giunti of harbouring republican sympathies. Less is known about the smaller Lyons branch of the firm, founded by Giacomo, nephew of Luca-Antonio, in 1520. The Giunti presses were not adventurous, but they seem to have been profitable. The Giunti emblem, based on the Florentine lily, adorned innumerable Latin liturgical texts and school books. At the same time, the Giunti stood out for their lack of scruple, even in a business known for sharp practice. The Lyons branch, with the connivance of Luca-Antonio, printed counterfeits of the Aldine classics. Luca-Antonio the Younger harassed rival printers and engaged in political intrigue to safeguard his near-monopoly of liturgical works. When that failed, he put new title pages on older, banned liturgical works in order to pass them off as new. PG

P. Camerini *Annali dei Giunti: Venezia* (2 vols 1962–63); D. Decia, R. Delfiol and L. S. Camerini *I Giunti tipografia di Firenze: Annali 1497–1625* (2 vols 1978)

Giustiniani, Bernardo (1408–89) Venetian statesman, humanist and historian. Born of a patrician family, he had a career mainly in diplomacy. His major work is *De origine urbis Venetiarum rebusque eius ab ipsa ad quadringentesimum usque annum gestis historia* (*History of the origin of Venice*; 1493). This follows classical models of the 'histories of peoples' and it expounds the mythology of the Venetians as lovers of liberty whose state, fortified by *virtù*, replaced the decayed Roman Empire, which had lost it. OL

P. H. Labalme *Bernardo Giustiniani: a Venetian of the Quattrocento* (1969)

Giustiniani, Paolo (1476–1528), born Tommaso, was an ascetic-mystical writer and Camaldolese reformer. A Venetian noble, humanistically educated, in 1505 he spurned profane studies for sacred ones and after a dramatic personal conversion entered the order of the Camaldolese Hermits in 1511. He and his fellow Venetian Pietro Querini established a distinct strict eremetical body within the order, which became the Monte Corona Congregation. In 1513, on the occasion of the Fifth Lateran Council, Giustiniani and Querini presented the *Libellus ad Leonem X* (*A tract for Leo X*), containing wide-ranging proposals for

church reform, including a programme for the education of intending clergy in sacred studies. Giustiniani's religious writings, still only partly published, are in the great contemplative tradition: *amor Dei* is the dominant motif. OL
Libellus J. Mittarelli and M. Costadoni eds *Annales Camaldulenses* IX (1773); J. Leclercq *Un humaniste ermite, le bienheureux P. Giustiniani* (1951)

Glory To have the distinction of one's deeds recognized in life and to be revered for them posthumously: this was glory. The nature of true *gloria* was much discussed, whether it must be connected with the public good, whether the actions that led to it must conform with Christian ethics, how it differed from notoriety. The concept did not exclude religious figures (the title of the church of the Frari in Venice was S. Maria Gloriosa), but it was overwhelmingly seen in terms of secular success and subsequent recognition, as determining the lifestyles of the potent and the form of their commemoration in literature, in portraits and on tombs. As such, it has been taken as a denial of medieval religiosity ('*sic transit gloria mundi*'), and thus a hallmark of Renaissance individualism; as a formidable influence on cultural patronage; and as spurring on men of action, as well as writers and artists, to surpass their rivals – including their counterparts in antiquity. JRH

Gonzaga family Landowners who ruled Mantua from 1328 (Luigi I elected capitano), raised by Imperial concession to the titles of marquis (1433) and duke (1530); the duchy of Monferrato was added by marriage arrangements (1531). They assumed a military role as condottieri and were notable patrons of learning and the arts; their stable régime extended into the Church (a succession of Gonzaga cardinals began with Francesco, 1461–83), and cadet branches ruled minor principalities (Bozzolo, Guastalla, Sabbioneta) in the 16c. Genetically unhealthy, the direct line ended with Vincenzo II (d.1627). DC
A. Sestan 'La storia dei Gonzaga nel Rinascimento' *Mantova e i Gonzaga* (1977) S. Brinton *The Gonzaga - Lords of Mantua* (1927)

Gonzaga, Federico II Marquis of Mantua 1519–40 (b.1500) Like his father a prominent military commander, and like his mother Isabella d'Este a compulsive patron of artists, impelled by illusions of dynastic grandeur. He

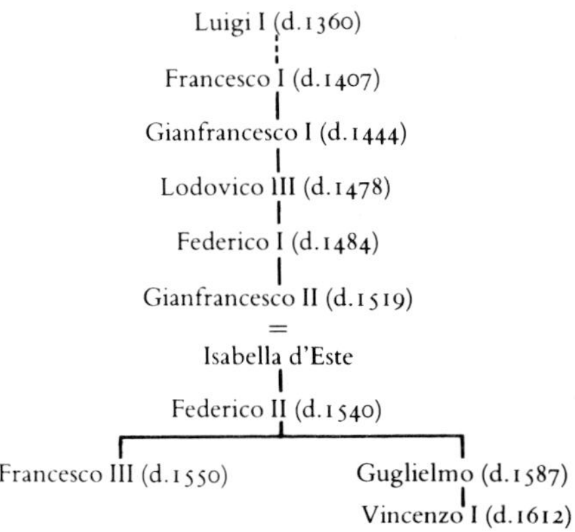

was godson to Cesare Borgia, and his childhood experiences included being a hostage at Pope Julius II's court for his father's loyalty (1510–13): here the indulgence of pope and cardinals replaced that of Isabella. A (lost) portrait of him in armour was painted by Raphael. He resisted Isabella's schemes for his marriage into the Palaeologo dynasty, and for years (to her disapproval) was associated with one Isabella Boschetti; in 1531, however, he married Maria Palaeologo and gained the succession to the duchy of Monferrato. From 1524 Giulio Romano worked for him, and the Palazzo del Tè grew from extensive stables into what may have been an amorous retreat for Boschetti, and eventually into a palatial hostel for distinguished visitors (Charles V stayed there in 1530 and 1532). Federico was appointed Captain of the Church (1521) and led Imperial troops in the siege of Pavia and the defence of Parma against Lautrec (1521–22); subsequently divided in his loyalties when Clement VII promoted the League of Cognac (1526), he remained nominally papal captain but allowed the Imperialist commander Frundsberg to pass the Po. His prudence was rewarded by appointment as captain of Imperial troops in Italy (September 1529) and the title of duke (1530). DC
J. Cartwright *Isabella d'Este* (1915); L. Mazzoldi *Mantova: la storia* II (1961); F. Hartt *Giulio Romano* (1958)

Gonzaga, Francesco I Signore of Mantua 1388–1407 (b.1366) successfully resisted the aggressions of Giangaleazzo Visconti (which included a plan to divert the city's natural defence, the river Mincio). Castello San Giorgio, Mantua, remains a monument of his defence buildings, and he built the church of S. Maria delle Grazie as a thanksgiving for relief from plague (1399). As Venetian captain-general, Francesco took possession of Verona and Padua (1405). His remarkable book collection included many French manuscripts. DC

G. Coniglio ed. *Mantova: la storia* I (1958)

Gonzaga, Gianfrancesco II Marquis of Mantua 1484–1519 (b.1466) was primarily a military captain. His finest hour was the battle of FORNOVO (July 1495), when he led the semi-victorious armies of the Italian League against Charles VIII. For long Venice's commander (1489–98), he had a less distinguished career subsequently: having entered Louis XII's service, he resigned just before the French defeat at the river GARIGLIANO (1503); he was dismissed by the Florentines (1505); he was Julius II's commander in his unopposed expedition against Bologna (1506), but in 1509, rather than benefiting from the victory of the League of CAMBRAI, was captured and imprisoned for a year by the Venetians. All the same, given the shortage of captains of princely rank and following, Venice seriously considered re-employing him. Short in stature and lacking the cultural avidity of his wife Isabella d'Este, who governed during his prolonged absences, he was overshadowed by her; this meant that his foreign policy was sometimes compromised by her Ferrarese interests. His new palace of S. Sebastiano near the Pusterla Gate of Mantua became his retreat; correspondence reveals that he appreciated topographical views and portraits of horses and dogs, but he also promoted choral and organ music in Mantua cathedral. DC

J. Cartwright *Isabella d'Este* (1915); L. Mazzoldi *Mantova: la storia* II (1961); W. Prizer 'La cappella di Francesco II Gonzaga e la musica sacra a Mantova' *Mantova e i Gonzaga* (1977)

Gonzaga, Lodovico Marquis of Mantua 1444–78 (b.1412) Educated by VITTORINO DA FELTRE, he appears to have espoused his precepts, becoming a just, pious, and learned prince. As a military captain he distinguished himself serving in the Milanese wars against Venice, even if (in jealousy of his brother Carlo) he temporarily deserted to Venice (1437–40): he became a firm ally and retainer of Duke Francesco Sforza. In later life a chronic invalid, he was portrayed with his wife Barbara of Brandenburg by Mantegna (whom he attracted to Mantua *c.*1458) as a model paterfamilias, though in fact he fathered many

The Madonna of the Victory (1495–96) by Mantegna, commemorating **Gianfrancesco II Gonzaga**'s success at Fornovo (detail) (Paris, Louvre).

A meeting of **Lodovico Gonzaga** and his son Cardinal Francesco Gonzaga in Mantegna's fresco cycle (Mantua, Ducal Palace).

illegitimate children. He was closely in touch with Medicean Florence (where he sponsored the building of the tribune of the Annunziata church), and had a highly informed interest in architecture which led to his employment of Luca Fancelli and Alberti upon Mantuan building projects, including the churches of S. Sebastiano and S. Andrea; the latter formed part of a scheme of urban improvement set in motion after a prestigious visit from the papal court (1459–60). Lodovico was much concerned to extend his authority, but by prudent and legal, rather than arbitrary, methods; most notably this included control over ecclesiastical foundations and patronage. DC

G. Mazzoldi *Mantova: la storia* II (1961); E. Marani and C. Perina *Mantova: le arti* II (1961); D. S. Chambers 'Sant'Andrea at Mantua and Gonzaga patronage 1460–72' *Journal of the Warburg and Courtauld Institutes* (1977)

Gothic, which may well have originated with Alberti as a derogatory term and which certainly corresponds to Vasari's '*maniera tedesca*' ('German style'), is properly the descriptive term for an artistic style which achieved its first full flowering in the Île de France and the surrounding areas in the period between *c.*1200 and *c.*1270, and which then spread throughout northern Europe. It is characterized by the hitherto unprecedented integration of the arts of sculpture, painting, stained glass and architecture which is epitomized in the great cathedrals of Chartres, Amiens, and Reims or in the Sainte Chapelle in Paris. In all the arts the predominantly planar forms of the Romanesque are replaced by an emphasis on line. There is a transcendental quality, whether in the soaring forms of the pointed arches or in the new stress on the humanity of Christ, which similarly distinguishes it from the preceding Romanesque style.

In thinking of Nicola (d. *c.*1284) or Giovanni Pisano (d. after 1314) there is some danger of forgetting what had happened in French sculpture half a century or more earlier, and likewise it is hard to remember that the spectacular achievements of early Renaissance art are a singularly localized eddy in the continuing stream of late gothic European art. By northern European standards few Italian works of art can be called gothic without qualification, and the story of 13c. and 14c. Italian architecture is as much one of resistance

Gothic: *the Madonna of the Annunciation* from the Orsini Polyptych of Simone Martini (Antwerp, Musée Royal des Beaux-Arts).

to the new style as of its reception, whether directly from France or through German or central European intermediaries. In sculpture and in painting, the Italian reluctance to distort the human figure, conditioned by a never wholly submerged awareness of the omnipresent antique heritage, gives a special quality to the work of even those artists such as Giovanni Pisano or Simone Martini who most closely approached a pure gothic style.

Nevertheless, the vitalizing role of Northern gothic art throughout the early Renaissance and the period leading up to it should never be underestimated. The artistic, like the cultural and commercial, interaction was continuous and much of the Italian achievement is incomprehensible if seen in isolation. It is not merely at the level of direct exchanges between one artist and another, or the influence of one building, painting, manuscript or piece of sculpture upon another, that the effects are to be felt. The streaming quality of line which is so characteristic of Brunelleschi's early Renaissance architecture surely reflects a sensitivity to the gothic contribution which is entirely independent of, and lies much deeper than, the superficial particularities of form.

The counterflow of influence and inspiration from South to North must likewise not be underrated. In particular, the contribution of Italian painters from Duccio and Simone Martini onwards is central to the evolution of the so-called International Gothic style developing in Burgundy, Bohemia and north Italy in the late 14c. and early 15c. JW

P. Frankl *The gothic* (1960); G. Henderson *Gothic* (1967); A. Martindale *Gothic art* (1967)

Gozzoli, Benozzo (active *c.*1444, d. 1497) Benozzo di Lese was an assistant of Fra Angelico. His major work was the continuous fresco of the Procession of the Magi (*c.*1459) in the chapel of the Medici Palace. Commissioned by Piero de' Medici, it takes Gentile da Fabriano's pageantry a stage further, populating almost the entire cortège with the Medici family and their associates. It must have been a constant reminder of the annual re-enactment of the original biblical procession by the Compagnia de' Re Magi, the most splendid and most aristocratic of the Florentine religious confraternities. The resultant blending of the secular and the religious would have been wholly foreign to Angelico, and prefigures the still more extreme fusion of the two in the works of Botticelli and Ghirlandaio. JW

A. Padoa Rizzo *Benozzo Gozzoli pittore* (1972)

A detail from **Gozzoli**'s fresco *The Procession of the Magi* in the chapel of the Medici Palace, Florence.

Grazzini, Anton Francesco (1503–84) One of the founders of the Florentine Accademia degli Umidi (later Fiorentina), where he took the name Lasca, by which he is often known, and in 1582 of the Accademia della Crusca. He is best remembered for his collection of short stories, *Le cene* (published 1756), written in a realistic, popular style, with emphasis on both comic and cruel *beffe*, presenting effective characterization and a lively portrait of grand-ducal Florence. He also wrote satirical poems and comedies (*La gelosia, La spiritata, La strega, La Pinzochera, La Sibilla, I parentadi, L'Arzigogolo*) which, alongside their more classical elements, also reveal popular aspects reminiscent of his *novelle*. LL

R. J. Rodini *A. F. Grazzini, poet, dramatist, and novelliere* (1970)

Gregory XII Pope 1406–15 (b.1336) Angelo Correr, a Venetian, was elected pope by the 'Roman' party in the Great SCHISM. His reluctance to resign his office in conjunction with his AVIGNON rival, Benedict XIII, led to his desertion by his cardinals (1408). In a despairing search for support Gregory handed over the Papal State to Ladislas I of Naples and became his virtual puppet. He was formally deposed as a perjured schismatic by the Council of Pisa (1409). Persuaded to acknowledge the authority of the Council of Constance, he resigned in 1415 and died 2 years later. JL

Grimani, Cardinal Domenico (1461–1523) Venetian churchman and collector. The son of Doge Antonio Grimani, he was a notorious ecclesiastical pluralist. His collection included an outstanding museum of antiquities (this now forms part of the Museo d'Antichità in Venice), Flemish and Italian paintings (some of those by Bosch are now in the Doges' Palace) and a great illuminated breviary (now in the Biblioteca Marciana). He left pictures and some of the antiquities to the Venetian state in 1523; the breviary passed to the state in 1593. OL

M. Perry 'Cardinal Domenico Grimani's legacy of ancient art to Venice' *Journal of the Warburg and Courtauld Institutes* (1978)

Doge Andrea **Gritti** by Titian (Washington, National Gallery, Samuel H. Kress Collection).

Gritti, Andrea (1455–1538) Battered as it is, Titian's portrait shows something of the spirit of this formidable Venetian patrician. After a time practising as a merchant, chiefly overseas, the crucial years of his preparation for the dogeship (1523–38) were those of the War of Cambrai. His bravery and expert knowledge as a military proveditor were such that in 1510 he was seriously proposed as commander-in-chief in the field. In 1512 he was taken as a prisoner to France, but returned in 1513 to be at once re-employed as proveditor general. His report of 1517 on the strategic defence of the terraferma was the basis for the Republic's programme of refortification during the rest of the century. Almost constantly occupied outside Venice in the field or in naval commands, as doge Gritti understandably showed impatience with the niceties of ducal procedure (he would, for instance, open dispatches without waiting for his councillors). The threat of Turkish attack, which materialized in 1537, kept criticism of his occasionally hectoring manner to a minimum. He was, however, the last person with such a militant career to be elected doge. JRH

Grotesques The name given to ornaments in paint or stucco composed from plants, animals (often fabulous) and human figures. The name is derived from the Italian *grotta* (cave): during the Renaissance such decorations were discovered underground in the remains of Roman architecture – the most notable example is Nero's Golden House – and they were widely imitated. Ghirlandaio, Pinturicchio, and in particular Raphael in the painted frames round the frescoes in the Loggie of the Vatican Palace, made use of this decorative form. LDE

Painted stucco of the **grotesque** decoration in Raphael's Vatican Loggie, Rome.

N. Dacos *La Découverte de la Domus Aurea et la formation des grotesques à la Renaissance* (1970)

Groto, Luigi (1541–85) Also known as Cieco ('the blind man') d'Adria (his birthplace): his blindness did not, however, prevent him from acquiring a vast erudition and from producing pastoral fables, poetry and plays. He wrote both tragedies – *Dalida* (1572), *Hadriana* (1578, based on Luigi da PORTO's short story of Romeo and Juliet) – and comedies – *Emilia* (1579), *Tesoro* (1580), *Alteria* (1584). The Mannerist traits found in his drama are prevalent in his *Rime* (1577); his verse is marked by extravagant stylistic affectation and luxuriant metrical artifice. He wrote in Latin, Venetian and Spanish as well as Italian. LL

V. Turri *Luigi Groto, il Cieco d'Adria* (1885); M. Ariani *Tra classicismo e manierismo: il teatro tragico del Cinquecento* (1974)

Guarini, Battista (1538–1612), a native of and teacher of rhetoric at Ferrara, served the Este court as diplomat and functionary until, on Tasso's disgrace, he came to replace him as court poet. His chief fame rested, then as now, on the pastoral play *Il pastor fido* (*The faithful shepherd*), in which he challenged – at much greater length – Tasso's *Aminta*. 'Here's *Pastor Fido*,' says a character in Ben Jonson's *Volpone* (1607); 'all our English writers, I mean such as are happy in the Italian, will deign to steal out of this author.' Scarcely less influential, both in and outside Italy, than this pastoral-tragical comedy was the controversy it led to, even before its publication in 1589, among literary purists who disliked the mingling of genres. *See* PASTORAL PLAY. JRH

V. Rossi *Battista Guarini ed il Pastor Fido* (1886); B. Weinberg *History of literary criticism in the Italian Renaissance* (1961)

Guarino da Verona (1374–1460), one of the founders of Renaissance EDUCATION, acquired his expertise in Greek during a stay in Constantinople 1403–08. He returned with a knowledge of the language perhaps unrivalled among contemporary Italians and with a collection of Greek manuscripts. He was invited to Florence as a teacher and spent 4 years there, 1410–14, leaving because of a quarrel with Niccoli, who was probably jealous of his superior knowledge of Greek. After attempts to establish himself at Padua and elsewhere he was summoned to Ferrara in 1429 by the Marquis Niccolò d'Este, as tutor to his son Leonello and professor at the university. Except for a period of employment as Greek interpreter at the Council of Florence (1438–39), he stayed at Ferrara for the rest of his life, making it famous as a centre of classical education.

Without original literary or philosophical gifts, Guarino was an utterly dedicated teacher of Latin and Greek. He promoted a thorough training in grammar, proficiency in writing verse as well as prose, knowledge of classical history and mythology, and practice in composing speeches on the model of CICERO. In his lectures he commented minutely on the texts of Latin authors. He had to defend himself against giving his pupils lectures on TERENCE when they should have been in church. His greatest innovation, however, was his insistence that Greek was of equal importance with Latin in the education of a gentleman. He translated Plutarch's *On the education of children* and revised Chrysoloras' Greek grammar. Through the impact of many distinguished pupils, through imitation by his contemporary VITTORINO DA FELTRE, and through the treatise on education composed by his son Battista, he was one of the most influential founders of the conception of a classical literary education. GH

R. Sabbadini *La scuola e gli studi di Guarino Guarini Veronese* (1896)

Guelfs and Ghibellines Italian political terms derived from the German *Welf*, a personal and thence family name of the dukes of Bavaria, and *Waiblingen*, the name of a castle of the Hohenstaufen dukes of Swabia apparently used as a battle cry. Presumably introduced into Italy 1198–1218, when partisans of the Emperor Otto IV (Welf) contested central Italy with supporters of Philip of Swabia and his nephew Frederick II, the terms do not appear in the chronicles until the Emperor Frederick's conflict with the Papacy 1235–50, when Guelf meant a supporter of the Pope and Ghibelline a supporter of the Empire. From 1266 to 1268, when Naples was conquered by Charles of Anjou, brother of Louis IX, the French connection became the touchstone of Guelfism, and the chain of Guelf alliances stretching from Naples, through central Italy, to Provence and Paris, underwritten by the financial interests of the Tuscan bankers, became an abiding feature of European politics. The Italian expeditions of Henry of Luxemburg (1310–13) and Lewis of Bavaria (1327–29) spread the terms to northern Italy, with the Visconti of Milan and the della Scala of Verona emerging as the leading Ghibelline powers. Attempts by Guelf propagandists to claim their party as the upholder of liberty and their opponents as the protagonists of tyranny rarely coincide with the truth: power politics, then as now, generally overrode ideology in inter-state affairs.

Factional struggles had existed within the Italian states from time immemorial, the parties taking a multitude of local names. In Florence, however, Guelf and Ghibelline were applied to the local factions which supposedly originated in a feud between the Buondelmonte and Amidei clans, *c.*1216. In 1266–67 the Guelf party, which had recruited most of the merchant class, finally prevailed over the predominantly noble Ghibellines; after this, internal factions in Florence went under other names, like the Blacks and the Whites who contested for control of the commune between 1295 and 1302. Meanwhile the Parte Guelfa had become a corporate body whose wealth and moral authority as the guardian of political orthodoxy enabled it to play the part of a powerful pressure group through most of the 14c. After the War of the EIGHT SAINTS, the influence of the Parte declined rapidly. Although its palace was rebuilt *c.*1418–58 to the designs of Brunelleschi, it had no part in the conflicts surrounding the rise of the Medici régime. JKH

J. K. Hyde *Society and politics in medieval Italy* (1973)

Guicciardini, Francesco (1483–1540) Florentine historian. A member of one of the best reputed of patrician families, he had a classical education, and after training in the law was sent as ambassador to Spain in 1511, an early beginning to a long career as an actor in the ceaselessly perturbed events of the age. Absent from Florence when the Medici returned in 1512, he was not excluded (as was Machiavelli) from their régime. Membership of the Signoria in 1515 was followed by posts under Pope Leo X: Governor of Modena in 1516, of Reggio in 1517, and of Parma in 1519. He became President of the Romagna in 1524, councillor to Clement VII in 1526, papal representative in Florence in 1530, and thenceforward a principal adviser to Alessandro de' Medici and, at the beginning of his reign, to Cosimo I. It was his subsequent exclusion from power by Cosimo that gave him the leisure to compose his *History of Italy*, a massive account of events in Italy from the first French invasion of 1494 to the death of Clement VII forty years later, which led Gibbon to rank him with Thucydides and Francesco de Sanctis to judge it 'from the point of view of intellectual power, the most important work to have issued from an Italian mind.'

Guicciardini's earliest historical work, the unfinished (and until 1859 unpublished) *History of Florence*, written in 1508–09, reflects his pride in his family's long connection with the city's government. Thereafter, his interest was deepened by his own immersion in public affairs and by an instinct to scrutinize not only what was happening among the protagonists of the political scene but also the way his own opinions and values were evolving as he watched them. This self-scrutiny led to the accumulation of maxims and reflections (*Ricordi*) on history, human nature and statecraft which constituted the moral and philosophical framework of his otherwise heavily factual later historical narratives. The first of these, *Florentine affairs* (*Cose fiorentine*, first published only in 1945), introduced another feature of his mature work: an acutely critical attitude towards, and an unprecedented use of, source material. The second, the *History of Italy* itself, added two further ingredients to his stature as a writer of contemporary history: a (for the time) unique cosmopolitanism, and a psychological interest that reflected his belief that history was shaped by the interactions of the passions of individuals – hence its largely unpredictable variety.

Though the servant of popes and dukes, Guicciardini was at heart the protagonist of a republic run by an élite of responsible citizens (a position argued in his *Dialogue on the government of Florence* of 1524–25), a conflict which held his observations and his convictions in literary balance. The *History of Italy* was published posthumously in 1561 and fairly quickly translated into Latin, French, German, Dutch, Spanish and English. *See* HISTORY AND CHRONICLE. JRH

R. Ridolfi *The life of Francesco Guicciardini* tr. C. Grayson (1967); M. Phillips *Francesco Guicciardini: the historian's craft* (1977); *The history of Italy* tr. and abr. S. Alexander (1969); *Maxims* . . . tr. M. Domandi (1965)

Guilds were essentially associations of masters in particular crafts, trades, or professions. In Italy they go back a long way; there is documentary evidence of guilds in 6c. Naples. In origin they were clubs which observed religious festivals together and attended the funerals of their members, but in time they acquired other functions. Their economic function was to control standards and to enforce the guild's monopoly of particular activities in a particular territory. Their political function was to participate in the government of the city-state. In some cities, notably Florence in the 14c., only guildsmen were eligible for civic office, thus excluding both noblemen (unless they swallowed their pride and joined, as some did), and unskilled workers like the woolcombers and dyers. In Florence in 1378 these groups demanded the right to form their own guilds, and there were similar movements of protest in Siena and Bologna.

Guilds were also patrons of art, commissioning paintings for guildhalls, contributing to the fabric fund of cathedrals and collaborating on collective projects like the statues for Orsanmichele at Florence. The guilds were not equal.

Ghiberti's statue of St Matthew commissioned for Orsanmichele by the **guild** of the *Cambio* (money-changers).

In Florence, the 7 'Greater Guilds', including such prestigious occupations as judges and bankers, outranked the 14 'Lesser Guilds', and in general the guild hierarchy was reflected in the order of precedence in processions. The great age of the guilds was the 13c. and 14c. The economic recession after 1348 meant fewer opportunities for journeymen to become masters, and greater hostility between master and man. The shift from trade to land in the 15c. and 16c. meant a decline in the social standing of the crafts. In some towns, such as Brescia and Vicenza, guild membership actually became a disqualification instead of a qualification for municipal office. The guilds lost their independence and became instruments of state control. In 16c. Venice, for example, they were made responsible for supplying oarsmen for the galleys of the state. *See* CIOMPI; ARTIST, STATUS OF THE. PB

V. I. Rutenburg 'Arti' *SI* V

Habsburg, house of Ruling house of Austria 1282–1918, tracing descent from Guntram the Rich, Count of Alsace and Breisgau in the mid-10c., whose grandson Werner built the castle from which the family derives its name. Rudolph I (d.1291) was the first Habsburg to be elected King of the Romans. It was the family's virtual monopoly of the title of Holy Roman Emperor from the election of Albert II in 1438 until 1806 which gave the Habsburgs an interest in Italy. Albert II was succeeded by Frederick III (1440–93), but during the Renaissance the two Habsburg Emperors of greatest significance from an Italian viewpoint were MAXIMILIAN I and his grandson CHARLES V, both of whom intervened actively in the peninsula. Charles V was the last Emperor to be crowned in Italy, at Bologna in 1530. At his abdication Charles divided his realms, his brother Ferdinand succeeding to the Empire, his son Philip II to Spain and the Italian territories. JH

A. Wandruszka *The house of Habsburg* (1964)

Hawkwood, John (*c.*1320–94) Known in Italy, because of the unpronounceability of his name, as Giovanni Acuto, Hawkwood was the last of the great foreign condottieri who not only fought the battles but also assisted with the diplomacy of their employers. Born in Essex, he started his military career in France; when the Hundred Years War was temporarily halted by the Peace of Brétigny in 1350, he passed with a band of similarly restless and ambitious troops, first to serve in Piedmont and then in Italy. In 1364 he was PISA's commander-in-chief in its war with Florence. Only after fighting thereafter in papal and then Visconti

Uccello's frescoed equestrian portrait of the English condottiere Sir John **Hawkwood** in Florence cathedral (detail).

pay did he take up (in 1377) the service in which he was to die, that of Florence. How far this was a reluctant precaution on the republic's part, an immobilization of its major bugbear in the recent anti-papal War of the EIGHT SAINTS, is unclear. What followed, however, was an unusually close bond between condottiere and government, particularly so once that government had become respectable in the eyes of a member of the military élite by purging itself of the popular element that had gained a voice after the CIOMPI revolt of 1378. Hawkwood symbolized his commitment by selling off the principality he had assembled at the expense of previous employers (based on Bagnocavallo and Cotignola, near Ravenna) and Florence granted him the status of citizen together with tax exemption for life. On his death, moreover, he was granted a state funeral and a frescoed monument in the cathedral. This was replaced 1436 by the present fresco by Uccello. JRH

J. Temple-Leader and G. Marcotti *Sir John Hawkwood* (1849)

Heresy, pre-Reformation The heretical movements affecting Italy between the mid-12c. and the mid-14c. had their main impact in an area covering the north-west of the peninsula and southern France: it is not possible to speak of distinct Italian and meridional French movements. The authentically Christian movements which were expelled from the Catholic Church must in the first instance be distinguished from Catharism, which represented an infiltration by the originally non-Christian dualist system of Manichaeanism; from the start, the Cathars were an anti-church. By contrast, the Waldensian, Spiritual and Joachimite movements appeared initially as vital manifestations of Catholicism; only after their condemnation by the ecclesiastical authorities do they seem to have developed notably eccentric doctrines and to have described themselves as the true Church in opposition to the institutional Church; they had a recognizable kinship with movements that remained within the pale of orthodoxy.

These Christian heresies had in common an attachment to the ideal of apostolic poverty, which came to be seen by the ecclesiastical authorities as a challenge to the institutionalized Church. The Waldensians or Valdesi (not to be confused with Valdesiani, the followers of Juan de Valdes (d.1541)) took their origin from the Poor Men of Lyons, founded by Peter Valdes or Waldo in the 1170s. They were distinguished by a strong attachment to the Bible and a desire to imitate Christ's poverty. At first approved by the Papacy as an order of laymen, they were condemned in 1184. Likewise condemned was the rather similar Lombard movement of the Humiliati. One stream of these remained as an approved order within the Catholic Church, while others merged with the Waldensians. The Waldensians came to teach that the sacraments could be administered validly only by the pure, i.e. only by Waldensian superiors or *perfecti* practising evangelical poverty. Alone among the heretical sects existing in Italy they were organized as a church, and regarded themselves as forming, together with brethren north of the Alps, one great missionary community. They spread all over western and central Europe but in the long term they came to be largely confined to the Rhaetian and Cottian Alps (the Grisons and Savoy). The Italian Waldensians in the 16c. resisted absorption by Reformed Protestantism.

The early Franciscans might be regarded as a movement, similar in character to the Poor Men of Lyons, which was won for the cause of Catholic orthodoxy. However, divisions within the order over the issue of poverty led to religious dissidence. The Spirituals held up the ideal of strict poverty as obligatory for Franciscans and, indeed, normative for churchmen; following the Papacy's recognition of the Franciscan order as a property-owning body in 1322–23, their position became one of criticism of the institutional Church as such. Their heresies came to incorporate the millenarian doctrines of the 12c. abbot Joachim of Fiore. He had prophesied a coming age of the Holy Spirit ushered in by Spiritual monks; his heretical followers prophesied a new Spiritual gospel that would supersede the Bible. Joachimite Spiritualists came to see the pope, head of the 'carnal Church', as Antichrist. The main impact of the movement upon the laity was in southern France; in Italy it was an affair of various groups of *fraticelli de paupere vita* (little friars of the poor life), mainly in the south. *See* REFORMATION. OL

G. Leff *Heresy in the later Middle Ages* (2 vols 1967)

Hermeticism A system of mystical and gnostic ideas based upon a group of Greek writings (called the *Corpus hermeticum*) falsely attributed to the mythical Greek god Hermes Trismegistus, who was identified with the

Egyptian god Thoth. Partially known in the Middle Ages, these writings were given a new life by the Latin translation of Ficino, first published in 1471. They were integrated into Ficino's neo-Platonic synthesis, and thereby were vastly influential into the 17c., when their spurious nature became increasingly evident. *See* PYTHAGORAS. CS

F. A. Yates *Giordano Bruno and the Hermetic tradition* (1964)

Hippocrates (?460–?377BC) His fame as a physician who approached practical MEDICINE in a philosophical manner brought respectful mentions of him from Plato and Aristotle, and was such that his name was attached not only to his own writings but to a *Corpus Hippocraticum* of some 60 surviving treatises. In Latin translations some of these works were known in the Middle Ages; more texts became known in the 15c. when, along with GALEN, Hippocrates became the guide to the study of anatomy, physiology, medication, diagnosis and clinical description, and dietary theory. His exposition of the theory of the 4 humours, an imbalance between which caused disease, had a hypnotic effect on diagnosis and prescription until the 17c. He was also the source of medical ethics. Best known today of the writings associated with him is the 'Hippocratic oath'. JRH

C. Singer *Greek biology and Greek medicine* (1922); *Hippocratic writings* ed. G. E. R. Lloyd, tr. J. Chadwick *et al.* (1978)

History and chronicle After Petrarch's intellectual (and emotional) apprehension of historical distance, of a past that *was* past and that had to be reconstructed in its own terms and was linked to the present by the individual's nostalgia and curiosity, the writing of history for the first time required an organizing sense of temporal perspective. With this was born a sensitiveness to anachronism, an increasing awareness that the past had its own manner which should not be confused with that of the present. Moreover, Petrarch wrote letters to the figures of Roman antiquity he most admired with a clear understanding that the civilization towards which the letters were launched had not been deliberately manipulated into being (as Dante had believed) by God as a suitable environment for a Christian revelation that would link it providentially as well as chronologically to the present. With a sense of time focused and demystified, historical writing was provided with a critical stance that could distinguish it from the medieval chronicle which, for all its fascination with personality and event, saw both as clay in the divine shaper's hand. 'History' was set on a different course from 'chronicle' – it might seem a more useful one. This has not turned out to be the case. Though modern historians primarily defer to such post-Petrarchan humanist historians as Bruni, Bracciolini, Pontano and Bembo, it is the chroniclers, Villani and Sanuto, who are used, and the men who combined the one-thing-after-another of the chronicler with the thoughtful interpretation of the historian – Corio, Machiavelli, Guicciardini, Paruta – who are read for pleasure as well as for information.

The irony arises from the deference to classical models common to the humanist avant-garde approach as a whole. By the early 15c. three had been established: Caesar as the model for the writing of recent and contemporary history, Sallust for the history of campaigns, Livy for that of institutions. It had also been established from classical authors (chiefly Cicero) that the historian's style should be dignified, that his subject matter should be political and military, and that his material should be so shaped, with the assistance of such literary devices as authorial interpolations and imaginary speeches, as to have a positive educative effect on the reader – to encourage him to follow the example of wise, and eschew that of evil men and to see the relevance of past to present affairs.

Thus, though classical precept (Cicero again) also stressed that the historian, unlike the chronicler, should explain 'not only what was done and said but also how and why', the impulse to improve on the chronicle by discussing what caused actions and events was largely cancelled out by a new subjectivity in the choice and presentation of material. So at the very moment when the urge to record what was happening (in diaries, family memoranda, biographies and civic chronicles) had never been stronger, the newly reinvented history put interpretation before record, and in putting fashion first became trapped by the very sense of time whose nature it had reconsidered. Moreover, although many Latin humanist historians were chancery officials or in other ways had access to governmental records, they preferred to reshape chronicles, and to reserve a comparative, critical examination of sources to the moment when the current of their interest could be plugged into its source of energy, their city's point of contact with the history of ancient Rome.

While Latin histories, chiefly concerned with form and message, continued to be written throughout the 16c., the vernacular chronicle had retained its vitality. It was the fusion of both approaches that, with the first half of the century (helped by a painful desire to explain why the wars from 1494 had brought such changes and humiliation in their train), produced a type of historical writing – interpretative, explanatory, yet liberally factual – which aroused the admiration of such successors as Sir Walter Raleigh and Sir Francis Bacon, and which retains its usefulness and fascination today: notably the Florentine histories of Machiavelli, Guicciardini (who in *c.*1528, in his *Florentine affairs*, at last pioneered the meticulous comparison of source material), Francesco Vettori and Nardi, Corio's history of Milan, Paruta's of Venice and, best of all, Guicciardini's *History of Italy*. For while these authors showed their loyalty to the chronicle's immediacy and variousness by using the vernacular, they reflected the humanists' contribution in an acknowledgment of the serious purpose of historical writing and of the author's deliberate choice in how he hands on a delineation of the past to posterity. *See* HUMANISM. JRH

D. J. Wilcox *The development of Florentine humanist historiography in the fifteenth century* (1969); F. Gilbert *Machiavelli and Guicciardini* (1965); N. Struever *The language of history in the Renaissance* (1970); G. Spini 'Historiography: the art of history in the Italian Counter-Reformation' in E. Cochrane ed. *The late Italian Renaissance, 1525–1630* (1970)

Holy League Any alliance which was aggressive in intent and had a pope as a signatory was likely to be dubbed a Holy League. The 3 most commonly so called are those of 1495, 1511 and 1571. The first comprised Ferdinand of Aragon, Maximilian I, the Duke of Milan, the republic of Florence and Pope Alexander VI. It was their forces that failed to defeat the invading French on their return journey from Naples at NOVARA. The second brought together, again in opposition to France, Maximilian, Venice, Ferdinand, Henry VIII of England and Pope Julius II – switching from his previous support of France. As well as relieving Venice from the united forces of the League of CAMBRAI, this League defeated the French at Ravenna in 1512 and, in the same year, forced Florence to take back the exiled Medici. The third was more accurately 'Holy' in that its signatories, Venice, Philip II of Spain and Pope Pius V, did combat the infidel, jointly defeating the Turkish fleet at LEPANTO. JRH

Pius V with Spanish and Venetian emissaries signing the **Holy League** against the Turks in 1571 (Siena, Archivio Comunale).

Homosexuality Whether the 'vice of Sodom and Gomorrah', as homosexuality was called, was particularly prevalent, especially in Tuscany (as contemporaries believed), we shall never know. What can be said is that the authorities of the period were preoccupied with sodomy, whether they ordered the guilty parties to be burned, hanged, whipped, fined or expelled. Moral reformers like S. Bernardino of Siena and Savonarola still thought that the laws did not go far enough. New statutes or decrees against sodomy were passed in Siena (1425), Venice (1496), and above all in Florence (1415, 1418, 1432, 1494, 1542). However, sodomy was not prosecuted all that often. In 1476 several Florentine artists (among them Leonardo) were accused of the 'unmentionable vice', but in the more permissive atmosphere of Rome Sodoma himself lived free from prosecution (though cf. SODOMA). PB

G. Ruggiero 'Sexual criminality in the early Renaissance' *Journal of Social History* (1974–75); M. Goodich *The unmentionable vice* (1979)

Horace (65–8BC) Quintus Horatius Flaccus, Latin lyric and satirical poet, known and admired since Petrarch. His *Ars poetica* was translated into Italian in 1536. JRH

Hothby, John (d.1487) A Carmelite monk who, in common with several other English musicians, settled in Italy, after travels in Spain, France and Germany. He spent many years in Lucca as *maestro di cappella* at S. Martino before returning to England, on the orders of Henry VII. He is mainly known as a writer of theoretical treatises in which he codifies the more sonorous style of descant over a *cantus firmus.* DA

Humanism is a 19c. coinage, invented to describe the programme of studies, and its conditioning of thought and expression, that was known from the late 15c. as the province of the *umanista*, the teacher of the *studia humanitatis* or arts syllabus in schools and universities. This had by then come to include the study of Latin (and to a much lesser extent, Greek) texts dealing with grammar, rhetoric, history, poetry and moral philosophy. Such a programme was secular, concerned with man, his nature and his gifts, but Renaissance humanism must be kept free from any hint of either 'humanitarianism' or 'humanism' in its modern sense of a rational, non-religious approach to life.

Much of the material for humanism had been latent in the Middle Ages in the form of well-known classical literary texts, those of VIRGIL, OVID, HORACE, Sallust, SENECA among them. What was needed to so redirect interest as to amount to a revival of imaginative understanding of these authors was, first, a new appreciation of their purely literary quality and an awareness of how they achieved their effects, then a clearer vision of the writers themselves and of the times in which they had lived. Interest of this sort is observable in Padua, Verona and Naples in the first third of the 14c. With Petrarch humanism is in being: sensitiveness to quality and purpose, an apprehension of personality and historical distance, an itch to restore the original quality of classical works by editing them, and to discover others that had lain neglected or forgotten in monastic libraries; finally an urge to emulate classical literary achievements that, by producing a form of ambition at odds with Christian otherworldliness, caused a perturbed mental stocktaking that was to make the relationship between the present and the ancient past an increasingly selfconscious one.

As text by text – Catullus, more CICERO, more LIVY, VITRUVIUS, QUINTILIAN – the imaginative reconstruction of the ancient world proceeded, its relevance became clearer. Their sense no longer obscure, their personalities restored, replaced in the context of their own society, the authors of antiquity presented a view of a civilization, vast in extent and time, which had not only the clarity of a clearly perceived remoteness but the wholeness of a completed cycle, from obscurity through Empire – first Greek, then Roman – to barbarian chaos. Though distant in time, this civilization was attractively near in space to a people whose ploughs turned up Roman coins and statues and whose southern lands contained Greek-speaking communities. And the combination enabled them to see the ancient world as a source of models from whom to learn about statecraft, the waging of war, the creation of works of art – and the more important art of bearing up under adversity. The challenge of these models was all the easier to accept because of the feeling of pride in contemporary cultural achievement such as was expressed in 1492 by Ficino: 'it is undoubtedly a golden age which has restored to light the liberal arts that had almost been destroyed: grammar, eloquence, poetry, sculpture, music.'

Recent formulations stress the theme of relevance: 'civic humanism' the role of authors like Cicero in encouraging the individual to participate in government; 'humanist educational theory' the preparation for a life of action; 'artistic humanism' the adaptation of classical forms; 'scientific humanism' the rehabilitation of ancient, especially Greek, texts as guides; 'utilitarian humanism' as an invitation to copy, as in military or agricultural affairs, methods that could help the present. But in the 16c., as in the 13c., the core of humanism was the private preoccupation of the *umanista* with getting his text right: unless the word 'humanism' retains the smell of the scholar's lamp it will mislead – as it will if it is seen as in opposition to a Christianity its students in the main wished to supplement, not contradict, through their patient excavation of the sources of ancient God-inspired wisdom. *See* EDUCATION; RHETORIC. JRH

P. O. Kristeller *The classics and Renaissance thought* (1955); R. Weiss *The spread of Italian humanism* (1964); C. Vasoli *Umanesimo e Rinascimento* (1969); L. Martines *The social world of the Florentine humanists 1390–1460* (1963); W. Ullmann *Medieval origins of Renaissance humanism* (1977)

Humour No culture that reached from Boccaccio's *Decameron* to the 'surprise' water jets of late 16c. gardens, via Lorenzo the Magnificent's carnival songs, Machiavelli's and Aretino's comedies, and such gently mocking paintings as the Bellini-Titian *Feast of the Gods*, can be seen as lacking in humour. Equally, humour without the tone of voice that nuanced it, or an understanding of reactions to it at the time, remains elusive.

The 15c. became selfconscious about the idea of humour. Cicero started this through his discussion (with examples) of humour in *On the orator*, that essential text for the Quattrocento humanist or would-be humanist. Pontano, in his *On conversation* (*c.*1499), both defined and illustrated humour, as did Castiglione in Book II of *The courtier*: 'what causes laughter is something incongruous and yet not really unpleasing.' While admitting puns (but not mentioning parody, a source of humour at the expense of the 'classics' – ancient and modern – of literature and art increasingly indulged in from the late 15c.), he stressed 3 main sources of that sense of humour which distinguishes men from other animals: the anecdote, the repartee and the practical joke. It may be frustrating when he tells us how frequently the assembled company laughed at the examples of each he provided. But that he took it for granted that examples would be welcome is understandable; 272 had been collected by Bracciolini between 1438 and 1452 (printed 1470); Poliziano in the 1470s collected 413, including a number of humorous or merely smart proverbs (not printed until 1548); the *Jokes and pleasantries* fathered by and on the jovial Tuscan priest Arlotto were published in *c.*1514. By the mid-16c. enough were in printed, manuscript or oral circulation for the professional man of letters Lodovico Domenichi to bring out in 1550 the first of 3 volumes of them. Thereafter, published humour, save of a guardedly ironic or licensed-target (i.e. at the expense of peasant or pedagogue) kind, became rarer. This was because both sexual *double entendre* or outright obscenity and anecdotes designed to deflate authoritarian figures became barred from an increasingly conformist press. Similarly impoverishing was the decline of heartfelt anticlericalism as the mood of Counter-Reformation took hold, and of Homeric laughter when mockery of the classical Gods (as in paintings of Vulcan's cuckoldry) came to imply a perilous domestication of them in a Christian's imagination.

Humour: dwarfs in Mantegna's fresco of the Gonzaga court (Mantua, Ducal Palace).

Renaissance selfconsciousness categorized not only the sources of humour but also its effects. Of jokes Castiglione wrote that 'there are some which are characterized by a certain modest humour and grace, others which have a hidden or obvious sting, others slightly indecent, some which provoke laughter as soon as they are heard, and others which do so the more they are thought about, others which cause blushes as well as laughter, and still others which arouse a show of anger.' The only sort of joke which he deplores is one that is deliberately ruthless, as 'the remark made to a man who had lost his nose, namely "Where, then, do you rest your spectacles?"' Here he was a reformer. The pleasure taken in scoring off others regardless of the humiliation caused was widespread. Many anecdotes and novellas from the 14c. onwards involved elaborately savage punishments, as it were, for gullibility. These, and the races which Jews, the (plebeian) aged and sometimes gipsies were forced to run as part of the Roman Carnival from the 1460s – as prostitutes were in Mantua and Ferrara – can cautiously be seen as a diversion of 'normal' society's insecurities and aggressiveness against misfits; while not uncharitable, society was not yet humanitarian.

The need for carefree humorous diversion at courts (including that of the Papacy until the 1530s) led to the employment of professional producers of mirth; calculating, as with jesters, or involuntary, as with simpletons – like the one that was convinced by a bored Mantuan court in 1506 that he had been appointed a bishop. The attitude to dwarfs was more complex. They were valued as exotic curiosities, as pets for casual fondling, as alarming but titillating evidence that nature could make mistakes. It is clear that at least some dwarfs found compensation in security and gratified vanity. Thanks to Giambologna's sculpture and Bronzino's twin portrait, front and rear of him in the nude, Cosimo I's dwarf Morgante is better known to us than most of the normally-sized members of his court. JRH

C. Speroni *Wit and wisdom of the Italian Renaissance* (1964); P. Barolsky *Infinite jest: wit and humour in Italian Renaissance painting* (1978); A. Luzio and R. Renier 'Buffoni, nani e schiavi dei Gonzaga' *Nuova Antologia* (1891); E. Tietze-Conrat *Dwarfs and jesters in art* (1957)

Hypnerotomachia Polifili (*The dream of Polyphilus*) A philosophical romance by the Dominican friar Francesco Colonna, published in Venice 1499. Its chief interest lies in the fine woodcut illustrations, especially in the architectural fantasies. OL

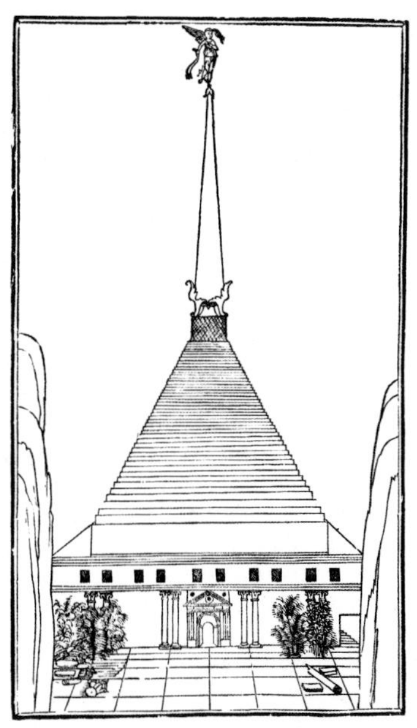

A woodcut from the **Hypnerotomachia Polifili**.

G. Pozzi and L. A. Ciapponi 'La cultura figurativa di Francesco Colonna e l'arte veneta' in V. Branca ed. *Umanesimo europeo e umanesimo veneziano* (1963); text ed. G. Pozzi and L. A. Ciapponi (1980)

Impresa Compared with that of more heavily feudalized and politically uniform countries, Italian heraldry, while it could produce an effective family trade mark or recognizable battle insignia, developed in an imprecise and *ad hoc* manner and never acquired the sophistication that derives from organized central control. What did engage the imagination and intellect in Italy was the device (*impresa*) in its purely personal form, as an image, usually accompanied by a motto, that expressed the individual's sense of what he stood for or aspired to or which associated him with some generally respected quality (concealed strength, faithful vigilance, etc.) or idea (the nature of Platonic love). The *impresa* in this form was inspired by Imperial Roman coins and came to characterize the reverses, or non-portrait sides, of medals from the 1430s. But it was not until the arrival of French nobles in the armies that invaded Italy from 1494, with their flaunting of personal emblems on bard and surcoat as well as family, heraldic devices on shield and banner, that the custom became widespread, expressed in woodcut and paint, and anthologized and explained in such works as Giovio's *Dialogo delle imprese* . . . (Rome 1555).

It was a form of self-expression for which the Italian imagination had become particularly well prepared thanks to the study of Egyptian hieroglyphs, cabbalistic musing over the significance of individual Hebrew letters of the alphabet, and a familiarity with classical literature that enabled a drawing of a bee and a bow to conjure up the poem of Theocritus in which Venus remarks to Cupid, when he complains of a sting, that he is the inflicter of a more grievous form of hurt. The *impresa* had also latent in it the appeal of being a visual riddle. Originally a serious, guarded self-revelation (Alberti's winged eye), it became a more general test of ingenuity, akin to the

The winged eye **impresa** on the reverse of Alberti's medal by Matteo de' Pasti (1446–50) (London, British Museum).

Victorian rebus, and finally – reflecting the recondite niggling of 16c. academies – a message from the scholar who invented it to the pundit who might spot its meaning. But by then, the mid-16c., the *impresa* was ceasing to be a personal device and had become almost indistinguishable from the emblem, that allied form of visually coded ideas that under Italian impetus swept through the cultivated European imagination well into the 17c. Albeit on a small and specialized scale, the *impresa* is a good example of Renaissance Italy's ability to receive, transform and re-export an idea. JRH

Individualism The troublesome notion that the Renaissance period in Italy was characterized by a new perception and display of man's individuality was launched by Jacob Burckhardt. In the Middle Ages, he wrote in 1860, 'man was conscious of himself only as a member of a race, people, party, family, or corporation – only through some general category. In Italy this veil first melted into air; an *objective* treatment and consideration of the state and of all the things of this world became possible. The *subjective* side at the same time asserted itself with corresponding emphasis; man became a spiritual *individual*.'

After a long vogue due to its inherent, romantic attractiveness, the notion came to be looked on with scepticism. The resentment of medievalists at the implied passivity of a period rich in such characters as William the Conqueror and Peter Abelard has been vocal. And Renaissance scholars have stressed the continuing strength of corporative attachments: family and kinship (*see* FAMILY STRUCTURE), CLIENTAGE relationships, GUILDS, parish organizations and CONFRATERNITIES, ACADEMIES – all representing familiar patterns of sought-after mutual support. Perhaps these ties were weakest in the 14c., when an unprecedented number of lives were alienated from their traditional backgrounds by emigration from the land to towns, and by an urban environment whose educational opportunities aided social mobility. Taking account, too, of the number who were engaged in a chancy and in some ways still *ad hoc* and experimental commercial and business life, it is possible to speak of a new individualism, and to see it, indeed (as has been suggested), as a burden. But thereafter such strains lessened. In some areas, for instance in the case of princes increasingly bound by the weight of their burgeoning bureaucracies, or CONDOTTIERI increasingly favoured for their inherited social standing and their ability to produce obedient subjects, the need and the opportunity to flourish 'individuality' diminished.

Our own perception of the men of the period is affected by the nature of the evidence: by an art that came to make them look more 3-dimensional and a literature that suggests an enriched subjectivity. It is hard to say how far these reflect an actual change in consciousness rather than changing conventions stimulated by an increased awareness of the art and literature of antiquity. Certainly among intellectuals a new sense of historical distance enabled the individual to 'place' himself in time. Portraits, tombs and inscriptions show a wish to be remembered with a new particularity. Humanist educators stressed the importance of developing the full potential of the human mind and body. And at the heart of these impulses towards self-definition was a literature concerned with the very nature of human individuality. It was Petrarch who brought together, in his *De remediis . . .* (*On the remedies of both kinds of fortune*), the Christian emphasis on man as made by God 'in our own image, after our likeness' and the Platonic notion that the human mind was in tune with the divine and could, if guided aright, seek and reach it. And to these views, which implied that everything else in creation had been made for man's use or contemplation, he added a third, this time derived from classical moral philosophy: that certain virtues – justice, moderation, magnanimity – were best nourished by use, and best studied in the authors who described those who had used them most notably.

This justified the study of the great men of action, soldiers or statesmen, of the past; indeed, the imitation of them, for to acquire fame was laudable if it were done to display the best qualities planted in men by God. Petrarch himself was uneasy about the relationship between a realization of the nature of individuality and cultivating it in practice – between the contemplative and active life. But with the topic launched, there was no stopping it, and by the time of Giannozzo Manetti's treatise *On the dignity and excellence of man* (*c.*1452) and Pico della Mirandola's pithier and more ecstatic *Oration* (1486) on the same theme, treatments of the subject had become a genre of their own. All the same, while its echoes may have suggested the wording of an epitaph, or stimulated artists and writers to see their own work in terms of creative genius and therefore express themselves with more confidence, or if a Machiavelli could see a purely personal intelligent energy or *virtù* as contending with a purely whimsical *fortuna*, a theory of individuality does not make a society as a whole more or less individual, nor provide opportunities for its members to stand out from others. *See* RENAISSANCE; ACTIVE V. CONTEMPLATIVE LIFE. JRH

C. Trinkaus *In our own image and likeness: humanity and divinity in Italian humanist thought* (1970); B. Wittkower *Born under Saturn: the character and conduct of artists* (1963); E. Cassirer *The individual and the cosmos in Renaissance philosophy* (1963); J. Pope-Hennessy *The portrait in the Renaissance* (1966)

Industry The leading industry of Renaissance Italy was clothmaking. In Florence in 1427, 38 per cent of the heads of household who declared an occupation were active in the textile industry, and the 10 most common occupations declared included weaver, wool merchant, carder, linen merchant and dyer. Como was another cloth town, and so was Cremona, which specialized in fustian. Lucca and Genoa were silk towns. Venice turned to clothmaking late, but produced nearly 25,000 'pieces' in 1600. Other important Italian industries included building, especially in Lombardy (it was the Lombard masons who took Renaissance architecture abroad); the manufacture of arms and armour, in Milan and Brescia; shipbuilding, in Venice and Genoa; glassmaking, soapmaking, and sugar-refining, all important in Venice, which also possessed Europe's leading PRINTING industry in the early 16c. The Papal State, however, had little industry, apart from papermaking at Bologna. As for the south, although weavers were at work in Naples, Catanzaro and elsewhere, the region as a whole (Sicily included) exported wool and raw silk and imported cloth.

Shipbuilding in the Venice Arsenal, an exception to the rule of generally small-scale **industry** (Venice, Museo di Storia Veneziana).

Industry was not confined to the towns, much as urban GUILDS would have liked this. Spinning (for women) and weaving (for both sexes) were common rural occupations. Forges, glassworks and even paper mills could be found in the mountains of 15c. Liguria. The organization of industry was usually small in scale. In Venice, no more than 6 looms were allowed under one roof. However, decentralization did not always mean independence. Weavers often hired their looms from cloth merchants and were in any case dependent on them for supplies of raw material. They were often paid in kind, a sure sign of dependence. In the cloth industry in particular, where the division of labour had given rise to 26 different occupations (including beating, sorting, washing, combing, carding, fulling, stretching, napping and shearing), an entrepreneur was clearly necessary to coordinate the different activities. However, the great fortunes of the period were not made in manufacturing but in trade and BANKING. Capitalism was commercial rather than industrial.

An example of state capitalism, and a major exception to the rule of small-scale industry, was the Venetian ARSENAL, a shipbuilding enterprise which employed some 1500 people, from ship's carpenters to sailmakers, and made use of something like assembly-line techniques. It might have been rivalled if Sixtus V had succeeded in turning the Colosseum into a cloth factory, as he planned to do, in order to set the Roman poor to work. State intervention in industry was normally confined to decrees ordering landowners to plant so many mulberry trees per acre, for the sake of silk production, or, in connection with the sumptuary laws, to prohibiting the import of foreign cloth or requiring officials to wear clothes which had been made locally. There was a trend towards the mechanization of industry, most obvious in the case of printing, but no industrial revolution. Changes in the performance of Italian industry 1300–1600 are difficult to measure, but the main trends seem to have been downward. Clothmaking, shipbuilding and printing all became increasingly vulnerable to competition from England and the Netherlands. *See* ECONOMY; TECHNOLOGY. PB

G. Luzzatto *An economic history of Italy* (1961)

Innocent VI Pope 1352–62 (b.1282) Étienne Aubert, jurist, one-time high official of the French crown, succeeded Clement VI, whose jewellery and works of art he was to sell in an attempt to restore the papal finances. He accepted the claim of the German Imperial electors that they should be free of any feudal dependence upon the Papacy. His appointment of ALBORNOZ as papal legate in Italy launched a long war throughout the peninsula in an attempt to revive the reality of the Papal State. *See* AVIGNON. JL

Inquisition Procedures for the prosecution of HERESY were first organized in the 1230s, primarily to combat the Cathars and Waldensians. In time, inquisitors extended their attentions beyond heresy to witchcraft (*see* WITCHES), blasphemy and sacrilege and these were again major areas of concern for the reconstituted inquisitorial tribunals of the 16c. Inquisitorial activity in Italy largely ceased in the 14c. but was revived with the Reformation. Paul III in 1542 provided for a new centralized organization, the Holy Office, with its headquarters in Rome, to supervise and coordinate the activities of inquisitorial tribunals elsewhere in Italy. Its first organizer was the hard-line zealot Giampietro Caraffa, later Paul IV. The tribunals in the Venetian dominions, which resumed activity from 1540, remained outside this system and Venetian subjects could not be transferred from them to Rome; here representatives of the lay power were present at proceedings and penalties were generally lenient. Inquisitors were always Dominicans or Franciscans, but local tribunals would include the bishop and the papal nuncio, where resident. The records of the Roman Holy Office were destroyed in 1559 in riots on Paul IV's death, and in general Inquisition trials in Italy have been little studied; we are best informed about tribunals in the Venetian dominions. OL

J. Tedeschi 'Preliminary observations on writing the history of the Roman Inquisition' in F. F. Church and T. George eds. *Continuity and discontinuity in Church history: essays presented to G. H. Williams* (1979); P. F. Grendler *The Roman Inquisition and the Venetian press* (1977)

Isaac, Heinrich (Henricus) (*c.*1450–1517) Composer. It is generally assumed that he was a German, though where north of the Alps he was born is unknown. In 1474 he was a pupil of the organist Squarcialupi in Florence, and around 1480 he probably entered the service of Ercole d'Este of Ferrara. Later in that decade he became organist of the cathedral of Florence and he was teacher of Lorenzo de' Medici's sons. He was a friend of many humanists, but it is difficult to trace their influence on his music, though his German *Lieder* do tend towards a simpler style akin to that of the later chanson. His main achievement was the composition of a series of motets for the church year, called the *Choralis Constanticus*, published many years after his death, in which he shows his mastery of the Franco-Flemish contrapuntal style, less smooth and more vigorous in rhythm than that of Josquin des Prez. The teacher of a whole generation of German composers, he more than anyone else was responsible for turning German music away from its conservative medieval forms to the newer Renaissance manner of Italy. DA

H. M. Brown *Music in the Renaissance* (1976)

Italian language Which were the languages of Renaissance Italy? At least 3 must be distinguished. Latin remained the dominant language of culture: up to the end of the 16c. more works were still written and published in Latin than in Italian. In everyday speech most people (certainly those who were not literate) would use their native dialects. These can be classified into about a dozen major regional groups: Piedmontese, Lombard, Venetian, Emilian, Campanian, Sicilian, etc., which differed from each other sometimes to the point of reciprocal unintelligibility. Even dialects belonging to the same group could vary widely between neighbouring villages. The relevance of this situation for the social and cultural history of Italy should not be underestimated. When we come to speak of Italian, the notion is problematic.

In Italy spoken Latin developed gradually into different local idioms; it is difficult to say when people started speaking an idiom we can call Romance rather than Latin. The first documents revealing an awareness of the coexistence of two languages are of the 9c.; the first dated text where an Italian vernacular is clearly distinguished from Latin is of 960; the first literary documents in the vernacular are of the 13c. These are not in 'Italian', but in different vernaculars: Sicilian, Umbrian, Lombard, Venetian, Florentine, etc. One hesitates to call them 'dialects' in this period, because the notion of dialect implies an opposition to some sort of standard or more prestigious language, in our case a national Italian language which only took root in the second half of the 15c. Only after that can one speak of dialect works, which are consciously opposed to Italian, and which emphasize their municipal character, their linguistic parochiality; some of these works are among the most striking products of the Renaissance, such as Beolco's plays in the dialect of the Paduan countryside. There are also plays in which certain characters or masks are identified by their use of stylized forms of dialects, foreign languages, or mock Latin.

The vernacular literature which proved most influential was Tuscan, particularly the works of the great 14c. Florentine writers Dante, Petrarch and Boccaccio. During the 15c. we find that humanist culture both restricted the literary possibilities of the vernacular, and transferred to it some of its own ideals (cf. Alberti and so-called vernacular humanism). The influence of Tuscan remained strong, although works produced in different parts of Italy kept their own distinct linguistic features, for instance with the northern koine of Boiardo's *Orlando innamorato*, with the Florentine of Pulci's *Morgante*, and with the southern variety apparent in the first version of Sannazaro's *Arcadia*.

It was in the early part of the 16c., with the wars and the great political crises which shook the whole of Italy, that the *questione della lingua* flared up. One thesis, usually referred to as that of the *lingua cortigiana*, and put forward by Castiglione and Trissino among others, claimed that the Italian language was to be supra-regional, that mixed but polished idiom spoken in the main courts (like Rome, Milan, Ferrara, Urbino) by the *cortigiani*, who notwithstanding their different origins used a basically national tongue. The Tuscans swiftly reacted, pointing out that this national language was in fact their own, i.e. Tuscan (or rather Florentine, as Florentine literati insisted). But Tuscan culture had lost its impetus and the position which prevailed was that codified by the Venetian Pietro Bembo in his *Prose della volgar lingua* (1525): as in Latin Virgil and Cicero were used as models, so vernacular writers must use the vernacular classics, Petrarch and Boccaccio, as their models; and to be born a Florentine in the 16c., it was argued, was no great help if your language was to be based on 14c. authors. This was the foundation on which the literary language was unified at all levels: from spelling to grammar and vocabulary. Ariosto revised his *Orlando furioso* (which was already far more Tuscan than Boiardo's poem), using for his final edition (1532) the rules set out in Bembo's *Prose*; and at the end of the century the Accademia della Crusca adopted Bembo's principles as the basis for its great *Vocabolario* (1612), which was to have such influence on the language of Italian literature. Non-literary works, on the other hand, private documents like letters and diaries, or even (particularly in the case of Venice) official state papers, such as historians are likely to consult in archives, still kept a much more regional, dialectal flavour.

This explains some important features of Italian: a literary rather than a spoken language, more suitable for poetry and rhetorically regulated prose than for science and everyday affairs, a language for an educated élite who would learn it from books rather than acquire it as a native idiom; but it was probably the only language which, given the historical conditions of a politically divided Renaissance Italy, could become a *national* (albeit literary rather than popular) language. It is only in the present

century that Italian is becoming the native language of Italians. *See* NATIONAL FEELING. LL
B. Migliorini and T. G. Griffith *The Italian language* (1966); A. Stussi 'Lingua, dialetto e letteratura' *SI* I

Jerome, St (*c*.345–*c*.420) Latin Church Father, born at Stridon, Croatia. He revised the old Latin Vulgate version of the New Testament on the basis of a Greek text and made a new translation of the Old Testament from the Hebrew. Jerome, who had studied under Donatus, was a good classical stylist and once dreamed that a voice from heaven accused him of being 'a Ciceronian not a Christian'. He was cited by early 15c. humanists, including Bruni, as proof that the study of pagan learning could be of value to the Christian. Iconography commonly depicts him during his 2-year period of retirement in the desert near Aleppo. OL

Jews Before 1300 there were relatively few Jews in Italy. Substantial numbers migrated from Germany in the 14c. and 15c. and from Spain and Portugal after their expulsion in 1492. There were some 35,000 Jews in Italy early in the 17c. They were particularly active in the loan business (from banking to pawnbroking), in the second-hand clothes trade, as goldsmiths and as physicians. They had always tended to live in their own quarters, but were compelled, in the 16c., to live in closed ghettoes, first in Venice in 1516 (in the old foundry area from which the term 'ghetto' derives), and later in Rome, Florence, and elsewhere. Jews were also compelled to wear distinctive clothing such as red or yellow hats. Anti-semitism was institutionalized in the Roman Carnival, in which Jews had to race naked and were pelted by bystanders. It was frequently whipped up by Franciscan preachers, quick to accuse Jews of ritual murder (as in the celebrated case of the infant Simon of Trent, found drowned in 1475), of desecrating the host, and of spreading plague. Anti-semitism seems to have grown during the Counter-Reformation. Paul IV and Pius V passed measures against the Jews, whose expulsion from Genoa and Lucca followed. Some of the Jews in Italy assimilated Renaissance culture.

Jews are burnt at the stake for the profanation of the Host: from a predella panel by Uccello (Urbino, Galleria Nazionale delle Marche).

Leone Ebreo, physician to Gonzalo de Cordoba in Naples, wrote, *c*.1501, his famous neo-Platonic *Dialoghi d'amore*. Conversely, some humanists studied Hebrew, among them Giannozzo Manetti and Giovanni Pico della Mirandola, an enthusiast for Christian CABBALA. But from 1548 Jews in Venice were not allowed to engage in printing books, and the burning in Rome in 1553 of the Talmud and other Jewish books effectively marks the end of an age of Christian-Jewish cultural cross-fertilization. PB
C. Roth *The Jews in the Renaissance* (1959); M. A. Shulvass *The Jews in the world of the Renaissance* (Eng. tr. 1973); B. Ravid 'The establishment of the *Ghetto Vecchio* of Venice' *Proceedings of the 6th World Congress of Jewish Studies* II (1975)

John XXII Pope 1316–34 (b.1244) Jacques Duèse, a Gascon, former chancellor of Charles II of Naples, was elected to the papacy as a stop-gap candidate, aged 72 and in bad health. The invigorating effect of power upon his constitution allowed him in fact a reign of 18 years. Certain apparent eccentricities in his pontificate – his conviction that numerous Italians (among them Dante) were seeking to encompass his death by magic powers, and his propagation of an heretical interpretation of the Last Judgment – are better considered as reflections of the character of his times than any indications of senility, for he remained to the last an able administrator. His pontificate was remarkable for his attack upon the Spiritual Franciscans – those of the order who sought an absolute rather than comparative poverty, and his condemnation as heretical of their view that Christ on earth led a life of absolute poverty.

Through his legate, Bertrand du Poujet, he waged a long and ultimately unsuccessful war (1316–34) in Italy in an attempt to recover control over the Papal State. At the same time, seeking to exploit rival candidacies to the throne of the Empire, he was involved in a protracted struggle with the Emperor Lewis IV of Bavaria. To finance the vast expenses of these conflicts he developed the bureaucratic, fund-raising machinery of the Curia to new heights of efficiency, and he can be seen as a principal architect of that papal fiscal development which was to arouse such profound hostility in Europe. *See* AVIGNON. JL

G. Mollat *The popes at Avignon, 1305–1378* (1963)

John XXIII anti-Pope 1410–15 (b.*c.*1370) The Neapolitan Baldassare Cossa (or Coscia) was elected pope by the Pisan party in the Great SCHISM largely as a result of the energy he had shown in defence of the Papal State as legate of Bologna. Under the attacks of King Ladislas of Naples he was forced to seek the protection of the Emperor Sigismund, who compelled him to adhere to the Council of Constance. Faced here with demands for his abdication, he fled (March 1415) and was thereupon indicted for a variety of crimes. 'The more scandalous charges,' writes Gibbon, 'were suppressed; the vicar of Christ was only accused of piracy, murder, rape, sodomy and incest.' Renaissance propaganda tended to extremes and these accusations, though sufficient to intimidate him into submission, were without substance. After a 4-year imprisonment he was released and created cardinal bishop of Tusculum. He died in the house of his friend Cosimo de' Medici (22 December 1419), and is buried in a tomb with effigy by Donatello and Michelozzo in the baptistery of Florence. JL

The bronze effigy on the tomb of the anti-pope **John XXIII** by Donatello and Michelozzo (Florence, Baptistery).

Josquin des Prez (*c.*1440–1521) The greatest composer of his generation. He was born in the Netherlands, and may have been a choirboy at St Quentin, but apparently began his adult career as a singer in Milan cathedral in the 1450s, remaining there until about 1473, when he became a member of the retinue of the Sforzas. He is next heard of in Rome, possibly having gone there in the wake of Ascanio Sforza on the latter's election as a cardinal. He was a member of the papal choir for several years from 1486. When he failed to obtain promotion to the post of *maestro di cappella* to the Duke of Ferrara, being considered both too temperamental and too expensive, he seems to have returned to the Low Countries, but he came back to Italy to be given the post at Ferrara at last in 1503. In the following year he left because of an outbreak of plague, to become Provost of Notre-Dame in Condé, where he remained for the rest of his life.

Josquin was the first composer in the history of music to be considered a genius in his own lifetime, a fact which marks the difference between the medieval attitude to music as a craft and the High Renaissance idea of music as an art. He was in fact a highly skilled composer in a contrapuntal idiom, capable of writing learned Masses using *cantus firmus* techniques, canon and most other devices. But he differed from other Netherlanders, notably his teacher Ockegham, in that counterpoint was a comparatively minor side of his interests, his genius being shown in the way he expresses the inner meaning of the texts he set (which commended him to humanistically inclined musicians) and in his capacity to follow the accentuations of the words, using textures which allow them to be clearly audible. If his major music was written for church use, he was also an attractive composer of chansons, in some of which he breaks away from courtly politeness. Martin Luther said of him: 'He is master of the notes; others are mastered by them.' *See* MUSIC. DA

E. Lowinsky *Josquin des Prez* (1976)

Raphael's portrait of the ageing **Julius II** (London, National Gallery).

Julius II Pope 1503–13 (b.1443) Ablest of the nephews of Sixtus IV, Giuliano della Rovere became Cardinal S. Pietro in Vincula on the elevation of his uncle in 1471. He was one of the most successful pluralists of his age, eventually accumulating 8 bishoprics and 1 archbishopric (Avignon) as well as numerous abbeys. As legate *a latere* to France (1480–82) he displayed his diplomatic skill by reconciling Louis XI and Maximilian of Austria. Being also largely responsible for the election of Innocent VIII (1484), he continued to enjoy considerable influence and, during the so-called Barons' War (1484–86), provided, with characteristic energy, for the defence of Rome from the armies of the King of Naples. After the election of his rival, Cardinal Borgia, as Alexander VI (1492), Giuliano retired to his fortress at Ostia. In 1494 he fled to France, hoping to obtain backing for the convocation of a Council to depose Alexander VI. This plan failed and Giuliano was reconciled with the Borgias (1498). In 1502, however, Cesare Borgia invaded the duchy of Urbino, whose heir-apparent was Francesco della Rovere, and Giuliano again retired to France, returning to Rome on Alexander VI's death (1503). On the death of Pius III, Giuliano himself became pope (1503).

His pontificate was an important one for the Papacy. Julius II, whom Machiavelli admired almost unreservedly, was responsible for reconstituting the Papal State into the form it retained for 4 centuries. He recovered the territories taken by Cesare BORGIA and reasserted papal authority over the Roman barons. He obtained the surrender of Perugia from Gian Paolo Baglioni and expelled Giovanni Bentivoglio from Bologna (1506). He joined the League of CAMBRAI and excommunicated Venice (1509), then, having recovered Rimini and Faenza, made peace (1510). Disturbed by growing French strength in Italy, he then allied with Venice, Spain and England in the Holy League. He attacked the Duke of Ferrara, occupied Modena (1510) and captured Mirandola (1511), himself playing an active part in the campaigns. The French recovered Mirandola and Bologna and in 1512 won the battle of Ravenna, but by 1513 their power in Italy had collapsed. Meanwhile, Julius had successfully backed the Medici restoration in Florence (1512). In 1511 Louis XII summoned the *conciliabulum* of Pisa. Julius who had a sincere, if sporadic, interest in church reform had already issued a bull against simony and was actively supporting missionary enterprises in the New World and the reform of the Benedictines. He, therefore, countered the French king's move by summoning the not unimpressive Fifth Lateran Council.

Julius was a financial genius and brilliant administrator. He carefully supervised all aspects of the papal administration, was responsible for defining the legal and procedural distinctions between lay and ecclesiastical cases, reorganized the college of notaries and began the system of strict annual auditing of the papal accounts. His monetary reforms, including the issue of the new silver *giulio*, helped avoid a papal bankruptcy. His enlightened patronage of the arts laid the foundations of the Roman High Renaissance. He expanded the Vatican library and began the papal collection of antique sculpture. He employed Michelangelo, Bramante, Raphael and other artists to celebrate the power of the Church and the truth of its doctrine. It was he who began the building of the new St Peter's and he who commissioned the Sistine ceiling from Michelangelo and the Stanze della Segnatura from Raphael.

Julius was criticized by his contemporaries, as he has been by subsequent historians, for his involvement in secular affairs. Yet his determined efforts to restore the Papal State were an honest attempt to rescue the Church from the control of any secular power, and he was the first Renaissance pope to attempt to eliminate both simony and nepotism. *See* PAPACY; WARS OF ITALY. JH

L. Pastor *The history of the popes* VI (1898); L. Partridge and R. Starn *A Renaissance likeness: art and culture in Raphael's Julius II* (1980)

Ladislas of Durazzo King of Naples 1386–1414 (b.1380) Acceding to the throne of Naples, aged 6, in 1386, Ladislas was crowned in 1390. He fought off his rival to the throne, Louis II of Anjou, from 1390 to 1399. From 1404, taking advantage of the confusion caused by the Great SCHISM, he seized Rome, Latium and Umbria. In 1409 he gained Cortona in southern Tuscany. Alarmed by these developments and claiming that he was seeking 'the kingdom of Italy', Florence united with his Angevin enemies against him. JL

A. Cutolo *Re Ladislao d'Angiò Durazzo* (1936)

Landini, Francesco (*c.*1335–97) Blind Florentine organist of whom very little is known beyond several mentions by contemporary writers. His surviving madrigals and *caccie* show a gift for vivid depiction of the verse. DA

Landino, Cristoforo (1424–92), Florentine humanist, was a prominent member of the circle of Lorenzo de' Medici and an important literary theorist. He was appointed to a chair of poetry and rhetoric at Florence in 1458. His *Disputationes Camaldulenses* (1474) gives an imaginative view of the new Platonists: it purports to record discussions held at the monastery of Camaldoli in which Lorenzo de' Medici and Alberti debate the active and contemplative lives, Alberti and Ficino discuss the question of the highest good, and Alberti gives an allegorical interpretation of Virgil's *Aeneid*. It probably conveys something of the current atmosphere. Landino was himself a mediocre poet: his greatest influence stemmed from his application of the new Platonism to a view of poetry as a source of divine wisdom. In 1481 he published an influential commentary on Dante's *Comedy*, presenting it as an allegorical poem and Dante as a Florentine patriot and opponent of the Papacy. *See* PLATO AND NEO-PLATONISM. GH

Landino lecturing: woodcut title page of his *Formulaio di lettere*, 1492.

Lannoy, Charles de (1487/8–1527) was one of the very few individuals ever to enjoy Charles V's friendship. After 1515 he was numbered among Charles's closest advisers, and served as a conscientious Viceroy of Naples, 1522–24. He played a notable part in all the fighting in northern Italy and, after the battle of PAVIA (1525), it was he who insisted on transporting the captured Francis I to Madrid. He was, however, opposed to the imperial attack on the Papacy in 1527, and bitterly regretted the SACK OF ROME. JH

Laurana, Francesco (*c.*1430–?1502) Nomadic sculptor from Dalmatia, first documented at work on the triumphal arch of the Castelnuovo, Naples, in 1453. Between 1461 and 1466 he worked for René of Anjou in France, and then went to Sicily, producing notable statues of the Virgin and Child. He later returned to Naples and then to France,

The marble portrait bust of Beatrice of Aragon by **Francesco Laurana** (Berlin, Staatliche Museum).

working at Marseilles and Avignon (1477–83). His is a vivid and realistic style which is at its best in narrative reliefs and in several portrait busts of court ladies, where his interest in abstraction of forms is remarkable. [24] CA

J. Pope-Hennessy *Italian Renaissance sculpture* (1958); W. R. Valentiner 'Laurana's portrait busts of women' *Art Quarterly* (1942)

Laurana, Luciano (1420/5–1479) Architect from Dalmatia (Yugoslavia) who worked at the courts of Mantua, Naples, Pesaro and, most importantly, Urbino, where from 1465 he supervised the building of the Ducal Palace, joining the earlier 15c. wing to the older buildings on the site. The square brick courtyard articulated with white stone columns, and the spacious vaulted apartments enriched with exquisitely carved door and fireplace surrounds, make the palace one of the most harmonious surviving 15c. architectural ensembles, embodying the principles of Alberti, who may well have advised Federico da Montefeltro on the project. CE

P. Rotondi *Il Palazzo Ducale di Urbino* (1950; abr. Eng. tr. 1964)

The courtyard of the Ducal Palace at Urbino, designed by **Luciano Laurana**.

Leo X Pope 1513–21 (b.1475) Born Giovanni de' Medici, second son of Lorenzo the Magnificent, Leo had been destined from childhood for ecclesiastical stardom. Piero, his elder brother, was to inherit Lorenzo's political position in Florence. Giovanni was to broaden the family's power base and bring it additional repute by becoming a prince of the Church. Lorenzo pushed his career untiringly, having him admitted into minor orders at the age of 8, and pulling every diplomatic string at his command to get him appointed to wealthy parishes and abbacies (including Montecassino) and secure the necessary permission for him to hold them jointly and *in absentia*. In 1489, when Giovanni was 13, Pope Innocent VIII promised to make him a cardinal. It was, Lorenzo wrote, 'the greatest achievement of our house', and he made it clear to Giovanni that while he was destined to serve the Church, at the same time 'it will not be difficult for you to aid the city and our house.'

Ebullient, cultivated and pliable, Giovanni had a natural flair for combining these roles with charm and shrewdness. Following Piero into exile in 1494, he fostered from Rome the Medicean fifth column in Florence and so commended himself to Julius II that he was given positions of responsibility that made him, in spite of his youth, *papabile*. In both roles he achieved extraordinary success. In 1512 his family was restored to power in Florence. In 1513, on Julius's death, he was elected pope and took the title Leo X. Seeing him thus favoured by fortune, it is hard to reject simply as hearsay the remark attributed to him (by a Venetian ambassador four years later): 'let us enjoy the papacy since God has given it to us.'

ʾortrait drawing of **Leo X** attributed to Giulio omano (Chatsworth, Devonshire Collection).

Leo's enjoyment of the papacy was obvious. e was able to indulge his taste for hunting and asting as well as his delight in offering the spitality of his court to men of letters and the holars and agents who added to his collection classical manuscripts. Bembo and Sadoleto ere among his secretaries, Cardinal Bibbiena as his treasurer general. Raphael continued to ork in the *stanze* of the Vatican and it was for eo that he designed the great series of tapestries r the Sistine Chapel. Leo hastened the process hereby ROME was being reshaped into a enaissance capital and did something, at least, prevent this being done mainly at the xpense of the materials that made up, still so mpressively, the monuments of ancient Rome. He urged on the building of the new St Peter's tarted by Julius II.

He did this by licensing the sale of indulgences. These were the indulgences that moved Luther to open criticism of the Church. He granted the title 'Defender of the Faith' (so oddly first used on British coinage by George I and still so cherished) to Henry VIII, not so long before his break with Rome. It would be hard to claim, however, that the magnitude of either threat could then have been foreseen. His Concordat of Bologna of 1516 gave Francis I almost as much as he wanted as far as control over the Church in France was concerned; but if the tie with Rome here became unduly elastic, at least it was not to break. Leo was a conscientious and, at the appropriate moments in the Church's calendar, devout and pious man. Insulated by the city and society he helped to create he was, perhaps, insensitive to the religious mood beyond it. What he never lost sight of beyond its walls was Florence, whose affairs he ran, at a distance and through deputies, with meticulous attention, while not failing to make the ex-rebel city pay for certain purely Roman concerns, such as the conquest of Urbino in 1517. From the repossession of the Milanese by the French in 1515 to their expulsion a few months before he died, Leo was not tested by the threat of large-scale wars in Italy. In this respect the time of his death was fortunate. In retrospect it was not unsuitable to describe his pontificate – like his father's period of control in Florence – as a Golden Age. *See* PAPACY. JRH

L. Pastor *The history of the popes* VII and VIII (1908); G. B. Picotti *La giovenezza di Leone X* (1927); E. Rodocanachi *Le pontificat de Léon X* (1931)

Leonardo da Vinci (1452–1519), the bastard son of a Florentine notary and the greatest, most wide-ranging genius in the history of Western art, was the man with whom Vasari rightly began the third and culminating section of his story of the equalling, and finally the overtopping, of the triumphs of antiquity by the arts of the Renaissance. Athletics, music, drawing, painting, sculpture, architecture, town planning, perspective, optics, astronomy, aviation; hydraulic, nautical, military, structural and mechanical engineering; anatomy, biology, zoology, botany, geology, geography, mathematics – the list of his interests is seemingly endless. The mass of notes and drawings in which he recorded his ideas and experiments are not just revealing of the workings of his own mind but vital for any understanding of the meaning of the Renaissance. It is no surprise that he should have said that 'a painter is not admirable unless he is universal'. He also said that 'impatience, the mother of stupidity, praises brevity,' and what he would have thought about an entry such as this can well be imagined.

Leonardo's artistic career is easily divided into 4 main periods. The first Florentine period lasts until his departure for Milan to work for Lodovico Sforza in 1482–83. He trained under and worked with Verrocchio, being enrolled as

The later version of **Leonardo**'s *Virgin of the Rocks* (London, National Gallery).

a master in the painters' guild in 1472, and his first major, independent work is the Verrocchiesque *Annunciation* in the Uffizi. The portrait of *Ginevra Benci* (?1474), the Munich and Benois Madonnas, and the great *Adoration of the Magi*, begun in 1481 and never finished (as is the case with many of Leonardo's projects), are the major products of this phase of his activity.

The Louvre *Virgin of the Rocks*, almost certainly begun in 1483, and the London National Gallery version – which, despite the innumerable controversies which have surrounded it, was almost certainly begun in the mid-1490s, left incomplete when Leonardo fled from the French invasion of Milan, and only completed after his return in 1506 – are, with *The Last Supper* (S. Maria delle Grazie), the surviving masterpieces from the first Milanese period, his bronze equestrian monument to Francesco Sforza having only reached the stage of an enormous clay model for the horse itself before it was destroyed.

In the second Florentine period Leonardo's major commission was for the great fresco of the *Battle of Anghiari* (1502–03), set as a pendant to Michelangelo's *Battle of Cascina* in the Council Chamber of the Republic. *The Mona Lisa* and the *Virgin and St Anne*, both in the Louvre, together with the cartoon for the latter (London, National Gallery), mark the flowering of his new sfumato style. Returning to Milan in 1506 to complete the National Gallery *Virgin of the Rocks*, he became Painter and Engineer to Francis I of France, but apart from work on the Trivulzio Monument, another major equestrian group, he appears to have concentrated more and more on his scientific pursuits. Indeed, the only surviving record of his late pictorial style is the Louvre *St John*. This was probably carried out after he left for Rome in 1513 and before he departed for France in 1517 to die in the château at Cloux that had been presented to him by the King.

That Leonardo's scientific, and above all his anatomical, discoveries did not themselves change the course of history is largely owing to the fact that they were not published during his lifetime, while his notes, which he left to Francesco Melzi, disappeared from sight until after the latter's death in 1570. Many of his inventions, such as the tank, were frustrated for lack of a prime mover, which steam or the internal combustion engine were later to provide. What was never frustrated, however, was Leonardo's unrivalled ability to cut down to the nub of the matter at hand; to lay down the principles of tank warfare; to see that the basic problem of anatomical drawing is the nature of the multi-layered 3-dimensional structure with which it deals, and to solve it by reducing muscles and tendons to lines of force; to solve the circulation problem of medieval towns by suggesting multi-level road and canal systems based on separation of function: at every point he separates out the essential features of the problems he faces and proposes radical solutions.

In almost every aspect of his life and work Leonardo stands at a parting of the ways, at a crucial moment of decision on the road towards the modern world. Insisting on the medieval concept of universality, he helped, by his insistence on observation and experiment and on the accumulation of factual knowledge, to render universality unobtainable and to usher in the modern world of specialization. Insisting on the genius of the artist and on his unique service to society, he went far to complete the process of freeing the artist from the secure, but humble, artisan status which he had enjoyed in the medieval world. He ushered in the modern age of the individual, socially mobile, entrepreneurial artist, free to prosper or to starve. He also epitomized the artist's new role, not merely as a manual worker, but as a thinker and a theorist.

In so doing he stands at the head of the development of the academies and schools of art. At the same time his concurrent development of purely manual, technical skills to a new peak of excellence was such that, in developing the artist's power to represent the natural world with an unprecedented degree of subtlety and precision, he also turned his pen or pencil into a seismograph that registered every tremor and each perturbation in the artist's inmost psychological being. Not only could Freud undertake an analysis of the cartoon for the *Virgin and St Anne*, but the road which leads towards the artist-scientist, the artist-illustrator and communicator, is also the road which leads towards the modern world of self-revelation, self-expression and self-isolation in the face of an often uncomprehending public. Indeed, as a draughtsman Leonardo carried the expressive potential of the individual drawn line further than any previous artist except Antonio Pollaiuolo, and the progress of his draughtsmanship from the early, parallel hatching, silverpoint style, through the curvilinear hatching style developed at the end of the first Milanese period, to the red and black chalk stippling of his late drawings provides the essential foundation for his development as a painter. In their range and in their significance for art and visual understanding, Leonardo's drawings are unparalleled.

As Leonardo endlessly insists, all his scientific work was in the service of an art in which the essential value, unlike that of scientific experiment, lies precisely in its uniqueness and its unrepeatability. He and his fellow artists, not the doctors of his day, having reached the limits of what could be achieved by external observation, turned to dissection and anatomy to extend their knowledge of the underlying forces and structures which condition the external appearances of the human figure. It was in the service of art that they developed a precision of draughtsmanship without which the rate of progress in the natural sciences in the centuries that preceded the invention of the camera would have been inconceivable. He lived, indeed, in that one magic moment in the history of Western civilization when art was at the forefront of the move into the modern scientific world, and budding science was the catalyst for supreme artistic achievement. *See* ARTIST, STATUS OF THE; SCIENCE. [27, 126, 209] JW

J. P. Richter *The literary works of Leonardo da Vinci* (1970); K. Clark *Leonardo da Vinci* (1958); L. D. Ettlinger *The complete works of Leonardo da Vinci* (1968); R. E. Popham *The drawings of Leonardo da Vinci* (1946)

Leone Ebreo (*c.*1465–before 1535) Portuguese Jew (*ebreo* is Italian for 'Jew') who, after living in Toledo from 1483–92, fled to Italy during the expulsion of the Jews from Spain. There he lived an unsettled life, practising as a doctor in Naples, Genoa, Rome and perhaps Venice. His *Dialoghi d'amore* (pub. 1535), which sum up and metaphysically extend the place Ficino and Pico had accorded to love as a path to divine understanding, acquired a European fame, appealing to temperaments as different as those of Cervantes and Spinoza. JRH

G. Saitta 'La filosofia di Leone Ebreo' *Filosofia italiana e umanesimo* (1928)

Leoni, Leone (*c.*1509–90) was a goldsmith, medallist and bronze sculptor of great brilliance, whose career ran parallel with those of Cellini and Michelangelo. In the 1530s he was producing medals in Padua (Bembo, Aretino, Titian) and Rome (for the Pope). In the 1540s he entered the service of Charles V, expanding his range to monumental portrait sculptures of the Habsburgs, mostly for Spain, *Charles V Restraining Fury* (1549–64), *Philip II, Mary of Hungary* and others (1553–55; Madrid, Prado). He also produced statues of the Gonzaga (Sabbioneta, Guastalla), the tomb of Gian Giacomo de' Medici (Milan cathedral), and a number of other reliefs and statuettes in bronze. Leoni's consummate skill in metal craftsmanship set a standard which influenced the course of sculpture and medallic art all over Europe, thanks to the wide sway of the Habsburg Empire. [79, 248] CA

J. Pope-Hennessy *Italian High Renaissance and Baroque sculpture* (1970); E. Plon *Leone Leoni et Pompeo Leoni* (1887)

Lepanto, battle of (7 October 1571) Naval victory of 208 galleys of the Holy League over 210 Turkish galleys plus lighter supporting craft, fought just outside the Gulf of Corinth.

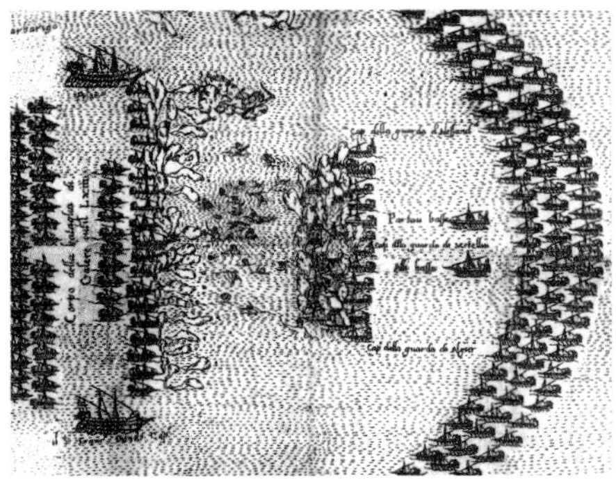

Detail from a plan of the formation of the Christian and Turkish forces during the battle of **Lepanto** in 1571.

Four of the seven **liberal arts** with their exponents, in Andrea da Firenze's fresco (Florence, S. Maria Novella, Spanish Chapel).

Resounding in terms of casualties (*c.*30,000 Turks as against *c.*9000) and prizes (apart from those sunk, 117 Turkish galleys were captured), but its effect on the balance of power in the Mediterranean was only moderate: in 1572 the dockyards of Constantinople produced a fleet almost as large as that of Lepanto. JRH

J. F. Guilmartin *Gunpowder and galleys* . . . (1974)

Leto, Pomponio (1428–98), extreme devotee of Roman antiquities, was a pupil of Valla. He gathered round him at Rome an Academy of pupils and fellow humanists, propagating an exaggerated devotion to Roman literature, names, pagan ceremonies, even early Roman methods of agriculture, which was temporarily suppressed by Pope Paul II in 1468 because of suspicions of irreligion and republicanism. Leto fled, returned and was imprisoned in S. Angelo but released after condemnation for paganism and pederasty. GH

V. Zabughin *Giulio Pomponio Leto* (1909–12)

Liberal arts These represented the subject matter of the secular 'arts' syllabus of the Middle Ages; first the preparatory *trivium* – grammar, rhetoric and dialectic, then the basis of a philosophical training, the *quadrivium*, comprising arithmetic, geometry, astronomy and music. By the 13c. each had been given a pictorial identity, together with identifying attributes (e.g. a measuring rod for geometry) and exemplars (e.g. Pythagoras for arithmetic, Tubal for music). While treated with a stylistic variety that reflected current pictorial concerns, whether with iconographic completeness (Andrea da Firenze in the Spanish Chapel at S. Maria Novella in Florence), or with narrative (Pinturicchio in the Vatican) or with the nude (Pollaiuolo's tomb of Sixtus IV in St Peter's), the theme was left remarkably intact by artists whose own activity (save through the mathematics of perspective) was excluded from it as manual rather than liberal. JRH

R. van Marle *Iconographie de l'art profane* II (1932); R. McKeon 'The transformation of the liberal arts in the Renaissance' in B. S. Levy ed. *Developments in the early Renaissance* (1972)

Ligorio, Pirro (*c.*1510–83) Neapolitan architect and passionate antiquarian, whose extensive notebooks and map reconstructing

Detail of the stuccoed and painted ceiling of the loggia of the Casino of Pius IV in Rome, by **Ligorio**.

the buildings of ancient Rome (1561) drew on an unprecedented array of archaeological sources (coins, inscriptions, excavations). Ligorio incorporated his researches into his buildings, like the Casino of Pius IV in the Vatican gardens (1558f.), a delicious retreat of pavilions and loggias around an oval courtyard, crammed with bizarre and erudite decoration. Apart from continuing and transforming Bramante's Cortile del Belvedere, Ligorio almost certainly designed the Villa d'Este at Tivoli (1560f.), in which the entire repertory of the Roman 16c. villa – fountains, staircase, ramps, water-organs, grottoes, a miniature reconstruction of ancient Rome – cascades in symmetrical profusion down the hillside. Sacked from St Peter's in 1565, Ligorio retired to Ferrara to pursue his eccentric researches. CE
E. Mandowsky and C. Mitchell *Pirro Ligorio's 'Roman Antiquities'* (1963); G. Smith *The Casino of Pius IV* (1977)

Lippi, Filippino (1457–1504) The son of Filippo Lippi, he entered Botticelli's workshop after his father's death. He does not appear to have gone with him to Rome in 1481 to work on the Sistine Chapel, but to have remained in Florence where, between 1481 and 1486, he painted his famous *Vision of St Bernard* (Florence, Badia). In 1484 he received a commission to complete the Brancacci Chapel in S. Maria del Carmine which had been left unfinished by Masaccio and Masolino half a century earlier. In 1487 he signed a contract to decorate the Strozzi Chapel in S. Maria Novella, a task which was promptly put off by his departure to Rome in 1488 to decorate the Carafa Chapel in S. Maria Sopra Minerva. By 1493 he was back in Florence and in 1495 he was commissioned to paint an Adoration of the Magi (Florence, Uffizi) to replace the unfinished work by Leonardo for a monastery outside Florence. The Strozzi Chapel was finally completed in 1502, two years before his premature death. His nervous, attenuated style derived from Botticelli's decorative and sensitive Quattrocento manner. LDE
K. B. Neilson *Filippino Lippi* (1938); L. Berti and U. Baldini *Filippino Lippi* (1957)

Lippi, Fra Filippo (active *c.*1432, d.1469) was an orphan placed in the Carmine in 1421, whose unfitness for his imposed religious life is summed up in his trial for fraud, his abduction of, and subsequent marriage to, the nun Lucrezia, and the birth of his son Filippino (1457–58), who also became a distinguished painter. Consistently patronized by the Medici and chiefly, though not exclusively, active as a panel painter, he marks the transition from the monumental gravity and apparent simplicity of the Masacciesque 1420s to the lighter, linear, and more overtly complex art of the mid-century, dominated as it was by the mature work of Donatello, and by sculptors such as Rossellino and Desiderio da Settignano. Like Donatello, Lippi investigated, in his own intensely personal way, the complicated interplay of space and plane, picture and frame, inherent in the new Artificial PERSPECTIVE. From his earliest dated work, the *Tarquinia Madonna* (1437), to his frescoes in the cathedral at Prato

The Vision of St Bernard by **Filippino Lippi** (detail) (Florence, Badia).

Filippo Lippi's Barbadori altarpiece (Paris, Louvre).

(1452) and his late and increasingly mystical Nativities, these investigations created a constant underlying motif to set against the more explicit theorizing of men such as Uccello or Piero della Francesca. JW

G. Marchini *Filippo Lippi* (1975)

Literature The centuries between 1300, the year that Dante chose as the now and forever of the *Divine Comedy*, and 1600, when Bruno was burned in Rome for heresy, produced a literature that made Italy, in this art as in others, an object of emulation throughout Europe. While the great Trecento writers epitomized late medieval civilization, they also foretold the passing of Gothic sensibility and scholastic specialization. Here began a shift in emphasis toward EDUCATION with a literary bent, based on the *studia humanitatis*, with a re-evaluation of secular antiquity and of the natural world that has gained for the Quattrocento and Cinquecento the disputed name of RENAISSANCE. The idea of a revival of classical values after a millennium of darkness was enunciated by Petrarch, with Dante and Boccaccio one of the '*tre corone*', the triumvirate who made Tuscan pre-eminent among regional vernaculars and set standards for Italian literature.

Dante's *Comedy* was imitated in such Trecento poems as Fazio degli Uberti's *Dittamondo*, but Petrarch's and Boccaccio's works, vernacular and Latin, had broader immediate influence. As a model of the man of letters, Petrarch used the forms of the medieval and classical past to map the Renaissance future. His *Rime* set a course for the love lyric, as his Latin letters and his cultivation of the eclogue, dialogue, epic and comic genres did for humanistic writers. Boccaccio gave literary form to the traditional collection of tales, creating a portrait of the mercantile class and urban society of medieval Florence, juxtaposed with nostalgic images of a feudal and courtly way of life that would continue to stir the imagination of Renaissance writers. The *Decameron* was followed by Sacchetti's *Trecentonovelle*, Ser Giovanni's *Pecorone* and other novella collections. Boccaccio's other works, in verse and in prose, were equally seminal: the range of his prose, from Ciceronian to popular, and his refinement of the narrative *ottava rima*, were as shaping of future literature as his Latin delvings into classical myth and history were. The desolating series of plagues, famine and economic crises that fell across the Trecento, affecting Boccaccio's and Petrarch's later works and those of the minor lyric *petrarchisti*, also encouraged vernacular devotional literature expressing worldly disillusionment and spiritual mission, none more fervently than the mystical and proselytizing prayers, letters and dialogues of St Catherine of Siena.

Although, from Petrarch's death in 1374 until Poliziano's début about a hundred years later, Italian verse was undistinguished, literary production in the Quattrocento was intense. The achievement of the first decades was the recovery of lost or corrupted classical texts, the philological and stylistic accomplishments of neo-Latin scholars and writers, and the establishing of the study of Greek literature. The allying of values of the humanistic movement with civic life and institutions begun by the Florentine chancellor Salutati was continued by such disciples as Bruni and Bracciolini, who made prodigious contributions to the restoring of texts and to the emergent discipline of historiography. The *signorie* of Milan, Ferrara, Mantua, the Kingdom of Naples and the Papacy also encouraged humanistic literature, sometimes with radical philological results like Valla's. By the late Quattrocento a new command of classical genres had been achieved, and in some centres, Ficino's Florentine Academy for one, humanistic literature became increasingly contemplative in character. The change in Latin style necessarily affected Italian literature, and some of the best neo-Latin pens also wrote the best vernacular literature: Alberti's Tuscan dialogue treatise *Della famiglia*, Sannazaro's *Arcadia* and Poliziano's *Stanze per la giostra*. Popular literature flourished in rustic lyrics, farces and municipal religious drama, forms also taken up for more sophisticated purposes by writers like Lorenzo the Magnificent. Masuccio Salernitano and his contemporaries answered a continuing demand for novellas. An especially vital form of popular literature was the Carolingian and Arthurian romance brought from France to Italy, where it gained new literary status in the *ottava rima* epic romance, represented by Pulci's *Morgante* and Boiardo's *Orlando innamorato*.

In the Cinquecento vernacular literature came fully of age, Trecento and classical examples having been assimilated for use in an 'illustrious' or polished modern language about which a debate, the '*questione della lingua*', raged. Competitive imitation of the classics was a principle of most literary enterprise and determined many characteristic High Renaissance fusions of materials and genres. Modern theatre was born in Ferrara and Florence from the union of Greek and Latin DRAMA with medieval narrative and spectacle. Machiavelli and Guicciardini summoned new historical visions from observation of contemporary events – politics and psychology collated with classical HISTORY – and Castiglione expanded Platonic and Ciceronian models of dialogue into an image of Renaissance courtly society. Ariosto's continuation of Boiardo's *Innamorato* brought to the epic romance some of the lessons learned from Ovid and Virgil and from Bembo's answer to the '*questione della lingua*'. The almost numberless lyric poets of the Cinquecento were also influenced by Bembo, as by the neo-Platonic theories of love of Leone Ebreo and his successors.

These ideas, and the spirit of religious reform, caused qualities inherent in the Petrarchan tradition to become more pronounced in the Cinquecento in the lyrics of Vittoria Colonna, Michelangelo and della Casa, reaching a philosophical extreme in those of Bruno, while its wit, conceits and potential for parody were exploited by Berni and later by Mannerists preparing the way for Giambattista Marino (1569–1625). Like the drama, to which it offered plots, the novella prospered. A trend toward the risqué and pithily dialectal, especially among Florentines such as Grazzini, was in contrast with the moral, tragic and sensational bent of Giraldi and Bandello. As ACADEMIES proliferated, anti-academies challenged the neo-classical literary establishment, a challenge made also by individual 'irregulars', fecund stylistic opportunists like Aretino, fantasists like Doni, self-taught and self-celebrating adventurers like Cellini.

The late Cinquecento is known as the age of criticism because of an explosion in theory sparked by the dissemination of Aristotle's *Poetics* in a restored text. Francesco Robortello's commentary (1548) was followed by the treatises of J. C. Scaliger, Castelvetro and others, laying the foundations for later neo-classical doctrines and for the modern 'science' of literary criticism. In this atmosphere Tasso composed, revised and defended the *Liberata*. The Council of TRENT organized Catholic response to the Protestant Reformation and conscripted writers into the service of the Church's re-unification policy, while the spread of PRINTING made literary communication more than ever effective and encouraged translations, anthologies and other means of cultural self-help.

The spirit of the times combined neo-medievalism, a reaffirmation of universals, with a neo-classical attachment to the formal and historical sophistication acquired by humanism and the vernacular literature of the preceding 2 centuries. Militancy and negation, often harbouring together, contributed to a literature of paradox, and the familiar rhetorical device of antithesis evolved into a state of mind. Although the extremes of within-form strain, of ornament, hyperbole and ingenious conceit, would not be reached until the 17c., the presence of these traits cause such disparate styles as Tasso's, Guarini's and Bruno's to be considered early examples of Baroque literature. *See* HUMANISM; ITALIAN LANGUAGE; CRITICAL THEORY OF LITERATURE; LIVY. LGC

V. Branca ed. *Dizionario critico della letteratura italiana* (1973); J. H. Whitfield *A short history of Italian literature* (1960); E. H. Wilkins *A history of Italian literature* revised ed. T. G. Bergin (1974)

Livorno (Leghorn) Most of the town planning exercises of the Renaissance were in the interest of expanding already flourishing cities (Ferrara) or policing frontier areas (Palma). Only at Livorno (Leghorn is the anglicization of the early Italian spelling Legorno) was a fishing hamlet transformed into a thriving commercial metropolis. The impulse came from COSIMO I, in a determination to provide better port facilities for Tuscan trade than those available at the largely silted-up port of Pisa. The momentum behind the quay construction, land reclamation and house building was maintained by the Grand Dukes Francesco and Ferdinand. By 1600 the city had a population of 5000. Ferdinand attracted settlers by offering 15 years' exemption from taxes and perpetual freedom of trade to all nations. With its moderate harbourage and warehousing charges, and its absence of all political dues, Livorno became one of the most internationally used ports of the Mediterranean, even if – given the speed and economy with which it was created, and its absence of social 'tone' – it was one of the least physically attractive. JRH

F. Braudel and R. Romano *Navires et marchandises à l'entrée du port de Livourne, 1547–1611* (1951)

Livy (50 BC–AD 17) Because of its great bulk, Livy's (Titus Livius') history of Rome from its foundation to AD 9 was separated into Decades in the manuscript tradition, and some of them disappeared. The recovery of Livy arose from the circumstances of the AVIGNON Papacy, when Italian clerics who followed the Curia received benefices in France. Thus Landolfo Colonna went to Chartres and tapped the rich cathedral library, which had survived the decadence of the feudal age and like other cathedral and abbatial libraries awaited the touch of a reviving interest. Landolfo brought to Avignon for Petrarch to inherit in 1328–29 the text of the *vetus carnotensis*, a manuscript of Livy which had in particular Books XXVI-XL in a better text than any other. Petrarch was able to put together Decades I, III and IV, leaving only a few books from the Vth Decade to be found and published in 1533. His splendid manuscript (now in the British Library), with its composite text, sometimes in Petrarch's own hand, brought together again almost all that survived of Livy. Not only was it the basis for Petrarch's loving and intelligent annotation – the first philological enquiry of the humanistic world: it was the start of the whole European tradition for the text of Livy and, by its passage to Lorenzo Valla's hands in the next century, it received in its turn the attentions of that prince among Quattrocento philologists, the fruit being his *Emendationes in T. Livium* (1448). After Valla came Poliziano. While these two have long been in evidence in the textual tradition of Livy, it is only now that scholars have begun to see the traces, and recognize the importance, of Petrarch's contribution.

So an author whom Dante may have had to take on trust, probably knowing little of him at first hand, came back as the main historian of Rome. Petrarch vies with Livy in his *De viris illustribus*, and if he vies with Virgil in the *Africa*, it is with material that comes from Livy. Equally important is the impact on Boccaccio, who, in the wake of Petrarch's reconstitution of the text, translated Decades III-IV, and who laid the foundations of his own prose style in the *Decameron* under the influence of Livy (with some help from his favourite author Apuleius). Thus Livy, at one remove, becomes the foundation-stone of the reigning Italian prose-style down to Manzoni.

Meanwhile, the virtues which Livy saw in the republican history of Rome became the examples which the Quattrocento admired. Of this universal admiration we may note 2 cases. In the preface to the Venice edition of 1470 the luck of Livy in having Rome for subject is equated with the luck of Rome in having Livy as its mouthpiece. And Valla, in the proem to his *History of Ferdinand of Aragon*, after listing a few of the innumerable examples (the Fabritii, Curii, Reguli, Decii), exclaims 'For as the Greeks availed by their precepts, so do the Romans, and, what is better, by their example.' Cosimo de' Medici sent Alfonso of Aragon a manuscript of Livy, and, though warned to beware of poison, Alfonso opened it and had Livy read to him. The climax of this reverence for Livy comes at the beginning of the 16c., with Machiavelli's *Discourses on Livy* (*c.*1516–19), which are still bathed with a republican admiration for these same examples from the time before Rome became corrupt under its Emperors. It was in the crisis of the late 1520s (the Sack of Rome, the fall of the Florentine Republic) that the appetite for Livy waned, and Tacitus came to take his place. Only a belated Machiavellian, Jacopo Nardi, in exile from Florence, continues in the 1540s with his devotion to Livy, completing a new translation soon to be swamped and forgotten amongst the commentaries on Tacitus. JHW

G. Billanovich 'Petrarch and the textual tradition of Livy' *Journal of the Warburg and Courtauld Institutes* (1951); J. H. Whitfield 'Livy → Tacitus' in R. R. Bolgar ed. *Classical influences on European culture 1500–1700* (1976)

Lodi, Peace of (9 April 1454) Confusingly, this term is used to describe not only the peace settlement between Venice and Milan signed at Lodi, but also the defensive league signed in Venice on 30 August between Venice, Milan and Florence, and the later adhesion of Alfonso of Naples and Pope Nicholas V, early in 1455, to what became a mutual non-aggression pact binding for 25 years on the 5 major Italian powers and the greater number of their satellites. Though disturbed by some threatening alignments (notably Florence and Milan against a Venice-Papacy-Naples axis) and local wars (such as the Papal-Neapolitan campaign against Lorenzo the Magnificent after the partial failure of the PAZZI assassination plot and the War of FERRARA), the Lodi guidelines did secure an unprecedented degree of peaceful coexistence in the peninsula until the beginning of the Wars of Italy in 1494. JRH

G. Soranzo *La lega italica 1454–5* (1924)

Tullio **Lombardo**'s relief of *Bacchus and Ariadne* (Vienna, Kunsthistorisches Museum).

Lomazzo, Giovanni Paolo (1538–1600) Milanese artist, poet and writer on the theory of art. In spite of his indifferent ability, he had many commissions for portraits and frescoes in and around Milan. He travelled widely and even went as far north as Antwerp before he became blind in 1572. His 2 treatises, *Trattato dell'arte* (1584) and *Idea del tempio della pittura* (1591), on which his fame rests, sum up the Mannerist theory of his day. LDE

A. Blunt *Artistic theory in Italy 1450–1600* (1956)

Lombardo family The most important family of sculptor-architects active in Venice during the High Renaissance. The father, Pietro (*c.*1435–1515), was responsible for introducing Tuscan Renaissance architectural and sculptural style into Padua (Roselli Monument, S. Antonio, 1467) and Venice (chancel of S. Giobbe, *c.*1474). His principal monuments in Venice are those to Pasquale Malipiero (d.1462) and to Pietro Mocenigo (d.1476) in SS. Giovanni e Paolo. Several other tombs and a number of buildings were created in collaboration with his sons Tullio (*c.*1455–1532) and Antonio (*c.*1458–?1516).

Tullio was a brilliant marble sculptor whose masterpieces are the tombs of Giovanni Mocenigo (d.1485) and Andrea Vendramin in SS. Giovanni e Paolo. Architectural frameworks based on Roman triumphal arches were populated with marble statues imbued with the classical spirit, e.g. *Adam* (now New York, Metropolitan Museum of Art). Tullio carved a number of independent classicizing reliefs, e.g. *Bacchus and Ariadne* (Vienna, Kunsthistorisches Museum). Both he and Antonio contributed narrative reliefs to the Chapel of St Anthony in the basilica at Padua. Antonio not only shared in the vast output of monuments from the Lombardo workshop, but also provided models for life-size bronze sculptures in the Zen Chapel (S. Marco, Venice) and probably for small statuettes as well (e.g. *Pomona*, Ohio, Cleveland Museum of Art). His major independent commission (1506–16) was a series of mythological marble reliefs for the Camerini d'Alabastro in the Castello of Ferrara for that great patron of art Alfonso I d'Este. Many are now in the Hermitage, Leningrad, while separate but related panels are to be found e.g. in the Victoria and Albert Museum in London. Antonio's style is equivalent to those of Giorgione and the early Titian, forming with them the Venetian High Renaissance. CA

J. Pope-Hennessy *Italian Renaissance sculpture* (1958); L. Planiscig *Venezianische Bildhauer der Renaissance* (1921)

Loredan family Leonardo (1438–1521), doge from 1501, presided, at first feebly but with mounting authority, over Venice in the most desperate period of its fortunes: the campaigns (1509–16) that followed the Venetian defeat at AGNADELLO. Pietro (1481–1571), doge from 1567, saw Venice into the first dramatic phases of the War of Cyprus. These careers brought

Doge Leonardo **Loredan** as portrayed by Giovanni Bellini (London, National Gallery).

but additional fame to a family prominent in Venice in previous centuries and which, in the person of another Pietro (d.1439), had notably contributed to both the military and the administrative extension of that mainland empire which was to arouse the jealousy of the allies of CAMBRAI in 1509. JRH

Lorenzetti, Ambrogio (active 1319, d.?1348) With Simone Martini and his own brother Pietro, Ambrogio dominated Sienese art after the death of Duccio. Like many Sienese artists he was also active in Florence. In his case the result was an unprecedented fusion of the two styles. He was possibly responsible for the two earliest surviving pure landscape panels since antiquity (Siena, Pinacoteca), and his frescoes of *Good and Bad Government* in the Palazzo Pubblico, Siena, constitute the most important remaining secular decorative scheme from the Europe of their time. Replete with classical allusions, they run the gamut from meticulous allegorical expressions of contemporary political ideals and realities to town and landscape panoramas so revolutionary that there is not the remotest contemporary parallel anywhere else. In Italy they remain unequalled, and only Pieter Bruegel in the mid-16c. eventually matches their combination of large-scale foreground detail and panoramic range. [95] JW

G. Rowley *Ambrogio Lorenzetti* (1958)

Lorenzetti, Pietro (active 1320, d.?1348) Often overshadowed by his brother Ambrogio, with whom he collaborated, he was a significant figure in his own right and a major innovator in the representation of interiors. His Polyptych of 1320 (Arezzo, Pieve) marks the first surviving attempt to use the actual frame as a fully integrated, 3-dimensional forward boundary of the architectural space. In his *Birth of the Virgin* (1342; Siena, Museo dell'Opera del Duomo), he carried the process further than any of his contemporaries, Ambrogio included. JW

E. T. de Wald *Pietro Lorenzetti* (1930)

Lorenzo Monaco (1370/1–1425), Sienese painter and illuminator, entered the Camaldolensian monastery of S. Maria degli Angeli in Florence. His *Coronation of the Virgin* (1414) and late *Adoration of the Magi* in the Uffizi, Florence, together with a haunting, dream-like *Journey of the Magi*, show him carrying late-14c. Italian Gothic style, reinforced by contact with the early work of Ghiberti and with the International Gothic combination of fantasy and intense realism, on into 15c. Florence, alongside the emergent Renaissance art of Donatello and Masaccio. JW

Lotto, Lorenzo (*c*.1480–1556) Painter born in Venice, whose restless life is clearly documented only from 1538, when he began to keep his *Libro di spese diverse*, or account book. He was then in Ancona. Previously he had worked in Rome, Bergamo and at various places in the Marche, and possibly in Tuscany, as well as in Venice. Highly responsive to the art of others, his style evolved through a series of fusions that contained the main influences of the moment, whether Venetian colour or Roman Mannerism, without ever losing its individuality. Not acquiring the nonchalance of an assured and familiar approach, his works, which mainly comprised portraits and altarpieces, often express a nervous force which catches his sitters in revelatory off-guard moments (*Portrait of a Young Man*; Venice, Accademia) or places his intent religious figures within a setting of cool, brilliant colour (St Lucy altarpiece, Biblioteca Comunale, Jesi). In spite of his considerable output, poverty, as well as the mental perturbation he had referred to in his will of 1548, led him in 1552 to seek admission to the Holy Sanctuary at Loreto, the place of his death. [265] JRH

Il libro di spese diverse ed. P. Zampetti (1969); R. Palluchini *L'opera completa del Lotto* (1975)

Louis I of Anjou King of Hungary 1342–82, King of Poland 1370–82 (b.1326) Under Louis 'the Great' Hungary conquered Dalmatia from the Venetians and achieved its widest-ever territorial extent. On the murder in 1345 of his brother Andrew, husband of Giovanna I of Naples, Louis proclaimed the guilt of the Queen, asserted his own right to the throne, and launched an ultimately unsuccessful invasion (1347–52). In 1380–82 he supported with Hungarian troops the revolt against Giovanna which brought his cousin Charles of Durazzo to the Neapolitan throne. JL

B. Hóman *Gli Angioini di Napoli in Ungheria (1290–1403)* (1938)

Louis II of Anjou (1377–1417) On the death of his father, Duke Louis I of Anjou (cousin of Louis I of Anjou, King of Hungary), in 1384, Louis II inherited his claim to the Neapolitan throne. With the aid of the French crown and the anti-Pope Clement VII, he invaded the kingdom in 1390 in an attempt to seize it from the young King Ladislas. Despite initial successes he was forced to return to France in 1399. In 1411 he invaded the kingdom again as the nominee of the Pisan popes, defeated Ladislas's army at the battle of Roccasecca (19 May), but was compelled through lack of money to withdraw to Provence 3 months later. *See* SCHISM, THE GREAT; NAPLES. JL

Louis XII King of France 1498–1515 (b.1482) When Charles VIII died without an heir, Louis, Duke of Orléans, succeeded as his next of kin. He had served with the invasion force of 1494 and succeeded also to Charles's ambition to prosecute the Angevin claim to Naples. To this he added the claim of his own house to the duchy of Milan, based on his grandfather's marriage to Valentina Visconti; for him the Sforzas were usurpers. Thus doubly committed, he turned what might have been an isolated French raid into the WARS OF ITALY.

His intervention in the peninsula fell into 3 phases. In 1499 he accompanied an army which occupied Milan without difficulty. Here, by prior agreement, he paid off Venetian neutrality by giving them the Milanese outpost of Cremona, and guarded his southern flank by promising aid to Florence in its war to regain Pisa. After his return to France Louis, alerted to Lodovico Sforza's determination to return to Milan with Swiss aid, sent reinforcements which enabled his Milanese army to defeat Lodovico at Novara in 1500: Lodovico spent the rest of his life a courteously guarded prisoner in France. In the same year Louis signed an agreement to partition Naples with Ferdinand of Aragon (the Treaty of Granada, 11 November). In 1501 another French army passed down a peninsular corridor left free by Italian allies (including Pope Alexander VI, anxious for French support for Cesare Borgia in the Romagna). The campaigns of Louis's army and Ferdinand's effectively ended Neapolitan independence. By 1503, however, the invaders had fallen out, and Spanish victories over the French at Cerignola and the Garigliano were accepted by Louis in 1504 as spelling the end of French ambitions in the south.

Barred from Naples, Louis opened the next phase of his intervention in Italian affairs with the first example of French aggression unjustified by legal claims. In 1508 he signed the Treaty of CAMBRAI and in 1509 he entered Italy with a new army that defeated the Venetians' forces at Agnadello, and occupied their territory as far east as Peschiera. As in 1499, with the immediate objective gained, Louis, neither a warrior nor a dedicated administrator, returned to France. When the instigator of the treaty, Julius II, turned his coat in 1510, Louis riposted in 1511 by calling a General Council of the Church to meet at Pisa – recently (1509) reconquered by his ally Florence – to depose the Pope. This turned out to be too ill-attended to be a major threat, but in 1512, outside Ravenna, a French army defeated that of Julius and his chief ally Ferdinand of Aragon who, now safely in command of Naples, was also concerned by France's position in northern Italy.

None the less, the death in the battle of Louis's brilliant young commander-in-chief, Gaston de Foix, coupled with a threat against Milan by Julius's allies the Swiss, led to an almost total withdrawal of French troops from Italy, leaving Louis with little to show for his Italian policy so far apart from garrisons in the *castello* of Milan and in a few cities in the western terraferma of Venice. Nor was the third phase of Louis's peninsular enterprises, initiated in 1513 with the support of his ex-enemy Venice and his ex-ally Spain, more successful: a renewed invasion of Lombardy was turned back at Novara. Coinciding with Henry VIII's campaign against Tournai and that of a Swiss army against Dijon, this defeat forced Louis into a turmoil of diplomatic activity before he was free to plan yet another invasion of Italy. He died before this could be accomplished.

By the French, who saw him as an authoritarian but fair monarch, he was dubbed 'Father of his Country'. The title sits oddly on a king who so consistently put Italian above domestic affairs and left France poorer in pocket and no richer in land than he found it. His obsession with Italy was initially encouraged by the most powerful of his ministers, the Archbishop of Rouen, Georges d'Amboise (d.1510), who hoped to make himself a powerful candidate for the papacy, and by Italian exiles like the commander-in-chief of the invasion of 1499, Gian Giacomo Trivulzio. But it was Louis himself who added such momentum to French involvement in Italy that his successor, Francis I, inherited it as a duty that had also become a habit. JRH

J. S. C. Bridge *A history of France . . . 1483–1515* III-V (1921–36)

Lucca In the early 14c. Lucca was, after Florence, the most prosperous and populous city in Tuscany. But in 1300 feuding between 'white' and 'black' GUELF families led first to the wholesale exile of the former and then to their unexpected return under the military aegis of the Ghibelline Uguccione della Faggiuola in 1314. On his withdrawal his authority passed to Castruccio CASTRACANI who, as *signore* from 1320, inflated Lucca's political power and territory into a serious challenge to Florence itself. After his death in 1328 the resumption of inter-family feuds made Lucca helpless to fend off the advances of would-be 'protectors' – Genoa, Parma, Verona, Florence, Pisa: Lucca was subject to each for a short period before a new period of stability commenced in 1369 when Lucca offered itself to the Emperor Charles IV in return for his guarantee of independence from any Italian power.

The city then reordered its constitution on broadly representative republican lines. However, the usual republican tendency towards oligarchy led to the domination of domestic politics by the supporters of two rival families, the Guinigi and the Forteguerra. In 1400 Paolo Guinigi was accepted as signore and Lucca ceased to be a republic. His rule lasted until 1430, when Francesco Sforza, acting for Filippo Maria Visconti but aided by the opponents of the Guinigi régime within the city, occupied Lucca. Once more a republic, the city uneasily maintained its independence from Florence during the war that continued until 1433 (a war whose failure contributed to the unpopularity of the ALBIZZI in Florence), and from its northern neighbours, though it was forced to concede territory: Carrara to the Malaspina, most of the Garfagnana (the region along and to the north of the river Serchio) to the Este. The city similarly preserved its independence first during the WARS OF ITALY and then from the pan-Tuscan ambitions of Duke COSIMO I of Florence. Its form of government, however, reflecting fears of worker revolt and conspiracies such as that of Francesco BURLAMACCHI, became less open to new blood and in 1556 turned into a closed oligarchy.

The city's chief industry was silkweaving, and successive waves of slump or domestic insecurity led Lucchese weavers to take their skills elsewhere, to Venice and to France, where they played an important part in developing the industry. Feeling vulnerable to Cosimo I's centralizing policy in Tuscany, and conscious of its dangerous reputation as a refuge for those out of sympathy with the Counter-Reformation, the city decided in 1561 to surround itself with new fortifications. They remain the best preserved of such defences. JRH

C. Meek *Lucca 1369–1400: politics in an early Renaissance city-state* (1978); M. A. Berengo *Nobili e mercanti nella Lucca del Cinquecento* (1965)

Lucretius (?94–55 BC) Latin author (Titus Lucretius Carus). His long poem in 6 books, *De rerum natura (On the nature of things)*, set out an interpretation of the universe in which gods had no place and man, though retaining free will and choice, was, together with his environment, the product of a mechanical assemblage of atoms. The poem also advanced the Epicurean view that pleasure, rightly viewed, could be pursued as the goal of a consciousness that would stop with death. Lucretius was known in the Middle Ages only through quotations by other authors: the discovery of a complete manuscript was the work of Poggio Bracciolini. Thereafter he was treated cautiously, as one of the few philosophizing ancients who could not be seen as purveying wisdom of which Christ would have approved: it was with a twinge of this realization that Ficino threw him (he says) into the fire. Bruno was perhaps the author most influenced by Lucretius as both poet and thinker. *See* EPICURUS. JRH

De rerum natura tr. R. C. Trevelyan (1936); J. H. Nichols *Epicurean political philosophy: the 'De rerum natura' of Lucretius* (1972)

Luini, Bernardino (*c.*1480–1532) represents 15c. Milanese tradition as transformed under Leonardo's influence. He was primarily a painter of narrative frescoes, both sacred and secular. His exposure to Leonardesque models produced an illustrative style of expressive clarity (as in the Brera *Dream of Joseph*, 1518–20), conservative in conception yet partaking of a certain modernity of appearance, that became extremely fashionable. His two fresco cycles for the della Robbia family (1520–25) both make this stylistic amalgam explicit and adumbrate the direction of his later development, which was worked out mainly in Milan, Lugano and Saronno. LP

A. O. della Chiesa *Bernardino Luini* (1960)

Luzzaschi, Luzzasco (*c.*1545–1607) Organist and composer. A pupil of Rore, he spent much of his life in the service of the Este family at Ferrara, where he was one of the few people who could play the *archicembalo* (see MUSIC) well. A competent madrigalist, he is famous as the composer of some trios for women singers of the Ferrara court which were precursors of monodic song, and also as the teacher of Gesualdo. DA

Machiavelli, Niccolò (1469–1527) Florentine political theorist and dramatist. After an adequate humanistic education, Machiavelli entered the bureaucracy of the republican government in 1498, chiefly being employed as secretary to the Ten of War, the committee responsible for the conduct of military and diplomatic affairs. This daily contact with affairs of state, supplemented by missions which took him to the courts of some of the chief actors in the political events of these years (Louis XII, Maximilian I, Julius II, Cesare Borgia), stopped abruptly with his dismissal in 1512 on the re-establishment of Medicean control over Florence. The closeness of his involvement with the previous régime and its titular leader, Soderini, and his suspected collusion in an anti-Medicean plot early in 1513, led to Machiavelli's bitterly regretted but permanent exclusion from government employment save for a trifling errand in 1521 and a temporary secretaryship (to a commission inspecting the fortifications of Florence) in 1526.

Living in enforced retirement on his farm in the small village of S. Andrea in Percussina, 7 miles S of Florence, he produced the works on which his renown is based: *Il principe* (*The prince*), 1513; *Discourses on the first decade of Livy*, 1513 or (more probably) 1516 to 1519; *Mandragola*, 1518; *The art of war*, 1519–20; *The history of Florence*, 1520–25. Of these, only *Mandragola* and *The art of war* were published before his death: *Il principe* was first published in 1532.

Machiavelli was an ardent if unscholarly student of the political structures and leaders of antiquity: for him HUMANISM meant access to lessons that could be applied in his own day. He was a natural, zestful writer, effective whether arguing a point of statecraft, describing in letters his somewhat rackety style of life, or composing his poetry (now unread) and his still most stageable plays; *Mandragola* is the finest comedy written in Italy before Goldoni, and *Clizia* (1524 or 1525) is scarcely inferior. The energy of his political writing was sustained by certain passionately held convictions: that his own experience qualified him as a pundit; that the unchanging nature of men and the recurrence of political and strategic situations meant that the present could and should learn from the past; that politics, a matter of dealing quickly with converging public contingencies, could not be dealt with in terms of a morality tailored to the individual and his long-term chances of salvation in Christian terms; that republics were preferable to princely governments when territorial limits were stable and the citizens politically mature enough to share selflessly the burdens of office; that native troops were vastly superior to mercenaries or to soldiers loaned by an ally; that political success depended upon vigilance, sensitivity to the purport of events, activism, a nicely calculated unscrupulousness.

Machiavelli was neither an atheist nor the advocate of trickery or cruelty for its own sake, but the equivocal relationship between the polemical tone of his personal convictions and his insistence that he is merely describing how things are, rather than how they ought to be, maintains today something of the power to shock that made him into the evil 'Machiavel' of political folklore in the late 16c. *See* POLYBIUS. JRH

R. Ridolfi *The life of Niccolò Machiavelli* tr. C. Grayson (1963); J. R. Hale *Machiavelli and Renaissance Italy* (1961; revised 1972); S. Anglo *Machiavelli: a dissection* (1969)

Maclodio, battle of (17 October 1427) A victory for the Venetians, under Carmagnola, over the Milanese, which won them the city and territory of Bergamo. The village lies 9 miles SW of Brescia, which had fallen to Venice in the previous year. JRH

Maggi, Girolamo (*c.*1523–72), scholar, poet and military enthusiast, was born at Anghiari, studied at the universities of Perugia, Pisa and Bologna, and settled as a proof-reader in Venice from 1560. He wrote a pioneering work on military engineering (1564), and he was unlike other amateurs of the art of war in that his manuscript treatise on machines and other inventions for the defence of Cyprus (1570) was so convincing that the Republic, after knighting him, sent him there. He was taken by the Turks when Famagosta surrendered in 1571, and died in captivity in Constantinople. JRH

Magic There seems to have been something of a revival of learned magic in Italy in the later 15c. Some of the 900 theses offered for debate by Giovanni Pico della Mirandola in 1486 defended the study of magic; for him, the power of the magus was an illustration of the dignity of man. His friend Ficino defended magic against criticisms and practised it himself: 'natural' magic, involving planetary influences, with a clear conscience, and 'ritual' magic, involving supernatural intermediaries, with some doubts about its compatibility with Christianity. Leading 16c. magicians included Giambattista DELLA PORTA, author of *Magia naturalis* (1558), Lodovico Lazzarelli and Bruno, the last two men being enthusiasts for the *Hermetica*, Greek texts attributed to the god Hermes Trismegistus and interpreted as instructions for the attainment of magical powers. This learned magic coexisted with, and possibly influenced, a popular magic about which less is known, concerned with love potions, abortions, finding lost property, telling fortunes, and protection against the evil eye. Its practitioners ran the risk of being accused of witchcraft. Enchanters and enchantresses, genuine or fake, good or evil, have a prominent place in Italian plays of the 16c., including Ariosto's *Il negromante*, Dovizi's *La Calandria*, Grazzini's *La strega* and Bruno's *Candelaio*. *See* CARDANO; HERMETICISM. PB

D. P. Walker *Spiritual and demonic magic from Ficino to Campanella* (1958); 'Magic and astrology in the civilisation of the Renaissance' in E. Garin *Science and civic life in the Renaissance* (1969); F. Yates *Giordano Bruno and the Hermetic tradition* (1964)

Malatesta family Landowners and warrior magnates of papal territory in the southern Romagna, providing one of the best examples of an opportunist *signoria* of the 14c. and 15c. rising to princely status, first sustained and then destroyed by both local and papal interests. Rimini was their power base and its revised statutes (1334) surrendered to Malatesta 'Guastafamiglia' ('destroyer of families') nearly all civic autonomy; but Malatesta control extended over other towns (e.g. Fano, Cesena, Pesaro) and inland territory. Granted a papal vicariate (1355), they provided a strong military and political arm to the Church for nearly a century. The breach came with the imprudent Sigismondo, deprived of all but Rimini (1463). In spite of the military renown of his son Roberto (d.1482), the family's power declined and money was lacking. The brutal Pandolfo V narrowly survived the dynasty's only recorded internal rebellion (1498) and was to lose the Venetian support on which he depended. After Pandolfo's deprivation by Alexander VI (October 1500), the Malatesta saw only two brief periods of restoration to Rimini (1522–23, 1527–28). DC

P. Jones *The Malatesta of Rimini*

Malatesta, Carlo I (1368–1429) Lord of Rimini from 1385 and by papal appointment rector of Romagna and military commander of the Church. He was active in stabilizing Lombardy after the death of Giangaleazzo Visconti and strove to end the Great Schism, receiving Gregory XII at Rimini (1408) and acting as proctor for Gregory's abdication at Constance (July 1415); subsequently he resumed his military career. His learned piety was reflected in severe edicts against blasphemers and idolators at Rimini, and may explain why at Mantua (his wife was Elisabetta Gonzaga) he had a statue of Virgil destroyed (1397) as a cult object. DC

P. Jones *The Malatesta of Rimini* (1974)

Malatesta, Sigismondo (1417–68) was accused of numerous depravities by Pope Pius II and has for long been held up as an archetype of the artistically-minded immoral Renaissance prince. Recently more moderate judgments have emphasized his prevailing weakness as imprudence inclining towards puerility. The illegitimate son of Pandolfo, Malatesta ruler of Fano, Sigismondo succeeded his uncle Carlo as signore of Rimini in 1432. His prestige as a condottiere was high during his years of service with Francesco Sforza and on behalf of Eugenius IV, and his advanced interest in military science is borne out by his patronage of VALTURIO and the many fortified buildings he commissioned, including the redesigned castle in Rimini which was also his residence. But Sigismondo's desertion of King Alfonso of Naples in 1447, added to his implacable hostility towards the neighbouring Montefeltro of Urbino and Sforza of Pesaro, tarnished

A pillar base with a relief portrait and elephant emblems of Sigismondo **Malatesta** by Agostino di Duccio (Rimini, Tempio Malatestiano).

his reputation, and his disregard of the peace terms (very unfavourable to himself) proposed by Pius II in 1459 brought upon his head excommunication, war and further censures, including a unique canonization to hell in April 1462. After the siege of Fano (1463) Sigismondo submitted to heavy penalties, including the loss of all his dominions except Rimini. Quixotically he then entered Venetian service against the Turks in southern Greece (1464–66), but died at Rimini.

The most scurrilous allegations against Sigismondo concerned sexual irregularities and impiety. In fact he was constant in his passion for Isotta degli Atti: it survived 2 marriages (the death of his second wife Polissena Sforza in 1449 gave rise to rumours of poison) and he married Isotta in 1456. About his irreligion there is little clear evidence. The design of the so-called Malatesta Temple in Rimini has never been fully explained, but profane decorative features appear to contain various, if enigmatic, levels of meaning. In 1447 Sigismondo had started the rebuilding of the church of S. Francesco in Rimini with a chapel to his name-saint, but by 1450 a more ambitious scheme was in progress; marble was brought from ancient sites and the opinions of Matteo de' Pasti and Alberti were sought. The façade, incorporating Roman arch motifs, was never completed, much less the cupola, though an arcade of niches to contain the funerary urns of famous men was built along one side, and side chapels within contain a diversity of sculptured motifs, including the celebration of Isotta and of the zodiacal powers. Work ceased in 1461. DC

P. Jones *The Malatesta of Rimini* (1974); M. Tabanelli *Sigismondo Pandolfo Malatesta* (1977); C. Ricci *Il tempio Malatestiano* (1924)

Manfredi family Lords of Faenza 1313–1501, papal vicars (from 1412) and counts of Val di Lamone. Their fortunes resemble those of other military signori of the Romagna. Astorgio II (1448–68) and Carlo II (1468–77) displayed interest in learning, the visual arts and urban improvements; Galeotto (1477–88) was assassinated, allegedly because his wife resented his lover; the young and popular Astorre (1488–1501), dependent on Venetian protection, was a victim of Cesare Borgia, who captured Faenza after a long blockade (April 1501): he was found murdered in Rome (June 1502). DC

J. Larner *The lords of Romagna* (1965); A. Medri *Il duplice assassinio di Galeotto Manfredi 1477–88* (1972); M. Mallett *The Borgias* (1969)

Mannerism is a stylistic term which, like all others, is the subject of more or less continuous controversy. Attempts to define it purely negatively as being anti-classical or anti-High Renaissance fly in the face of the historical facts, since many of its sources lie in the work of Raphael, and of Michelangelo, who was himself a leading creator of early Mannerist

Michelangelo's **Mannerist** use of classical elements in the vestibule of the Laurentian Library, Florence.

Mannerist poses and elegant refinement in Salviati's *Charity* (Florence, Uffizi).

architectural and sculptural form. The difficulty with basing a definition on Vasari's use of the term '*maniera*', on the other hand, is that his use of it is shifting and occurs in innumerable different contexts. To see Mannerism simply as the 'stylish style' is somewhat tautological and does not make clear how it differs from many other styles, such as International Gothic, which are characterized by extreme stylishness, by elongation of the human figure, and so forth.

In Italy, following in the wake of Raphael and Michelangelo, the leading painters working in the newly developing style included Giulio Romano (most notably in the architecture and decoration of the Palazzo del Tè, Mantua, where he was assisted by Primaticcio), the Florentines Pontormo, Rosso, Bronzino and Salviati, the Sienese Sodoma and Beccafumi, together with Parmigianino, Barocci, and Taddeo and Federico Zuccaro. Vasari was himself both painter and architect and, together with Serlio, Sanmicheli, Buontalenti, Vignola, Ligorio and many others, developed varying architectural aspects of the style, while in sculpture Cellini, Ammannati and Giambologna stand as the supreme exponents of Mannerism. Rosso and Primatticcio carried the new art into France under Francis I, founding the First School of Fontainebleau, and subdivisions of Mannerist style were developed throughout Europe, with particularly notable results in Antwerp and the Netherlands, though many of these widespread local schools are hardly Mannerist in the Italian sense of the word.

Mannerism properly so called develops directly out of the High Renaissance and represents a whole series of mutually exclusive experiments which take one or more aspects of High Renaissance style to their extreme limits. Where High Renaissance artists damp down the paradox created by the very act of 3-dimensional representation on a 2-dimensional surface, treating it only as the necessary starting point for their work, many Mannerist painters, such as Salviati, make the paradox itself the central focus of their interest. Similarly, Giulio Romano questioned the otherwise generally accepted structural role of applied architectural features such as columns, pilasters, entablatures and the like, paradoxically drawing attention to the absence of any real loadbearing function. In architecture and in painting alike, double function and calculated ambiguity are everywhere. There is continual tension between form and content, between the real and the ideal, between the intensely naturalistic and the intensely artificial, between the scale of what is represented and the frame which closes round it and cuts, often arbitrarily, into it. In all its aspects, Mannerism is a calculated, highly sophisticated style, founded on supreme technical competence.

All too often Mannerism, which has much in common with the creative diversity of 20c. artistic style, is seen merely as a negative interlude before the development of the Baroque. In fact it is, together with the High Renaissance, one of the major conditioning factors for the new 17c style. As Giambologna's freeing of sculpture from the straitjacket of the Michelangelesque block, however creative that confinement may have been in its own day, is important to Bernini, so the disruption of the mathematically measured and therefore limited perspectival space of High Renaissance painting, with its omnipresent insignia of the squared pavement, is essential to the development of the dynamic, free-flowing, limitless space of the Baroque. JW

E. Battisti *Rinascimento e Barocco* (1960); J. Shearman *Mannerism* (1967)

Mantegna, Andrea (active 1441/5, d.1506) The leading painter of north Italy before his brother-in-law Giovanni Bellini diverted Venetian, and with it much of north Italian, art along new paths, Mantegna is a paradigm of the Renaissance artist-archaeologist-antiquarian. His earliest major works were the now largely ruined frescoes of the Ovetari Chapel in the Eremitani, Padua (1459). His interest in classical archaeology, in sculptural form, and in the bold use of the new, scientific Artificial PERSPECTIVE are already apparent, the two lowest scenes of the life of St James being among the few Renaissance frescoes to be realistically foreshortened as if seen from below. The sculpture of Donatello was a major influence from the start, and Mantegna's S. Zeno altarpiece, likewise dating from the late 1450s, is probably the closest surviving record of Donatello's dismembered sculptural altarpiece for the Santo, Padua. It is also a masterpiece in its own right, and arguably the most spectacular 15c. Italian altarpiece to have survived complete. The architectural grandeur of the frame, derived through Donatello from Alberti, its coordination with the deep pictorial space, the brilliance of the colour and the combination of monumental sculptural form with intricacy of decorative detail, make it an unforgettable sight as it stands in the no less spectacular Romanesque surroundings of S. Zeno, Verona.

From 1460 onwards Mantegna was painter to the Gonzaga court in Mantua, and his employment by the scholarly Marquis Lodovico GONZAGA who, with his interest in history and in Latin literature, was himself an antiquarian and bibliophile and perhaps the most important pupil of the humanist VITTORINO DA FELTRE, confirmed the archaeological and antiquarian bent undoubtedly first encouraged in Mantegna by his master and adoptive father, Squarcione. A superb draughtsman, he maintained his brilliantly hard, linear style and bright, non-atmospheric colour to the end, resisting all the blandishments of the developing Venetian painterly style. He was of great importance in the early history of engraving, transferring his powerful pen style directly to the new medium. His engraving of the *Sea Gods* was copied and transformed by Dürer in the process of his development of new techniques adapted to print making. So powerful were his sculptural interests that many of his works are in grisaille imitating marble or bronze relief.

Mantegna's engraving of the *Battle of Sea Gods*, c.1490.

His interests in portraiture and in illusion are combined in the frescoed decoration of the so-called Camera degli Sposi (completed 1474) in the Ducal Castle at Mantua. There the Gonzaga family and its retinue are seen assembled beneath a vaulted ceiling, decorated with imitation stuccoes focused on Imperial Roman portrait medallions, and pierced dramatically at its centre by an illusion of a circular balcony open to the sky. This remarkable invention is the forerunner of Raphael's work in the Vatican Loggia, of Correggio's cupolas in Parma and, after them, of the Baroque ceiling paintings of 17c. Rome. It was for the Ducal Palace that Mantegna also painted (*c.*1486) the 9 great canvases of the *Triumphs of Caesar*, now restored and on display at Hampton Court. These are perhaps the most extreme and the most quintessentially personal of all his major works, combining as they do his interest in the archaeological recreation of antiquity, his love of foreshortening and perspective and, not least, his enthusiasm for the pictorial bas-relief. [161, 172, 221, 337] JW

E. Tietze-Conrat *Mantegna* (1955); A. Martindale *The triumphs of Caesar* (1979)

Mantua enjoyed 3 centuries of security under the GONZAGA family's domination, from 1328 to the siege and sacking of the city by Imperial troops (1629–30). Its physical situation was an advantage: though surrounded by the flat fertile plain of eastern Lombardy it was protected on 3 sides by swampy lakes through which the river Mincio flows on its way from Lake Garda to join the Po at Governolo. On its western side, the direction of rapid expansion in the 13c., walls and gates protected it, while beyond was the defensive perimeter of the Serraglio.

Mantua stood between the expanding frontiers of Milan and Venice, and it was in the interests of both to see an autonomous Mantuan territory, guaranteeing, even if it taxed, their riverine trade, its rulers available for hire to either side as military commanders. Its traditionally Imperial connection remained important, as it did for few other Italian cities by the 15c.; when German Emperors travelled to Rome it was an obvious stopping place; the Imperial titles and German marriages of the Gonzaga strengthened the links; Federico Gonzaga and his brother Ferrante supported and served Charles V, assuring Mantua's autonomy in spite of the Emperor's domination of northern Italy by 1529. Its laws, taxes and the institutions of civic government, the Councils of 400 and 20, upon which the Gonzaga still depended for the elective title of capitano in the early 15c., had long been under the dynasty's control (Francesco I promulgated revised statutes in 1404), but the régime seems to have enjoyed a consensus of support and the approval of leading families and citizens. The administration of Cardinal Ercole Gonzaga (1540–50) introduced many measures for greater efficiency.

In 1500 Mantua had *c.*25,000 inhabitants, and the number was growing, in spite of the unhealthiness of the place (Petrarch's characterization of it as foggy and frog-infested was endlessly repeated). It was essentially the centre of a prosperous agricultural and stockbreeding economy, though cloth production (woollens and later silk) had revived in the second half of the 15c.; the court also provided extensive employment, not least for building trades. The cathedral was refaced (*c.*1400) for Francesco I and its interior reconstructed according to plans drawn by Giulio Romano (1545). S. Andrea, a Benedictine monastery church which possessed a venerated relic of Christ's blood, was refounded as a secular church by Marquis Lodovico (1472): rebuilding started on a colossal scale, inspired by Alberti and forming part of general improvements to the town centre (street paving, a zodiacal clock and restoration of the communal palace). Other major churches enjoying Gonzaga benefaction were Alberti's S. Sebastiano in the 1460s, Bertani's S. Barbara adjoining the palace, (1562–64), and the Jesuit church of S. Trinita (founded 1591). But the most continuous projects of building and decoration were in successive additions to the main Gonzaga residence to the east of the town; 2 suburban palaces on its western side (in the early 16c.: S. Sebastiano and the Tè); and many more in the vicinity of Mantua and in other parts of its territory.

The growing prestige of the Gonzaga dynasty combined with the town's situation to make Mantua an important rendezvous for political events, particularly the visit of the papal court with Pius II (1459–60) which, if it failed to promote the intended crusade, still facilitated many cultural influences. Charles V visited it twice (1530, 1532). Mantua was not a university city, nor did it become a notable centre of printing, but thanks to Gonzaga patronage the school of VITTORINO DA FELTRE stimulated a generation of literate rulers and court officials, and many writers benefited from Gonzaga protection (Platina, Castiglione, Tasso, etc.). Neither did it have distinctive workshop traditions of its own in the plastic arts, but the Gonzaga drew widely upon those of elsewhere, particularly the Veneto. DC

Mantova: la storia, le lettere, le arti (9 vols 1958–63); *Cività mantovana* (1966–)

Marco Polo (1254–1324) Venetian author of *The description of the world (Divisament dou monde)*, the most extensive and factual of the accounts written by westerners of the Orient during the Mongol peace, reflecting Marco's experience 1271–92 as a roving official in the service of Kubla Khan. Circulating widely in the original French, Latin and many vernaculars, it was often regarded as a book of tall stories (hence his nickname 'Il Milione'), but the hearsay description of Japan as an island rich in gold 1500 miles east of China provided the lure for Columbus's great design. JKH

Fr. text *Il Milione* ed. L. F. Benedetto (1928); Eng. tr. R. Latham *The travels* (1958)

Marenzio, Luca (*c.*1553–99) Composer of madrigals. Born at Coccaglio near Brescia, he entered the service of Cardinal Luigi d'Este in 1578 and lived in Rome, also visiting Ferrara with his patron. In the early 1580s he was the most popular and fluent contemporary composer of secular music, writing in an easily singable style which fitted the pastoral verse of Sannazaro and his followers. About 1587 he began to compose more serious madrigals, and in the 1590s he became one of the more conservative members of the avant-garde group whose most famous member was Monteverdi. He spent a period in Florence and was in Poland for a short time, returning in the later 1590s to Rome, where he died, his early compositions still famous throughout Europe, with particular influence in England. DA

D. Arnold *Marenzio* (1965); A. Einstein *The Italian madrigal* (1949)

Marignano, battle of (13–14 September 1515) At the village of Marignano (now called Melegnano), a little to the SE of Milan, a French invading army led by Francis I, with some Venetian assistance, defeated an army raised by Pope Leo X and Massimiliano Sforza, Duke of Milan. The latter's strength lay in its Swiss infantry, acting as allies and, indeed, sponsors of Massimiliano's shaky control over the Milanese. Francis's victory led to a fresh occupation of Milan (and subsequently of Genoa), and a permanent tarnishing of the up till then almost unchallenged superiority of the SWISS as foot soldiers, signifying the end of their pretensions to intervene in Italy as a political power. After a Franco-Swiss settlement in the following year the Confederation accepted a border with Milan which is largely the one that exists today, and henceforward the Swiss took part in the Wars of Italy simply as mercenaries.

E. Usteri *Marignano* (1974)

Marsuppini, Carlo (1399–1453), native of Arezzo, was a member of the early Florentine humanist circle. He was highly respected for his command of Greek, and his friends secured the chair of Greek for him, to replace the alien Filelfo, in 1431. No original or prolific writer, his inclinations were typical of the Florentine-Roman circle. He was for a time a papal secretary, at the end of his life Chancellor of Florence; he was suspected of paganism but his translation of Book I of the *Iliad* into Latin was applauded by Pope Nicholas V. GH

Martin V Pope 1417–31 (b.1368) Oddone Colonna was elected pope by the Council of Constance. An astute reactionary whose façade of patrician *bonhomie* concealed a strong will to dominate, he devoted his pontificate to the recovery of that Roman authority which had been so damaged in the course of the Great SCHISM. His greatest success lay in the restoration of the Papal State. Preserving a prudent neutrality in the conflicts between Florence and Milan, exercising skilful diplomacy and duplicity, always at war, he had by the end of his pontificate established a large measure of control over the State. Yet this achievement was marred by his policy of large-scale nepotism on behalf of the Colonna family, which did indeed greatly strengthen his own rule but was to prove a considerable embarrassment to his successor.

Faced with the conciliar movement, whose ideal – the subjection of the papal monarchy to the control of Councils – had seemed to triumph at Constance, Martin again fought back vigorously. In response to the decree 'Frequens', which required the summoning of regular General Councils of the whole Church, he convened the Council of Pavia-Siena (1424–25). But he refused to attend it in person and through his legates sowed such divisions among its already disunited representatives that it achieved nothing. Yet its failure led only to repeated demands for another Council and Martin was forced to announce the summoning of a new assembly for 1431 at Basle. At the beginning of that year he died of an apoplexy, leaving to Eugenius IV the many problems which that body was to provoke. *See* COUNCILS OF THE CHURCH. JL

L. Pastor *The history of the popes* I (1899); P. Partner *The Papal State under Martin V* (1958)

Martinengo family It was above all in the 16c. that this Brescian family, or rather clan of interrelated families, provided Venetian armies, in peacetime as well as in war, with a steady supply of condottieri and infantry captains. Girolamo (d.1570) and Marcantonio (d.1595) were also prominent among Venetian military engineers. JRH

Martini, Simone (active *c.*1315, d.1344) The Sienese painter and probable pupil of Duccio came closer than any other major Italian painter to developing a fully gothic style, and his influence on the subsequent development of the International Gothic is incalculable. Although he is famous for his harmonies of line and colour, his work is highly influenced by that of the Sienese sculptors and his early masterpieces, the frescoed *Maestà* (1315; Siena, Palazzo Pubblico), derived from Duccio's altarpiece, and the *St Louis* (1317; Naples, Capodimonte) were full-blown political manifestos. His *S. Caterina Polyptych* (1319; Pisa, Museo

Nazionale) inaugurates the era of the fully architectonic gothic altarpiece. Among his most famous later works are the *Annunciation* (1333; Florence, Uffizi), which he carried out with Lippo Memmi, and the frontispiece, with its laudatory rhyme, which he illuminated for Petrarch's Virgil manuscript. The underdrawings of the frescoes in Notre-Dame les Doms in Avignon, where he died, reveal the quality of these largely perished works. His outstanding masterpiece, however, is the frescoed decoration of the Chapel of St Martin in S. Francesco, Assisi, for which he also probably designed the marble decoration and stained glass, creating one of the surviving jewels of Italian 14c. art. [162] JW

G. Paccagnini *Simone Martini* (1955); M. C. Gozzoli *L'opera completa di Simone Martini* (1970)

Martire, Pietro *See* ANGHIERA, PIETRO MARTIRE D'

Martyr, Peter *See* VERMIGLI, PETER MARTYR

Masaccio (1401–*c*.1428), born Tommaso di Ser Giovanni di Mone, was, with Brunelleschi and Donatello, one of the triumvirate who, upon foundations laid a century earlier by Giotto and the Pisani, established the renaissance of the arts. They, in their turn, formed the school in which Raphael and Michelangelo studied. In either case it would be folly to ignore the intervening decades, yet these century-long pauses and returns, endemic in the history of Italian art, lie at the very heart of its achievement. Just as Giotto and the Pisani took their art as far as it could possibly be taken within the technical and conceptual framework of their day, so did Masaccio in his short life. It was only after enough time had elapsed for a new framework to evolve that age-old artistic problems could be seen from a fundamentally fresh viewpoint, and that further, radical developments became possible. Masaccio's current fame is founded on three works, all painted in the last 4 years of his life. They are the Pisa Polyptych, now dispersed between London, Pisa, Naples and Berlin, the frescoes of the *Lives of SS. Peter and Paul* in the Brancacci Chapel in S. Maria del Carmine, Florence, and the fresco of the *Trinity* in S. Maria Novella.

In all periods of growing or renewed interest in the accurate delineation of the structure and volume of the human figure, from 5c. BC Greece to 13c. France or Italy, it is usual to find the sculptors in the lead, since their medium is naturally 3-dimensional, whereas the painter has to struggle to create even a semblance of 3-dimensionality on what is inescapably a 2-dimensional surface. It is therefore no surprise that Masaccio's massively monumental figures with their powerful, often brooding personalities and soft, heavy draperies depend at every turn on Donatello's immediately preceding sculptures, from the *St John the Evangelist* and the *St Mark* to the *Jeremiah*, and to the *Habbakuk* which was begun, but not completed, in Masaccio's lifetime. Similarly, the magnificent architecture of the *Trinity* gives gravity and grandeur to the graceful forms of Brunelleschi's Ospedale degli Innocenti. Undoubtedly it was also Brunelleschi's invention of Artifical PERSPECTIVE that provided Masaccio with the new conceptual framework and the technical means for the creation of a revolutionary and typically Renaissance art. The new perspective introduced a scientifically accurate way of creating an illusion of 3-dimensionality which was precisely dependent on the assumed position of the onlooker in real space. It also provided a means of organizing the composition and of directing the spectator's attention within the unified pictorial space. The vanishing point of the buildings in Masaccio's *Tribute Money*, for example, lies in the head of Christ and therefore gives the central figure additional, all-important emphasis.

Because such things are easily described and because the element of illusion provided writers, from PLINY onwards, with a standard cliché with which to praise whatever was considered good in art, it is upon this aspect of Masaccio's work that critics from Vasari onwards tend to dwell. There had, however, already been an element of spatial illusion in the art of Giotto and of his contemporaries and immediate followers. What there was not was light. Buildings were, it is true, often lit from the direction of a particular window in a church or chapel, but the creation of seeming 3-dimensionality in the figures was so taxing that in them the light and shade was invariably distributed *ad hoc*, according to the immediate problems raised by each particular form. What strikes the eye immediately when one enters the Brancacci Chapel is the unifying golden light that floods through the frescoes, over figures and architecture alike, as if from a single source that could at any moment be eclipsed; the

The Madonna and Child: the central panel of **Masaccio**'s now dispersed Pisa Polyptych (London, National Gallery).

harmony with the evening light that streams through the window above the altar is complete, and it is this that separates the *Madonna* in the Pisa Polyptych from the neighbouring Trecento paintings in the National Gallery in London and that gives reality to Masaccio's new understanding of anatomical structure, long before the onlooker is close enough to become aware of perspectival niceties. Light, as much as the new perspective unity and the emphasis on structure and proportion, separates Renaissance art from that of the preceding centuries and enables St Peter in the *Shadow Healing* to work his miracle without the need for so much as a sidelong glance.

In the final analysis, however, it is not the mechanics of light or perspective that clinch Masaccio's place in history. He owes that to his grasp of human personality, rivalled only in the work of Donatello, and to his ability to portray the reaction of the individual to the impact of great spiritual events with a gravity and a grandeur that is unforgettable. JW

L. Berti *Masaccio* (1967)

Masolino, Maso di Cristofano Fini, il (active *c*.1423, d.1447), a sadly under-appreciated Florentine painter, is one of the leading casualties of art historical earnestness. His misfortunes stem from his collaboration with Masaccio in the Brancacci Chapel. His frescoes are too often seen as attributional problems rather than as works of art, 'the good bits' being attributed to Masaccio's hand or influence. As is confirmed by his works in Castiglione d'Olona and in S. Clemente, Rome, he is, in fact, a delightful artist, strongly reflecting contemporary International Gothic trends. Above all, however, he was fascinated by the new Artificial PERSPECTIVE and is one of the earliest painters to take exuberant delight in using it to punch perspectival holes through the wall, creating space for the sheer joy of it. Airy Renaissance colonnades sweep like express trains straight back into deep space; boxed interiors reveal the abstract grid on which the new spatial geometry is based, and through them all his graceful figures promenade, oblivious. JW

Masuccio Salernitano (?1410–?1475) Pen name of Tommaso Guardati of Salerno, who was connected with humanists of the Aragonese court and became secretary to Roberto Sanseverino, Prince of Salerno. His *Novellino* is a collection of 50 stories, divided into 5 themes, in a Boccaccian tradition, although it is Masuccio himself telling the tales, each one being addressed to a member of the Aragonese court. They have a southern dialectal linguistic colouring and a tendency

Woodcut from the *Novellino* by **Masuccio Salernitano**, printed in Venice in 1492, showing the author presenting his book to the dedicatee.

towards anti-clerical and anti-feminist satire, combined with comic or grotesque features. LL
Il novellino ed. G. Petrocchi (1957); G. Petrocchi *Masuccio Guardati e la narrativa napoletana del Quattrocento* (1953)

Mathematics To the men of the Renaissance this was a subject with a curiously ambivalent connotation. On the one hand, the 15c.'s intellectual hero, PLATO, had stressed its importance for the training of the mind, and hence some mathematics, including elementary geometry and practical aspects like surveying, was a part of humanist education. On the other hand, mathematics also meant such esoteric subjects as number mysticism, cabbalistic divination and astrology. The term 'mathematician' might designate a practitioner of either branch – or of both (as with CARDANO). Non-mystic mathematics was a complex subject: the ordinary educated scholar learned geometry (as every university graduate had done during the Middle Ages), number theory ('arithmetic'), the theory of music and elementary mathematical astronomy, the 4 sciences of the quadrivium, while in the 16c. vernacular translations of EUCLID extended knowledge of geometry to the less well educated. Higher mathematics was for the few.

In the 16c. humanist mathematicians like BOMBELLI and COMMANDINO translated the more difficult Greek mathematicians into Latin, and the simpler ones into Italian. New editions of ARCHIMEDES profoundly affected both pure mathematicians and mathematical physicists. Translations of Apollonius opened the way for the study of conic sections, as those of Diophantos did for number theory, but the liveliest developments were in the solution of cubic equations, a legacy of Arabic mathematics (cf. CARDANO and TARTAGLIA). In applied mathematics the medieval legacy was exploited in such works as PACIOLI's summary of practical, mercantile arithmetic, while there were many manuals on surveying, fortification and gunnery. Greek geometry opened new possibilities: the most important was the study of PERSPECTIVE, which was central to painting in the 15c. and 16c.; it is not surprising that Leonardo cooperated with Pacioli. A lesser example is BIRINGUCCIO's understanding of how to 'figure' a bell-mould. Mathematics was central to cartography, which provided another area for cooperation between artist and scholar after the rediscovery of PTOLEMY's *Geography* (1410), and engineers like RAMELLI regarded their profession as a branch of mathematics.

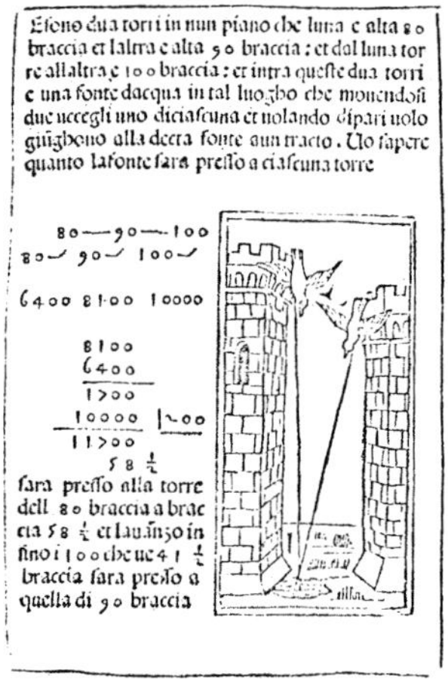

Mathematics: a surveying exercise from Filippo Calandri's *De arimethrica*, published in Florence in 1491.

Just as pure mathematics was encouraged by the 15c.'s worship of Plato, so the magical aspects of mathematics were encouraged by the same century's addiction to neo-Platonism, Pythagoreanism and HERMETICISM. These all encouraged the belief that the ancients had approved the mystic applications of geometry and number theory, giving hardly-needed encouragement to the rampant astrology and number mysticism of the age. The line between rational and irrational remained difficult to draw: Pacioli studied both the 'Platonic' (regular) and the non-regular solids theoretically, at the same time as others studied them mystically. It was difficult to determine which approach would be more fruitful. *See* CABBALA; PLATO AND NEO-PLATONISM; PYTHAGORAS. MBH
P. L. Rose *The Italian renaissance of mathematics* (1975)

Mattioli, Pierandrea (1500–77) Botanist. At Padua he studied languages, mathematics, philosophy and medicine, but his interests were primarily botanical. He travelled extensively in Italy collecting plants. His *Di Pedacio Dioscoride anazarbeo liber cinque* (1544) is an Italian version of Dioscorides' *Materia medica*. Appearing in many expanded versions in Italian and Latin, it was the most important of Italian herbals. MBH

Mauro, Fra (d.1460) Almost nothing is known of the life of this friar of Murano, in the Venetian lagoon, save that his cartographical skill and the up-to-dateness of his geographical knowledge were such that King Alfonso V of Portugal commissioned a world map from him. This and all his other works have disappeared, save for a world map in the Marciana Library of Venice which, better than any other in existence, shows the dimensions of the world as they were known up to the eve of its completion by assistants shortly after Mauro's death. JRH

T. Gasparrini Leporace *Il mappamundo di Fra Mauro* (1956)

Maurolico, Francesco (1494–1575) Sicilian mathematician and writer on optics. After a humanist education he took orders (1521) and later became a Benedictine monk and mathematical tutor. He wrote commentaries on several late Greek mathematicians (including Apollonius), but is best known for his *Photismi de lumine et umbra* (written in 1521; published only in 1611). This deals with the rainbow, vision, lenses and photometry, and is novel for its mathematical and physical adumbration of the Arabic view that light emanates from a body on a point-to-point basis, in contrast to the Greek view that light rays emanate from the eye. MBH

Maximilian I (1459–1519) For Italian history, the most significant moment in Maximilian's career was his death. This brought his grandson Charles to succeed him as Emperor, adding his kingdom of Spain to Maximilian's hereditary Habsburg territories in Austria and the Tirol, and those he had acquired in Burgundy and the Netherlands through his marriage in 1477 to his first wife Mary (d.1483), daughter of Duke Charles the Bold of Burgundy. It was the Spanish connection with Germany that made CHARLES V intent on occupying Milan as a bridge between the two halves of his Empire and that led to the preponderance of Habsburg power in the peninsula.

Maximilian had been granted the title King of the Romans, or Emperor Presumptive, in 1486, a title which took added meaning within Germany, as well as in Austria, when his father, the Emperor Frederick III, died in 1493. Strictly speaking, the title Holy Roman Emperor could only be assumed after coronation by the pope. Maximilian was never so crowned, extracting (from Pope Julius II) only the right to call himself Emperor Elect. All the same, he was, and is, known as the Emperor Maximilian.

Most of his reign was occupied with diplomacy and war aimed at giving substance to his claims to authority in Germany and Switzerland and at combating French claims to much of his inheritance by marriage. It was antipathy to France that first turned his attention to Italian affairs. First he gave nominal support to the League of Venice of 1495, which was designed to counter the early successes of CHARLES VIII in the peninsula, a matter of personal concern to Maximilian because of his marriage in 1494 to Bianca Maria Sforza, niece of Duke Lodovico of Milan. Another jolt to his semi-legal, semi-possessive attitude to the by now vague Imperial pretensions to suzerainty over northern Italy came with LOUIS XII's conquest of Milan in 1499 and his subsequent subjection in 1507 of Genoa, whose government had turned to Maximilian as its natural protector. Powerless to help physically because of the lack of support in Germany for projects that were now thought of as purely of antiquarian interest, Maximilian resolved at least to buttress the credibility of his title by being crowned in Rome.

In 1508, however, the Venetians, fearing a resumption of the Imperial claim to the area of Lombardy they had conquered in the first half of the 15c., defeated the army he had (with great difficulty) mustered to accompany him. It was while still smarting from this rebuff that he was persuaded to join the League of CAMBRAI, leading, in the wake of the French victory at Agnadello, another painfully raised army to an unsuccessful siege of Padua in October 1509. Called away by other challenges to his authority, both within Germany and in the zone of his uneasy western inheritance (which led him to war in northern France as an ally of Henry VIII of England in 1513), as well as by checks to his expectations in the dynastic hunting grounds of Poland and Hungary, Maximilian's next and last Italian intervention was a hurried and insufficiently supported campaign in 1516 aimed at dislodging the French from Milan, conquered by Francis in the previous year.

This account, centred on Italy, can do no justice to a character at once ardent and ineffectual, chivalrous and highly cultivated, innovative but trapped by the glamour of an impressive but administratively ramshackle inheritance. *See* EMPIRE, HOLY ROMAN. JRH

M. Wiesflecker *Kaiser Maximilian I* (1971–); R. G. D. Laffan 'The Empire under Maximilian I' *New Cambridge modern history* I (1957); N. Rubinstein 'Firenze e il problema della politica imperiale in Italia al tempo di Massimiliano I' *Archivio Storico Italiano* (1958)

Medals The medal came to artistic maturity within a remarkably short time of its introduction in 15c. Italy. This was partly because ancient Roman coins, which were beginning to be reverently collected, suggested (on a smaller scale) its form: profile portrait bust on the obverse, a different design on the reverse, an inscription running round the rim. Like the finest Imperial coins, the medal's purpose was commemorative. Without monetary value, and of non-precious metal (bronze or lead), it was a way of circulating a likeness to a chosen few; it anticipated the use of miniatures and was indeed frequently worn round the neck. And while the reverse could record a historical event or make a propaganda point related to its subject's career, more commonly it bore a design that purported to convey the 'essence', as it were, of the person portrayed on the other side.

Given the admiration for the men and artefacts of ancient Rome, the stress on individual character, the desire for fame and the penchant for summing up temperament in symbols and images, it is easy to understand how quickly the fashion for commissioning medals spread. Its pioneer executant was PISANELLO. The precedents before he began to cast medals in 1438–39 had been few and excessively coin-like. Within 10 years he had established the form the medal was to retain until the influence was registered of the reverseless, hollow-cast and wafer-thin medals of the 1560s and 70s made by Bombarda (Andrea Cambi). Pisanello's approach was first echoed by the Veronese Matteo de' Pasti (d.1467/8). It was, perhaps oddly, not until the works from 1485 of Niccolò Fiorentino (Niccolò di Forzore Spinelli, 1430–1514) that Florence produced a medallist of the highest calibre. Other specialists in the medium included Sperandio (Sperandio Savelli, *c.*1425–1504), L'Antico (Pier Jacopo Alari Bonacolsi, *c.*1460–1528), Caradosso (Cristoforo Caradosso Foppa, 1452–1526/7). The work of these men, and of the many, often

A preparatory drawing by Pisanello (1448) for his **medal** of Alfonso I of Naples (Paris, Louvre).

The lead **medal** of Alfonso designed by Pisanello (1449) (Washington, National Gallery, Samuel H. Kress Collection).

anonymous, who reflected them, is still coveted because it avoided the two medallistic errors: making a medal look like either an enlarged piece of money or a small sculptured plaque. *See* IMPRESA. JRH

L. Goldscheider ed. *Unknown Renaissance portraits* (1952); G. F. Hill and G. Pollard *Renaissance medals from the Kress collection* (1967)

Medici family The Medici started arriving in FLORENCE as immigrants from the nearby valley of the Mugello in the 13c., only becoming firmly identified with political influence and great wealth in the lifetime of Giovanni di Bicci (1360–1429). It was his son Cosimo who from 1434 became the leading figure in the city, a role intensified by Cosimo's son Piero and grandson Lorenzo. Periods of exile (1494–1512 and 1527–30) were followed by the family's near-absolute control of Tuscany as dukes and grand dukes, a process eased by the careers of two Medici popes, Leo X and Clement VII. Alternately praised as patrons and blamed as tyrants, the family has had a stormy historiographical career. It is unclear whether the *palle* (balls) on their coat of arms originated as pills (*Medici:* 'doctors') or coins (a reference to the banking origin of their fortune). JRH

G. Pieraccini *La stirpe dei Medici di Cafaggiolo* (4 vols 1947); J. R. Hale *Florence and the Medici: the pattern of control* (1977); K. Langedijk *The portraits of the Medici: 15th-18th centuries* (2 vols 1980)

Medici

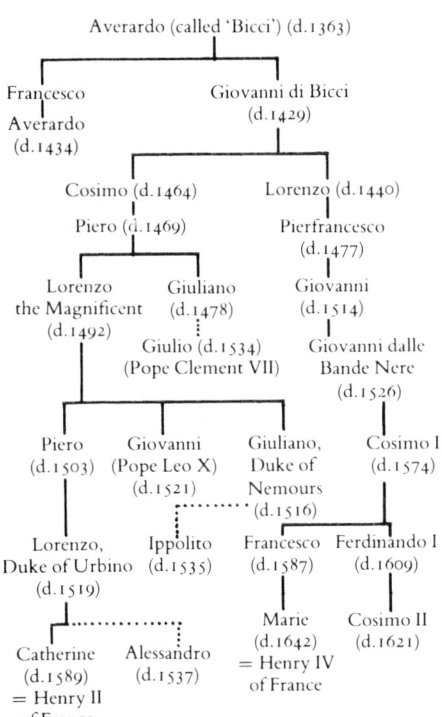

Medici, Cosimo de' (1389–1464) From 1434, when he was recalled from the exile to which he had been sentenced in the previous year, Cosimo's influence in Florentine governing circles was so dominant as to create a feeling that, without a member of his family to give the lead, Florence would relapse into a damaging political free-for-all. He thus became the founder of a dynasty that, fairly covertly in the 15c., openly in the 16c. and 17c., directed the fortunes of Florence. To achieve this in a city where wealth was granted more authority than breeding required a fortune. This Cosimo inherited from his banker father Giovanni, and, inheriting too a flair for business, he increased it. Shrewd in his choice of partners and managers, methodical as a book-keeper and imaginative as an investor, Cosimo derived his wealth from commerce and industry as well as from banking, and it brought him both an involuntary respect and the means of buying more; given the city scale of most Italian statecraft, it is not without reason that he has been compared to the 'boss' of Chicago or Dallas ward politics or the 'padre' of a power zone of the Mafia. Aided by his father (d.1429) and supported by his banker cousin Averardo (d.1434), Cosimo had left behind on his banishment (by the then dominant Albizzi régime) a party which lost no time in bringing him back, and thereafter hardly faltered in seeing him as the continuing guarantee of protection from governmental decisions that would hurt their persons, profits, or standing within the city.

To high ability as a financier, and to genius as a party manager, Cosimo added two qualities that distinguish him from others who had mastered the practical details that ensured a successful political career. As a politician he had a vision that looked beyond Florentine Tuscany. This was helped, indeed necessitated, by the conduct of a firm with international interests. But it was more than just business acumen that eventually persuaded his political colleagues to give him a fairly free hand in actually negotiating, as well as determining, the city's foreign policy – and that led them to accept the opinion of foreign princes that Cosimo was really the ruler of Florence. (They watched his encouragement, and later support of, Francesco SFORZA's takeover of the duchy of Milan with considerable reserve before accepting it as in Florence's interest.)

The second 'extra' quality is less tangible: Cosimo's respect for, and indeed dependence on, the qualities of pure intellect possessed by others. It was not just a shrewd deference to the ideal of patronage that made him buy manuscripts and found libraries (at S. Marco, at the Badia of Fiesole, and his own – now known as the Laurenziana, not from his grandson, Lorenzo the Magnificent, but from the church of S. Lorenzo which houses it), support scholars of the calibre of Argyropoulos and Marsilio Ficino (to whom he gave his start in life), and take so strong an interest in Donatello and Michelozzo (who designed his palace). Patronage involved status if the right horses were backed, and Cosimo was ambitious for himself and his descendants. All the same, there is evidence that Cosimo sensed a genius in others that was derived from values beyond (though not irrelevant to) his own aspirations, which marks him as more than simply abreast of what his society had to offer.

His political role is described under FLORENCE. His character remains unfocused though far from enigmatic, as far as his contemporaries reveal it: indeed, the emphasis these place on his patriarchal simplicity of manner and homespun wisdom expresses the desire to domesticate a many-fronted energy that was to be rivalled by none of his descendants. JRH

C. S. Gutkind *Cosimo de' Medici, Pater Patriae* (1938)

Medici, Lorenzo de' (1449–92) Lorenzo's father Piero had, in the short time left to him by his invalidism (1464–69), weathered the natural reaction against Medicean political leadership – the dominant position obtained by his father Cosimo. Though Lorenzo was only 20 at the time, therefore, the leading families in Florence were prepared to rally behind his family's reputation and his own wealth rather than return to the free-for-all factionalism that had ruined so many fortunes and reputations in the past. Lorenzo has come to be known as 'the Magnificent'. *Il magnifico* was, in fact, no more than a common title of respect accorded to anyone who was in a position of political authority without being of princely blood. That Lorenzo should be singled out in this way reflects 2 factors: the WARS OF ITALY initiated so long and sad a story of Italian humiliations that he was seen by a later generation of Florentines as having presided over a period of peace, plenty and confident magnificence; and non-Italian historians of the 19c. caught this tone of

Terracotta bust of **Lorenzo de' Medici** by Verrocchio (Washington, National Gallery, Samuel H. Kress Collection).

laudifying nostalgia and fitted it into their own vision of a man who, as they saw it, was single-handedly responsible for the last great phase of Florentine cultural leadership – the age of Ficino and Pico della Mirandola, of Filippino Lippi, Botticelli, Verrocchio, the aspiring Leonardo and the tyro Michelangelo, of Poliziano, Pulci – and of Lorenzo the poet-patron himself.

Lorenzo's political role is reviewed under FLORENCE. His role as the magician who conjured up the talents that contributed to the intellectual and artistic image of Florence in the late Quattrocento can be assessed briefly. He responded, as a highly intelligent and carefully educated young man might, to quality, whether shown in intellectual speculation or in artistic endeavour. But as a patron of the arts his role was to encourage others to employ the city's artists rather than to commission works from them himself. He arranged for Giuliano da Sangallo to work for the King of Naples. It was his cousin Lorenzo di Pierfrancesco de' Medici who obtained *Primavera* and *The Birth of Venus* from Botticelli, his business associates who paid Ghirlandaio for the fresco cycles in S. Trinita and S. Maria Novella. The latter cycle cost only a tenth of one of Lorenzo's own most cherished purchases, the antique Tazza Farnese.

His preferred taste, backed by his own pocket, was for the more private forms of art represented by works of this sort; for small, precious objects: ancient vases, cups, cameos, jewels and bronze statuettes. He did commission Giuliano da Sangallo to remodel one of his favourite country retreats, the farm at Poggio a Caiano, and Perugino, Ghirlandaio, Botticelli and Filippino to decorate another, his villa at Spedaletto (near Arezzo: the frescoes have disappeared).

He was a leader indeed in that growing taste for country life which, together with the jousts he sponsored, was part of a more general leadership of the Florentine patriciate towards a style of life closer to that of the aristocratic north. Outside his political role, in which he was painstaking and careful not to push too far the licence granted – increasingly grudgingly on the part of many – to his family to act independently, and outside his role as banker, which he neglected, Lorenzo's interests suggest that inside the statesman and party manager was a reflective scholar-prince longing to get out. Yet he remained a steady and loving centre of his family, and though more places might be laid at table for visiting dignitaries and for artists and men of letters than in other Florentine households, the palace in the Via Larga cannot be seen as in any sense the nucleus of a court. He was absorbed by, and ambitious for, his family, just as his father and grandfather had been, and he did nothing that contributed more to the perpetuation of his family name than when he obtained in 1489 Pope Innocent VIII's promise of a cardinalcy for his son Giovanni, the future Leo X. JRH

C. M. Ady *Lorenzo dei Medici and Renaissance Italy* (1960); E. M. Gombrich 'The early Medici as patrons of art' in E. F. Jacob ed. *Italian Renaissance studies* (1960); A. Chastel *Art et humanisme à Florence au temps de Laurent le Magnifique* (1959); *Lettere* ed. N. Rubenstein (3 vols to date, up to 1479; 1977–79)

Medici *See* COSIMO I DE' MEDICI

Medicine Renaissance medical practice was mainly a continuation of a well-established medieval profession. The 15c. or 16c. physician in his long gown was a university 'doctor', trained in a tradition now several centuries old, following the precepts of the Graeco-Arabic textbook, familiar with concepts of disease, diagnosis and treatment long sanctified. Renaissance physicians seem to have been more influenced by certain aspects of HIPPOCRATIC medicine than their predecessors: for example, more 'casebooks' (both medical and surgical) survive from the 15c. and especially the 16c. than for all the preceding centuries.

Medical and (specifically) surgical practice were, however, much influenced by 15c. technology. Gunshot wounds, first experienced in the 14c., became far more common, and new surgical techniques were needed: new instruments for the extraction of bullets and new methods of treating the wounds. All nations had army surgeons who pioneered new treatments; the best known Italian representative is Giovanni da VIGO. The explorations of the late 15c. (only possible because of improved ships) brought new diseases, in particular the 'new disease of the armed forces', *lues venerea*, syphilis (after FRACASTORO's poem about an unfortunate shepherd of that name stricken by the disease). Although authorities differ, it is probable that syphilis came to Europe with the returning sailors of Columbus's fleet – a case was reported in Madrid soon after their return, and an outbreak occurred in the Spanish troops at Naples in 1495. Since the disease was characterized by external lesions it was treated

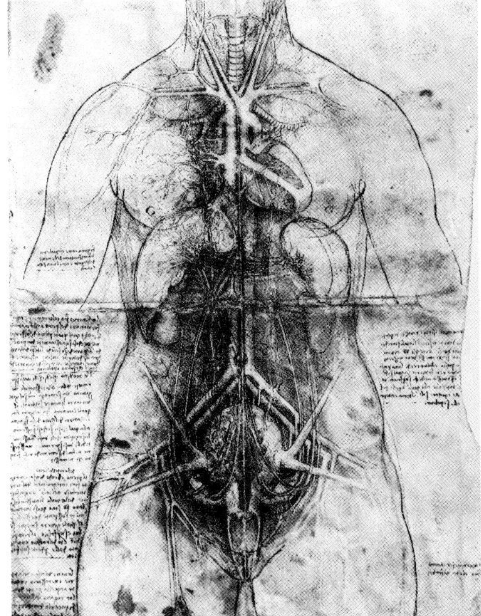

Medicine: a descriptive anatomical drawing of the principal organs of a woman by Leonardo (Windsor, Royal Library).

(by surgeons) with mercury ointment, and later by ingestion of mercury compounds, the only alternative being guaiacum, a wood from South America used on the principle that nature must have an indigenous cure for an indigenous disease. Contemporary chemistry provided calomel or 'dulcified mercury' – an apparently safe form of mercury – for ingestion. PLAGUE continued. So did, in a highly contagious form, a newly-characterized pestilence, typhus, well described by CARDANO and Fracastoro, commonly associated with armies, who spread the disease widely.

Medical science – the investigation of anatomy and physiology – greatly outdistanced medieval knowledge under the twin stimuli of art and humanism. Leonardo was only the most thorough of artistic explorers of anatomy, with a view to the improvement of naturalism in painting and sculpture. Surface anatomy was widely taught in artists' studios, and many artists assisted at dissection. The rediscovery and translation of GALEN's *Natural faculties* (1523) and *Anatomical procedures* (Venice 1531) powerfully stimulated an interest developed from the study of his *On the use of the parts*, widely known only about 1500. The anatomical school at Padua, founded by VESALIUS and kept going by Realdus COLUMBUS, EUSTACHIO, FALLOPPIO, FABRICIUS and others, made Italian universities, and Padua especially, international centres for anatomical and physiological research and teaching. MBH

W. P. D. Wightman *Science and the Renaissance* I (1962)

Melozzo da Forlì (1438–1494), an artist of formidable ability, especially in illusionism, is mentioned in verses by Giovanni Santi (Raphael's father) on the painters of his day as being unsurpassed in perspective. Much of his *oeuvre* has been destroyed, and nothing is known of his early life. He was certainly in touch with Piero della Francesca and at the court of Urbino 1465–76. His work in the sacristy of S. Marco in Loreto is an outstanding testament to his skill, as are the few remains of his fresco for the dedication of the Vatican Library and the church of SS. Apostoli in Rome. Correggio's cupola decorations for S. Giovanni Evangelista in Parma are directly derived from the latter. [256] LDE

Mercenaries By the 14c., though citizens were still legally liable for military service, they were seldom called on save in a local police function. Wars were fought by men recruited by hired contractors, CONDOTTIERI in the case of cavalrymen, *contestabili* in that of infantry commanders, though until the 16c. the distinction was not clear: a single contractor frequently produced, and led, a force of both horse and foot. The advantages of the system were clear, The core, and often the great majority, of the hired force were professionals, trained and experienced in a way no force of hurriedly mustered civilians could be. A mercenary army did not call merchants from their desks or craftsmen from their shops: business in wartime could proceed as usual. The availability of mercenaries meant that governments did not have to take the risk of entrusting their own subjects with arms that could be turned against them.

The disadvantages of the system were, however, also clear. The holder of a military *condotta* (contract, hence 'condottiere') required regular pay to pass on to his workforce, and both psychologically and for technical reasons governments found it hard to translate war taxation into actual cash. The mercenary could blackmail or even turn against his employer as well as serve him – as when Francesco Sforza took over the government of Milan in 1450 and established a new dynasty there. Such cases, however, though perturbingly dramatic, were few. Finally there was the belief that mercenaries fought in order to fight another day, conserving their capital (their men, mounts and equipment) rather than taking the risks felt to be justified by the ideology or need of their employer.

By the 15c. the mercenary system was, in spite of the jolt given to potential employers by the behaviour of Sforza, institutionalized in a manner that gained general if guarded approbation. The foreign adventurers who had contributed so much to its reputation for irresponsibility had mostly disappeared. The division of Italy into rich areas (Lombardy, the Veneto, Tuscany) and poor (the Marche, Romagna and Campagna and Naples) made it logical that the former should employ needy men from the latter. Rulers who were also mercenary commanders, like those of Mantua, Ferrara and Urbino, gave the system respectability. Employers, notably Florence, Milan and Venice, extended the earlier practice of giving land on feudal terms to captains who could be relied on to serve them, thus providing

Mercenary captains receiving their pay: from a painted book cover, 1464 (Siena, Archivio di Stato).

themselves with the nucleus of a standing army that could, in wartime, be built up through subsidiary contracts. In the 16c. the main Italian states had forces which comprised a small permanent garrison force, a number of resident military contractors responsible, in person or through agents, for collecting large forces in wartime, and native militias bound (in return for peacetime tax and arms-carrying privileges) to back up armies or garrisons in times of emergency.

From the early Quattrocento, however, this commonsense evolution has been accompanied by objections from scholarly or quasi-learned authors who insisted that the only reliable soldier was the citizen-in-arms. The defence of the native, as opposed to the hired, soldier was taken to an extreme by Machiavelli, who falsified the record of Florence's past wars to show that mercenary wars were 'bloodless' and against the employer's interest. Propounded in *The prince*, emphasized in *The art of war* and consolidated in *The history of Florence*, this thesis launched the notion of chessboard warfare that has only fairly recently been shown to be intriguing, but wrong. JRH

M. E. Mallett *Mercenaries and their masters* (1974); C. C. Bayley *War and society in Renaissance Florence* (1961); W. Block *Studien über die sogennanten 'unblutige Schlachten'* (repr. 1965)

Merulo, Claudio (1533–1604) Organist and composer. He was born at Correggio and became organist at Brescia cathedral in 1556, before being appointed organist at St Mark's in Venice in the following year. There he remained until 1584. Two years later he entered the service of the Duke of Parma, continuing as organist of the Steccata confraternity's church until his death. A marvellous composer of virtuoso toccatas in an improvisatory manner, he wrote a substantial corpus of keyboard music, usually showing his mastery of embellishment. He wrote some excllent madrigals and some impressively sonorous church music, including works in the Venetian polychoral manner. DA

Michelangelo Buonarroti (1475–1564) Sculptor, architect and poet: he himself wanted to be known as a sculptor. Unlike many contemporary Florentine artists he came from a family of some social standing, and only after initial parental opposition was he apprenticed in 1488 to Ghirlandaio. He stayed with him only briefly, however, and is supposed next to have joined Bertoldo di Giovanni, who allegedly trained young sculptors among the antiques collected by the Medici in a garden near S. Marco. This ought to be treated with caution. At the time the Medici did not own a notable collection of classical statues and Bertoldo worked exclusively in bronze. When in his old age Michelangelo insisted to his biographer Condivi that he was really self-trained, he may well have spoken the truth. He went round Florentine churches sketching after Giotto and Masaccio, as is proved by surviving drawings. The technique of fresco he would have picked up in Ghirlandaio's workshop, and the handling of the sculptor's tools he learned by borrowing a mason's implements, as Condivi mentions.

From 1490 until Lorenzo de' Medici's death in 1492 Michelangelo lived in the Medici household, where he would have met the leading intellectuals and neo-Platonists of Florence: Ficino, Landino and Poliziano. But he also must have listened, as everyone in Florence would have done, to Savonarola's sermons and studied the friar's writings. To this period belong his earliest surviving works which, in their sharp contrast, already indicate his lifelong preoccupations. Both are marble reliefs. The *Battle of Lapiths and Centaurs* (Florence, Casa Buonarroti), a classical subject suggested by Poliziano, is deeply carved in the manner of a Roman sarcophagus, while for the profoundly felt *Madonna of the Stairs* (Florence, Casa Buonarroti) he uses Donatello's shallow carving technique, the so-called *relievo schiacciato*.

This intriguing contrast in classical and Christian subject matter is evident once again in Michelangelo's first monumental creations, both made in Rome, where he had gone to escape from trouble-ridden Florence after the expulsion of the Medici. In 1496 he carved for Jacopo Galli his drunken *Bacchus* (Florence, Museo Nazionale), thought by some contemporaries to be 'a remarkable piece of antique art'. In contrast the *Pietà* (Rome, St Peter's), a commission from a French cardinal completed by 1499, is a serene, deeply moving piece of Christian devotional art. The motif of the dead Christ lying across his mother's lap is German in origin, but Michelangelo has transformed the harsh realism of the north into a classical and restrained pyramidal group.

After his return to Florence in 1501 Michelangelo carved the huge figure of *David* (Florence, Accademia) which in 1504 was placed outside the Palazzo Vecchio. David had long been a favourite with the Florentines, the virtuous fighter for freedom against superior odds. Two unfinished marble tondi of the Virgin and Child (one in the Royal Academy, London) and his first paintings also date from this period. Though the *Doni Tondo* (Florence, Uffizi), showing the Holy Family, was clearly influenced by the *Virgin and Child with St Anne* (cartoon London, National Gallery; painting Paris, Louvre), on which Leonardo was working in Florence at that time, the hard, sculptural handling of the figures is Michelangelo's own. The commission for a fresco with a scene from Florentine history, the battle of Cascina, to be done for the Council Hall, was never executed, and we only have some of the master's drawings and a copy of a cartoon, a group of bathing soldiers roused by the battle alarm (Holkham Hall, Norfolk). This is an important work showing how deeply Michelangelo was absorbed in saying everything through the human figure alone.

The execution of the fresco was prevented by Pope Julius II's ordering Michelangelo to Rome in March 1505 to work on his tomb. This task was a binding preoccupation for 30 years, and the grandiose scheme for a free-standing monument with some 40 figures to be placed in St Peter's was reduced to increasingly modest dimensions in subsequent contracts. The rather dull structure that finally emerged (S. Pietro in Vincoli) was put together by Michelangelo's pupils: it is, however, redeemed by one of his greatest sculptures, the *Moses*. Among the scattered completed (or more often uncompleted) sculptures for the tomb are the two so-called *Slaves* (Paris, Louvre). He himself spoke ruefully of 'the tragedy of the tomb'.

After a quarrel with the Pope he left Rome, but was recalled in 1508 to paint the vault of the Sistine Chapel in the Vatican, a task which he at first resisted. Apart from some technical help he insisted on executing this gigantic work alone and unobserved. The walls of the chapel had been painted with scenes from the lives of Moses and Christ at the time of Julius's uncle, Sixtus IV, and to these Michelangelo now added on the ceiling the biblical story from the Creation to Noah, the stories running from the altar towards the main entrance. These are set in an architectural framework which divides the ceiling into large and small fields, with nude youths at the 4 corners of each panel, the *ignudi* – purely decorative figures of great beauty without any iconographic significance. Along the sides alternate the figures of 7 prophets and 5 sibyls, and in the lunettes above the windows are the ancestors of Christ. Walls and ceiling seen together form a coherent account of Christian world history, to which the *Last Judgment* on the altar wall (1536–41) was to form the logical conclusion. Commissioned at first by Clement VII and after his death by Paul III, this fresco rising from floor to ceiling makes of the Last Judgment an emotion-laden dramatic event of an intensity and force never equalled.

Michelangelo's first commissions for architecture came from the Medici. His designs for the façade of S. Lorenzo came to nothing, but from 1520 on he worked for Cardinal Giulio, later Clement VII, on the mausoleum for members of the family, still incomplete when he left Florence in 1534 for ever and settled in Rome. The shape and decoration of the chapel reflected its liturgical function as the setting for services for the dead. The effigies of Giuliano and Lorenzo turn towards the Madonna. The figures of *Day, Night, Dawn* and *Dusk* represented earthly time; the figure of the Virgin suckling her child, the Saviour, and a fresco of the Resurrection that was to be painted above her, told of eternity. There is nothing neo-Platonic in this chapel (as has been claimed) and it is – like all religious works of Michelangelo – imbued with a devout Christian spirit. Indeed, only in some late sonnets and allegorical drawings done for his young and deeply loved friend Tommaso Cavalieri does an overt neo-Platonism surface in his work. While this work was in progress Michelangelo also designed the Laurentian Library at S. Lorenzo – with its (later) triple stairway flooding into a vestibule whose architectural components flagrantly contradict the function expected of them, a forerunner of the architecture of Mannerism.

In January 1547 he was appointed architect of the new St Peter's, begun by Bramante in 1506; his most significant contribution was the huge dome, somewhat modified in execution from his original design. Between 1542 and 1550 he painted for Paul III frescoes in another chapel of the Vatican, the Cappella Paolina, showing the *Crucifixion of St Peter* and the *Conversion of St Paul*. These images, with their stress on suffering and miraculous conversion, eschewing all conventional beauty of form, show something of the spirit of the Counter-Reformation. Late in the 1530s he had met Vittoria Colonna: he dedicated to her his most fervent religious sonnets and made for her his most moving drawings, such as the *Crucifixion* in the British Museum or the *Pietà* in the Isabella Stewart Gardner Museum in Boston. In fact, just as at the beginning of his career, the Pietà became an absorbing subject for him. The group now in the cathedral of Florence had been destined for his own tomb, and the *Pietà Rondanini* (Milan, Castello) was still in his studio at the time of his death.

No brief account of Michelangelo's work can do justice to the beauty and pungent originality of his style, which led him to be called 'divine' and to be associated with the quality of *terribilità*, or awesome power. In no other Renaissance artist, not even in Donatello or Leonardo, was passionate feeling so identified with the manual activity of giving material form to ideas. Whether in the finished, polished earlier works (the St Peter's *Pietà*, the *David*) or in the dragging, spiritually labouring forms of his late, to us perhaps most evocative, works, the sense of fusion between mental and physical creation has never been more cogently communicated; it is not just sentiment that makes the stretching out of God's hand to Adam's on the Sistine ceiling a symbol of his work. His reputation in his lifetime was immense; doggedly determined to abide by the pace of his own cogitations and the few patrons to whom he chose to be (at times miserably) loyal because they stirred him creatively or left him more or

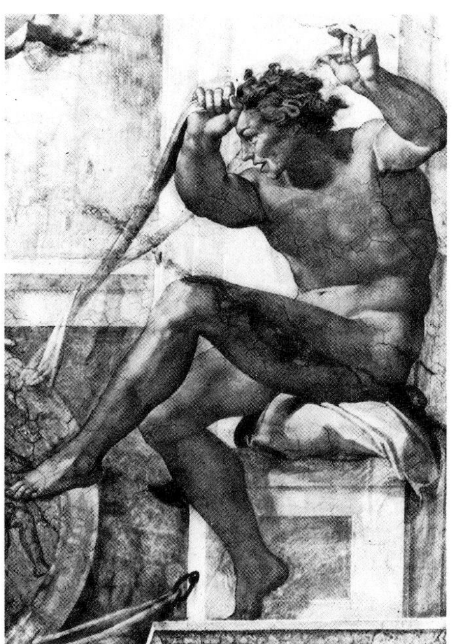

One of **Michelangelo**'s *ignudi* in the Sistine Chapel.

less alone, he satisfied few of the requests made to him. For VASARI he was the culmination of a process whereby, generation by generation, art had not only met the challenge of ancient achievement and the models supplied by nature itself, but gone beyond them. No one, as the elaborate exequies carried out in Florence (the Florence of Cosimo I, whose repeated blandishments had failed to tempt him from Rome) on his death were designed to make clear, had done so much to make loom above the vast assemblage of individual works of art the concept of Art. [73, 78, 197, 267, 319] LDE

C. de Tolnay *Michelangelo* (5 vols. 1969–71); H. von Einem *Michelangelo* (1973)

Michelozzo di Bartolomeo (1396–1472) Florentine sculptor and architect whose dependable efficiency endeared him to Cosimo de' Medici. First heard of assisting Ghiberti with bronzeworking, by 1425 Michelozzo was in partnership with Donatello on important tombs for Florence (Pope John XXIII, Baptistery) and Naples (Brancacci, S. Angelo a Nido). For both Michelozzo supplied the architectural scheme (updatings of traditional types) and much of the sculpture: the stiff poses and

Michelozzo's Medici Palace in Florence.

Romanizing features reappear in the astonishingly *all'antica Leavetaking* relief for the humanist tomb of Aragazzi in Montepulciano (1428f.) After the Prato pulpit (1428f.), a joint commission with Donatello, Michelozzo became increasingly engrossed in a large architectural practice, especially for Cosimo de' Medici. The Medici Palace itself (1444f.) was seen by contemporaries, despite its traditional features, as 'comparable to the works of the Roman Emperors' (Flavio Biondo). In the courtyard here and at S. Marco (1430s) Michelozzo employs a basically Brunelleschian vocabulary without Brunelleschi's strict proportions, modular elements, or novel vaulting types. By contrast, Michelozzo's references to antiquity are often more varied and direct. His most controversial building remains the round choir of SS. Annunziata (1444f.), close to the 'Temple of Minerva Medica' in Rome, and making little concession to the liturgical need to separate clergy and laity. Later alterations and the possible participation of Alberti have obscured Michelozzo's role in the design. Outside Florence, both in his buildings at Montepulciano (S. Agostino, 1437f; Palazzo Pubblico, 1440) and in his villas for the Medici (Trebbio, Cafaggiolo, Careggi) Michelozzo tended to revert to a hybrid style where traditional forms (polygonal piers, gothic arches) stand in 'allusive contrast' (Haalman) to *all'antica* elements. [179, 336] CE

H. Caplow *Michelozzo* (1977)

Milan became the most successful and powerful example of signorial government, by contrast with republican Florence, Venice or Genoa. Although it was not situated on any navigable river, its fertile surroundings and its accessibility – from the rivers Po, Adda and Ticino, Lakes Como and Maggiore and the Swiss transalpine passes – ensured its economic growth. Milan's wealth, populousness and industry were described in detail by Bonvesin da Riva (*c.*1288) just when the VISCONTI dynasty was prevailing over the autonomous commune and the rival dynasty of the della Torre. This control became an established *signoria* with Matteo I (captain-general and Imperial vicar, 1311) and remained hereditary until 1447. The expansionist aims of the Visconti, going far beyond control of neighbouring Lombard cities, reached a peak with Giangaleazzo (1385–1402), whose dynastic pretensions were gratified by the Imperial grant of a dukedom (1395) and the marriage (1387) of his daughter Valentina to Louis, Duke of Orléans – the fatal cause of later French claims to Milan.

If the Visconti's policy of north Italian hegemony and princely grandeur (the court of Giangaleazzo had no equal in lavishness outside France or Burgundy) was conceived in their own name and interest rather than Milan's, the city was undoubtedly the beneficiary. Although highly taxed and without powerful guilds or free civic institutions (after 1396, when the statutes were revised, the Council of 900, anyhow ineffectual, was nominated: the main organs of government were the ducal Consiglio Segreto and Consiglio di Giustizia), it retained an exceptionally dynamic economy. Manufactures included textiles (woollen cloth, cotton fustians, luxury silks) and metalwork, particularly armour and armaments. Health regulations which controlled plague were advanced and effective in the second half of the 14c. and communications were improved by canals (the Naviglio Grande, linking Milan to the Ticino, was promoted by Giangaleazzo). Such advantages may help to explain the acceptance of a princely authority which was sometimes brutal and arbitrary and not always triumphant in its many wars: Giangaleazzo's death suddenly halted Visconti expansion into central Italy and Filippo Maria (1412–47) had little success in reversing the mainland advances of Venice.

Petrarch praised the régime of his patron Archbishop Giovanni Visconti (d.1354), and a century later Pier Candido Decembrio, one of the humanists in Filippo Maria's employment, described Milan as preferable to Florence in form of government, site, climate and other amenities. The interlude of free civic government (the AMBROSIAN REPUBLIC, 1447–50) was not successful, lacking support among the socially and economically powerful of Milan, and, against the background of Venetian aggression, witnessing the disaffection of formerly dependent cities. The SFORZA dukes who followed (1450–99) needed to pursue a more cautious external policy – the alliance with Medicean Florence was paramount for Francesco Sforza, and dependent relations had to be forged with the dominant families of the duchy's subject towns. In essence, however, theirs was a continuation of Visconti methods: the use of professional administrators and of a body of *ad hoc* inner experts under Lodovico called the '*deputati del denaro*'. It is significant that the assassination of Galeazzo Maria (1476) provoked no civic uprising and that even Lodovico, on his brief return from exile (February–April 1500), was welcomed.

The Sforza personified continuity, not least in their building works: the enormous Milan cathedral, promoted by Giangaleazzo (1387) though officially entrusted to its autonomous *fabbrica* (works office), nearly reached completion, apart from the façade, under Lodovico Sforza; Francesco restored the Castello di Porta Giovia (of which the present Castello Sforzesco is a 19c. reconstruction); canal building continued, notably the Martesana, connecting Milan with the river Adda. Under Francesco, however, the new connection with Medicean Florence was also expressed in Milanese building: particularly the Ospedale Maggiore by Filarete and the (destroyed) Medici Palace, the seat of the Medici bank, whose manager Pigello Portinari (d.1468) is commemorated by his chapel in S. Eustorgio. Lodovico, the discerning patron of Bramante, had the churches of S. Maria presso S. Celso and S. Maria presso S. Satiro built, S. Maria delle Grazie completed, and a new cloister constructed for S. Ambrogio, the monastery of Milan's patron saint. His concern for the historical past of Milan is shown by his commission to CORIO to write its history.

Possession of Milan had been for the Visconti and the Sforza the key to their predominance in northern Italy. Its importance was even more apparent in the 16c. It was the capital of the French government of occupation set up by LOUIS XII, lasting from 1500 to 1521 (apart from an ineffectual interval under Massimiliano Sforza (1512–15), backed by the Emperor Maximilian). Thereafter it became the main prize fought over by FRANCIS I and by CHARLES V, whose control was first exerted through the puppet Duke Francesco II Sforza (1521–35). It suffered enormously from the effects of warfare, particularly in the siege of 1526. Direct rule by Imperial governors, backed by occupying Spanish troops, started in 1535. The extent of oppression should not be exaggerated: the governor's authority was counterbalanced by a professional civil service, and some degree of opinion could be expressed through the Senate or by direct appeal against misgovernment to the Emperor. Thus Ferrante Gonzaga, Governor 1546–55, who had immense and costly bastioned fortifications constructed, was removed from office as a result of protest and subsequent investigation. Industry and population figures recovered (a total of 90,000 in an ecclesiastical census of 1576 corresponds roughly to late 15c. estimates). *See* BORROMEO, CARDINAL CARLO. DC

Storia di Milano Fondazione Treccani degli Alfieri V-IX (1955–61); D. Muir *A history of Milan under the Visconti* (1924); C. M. Ady *A history of Milan under the Sforza* (1907); F. Chabod *Il ducato di Milano e l'impero di Carlo V* (2 vols 1961–71)

Mino da Fiesole (1429–84) Florentine marble sculptor who was influenced by Desiderio da Settignano and Antonio Rossellino, though his carving is drier and his figures stiffer and less natural. His earliest dated work is also the earliest dated Renaissance portrait bust, depicting Piero de' Medici (1453). Mino carved at least six other good busts and produced a number of tombs and tabernacles in Florence; he is probably identical with a prolific sculptor active in Naples and Rome in the 1460s and 1470s who signed himself Mino del Reame. While superficially attractive, his sculpture lacks genuine emotion and frequently degenerates into naïve sentimentality. CA

C. Avery *Florentine Renaissance sculpture* (1970); J. Pope-Hennessy *Italian Renaissance sculpture* (1971)

Self-portrait in a convex **mirror** by Parmigianino (Vienna, Kunsthistorisches Museum).

Mirrors Mirrors of glass 'silvered' on the back began to supplement those of polished metal in the 14c., though it was only in the 16c. that high-quality glass ones were made (at Murano) on a scale that made them one of Venice's chief luxury exports. The connection between the increasing use of mirrors and the art of make-up (the mirror was a familiar symbol of vanity) and personal cleanliness is unexplored, but they had an influence on the development of the self-portrait in painting: Vasari assumed that Simone Martini (d.1344) 'painted himself with two mirrors in order to get his head in profile'. Parmigianino (d.1540) took self-scrutiny to a thoroughly introspective level in his *Self-portrait in a* (convex) *Mirror*. JRH

Missaglia family From the 14c. they practised as makers of fine armours and weapons in Milan. With Tommaso and, on his retirement in *c.*1451, with his son Antonio (d. *c.*1495) the family acquired a European reputation for producing what were, in terms of beauty as well as of practicality, the finest armours in existence. Having become wealthy in goods and enfeoffed land the family withdrew from trade on Antonio's death. Their place was taken by a family only slightly less famous, the Negroli, who maintained Milan's reputation as a fine armaments centre to the late 16c. JRH

Monte, Guidobaldo, Marchese del (1545–1607) Soldier and mathematician. He was a friend and pupil of Commandino and for 20 years a patron, teacher and friend of Galileo; his interest in Archimedean mathematical physics was influential. His *Liber mechanicorum* (Pesaro 1577, Italian ed. 1581) was seen by contemporaries as the greatest work on statics since the Greeks. He also wrote on the calendar, on perspective, on astronomy and on mathematical instruments. MBH

Montefeltro family From the 13c. members of this family exercised an increasingly steady control over Urbino from their pinnacle fortress of S. Leo in the mountainous region of the Romagna, whence they took their name. The poverty of the area, however, forced the Montefeltro counts to be absent for long periods earning money as condottieri or as podestà or capitani of other cities; frequently their lands were overrun by neighbouring signori acting on their own part or as agents of the Papacy. Stability was first achieved under FEDERICO (1422–82), signore from 1444, created duke in 1474. His son Guidobaldo died without an heir in 1508, leaving the duchy to Francesco Maria della Rovere. JRH

J. Dennistoun *Memoirs of the dukes of Urbino* (1909); G. Franceschini *I Montefeltro* (1970)

Early armour by the **Missaglia** family, 1380–90 (Tyrol, Churburg Castle).

Montefeltro *See* FEDERICO II DA MONTEFELTRO

Montemurlo, battle of In July 1539 the newly appointed Duke of Florence, the young COSIMO I, dispatched a force under Alessandro Vitelli which defeated near Pistoia the advance guard of an army raised by anti-Medicean exiles. The news led to the retreat of the main body, and the victory (commemorated by the column in Piazza S. Trinita) was seen then and since as both assuring the continuation of the ducal régime and encouraging Cosimo's insistence on being his own, and not his older councillors', man. JRH

Moretto da Brescia (*c.*1498–1554) The popular name of Alessandro Bonvicino, who was, together with Romanino, the chief painter of early 16c. Brescia. Many altarpieces by Moretto survive there, showing the influence of Titian (with whom he may have trained), but his style, characterized by Vasari as 'of great diligence', and perhaps influenced by Savoldo, is more typical of Lombardy in its attention to detail and relative flatness. A small group of striking portraits, influential for Moretto's main pupil, Moroni, includes the earliest known Italian full-length (1526; London, National Gallery). AB

G. Gombosi *Moretto da Brescia* (1943)

Morone, Girolamo (1470–1529) Legally trained, this Milanese civil servant and diplomat combined local patriotism and loyalty to the Sforza with a commonsense acceptance of the *status quo* of the moment. He was thus accepted as an essential public servant through the succession of régimes that governed Milan 1499–1515. Failing then to commend himself to the French, he joined the exiled Sforza and, from 1521, supported Charles V's campaigns against the French in the Milanese. The Imperial victory at Pavia in 1525, however, led him to promote the 'Morone conspiracy'. This envisaged the ousting of the Imperial presence from Italy. The kingdom of Naples was to be taken over by Charles's great general Ferrante, Marquis of PESCARA, who was known to resent the Emperor's lack of gratitude for his services. The next move was to be military action which would make Duke Francesco II Sforza the actual ruler of Milan, rather than Charles's puppet. All this was to be done with at least the tacit agreement of Pope Clement VII and Venice. As High Chancellor of Milan, Morone was a man to take seriously, and Pescara did waver when offered the crown of Naples. He then, however, passed on the details of the plot to Charles, who ordered the imprisonment of Morone. Pescara died shortly afterwards, and Charles not only honoured the wish expressed in his will that Morone should be freed, but relied on his cooperation during the campaigns that followed the anti-Imperial League of COGNAC. The combination in Morone of Trimmer, local patriot and Italian visionary has not yet been traced in any adequate biography. *See* MILAN; WARS OF ITALY. JRH

Moroni, Giovanni Battista (*c.*1520–78), painter chiefly celebrated for his portraits, was born near Albino, not far from Bergamo, and trained in Brescia in the studio of Moretto. His later years were passed in and around Bergamo. Moroni's many religious paintings derive from Moretto's, but as a portraitist he showed from the start much sharper observation of human character and a more fluent and descriptive technique. Such masterpieces as *The Tailor* (London, National Gallery) and *Gian Girolamo Grumelli* (*Il Cavaliere in Rosa*; Bergamo, Moroni Collection) place him among the greatest of all specialists of the portrait. AB

M. Gregori *Giovan Battista Moroni* (1979)

Music played an important part in the cultural life of Italy during the 3 centuries from 1300, although it is only possible to apply the word 'Renaissance' to the music of the 125 years up to 1600 with any real meaning. The 2 broad features of the period are the exchange in the importance of religious and secular music, and the development of an indigenous Italian school of composers after a period of foreign domination.

In 1300 the most important music was emanating from France. It was complex and polyphonic, in a manner developed from the so-called Ars Nova, in which new concepts of musical notation opened the way to a very sophisticated musical style. In France this affected both religious and secular music. Italy seems to have been little influenced by these advances for some time, and it was only *c.*1330 that a distinctive school of composers emerged. These seem to have worked mainly in the north, notably at Padua and Bologna (significantly, university towns), Verona, Milan and Florence. They wrote principally in two secular genres. The *caccia* was strongly influenced by the French *chace*, and consisted of a poem in which the incidents of the hunt (and, by analogy, other scenes of common life) were vividly depicted. The music, appropriately, was in the form of a canon, in which one part follows another with identical music, a third part being left free to accompany the other two. The madrigal was a setting of a poem with several 3-line strophes, all set to the same music, followed by a 2-line refrain, set to a different rhythm. The Italian penchant for melody is already shown in the way the upper part is often more florid than the accompanying lower ones, implying the attainment of a certain virtuosity. To these genres the most famous Italian composer of the 14c., LANDINI, added the polyphonic *ballata*, often in a simpler style, with both parts (one of which might be vocal, the other instrumental) in roughly the same rhythm, as in the well known 'Ecco la primavera'.

For most of the century there is little religious music, the main surviving examples being composed around 1400 by Matteo da Perugia, *maestro di cappella* at Milan cathedral and a favourite of Pope Alexander V. The return of the popes from AVIGNON undoubtedly helped to stimulate an interest, but there was no substantial tradition: the singers in the papal chapel were often foreigners, more especially products of the cathedral and monastic song schools of France and the Low Countries. They were to some extent affected by the Italian tradition: they tended to simplify the complicated contrapuntal style which they had adopted for their native employers, and also took to splendid sonorities for the ceremonial and homage motets with which they praised patron saint or duke. But Italian vernacular song did not maintain the impetus of the 14c., for the major composers preferred to compose to French texts.

Settings of the Italian vernacular were, however, not unknown. They were generally improvised by musician-poets, some of them intellectuals such as Leonardo Giustiniani (*c.*1398–1446) and FICINO, who sang, accompanying themselves on a lyra viol (a kind of bowed instrument with a curved bridge which allowed chords to be played). The music they sang is lost, but we can reconstruct it to some extent through the music of the frottolists of the period 1480–1520. This is simple and written in stereotyped rhythmic patterns, with repeated sections adapted to different kinds of verse structures. Thus virtually all sonnets (for example) could be sung to the same music, this being generally written so that it might be performed by a solo singer accompanied on a lute, or, in some of the more complex pieces, by a group of viols. This indigenous growth, practised especially at the Mantuan court by TROMBONCINO and CARA, attracted some of the foreigners, such as JOSQUIN DES PREZ, who still tended to fill the most important posts in both court and cathedral, and as a result were inclined to make the music more contrapuntal and therefore less easy to adapt to all examples of a verse pattern.

By this time it was becoming fashionable for intellectuals to discuss the ideas on music held by the ancient Greeks. The total lack of any of the original music made the problem of recreating what had been, by all classical accounts, much more emotionally powerful than most of the music then current, to say the least, hard to resolve. The consensus was that words and music had to be combined in some meaningful way to give a total experience that neither could realize separately. The immediate attempt to fulfil this criterion was through the madrigal: nothing to do with the 14c. genre, but a kind of much enriched FROTTOLA, except that now the music could only be sung to one poem, and there was an attempt to give the finest shades of verbal meaning a musical equivalent. This was only possible if some sort of musical symbolism was created and here too Greek theory was followed, in which the use of different modes and *genere* (scale and melodic patterns) were held to give rise to different emotions. Various experimental recreations of these Greek scale patterns were tried, notably at Ferrara, where the concept of chromaticism was investigated with the aid of a harpsichord called the *archicembalo*, which was provided with extra keys and strings to cope with very complicated systems of tuning. Such experiments largely foundered because Greek music had been monophonic, whereas 16c. music was essentially harmonic. Nevertheless they created a wide variety of new resources, both in melody and harmony, which were put to good use for the remainder of the century.

The rise of serious vernacular music meant that, although many of the first generation of madrigalists (*c.*1530–50) were Netherlanders, from the middle of the century native Italian composers were much in demand and occupied the cream of court posts as *maestri di cappella*,

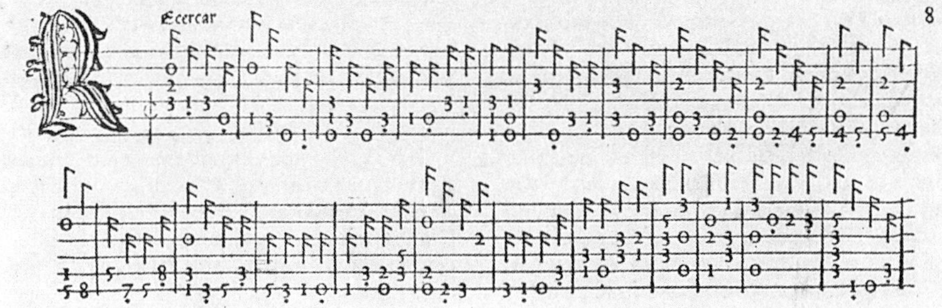

Lute **music** printed from movable type by Petrucci in 1508.

and increasingly also those in large cathedrals and basilicas. This movement was encouraged when the Council of TRENT, discussing church music in some detail in 1562, decided that one major concern must be the audibility and expression of the words of the Mass – not very different from the preferred views of the humanists. Thus such native composers as PALESTRINA in Rome and Vincenzo Ruffo (*c.*1510–87) of Verona began to produce church music which was much simpler in texture, but very splendid in sonority. As a corollary of the madrigal, a vogue grew for the motet, a non- or para-liturgical piece in which the words were freely chosen, often specially so that the musical symbolism developed in secular music could be deployed here also (a difficult matter when setting the more abstract Ordinary of the Mass). An enormous demand for both secular and religious music was made possible by the invention of a method of printing music from movable type in 1501 by the Italian Ottaviano PETRUCCI (1466–1539), later developed by Antonio Gardane (died *c.*1570). The Venetian publishing houses were soon turning out a very considerable quantity of such music, much of it in elegant volumes; they were followed by usually less skilled but nonetheless efficient houses in Milan, Rome and several smaller cities. This widespread dissemination of music in turn helped to create a very sophisticated audience and by the last 25 years of the 16c. musical style had evolved to a peak of expressiveness in a huge variety of genres.

In secular music, the madrigal's greatest practitioners, MARENZIO, Monteverdi and GESUALDO, may appropriately be called Mannerists. They set exquisite texts, often pastoral in subject-matter in the manners of Sannazaro, Tasso and Guarini; and used a complex set of symbols to mirror each passing mood of the verse. The result is often restless and full of strong contrasts. It uses supreme artifice: melody which sometimes follows the speech rhythms of the verse rather than the measured metres of the older contrapuntal music; complex contrapuntal passages, where the words are obscured, alternating with homophonic passages, where they are clear; extreme dissonance, sometimes juxtaposed with the most simple consonance; chromaticism brought in to colour the by now straightforward diatonicism which had almost replaced the medieval modal system. Such music does indeed *muovere gli affetti* – move the whole man – fulfilling the Greek and humanist demand.

Together with such seriousness (the aim of the madrigal), many lighter forms emerged. The *villanella* or *villanesca* started as a popular Neapolitan dialect song, soon took to guying the sentimental madrigal, and finally became somewhat more respectable, ending as the *canzonetta*, defined by Thomas Morley (1557–1602) as 'the counterfeit of the madrigal'. Dialect and anti-sentimental verse were used in the *giustiniana* and the *mascherata*, in which such butts as foreigners, Jews, old impotent men and members of the lower orders were depicted as vividly as in the etchings of Callot; and these were joined together into 'madrigal comedies' (the most famous of which is VECCHI's *L'Amfiparnaso* of 1597), telling a story in the manner of the *commedia dell'arte*.

Little, it may be noticed, has been said about purely instrumental music, which was less practised in Italy than in either Germany or

England, presumably because Renaissance philosophizing was concerned with the conjunction of words and music. But many varieties of instruments were in common use, played by the town musicians, or *piffari*, who mastered all kinds of flutes and recorders, shawms and bassoons, cornetts and sackbuts or trombones to play dance music, while the nobility played viols and lutes in chamber music. In civic and religious processions the confraternities had musicians who played *viole da braccio*, and the cathedrals hired the *piffari* to make their choral music still grander. All in all, by 1600, Italy had become the centre of the musical world, a position it was to maintain for nearly a century and a half. DA

F. Blume *Renaissance and Baroque music* (1967); H. M. Brown *Music in the Renaissance* (1976); G. Reese *Music in the Renaissance* (1954); G. Abraham *The concise Oxford history of music* (1979)

Myth of Venice The phrase is used to summarize the image of Renaissance Venice in the eyes of its admirers – an image nourished by propagandistic analyses of the Republic by its own publicists. The image was suggested from the mid-15c. and expressed with full maturity in the publications of Contarini and Giannotti in the 1540s. It contained 3 main components. One was stability: while other states changed their mode of government as a result of foreign conquest or internal revolt or crisis, Venice remained unvanquished and its republican institutions virtually unchanged. The second and third sought to explain this stability. On the one hand the constitution of Venice was seen to be 'perfect' in that it ideally combined the 'best' Aristotelian forms of government: by one good man (the doge), by a beneficent élite (the senior patricians of the Senate), and by the responsible many (the membership of the Great Council); on the other, Venice had discovered the secret of preserving harmony between interest and income groups, between governors and governed, the key to this being an impartial justice.

The **myth of Venice**: a popular Venetian print of 1502 showing the 'Triumph and Glory of the Venetians'.

Thus constituted, the image was made all the more glamorous by the city's strangeness of setting, surrounded and penetrated by water, and by the beauty of its fabric. Each component contained an element of exaggeration (hence 'myth'), but in comparison with every other Italian state and, indeed, most European ones, the political and constitutional stability and the social harmony of Venice were dramatic enough for the image to carry a conviction that lasted beyond the Renaissance: Venice was cited as a model by the Dutch, seeking independence from Spain, by the English, thinking of substitutes for a monarchy chopped off with Charles I's head, and by the Founding Fathers of the independent states of America. JRH

Mythology never dies. Fulgentius allegorized it in the *Mythologicon* early in the 6c. AD, and the Middle Ages held on to it in the same disguise. Exceptionally, Dante, in the *Convivio*, suggested that the angels could be equated with Plato's Ideas, and both with the pagan gods (even though the gentiles had not well understood the nature of the divine). It may have been this that enabled him to use the pagan gods within the *Comedy*, in their own guise, and without allegory. But it was not until Boccaccio, in his later years, and particularly in the *Genealogia deorum* (*Genealogy of the gods*; worked on over the last 25 years of his life, from 1350 to 1375), that any systematic effort was made to map the mythological territory. Boccaccio did this with a mixture of rashness and caution. Thinking of the classical gods as all demons, he looks under the ridiculous surface for what prudent men may have hidden. In accordance with the medieval habit, he is not afraid to look for a plurality of lessons. So when Perseus slays the Gorgon, the moral sense is the victory of virtue over vice, the allegorical sense is mind rising superior to mundane delights and turning to celestial ones, and the anagogical sense is the ascent of Christ to the Father through the conquest of the prince of darkness. This is the cautious side, and it accounts for a lot of tedium in the work. The rash side lies in Boccaccio's assertion that he goes to the source, and neglects the secondary streams. In reality he picks up his information at the most available levels. He follows no system. He accumulates all that he can but lacks a critical sense to sift the authority of his informants. His is a medieval encyclopaedia, though the fullness of its information prolonged its life into the Cinquecento.

What survives today from the *Genealogy of the gods* is Boccaccio's belief in, and defence of, poetry (Books XIV–XV). Petrarch was, as a more practised scholar, more critical. He never compiles, or allegorizes; he notes the aberration of belief in a multiplicity of gods, but finds it hard to think that this was really the sense of the great minds of antiquity. Who could venerate adulterous and deceitful gods? So he looks for the evidence of monotheism in the ancient writers (particularly in Cicero), and makes the plurality of gods the fault, not of poetry itself, but of men, so as not to prevent new poets in another age, with another frame of mind and better grace, combining mythologizing eloquence with Christian piety. The other main development of the first half of the Quattrocento was the licence given by ALBERTI in the *De pictura* (1435) to paint other subjects than religious ones; and the main surprise is how little the painters of the Quattrocento availed themselves of this permission. It was not until the 1470s that Poliziano, in the *Stanze per la giostra*, gave a pictorial treatment to the Realm of Venus; and it was equally in the 1470s that Botticelli painted the *Birth of Venus* and the *Primavera*. When Aby Warburg first looked for the sources of Botticelli's pictures (in 1893) he found them near at hand in Poliziano, and behind Poliziano in OVID and CLAUDIAN; when his successor Ernst Gombrich returned to the problem (in 1945) he was inclined to seek a meaning in the neo-Platonism of FICINO, with Venus as *Humanitas* and not as pagan sensuality. And it is possible that the exceptional nature of these pictures – unparalleled elsewhere in Italy – admits rather of an allegorical than of a pagan meaning.

If we look beyond Botticelli to the most classically minded of his contemporaries, Mantegna, we see how small a place the pagan gods have in his painting. Only the pictures for

Mantegna's *Minerva Driving out the Vices*, part of the **mythological** decorative scheme for Isabella d'Este's Studiolo (Paris, Louvre).

the Studiolo of Isabella d'ESTE prefigure a change of mood that took place in the early 1500s, and one of them, *Minerva Driving out the Vices*, has a theme which still moralizes, as do the celebrated *Stanze* of Raphael in the first decade of the 16c. Surprisingly it is Giovanni Bellini, whose whole *oeuvre* is Christian, who in his last picture (1515) paints a *Toilet of Venus* which is clearly for its own sake, and which matches the Dresden *Venus* of Giorgione: both foreshadow (with Bellini's *Feast of the Gods*) the Venetian concern with Ovidian material throughout the Cinquecento. Meanwhile it was halfway through the century before Vincenzo Cartari (1556) at last produced a new handbook to replace Boccaccio with a visual repository, *Le imagini dei dei degli antichi* (*Images of the gods of the ancients*), which we may take as a sign that it was art rather than literature that fed most avidly on classical mythology. JHW

J. Seznac *La survivance des dieux antiques* (1940); A. Warburg *La rinascita del paganesimo antico* (1966); E. Gombrich *Symbolic images* (1972)

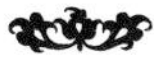

Nanni di Banco (*c.*1384–1421) A transitional Florentine sculptor who vied with Ghiberti and Donatello over the statuary for the cathedral and Orsanmichele. His *St Luke* (1408) shows him trying to imbue a figure in gothic drapery

with a classical spirit, an attempt that succeeds better in his group of *Four Saints* for Orsanmichele, looking like Roman senators discoursing. His greatest project was the completion of the Porta della Mandorla of the cathedral with a narrative relief of the *Assumption of the Virgin* (1414–21). This still retains a gothic flavour. CA
C. Avery *Florentine Renaissance sculpture* (1970); J. Pope-Hennessy *Italian gothic sculpture* (1970); H. W. Janson 'Nanni di Banco's *Assumption of the Virgin* on the Porta della Mandorla' *Studies in Western Art* (1963)

Naples, kingdom of With the revolution of 1282 against Charles I of Anjou (the 'Sicilian Vespers'), the southern Italian mainland and the island of Sicily, hitherto ruled as a united 'kingdom of Sicily', split into 2 separate states. The island became known as the kingdom of Trinacria, the mainland, from its capital, as the kingdom of Naples. Although the legality of this division was never accepted by the Angevin rulers of Naples, who continued to speak of themselves as 'kings of Sicily', the two realms were only for a few brief years to be reunited in the Renaissance period.

As a result of fiscal policies which prevented the growth of a powerful native merchant class, the mercantile economy of the kingdom of Naples, which in the 11c. had shown strong possibilities of development, was profoundly backward in comparison with those of the Tuscan and Lombard cities by the mid-13c. In the 14c. almost all trade and banking were in the hands of north-Italians, particularly Florentines. At the same time – outside certain limited areas such as Sulmona, Campania and coastal Apulia, which did indeed produce large surpluses of corn for export – agriculture was cursed by poor soil and climate. The social structure of the realm corresponded to this economy. A few powerful noble houses, allied to the crown by blood or service, held broad estates (*latifundia*). Beneath them, and like them mainly of northern French or Provençal descent, stood a great number of lesser nobles, living often on fiefs fractioned through inheritance, and resentful of their comparative poverty. Below these were a mass of workers upon the land, living close to subsistence and untouched by those changes in farming techniques that were coming to the north of Italy. All enterprise in the kingdom centred on the capital, the city of Naples, which had a population of perhaps 30,000 at the beginning of the 14c., 60,000 at the beginning of the 15c., and a remarkable 280,000 in 1595. No figures exist for the kingdom as a whole until the beginning of the 16c., when the total population was 1 million: in 1595 it was 2.1 million. In the capital, wealth could be achieved not through commerce but only through royal bounty. It was a society destined to be split by the rancour of disappointed nobles and pervaded by the violence of the rural poor.

The difficulties of ruling such a kingdom were compounded above all by the revolt of Sicily in 1282. This led to a hundred years of war, in which the mainland monarchs sought to recover the island. Against these problems Charles II (1288–1309) and Robert I (1309–43) struggled with some degree of success. But with the accession of GIOVANNA I (1343–82), royal power dissolved. The Great SCHISM aggravated the condition of the kingdom by throwing up 2 rival houses as pretenders to royal authority; the second house of ANJOU and the line of DURAZZO. In the contest Charles III of Durazzo (1382–86) triumphed. His son LADISLAS (1386–1414), taking advantage of the disturbances brought by the Schism, was even able to gain what to some contemporaries appeared as a position of brief predominance in peninsular politics. With the reign of his sister, Giovanna II (1414–35), whose over-rapid transfers of affection between her husband and various lovers brought confusion, internal anarchy was renewed.

At her death RENÉ of Anjou waged war with Alfonso V, King of Aragon, for the succession. The victor was ALFONSO (I of Naples, 1442–58), who proceeded to embark upon an ambitious foreign policy. This could be sustained only through the support of the kingdom of Aragon and through large concessions to an already powerful baronage, men whom Machiavelli was justly to describe as 'enemies of all civil order'. The fruits of such a policy were revealed at Alfonso's death when his Aragonese possessions passed to his brother and Naples was inherited by his illegitimate son, FERRANTE I (1458–94). Ferrante was able to maintain himself in power only by a ruthlessness which alienated all loyalty. When CHARLES VIII invaded the kingdom in pursuit of the Angevin claim (1494), Ferrante's 3 successors, in their brief reigns, could muster no native support. It was in these circumstances that Ferdinand II of Aragon first partitioned Naples with LOUIS XII of France (Treaty of Granada, 11 November

1500) and then took over the whole of the kingdom (1502–04). Thenceforth, until the beginning of the 18c., Naples was to be a viceroyalty of the Spanish kings.

Despite the economic backwardness of the kingdom, in periods of comparative stability the kings were able to tax their subjects heavily. In 3 eras royal wealth promoted a notable cultural flowering. The first was the age of Frederick II, among whose achievements was the foundation of the university of Naples (1224). The second was the early period of Angevin rule (1266–1343), which saw the adornment of the city of Naples, the enlargement of its perimeter, the building of Castel Nuovo and of, among other churches, S. Maria Donnaregina and S. Chiara. The third was seen with the humanist patronage offered by Alfonso I and the renewal of the capital by his grandson Alfonso in the 1480s. With the Spanish conquest, however, cultural life withered to isolated figures – Bernardino Telesio, BRUNO, and Tommaso Campanella – who founded no schools. JL

E. Pontieri ed. *Storia di Napoli* II–III (1975–76); F. Sabatini *Napoli angiovina* (1975); B. Croce *Storia del Regno di Napoli* (4th ed. 1953)

Nardi, Jacopo (1476–1563) wrote in the 1550s a somewhat rambling history of Florence up to the eclipse of the Republic's last hopes in 1537. He had belonged to the literary circle of the RUCELLAI Gardens, where he knew Machiavelli, and held various minor offices. The earlier part of his history is mainly second-hand, but in 1512 and 1527 Nardi took an active part in revolutionary events and his personal recollections stir it into life, as they do throughout the period of the Last Republic, his commitment to which brought about exile in 1530. DC

A. Gelli *Istorie della citta di Firenze di Iacopo Nardi* (2 vols 1858); R. von Albertini *Firenze dalla repubblica al principato* (1970)

National feeling No one who knows Italy today, over a century since the establishment of Italian political unity, can expect to find much evidence that a shared feeling of national identity was present in the Renaissance. How could it have been? By the 14c. a multitude of territorial nuclei had painfully and proudly constituted themselves as socio-political entities, pushing outwards against neighbours (and therefore enemies) until they were forced to stop. City-states, civic estates, mini-empires: by whatever name they are called, the urban-based independent powers of the peninsula, whether as small as San Marino or as large as Florence, had striven to occupy spaces whose emotional significance they were not prepared to jettison by mentally assigning them to a larger whole.

The peninsula was not a closed world, neither were the rivals within it of a piece. Much of it was in theory, and in practice when it was convenient to individual cities, subject to the authority of the German Holy Roman Emperors. Angevins and Aragonese contested their rights to a third of the peninsula, the kingdoms of Naples and Sicily. In the centre was that giant anomaly the Papacy, with its wide and resentful Papal State: a GUELF answer, to cities in need of an ally, to the Ghibelline support invoked by their rivals. The most enlightened (in the sense of least parochial – or campanilistic) response to common danger was a common determination to sink differences – for the moment. Thus the Peace of LODI of 1454 rationalized a point of internal mutual exhaustion. Thus the alliances, Holy or otherwise, of the generation after 1494 sought to check, stage by stage, the incursion of foreign forces.

Humanist research, by disinterring the geopolitical unity as well as the dominant ideas of ancient Rome, did launch the concept of shared inheritance. Petrarch could lament the lacerated condition of 'Italy'. Armies from 1494 could fight with the word as a rallying cry. Machiavelli, with desperate flattery, could claim (in the last chapter of *The prince*) that all Italy was awaiting the leadership of a Medicean dictator-legislator to oust the 'barbarian rule' of France and Spain. Guicciardini, from the viewpoint of an ex-papal and therefore to some extent international functionary, could move from a Florentine history to a *History of Italy*

But to call others barbarians because they did not have the civilizing spirits of ancient Rome on tap in their cellars was an appeal to a common nostalgia, not a call to common action. The alliances formed from 1494 were not to liberate occupied territories but to protect those who were still free, and – once the danger seemed to have gone – they fell apart. Though Italians travelled widely and resided in other Italian cities as exiles or artists or merchants, they formed no business partnerships and very few marriage alliances with their alien hosts, whose manners and language they often mocked – and, if they were Tuscan publishers, strove with earnest tactlessness to correct. Even before the divisive effect of Spanish occupation in Milan and Naples had had time to make itself felt, Italian national feeling proved no more than a momentary stirring in the sinews or the brain in response to challenge by *alieni*, 'outsiders'; not *stranieri*, 'foreigners': that was a term Italians mainly reserved for describing one another. *See* CAMPANILISMO; ITALIAN LANGUAGE; WARS OF ITALY; CONSTITUTIONS. JRH

V. Ilardi '"Italianità" among some Italian intellectuals in the early sixteenth century' *Traditio* (1956); B. Croce *La Spagna nella vita italiana durante il Rinascimento* (1941)

Nature Men's response to nature, in the sense of the natural world, can be gauged only partially through the evidence for it; painting, literature, the design of gardens, the siting of houses were all subject to convention. In painting, landscape was long subordinate to figures, but from Ambrogio Lorenzetti's *Good government* (1337–39) there was a growing tendency to give the illusion of a real tract of countryside rather than to create a decorative assemblage of individually observed details. Linear perspective helped in the organization of such scenes, and once landscape had become unified it could be used to express a personal feeling – for a particular time of day, perhaps, as with Piero della Francesca or Mantegna, or a particular mood, as with Giovanni Bellini and Giorgione. Later, the work of painters like Niccolò dell'Abbate and Jacopo Bassano reflected a taste for paintings in which landscape so dominated the figures as to be in effect the true subject. In decorative cycles like those of Veronese at Maser the pleasure of linking the painted nature on the walls to the real nature outside also helped the development of landscape painting as a genre. This whole process may have been helped by a change in artists' self-consciousness: from being doomed to produce inferior copies of what God had created to being able to sense, and indeed actively share in, this creativity. The work of artists, moreover, came to be seen in terms of a fruitful rivalry with nature. 'In your hands lies hidden the idea of a new nature,' Aretino wrote to Michelangelo in 1537. And in writing to Titian in similar terms he made it clear that it was not just the human figure but landscape too that could be created anew. But as landscape painting becomes more subjective, idealized or

Giambologna's sculptural allegory of the wild **nature** of the Apeninnes, *c.*1580, at Pratolino.

mannered, it reminds us, as forcibly as the symbolic landscapes of Giotto and Duccio, that the artist's is not a true indicator of the ordinary individual's view of the countryside.

And though from Petrarch onwards writers expressed the solace they found in the countryside and the joy they took in its meadows and woods and streams, its birds and flowers, there is usually enough artifice – reacquaintance with classical pastoral poetry, a quickened response to the northern chivalric pleasure in the quest and the hunt, the antithesis between country and city – to put us on our guard. However, the pleasure in the countryside expressed in Pius II's autobiographical *Commentaries* is patently genuine, and it was echoed in his choice of a site for his palace at Pienza, with its wide view towards Monte Amiata. Indeed, though there were reasons of landlordship and escape from the summer diseases of the city to live in the countryside, the landscape so liberally sprinkled with castle-villas in Gozzoli's frescoes in the Medici Palace suggests that residence there was found pleasant as well as useful. And as the villa gradually lost its defensive aspect from the 1470s, this other aspect becomes increasingly pronounced.

It is, however, from the development of the garden that clearer evidence of feeling for the countryside can be derived. The 14c. ideal was a walled enclosure within which selected fragments of nature, flowers and shrubs, were carefully arranged to be inspected from paths or through the open sides of pergolas and arbours, and assiduously watered. Real nature, with its footpads, its droughts, and the unacceptable immensities of its forests and mountains and coastlines, was excluded. From the 15c. the addition of a grove or *boschetto* conceded to a taste for something more natural but still safe enough for the perambulations of ladies (a chief motive behind garden design). In the 16c., the alarm felt in confronting real nature at its rawest was harmlessly converted into a *frisson* through the introduction, into slightly wilder areas of gardens, of grottoes, hydraulic tricks, artificial mountains, vast rocks and sculptures referring with grotesque relish to the untameable forces of the world outside. These themselves remained 'off limits' to the sympathetic imagination until the Romanticism of the 18c. JRH

J. Bialostocki 'The Renaissance concept of nature and antiquity' *The Renaissance and Mannerism* (12th International Congress of the History of Art; 1963); A. R. Turner *The vision of landscape in Renaissance Italy* (1966); D. R. Coffin ed. *The Italian garden* (1972)

Nepotism The accusation levelled against the popes of the Renaissance from Sixtus IV to Paul III (with Alexander VI as an especially opprobrious case), that they appointed nephews (*nipoti*) and other relations to clerical and administrative positions of importance, is as true as it is notorious. This sort of favouritism was an abuse of power. It subordinated spiritual fervour or trained bureaucratic competence to the accidents of relationship. But popes were temporal rulers of a large part of Italy as well as spiritual leaders: other rulers did not hesitate to use members of their own family as military commanders or policy advisers. Popes, moreover, were usually old when elected, surrounded by the supporters of their ex-rivals, confronted by a plethora of Vatican staff members either self-interested or in foreign pay. To conduct a vigorous personal policy it was not unnatural that popes should promote men of less questionable loyalty. JRH

Neri, S. Filippo (1515–95) Founder of the Oratorians. Born in Florence, where he was a devotee of Savonarola's memory, he lived in Rome from 1533 until his death. As a priest, he founded an oratory or confraternity for young men, and out of this pastoral experience grew the idea for the Congregation of the Oratory, a community of priests approved by the Papacy in 1575 with its base in S. Maria in Vallicella. He was a man of aesthetic sensitivity. Palestrina, who was one of his followers, composed musical settings for the afternoon cycles of Scripture readings and song which he instituted – hence the term 'Oratorio'. OL

L. Ponnelle and L. Bordet *St Philip Neri and the Roman society of his times* tr. R. F. Kerr (1933)

Niccoli, Niccolò (1364–1437), one of the most important but most elusive members of the Florentine humanist circle, wrote practically nothing but exerted much influence. He appears first in dialogues by Bruni composed about 1401, maintaining the extreme classicist pose which he retained to the end. His passion for all aspects of ancient culture led him to form an outstanding library, the fruit both of searches which he encouraged for existing manuscripts, and of his own extensive work as a painstaking copyist with a keen interest in humanist script. After his death his books became the basis of the public library established by Cosimo de' Medici at S. Marco. He also had a keen interest in classical art, coins and other antiquities, which he collected. Though evidence is scanty, he was probably an important inspirer of classical taste in architecture and sculpture in the school of Brunelleschi and Donatello. GH

G. Zippel *Niccolò Niccoli* (1890)

Niccolò da Tolentino (*c.*1350–1435) On his death the condottiere Niccolò Mauruzi della Stacciola was given a state funeral in Florence cathedral in the presence of Pope Eugenius IV. To this honour was added the equestrian fresco monument by Andrea del Castagno in 1456. To earn this posthumous fame he had, after serving as a career soldier in southern Italy, been employed by Florence from 1426 in a particularly acute phase of their war with Filippo Maria Visconti. Among Niccolò's most notable actions was his contribution to the victory at MACLODIO in 1427. He became the republic's commander-in-chief in 1431. His defeat by Niccolò Piccinino in the year before his death made Florence's homage seem all the more generous. However, as in the case of HAWKWOOD, Florence was showing that it could offer posthumous fame as well as cash in return for loyalty. JRH

Nicholas V Pope 1446–55 (b.1397) Tommaso Parentucelli was educated at Bologna. The first ardent admirer of humanism among the popes, a friend of Cosimo de' Medici, Bruni and Bracciolini, he was persuaded that papal authority might be renewed through extensive patronage of learning and by the creation of a worldly magnificence in Rome and the papal court. Summoning Alberti, Fra Angelico and Gozzoli, he considered ambitious schemes for the town planning of Rome, restored its walls, added to Castel S. Angelo and reconstructed the Capitol. In a characteristic pursuit of modernity he began the destruction and planned the rebuilding of the time-hallowed basilica of St Peter.

As a patron of humanists, his particular interests were found in translation from Greek works, particularly Aristotle, the historians, and the Church Fathers. He gave liberal rewards to scholars, among whom were the exiled Greeks Bessarion, George of Trebizond and Theodore of Gaza, and the Italians Valla, Filelfo and Gianozzo Manetti. A compulsive book-collector, he can be seen as the true creator of the Vatican library. It was ironic that Nicholas should have faced the ineffectual conspiracy (January 1453) led by PORCARI which, seeking the freedom of Rome from the popes, was largely the fruit of humanist rhetoric on republican themes: ironic, too, that with the triumph of Greek at the papal court Constantinople should finally fall to the Ottomans. Nicholas, who had made no move to assist the Byzantines before the conquest, declared a crusade (September 1453) once it had taken place, but in the 18 months before his death came to realize that it evoked no response. JL

L. Pastor *History of the popes II* (1906)

Novara, battle of (6 June 1513) The town is 27 miles W of Milan. Here a French army, *en route* to oust Massimiliano Sforza from Milan, was defeated by the Swiss troops protecting him and forced to retire. JRH

Obrecht, Jacob (1450–1505) One of many Netherlands musicians of his generation to be employed in Italy. He was master of the choristers in Utrecht about 1475, where Erasmus may have been one of his pupils. He worked in several other cathedrals in the Low Countries before accepting an invitation to spend several months at the Este court at Ferrara in 1487. He went back there in 1504, to die in the outbreak of the plague from which JOSQUIN DES PREZ had fled. Although a master of the contrapuntal style of church music, he is now best known for his songs, written in a more obviously popular vein, even to the point of sometimes using folk melodies. DA

H. M. Brown *Music in the Renaissance* (1976)

Occasio (Latin for 'opportunity') An example of the classically-influenced enrichment of the medieval tendency to personify virtues and vices like Hope or Sloth. *Occasio* was, like FORTUNA (to whom she served as short-term antidote), portrayed as a woman. She was shown as unstable, often riding a wheel or globe, with a flying forelock but the rest of her head slippery with baldness – capable of being restrained and bent to one's will only if grabbed on her approach. Hence 'seize time by the forelock'. JRH

Ochino, Bernardino (1487–1563) Sienese preacher and Protestant theologian. He first joined the Franciscan Observants and then the Capuchins, whose first Minister General he became. The Franciscan ideal was a major element of his spirituality, his ultimate concern being total personal conversion to Christ's example. His career as a preacher in Italy was triumphant. In the 1530s he was connected with Juan de Valdes and developed Protestant sympathies, but he avoided a break with the Catholic Church until, in 1542, he fled to Geneva. He subsequently lived in Germany, England and Poland, dying among Italian Anabaptists in Moravia. OL

R. H. Bainton *Bernardino Ochino, esule e riformatore senese del Cinquecento (1487–1563)* (1940)

Opera A genre invented in the last decades of the 16c. but discussed and preceded by like forms for many years before. It came from the essentially Renaissance desire to recreate Greek tragedy, which was, it was held by some intellectuals, sung throughout, and its origins date back to Poliziano's *L'Orfeo* of *c.*1480, which certainly included songs, perhaps improvised in the manner of a frottola. The music survives for episodes in several later plays, notably Agostino de' Beccari's (*c.*1510–90) *Il sacrificio*, produced in Ferrara in 1554, for which Alfonso della Viola composed some simple choruses and alternating chants for priests in a scene of religious ritual. More significant than these are the lavish *intermedii* given between the acts of plays for wedding celebrations at Florence. These *intermedii* were tableaux vivants, each taking a theme such as *The harmony of the spheres* or *The victory of Apollo over the serpent* (both included in the Florentine *intermedii* for the wedding of Ferdinand I to Christina of Lorraine in 1589). These themes were illustrated with songs, choruses and sometimes dancing, using virtuoso singers and a vast ensemble of voices and instruments. They were not essentially dramatic, being rather static evocations of a mood, but they gave musicians practice in composing 'situation music' which was to be an essential ingredient of opera.

The possibility of writing continuous music for a real drama came with the discussions about the nature of Greek singing by a number of intellectuals interested in humanist ideas. These men, of whom the best known were Girolamo Mei (1519–94) and Giovanni Bardi, Count of Vernio (1534–1612), are usually referred to as the Camerata. The consensus from which practical experiments in revival arose was that drama should be performed in a kind of speech-song, in which natural rhythms should predominate, even at the expense of regular rhythmic patterns. Rather than the wide range of musical parts, the inflexions should represent the narrow pitch ranges of speech. Ornaments were allowed for the expression of emotional words but were not to be applied indiscriminately. To allow freedom of rhythm, the voice was to be only lightly accompanied by lutes or harpsichords.

The first operas to be given as the result of these discussions were performed in Florence, with texts by Ottavio Rinuccini (1563–1621) and music by the court musicians PERI and CACCINI. The former's *La Dafne* was given in Carnival in 1598 at the Palazzo Corsi. The music is lost except for small extracts, but from Rinuccini's verse and some descriptions it seems to have been close to the earliest surviving opera, Peri's *L'Euridice* (which also had certain pieces of music by Caccini), produced in 1600. Caccini's own setting of the text was performed 2 years later. All are settings of the Orpheus story turned into a pastoral, with the happy ending or *lieto fine* which became the *sine qua non* of opera for the next 2 centuries. The music intersperses the speech-song or recitative with short, attractive songs (Caccini especially

Print of Buontalenti's set for *The victory of Apollo over the serpent*: an example of an *intermedio*, one of the precursor genres of **opera**.

introducing elements of vocal display). There are also some simple choruses, but the small instrumental ensemble, consisting mainly of accompanying instruments, allowed no overture or lengthy instrumental interludes.

There is little evidence that these Florentine operas stimulated any widespread emulation, but the Duchess of Mantua was certainly at the marriage celebrations at which Peri's *L'Euridice* was given, and 2 notable operas produced a few years later at Mantua were to establish the genre. These were both by Monteverdi (1567–1643). *L'Orfeo* (1607) sets another reworking of the subject by Striggio. The published libretto shows that this was conceived as a true tragedy, although the vein is pastoral and in the event the *lieto fine* was adopted. The music was composed rather in the *intermedio* tradition, using a large ensemble which allowed for separate instrumental pieces, a toccata or overture, preludes and postludes to acts, ritornellos to precede and punctuate arias, and dances. The instruments are used with the greatest imagination to convey the moods of the dramatic situations, and the vocal music has a smaller proportion of recitatives and many more set pieces. The production was on a sumptuous scale, involving stage machines. This success was followed by *L'Arianna* (1608), the music of which is lost with the exception of the climactic 'Lament', the first operatic scena which rapidly became a popular hit. Thereafter the future of opera was assured. DA

For bibliography see MUSIC.

Orcagna, Andrea (active *c*.1343, d.1368) Andrea di Cione Arcagnolo, painter, sculptor and architect, was, with his brothers Jacopo and Nardo di Cione, the most important and influential artistic figure in mid-14c. Florence. His Strozzi Chapel altarpiece (1354–57, S. Maria Novella) is one landmark, the sculptured tabernacle which dominates the interior of Orsanmichele another. In both of them the tension between line and volume, spatial realism and decorative design, hieratic and representational concerns is of primary interest. He was capomaestro of Orsanmichele by 1356 and of the cathedral of Orvieto in 1358, and was active in many ways in competitions and commissions connected with the building of Florence cathedral. This combination of talents and wide-ranging expertise was an accepted phenomenon in Italian society from the late 13c. onwards, culminating, in the High Renaissance, with Michelangelo. JW

R. Offner *A critical and historical corpus of Florentine painting* Section IV, Vol. I (1962)

Orléans, house of The second house of Orléans was founded by Louis I, Count of Turenne, brother of Charles VI of France, who created him Duke of Orléans in 1392. He married Valentina, daughter of Giangaleazzo Visconti, receiving as dowry the County of Asti. It was a match which provoked certain tensions at court in that Charles VI's queen, Isabelle, was a grand-daughter of Bernabò Visconti, whom Valentina's father had dispossessed. Louis was murdered by John the Fearless, Duke of Burgundy, in 1407. His son Charles, captured at Agincourt and held prisoner in England 1415–40, was a graceful poet in French and English. On the death of Filippo Maria VISCONTI (1447) he had the best legal claim to the inheritance of Milan, and troops of Charles VII moved to Asti in an attempt to assert his rights. But rival pretenders and the creation of the AMBROSIAN REPUBLIC frustrated his ambitions. Louis XI, allied with the usurping duke, Francesco SFORZA, tried unsuccessfully to induce him to relinquish his claims and to sell Asti. At his death in 1465 Charles left his rights in the duchy of Milan to his son, who became LOUIS XII of France in 1498 and moved to claim his inheritance in Italy in 1499. JL

Second house of Orléans
(and claim of French royal house to Milan)

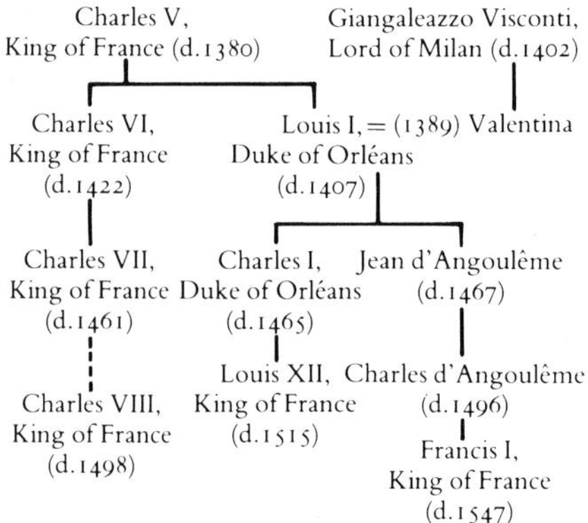

Orsini family Leading family of Roman barons which included Popes Celestine III, Nicholas III and Benedict XII, as well as numerous other churchmen, statesmen and soldiers. The Orsini first came to prominence in the 12c. Pro-papal, although only in so far as this suited their own interests, and pro-Venetian, the Orsini were inveterate opponents of the COLONNA. They held vast territories to the north of Rome, including the independent county of Pitigliano, which involved them in constant border disputes with Siena. Particularly favoured during the pontificates of Gregory XI, Sixtus IV and Innocent VIII, the Orsini were attacked at the time of Alexander VI by Cesare Borgia, who took their strongholds of Trevignano and Bracciano, but they recovered rapidly under Julius II and Leo X. The family provided many of the leading condottieri of the 15c. and 16c., and Lorenzo Orsini of Ceri (d.1536) defended Rome and Castel S. Angelo in 1527. JH

G. B. Colonna *Gli Orsini* (1955)

Otranto Apulian port whose name is identified with the shock produced by a Turkish naval expedition which captured it in August 1480 and held out against an infirmly conducted siege until September 1481. This brought home, as the fall of Constantinople in 1453 had not, the threat of the Turkish presence in the Mediterranean. JRH

Ottoman empire Among the migratory waves of Turkish (or Turcoman) peoples who from the 11c. moved from Central Asia into the Islamic zone of Asia Minor, only one, that of the Ottoman Turks, was to have a direct influence on Italy. The empire (as it came to be)

took its name from Osman (Uthmān), emir (*c.*1281–1326) in northern Anatolia and victor in 1301 over a Byzantine army sent across the Bosphorus to dislodge him from his siege of the Christian outpost of Nicaea. Within the Islamic world it was the Turks who most forcibly represented the notion of the *jihad* or holy war. The Christian word 'crusade' is not an equivalent: it signified recovery of lands lost. *Jihad* meant extension, conquest and thus, as a secondary and not necessarily immediately enforced consequence, the gaining of souls through conversion.

Osman's realm, though small, faced Christian territory. As a springboard for *jihad* it attracted – an attraction confirmed by the victory of 1301 – immigrants from adventurous non-Turkish Islamic peoples in whose vision of the faith the idea of *jihad* had a predominant appeal. The military strength of Osman and his successors was not therefore limited to members of his own race. And as they extended more deeply into Europe, strengthening their armies and administration with carefully re-educated Christian boys taken as living tribute, they fought, colonized and negotiated their way east and south as well, becoming the masters not only of south-east Europe but also of the ports in the Levant and Egypt on which European trade depended.

The rise of the Ottoman empire coincided with the period of the Renaissance in Italy. It was in 1352 that the Ottoman Turks first crossed the Dardanelles. Taking advantage of the weakness of Constantinople and the mutual jealousies of the satellite dynasties within the Byzantine Empire, by 1400 they had either occupied or reduced to vassal status Greece north of the Peloponnese, southern Albania, Bulgaria and Serbia: the Balkans, that is, between the Gulf of Corinth and the lower Danube. Checked from 1401 first by Tamerlane's invasion of Anatolia and then by civil wars, the Turks returned to consolidate their control of the Balkans only in the 1430s, extending it with the conquest of Constantinople by Mehmed the Conqueror (1451–81) in 1453. Later campaigns led to fresh conquests: the Peloponnese mainland (Morea) (1460); southern Albania (by 1479); Bosnia (1463). In 1478 the first direct contact with Italy was made with raids deep into Friuli.

In 1480 a new, naval phase of *jihad* began with an unsuccessful attempt against the headquarters of the Knights of St John in Rhodes and an occupation of the Italian port of Otranto and its hinterland, which lasted from August 1480 to September 1481. In 1499–1501 the Turks not only defeated a Venetian fleet off Zonchio (Navarino, or Pílos) but also took the Republic's Peloponnese ports of call Modon (Methóni) and Coron (Koróni). These events took place in the reign of Bayezid II (1481–1512). Under his successor, Selim (1512–20), Ottoman conquest resumed: this time in the Levant, Syria succumbing in 1516, Egypt in 1517. In that same year the keys of the Holy Cities, Mecca and Medina, were sent to Selim in acknowledgment that the faith of Islam and the authority of the descendants of Uthmān were now identified.

Jihad had gained a new meaning and Suleiman (1520–66) acted in its spirit. Despite the problems set by increasingly long lines of communication and by an empire constantly threatened on two fronts, Christian and Persian, he moved into what was then Hungary, capturing Belgrade in 1521 and, after his defeat by a Christian army at Mohacs (just over the present Hungarian frontier) in 1526, occupied Buda. In 1529 he set siege to Vienna, but in calling it off after 3 weeks acknowledged that Austria was beyond the feasible limit of Ottoman control from Constantinople. By then, however, he had broadened his control of the Mediterranean nearer home by taking Rhodes in 1522. From then the balance of Christian–Ottoman power fluctuated north of the Balkan Danube: the Ottoman grip being firm on Moldavia and Wallachia, weakly contested in Transylvania, frequently effectively challenged in Hungary. In the Mediterranean, failure to take Malta, the new headquarters of the Knights of St John, in 1565 was balanced by the conquest in 1571 of Cyprus from Venice. From later in that decade, however, the earlier extension of Turkish authority among the Barbary coast emirates from Tripoli to Algiers, which had supplemented Ottoman fleets and harassed Christian merchant shipping, was balanced by the incursion into the Mediterranean of pirate-traders from northern Europe.

CRUSADE had failed to stop the Ottoman from becoming an alien European power. As far as the Italians were concerned the two states most closely involved through their trade were Genoa and Venice, though in the 16c. Spanish Naples and Sicily, the maritime states of the Church, and Tuscany had to embark on expensive programmes of coastal fortification. Genoa lost every colony it had in the Black Sea, the Levant and the Aegean (except Chios) in the 14c. and 15c. – but found ample compensation in the 16c. by acting as bankers and commercial middlemen to Spain's *jihad*-like conquest of an empire overseas. Venice, after the war of 1499–1502, settled for coexistence when possible, went to war (1537–40, 1570–73) when not. These wars and the annual cost of garrisons and fortifications, taken together with the higher insurance rates charged on cargoes passing through waters increasingly infested with Turkish pirates, were certainly among the causes of the Republic's decreasing net income from its empire and the trade that had brought it into existence.

When to Venice's 15c. pacts with the Ottomans was added in 1536 France's anti-Spanish alliance with them, the Turks came to be accepted, if warily, as part of the European diplomatic family. Though Mehmed the Conqueror had invited Giovanni Bellini to Constantinople and briefly welcomed western scholars like Ciriaco d'Ancona, coexistence led to no influential cultural cross-fertilization, no bridging of the gulf dividing the two faiths. Moralists and political thinkers could invite their readers to learn from the military discipline and ardent public spirit evinced by the Turks, but the image of raping, impaling fanatics remained very close to the surface of the popular mind. JRH

H. Inalcik *The Ottoman empire, the classical age 1300–1600* (1973); P. Coles *The Ottoman impact on Europe* (1968); D. M. Vaughan *Europe and the Turk* (1954)

Ovid (43 BC–AD 17) Even more than Virgil, Ovid (Publius Ovidius Naso) survived undimmed at the start of the Renaissance period: indeed, the diffidence which had been felt towards him relaxed from the 10c., and the swell of his popularity carried him to an Ovidian Age (12c. to 13c.). This recognized two sides to Ovid, the most complete mythographer and the master of erotic teaching. This acceptance of Ovid required a vast effort of the imagination. While the moralists sharply condemned Ovid as immoral, others laboured to allegorize and Christianize the *Metamorphoses*: the surface, says the author of *Ovide moralisé* (1305), is *droite bogrerie*, but the hidden meaning – Myrrha as the Virgin Mary, or Iphigenia as Christ – is a different thing. In this picture Dante strikes another note: his overriding thesis, of the providential nature of Rome and its monarchy, leads him to accept Ovid as the equal of Virgil, and he takes the figures of his *Metamorphoses* as solid realities who can find entry into his other world. There is no moral condemnation for Ovid in Dante, and an avid use of his material all through the *Comedy*.

Apollo and Daphne, an episode from **Ovid**'s *Metamorphoses*, attributed to Antonio Pollaiuolo (detail) (London, National Gallery).

This was from a medieval basis, and does not imply a new humanist appreciation. Petrarch, significantly, returns to a stern condemnation of Ovid. He finds the *Ars amatoria*, especially, a mad work, and cause enough for Ovid's exile. Boccaccio swings both ways: an eager reader of Ovid, he pays tribute to him as a most noble poet in the *Filocolo*, where the spirit of Ovid's love poetry finds abundant expression; he vies with him in the *Fiammetta*, which is, as it were, a prose rival to the *Heroides*; and later he pillages Ovid in his encyclopaedic works, the *De claris mulieribus* (*On famous women*) and the *Genealogia deorum*. But in his latter and repentant state Boccaccio also reproaches Ovid with being an effeminate and lascivious poet.

For humanism Ovid does not represent a problem, nor is he an exclusive model for imitation. For instance, the *Cinthia* of the young Enea Silvio Piccolomini shows by its title that Propertius is as much an antecedent as Ovid. Doubtless Ovid remains as a universal ingredient, the main supplier still of mythological lore (witness those triumphant scenes of *Orlando furioso*, with Olimpia abandoned like Ariadne, or Angelica chained naked to the rock). It is these last that point towards the real triumph of Ovid in the Renaissance. From the *De pictura* of Alberti (1435) comes the sanction of antique subjects as a new ingredient of painting, and who can supply them better than the Ovid of the *Metamorphoses*? Titian is round the corner, with those splendid *poesie*, *Diana and Actaeon*, *Venus and Adonis*, *Diana and Callisto*. *See* MYTHOLOGY. JHW

Pacioli, Luca (*c.*1445–1517) Mathematician. His early life was passed in the service of a Venetian merchant, Antonio Rompiasi; in the 1470s he became a Franciscan friar and pursued theological studies. He was then a travelling teacher of mathematics until in 1497 he went to Milan at the invitation of Lodovico Sforza: there he worked with Leonardo da Vinci. In 1500 he went to Pisa and lectured on Euclid, of whose *Geometry* he produced a Latin edition in 1509. His *Summa de arithmetica, geometrica, proportioni et proportionalita* (Venice 1494) is, as its name implies, an encyclopaedia of number theory and (geometrical) proportion, but it is chiefly concerned with practical arithmetic (including book-keeping by double entry) and algebra. His *Divina proportione* (Venice 1509), on mathematical and artistic proportion, includes a discussion of regular and irregular solids; some illustrations are by Leonardo. MBH

Paciotto, Francesco (1521–91) of Urbino is notable as one of the last men whose interest in classical architecture (the monuments of Rome) and architectural theory (VITRUVIUS) led to a versatile career as a designer of fortifications and of palaces, villas and churches. He also exemplifies the influence of the Habsburg presence in Italy, for from the service of their clients the dukes of Parma he was called in 1558 to work in Flanders; after a term with the Duke of Savoy (1561–62) he went to Spain itself, where his designs for the Escorial have been thought to have brought to Spanish architecture a sobriety influenced by his work as a military engineer. JRH

G. Kubler 'Francesco Paciotto, architect' *Essays in memory of Karl Lehmann* (1964)

Padua The city's essential character was firmly developed by the time it was forced, in order to counter pressure from the DELLA SCALA lords of Verona, to offer itself in 1318 to Jacopo da Carrara, first as capitano and then as the first of a succession of CARRARA signori. It was a thriving and populous market town, whose wealth was displayed in the great pilgrimage church, containing the miracle-working bones of St Anthony; the Palazzo della Ragione, enclosing one of the vastest of medieval halls; the Scrovegni Chapel, decorated with Giotto's best-preserved frescoes; and the university, already attracting students not only from other parts of Italy (its only rival of comparable status being Bologna) but from beyond the Alps.

In 1405 Venice absorbed Padua in its successful bid for a mainland empire, and henceforward its history was that of a Venetian subject city. The Republic, however, left the machinery of municipal government more or less intact, and the patrician rectors, responsible to the capital for maintaining law and order, military security and the extraction of the portion of the tax and toll revenues due to Venice, were chosen with the special dignity attached to this particular possession in mind. Padua's revolt in 1509, which took advantage of Venice's apparent helplessness before the allies of CAMBRAI, was its last. After forcible reoccupations and wholesale banishment of and confiscation from the rebels, Venice resumed the light hand with which it had governed before.

Though, apart from Mantegna, no subsequent artist produced work of the stature of the visitor Donatello's *Gattamelata* and altar in S. Antonio, Padua's continuing growth and prosperity in the 16c. was not simply that of a provincial town. As well as its infantry garrison, it held the headquarters of the Republic's cavalry. Taking advantage of this and of the chivalrous tastes of many of the university's students, riding masters established schools of equitation which put Padua on the route of young aristocrats travelling to be 'finished'. There were a number of learned or literary societies and a flourishing musical life which produced, among more important things, the form of dance music known as the *padovano*. JRH

J. K. Hyde *Padua in the age of Dante* (1966); A. Pino-Branca 'Il comune di Padova sotto la Dominante nel secolo XV' *Atti del Reale Istituto Veneto* (1933–34; 1936–37; 1937–38)

Palaces (large urban dwellings: *palazzo* in Italian carries no regal connotations) Alberti described the palace as a city in little, and, like cities, Italian Renaissance palaces vary in type according to differences of climate, tradition and social structure. On to these regional stocks were grafted new architectural strains, reflecting theoretical reinterpretations of antiquity and individually influential examples.

The atrium and peristyle house described by VITRUVIUS and now known from Pompeii did not survive antiquity, and much of the interest of Renaissance designs lies in creative misunderstandings of Vitruvius's text. Medieval palace architecture probably inherited the *insula* type of ancient apartment house, related to the modest strip dwellings which never disappeared from Italian cities. In Florence a merchant palace developed from fortified beginnings, with vaulted shop openings on the ground floor, and the main apartments above, reached by internal stone staircases opening from an inner court. Renaissance developments regularized without changing the essential type, although large cloister-like courtyards were introduced, while shops came to be thought undignified. At MICHELOZZO's Medici Palace (1444f.) a square arcaded courtyard with axial entrance lies behind a façade of graduated rustication, with biforate windows, a classical cornice replacing the traditional wooden overhang. The apartments on the *piano nobile* formed interconnecting suites of rooms of diminishing size and increasing privacy. The classical orders which ALBERTI introduced to the façade of the Palazzo Rucellai (*c.*1453f.) were not taken up by the conservative Florentines, who continued to build variations on the Medici Palace (Palazzo Pitti; Palazzo Strozzi). In the 16c. rustication was reduced to quoins and voussoirs, and large windows appeared on the ground floor, 'kneeling' on elongated volutes.

Palaces: a pen and ink drawing of Bramante's 'House of Raphael' in Rome (London, RIBA).

At Urbino the Ducal Palace (1465f.) reflected Alberti's recommendations for the princely palace, and was in turn influential on late 15c. palaces in Rome (e.g. the Cancelleria). A harmonious Florentine courtyard and ample staircase replace the embattled spaces of medieval seigneurial castles, of which vestiges remain only in the towers flanking the balconies of the duke's private apartments, designed as a scholarly retreat. In the absence of a merchant class or a cultured nobility in 15c. Rome, the architectural pace was set by the papal court. Papal incentives to build, and large households, meant less compact plans for cardinals' palaces, often built next to their titular churches. Renaissance forms appear in the unfinished courtyard of the Palazzo Venezia (1460s), with its arcade system derived from the nearby Theatre of Marcellus, and in the delicately ordered stonework of the Cancelleria (1485f.) In the 16c. vestigial corner towers and shops disappear from cardinals' palaces, and Antonio da SANGALLO's Palazzo Farnese (1516f.) introduces symmetrical planning and Vitrivuan elements, like the colonnaded vestibule, behind a sober Florentine façade, enlivened by Michelangelo's cornice. A smaller palace type supplied the needs of an enlarged papal bureaucracy, more ambitious for display than for domestic accommodation. Bramante's 'House of Raphael' sets the façade style not only for this new type, but also for Renaissance houses all over Europe. Raphael and Peruzzi made ingenious use of difficult sites (Palazzo da Brescia; Palazzo Massimi), and their sophisticated façades flattered the architectural pretensions of patron and pope (e.g. Palazzo Branconio dell'Aquila).

Movement of patrons and architects, especially after the SACK OF ROME, meant a diffusion of Roman forms to central and northern Italy, where SANMICHELI's palaces in Verona, and PALLADIO's in Vicenza, adapted Roman types to suit local conditions. Palladio's 4-columned atrium is a Vitruvian solution to the traditionally wide Veneto entrance hall, and his plan for the Palazzo da Porto-Festa contains explicit references to Vitruvius's House of the Greeks. In Venice, defended by its lagoon and a stable political system, the hereditary aristocracy built palaces open to trade and festivity on the Grand Canal. The traditional Venetian palace has a tripartite structure: long central halls above entrance vestibules used for unloading merchandise are lit on the canal façade by clusters of glazed windows (rare elsewhere), and at the back from small courts with external staircases (as in the Ca' d'Oro). CODUSSI's palaces introduced biforate windows and a grid of classical orders into the system, while SANSOVINO's Palazzo Cornaro retains vestiges of the Venetian type (small courtyard; tripartite façade) despite its Bramantesque coupled orders and licentious window surrounds. Other cities, like Genoa, evolved influential types. Through engravings and the illustrated treatises, Italian Renaissance ideas of palace planning, originally evolved in response to specific conditions, came to be applied all over Europe. CE

R. Goldthwaite 'The Florentine palace as domestic architecture' *American Historical Review* (1972); C.L. Frommel *Die romische Palastbau der Hochrenaissance* (3 vols 1973)

Palestrina, Giovanni Pierluigi da (*c*.1525–94) The most important composer of church music in Italy in the later 16c. Born in Palestrina in the Sabine Hills, he was first a choirboy in the cathedral there before joining the choir of S. Maria Maggiore in Rome. He returned as organist to Palestrina cathedral in 1544, and on the election of his bishop as Pope Julius III he was appointed director of the Cappella Giulia. Thereafter he spent most of the rest of his life in Rome, in charge of music at S. Maria Maggiore for some 6 years after 1561, and of the Cappella Giulia from 1570 to the end of his life. In the intervening years he was in the employ of Cardinal Ippolito d'Este, spending his summers at Tivoli. He married twice, his second wife inheriting a leather and fur business, which Palestrina ran most efficiently and which made him unusually secure financially.

Palestrina's music is best seen as representing the ideals of the COUNTER-REFORMATION. He devoted most of his energies to the provision of liturgical music, setting the Ordinary of the Mass over 100 times. Although the story of his 'saving church music' after the bishops of the Council of TRENT wished to abolish all elaborate music is apocryphal, in principle it contains much truth. Palestrina shows how music could reflect the meaning of words while not essentially obscuring their audibility. He wrote, without the aid of the instruments so often used in Venice, sumptuous music which exploited to the full the sonorities of which the unaccompanied choir is capable; and the grand-scale masses of his later years show a strange mixture of purity (in harmony, where dissonance is now carefully controlled; and in melody, based on the smoothness of plainsong models) and sensuousness (in sound). His music became the model for many generations of Roman composers. DA

J. Roche *Palestrina* (1971)

A page of music in **Palestrina**'s own hand (Codex 59, Rome, St John Lateran).

Palladio, Andrea (1508–80) Vicentine architect of worldwide influence. Trained as a stonemason in Padua, by 1524 Andrea di Pietro della Gondola was working in Vicenza. His most important early contact was with Trissino, the humanist patrician and architectural amateur, who introduced the vocabulary of

The portico of **Palladio**'s Villa Foscari (La Malcontenta), near Fusina on the Brenta.

Serlio together with rational planning into his villa at Cricoli (*c.*1535f.). Also crucial for Palladio were Veneto building traditions, the workmanlike classicism of Sanmicheli, Falconetto's buildings for Alvise Cornaro, Serlio's treatises, and local antiquities in Verona. The first of many visits to Rome, in 1541, brought first-hand experience of High Renaissance architecture and the major ancient buildings. Although Palladio reinterpreted ancient architecture in his own image, his accurate reconstructions are still useful to archaeologists.

In 1546 the relatively inexperienced architect won the commission to reface the Vicentine town hall, since known as the Basilica, for which ideas by the much better-known Giulio Romano and Sanmicheli had been rejected. Palladio captured the aspirations of the Vicentine patriciate with his grand but flexible system of superimposed stone colonnades punctuated by arches, which concealed the irregularities of the medieval building. This success brought his adoption as architect to the tightly-knit, though feuding, Vicentine ruling class. Palladio gave architectural expression to the Vicentines' land-based prosperity in his villas, cheap and functional farm buildings as well as elegant romanizing structures. Palladio's villas are hierarchical organizations of rooms of different size and height around a central hall, raised up on basements and fronted by porticoes. Initially influenced by Giulio Romano and Sanmicheli as well as by the Roman baths, Palladio developed his mature villa types in the 1550s and 60s, with buildings like the Villa Badoer, the Villa Emo, and the Villa Barbaro at Maser. Here, for Venetian noblemen turning to agricultural investment and land reclamation, he linked the farm buildings by straight or curved service loggias to a central block with temple-front portico. A 2-storey type was used for suburban sites (Villa Cornaro, Piombino d'Este; Villa Pisani at Montagnana; Villa Foscari, La Malcontenta). Palladio's most famous villa, the Rotonda, is really a suburban palace. Its round-domed hall and four identical porticoes commanding panoramic views relate to reconstructions of ancient hill-top complexes in Verona and Palestrina.

Despite economic roots in the land, the Vicentines conducted their life of social display and intrigue from urban palaces. Here Palladio's designs combined High Renaissance types with ideas adapted from the Vitruvian house to suit local conditions (e.g. Palazzo da Porto-Festa). Later palaces employ the giant order (Palazzo Valmarana) or ornate stucco surfaces (Palazzo Barbaran), also found in his most unorthodox building, the Loggia del Capitaniato (1576f.). The Teatro Olimpico, built for the Vicentine academy, sums up the intellectual aspirations of the Vicentine patriciate, whose sculpted portraits as togaed Romans appear on the proscenium. Although a blind alley in the history of stage design, it is the most scholarly combination of Vitruvius's enigmatic text with the ancient theatre remains.

After Sansovino's death Palladio could command commissions in Venice itself. Though projects for rebuilding the Rialto Bridge and the Doges' Palace foundered, the two Venetian churches, S. Giorgio Maggiore (1566f.) and the Redentore, are among his finest works. Sequences of differentiated vaulted spaces seen through columnar screens evoke the Roman Baths, while preserving Counter-Reformation simplicity and type of plan. Their façades are the most successful Renaissance attempt to apply temple-front systems to churches with naves and side chapels. The interlocking pediments of the Redentore façade both reflect the structure of the church behind and brilliantly exploit the scenographic site, where Venice annually celebrates deliverance from the plague of 1576–77.

Palladio's *Quattro libri dell'architettura* (1570) synthesize Alberti and Vitruvius into a readily comprehensible architectural system. By illustrating domestic architecture with his own buildings, Palladio ensured the wide diffusion of his models, which resulted in the 18c. Palladian movements in England, Ireland and America. Large quantities of his drawings, including a series of antiquities intended for later publications, were brought back from Italy by Inigo Jones, and still survive. CE

J. S. Ackerman *Palladio* (1966); H. Burns *et al.* *Andrea Palladio* (1975)

Palma Giovane (1544–1628), a great-nephew of Palma Vecchio, was the leading Venetian painter after the death of Tintoretto (1594). After training with his father, who in turn had been a pupil of Palma Vecchio's assistant Bonifazio Veronese, Palma Giovane assimilated the work of Tintoretto and, in a debased though competent imitation of his manner with overtones of the work of Veronese and others, became an enormously prolific painter and draughtsman. He specialized in large-scale narrative and allegorical canvases, many of which he painted in succession to Tintoretto for the decoration of the Sala del Maggior Consiglio of the Ducal Palace. [67] AB

N. Ivanoff and P. Zampetti *I pittori bergamaschi, il Cinquecento* III (1979)

Palma Vecchio (*c.*1480–1528) The popular name of Jacopo Negreti, who was, after Titian, the leading painter in Venice between 1510 and his death. One of several painters, including Giovanni Cariani and Andrea Previtali, born in or near Bergamo who settled in Venice, Palma established a flourishing practice there which ultimately devolved upon his great-nephew, Palma Giovane. Palma's style was deeply indebted to Giorgione and the young Titian, though he specialized in more modest compositions (principally representations of the Holy Family in landscape settings, a 16c. variant of the traditional Venetian Madonna painting, which his pupil Bonifazio Veronese continued to develop) and in idealized representations of courtesans, lightly disguised as goddesses – the equivalent of modern 'pin-ups'. Palma was also an accomplished portrait painter (*Portrait of a Poet*, London, National Gallery) and the author of a scattering of altarpieces, of which the most famous is the S. Barbara altar (S. Maria Formosa, Venice). [105] AB

G. Mariacher *Palma il Vecchio* (1968)

Palmieri, Matteo (1406–75) A member of a reasonably prosperous Florentine mercantile family, Palmieri secured a sound humanist education and, while filling important positions in government, wrote historical works, a long religious poem, *La città di vita*, and above all the work for which he is remembered, the vernacular treatise *Della vita civile* (1531–38). Though it is couched in the form of a discussion between 4 men (including the author) who have, as in the *Decameron*, moved into the country to avoid the plague-stricken city, there is no doubt about Palmieri's partisanship as they debate the preparation for and pursuit of the active life of responsible and measured civic involvement, as against the life of refined scholarly contemplation. Heavily dependent on CICERO and QUINTILIAN, it is an early but notable example of the tradition of didactic works describing the intellectual and moral formation of the politically useful man that culminated in Castiglione's *The courtier*. While arguing that a republic provides the best setting for such a man, Palmieri urged a fairer distribution of offices and taxes than then obtained in Florence. *See* ACTIVE V. CONTEMPLATIVE LIFE. JRH

La vita civile ed. F. Battaglia (1944); A. Buck 'Matteo Palmieri als Repräsentant des florentiner Burgerhumanismus' *Archiv für Kulturgeschichte* (1965)

Panormita *See* BECCADELLI, ANTONIO

Papacy Papal rule had 3 aspects. As successors to St Peter, the disciple charged with the fulfilment of Christ's mission on earth, and as men uniquely privileged to interpret and develop Christian doctrine, the popes were both the leaders and the continuators of a faith. Then, thanks to their possession of the Papal State, the popes were the rulers of a large part of Italy. To maintain their authority, enforce law and order, extract taxes and check incursions from rival territories they had to act like other, secular rulers, becoming fully enmeshed in diplomacy and war. The third aspect was administrative. The popes were the heads of the largest bureaucracy in Europe, maintaining contact with local churches through the making or licensing of appointments, the management of clerical dues and taxation, the receipt of appeals in lawsuits conducted in terms of the Church's own canon law.

A number of matters, notably the making of appointments to especially wealthy sees and abbacies, or the incidence of taxation, could lead to conflict with secular authorities. This in turn led to the practice whereby monarchs retained the services of cardinals sympathetic to their national policies, so that they might have a voice at court, as it were, to influence popes in their favour. The choice of popes became increasingly affected by the known political sympathies of cardinals, and the pressure and temptations that could be applied to them. So onerous, various and inevitably politicized an office was not for a saint. The pious hermit Celestine V had in 1294 crumpled under its burden after only a few months.

The identification of the Papacy with ROME, which seems so inevitable, was long in doubt. The insecurity of the shabby and unpopulous medieval city, prey to the feuds of baronial families like the ORSINI, COLONNA and CAETANI, had already forced the popes from time to time to set up their headquarters elsewhere in Italy. For the greater part of the 14c. (1309–77) the Papacy functioned out of Italy altogether, at AVIGNON, building there (especially the huge Palace of the Popes) on a scale that suggested permanence. Though they were by no means in the pockets of their neighbours the kings of France, criticism of undue influence steadily mounted. Provence ceased to be a comfortingly secure region as the Hundred Years War between England and France proceeded. Finally the breakdown of central authority in the Papal State, despite the efforts there of such strenuous papal lieutenants as Cardinal ALBORNOZ (in 1353–67), prompted Gregory XI to return to Rome in 1377.

The period of authority and cultivated magnificence associated with the Renaissance Papacy was, however, to be long delayed. The return to Rome was challenged by a group of cardinals faithful to France. On Gregory's death in 1378 their election of a rival or anti-pope opened a period of divided authority, further complicated in 1409 by the election of yet a third pope. This situation deepened the politicization of the papal office (for support to the rivals was given purely on the basis of the dynastic conflicts in Europe) and confused the minds, if it did no serious damage to the faith, of individuals. But the remedy was another blow to the recovery of papal confidence and power. To resolve the problem of divided authority, protect the faith from the extension of heresy (especially in the case of the Bohemian followers of John Huss), and bring about an improvement in the standards of education and deportment among the Church's personnel, it was at last resolved to call together a General Council of the Church. It was argued that such a council, which met at Constance 1414–18, would, by being representative of the Christian faithful as a whole, possess an authority which, in the eyes of God, could supersede that of a pope. In this spirit Huss was tried and executed, a number of reforms relating to the clergy were passed and, above all (for this was the only measure with permanent consequences), two of the rival popes were deposed and the other forced to abdicate, Martin V being elected by a fairly united body of cardinals.

There remained, however, the challenge to his authority represented by the conciliar theory itself: that final authority could be vested as well in a group (if properly constituted) as in an individual. This view was expressed again by the Council of Basle, which lasted from 1431 until as late as 1449. Not until 1460 did a pope feel strong enough to make rejection of the theory an article of faith, as Pius II did in his bull 'Execrabilis'. By then, however, in spite of further absences from Rome, notably that of Eugenius IV (1431–40), who governed the Church chiefly from Florence, the acceptance of the city as the most practical – as well, from the point of view of its religious associations, the most appropriate – base for the Papacy had been made clear in the plans of Nicholas V for improving it. Thenceforward the creation of a capital commensurate with the authority of the institution it housed continued steadily. As at Avignon, fine buildings and a luxurious style of life were, as such, considered perfectly suitable for the role played by the head of the Church: a view exemplified in episcopal and archiepiscopal palaces all over Europe. However, the creation of a cultural capital, through lavish patronage of artists, scholars and men of letters, as well as a governmental one, not only contributed to an atmosphere of worldliness that aroused criticism, but may also have diverted the popes from registering the true import of the spiritual movements that were to cause the Reformation conflict of faiths. The fortunes of the Papacy from its return to Rome can be followed in the biographies of its outstanding representatives. *See* MARTIN V; EUGENIUS IV; NICHOLAS V; PIUS II; SIXTUS IV; ALEXANDER VI; JULIUS II; LEO X; CLEMENT VII; PAUL II; PAUL III; PIUS V; GREGORY XII; SIXTUS V; CLEMENT VIII; *also* COLLEGE OF CARDINALS; COUNCILS OF THE CHURCH; HERESY; SCHISM, THE GREAT; TRENT, COUNCIL OF. JRH

L. von Pastor *History of the popes* I–XXIV (1923–33); R. Aubenas and R. Ricard *L'Eglise et la Renaissance 1449–1517* (1950); P. Partner *The lands of St. Peter* (1972); G. Carocci *Lo stato della chiesa nella seconda metà del secolo xvi* (1961)

Paragone ('comparison') In an art historical context *paragone* refers to debates concerning the respective worthiness of painting and sculpture. The first protracted discussion was compiled from passages scattered through the notebooks of Leonardo da Vinci. It is one of the topics dealt with in Castiglione's *The courtier*, and in 1546 Benedetto Varchi even sent a questionnaire on the subject to sculptors (including Michelangelo and Cellini) and painters (including Pontormo and Vasari). Apart from demonstrating an aspect of the interest taken in the arts, it acted as a stimulus to the development of the language and concepts through which art could be appraised and understood, as did the parallel discussion of the respective merits of painting and poetry. JRH

I. A. Richter *Paragone: a comparison of the arts by Leonardo da Vinci* (1949); J. White 'Paragone: aspects of the relationship between sculpture and painting' in C. Singleton ed. *Art, science and history in the Renaissance* (1967)

Parma The history of Parma exemplifies all the features that make urban history in this period so confusing. With its situation on the northern fringe of the Papal State and with Germany not so far away, GUELF AND GHIBELLINE rivalry had a particularly clear political significance in Parma, which in times of crisis offered itself now to pope, now to Emperor. Plagued by internal dissensions prompted by the rival da Correggio and Rossi families, situated within the fields of power emanating from the VISCONTI of Milan and the DELLA SCALA of Verona, at few moments before 1346 was the city, or did it feel safe to be, an independent commune. From that date Parma became subject to the dukes of Milan, first the Visconti, then, after a last brief interval of independence (1447–49), the SFORZA, while it nonetheless retained considerable freedom to govern itself. With the WARS OF ITALY came another period of confusion. In 1500 Parma was occupied by the French. In 1512, after the French retreat after the battle of Ravenna, Parma was brought back into the Papal State – only to be handed over to France in 1515 by Leo X. In 1521, however, Leo retook the city and it remained a papal possession until, in 1545, Paul III linked it to Piacenza as an independent duchy for his bastard son Pierluigi Farnese, whose descendants ruled there until the 18c.

With a modest population (some 15,000 in *c.*1500), a primarily agricultural economy, and a troubled or dependent political status, the city developed only slowly after the building of its major monuments, the cathedral, baptistery, town hall and bishop's palace, in the 13c. S. Giovanni Evangelista was begun in the ominous year 1494, and the great church of S. Maria della Steccata in 1521. In the 1520s too the work of Correggio and Parmigianino (a native of Parma) established for the first time a style that could be recognized as a distinctively local one. But it was only with the creation of the duchy that a court began to act as the focus of cultural life and, even before the building of the beautiful Farnese Theatre from 1628, the centre of that life was above all musical. JRH

A. Quondam ed. *Le corti farnesiane di Parma e Piacenza, 1545–1622* (2 vols 1978)

Parmigianino, Francesco Mazzola, il (1503–40) Born in Parma (whence his familiar name), the son of a painter, Parmigianino's own career was initially shaped by the works he saw there by Correggio. He went on to work in Rome and Bologna. A draughtsman of great virtuosity and a colourist who put sensuous delight above the accurate record of appearance, by the time of his later works (*Madonna, Child and Saints*; *Madonna dal Collo Lungo*; both Florence, Uffizi) he had come also to subordinate human proportion and spatial logic to an overall effect of gleaming exquisiteness, charged with a chilly sexuality. In his portraiture, however, 'style' never swamped sympathy; his *Antea* (Naples, Capodimonte) is

Parmigianino's studies of nudes for the ceiling of S. Maria della Steccata in Parma (1531–39) (London, British Museum)

one of the 16c.'s tenderest portraits, as well as perhaps its loveliest. [216, 347] JRH

S.J. Freedberg *Parmigianino: his works in painting* (1950)

Paruta, Paolo (1540–98) was a Venetian patrician whose tenure of a long and increasingly weighty series of public offices could well, had he not died prematurely, have ended in his becoming doge. He wrote 2 officially commissioned political histories which, thanks to his access to documents, retain their value: a history of Venice, 1513–52, and an account of the War of Cyprus, 1570–73. More revealing of his own reactions to public events are 2 works he wrote on his own initiative. The first, *Della perfezione della vita politica*, published in 1579 but written previously, is a treatise in dialogue form set in 1563 at TRENT, during the closing session of the Council. The protagonists represent the two sorts of men present, clerics and politicians, and the arguments range widely over human nature and its fitness for development within those familiar polarities: celibate religious contemplation and active immersion in family and civic life. Paruta's voice is clearly given to the latter alternative, which he defends all the more firmly for the threat posed by the Counter-Reformation Church to the secularist and independent tone of life in his own city.

In the second work, the *Discorsi*, he took up the issues raised in Machiavelli's *Discourses on Livy* (though covertly, as it was on the Index) and cautiously pondered the lessons of history, the example of ancient Rome, the bases of political action, the nature of the ideal state and the functions of its subjects. As the products of a conservative and defiantly patriotic temperament which was yet subtle and self-doubting, these works have a fascination of their own. They are increasingly studied, however, for two additional reasons: the interest of seeing issues that had concerned Florentines from Bruni and Palmieri to Machiavelli and Guicciardini re-emerging in a different time and place; and the evidence they provide of the state of mind in which the Venetian patriciate approached the Republic's religious and political crisis of the early 17c. JRH

W.J. Bouwsma *Venice and the defence of republican liberty* (1968)

Pastoral play (*favola* or *tragicommedia pastorale*) Dramatic form invented and achieving a great vogue in the Cinquecento, praised by its adherents as the ideal mixture of tragedy and comedy, superior to either. After Marc' Antonio Epicuro's *Mirzia* (1535), Giraldi's *Egle* (1545), Agostino Beccari's *Il sacrificio* (1554) and other Arcadian plays had prepared the way, Tasso's *Aminta* (1573) attracted many imitations, the most famous of which, Battista Guarini's *Il pastor fido* (1589), set off a critical polemic about tragicomedy. Usually in 5 acts of unrhymed and rhymed verse of 11 and 7 syllables, with unity of time and place, pastoral plays concern the loves of Arcadian shepherds and nymphs, sometimes intended to refer to well-known courtiers and intellectuals, and often governed by neo-Platonic or disguised Christian allegory. Song contests, praises of landscape, musing on the Golden Age and comparisons of the court with the country are standard topics. The typical denouement demonstrates the power of love, one feature that made the genre fashionable as a wedding entertainment. LGC

E. Bigi 'Il dramma pastorale del '500' in Accademia Nazionale dei Lincei' *Il teatro classico italiano nel '500* (1971); L.G. Clubb 'The making of the pastoral play' in J. Molinaro ed. *Petrarch to Pirandello* (1973)

Patrizi, Francesco (1529–97) Philosopher, born in Cherso (Istria). He served several Venetian nobles as secretary and administrator and was professor of Platonic philosophy at the universities of Ferrara and Rome. His main philosophical debt was to the Platonizing schools of late antiquity, and he was remarkable among systematic philosophers of the Renaissance for his hostility to Aristotle, this being manifest even in his theory of poetry. His major work is *Nova de universis philosophia* (*A new philosophy of the world*; 1591), which posits the cosmos as an emanation of God permeated by a world soul; its universal principle is light (by contrast with the Aristotelian principle of movement). Also of special interest are his *Della historia* (1560) and *Della retorica* (1562). OL

P. O. Kristeller *Eight philosophers of the Italian Renaissance* (1974)

Patronage Axiomatic as the notion that Renaissance culture flourished in an atmosphere of patronage is, it remains a vague one. Not only does the functioning of cultural patronage (its social and political equivalent is described under CLIENTAGE) remain inadequately charted, but its nature is still obscured by a misleading glamour. How far contemporary values distinguished between the selective employment of a gifted secretary or accountant and an effective author or musician sufficiently to justify our using the term 'employment' in one case and 'patronage' in the other is uncertain. There were 3 forms of cultural 'patronage'. One was paying for a specific object because convention called for it (a painting for an altar, a set of Latin verses to welcome an illustrious guest, a grander house); this was a simple, if discriminating, shopping operation. The second was the deliberate support of an individual's career because he represented a potential accomplishment that might otherwise be stultified. The third was the support of some form of cultural expression because of a belief in its value for its own sake.

Though there came to be a certain amount of *ad hoc* art dealing and the occasional pushing of an artist's work by his friends, painters and sculptors (and necessarily architects) from the 14c. to the 16c. waited for commissions before putting expensive materials to use. 'On spec' production was limited to the most routine grade of workshop objects, mainly religious. But the demand for their works was such that artists of repute, though welcoming security, normally did not need it in the form of exclusive, retained employment. Nor did any art purchaser have so many altars, niches or building sites that he needed the total output of an artist, or to tie him by a contract that forbad him to accept commissions from others. So, though an artist might find it profitable or challenging to work for some period for one employer, or an employer might wish to monopolize for a while an exceptional talent or retain a first call on the products of a congenial group of artists, there was on the whole an interplay of mutual advantage that made patronage of the second type episodic and in no true sense an explanation of an artist's development.

The 'court' artist on a long-term contract was in any case usually an artist-of-all-work, turning his gift for design from a portrait or altarpiece to a parade costume or the layout of a garden. Such creative interplay as there was between Pope Julius II and Michelangelo, which may have actually enhanced the quality of an artist's work, was a rare phenomenon. There was, indeed, a sense in which employers were the suitors to, rather than the employers of, outstanding artists, and this casts another doubt on the significance of 'patron'; as Michelangelo liked to work for popes, so Titian liked to work for monarchs, but does this make Julius II or Paul III or Charles V or the Duke of Urbino patrons rather than favoured customers? In the 16c. artists themselves further clouded the issue by seeking paid sinecures (Sebastiano del Piombo's post in the papal chancery, Cellini's in the Roman mint), but that phenomenon is nearer to clientage than to patronage.

From the time of Giotto those commissioning works of art had been selective. From the late 15c. the social and intellectual status of the artist began to rise, a process aided by competition for the work of the best among them. Increasingly it became a source of pride to possess works by men of wide repute, and expenditure on art came to be seen as one of the pleasing duties of the powerful. But art patronage by 1600 was little touched by the notion of Art; art pleased, recorded, diverted, impressed, commemorated, taught (especially in the religious context), but its essence was as yet hardly detached from its immediate purposes. Though there is evidence of pride in the possession of good contemporary paintings from the late 15c., collecting, and the opening of collections as a source of inspiration, was – as in Lorenzo de' Medici's garden or Sixtus IV's Vatican – largely restricted to antiquities; the notion of art for Art's sake originated in a regard for the works of men beyond the reach of patronage.

In the case of musicians and composers, patronage has also to be seen in terms of a period when supply and demand were in an equipoise that needed no idealistic or quixotic form of patronage. Though the idea of Music was (because of its place in the academic arts syllabus and its recognized power to move men's feelings) more readily separated from the mass of its executants than was the idea of Art, employers, whether town councils, cathedral chapters or individuals, did not see themselves as doing more than competing for the man best able to yield the most fashionably desirable results.

And literature? Here, payments were made mostly with an eye on the past – the scholar's ability to resurrect, dust off or translate the revered texts of antiquity, or on the future – the perpetuation of names through an inscription, a history, a biography or, more rarely, an imaginative work (Poliziano's *Stanze*, Ariosto's *Orlando furioso*) whose allusions identified it with the sponsor's family. The retained writer, like the court artist, was expected to be a maid-of-all-work: in his case tutor, pageant-librettist, chronicler, sometimes diplomat. Self-expression was a spare-time activity; from Dante and Petrarch to Tasso and Bruno, patronage was extended to 'letters' rather than to Literature. The financial side of printing remains obscure, but the attention-calling device of the dedicatory letter reinforces the impression that creative self-expression was not yet considered worthy, for its own sake, of consistent support. JRH

'The early Medici as patrons of art' in E. H. Gombrich *Norm and form* (1966); R. Weiss *The Renaissance discovery of classical antiquity* (1969); N. Bridgman *La vie musicale au Quattrocento* (1964)

Paul II Pope 1464–71 (b.1417) A wealthy Venetian, Pietro Barbo owed his education and early advancement to his uncle, Eugenius IV. He was a cardinal at 23. Much of his income from a growing collection of benefices was used to build up another collection, of ancient coins (the finest holding then in existence), small bronzes, cameos and engraved gems, in all of which he took the interest of a scholarly antiquarian. Much of this collection passed after his death into that of Lorenzo the Magnificent.

As pope he tried as hard as Pius II had done to gain support with which to check the Turks' advance into the Balkans, but achieved no success in spite of their occupation of Albania and, in 1470, their conquest of the Venetian Aegean island of Negroponte (Euboea). He won more backing for campaigns against the heretical King of Bohemia, George Podebrady, but this was because the succession to the Bohemian throne was a nearer (and in the eyes of the European powers a purely secular) issue. He scored a diplomatic triumph by persuading Louis XI of France to abrogate the 1438 Pragmatic Sanction of Bourges, which had seriously curtailed papal authority (appointments, taxation) in France. He made strenuous attempts to reimpose direct control over some of the more renegade parts of the Papal State (Anguillara, Rimini) but died with the honours undecided. Indeed all these issues – crusade, heresy, Catholic obedience – were of such long duration that what happened between 1464 and 1471 has the interest merely of episodes. It is tempting, therefore, to concentrate on 2 local issues, one because it was novel and of great symbolic interest, another because of its contributions not only to the nature but also to the image of Roman life.

The former was the first overt clash between Christianity and the humanistic cult of the pagan past. Paul opened his reign by dismissing many of the humanists who had been appointed to positions in the chancery by his predecessors. Though this was done in the interest of restoring control over the selection of staff to the papal vice-chancellor, it prompted a defiantly vigorous complaint amounting to the first claim by humanists that their brains and eloquence defined them as a separate and essential caste – albeit within this local context. Their continuing resentment led to Paul's prosecution of the deliberately provocative academy they then formed (especially identified with Leto and Platina) and to his pronouncement in 1468 that the study of classical authors of deistic, Epicurean or immoral tendencies should be barred: this, at least, appears to have been the drift of an inadequately documented policy.

The second issue concerned Paul's fostering of ROME as a permanent and worthy home of the PAPACY. He increased the ornateness of papal ceremonies and processions, encouraged the proliferation of carnival festivities, stimulated the pilgrim traffic by offering more lavish indulgences, restored ancient monuments and medieval churches and stimulated new buildings, notably through the example of his own vast palace, now the Palazzo Venezia. JRH

L. Pastor *The history of the popes* IV (1894); R. Weiss *Un umanista veneziano: Papa Paolo II* (1958)

Paul III Pope 1534–49 (b.1468), one of the most successful of popes and a man of real creative genius, was born Alessandro FARNESE and enjoyed all the benefits of a fine humanistic education in the ambience of Lorenzo the Magnificent and at the university of Pisa. To gratify his mother he embarked on an ecclesiastical career in which promotion came almost too readily. He was appointed apostolic protonotary (1491) and cardinal (1493) by Alexander VI, and because of that pope's supposed liaison with his sister was immediately dubbed 'the petticoat cardinal'. He received the first of 16 bishoprics in 1499. Clement VII had a great regard for Farnese, who shared his political views as well as his humanist tastes, and effectively selected him as his successor.

Paul's pontificate was among the happiest in the history of ROME. As cardinal he had already begun the construction of the Farnese Palace in the city. As pope he was responsible for continuing or initiating most of the major urbanizing programmes of the 16c., in particular the levelling and widening of the streets and the opening up of new public squares. In the Papal State he reasserted papal authority, seriously eroded after the SACK OF ROME, and employed Sangallo the Younger on a series of major refortification projects, including the building of the Rocca Paolina at Perugia.

Although no puritan and the father of at least 4 bastards, from the beginning of his career Paul was concerned about the condition of the Church and always sympathized with the reforming party within it. As bishop of Parma he had introduced a much stricter system of administration, which was widely imitated. Within weeks of his election as pope he was ordering his cardinals to adopt a more modest lifestyle and the new cardinals he appointed were all known for their enthusiasm for reform. In 1537 several of them sat on Paul's commission on church reform – the *Consilium de emendanda ecclesia* – whose report, highly critical of the Church, was accepted immediately by the Pope and published in 1538. Paul actively encouraged the Barnabite and Theatine orders, suggested the foundation of the Somaschi, and protected the Roman Oratory. He was an enthusiastic promoter of foreign missions. His greatest contribution to church reform, however, was the summoning of a General Council, which, entirely owing to the Pope's zeal, finally met at TRENT for the first time in 1545.

Paul III triumphant over Protestants and Turks in Salviati's fresco cycle in the Farnese Palace, Rome.

In international affairs Paul's ideas were dominated by the need to bring peace to Europe in order to promote church reform and halt the Ottoman advance. It was partly thanks to his efforts that Spain and France agreed to a suspension of hostilities by the Truce of Nice (1538). He was less successful in his dealings with the Papal State, partly because the resentment caused by his centralizing policies provoked the revolt of Perugia and a rebellion by Ascanio Colonna, known as the SALT WAR (1540–41), and partly because of his inability to resist the demands of NEPOTISM. Although there is no evidence that Paul normally subordinated the interests of the Church to those of the Farnese family, his favourite child, Pierluigi, was created Duke of Parma and Piacenza, and his grandson Ottavio was invested with Camerino; Castro was given to Ottavio's brother, Orazio.

Totally attuned to the cultural climate of his age, Paul always retained a love of arts and letters. As pope he surrounded himself with scholars and writers, and few have been more assiduous in their care for the Vatican library. He was a great friend to the university of Rome and an enthusiastic promoter of the printing industry. He was equally generous in his

patronage of artists, and as pope was responsible for giving Michelangelo the commission for a design for the new St Peter's. JH
E. N. Rocca *I Farnese* (1969)

Pavia, battle of (24 February 1525) Francis I invaded Italy late in 1524 and his army settled down to besiege Pavia as a preliminary to an assault on Milan. An Imperialist army (representing Charles V) came to the city's relief in February and Francis, concerned by the effects of the winter on the morale of his troops, accepted battle and was himself captured in a defeat that has been compared to Agincourt in terms of losses among the French nobility. JRH
J. Giono *The battle of Pavia* (1965)

Pazzi family On Holy Saturday a dove whizzes from the altar of the cathedral in Florence, down the nave and into the ox-drawn *carro*, laden with fireworks, waiting outside. Legend has it that the resulting explosions commemorate the sparks created by stones brought back from the Holy Sepulchre by a Pazzi knight who had accompanied the First Crusade. Certainly family hauteur contributed to the animosity felt by this always noble and, since *c.*1400, prosperous banking family towards the Medici. Fortified by the tacit support of the most important client of their bank, Pope Sixtus IV, who was also anxious to see the fall of Medicean ascendancy, Francesco and Girolamo in 1478 organized a plot to assassinate Lorenzo the Magnificent and his brother Giuliano in front of that same altar after Mass. Though Giuliano was stabbed to death, Lorenzo escaped; the Florentines paid no heed to the urging of the conspirators towards revolt and the Pazzi were virtually submerged by a wave of executions and sentences of exile. Though individual members of the family acquired some prominence again in the 16c., 1478 ended their prominence as a clan. JRH
H. Acton *The Pazzi conspiracy* (1979); A. Poliziano *The Pazzi conspiracy* (1478/79), tr. in B. C. Kohl and R. C. Witt ed. *The earthly paradise* (1978)

The attack on Lorenzo and Giuliano de Medici during the **Pazzi** conspiracy, commemorated on a coin by Bertoldo di Giovanni (Washington, National Gallery).

Pegolotti, Francesco Balducci Florentine merchant associated with the BARDI company, which he served in Antwerp, London and Cyprus 1310–47, who compiled the merchant handbook known as *La pratica della mercatura* (*c.*1340). Details are given of weights and measures, currencies and merchandise, for trading centres ranging from London to Tabriz and from Seville to Tana, on the Black Sea, whence he outlined the route to Cathay 'most secure by night and day according to the merchants who have used it.' JKH
La pratica della mercatura ed. A. Evans (1936)

Peri, Jacopo (1561–1633) Composer of the first real OPERA. Born of a well-to-do Florentine family, he studied music seriously with the organist of Florence cathedral, and himself became organist and singer to various churches and confraternities. In the 1580s he became a court singer to the Medici, composing some music for the *intermedii* for *La pellegrina* in 1589. He wrote *La Dafne*, the first dramatic entertainment to have continuous music (now lost except for small extracts), given in the Palazzo Corsi in 1598, with more success than the more famous *L'Euridice* (1600), possibly because of his colleague Caccini's insistence on contributing songs to the latter. He was in indifferent health for much of his later life but wrote a good deal of theatre music, none of which survives; an attractive book of songs, *Le varie musiche* (1609); and Easter music for S. Nicola at Pisa. One of his 10 children, Dino, was a gifted pupil of Galileo Galilei. DA
H. M. Brown 'An introduction to Jacopo Peri's *Euridice*' in E. Cochrane ed. *The late Italian Renaissance* (1970)

Perino del Vaga (1501–47) played a major role in the formation of a *maniera* decorative style in Rome. In his illusionistic prophets in the Pucci Chapel (Trinità dei Monti, Rome; *c.*1525–26) Perino reconciled two major elements of High Renaissance classicism – Michelangelo's expressive power and Raphael's *grazia*. A concern for Raphaelesque space and substance is tempered by the introduction of Parmigianino's stylized figure canon and rhythmic surface pattern in paintings for Andrea Doria's Palazzo dei Principi (Genoa, *c.*1527–33). Designs for the Pauline apartments (Rome, Castel S. Angelo; begun 1545) reveal renewed allegiance to figural plasticity based upon Michelangelesque models, but a plasticity that is now effectively subjugated to the demands of ornamental design. LP

B. Davidson *Perino del Vaga e la sua cerchia* (1966); R. Harprath *Papst Paul III als Alexander der Grosse* (1978)

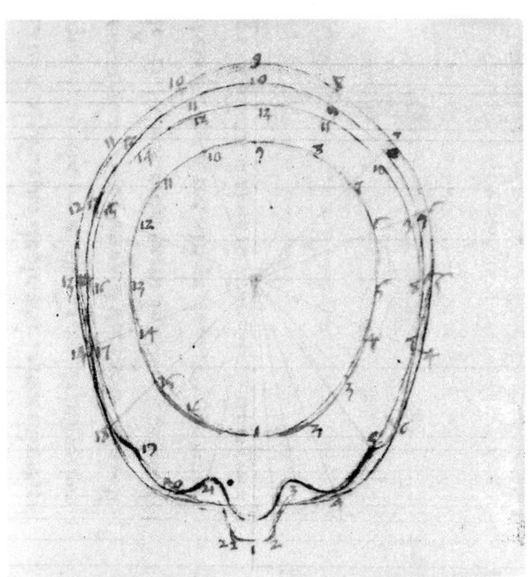

Perspective study from Piero della Francesca's *De prospectiva pingendi.*

Perspective is, as far as art is concerned, any organized method of representing the 3-dimensional world on a 2-dimensional surface. It is likely that the first system using a vanishing point to which all orthogonals, or lines at right-angles to the pictorial surface, recede was developed in antiquity. The modern history of perspective begins, however, in the late 13c. and 14c. in Italy with the growth of a new interest in naturalism, which caused artists such as Giotto to look closely at the actual appearance of solid objects and to search for empirical means of representing them convincingly. This led, for a time, to a tendency to show objects in oblique settings corresponding to what can be seen if one looks directly at a cubic object of which more than one side is visible. A compositionally easier method to control was, however, the foreshortened frontal system in which one side remains undistorted, parallel to the picture plane, as, for instance, in the work of Duccio, and of course in the developed, theoretically based Artificial Perspective system developed by Brunelleschi in the early 15c. and first described in abbreviated form by Alberti.

By the mid-14c., however, artists had already observed that in a properly foreshortened squared pavement or coffered ceiling the diagonals of squares all recede to single points, known as distance points, which lie on the same horizon line as the vanishing point. This led to the workshop system largely used in northern Europe during the 15c. and also certainly popular in Italy alongside the Albertian Artificial Perspective system. The distance point construction adds the essential feature of the proportional diminution of the transversals of the squared pavement and, of course, in the size of any objects placed on it.

In the fully developed theoretical system, first laid out in its full rigour by Piero della Francesca, the position of the vanishing point is determined by the position of the spectator's eye, and the degree of foreshortening and the rapidity of the proportional diminution of objects is conditioned by the spectator's assumed distance from the picture plane. If all the conditions for correct viewing are fulfilled, and these include looking with one eye only and not moving the head, the foreshortening of the picture plane itself takes care of all lateral and vertical foreshortening and the objects shown on it are represented with a scientific accuracy which makes them correspond exactly to what would appear if real objects and a window pane were substituted for the painted suface. It is this system which leads on to the illusionism of artists such as Mantegna and Correggio, and beyond them to the ceiling painters of the Baroque.

Pure illusionism was, however, relatively seldom the aim of Renaissance artists and they were perfectly well aware that the theoretical viewing conditions would virtually never be met. People move about and, in any case, in nearly all frescoes and altarpieces the vanishing point would be placed far above the spectator's head. Similarly the advantages of being able to carry out the whole construction on the final surface meant that the distance points were often placed at the edges of the painting, giving a viewing angle of 90 degrees and an impossibly short viewing distance amounting to only one half of the width of the painting.

From the start, therefore, artists such as Uccello and Leonardo were evidently looking for alternative systems which would take account of the onlooker's freedom of movement and of the normal ways of looking at things, as well as of the desirability of breaking down the parallelism between the rectangle of the frame and the undistorted rectangular surfaces of the buildings and so forth which were represented. This parallelism effectively defeats the perception of the lateral and vertical foreshortenings seen in the natural world and essential to the Artificial Perspective system.

For these and many other reasons, therefore, the Artificial Perspective of the Renaissance was arguably more important in artistic terms as a method of controlling the spectator's attention and as an organizational and compositional device than as a means of creating actual illusions. It related the real and pictorial worlds in a new way. It gave the observer a central position analogous in a way to the central position of man in the neo-Platonic universe. It united the proportionality of the pictorial world to that of music and architecture, and of man himself, indeed to that of the divine mathematics of the universe on which all beauty depended and from which all natural objects were to a greater or lesser degree a departure. In the short period of its domination of the artistic scene it generated untold excitement and, in conjunction with the observation of light and of atmospheric perspective, provided the essential framework for the supreme achievement of Renaissance art. JW

L. B. Alberti *Della pittura* ed. L. Mallé (1950); Piero della Francesca *De prospectiva pingendi* ed. G. Nicco-Fasola (1942); W. Abbot *The theory and practice of perspective* (1950); J. White *The birth and rebirth of pictorial space* (1967)

Perugia On an eminence close to the Via Flaminia and dominating routes to Tuscany and the Marche, Perugia was integrated into the Papal State at the beginning of the 13c. and was ruled, internally (1303–1540), by its College of the Ten Priors of Guilds. In the 14c. it was beset by FACTION conflict, frequently at war with neighbouring communes, often in revolt against the Papacy. It passed under the lordship of Giangaleazzo Visconti (1400–02), of King Ladislas of Naples (1408–14), and of the condottiere Fortebraccio (1416–24), and was then ruled by the Ten Priors, dominated by a few oligarchical houses, working in general harmony with papal legates. Most powerful of the local families was the Baglioni, who, however, never attained *signoria* over the commune. The city's limited autonomy was abolished by Pope Paul III following a revolt against the imposition of a new salt tax in 1540. There was a population of perhaps 45,000 in the city and contado at the beginning of the 15c., perhaps 20,000 in the city and 46,000 in the contado in 1551.

Perugia was the seat of an important university (founded 1308) in which two great 14c. jurists, Bartolus of Sassoferrato and Baldo Ubaldi, held chairs. Up to the mid-15c. its numerous artists were largely influenced by the Sienese school; thereafter, of the painters whose names are most closely associated with the city, Perugino, Pinturicchio and the young Raphael, the last two are better considered as offshoots of Florentine rather than Umbrian traditions. In architecture gracious gothic forms (in the Palazzo dei Priori, the Fontana Grande of the Pisani, the Loggia di Braccio) prevailed until in the mid-15c. Agostino di Duccio introduced Renaissance styles (façade of S. Bernardino, Porta S. Pietro, Palace of the Capitano del Popolo, Palace of the Old University). *See* SALT WAR. JL

C. F. Black 'The Baglioni as tyrants of Perugia, 1488–1504' *English Historical Review* (1970)

Perugino, Pietro Vanucci (active *c.*1472, d.1523), the Umbrian painter, is one of the harbingers of the High Renaissance. Static, non-dramatic, gently classical in pose and clothed in soft, relatively heavy material falling in simple folds, his figures mark the changeover from mid-century linearity. His pictorial architecture is likewise characterized by uncluttered, grave simplicity and the eschewing of unnecessary details. Unlike the great Florentines, who spread their figures throughout the pictorial space, Perugino almost invariably sets them in a foreground screen, behind which ranges deep, often empty, architectural or

Part of **Perugino**'s fresco of the *Donation of the Keys* in the Sistine Chapel, Rome.

landscape space, as in his most famous work, the fresco of the *Donation of the Keys* (Rome, Sistine Chapel).

His innumerable altarpieces exemplify the extension of the medieval workshop into the Renaissance. Drawings from the life, usually of studio assistants, were used to fix poses, which were then combined and recombined, this head on that body, pose repeated, pose reversed, with this attribute or that, in seemingly endless simple permutations to satisfy the demand for his sweetly pious altarpieces of the Virgin and Saints. The story of Raphael's early years before he went to Florence is largely concerned with the absorption and supersession of the rigidities of Perugino's workshop methods and compositional principles. JW

E. Camesasca *Tutta la pittura del Perugino* (1959)

Peruzzi, Baldassare (1481–1536) Sienese painter and architect of great originality, whose lack of worldly success was attributed by Vasari to his 'timidity and excessive modesty'. From *c.*1503 Peruzzi worked in Rome, until forced by the SACK OF ROME in 1527 to base himself in his native Siena: his last years were spent once more in Rome. As a painter he mastered Raphael's new monumentality without losing his own Sienese Quattrocento grace (e.g. Ponzetti Chapel, S. Maria della Pace, 1516). His distinctive pictorial contribution was in painted architecture (*Presentation of the Virgin*, S. Maria della Pace, *c.*1520), perspective (*Sala delle Prospettive*, Farnesina, 1516) and stage design. His perspectival stage sets incorporating a variety of ancient and modern buildings were the basis for Serlio's publication of the Vitruvian Tragic and Comic Scenes.

Probably trained in architecture under Francesco di Giorgio, Peruzzi developed a fastidious and discriminating approach to the 'beautiful manners in ancient buildings' (Cellini), rejecting Vitruvian dogmatism. His first building after the move to Rome was the Farnesina (1505f.), a U-shaped suburban villa with a double loggia between projecting wings, reminiscent of the Villa Le Volte in Siena, also for the Chigi family. The severity of the Farnesina's external system of superimposed Doric pilasters would have been relieved by the now lost grisaille decoration, a medium in which Peruzzi excelled. As co-architect of St Peter's under Sangallo the Younger, Peruzzi produced many brilliant experimental designs, showing the same tendency as at S. Petronio, Bologna (1521–23) and S. Domenico, Siena (1532) to pursue inventive alternatives, explored in virtuoso draughtmanship, rather than concentrating on a single solution.

His masterpiece, the Palazzo Massimo alle Colonne (1532f.), makes most ingenious use of an irregular site, with its curving façade and off-

The curved façade of the Palazzo Massimo alle Colonne in Rome, designed by **Peruzzi**.

centre courtyard where no two elevations are alike, instead of imposing awkward symmetries *à la* Sangallo. The highly original façade, with its complex rhythm of open and closed orders on the ground floor and bizarre window surrounds above the *piano nobile*, should not be seen as a rejection of antiquity, but as characteristic of Peruzzi's search for a more beautiful ancient 'manner'. Via Serlio's books, which used his unpublished theoretical writings, Peruzzi's ideas and individual solutions, such as the oval ground plan, entered the international language of Renaissance architecture. CE

C. L. Frommel *Die Farnesina* (1961); — *Baldassare Peruzzi als Maler und Zeichner* (1967–68)

Pescara, Ferdinando Francesco d'Avalos, Marquis of (1489/90–1525), the husband of Vittoria Colonna and a poet, is also remembered for his military career in the service of Charles V. He led the light cavalry at Ravenna (1512), captured Milan (1521) and Genoa (1522), and was chiefly responsible for the Imperial victory at Pavia (1525). Among the most hispanicized of Italians, his many services to Charles V went largely unrewarded; none the less, when offered the throne of Naples if he would join Girolamo Morone's anti-Imperial conspiracy, he chose to reveal the plot to Charles, arrested MORONE, and occupied Milan (1525). *See* WARS OF ITALY. JH

Pescara *See* VASTO, ALFONSO D'AVALOS DEL

Petrarch (1304–74) Francesco Petrarca (originally Petracchi) was born at Arezzo, the son of a Florentine notary banished by the 'Black' Guelfs (*See* GUELFS AND GHIBELLINES). After a few years at Incisa in the Valdarno, the family moved in 1311 to Provence, following in the wake of the Avignonese Papacy. In spite of extensive travels in Italy and France, Petrarch's base until 1353 was Provence and above all the villa which he acquired at Vaucluse. After a grounding in grammar and rhetoric from the Tuscan Convenevole da Prato, Petrarch was made to study law at Montpellier and Bologna, but abandoned it for a freer life in AVIGNON. Here in the church of St Clare, on 6 April 1327, he saw the woman he calls Laura, about whom we know little more than that he loved and celebrated her in his Italian poetry and in some of his Latin writings. But Petrarch also inserted himself into the nascent humanism of the papal court, and already in his twenties was committed to the study and emendation of ancient texts, particularly Livy, though he also studied the poets and to some extent the Church Fathers.

In 1330, probably for financial reasons, he took minor orders, and began to receive benefices, as well as protection and friendship, from the COLONNA family: but, though committed to celibacy and the tonsure, he performed merely nominal duties, and his position did not prevent the birth of a son, Giovanni, in 1337, and a daughter, Francesca, in 1343. During the 1330s and 1340s Petrarch wrote Italian poetry, but also became a pivotal figure for humanist culture. He made available neglected texts, particularly CICERO's *Pro Archia*, found at Liège in 1333, and Cicero's letters, which he found at Verona in 1345, and which led him to make collections of his own letters (*Familiares* and, towards the end of his life, *Seniles*). And he embarked on a number of innovatory works – a series of biographies, initially of famous Romans (*De viris illustribus*), an epic, the *Africa*, based on the life of Scipio Africanus, and a major historical work, *Rerum memorandarum libri* (*Of memorable things*). None of these was completed, in spite of further work on the first two: but the *Africa* and Petrarch's reputation were sufficient to win him the Poet Laureate's crown, which, after an examination in Naples by Robert of Anjou, he delightedly received on the Capitoline on 8 April 1341, the first modern poet to do so.

The coronation was the extreme point of Petrarch's 'Roman' orientation, though he went on to give his support to COLA DI RIENZO's attempt to restore the ancient constitution of Rome. Difficulties with the Colonna and Cola's failure in 1347 led him to withdraw from active political involvement and to accept the power and patronage of the princes of the day, somewhat to the dismay a little later of friends in republican Florence (who included, from 1350 onwards, Boccaccio). But the 1340s also saw him writing poems in Italian in which an already noticeable existential uncertainty becomes more insistent, and in addition works in Latin which attempted to reconcile humanistic study with Christian practice (*De vita solitaria*, 1346); or else to reject the former for an ascetic form of the latter (*Secretum*, 1342–43). The crisis was accentuated by the death of Laura in the plague of 1348, but continued unresolved except in aesthetic or literary terms. However the fluctuations in Petrarch's thought enabled him to create in his writings a complex, slightly fictional self-portrait, which is also a document of the equally complex shifts in the culture of his time.

From 1353 onwards Petrarch lived in Italy, first in Milan under the patronage of the Visconti, and then in Padua, Venice and Pavia: he spent the last 6 years of his life at Arquà in the Euganean hills, where Francesco da Carrara had given him some land. It was there that he died and was buried. In these years Petrarch continued work on writings begun earlier, wrote the influential dialogues of *De remediis utriusque fortuna* (*Remedies against both kinds of fortune*), and completed a number of invectives defending himself and the studies he favoured against criticism, the most important of which, *Invective contra medicum* (*Invectives against a doctor*), had been begun in Provence in 1352. Though he never finished his allegorical *Triumphs*, the great body of his Italian poetry, the *Rerum vulgarium fragmenta* (*Fragments of vernacular poetry*), better known as the *Canzoniere*, was given what appears to be its final form not long before his death.

This poetry (and beyond one trivial letter no Italian prose by Petrarch survives) had enormous influence on European literature: though he did not invent the 'Petrarchan' sonnet or introduce other striking novelties, he created a synthesis of preceding vernacular traditions that was new in its subtlety, musicality, cohesion and classicism. This is a poetry which has held its fascination. It seems to have a unique formal perfection, to explore the hidden riches of a select but not *recherché* language, and yet, for all its clarity, intelligence and at times playfulness, to be enticing and elusive. Given the example of Dante, his emphasis on Latin culture (in spite of efforts to the contrary he had no Greek) may seem regressive; yet it was the scope and depth of Petrarch's practice as a Latin scholar and writer that provided the essential material and the primary example for the flowering of humanism in the next century. For those strands in his thought which have led to his being dubbed 'the first modern man' *see* HUMANISM; HISTORY AND CHRONICLE; RENAISSANCE; ITALIAN LANGUAGE. [321] PH

E. H. Wilkins *Life of Petrarch* (1961); U. Bosco *Francesco Petrarca* (1961); A. Enzo Quaglio *Francesco Petrarca* (1967)

Petrucci family In 1487 Pandolfo Petrucci, then 36, seized the government of Siena at the head of the Noveschi faction. He assassinated his wife's father and encouraged the Magione conspiracy against Cesare Borgia: he was admired by Machiavelli. He abdicated in favour of his son Borghese, and died in 1512. Borghese and his brother Fabio were expelled in 1516 and replaced, through the influence of Leo X, by Rafaello Petrucci (d.1522). Fabio's brief return to power, 1522–24, ended the family's prominence. JL

U. Mondolfo *Pandolfo Petrucci* (1899)

Petrucci, Ottaviano (1466–1539) The first commercial music printer. Educated at the humanistic court of Urbino, he settled in Venice about 1490 and in 1498 obtained the privilege to print music, including keyboard and lute tablatures. He founded a publishing house with 2 partners and in 1501 produced his earliest collection of songs, the *Harmonice musices odhecaton*, using a 3-stage method, printing first the lines, then the notes, and finally the verbal text and any other non-musical material. During the next few years he produced a large number of volumes, containing FROTTOLAS and much church music, all of them extremely elegant: indeed, they included some of the finest of all examples of music printing. The War of the League of Cambrai caused him to leave Venice around 1510, and he returned to his native town of Fossombrone, where he continued to print music, though in less elegant, more commercial books. He returned to Venice in 1536 at the request of the Senate, but printed Latin and Italian authors, music now being produced in a 2-stage process by Antonio Gardane. [219] DA

Philip II King of Spain 1556–98 (b.1527) In 1554 the weary Emperor Charles V made his son Philip ruler of Naples and Sicily, in 1555 of the Netherlands, in 1556 of Milan and of Spain itself. In 1558 Charles died and Philip became fully responsible for Spain's possessions in Europe and in Mexico, Peru and the Caribbean. Even without the Habsburg lands in Germany, which had passed to Charles's brother Ferdinand in 1556 and which (together with the Holy Roman Emperorship) remained in his branch of the family, Philip's domains were enormous: 'God has turned into a Spaniard,' ran the Italian saying. Philip, who chose to run his empire from his study in the Escorial (getting through

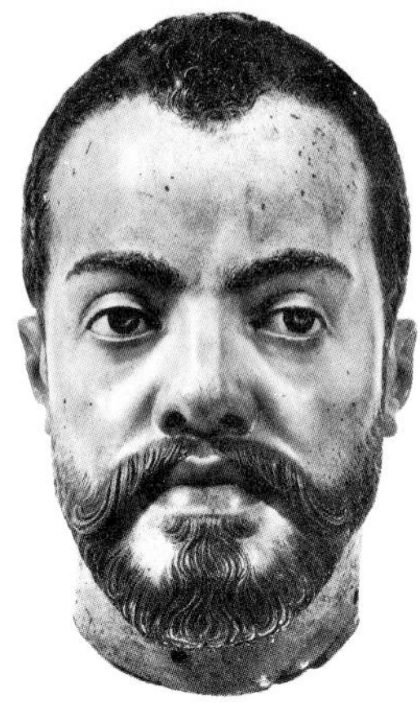

Enamelled silver head of **Philip II** by Leone Leoni (Vienna, Kunsthistorisches Museum).

as many as 400 documents in a day), never visited Italy. He was content that his provinces there should be run by viceroys who communicated with him through his special council for Italian affairs. His power could be felt, however, not only through Naples and Milan, but also through his close supporter Genoa, and as the 'most Catholic King' he exerted a force on the Papacy and, through the Council of TRENT, whose session of 1562–63 he had been primarily responsible for calling, on the tone of religious life in Italy.

Preoccupied with the Turks' threat to Sicily and to Spain itself from their satellite bases in North Africa – whence aid could so easily be sent to his disaffected Morisco subjects in Granada; forced to cope with rebellion and finally war in the Netherlands; fearful of any aid from England that might give backbone to his chief potential rival, France – Philip was not inclined to alter the Spanish position in Italy as it had been left at the Peace of CATEAU-CAMBRESIS. He needed Naples. He taxed it heavily: 'you cannot imagine a method of extracting money from subjects which has not been used in this kingdom,' as a Venetian ambassador remarked; and, besides, Spain had always needed wheat from southern Italy. He needed Milan, the crossroads of his military support systems, whence Spanish troops, disembarked at Genoa, could move north up the 'Spanish Road' he controlled, via Savoy, Franche-Comté, Alsace, Lorraine and Luxemburg to the Netherlands – or move east, north of the Veneto, to assist his fellow-Habsburgs in their endless struggle to keep Hungary from the Ottoman Turks.

In practice it was only Venice which felt the Madrid-Milan-Vienna axis as a constant threat to its independence, and the Republic was well aware that Philip's participation in the Holy League which led to the victory of Lepanto made him no more than a reluctant and a temporary ally. But Philip none the less took the precaution, through his agents in the peninsula, of immobilizing Italian princes (like the dukes of Urbino) whose subjects could be used in wars to the disadvantage of Spain, by pensions, stand-by contracts or honours. This was part of the caution and the unremitting attention to detail that would, had he not been the 16c.'s greatest monarch (for his territories, in the New World as well, became even greater than had been those of Charles V), have made him its greatest civil servant. JRH

Geoffrey Parker *Philip II* (1978); J. C. Davis *The pursuit of power: Venetian ambassadors' reports ... in the age of Philip II* (1970); H. Koenigsberger *The government of Sicily under Philip II of Spain* (1951)

Piccinino, Niccolò (1386–1444) Born the son of a butcher at Callisciana, near Perugia, to avoid the life of a tradesman he joined a local man-at-arms as his page and before long was qualified to serve as a cavalryman himself. In 1416 he joined the band of Braccio da Montone, taking over the command of his men on his death in 1424 after the battle of Aquila. With this nucleus to sell he was employed first by Florence and then from 1426 by Filippo Maria Visconti, who relied on him in his series of wars against Venice and Florence. His frequent success in the field, however, was echoed in the growth of his own territorial ambitions and in the intensification of his personal vendetta with Venice's commander, Francesco Sforza. Fearing that Piccinino was putting his own interests before Milan's, Filippo Maria tried to woo Sforza from Venice with the offer of marriage to his bastard daughter Bianca Maria. While Piccinino was still feeling alarm at this move (even though Francesco did not follow up the marriage by changing sides), his standing was worsened further by a defeat at Sforza's hands in 1443 at Monteloro. Whether or not these setbacks worsened the effects of the dropsy he suffered from, he only survived them by a year, passing on both his feud with the Sforza and his dropsy to his condottiere son Francesco, who commanded the forces of the Ambrosian Republic of Milan but died of the disease in 1449. JRH

E. Ricotti *Storia delle compagnie di ventura* II (1844)

Piccolomini *See* PIUS II

Pico della Mirandola, Gianfrancesco (1469–1533) Philosopher. He spent much of his life defending his claim to the principality of Mirandola against his brothers. The two great influences on his thought were his uncle, the philosopher Giovanni Pico della Mirandola, whose biography he wrote and whose works he edited, and Savonarola, of whom he was a leading defender. His major work was *Examen vanitatis doctrinae gentium* (*The emptiness of pagan philosophy*; 1520). This was an attack on Aristotle in the first instance, but also more generally on the claims of any philosophical school to have arrived at truth. Gianfrancesco attacked the philosophers on their own ground, deploying philosophical tools to demolish their claims; here he made particular use of the sceptical arguments of Sextus Empiricus, being one of the first of a line of Christian fideists to do so. *See* SCEPTICISM. OL

C. B. Schmitt *Gianfrancesco Pico della Mirandola (1469–1533) and his critique of Aristotle* (1967)

Pico della Mirandola, Giovanni (1463–94) was born into a family of Lombard noblemen. He was destined for a career in canon law but was diverted early into philosophy, which he studied at Ferrara, Padua, Florence and Paris. From an early point his approach was distinguished by an interest not only in the Greeks but also in the Arabic tradition of AVERROES and others, and in medieval Jewish philosophy. He broke into the public scene in 1486 with the publication in Rome of his 900 *Conclusiones*. Some of them were condemned by a papal commission. Pico composed an *Apology* in their defence, dedicated to Lorenzo de' Medici, which led to orders for his arrest. Escaping to France, he was imprisoned but released after diplomatic intervention by Lorenzo and others. Back in Florence he dedicated the *Heptaplus*, a sevenfold interpretation of Genesis, to Lorenzo in 1488. He then remained in the Florentine Platonic circle, dedicating *De ente et uno* (*On being and the One*) to Poliziano in 1492 and leaving an incomplete *Disputationes adversus astrologiam* (*Disputationes against astrology*). He was associated with Savonarola but died in 1494 before the latter's hey-day.

Though friendly with the Florentine Platonists, Pico was not a pupil of Ficino and differed from them markedly in interests and inclinations. His acceptance of aspects of Averroes's thought was one difference, another his keen interest in and use of Jewish CABBALISM. Pico was not concerned only with PLATO, neo-Platonism and HERMETICISM; he was interested in a still wider synthesis of non-Christian ideas. The difference is brought out by Pico's best-known work, the *Oratio de dignitate hominis* (*Oration on the dignity of man*), where he denies the neo-Platonic proposition that man is an intermediary between the earthly and divine worlds. He is outside this hierarchy and possesses an unlimited capacity for spiritual self-development. The value of philosophical truth is its capacity for cleansing the human soul and assisting its perfection.

In his *Conclusiones* Pico extends the notion that all philosophies contain valuable truth, to make it embrace the Arabs and the Jews. He is thus the most spectacular early exponent of religious and philosophical syncretism. He maintained that the conceptions of being and unity in Aristotle and Plato were, contrary to the neo-Platonist view, essentially the same. He extended the idea of a primitive fund of divine wisdom, from the Hermetic writings to Jewish cabbalism, which he thought enshrined an authentic tradition of learning essential for the interpretation of the Bible. He promoted the allegorical interpretation of the Greek myths but he was opposed to conventional ASTROLOGY, attacking it vigorously as an enemy of religion in his last book. GH

E. Garin *Giovanni Pico della Mirandola* (1937)

Pienza Between 1459 and 1464, the year of his death, Pope Pius II rebuilt his village birthplace, Corsignano, and, having equipped it with a cathedral, a bishop's palace, a town hall and a palace for himself, renamed it Pienza as his own architectural monument. Built to designs planned and supervised by Bernardo Rossellino in close consultation with Pius himself, this tiny city is the earliest example of symmetrical Renaissance town planning. Only a few houses had been built, enough to suggest the relationship of the street grid to the central piazza, when Pius died. Its remote site has kept Pienza singularly unspoiled. JRH

E. Carli *Pienza, la città di Pio II* (1967)

The Dream of Constantine from **Piero della Francesca**'s fresco cycle in S. Francesco, Arezzo.

Piero della Francesca (active 1439–78, d.1492), born and subsequently active in the small Umbrian town of Borgo S. Sepolcro, is first recorded working in Florence with Domenico Veneziano on the lost frescoes of S. Egidio. His great follower Seurat notwithstanding, and despite the existence of artists such as Poussin and Vermeer, Piero's work represents the supreme example of the application of pure mathematics to the portrayal of the human form and personality in its relationship to its architectural and landscape surroundings. The timelessness and stillness of his figures, their extreme simplification, the geometrical purity evident in their contours and their volumes, the overt relationships established between their columnar, monumental forms and those of the architecture which surrounds them, are not a matter simply of an imposed stylization. They are the end-product of a quintessentially Renaissance attitude.

Piero, himself a profound theorist, wrote two treatises directly relevant to the history of art, the *De prospectiva pingendi* and the *De quinque corporibus regularibus* (*On the five regular bodies*). In the former he showed how, by means of strictly plotted coordinates, exactly the same rules of mathematical foreshortening could be applied to a human head as to a cube or a Corinthian capital. Extreme simplification is therefore a necessary, and not an accidental, aspect of his art. For Piero, as for Plato and for contemporary neo-Platonists, all natural beauty is founded on the unsullied perfection of pure form, devoid of incidental imperfection. For him, as for Vitruvius, man is the measure of all things, and the mathematical proportions of his architecture derive from the mathematical relationships of his own harmonious body.

None of this would matter much in the history of art, as opposed to the history of ideas, if it were not brought to life by intense powers of natural observation, by consummate skill, by a sense of light and colour derived from Domenico Veneziano, by a Donatellesque feeling for sculptural form, and by a sensitivity to void and solid, interval and accent, which is Piero's own. For Piero the perspectivist, as for Seurat and Mondrian after him, the eye and not the ruler provided the actual artistic measure. Nevertheless, the omnipresent pricked contours in his frescoes seem to show that it was probably he who, in his search for perfection in the transfer from design to final execution, made the transition from the partial to the full-scale, overall cartoon.

In so doing he opened the way for Leonardo, Raphael and Michelangelo and forged the final weapon in the armoury of the Renaissance artist. From the early *Madonna della Misericordia* altarpiece in Borgo S. Sepolcro (commissioned 1445), to the *Flagellation* (Urbino, Palazzo Ducale), the frescoes of the *History of the True Cross* in S. Francesco, Arezzo, the portrait of his great friend and patron Federigo da Montefeltro and his wife Battista Sforza (Florence, Uffizi), and the late *Madonna and Saints* (Milan, Brera), with its increasing recognition of Flemish media and techniques, his working life is punctuated by a flow of acknowledged masterpieces. For a man who studied relationships of colour with the same intensity as he studied those of space and plane, uniting figures, architecture and landscape in a single complex web of repetitions and progressions, the failing eyesight of his last years must have tried him sorely. [243] JW

K. Clark *Piero della Francesca* (1969)

Piero di Cosimo (1462–1521) According to Vasari, Piero was the son of a Florentine goldsmith and was apprenticed to Cosimo Rosselli, with whom he went to Rome to work in the Sistine Chapel. The only 2 known dates for his career are both in 1504, when he served on the committee for the placing of Michelangelo's *David* and matriculated in the painters' guild. His early works show the influence of the main Florentine painters of his youth: Filippino Lippi, Leonardo and Ghirlandaio. But his interpretations and, more particularly, his subject matter (*Discovery of Honey*) are all his own. Vasari claims that he was strange from an early age and grew progressively odder as time passed, ending up by existing on hard-boiled eggs which he prepared when he made glue. Certainly his iconography is highly idiosyncratic and his interpretation of mythological subjects and allegories is unorthodox. LDE

R. L. Douglas *Piero di Cosimo* (1946)

Pigafetta, Antonio (before 1491–?1526) was from an aristocratic family of Vicenza and had possibly seen galley service with the Knights of St John before he set off in 1519 with Magellan, as a volunteer, on his voyage round the world: little else is known of him before this date. Early in 1519 he was at Barcelona, in the train of a Vicentine who was papal representative to the Spanish court. Hearing of the preparations for the voyage, he went to Seville, and must have appealed to Magellan as a cultivated companion who could be useful with a sword. The strong mutual regard between the two emerges clearly from Pigafetta's narrative. He was wounded at Magellan's side when he was killed by natives in the Philippines, and was one of the few survivors of that first, 3-year circumnavigation of the globe. His account, completed early in 1525, is the fullest source for our knowledge of the voyage, and its wealth of detail about places, products and people makes it an important contribution to our knowledge of South America and of the Pacific islands encountered in its course. JRH

Magellan's voyage round the world ed. J. A. Robertson (3 vols 1906)

Pinturicchio, Bernardo, il (1454–1513) Born Bernardino di Betto in Perugia, he came to Rome with Perugino for the decoration of the Sistine Chapel. He was a great favourite with the Curia: his most extensive papal commission was the famous Borgia apartments of Alexander VI (now the Museum of Modern Religious Art in the Vatican). His splendid use of colour and gold (which gained him his nickname) and his continuing use of a 15c. style in disregard of the innovations being made in art around 1500 earned him a hostile biography from Vasari, who even claimed that Raphael did the cartoons for Pinturicchio's last great commission, the decoration of the Piccolomini Library in Siena. Since the contract was signed in 1502 and work continued sporadically until 1508, this is impossible, though it is more than likely that Raphael did serve in his workshop briefly during this period. Pinturicchio made one last trip to Rome in 1507 to decorate the choir of S. Maria del Popolo for Julius II, and then returned to Siena, where he worked until his death. [23, 254] LDE

E. Carli *Il Pintoricchio* (1960)

Piracy In the sense of freelance robbery at sea, piracy was an endemic hazard. However, it took other forms. Under letters of marque, granted to merchants who had been robbed of goods either at sea or in a foreign port, goods of an equivalent value could be seized in reprisal; a system that in practice amounted to piracy-by-licence. 'Interloping', the irruption of foreign trading vessels into waters considered legally or by tradition 'personal' to a particular power, was treated as piracy by them and the heavy armament of the interloping vessels demonstrated their acceptance of this description, in effect if not in theory. Again, difference of faith or creed could be pleaded as legitimate cover for theft by sea and pillage by land. And, finally, whole populations could become dependent on the profits of piracy, promoting the notion of a pirates' nest into a deliberate and justifiable economic policy.

All these factors contributed to the making of patterns of violence between periods of formally declared war. In the Mediterranean, all combined with particular virulence in the 16c. The expansion of Ottoman seapower led to unofficially sponsored seafights and land raids (hence the string of coastal forts down the Tuscan and south peninsular coasts), and to the development of what were virtually corsair states in North Africa based on Algiers, Biserta and Tripoli. At Senj, on the north-east Adriatic coast, the entire economy and way of life of the USCOKS was dedicated to piracy. From the mid-

1570s Dutch and English vessels interloped in the Levant trade with guns blazing. Even galleys of the two 'crusading' orders, the Knights of Malta and the order of S. Stefano, were capable of preying on Christian shipping. Venice, vulnerable because of the proximity of Senj and of Ottoman bases in Albania and the Morea, its dependence on trade with the Levant, and its self-inflicted abstention from reprisal in the cause of neutrality, suffered particularly heavily. Piracy in the late Renaissance moves from the annals of crime into the mainstream of economic and political history. JRH

G. Fisher *Barbary legend: war, trade and piracy in North Africa, 1415–1830* (1957); A. Tenenti *Piracy and the decline of Venice 1580–1615* (1967)

Pisa Though Pisa's leading role as a sea power had been removed by the Genoese destruction of its fleet at the battle of Meloria in 1284, the city – together with its separate harbour area at the mouth of the Arno, Porto Pisano – remained the busiest port in Tuscany. Even when the harbour silted up, necessitating the development of LIVORNO from the mid-16c., much of the new port business was run, via agents, from the statelier, pleasanter and less malarial Pisa; in addition, goods unloaded at Livorno were brought to Pisa by canal for warehousing and redistribution. Thus the city retained a modest commercial vitality, supplemented, as in the previous centuries, by a vigorous tanning industry and the production of soap and hats. Pisa was a populous medieval city (some 40,000 inhabitants *c.*1300), whose politics were as factious as in other 14c. communes where GUELF AND GHIBELLINE, magnate and merchant feuds led to alternate phases of self-rule and surrender to the authority of an outsider. It was, none the less, only after a bitterly contested campaign that the city fell to Florence in 1406. Only in 1421 did Porto Pisano follow, purchased from Genoa, which, brought in as an ally by Pisa, had refused to yield it after the conquest.

With the acquisition at last of a major port, Florence's Tuscan hegemony was assured. Florentines went to live there and bought land in Pisan territory. Tax concessions and rent-free housing were designed to attract foreigners. Medicean interest in the city culminated in Lorenzo's revival of the *studio* (or university) in 1472. This was achieved by stripping the *studio* of Florence itself of several of its faculties, and was supported by a temporary ban on Florentines studying elsewhere. In 1495 the Pisans took advantage of Charles VIII's leaving a garrison in the city as a guarantee of Florence's goodwill on his return from Naples, and revolted: only in 1509, after a long and costly war, was the city retaken.

The war, sideshow as it was in the context of peninsular affairs, is memorable on a number of scores. It confirmed Machiavelli's distrust of mercenary troops. It committed Florence to the French alliance (as a second source of troops) which contributed heavily to the downfall of the republican régime of 1494–1512, and it demonstrated the lengths to which Florence was prepared to go, for reasons of prestige and landholding as well as of commerce, to regain the most prized of all its subject cities. It therefore plays a lengthy part in Guicciardini's *History of Italy*. 'There was' (according to Macaulay in his essay on Lord Burleigh) 'a criminal in Italy who was suffered to make his choice between Guicciardini and the galleys. He chose the history. But the war of Pisa was too much for him. He changed his mind and went to the oar.'

Though the evidence is unclear, the population of Pisa, which had not recovered quickly after the Black Death of 1348 and had been further thinned by exile and war up to 1406, and emigration to escape Florentine control thereafter, suffered another loss through emigration in the 16c. Though the Florentine grand dukes restored the university, set afoot drainage and water-supply schemes and made Pisa the base of the new crusading order of S. Stefano, Pisa remained a provincial centre in which there was a reasonably high standard of living but no reserve of talent or enterprise to revive the commercial or cultural activism of the 14c. The great flourishing of Pisan architecture was over by the 14c., with the completion of the cathedral-baptistery-Leaning Tower complex (though the last was not yet completed), and the beginning in 1278 of the Camposanto. However, the church of S. Maria della Spina (1320s and 30s) beautifully exemplifies the last flickers of a distinctively 'Pisan' style. Sculpture, too, after the death of the last great member of the Pisano family, Giovanni, in *c.*1314, declined in quality. Pisa was never a centre of painting. More and more, Pisa came to resemble a provincial Florence. The most creative talent of the 16c. was provided by a native: Galileo, who taught at

Pisa from 1592 to 1610 and established his European reputation there. JRH

D. Herlihy *Pisa in the early Renaissance* (1958); M. E. Mallett 'Pisa and Florence in the fifteenth century' in N. Rubinstein ed. *Florentine studies* (1968)

Pisanello, Antonio Pisano, il (active *c.*1415–*c.*1455/56) was probably the most famous Italian artist of his day. His achievements are recorded in the work of some dozen leading poets and literary figures, including Biondo and Guarino da Verona. He was the virtual originator of the Renaissance MEDAL and the supreme exponent of this form in the mid-15c. In its own way, his work has never been surpassed. Giovanni Francesco Gonzaga and Filippo Maria Visconti (1441), Francesco Sforza, Lionello d'Este (1442), Sigismondo Pandolfo Malatesta (1445), Vittorino da Feltre, Alfonso I (1449, Naples), Lodovico and Cecilia Gonzaga and John VIII Palaeologus are some of the great names for whom he created medallic masterpieces.

As a leading exponent of the International Gothic style, influenced by Stefano da Zevio and Gentile da Fabriano, whose frescoes in the Doges' Palace, Venice, he continued (1415–22), he was a painter of supreme, decorative, courtly splendour. That splendour was, however, firmly based on acute natural observation, and his drawings in the Codex Vallardi (Paris, Louvre), in this respect outranking even those of Jacopo Bellini, testify to his powers. His watercolour drawings of birds and animals remain among the most sensitive and subtle in the whole history of the genre, and his delicately tinted costume studies with their peacock-strutting figures are, quite simply, ravishing. [106, 206, 340] JW

G. A. dell'Acqua *L'opera completa del Pisanello* (1922); G. Paccagnini *Pisanello* (1973)

Pisano, Andrea (active *c.*1290, d.1348) is noted for the bronze south doors of the baptistery in Florence, commissioned in 1329, which show the influence of French gothic metalwork in their delicate, rhythmic forms. Andrea became Master of the Works at Orvieto cathedral in 1347. SJ

Pisano, Nicola (active *c.*1258–78) Regarded as the founder of modern sculpture. With his son Giovanni (active *c.*1265–*c.*1314) he revived the

Panel of the Nativity from the sculptured pulpit of **Nicola Pisano** in the baptistery at Pisa.

realism and dignity of Roman carving in a series of elaborate pulpits in Siena, Pisa and Pistoia. The treatment of features and the layout in the pictorial panels of the Pisa baptistery pulpit (*c.*1260) by Nicola are like the antique sarcophagi in the Campo Santo. Giovanni was responsible for the monumental statuary on the exterior of the Pisan baptistery and the cathedral in Siena. SJ

Pitti family The Pitti were brought to prominence among Florentine merchant families with the support given by Luca (1395–?1470) to Cosimo de' Medici. It is not clear how he accumulated the money necessary to build the Palazzo Pitti (this was in his time, however, only 7 bays wide). Tempted in 1466 to join the anti-Medicean conspiracy to oust Piero de' Medici from the dominant position he had inherited 2 years previously, Luca backed down in time to save his skin but not his

Painting by Giusto Utens of the **Pitti** Palace as it was built in the 15c., with Medici extensions to the rear (1599) (Florence, Museo Topografico).

reputation. He died distrusted by all parties, nor was any power subsequently exercised in Florence by the Pitti apart from Jacopo (1519–89), a senator and a historical and political writer of some note, who watched his master Cosimo I purchase, extend and move into his family's palace. JRH

Pius II Pope 1458–64 (b.1405) Enea Silvio Piccolomini was one of 18 children born to an unprosperous branch of one of Siena's leading families. Intellectually gifted and ambitious, he took every advantage of the humanistic teaching available in Siena. Facility as a latinist, charm and a vigorous pliability fostered a career as secretary to a series of prominent ecclesiastics, which led to his being entrusted with considerable administrative and diplomatic responsibilities. By 1442 he had become the chief spokesman for the rump of bishops who refused obedience to Pope Eugenius IV, and in that year he was crowned poet laureate by the Emperor Frederick III and employed as one of his own secretaries. In 1446 he took Holy orders. Hitherto he had played his part in ecclesiastical affairs as a layman and acquired a modest reputation besides as a man of letters with poetry, a comedy and a mildly erotic novella, *The tale of two lovers* (all written in Latin). From the Empire he now turned to service first with Eugenius IV, then with his successors Nicholas V and Calixtus III, acquiring a bishopric and the cardinal's hat which admitted him to the conclave that followed Calixtus's death in 1458.

While his reaction to his election as Pius II did not involve a dramatic 'conversion' from his career as womanizer, genial belletrist and place-seeker (for he had displayed a steadier and soberer sense of purpose from 1446), the intensity with which he sought to further the temporal and spiritual interests of the Papacy took his contemporaries by surprise. He trenchantly denounced the calling of General Councils aimed at displacing the authority of a pope. He took up the struggle, commenced by Martin V, to regain effective control within the Papal State. He succeeded in diluting the control which the French monarchy (by the 1438 Pragmatic Sanction of Bourges) had come to exercise over church affairs in France. Above all, he tirelessly but vainly attempted to gain European support for a crusade against the Turks, who had so recently (1453) conquered Constantinople. With little hope of support, but determined to set an example, he was waiting at Ancona for the little naval aid he had been promised when his health, which had been poor for some time, suddenly took a turn for the worse, and he died there.

Enea Silvio Piccolomini, the future **Pius II**, at the court of James I of Scotland: from Pinturicchio's fresco series in the Piccolomini Library at Siena.

Pius's chief interest as a patron of the arts was the transformation of the Sienese village where he was born, Corsignano, into the rationally planned miniature city of Pienza. He had no time to continue even the more serious of his previous learned interests as historian (of the Council of Basle), biographer (*On the famous men of his day*), educational theorist (*On the education of boys*), above all as topographer and historical geographer (*On Europe, An account of Bohemia, On Asia*). These three were the major contribution to the subject since antiquity: *On Asia*, indeed, was one of the sources carefully studied by Columbus.

Fortunately abstention from pondered scholarship made him all the more determined to continue his *Commentaries*. Though written in the third person, this Latin account of his own life and thoughts is not just the only autobiography of a pope, but the frankest and most immediate of self-revelations written in the Renaissance before the *Autobiography* of Benvenuto Cellini. His training as a topographer enabled him to express his delight in towns and countryside, and his depiction of

individuals and political situations also owed much to his earlier interests. He veils nothing (it seems) of his ambitions and indiscretions, and produces a startling inside picture of the Church (including a vivid account of the corrupt practices employed in the conclave of 1458). Thanks to this work he is of all Renaissance popes the one who can best be known and, perhaps in part for this reason, is not among those who are most admired. JRH
Memoirs of a Renaissance pope: the commentaries of Pius II tr. F. A. Gragg (1959 and later eds); R. J. Mitchell *The laurels and the tiara* (1962)

Plague, which had been extinct in Italy from the 8c., returned along eastern trade routes to strike the peninsula, and thereafter all Europe, in October 1347. During 1348 the Black Death, comprising the bubonic and still more deadly septicaemic and pneumonic forms of the disease, swept town and countryside in a series of attacks whose horror was strikingly portrayed by Boccaccio in his preface to the *Decameron*. Thenceforward, though in less widespread, more sporadic outbreaks, plague recurred periodically until the 18c. Thirty per cent of the population of Venice died in the outbreak of 1575–77, for instance, which was commemorated by Palladio's church of the Redentore. Preventive measures included the boarding up of infected families, the isolation of sufferers in plague hospitals, the burning of 'infected' clothing, but none worked or mitigated the feeling of hopelessness. The plague's social effects are an object of controversy. It seems probable, however, that during the second half of the 14c. plague reduced the population of Italy by a half and at certain centres, such as Florence and Genoa, sharply accentuated an economic depression which had already set in during the 1340s. In the 15c., despite regional variations, it is unlikely that population began to rise significantly before the 1470s.

San Rocco by Bartolomeo della Gatta: a panel commissioned during the **plague** of 1477–79 in Arezzo (Arezzo, Pinacoteca).

Large claims have been made in the field of the arts and of human sensibility for the influence of plague. In Florence and Siena from 1348 to 1380, religious feeling and the art which mirrors it seem to assume more sombre forms and to reflect less the human and more the divine, transcendent and threatening aspects of faith. Yet the black rat and its plague-bearing flea could find a more hospitable environment in the hovels of the poor than in the stone-built houses of wealthy patrons of the arts (who, moreover, were often able to remove themselves from areas where plague had broken out). For this reason, perhaps, it is difficult to find, outside Tuscany, evidence of cultural change which could be attributed to plague, and in the Italy of the 15c. and 16c. the main effect of the disease in art is to be found only in the frequent portrayal of the plague saints, Rocco and Sebastian. It is none the less interesting to recall that it was against a stark background of continual menace from plague that the human achievements of the Renaissance came into being. *See* ECONOMY. JL
M. Meiss *Painting in Florence and Siena after the Black Death* (1951); E. Carpentier *Une ville devant la peste: Orvieto et la peste noire de 1348* (1962); E. Rodenwaldt *Pest in Venedig 1575–77* (1953)

Platina (1421–81) was a Lombard humanist, born Bartolomeo Sacchi, who became a papal abbreviator (drafter of briefs) under Pius II. Paul II's policy of reducing the secretariat led to Platina's dismissal. When he responded with an attack on the Pope invoking the threat of a General Council of the Church he was imprisoned. Association with Leto's allegedly subversive Roman academy led him to be

Sixtus IV conferring on **Platina** the librarianship of the Vatican: fresco by Melozzo da Forlì of *c.*1477 in the Vatican, Rome.

imprisoned again and accused of paganism. More favoured under Sixtus IV, he then composed his *Lives of the popes* and used the opportunity to paint an unfavourable picture of Paul. GH

Plato and neo-Platonism The Renaissance revival of Platonism and neo-Platonism was one of the characteristic intellectual features of the age. In fields ranging from literature (Castiglione and Ronsard) to science (Bruno and Galileo) it exerted a great influence in all parts of Europe from Portugal and Scotland to Hungary and Poland. The founder of one of the 2 most influential ancient schools of philosophy, Plato (428–348 BC) was born at Athens. A student of Socrates, he continued to develop his philosophy after the master's death in 399, and was in turn the teacher of Aristotle. Writing in a forceful and compelling style mostly cast in dialogue form, Plato was the author of some 30 works of lasting fame including the *Republic*, the *Symposium*, *Phaedrus*, *Phaedo*, *Philebus*, *Timaeus*, *Theatetus* and the *Laws*.

Plato's philosophy has a distinctly otherworldly character, emphasizing the spiritual and non-material aspects of reality. In contrast with Aristotle, he gives knowledge and philosophy an intuitive and intellectual basis, not so much dependent upon sense experience as on inspiration and direct mental contact with the supra-sensible sources of knowledge. Thus empirical science does not have a central role in Plato's thought, though mathematics is consistently stressed as being an important gateway to the natural world. Such themes as poetic inspiration and harmony, as well as the rigorous analyses of central moral doctrines such as justice and happiness, have ensured that his works were widely read for many centuries. Rather unsystematic, with many internal contradictions and points left unresolved, his works were already subjected to critical analysis and amplification by his earliest followers. PLOTINUS, the greatest of his ancient disciples, systematized and added to what Plato had done, turning the tradition in an even more mystical and spiritual direction, while at the same time giving the philosophy a more coherent form. 'Neo-Platonism' resulted from these modifications and those of other ancient Platonists.

Only a small proportion of Plato's works was known during the Middle Ages in western Europe, though indirect knowledge of Platonic doctrine through many late ancient sources secured a significant *fortuna* down to the 15c. Petrarch favoured Plato over Aristotle as an authority and set the tone for the great Renaissance revival of interest in Platonism. The real re-emergence of Plato began around 1400, when Greek manuscripts of most of his works came into Italy from Constantinople. Latin translations of several works were made in the early 15c., but only with Ficino were the entire writings first made available in Latin (published 1484). Ficino was also the founder of the informal Platonic Academy which met at the Medici villa at Careggi, near Florence. Ficino's interpretation went far beyond what could be found in the text of Plato, and he utilized many other writings, including those of Plotinus, Iamblichus, and Proclus and a range of pseudonymous texts, among them those attributed to Hermes Trismegistus and Orpheus, and the Chaldaic Oracles, all of which he also translated into Latin. He emphasized the close kinship between the Platonic philosophy and the Christian religion, seeing them as parallel paths to the truth connected at source, and holding that Plato had

had access to the Pentateuch and absorbed some ideas from it: he agreed with Numenius (2c. AD) that Plato was a 'Greek-speaking Moses'.

Ficino's translations of Plato and the neo-Platonists were reprinted frequently and were the standard sources for knowledge of Platonism for several centuries. Among his Italian followers Giovanni Pico della Mirandola and Francesco da Diacceto (1466–1522) were perhaps the most important, and Agostino Steuco (*c.*1497–1548) developed Christian Platonism into a 'perennial philosophy'. The impact of Ficino's work gradually made itself felt beyond the confines of Italy, for example with Symphorian Champier (*c.*1472–*c.*1539) and Jacques Lefèvre d'Étaples (*c.*1460–1536) in France and John Colet (*c.*1467–1519) and Thomas More (1478–1535) in England.

The first Greek edition of Plato's works was published by Aldus at Venice in 1513, but the later edition published at Paris in 1578 by Henri Estienne achieved perhaps even greater fame. A new Latin translation, prepared by Jean de Serres (1540–98) to accompany Estienne's edition, partially, but not completely, replaced Ficino's. There was no complete translation into a vernacular language during the Renaissance, though various dialogues were rendered into Italian and French, the translations of Louis Le Roy (d.1577) becoming particularly popular. Unlike the case of Aristotle, the interest in Plato and neo-Platonism was largely outside the universities. It was especially in a number of academies in France and Italy that there was a focused reading of Platonic texts. The numerous editions and translations show that there was a wide general demand for his writings. Plato was read in the universities, if on a very limited scale: for example various dialogues were read from time to time as part of Greek courses. In the 1570s special chairs of Platonic philosophy were established at the universities of Pisa and Ferrara. The latter was held for 14 years by Francesco Patrizi of Cherso, one of the most forceful and original Platonic philosophers of the Renaissance. CS

P. O. Kristeller *Eight philosophers of the Italian Renaissance* (1964); E. N. Tigerstedt *The decline and fall of the Neoplatonic interpretation of Plato* (1974); D. P. Walker *The ancient theology* (1972)

Plautus, Titus Maccius (before 251–184 BC) Through the Middle Ages words about the theatre survived but the theatre itself vanished, to be recreated in a very different place and guise with the SACRA RAPPRESENTAZIONE. Born in the church and moving out into the piazza, this was independent of that non-existent building, the theatre. Meanwhile an author like Plautus had an awkward passage. Eight of his plays were extant in the 14c., and it was not till 1425 that Nicholas Cusanus found a manuscript at Cologne containing 12 more, which he ceded to Cardinal Giovanni Orsini at Rome in 1429. Even then, the new comedies were jealously guarded, and the text remained defective: there was, for instance, a big gap at the end of *Aulularia* and at the beginning of the *Bacchides* which has never been filled, even with Mai's discovery of a palimpsest at the beginning of the 19c. Though Alberti, in the *De re aedificatoria*, considered the theatre as a (possible) building, there were still no theatres in the Quattrocento.

Such plays as there were were Latin derivations from Plautus, of which the most noteworthy is the *Chrysis* (1444, but only printed in our own century) of the young Enea Silvio Piccolomini. Florence staged a Plautus comedy in 1476, and in 1486 the Estes at Ferrara mounted the *Menaechmi*. This was the fruit of the enthusiasm of Ercole d'Este, and from 1486 there was an unbroken run of performances of plays by Plautus and Terence (except for the years 1494–98). The young Ariosto both acted in these, and himself translated from Plautus and Terence for performance at the Este court, although his versions have not survived. His own comedies, beginning with the *Cassaria* (1508) – its title echoing the *Aulularia* from Plautus – are a free adaptation of the tradition of comedy: as Plautus and Terence were to their Greek predecessor Menander, so Ariosto is to Plautus and Terence; and with this takeover of classical comedy the *sacra rappresentazione* disappeared, and the modern stage-play was born.

In Florence Machiavelli wrote the *Mandragola* (1518), which infused the native spirit of the *beffa* into this stereotype of comedy, and he also freely adapted the *Casina* of Plautus for his own *Clizia* (1525). Machiavelli, it could be said, is more Plautine than Terentian: just as the language of Plautus is more primitive than that of TERENCE, so the spirit of his plays is harsher, the social conditions rougher at their edges, the outcomes not tailored to a moral pattern. Between them, however, Plautus and Terence, as re-presented by Ariosto and Machiavelli, dominated comedy both in the 16c. in Italy and in Europe generally until the 19c. JHW

R. Sabbadini *Le scoperte dei codici antichi* (1905); E. S. Piccolomini *Chrysis* ed. E. Cecchini (1968)

Pliny the Elder (AD 23–70) Gaius Plinius Secundus was the great and pioneer encyclopaedist of the ancient world. His major surviving work, the *Historia naturalis*, included, in his own phrase, '20,000 matters worthy of consideration.' Containing accounts of the then state of knowledge and hearsay about such matters as geography, zoology, botany and agriculture, medicine and minerals, and incorporating much material from other, especially Greek, sources that were subsequently lost, his book was an important influence on much Renaissance writing on technical and scientific subjects. Of particular interest was the account the *Historia* contained of the development of art, especially after its translation into Italian in 1473. It was from Pliny that men learned the terms by which works of art could be judged and categorized, in ways hardly modified until the mid-16c. From him artists could discover classical precedent for their own chief concerns, whether it was to obtain a greater illusion of reality, to combine aspects of what was real into an ideally harmonious effect, or to justify a preoccupation with mathematics, without whose aid, Pliny reported Pamphilus as saying, 'art could not attain perfection.' Conscious of their inferior social status, artists could take comfort from the respect Pliny said they were accorded by the Greeks, especially – for much of Pliny's account was in the form of agreeably told anecdotes – from the deference shown by Alexander the Great to Apelles: handing over to him no less a gift than his mistress Campaspe, with whom the painter had fallen in love while painting her in the nude (another instance, this, of Pliny's usefulness to artists seeking a defence of their subject matter). Pliny was stifled to death by fumes during an eruption of Vesuvius. *See* ARTIST, STATUS OF THE; CRITICAL THEORY OF ART. JRH

C. G. Nauert 'Humanists, scientists and Pliny: changing approaches to a classical author' *American Historical Review* (1979); *The Elder Pliny's chapters on the history of art* tr. K. Jex-Blake (repr. 1968); 'The Renaissance concept of artistic progress' in E. H. Gombrich *Norm and form* (1966)

PLINII NOVECOMENSIS IN LIBROS NATVRALIS HI
STORIE PROHEMIVM FOELICITER INCIPIT
IBROS NATVRALIS HISTORIE NO

Pliny at work, from a 15c. manuscript of his *Historia naturalis* (Vienna, Osterreichische Nationalbibliotek).

Plotinus (*c.*AD 204–70) Egyptian pagan philosopher who wrote in Greek and was the most important follower of PLATO in antiquity. His writings comprise 54 brief philosophical treatises, combined in a single work entitled *Enneads*. Plotinus systematized Plato's philosophy, incorporating into his synthesis much material from other ancient philosophical and religious traditions. Mystical in tone and intuitive to an extreme degree, Plotinus' neo-Platonism emphasized the absolute transcendence and uniqueness of God and the spiritual possibilities of man, who participates in the divine essence through thought. Influential in antiquity, e.g. in the works of St Augustine (354–430) and Pseudo Dionysius (5c. AD), the *Enneads* were not known directly during the Middle Ages. The Greek text was recovered in the 15c. and translated into Latin by Ficino, who also added an extensive commentary (first printed in 1492). The first edition of the Greek text appeared at Basle in 1580. Plotinus' works were widely read during the Renaissance, adding an important and highly speculative nuance to the neo-Platonic interpretation of Plato. CS

E. Garin *Rinascite e rivoluzioni* (1975)

Plutarch (*c.*AD 46–120) The *Lives* of Plutarch are the main repository of biographies of the heroes of the ancient world. As such they were looked forward to, and so eager was Coluccio Salutati that he did not wait for them in Greek, but translated in 1396 an Aragonese version which itself depended on a Rhodian scholar's translation into modern Greek. This did not have much circulation outside Florence, or much use even by Coluccio, for the good reason that a Greek manuscript of Plutarch soon became available, and the best humanists of the early 15c. devoted their energies to making Latin versions of single biographies. Bruni opened the series with the lives of Brutus and Cicero, key figures in the humanist approach to antiquity. Guarino da Verona and other prominent scholars added to the list, and partial collections were put together, without regard to the structure of Plutarch's work as a whole. Thus by 1435 it is possible to find a collection with 29 latinized biographies, and parallel with this activity comes the extraction of *Flores Plutarchi de dictis sapientium*, the humane lessons of Plutarch's political wisdom culled from the sayings of his heroes.

This piecemeal effort only reached completion in the 1460s, and already there was felt the need to find an easier approach to so vast a text. So the Milanese humanist Pier Candido Decembrio set himself to produce an *Epitome* of all the *Vitae parallelae* (in which Greek and Roman heroes are coupled as analogous counterparts). He began this ambitious project promisingly, studying the Greek text from 1432–37, and criticizing the translators into Latin. But he ended by relying on their by no means flawless versions, and since it was hard to collect them all, his task was never completed. But in 1470 at Rome there appeared a complete edition of all the *Lives*, still in their varying Latin form, and so it was easier for Decembrio's successor, Dario Tiberti, to aim at a new epitome of the whole. Tiberti's *Epitome*, published at Ferrara in 1501, was dependent as before on the Latin versions but made Plutarch accessible to the general reader in Italy, and, when reprinted at Basle in 1541, to Europe also.

The *editio princeps* of the Greek text was published by Aldus in 1519. The other side of Plutarch's vast *oeuvre* is the *Moralia*, 'than which nothing holier can be found'. Erasmus's judgment accords with the reputation of Plutarch as the most proto-Christian of Greek writers. Aldus published the Greek text in 1509. In 1410 Guarino da Verona translated the treatise on education from the *Moralia* into Latin, so that, at the same time as scholars were seizing on individual biographies, Plutarch was becoming one of the basic texts of humanist EDUCATION, with its belief in the harmonious development of the individual. JHW

G. Resta *Le epitomi di Plutarco nel Quattrocento* (1962)

Poison In Jacobean England, Italy was seen as (among other things) the land of poisoners. In John Webster's 2 tragedies alone, Italians poison their victims through the leaves of a book, the lips on a portrait, the pommel of a saddle and an anointed helmet. There was some fire under this fantasticated smoke. Poison (usually some form of arsenic) was licensed by governments – the evidence is fullest for Venice – for use in political assassinations, or in war through the contamination of wells in enemy territory. There is no evidence that the latter technique ever worked. Nor is there conclusive proof that poison worked in cases of assassination, though both prudent lawyers and contemporary historians (Guicciardini thought that the blackened and bloated corpse of Pope Alexander VI showed that he had been poisoned) took the possibility for granted. Poison was used in cases of ordinary murder but the singling out of Italians as specialists in this crime must be attributed to anti-Catholic and North *v.* South prejudice. JRH

V. Lamansky *Secrets d'état de Venise* (2 vols 1884; repr. 1968)

Pole, Cardinal Reginald (1500–58) Scholar and churchman. Born in England of the blood royal, he spent most of his life in Italy, first as student, then as exile. He was a member of the papal reform commission of 1536 and in 1541 was appointed Governor of the Patrimonium Petri, resident at Viterbo. Here he belonged to a major circle of Evangelicals. Ironically this religious moderate, who lay under suspicion of heresy at the time of his death, was Archbishop of Canterbury during the Marian reaction. *See* EVANGELISM. OL

D. Fenlon *Heresy and obedience in Tridentine Italy: Cardinal Pole and the Counter Reformation* (1972)

Polidoro Caldara da Caravaggio (*c.*1500–43) One of the pioneers of Mannerism, famous for his monochromatic frescoes (now mostly lost) which illusionistically encrusted palace façades in Rome with vast friezes of sculpture *all'antica*, as at the Palazzo Ricci (*c.*1524–25). The rhythmic grace, sculptural power and anatomical vigour of their style owed more to Polidoro's passionate temper than to the example of antiquity. A similar blend of poetic genius and inspiration from ancient art produced his important contributions to the history of landscape painting in the church of S.

Silvestro al Quirinale (*c.*1525). Following the Sack of Rome in 1527, Polidoro went south, finally settling in Messina, where his style became increasingly eccentric (e.g. *Road to Calvary*, Naples, Capodimonte). LP

A. Marabottini *Polidoro da Caravaggio* (1969)

Poliziano (1454–94) Angelo Ambrogini derived his humanistic name (often given in English as Politian) from Montepulciano, where he was born into a bourgeois family already connected with the Medici. After the murder of his father in 1464, he moved to Florence, began to study and to write, particularly Latin verse, and eventually won the protection of Lorenzo de' Medici: in 1475 he was appointed tutor to Lorenzo's son Piero and went to live in the Medici household. In this period he associated with the leading scholars and thinkers of Florence (Argyropoulos, Ficino, Landino), but, rather than towards neo-Platonism, his talents were directed to philology and to the writing of poetry in Latin and Italian. In 1475 he began his *Stanze per la giostra del Magnifico Giuliano* (*Verses for the joust of Giuliano the Magnificent*), part of which may be connected with Botticelli's paintings, but broke off the poem on the death of Giuliano in the PAZZI conspiracy of 1478, of which he wrote a history on the Sallustian model.

Poliziano with Lorenzo de Medici's son Piero, from Ghirlandaio's fresco cycle in the Sassetti Chapel, S. Trinita, Florence.

Doubts about the stability of Lorenzo's rule and the hostility of Clarice Orsini, Lorenzo's wife, led him to quit Florence for Mantua in 1479. There, for Francesco Gonzaga, he wrote *La favola d'Orfeo*, the first pastoral drama in Italian; but in 1480 he returned to Florence to receive from Lorenzo the chair of Greek and Latin eloquence in the *studio*, which he held until his death, continuing his researches into the more recondite and refined areas of Greek and Latin literature and culture, fruits of which were the erudite *Miscellanea*, the verse *Sylvae* (*Groves*), recited as prolusions to his academic courses, and a body of Greek epigrams that show him to have been the first Italian humanist to have had a real mastery of the language. Not a profound thinker, Poliziano continues to be admired as the greatest textual scholar of his age and as a poet who brought a new delicacy and music to the Italian lyric, blending, particularly in the *Stanze*, classical and vernacular modes with a lightness and sureness of touch characteristic of the best creations of Laurentian Florence. PH

E. Bigi *La cultura del Poliziano e altri studi umanistici* (1967); I. Maier *Ange Politien: la formation d'un poète humaniste, 1469–1480* (1966)

Pollaiuolo, Antonio di Jacopo Benci (active *c.*1457, d.1498), the Florentine goldsmith, painter, sculptor, embroidery designer, engraver and, above all, draughtsman, who shared a workshop with his less talented brother Piero, was a key figure in laying the foundations for the High Renaissance. He was, as Vasari notes, one of the first artists to undertake dissections to reveal the underlying structures that control the external appearance of the human form. His *Martyrdom of St Sebastian* (London, National Gallery) is laid out like an anatomical textbook, and its Arno valley background marks an equivalent advance in the observation and portrayal of landscape. His monumental engraving of the *Battle of the Nudes*, with its return-line hatching, represents a key moment in the transition from pen or silverpoint drawing to specialized engraving techniques. His small bronze *Hercules and Antaeus* (Florence, Bargello), like his two small *Hercules* paintings (Florence, Uffizi), stands at the head of developments for which Italy became famous.

Pollaiuolo's bronze group of *Hercules and Antaeus* (Florence, Bargello).

Pollaiuolo's most striking achievement of all was, however, the development of a penmanship in which swiftness was combined with startling precision, creating a form-following, form-defining contour which, unlike the generalizing contour of ancient or of medieval art, is so powerful that it is fully capable of suggesting internal volumes without recourse to hatching or shading. This technique, shared by Leonardo, marks the first time in human history that the full potential of the single drawn line, with its thickening and thinning, its change of tone and direction and its continuities and discontinuities, is exploited to the full to give precise anatomical information. Not until Matisse and Picasso is this potential taken further. [230, 300, 303] JW

L. D. Ettlinger *Antonio and Piero Pollaiuolo* (1978)

Polybius (?c.203–c.120 BC) Greek historian who wrote a history of Rome's rise to Empire from 220 BC to 144 BC, based on wide political and military experience and on extensive travel. Only the first 5 of the 40 books that comprised it remained intact: the others survived in incomplete or excerpted (e.g. in Livy and Plutarch) form. Apart from the narrative, of particular interest to Renaissance students of antiquity were his praise of the Roman constitution as a 'mixed' form, his suggestion that 'pure' forms tended to degenerate, his description of Roman and Greek (Macedonian) military methods, and the prominent role he gave to human character and to Fortune in shaping events.

The most famous example of his influence in the Renaissance is the one critics have long seen at the outset of Machiavelli's *Discourses on Livy*, where there is an unacknowledged borrowing from Polybius in the notion of a cycle of events through which a state proceeds. And because Machiavelli shared Polybius' admiration for the Roman constitution (which allowed Rome to escape from the wheel of fortune) there are other borrowings from Polybius in Book I of the *Discourses*. The problem is that the relevant section in Polybius had not been translated into Latin in Machiavelli's lifetime (1469–1527), and that it has been generally accepted that he knew no Greek.

Niccolò Perotti translated Books I–V of Polybius into Latin for Pope Nicholas V in 1452–53, and this was printed in 1473 and reprinted before the end of the century. Moreover, Perotti gives prominence to a statement on the missing books, and closes with the notice of what was coming in Book VI, its concern with the Roman constitution (there are actually extant two fragments of this Book, one on the militia, one on the constitution of Rome). When J. H. Hexter put forward a solution in 1956 it was via Janus Lascaris (1445–1534) and the Rucellai Gardens, where Machiavelli was a habitué in the years after 1515. But there were manuscripts of Polybius in Florence, notably in the Medici library, and other friends of Machiavelli might have satisfied his curiosity, when that had been aroused by his reading of Perotti. And though the question of Machiavelli's knowledge of Greek has not been reopened recently it should be noted that the manuscript of Lucretius which ends with the subscription of Niccolò Machiavelli as scribe also carries the indication *telos* in Greek characters. Perhaps that is too slight to build on, but the suggestions that Machiavelli learnt what he needed to know about Polybius Book VI in the Rucellai Gardens, more probably from his philhellenic Florentine friends than from Janus Lascaris, remain valid, and reinforce the view that the whole of the *Discourses* were written after 1515, and do not in any part precede *The prince* (against the old view that Machiavelli had broken off the composition of the *Discourses* in 1513 in order to write *The prince*).

Later in the 16c. it was chiefly for his account of military campaigns and the lessons to be learned from these, and from ancient military formations and the layout of armed camps, that Polybius (translated into Italian in 1546) was read; it was in this spirit that Palladio, shortly before his death, designed 39 etchings of battles, marches, sieges and armies to accompany a reissue of this translation. JHW

A. Momigliano 'Polybius' reappearance in Western Europe' *Polybe: entretiens sur l'antiquité classique* XX (1974)

Pomponazzi, Pietro (1462–1525), one of the most notable Aristotelian philosophers of the Paduan school, taught principally at Padua (until 1509) and at Bologna (from 1512). In 1516 he published his most famous book, *De immortalitate animae* (*On the immortality of the soul*). Its argument starts from the long-debated question whether the immortality of the soul could be proved by rational argument along Aristotelian lines. Pomponazzi disagreed with the solution of AQUINAS, which took Aristotle to be susceptible of interpretation to conform with Christianity. He also disagreed with AVERROES's view that the body left the soul after death to join a universal intellect. His solution was that the soul was partly tied to the body, but also participated in immortality to the extent that it was capable of reason and the understanding of eternal abstractions. In the same book he argued against the view that the immortality of the soul was necessary to morality. Against this he put the Stoics' acceptance of virtuous activity as its own reward and the end of temporal life; and STOICISM seems in general to have been the outlook on life which he found most congenial.

He was much attacked for these theories on religious grounds. Though he did not agree with Averroes, he belonged in a general way to the 'Averroist' tradition, strong at Padua, which separated religious conviction from philosophical demonstration. There is no evidence that he doubted the immortality of the soul as a matter of faith, even though he thought it unprovable. He also left two important works to be published posthumously: *De incantationibus* (*On enchantments*) and *De fato* (*On fate*). In the first he argued, with much offence to orthodox opinion, that many apparently supernatural events had natural explanations. GH

A. H. Douglas *The philosophy and psychology of Pietro Pomponazzi* (1910); Bruno Nardi *Studi su Pietro Pomponazzi* (1965)

Pontano, Giovanni (or Gioviano) (1422–1503), a humanist and man of action of unusually varied gifts, entered the service of Alfonso I of Naples in Tuscany and from 1447 was established as a royal secretary, becoming the central figure in the Neapolitan Academy. Classicist enthusiasm led him to adopt the name Jovianus (in an Italian version) in place of his baptismal Giovanni. He played an important part in war and politics under Ferrante and had a major diplomatic role in the War of Ferrara. Though a dominant figure in the administration of the kingdom until the invasion of Charles VIII of France, he accepted the French victory (1495) over Naples in a spirit of political realism and was therefore out of favour at the coming of Ferdinand II.

Pontano was a prolific writer of Latin prose and verse. Some of his compositions were merely extensions of conventional humanist themes: to this class belong philosophical essays on fortitude, fortune and other such topics. He also wrote a substantial piece of humanist history in the *De bello napoletano*, which chronicles the mid-century Aragonese-Angevin struggle in which he had taken part. His literary genius was expressed in more imaginative works. His dialogues and stories included for example *Asinus*, in which he portrayed himself amid the festivities following the peace of 1486 incongruously enamoured of an ass, allegorizing his own relationship as the architect of peace with an ungrateful king. His poetry includes delightful celebrations of nature and of love, both sensual and tender. His erotic poetry, his extreme devotion to ASTROLOGY and the indifference to Christian values revealed in his dialogues: these were aspects of an independent genius which exhibited the remarkable potentialities of the new Latin and contributed to the emerging atmosphere of Renaissance literature. GH

A. Altamura, *L'umanesimo nel mezzogiorno d'Italia* (1941)

Pontelli, Baccio (1450–92/4) 'Architect of Florence', as he described himself on an

Pontelli's fortress and church façade at Ostia.

The Deposition by **Pontormo** (Florence, S. Felicita).

inscribed stone in his major work, the fortress at Ostia. He was trained as a woodworker specializing in intarsia. Quickness of technical apprehension and responsiveness to the ideas of men concerned with the design of buildings (like Francesco di Giorgio) led to his employment as papal adviser or planner of fortifications in the Marche: Osimo, Offida, Iesi, Senigallia. He also rebuilt the church at Ostia and may have designed the porticoes of S. Pietro in Vincoli and SS. Apostoli in Rome. JRH

G. de Fiore *Baccio Pontelli* (1963)

Pontormo, Jacopo Carucci, il (1494–1556) is, in the intensity of his vision, perhaps the strangest and most moving of all the early Mannerist painters. He was born near Empoli and was active in Florence. Solitary and increasingly withdrawn, he reveals his obsessive and deeply neurotic character in the diary he wrote in the last years of his life. He was profoundly influenced by Leonardo, by Michelangelo, and by his master, Andrea del Sarto, and his work shows clearly how the new Mannerist tendencies depended on and grew out of the High Renaissance. His art is founded on superb draughtsmanship and his most extreme distortions and elongations of the human figure are based on a complete mastery of anatomy and of straightforward naturalism, as can be seen in his delightful early *Vertumnus and Pomona* in the Medici villa at Poggio a Caiano (1520–21). This was followed almost immediately by his thoroughly Mannerist Passion cycle in the Certosa del Galluzzo outside Florence. This cycle reflects the influence of Dürer's prints, and with it the increasing impact of the reproductive processes which so profoundly altered and accelerated the development of modern art. Pontormo's undoubted masterpiece and one of the greatest of all Mannerist paintings is his *Deposition* in S. Felicita, Florence. Strange, brilliant, light-toned colours combine delicacy with power in the creation of an ethereal, otherworldly quality, matching and intensifying the way in which the boldly distorted, frequently androgynous figures are made to transform the particularities of a religious event into a timeless, ritual ballet. JW

F. M. Clapp *Jacopo Carucci da Pontormo* (1916); L. Berti *L'opera completa del Pontormo* (1973)

Population Reliable population figures are lacking. Surveys of specific territories were often undertaken in the 15c. and 16c. to determine the number of 'souls', 'hearths', or 'mouths' there, according to whether the enquiry was carried out by ecclesiastical or civil authorities, concerned with Easter duties, taxes, or the danger of famine. However, lists of 'souls' omit Jews (and sometimes children). Figures for 'hearths' are difficult to transform into figures for individuals because household size varied from place to place and changed over time, though a multiplier of 4.5 is a useful approximation. There is also some direct and indirect evidence for the size of town populations, notably baptismal registers (which survive in Siena from 1381) and the changing area enclosed by the walls. It is likely that the population of the peninsula increased sharply in the 12c. and 13c., and that it began to press on the means of subsistence soon after 1300.

Undernourishment lessened resistance to PLAGUE and about a third of the population succumbed during the Black Death of 1348. Recovery was slow. In 1400 there were something like 8 million Italians, far fewer than in 1300; in 1500, about 10 million; and in 1600, 12 to 13 million. In other words, there was a population 'explosion' in the 16c. as there had been in the 13c., so that population pressed on the means of subsistence once more, with similar results. If they were less destructive than the Black Death, the plagues of 1630–31 (in north Italy) and 1656 (in Rome and Naples) were still extremely serious.

The regional distribution of the 9 million Italians of *c.*1450 was as follows: Liguria, *c.*400,000; Piedmont, *c.*600,000; Tuscany, *c.*600,000; Lombardy, *c.*750,000; the Veneto, *c.*1,600,000; the Papal State, *c.*1,600,000; Naples and Sicily, *c.*3,600,000. Population density was highest in Lombardy, where AGRICULTURE was most productive; there were 100 to 120 inhabitants to the square kilometre in 1600. A higher proportion of the population of Italy lived in towns than anywhere in Europe except for Flanders. The biggest city was Naples, with over 200,000 inhabitants in 1550, but urban density was greatest in the north, with Venice (*c.*160,000), Milan (*c.*70,000), Genoa, Bologna, and Florence (*c.*60,000 each), Verona (*c.*50,000), etc. In 1550 there were about 40 Italian towns with a population of 10,000 or more, and they accounted between them for some 13 per cent of the population. Most of the leading artists and writers of the period came from one of these 40-odd towns. No cities, no Renaissance. PB

K. J. Beloch *Bevölkerungsgeschichte Italiens* (3 vols 1937–61); A. Bellettini 'La popolazione italiana' *SI* V

Porcari, Stefano (*c.*1400–53) was a would-be restorer of Rome's republican liberty, whose motivations have still to be made clear. He belonged to a Roman patrician family and for long enjoyed papal favours. In 1427–28 he was Capitano del Popolo in Florence, and may have been influenced by Florentine political ideas and rhetoric; some of his own orations survive. But after the 1434 Roman rising against papal government he was employed by Eugenius IV as a mediator (presumably uncommitted) and he continued to hold offices in the Papal State; his active participation in the tumult which followed the death of Eugenius in 1447 has not been adequately proved. However in 1448 Porcari was exiled to Bologna, whence he absconded early in January 1453 to promote a Roman conspiracy whose aims were the capture of Castel S. Angelo and of Pope Nicholas V and the proclamation of Porcari as Tribune. The plot failed and Porcari was hanged. DC

O. Tommasini 'Documenti relativi a Stefano Porcari' *Archivio della società romana di storia patria* (1880); M. Miglio '"Viva la libertà et popolo de Roma", oratoria e politica a Roma: Stefano Porcari' *Archivio della società romana di storia patria* (1974)

Pordenone, Giovanni Antonio, il (1483/4–1539) Giovanni de' Sacchis, born at Pordenone in the Veneto, later settled in Venice and briefly eclipsed Titian as the main painter active there. More obviously than Titian, Pordenone was affected by the monumental character of contemporary art in Rome, and his most famous works, frescoes at Treviso (in part destroyed) and in Cremona and the neighbourhood, approach Correggio in their daring illusionism, which is allied to a rapid – even coarse – handling of paint. From 1527 until his death Pordenone worked mainly in Venice, where a few altarpieces survive (notably that of S. Lorenzo Giustiniani in S. Giovanni Elemosinario, about 1535–36). AB

B. Molajoli *Mostra del Pordenone* (1939)

Porto, Luigi da (1485–1529) Best known as the author of the most attractive of the versions of the Romeo and Juliet story that influenced Shakespeare (*Giulietta e Romeo*, written 1524, published 1530). He was born into a leading family of Vicenza, was educated privately, possibly spent some time at the court of Urbino, and became the friend of some of the leading literary men of the day, among them Bandello and Bembo. He was also a soldier in a brief career that turned his attention to the writing of history.

After the defeat of AGNADELLO in 1509, Vicenza was occupied by a German army acting on behalf of Maximilian I. Collaborators at first, the da Porto found their new masters harder to bear than their old ones, and Luigi applied for and was granted a contract to command 50 horse in Venice's much depleted army. He took part in a number of engagements in the Veronese and in Friuli. He was wounded in the throat in 1511, took long to recover, and never fought again. Moved by feeling he was an actor within a historical drama of unprecedented significance, he wrote a series of letters, at first primarily about his own experience but increasingly with the aim of leaving a record of events in the Venetian terraferma 1509–24. His *Lettere storiche* (*Historical letters*) thus form a source of considerable value, while they retain, in spite of the revision he subjected them to, a spontaneity and a personal flavour which make them a delight to read. The personality that emerges, especially in his – as it were – dispatches from the front, is very much that of Castiglione's courtier: skilled and brave in arms, he preferred skirmishes in which the individual could shine to the anonymous mass of battle; when the sword was idle he picked up his pen to indite poems to his cruel mistress. Displaying learning, he none the less drew on it gracefully and modestly. JRH

Lettere storiche ed. B. Bressan (1857)

Portrait The Roman portrait bust survived in the form of life-sized reliquaries of saints, but it was in 15c. Florence that the individual features and character of a contemporary sitter were accurately recorded by sculptors such as Donatello, Desiderio da Settignano, Mino da Fiesole and the Rossellino. A similar degree of realism occurs in 15c. tomb sculpture.

The equestrian portrait, based on antique statues such as the Marcus Aurelius monument (Rome, Campidoglio), was revived in the 14c. Two examples in fresco are Simone Martini's *Guidoriccio* (*c.*1328; Siena, Palazzo Pubblico) and the posthumous portrait of *Sir John Hawkwood* (1436; Florence, cathedral) by Uccello, which gives the illusion of a 3-dimensional statue seen from below. The Venetian Republic ordered imposing monuments from Donatello (1447; *Gattamelata*, Padua) and Verrocchio (1479; *Colleoni*, Venice), whilst other statesmen ordered their own images to be erected in public places, directly relating themselves to the military heroes of ancient Rome. Another form of political portraiture derived from antiquity was the commemorative portrait MEDAL designed by artists such as Pisanello.

Lorenzo Lotto's **portrait** of the collector Andrea Odoni (Royal Collection).

The carved or painted profile portrait became popular in the 1450s. The realism of the clear, flattened image, painted under the influence of Flemish examples by the Pollaiuolo brothers, Piero della Francesca and Botticelli, was superseded by the three-quarter and frontal portrait, psychologically more complex, such as Leonardo's enigmatic *Mona Lisa* (Paris, Louvre) with her momentary smile or Andrea del Sarto's arresting *Portrait of a Man* (London, National Gallery). The 16c. portrait became generalized, Lotto's *Andrea Odoni* (1527; Royal Collection) being an idealized concept of a collector rather than an individual. Group portraits, decorating whole rooms, include the narrative scenes of the Gonzaga court painted by Mantegna (completed 1474; Mantua, Palazzo Ducale) and the elaborate schemes commissioned by the Farnese family in Rome from Vasari (1546; Palazzo della Cancelleria) and Salviati (after 1553; Palazzo Farnese). Portraits were also incorporated into religious narratives, as in Ghirlandaio's fresco cycle painted for Giovanni Tornabuoni in S. Maria Novella, Florence (1486–90). SJ

J. Pope-Hennessy *The portrait in the Renaissance* (1966)

Poverty, relief of The traditional medieval attitude to poverty was that it was a holy state. Monks and friars took a vow of poverty. The poor were 'God's poor', deserving of the '7 works of temporal mercy' (feeding the hungry, visiting the sick, helping prisoners, etc.). Professional beggars were officially tolerated, although their deceits were well known. Poor relief was left to the Church and to private enterprise. Monasteries fed the poor who came to their gates. Individuals founded 'hospitals' to look after the sick, orphans, foundlings, pilgrims and so on. CONFRATERNITIES, like the Buonomini di S. Martino in Florence, or the *scuole grandi* in Venice, distributed alms, tending to give priority to the so-called *poveri vergognosi*, the 'shamefaced poor' (who sometimes wore a mask to beg), in other words distressed gentlefolk. Municipal intervention was limited to the establishment of *monti di pietà*, public pawnshops lending money at lower rates of interest.

The POPULATION explosion of the 16c. and the consequent series of subsistence crises encouraged the development of more systematic and more discriminating poor relief, and of attitudes to the poor which were more practical but less humane. In Venice, Florence and elsewhere the authorities now intervened. They encouraged private charity but added measures of their own. They distinguished between local poor, to be helped by their own parish, and 'foreign' poor, to be expelled; between the sick poor, to be hospitalized, and work-shy vagabonds, to be sent to workhouses or to the galleys. Begging was generally forbidden. It was not possible to enforce these measures on a regular basis, but all the same they mark a turning point in the history of attitudes to poverty as well as in the history of the social services. PB

B. Pullan *Rich and poor in Renaissance Venice* (1971); R. Trexler 'Charity and the defense of urban élites' in F. C. Jaher ed. *The rich, the well born and the powerful* (1973)

Preachers The field of preaching was dominated by the religious orders, primarily the mendicants. Quite apart from the notorious incompetence of the secular clergy, members of regular orders were the acknowledged masters of pulpit oratory, of the sermon as an art form. This pre-eminence was not challenged even in the 16c., when reformers called for the secular clergy engaged in the pastoral ministry, bishops

S. Bernardino **preaching** in the open air of the Piazza del Campo in Siena; detail of a painted panel by Sano di Pietro in Siena cathedral.

especially, to discharge their preaching duties. The great preaching events of the year were still the Lenten sermons given by friars or monks of repute; star preachers journeyed all over Italy. The major collections of sermons published in the 16c. came from friars or monks, several of whom became bishops; sermons of bishops not drawn from the orders are hard to find.

Outstanding preachers of the 15c. whose sermons are extant are the Franciscans S. Bernardino da Siena and Bernardino da Feltre (d.1494), together with the Dominican Savonarola. For the 16c. there are the Capuchin Ochino; the Franciscans Franceschino Visdomini (1514–73), Cornelio Musso (1511–74), bishop of Bertinoro and Bitonto, and Francesco Panigarola (1548–94), bishop of Asti; the Augustinian Canon Gabriele Fiamma (1533–85), bishop of Chioggia; and, from the secular clergy, Borromeo. The call to repentance was a major feature of Lenten sermons: here Bernardino da Feltre stood out for his harsh, minatory exhortations; Savonarola and Musso, in their appeals for communal religious renewal, took on the dramatic rolė of Old Testament prophets as if laying claim to divine inspiration. Mendicants of the 15c. castigated the vices of society, not least those of statesmen and prelates, but 16c. ones were more cautious here.

The styles of S. Bernardino da Siena and Bernardino da Feltre were earthy, abrasive even; Savonarola's by contrast was cultivated and his last sermons were complex and arcane; Ochino's unadorned style was peculiarly limpid and conveys a winged emotionality. The sermons of Visdomini, Musso and Panigarola on the other hand often strain after emotional effect by accumulation of rhetoric and largesse of poetic vocabulary; Panigarola is particularly noted for his literary conceits and has been viewed as a significant precursor of the literary Baroque. Fiamma's sermons, however, are not florid in style; his forte was allegorical explication of scriptural references. The flow of Borromeo's grandiose and sometimes emotive style shows how he, by contrast with the mendicant preachers, was versed in classical and patristic rhetoric. In general 16c. sermons were very free in their formal organization and in no way bound to the principles of construction laid down in medieval preaching manuals. OL

J. W. O'Malley *Praise and blame in Renaissance Rome: rhetoric, doctrine and reform in the sacred orators of the papal court c.1450–1521* (1979)

Prefiguration Typology – the notion that aspects of the life and mission of Christ were in many respects prefigured or foreshadowed in the Old Testament – had become popularized visually by the 14c. through versions of works like the *Biblia pauperum* with their pairs of illustrations: Brazen Serpent/the Crucifixion, Moses receiving the tablets of the Law/the Sermon on the Mount, Joseph sold into captivity/the betrayal of Christ, the temptations of Adam and Christ, Noah's Ark prefiguring the Church as a means of human salvation, and so forth. Strengthened by the 15c. wish to find anticipations of Christian teachings in the ancient world (e.g. the Sybils as the pagan counterparts of the Prophets), this fascination with parallels gave rise to whole cycles, like the frescoes on the walls of the Sistine Chapel showing scenes from the life of Moses answered by scenes from that of Christ, as well as providing some extremely recondite reasons for the choice of Old Testament subjects. The New Testament references in these would, however, have been caught at the time because of the continued popularity of typological analogies in sermons and devotional literature. JRH

L. Réau *Iconographie de l'art chrétien* I (1955); L. D. Ettlinger *The Sistine Chapel before Michelangelo* (1965)

Presentation drawings Evolving naturally as a consequence of contemporary workshop practice, these highly finished drawings, intended as complete works of art in themselves, seem to have first assumed an importance in the *bottega* of Verrocchio. They acquired under Leonardo and especially Michelangelo the role of high art for a privileged few. That the recipients of these drawings studied them carefully is made clear in contemporary letters, again indicative of the purpose they served. The term is perhaps a little too freely applied. JC-S

Prevesa, battle of (27 September 1538) Prevesa is on the west coast of Greece, just north of the island of Leukas. Here a Venetian-Spanish-Genoese galley fleet was badly mauled by a Turkish fleet under Khaireddin Barbarossa. It was the major naval engagement of the Turkish War of 1537–40. JRH

Michelangelo's *Christ on the Cross*, believed to be a **presentation drawing** for Vittoria Colonna (London, British Museum).

Primaticcio, Francesco (1504–70) became the most influential representative of Italian painting in 16c. France. Trained under Giulio Romano in Mantua, in 1532 he began working for Francis I in Fontainebleau, where his collaborator was his fellow-Italian Rosso. Their distinctive style, Mannerist in character, has given them the label 'First School of Fontainebleau'. He evolved a highly sophisticated type of decoration, combining painting and stucco in high relief. He visited Rome on behalf of Francis I to buy antiques and casts. He was also active as an architect at Fontainebleau. LDE

A. Blunt *Art and architecture in France 1500–1700* (1970)

Printing Long before the end of the incunable period (1499), Italy had become the most important publishing country in Europe. Italy's wealth, its paper production, its many cities and its large and literate population were fertile ground for the new invention. Immigrants from Germany printed the first books in Italy in the monastery of SUBIACO (near Rome) in 1465, in Rome in 1467, and at Venice in 1469. Church sponsorship helped establish the Italian press, but independent entrepreneurs soon dominated. Venice's commercial pre-eminence and its distribution network, probably the best in the world at the time, made it an attractive focus for printing. Before long Venice became Europe's first city of printing; Venice published about 3,750 incunable editions and Paris, the second city, about 2,200. In the 16c., about 500 different Venetian publishers produced over half the books printed in Italy, and exported them throughout Europe. Florence, Rome and Milan were flourishing centres, and most smaller cities had one or more important printers.

Italian publishers printed all kinds of subject matter. But Italy, as the first home of the Renaissance, printed more Latin and Greek classics and contemporary humanistic works than northern Europe in the incunable period. ALDUS won intellectual respectability for printing among the learned, and his elegant editions of the Greek and Latin classics encouraged scholarship. The GIUNTI press of Venice almost secured a European monopoly of liturgical works. In the 1540s and later, the GIOLITO press played a key role in encouraging and publishing vernacular literature.

Most publishers who succeeded in establishing their presses probably began with enough capital to sustain the high initial cost of production and large inventory of books, until sales made their investment profitable. Some books were subsidized by author or patron, but publishers also printed at their own expense, and even supported authors until reprints made the venture profitable. As a new industry, printing escaped restrictive guild regulation. This left much opportunity for initiative, but at the same time copyright protection did not extend beyond the city's walls and sometimes had little force within. Press runs were relatively small, about 1000 copies, but reprints or slightly revised editions were common. The price of books varied greatly. Short vernacular tracts or school books of a few pages sold for the very low price of 2 or 4 *soldi*, within the means of most of the population. But large folio volumes of Latin classics or professional works might sell for the very high price of 1 or 2 ducats, i.e., 124 or 248 *soldi*.

Intricate business ties, frequent quarrelling, and matrimonial alliances characterized the closely knit printing industry. Economically and socially, successful publishers fitted comfortably into the middle-class world of merchants and professionals. They were seldom rich, but usually securely above the struggle of lower-class life. All the same, the many who printed one or a handful of titles before failing, for lack of funds or other reasons, serve to remind us of the hazards of the business.

Church and state largely ignored the press until the Reformation. Local governmental indices of prohibited books appeared in the late 1540s, and censorship became effective with Paul IV's Index of 1559 and the Tridentine Index of 1564. CENSORSHIP halted the printing of some authors and titles, but did not completely stop the importing of banned books from northern Europe. Contrary to an older view, censorship did not ruin Italian publishing, but encouraged printers to publish more religious books. The printers continued to prosper. However, by the end of the 16c. the quantity as well as the physical and intellectual quality of Italian books had declined. Now Paris printed more books than Venice. The decline of major publishing firms, strong foreign competition, the shift of the commercial axis of Europe from the Mediterranean to the Atlantic, and the growing expertise of northern European scholars combined to make the difference. *See* TECHNOLOGY. PG

R. Hirsch *Printing, selling and reading 1450–1550* (2nd ed. 1974); P. F. Grendler *The Roman*

Inquisition and the Venetian press 1540–1605 (1977)

Priuli, Girolamo (1476–1547) Patrician Venetian merchant who wrote an informative and polemical secret diary 1494–1512, which survived except for part of 1506–09. Practising as a banker between 1507 and 1517, he suffered heavy losses in the war calamity of 1509, blame for which he ascribed partly to God's wrath with Venice and partly to the incompetence of its rulers. He lived obscurely after going out of business, and never married, but was sufficiently wealthy to provide several churches with furnishings. DC

R. Fulin 'Girolamo Priuli e i suoi diarii' *Archivio Veneto* (1881); *Diari* (up to October 1509) ed. A. Segre and R. Cessi *Rerum Italicarum Scriptores* XXIV (1912–19)

Professions The word *professione* meant simply 'occupation'. Tommaso Garzoni's *Piazza universale di tutte le professioni del mondo* (1585) goes from princes and humanists to innkeepers and beggars. But these occupations did have a hierarchy, and an important distinction, going back (as Renaissance writers well knew) to classical times, was that between the high-status 'liberal' occupations which a gentleman might practice, and the low-status 'mechanical', 'servile' or 'illiberal' ones, associated with the common people. There was considerable disagreement over which occupations should be considered liberal. Excluding the clergy (an 'estate' rather than a profession), and writers (since writing was usually a part-time activity), we may concentrate on the following 5 occupations which claimed to be liberal in this period, with varying success.

(1) Lawyers, and in particular judges and advocates, were members of a highly respected occupation. They were trained at university. They were given the title 'Messer' like knights. Noblemen often studied law and were not ashamed to practise it. In some cities, such as Padua, lawyers were civic leaders, though elsewhere, in Lucca for example, they were excluded from the town council, probably from fear of the experts taking over. Notaries, however, had a lower and more ambiguous status. They were addressed as 'Ser', like merchants. Some went to university but others learned their business by apprenticeship. They were too numerous to be respected: 8 notaries per 1000 people in Florence in 1427. In some cities, such as Florence, all lawyers, from judges to notaries, were members of the same guild; in others, such as Bologna, the notaries had a guild but the judges were organized in what was more grandly entitled a 'college'. The social distance between the two groups was increasing in the 16c. Both groups played key roles in administration; there was no separate profession of 'civil servant'.

Professions: the legist Filippo Lazzari lecturing to his students, from a marble relief on his tomb, 1468 (Pistoia, San Domenico).

(2) Like the legal profession, the medical profession was divided. Physicians were trained at university and generally had a high status, despite suggestions that their occupation was illiberal. Surgeons, however, had the low status generally associated with manual work, however skilled, in this period. They often combined their job with that of barber. The social distance between physicians and surgeons, like that between judges and notaries, seems to have increased in the 15c. and 16c. Physicians were not numerous; there was only 1 to every 10,000 people in Tuscany *c.*1600. Most of the sick must have dosed themselves or gone to the wise woman.

(3) Merchants who confined themselves to wholesale trade were generally considered respectable. In Florence, Venice and Genoa, some patricians were still involved in trade in 1600, though fewer than a century earlier, partly because the status of merchant was declining. Elsewhere in Italy it had never been high, even if the wealth it brought might command respect. As in Cicero's Rome, retail shopkeeping was always considered illiberal.

(4) Teachers had a more ambiguous status. Some university teachers, especially professors of law, were well paid; others, including the 'humanists' who taught grammar, rhetoric, etc., were not. Schoolmasters or 'pedants' had a rather low status, whether they were private tutors in wealthy families, worked for a town council, or remained independent by taking pupils at so much a head.

(5) Artists were generally considered to be mere craftsmen, hands rather than brains. But from Giotto onwards, if not before, some painters and sculptors did achieve respect. By the 16c. a gulf had opened between the high-status minority, including Raphael, Michelangelo and Titian, and the majority of their colleagues, who were still treated as craftsmen. *See* ARTIST, STATUS OF THE; CLASS, SOCIAL. PB

L. Martines *Lawyers and statecraft in Renaissance Florence* (1968); C. M. Cipolla *Public health and the medical profession in the Renaissance* (1976)

Ptolemy (2c. AD) Astronomer of Alexandria. Of the 3 books by him known to the Renaissance, 2 (the *Almagest* and the *Tetrabiblos* or *Quadripartitum*) were known from the 12c.; the third, the *Cosmography* or *Geography*, was discovered by Jacopo Angelo *c.*1406, and was extremely well known after 1410. The *Almagest* (a Latin corruption of an Arabic corruption of the Greek title, *Mathematical synthesis*) is a great synthetic work on mathematical astronomy which attempts to present in detail a mathematical description of the solar system. Ptolemy based it on the work of his predecessors, but added to it considerably himself. It was the basis for Arabic mathematical astronomy. Although available in Gerard of Cremona's translation from the late 12c. (printed 1515), it was less studied in detail than its Arabic commentators before the later 15c., principally because it is mathematically difficult. No sooner had it been mastered than attempts were made to supersede it; Copernicus's great work follows the *Almagest* in form chapter by chapter. The 'Ptolemaic system' is essentially the geocentric solar system.

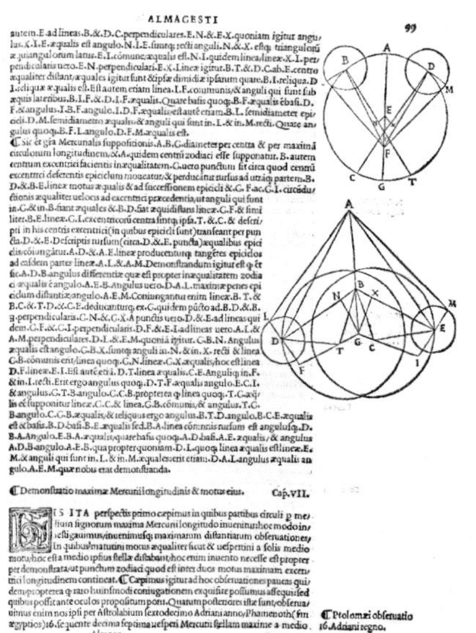
ALMAGESTI 99

Demonstratio maximæ Mercurii longitudinis & motus eius. Cap. VII.

Ptolomæi obseruatio 16. Adriani regno.

Almage. n 3

A page from an edition of **Ptolemy**'s *Almagest* printed in 1528.

Ptolemy himself regarded the *Tetrabiblos* as 'applied' astronomy. In fact a treatise on the theory and practice of astrology, it was extremely popular in the Renaissance, although a relatively advanced work on the subject. His *Geography*, even more popular in the 15c., revolutionized cartography even though it was transmitted without maps. It summarized Greek geographical knowledge and provided the basis for the theory of projection, previously unexplored in western Europe. Mathematicians and artists (like Crivelli) cooperated to produce maps according to Ptolemy's directions, so that editions of his work were technically advanced even though their geographical information was antiquated. The new discoveries were incorporated into maps on his projections about 1500; not until half a century later were his cartographic techniques improved upon. His *Optics*, which goes further than Euclid into the study of refraction, was not known to Renaissance scholars except by reputation. MBH

Dictionary of Scientific Biography (1970–80)

Pulci, Luigi (1432–84) A Florentine friend and dependant of Lorenzo de' Medici, Pulci was a bizarre and undisciplined writer, eventually suspected of heresy and sorcery and denied Christian burial. His literary fantasy tended towards the comic and the grotesque; and he developed a fascination for popular Tuscan language which produced a hyperbolic glut of idiomatic expressions. In the chivalric epic *Morgante* (1478 and 1483), Pulci simply rewrote two anonymous popular sources: one a

rambling series of adventures involving Charlemagne's paladins, the second telling the classic story of Roland's betrayal and death at Roncesvaux. Pulci's technique was to follow the narrative framework of his originals, but to allow verbal and imaginative digressions to play themselves out to the point of exasperation, most notably in the episode of the giant Morgante and the scurrilous half-giant Margutte. The result is inevitably uneven, but occasionally moving and often hilarious. RA
Morgante ed. F. Ageno (1955); D. de Robertis *Storia del Morgante* (1958); M. Davie 'Pulci's Margutte episode re-examined' *Italian Studies* (1978)

Pythagoras (*fl. c.*530 BC) Founder of a quasi-religious secret brotherhood in south Italy in which mathematics played an important role. To the historical Pythagoras of Samos is attributed the theory that number is the key to the universe. The Pythagoreans founded number theory (arithmetic), established the methods of geometrical argument, and developed the theory of proportionality (harmony). To the Renaissance, Pythagoras represented the perfection of mathematical and mystical learning (see HERMETICISM), and Pythagorean number theory was equated with neo-Platonic and cabbalistic number mysticism. Thus Lorenzo de' Medici persuaded Ficino to interrupt his translation of Plato so that he might translate Hermes Trismegistus. The Pythagoreans, who may first have held the universe – and hence the earth – to be spherical, were also (wrongly) thought to have held the heliocentric theory of the universe; hence Copernicus was often said to have 'revived' Pythagoreanism. MBH
J. A. Philip *Pythagoras and early Pythagoreanism* (1966)

Adam and Eve, relief panel from Jacopo della **Quercia**'s portal of S. Petronio, Bologna.

Quercia, Jacopo della (?1374–1438) The most important Sienese sculptor of the early Renaissance. He is first recorded in 1401, when he submitted a trial panel (lost) for the competition over the bronze doors for the Florentine baptistery. His tomb of Ilaria del Carretto (Lucca, *c.*1406) shows an interest in the Antique in the putti with garlands on the sarcophagus, while the drapery on the effigy is still late gothic in feeling. The same is true of Jacopo's Trenta family altar (S. Frediano, Lucca, 1422), where the framework is still gothic. His masterpiece in Siena was the Fonte Gaia in the Campo (1408–19), a public watering place surrounded with marble reliefs and crowned with statues: the voluptuous female and sturdy male figures are influenced by the Antique and in turn affected Michelangelo. Quercia's other principal commission was the font in the baptistery of Siena cathedral, where, because of his dilatoriness, he was obliged to collaborate with Donatello and Ghiberti. Unlike them, he seems to have resisted the appeal of scientific perspective, preferring medieval approximations, while his drapery style is heavy and blanket-like. His later work was on the portals of S. Petronio, Bologna, where he carved a very impressive series of panels in relief. He also carved in wood in 1421 a fine pair of statues showing the *Annunciation* (Collegiata, San Gimignano), which are central in the Sienese tradition of wooden pigmented sculpture. CA
J. Pope-Hennessy *Italian gothic sculpture* (1970); A. C. Hanson *Jacopo della Quercia's Fonte Gaia* (1965); C. Seymour jr. *Jacopo della Quercia* (1973)

Quintilian (*c*.AD 35–95) Petrarch, in his epistle to Quintilian, lamented that 'he came torn and mangled to my hands' and, though a complete *Institutio oratoria* (*The education of an orator*) existed in France before 1396, diffusion only followed Bracciolini's discovery of the whole text at St Gall in 1416. Through the Middle Ages Quintilian (Marcus Fabius Quintilianus) had been taken alternately as educator, rhetorician and moralist, but the early 15c. interest is overwhelmingly in Quintilian as educator, on the basis of the first 2 books of the *Institutio oratoria*, and in the light of the invocation by Martial to the 'supreme moderator of the restless Roman youth'. Since these 2 books were in the mutilated text available to Petrarch, they were able to influence Vergerio's *De ingenuis moribus* and form the basis for the whole system of education adopted by Vittorino da Feltre.

Later writers on education, such as Enea Silvio Piccolomini, or Filelfo, or Alberti in the first book of the *Famiglia*, also echo Quintilian; and Palmieri, in the first book of the *Vita civile*, depends for half his text directly on Quintilian, though without mentioning him. In evaluating the influence of Quintilian in the 15c. two considerations should be borne in mind: the first, that Quintilian has no empty art of words to sell, and his programme for the perfect orator ('the good man skilled in speech') is based on knowledge and virtue; the second, that after his initial books, which lay the basis for the education of the orator from the cradle on, and so could be taken for a general theory of education, Quintilian applied himself to the problem of forensic oratory. Although the humanists of the 15c. have often been taken as empty imitators of ancient rhetoric, they did not follow Quintilian here.

Lorenzo Valla's youthful comparison of Cicero and Quintilian (favourable to the latter) has been lost, but his reverence for Quintilian did not dim his respect for Cicero. The former he quotes in the *De voluptate* as 'more than a witness, an earthly oracle', while Cicero's example is praised in the *Elegantiae* as giving bones and sinews to one's discourse. And indeed Quintilian's deep respect for Cicero is patent throughout the *Institutio oratoria*. This is not surprising, for he saw the corruption of the eloquence of his time, and wrote with the express purpose of correcting its vices.

This required a united effort, the collaboration of the family and of the best of educators, and this is why Quintilian devises a complete course of education: after the first steps, the technical presentation (invention, disposition, locution, memory, pronunciation or action) and, in Book XII, after the art of oratory, his general reflections on the qualities of the ideal orator, and the ingredients of his culture. It was a fortunate thing that the only systematic pedagogical treatise of antiquity to be preserved should have been one in which Quintilian traces the path towards an ideal educational goal, where the skills of the orator are not divorced from the other tasks of forming his mind and developing his virtues. Neither Cicero nor Quintilian can be made the auxiliaries, or the basis, of an accusation of empty rhetoric against the Quattrocento. JHW

R. Sabbadini *Le scoperte dei codici antichi* (1905)

Ragusa (Dubrovnik) This port on the southern Dalmatian coast was a Venetian protectorate from 1205 to 1358, acquiring a considerable hinterland and a thriving coastal and, especially with Ancona and Otranto, trans-Adriatic traffic; Venetian authority, represented by a patrician rector with the title of count, was light, leaving the city's government largely in its own hands. In 1358 Venice lost its Dalmatian ports to Hungary by the Peace of Zara. In 1409 the pretender to the Hungarian throne, Ladislas of Naples, sold his presumptive title to them and Venice, taking advantage of the confusion within Hungary, had reoccupied them by 1420 – apart, that is, from Ragusa, which had refused to acknowledge Ladislas, and subsequently had obtained sufficient support from Hungary to dissuade Venice from attempting to renew the protectorate by force.

Thereafter, Ragusan and Venetian shipping coexisted in the Adriatic, not without friction at times, especially after 1526, when Ragusa paid an annual tribute to Constantinople to retain trading rights in Turkish waters. Ragusa's importance as a shipbuilding and commercial centre, the demand for Ragusan vessels and crews to work under charter, and a deliberate policy of offering refuge to refugees (often men of rank and substance) from the Turkish occupation of the Balkans and to exiles from Italy (Piero Soderini in 1512, for instance) helped foster schemes for street planning and palace building and the commissioning of works of art that can not unrealistically be referred to as the Ragusan renaissance. JRH

L. Villari *The republic of Ragusa* (1904); B. Krekić *Dubrovnik in the 14th and 15th centuries* (1972); M. Aymard *Venise, Ragusa et le commerce du blé pendant la seconde moitié du XIVe siècle* (1966)

Raimondi, Marcantonio (active *c.*1500, d.1534) was born near Bologna and apprenticed to Francia, but worked principally in Rome *c.*1510–27. He is, in one major respect, the most important of all Italian Renaissance engravers. He, more than any other man, including Dürer, whose woodcut *Life of the Virgin* he plagiarized in 1505, established engraving as a reproductive medium. The highly developed, but also highly simplified, cross-hatching technique which he evolved allowed accurate copies of works of art to be made as part of a workshop process. His engravings disseminated a knowledge of Raphael's major works, not to mention those of Giulio Romano and others, almost instantaneously across Europe. The ease and speed with which stylistic and iconographic knowledge could be spread was transformed, and a new era in the history of art, to last until the advent of photography, was inaugurated. JW

H. Delaborde *Marc Antoine Raimondi* (1888)

Ramelli, Agostino (*c.*1537–*c.*1608). Engineer, first in the service of Gian Giacomo de' Medici, Marquis of Marignano, then in that of the future Henry III of France. He was at the siege of La Rochelle in 1572 (where he was briefly captured), and settled in France. His great work *Le diverse et artificiose machine* (*Various and ingenious machines*; Paris 1588) was printed in Italian and French (on facing pages) and is the most beautiful of Renaissance 'machine books'. It is partly original, partly a compilation from others (including probably Leonardo), and includes pictures and descriptions of water-raising devices, mills, cranes, dams, automata, military bridges and machines. [313] MBH

Le diverse et artificiose machine Eng. tr. M. T. Gnudi, ed. E. S. Ferguson (1976)

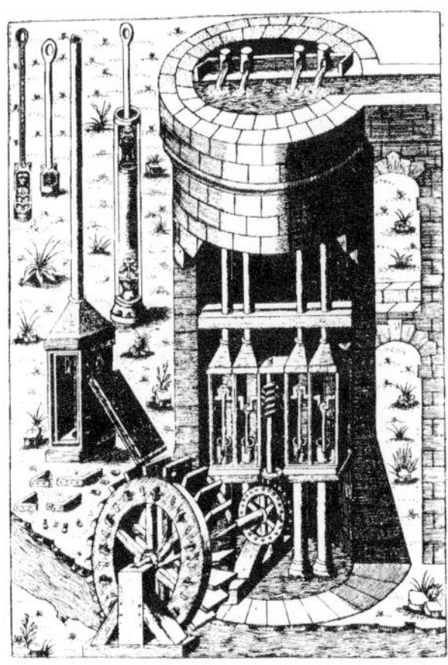

Ramelli's suction pump driven by a waterwheel, from *Le diverse et artificiose machine*, 1588.

Ramos, Bartolomé de Pareja (*c.*1440–after 1491) Spanish musical theorist who, after lecturing at Salamanca, settled in Italy, living in Florence probably in the 1470s, in Bologna about 1480, and later in Rome. He was one of those who advocated moving away from medieval techniques, more particularly in methods of tuning: some hold that he was a protagonist of something like modern equal temperament. DA

Ramusio, Giovanni Battista (1485–1577) With the 3 massive volumes *Delle navigationi et viaggi* (1550–59) Ramusio became the founder of the history of geography and the inspirer of Hakluyt and later collectors of voyage and travel narratives. Born in Treviso, he studied at the university of Padua and, like his contemporary and lifelong friend Fracastoro (to whom his collection was dedicated), he was stimulated by the atmosphere there to add a scientific interest to his study of Latin and Greek. In his case it was geography, and his *Navigationi* reflect not only a voracious appetite for narratives (and an ability to translate them from French and Spanish) but also a wide reading across the whole range of descriptive geography produced from antiquity to his own day. The work covers Africa, Asia and the New World and includes histories and descriptions of the territories covered as well as narratives of travel. In the 'discourses' which intersperse the work Ramusio shows a wide interest in the products of the countries he deals with, and the trade in them, and he also shows a taste for speculation, as when he discusses the possible causes of the inundations of the Nile. When to this is added his concern for the accuracy of the maps he prints he emerges as far more of an all-round geographer than the title of his work might suggest. It was compiled in the intervals of a busy public career in the Venetian chancery. After travelling as secretary to a number of patrician ambassadors he was appointed in 1515 to the important and burdensome post of secretary to the Senate. Ramusio did not drop his literary interests, editing Quintilian and the third decade of Livy's history of Rome for the Aldine press, and maintaining his youthful friendship with Bembo. When he died he had been for some years secretary to the Council of Ten. JRH

A. del Piero *Della vita e degli scritti di Gio. Battista Ramusio* (1902)

Feed My Sheep, one of **Raphael**'s Sistine Chapel cartoons (London, Victoria and Albert Museum, Royal Collection).

Raphael (1483–1520) Perhaps the most influential and certainly the best-loved artist of the High Renaissance, Raffaello Sanzio was born in Urbino, the son of a mediocre painter, Giovanni Santi. In spite of many likeable myths created in the 19c. there are no known 'portraits' of the young Raphael, either in the work of Santi or in that of Raphael's teacher, Perugino. Very little in fact is known about Raphael until his arrival in Rome in the latter part of 1508. His earliest documented work is an altarpiece, commissioned in 1500, of which little is left. He must have joined Perugino's workshop after his father's death in 1494 and by 1502/3 was receiving large commissions from patrons in Città di Castello and Perugia. He was active in Florence between 1504 and 1508, and also maintained ties with Urbino and Perugia, an indication of his popularity and his mobility.

He appears to have arrived in Rome in the autumn of 1508, where he was employed by Julius II in the decoration of the papal apartments, starting with the Stanza della Segnatura (completed *c.*1511), and by Agostino Chigi in his villa in Trastevere. In these two places he met such artists as Sebastiano del Piombo, Bramante, Sodoma, Lotto, Peruzzi and of course Michelangelo, who disliked him intensely and accused him of stealing his ideas from the Sistine ceiling. Indeed, Raphael was deeply influenced by Michelangelo and his style developed in Rome from Florentine elegance to classical monumentality, with great articulation of the muscles and more interest in complex poses of the body – reflections of the Ignudi in the ceiling of the Sistine Chapel. This greater monumentality is reflected in his frescoes for the Stanza dell'Eliodoro (1511–14). Although the Sistine ceiling was not completed until 1512, the scaffolding was removed in August 1511 to celebrate the feast of the Assumption of the Virgin, and it is most probable that Raphael saw it at this time, rather than sneaking in with Bramante behind Michelangelo's back as Vasari claims.

After Julius's death in 1513, Raphael became the favourite artist of Leo X. He was engaged not only to continue the decoration of the Stanze but also to serve as architect of St Peter's after the death of Bramante (1514), and as Superintendent of Antiquities. The latter appointment is particularly interesting in so far as it reflects the growing concern about the destruction of the past as Rome was being rebuilt and expanded in the 16c. In addition to all this Raphael continued to work for Chigi, decorating his chapels in S. Maria della Pace and S. Maria del Popolo (both left unfinished at his death) and designing a fresco cycle with the story of Cupid and Psyche for his villa.

His last great commissions were the cartoons for the tapestries for the Sistine Chapel (London, H.M. The Queen; on loan to Victoria and Albert Museum) and the *Transfiguration* (Rome, Vatican) commissioned by Cardinal Giulio de' Medici, later Pope Clement VII. Raphael died quite suddenly on Good Friday 1520, with many of his commissions left incomplete. He had, in his last 7 years, accepted so much work that he was unable to finish many tasks, even with a large and able workshop. He appears to have designed much of what was put out under his name, but left a good deal of the execution to his assistants, a fact which has kept art historians occupied attributing works to various hands.

Raphael has left an indelible mark on art. He revolutionized portrait painting with his *Julius II* (1512; London, National Gallery) and epitomized the style which has come to be known as High Renaissance. He had the ability to absorb the achievements of others and turn them into something profoundly his own. He has suffered recently from a reaction against the 'sweetness' of his imagery, a concept which is in fact an invention of the 19c. Works such as the portrait of Castiglione (Paris, Louvre) or the massive figures in the tapestry cartoons reveal a command of form that is awe-inspiring and intellectually challenging. Perhaps Raphael's greatest achievement is that he appeals on all levels and makes something profoundly deep and complex appear simple and comprehensible. [35, 73, 180] LDE

L. Dussler *Raphael: a critical catalogue of his pictures, wall-paintings and tapestries* (1971); J. Pope-Hennessy *Raphael* (1970)

Recreations, games Physically competitive games were popular. The nobles had their hunts, jousts and tournaments, and running at the ring, or quintain, while ordinary townsmen had their mock-battles, like the *gioco del ponte* at Pisa and the *guerra dei pugni*, also fought over a bridge, between the Castellani and the Nicolotti of Venice. Somewhat less violent were ball games like *calcio* and *pallone*, which attracted crowds of spectators in Florence (Piazza S. Croce) and Venice (Campo S. Stefano). Tennis arrived in Italy from France in the late 16c. Races (of men, women, horses, buffaloes, gondolas, etc.) were also a common form of sport. The *palio* of Siena goes back to the 13c. Games of chance were also popular, though frequently condemned by the authorities in Church and state because they led to betting, brawling and blasphemy. Men also wagered on the results of mock-battles, the sex of unborn babies, the outcome of elections of popes and doges, and on games of cards, which were coming to replace dice among the upper classes in the 16c. Chess was played throughout the period, with something like the notion of the chess 'master' from the mid-15c. The conservatism of children's games is well known. In Renaissance Italy, children (and to a greater extent than later, adults) played hide-and-seek (*sconder il vesco*), blind man's buff (*Maria orba*) etc. But what we call 'parlour games' were a relatively new development in 16c. Italy, their formalization and standardization being encouraged by printed guides. Some were contests in verbal skill, others were concerned with telling fortunes, devising emblems or answering questions about courtly love. The conversations in Castiglione's *The courtier* were the result of a search for amusement in the after-dinner hours. PB

Recreation: a horse race in the streets of Florence on a 15c. painted panel (Cleveland, Museum of Art).

I. Ringhieri *Cento giochi liberali* (1551); W. Heywood *Palio and ponte* (1904)

Reformation Historians of European Protestantism commonly distinguish between 'magisterial' and 'radical' Reformations. The 'magisterial' Reformations were the ones which established state churches, assuming an identity between visible church and civil community. They accepted the Nicene Creed as canonical. By contrast, the so-called 'Anabaptists' or 'sectarians' asserted that the only true Church was one composed of people who had made a personal decision for Christ and lived regenerate lives; hence it was a 'Church apart', outside society. Baptism was the testimony of personal conversion and therefore only applicable to adults; hence the epithet 'Anabaptists' (re-baptizers) applied by contemporaries. Commonly they were pacifists and refused to hold civil office. The Spiritualists stressed the interior nature of personal conversion, contrasting the spirit with outward observance; they spurned ecclesiastical organization, including the strict church discipline of the Anabaptists; there were some ecumenical figures who remained enigmatically poised between Spiritualism and Catholicism or conservative Lutheranism. Indeed one derivation of Spiritualism was 'Nicodemism', the position that it was permissible to conform outwardly to the practice of the Catholic Church or other 'unreformed' churches. The Anti-Trinitarians or Unitarians rejected the Nicene doctrine of the Trinity as irrelevant to the Christian life and denied full divinity to Christ. Anabaptists, Spiritualists and Anti-Trinitarians generally regarded Christ's mission as having been to reveal a way of life; they were largely indifferent to the doctrine of justification by imputation and through faith that was central to the theologies of the great magisterial reformers.

With regard to Italian religious dissent, it is helpful to follow the terminology of Delio Cantimori, who used the term *eresia* to cover radical strains, reserving the term *Riforma* (Reformation) for currents which can be aligned with the general theological positions of the great magisterial doctors such as Luther, Melanchthon, Bucer, Zwingli and Calvin. It should be noted, however, that the epithets *Luterani* and *Ugonotti* were terms of abuse which did not indicate any precise theological positions. Further, there were scarcely any organized Protestant churches apart from the Anabaptist networks and the ancient Waldensian communities. There were especially important movements of *La Riforma* in Lucca, Modena, Bologna and Vicenza around the 1540s. Distinguished Italian exiles who were accepted among the ranks of the transalpine magisterial theologians were Vermigli, Pietro Paolo Vergerio the Younger (1497–1565), Girolamo Zanchi (1516–90) and Ochino. The outstanding literary product of *La Riforma* was the *Beneficio di Giesù Cristo crocefisso verso i cristiani* (*The generosity of Christ crucified*), first published in Venice in 1543; it was composed by a Benedictine, Dom Benedetto da Mantova (evidently B. Fontanini), and revised stylistically by Marcantonio Flaminio. This book was rooted in the theological traditions of the Cassinese Benedictines, which were based heavily on St Augustine and St Bernard. Another influence was the Spaniard Juan de Valdes (d.1541), who founded a circle in Naples in the 1530s. Dom Benedetto's contribution was to have fused Valdesian spirituality with a profound knowledge of Scripture enriched by readings of northern Protestant theologians. The frontiers between *La Riforma* and Catholic orthodoxy were ill-defined before the Council of Trent and the *Beneficio* was warmly received by 'Catholic Evangelicals' (*See* EVANGELISM).

Reformation: title page of a Papal bull *Contra errores Martini Lutheri*, issued in Rome in 1521.

The interest of Italian religious dissent lies especially in the *eretici*. The main pioneers of Unitarianism were Italians, notably Lelio Sozzini (1525–62) and his cousin Fausto (1539–1604), who was the major theological formulator (hence the term 'Socinianism' commonly applied to early Unitarianism); it was Italians who founded the great Unitarian centres in Poland. Anabaptism was a popular movement which initially spilled over from the Tyrol into the Veneto. Italian Anabaptism was broadly similar in character to the mainstream transalpine varieties but in time showed a more marked tendency towards Anti-Trinitarianism. This may have attracted many adherents of Jewish descent.

The choice between dissimulation and exile imposed itself as repression mounted from the 1540s, while Calvin called upon believers to come out of Babylon, attacking Nicodemists. Nicodemism was a significant Italian phenomenon after 1550. It was not necessarily an affair of opportunism; it could be a reasoned position, being as such first disseminated from Strasbourg and being taken up especially by Spiritualists and Anti-Trinitarians including Giorgio Rioli alias Siculo, Camillo Renato,

Lelio Sozzini and some followers of Valdes. Major Italian exile communities developed at Geneva, Zurich and Chiavenna. However, the burning of the Spanish Anti-Trinitarian Servetus at Geneva in 1553 caused a crisis among Italian religious dissenters over the issue of emigration and strengthened the case for dissimulation. *See* HERESY. OL

D. Cantimori 'Italy and the Papacy' in *The new Cambridge modern history* II (1958); —*Prospettive di storia ereticale italiana del Cinquecento* (1960); A. Olivieri *La Riforma in Italia: strutture e simboli, classi e poteri* (1979); Paolo Simoncelli *Evangelismo italiano del Cinquecento* (1979)

Religious orders and congregations An order is a body of men or women bound by solemn vows and following a rule of life, e.g. the great orders of monks, hermits, canons regular, friars and nuns, or the Jesuits. A congregation may be either a subsection of an order, or a body of persons bound by simple vows and generally having a looser structure than an order. Among the old orders there was both fusion and fission. Among the contemplative orders, originally autonomous houses tended to group themselves into congregations, presided over by chapters general. A major stimulus to such reform movements was concern for mutual defence against the abuse of commendams, i.e. the grant of abbacies 'in trust' to non-resident outsiders to the order. At the same time, there was dissidence and fractionalization in almost all of the old orders and congregations, the great issue of contention being the strict observance.

The Benedictines, who had no overall organization originally, were mostly grouped into congregations by the 16c. The Silvestrines, Celestines and Olivetines were old congregations. That of S. Giustina, Padua, which was to become the main Italian one, developed from 1419 under the leadership of the Venetian Lodovico Barbo. He was particularly concerned to develop sacred studies and eventually there were certain designated houses of study for the entire congregation, the most notable being S. Benedetto, Mantua. In 1504, having absorbed St Benedict's original monastery, it became the Cassinese congregation. The Camaldolese were an offshoot of the Benedictines. Founded by St Romuald *c.*1012, they followed a distinctive eremetical rule of life, rather on the model of Eastern monasticism, with hermitages linked to matrix

Saintly members of various **religious orders** depicted in Fra Angelico's fresco *The Coronation of the Virgin* in the convent of S. Marco, Florence.

monasteries. In the second decade of the 16c. Paolo Giustiniani led a movement for a revival of the strict eremetical ideal; hence the formation of the Monte Corona congregation.

Canons Regular of St Augustine follow a rule and are basically monks; they are to be distinguished from secular canons who serve cathedral and collegiate churches. Two major congregations arose from reform movements in the 15c.: that of S. Salvatore, Bologna (1419), and the Lateran one (1446) which grew from S. Maria di Fregonaia, Lucca. A body genuinely monastic and contemplative in spirit, although technically of secular canons, was the congregation of S. Giorgio in Alga, Venice (1404), whose foundation is especially associated with Gabriel Condulmer (later Eugenius IV) and S. Lorenzo Giustiniani, the great patriarch of Venice. The Hermits of St Augustine and the Carmelites were originally contemplative eremetical orders which turned to the active life of friars. The Hermits of St Jerome (Hieronymites or Gerolimini) appeared from the 15c. and included the Fiesole and Lombard congregations and that of Pietro Gambacorta of Pisa.

The Friars Minor (Franciscans) had been split after their founder's death by disputes between the Spirituals, with their ideology of an absolute apostolic poverty, and their more institutionalized brethren, the Conventuals. After the repression of the Spirituals, the great dispute in the order was primarily a legalistic one: the division was between the Conventuals, whose friaries were corporate property-owners, and the generally moderate Observants, whose friaries were technically non-property owning, their resources being in the hands of trustees. 'The Observance' did not necessarily designate a very straitened rule of life but in the 15c. a strict movement of the Observance developed whose leading figures were S. Bernardino of Siena, S. Giovanni da Capestrano and Giacomo della Marca. In 1517, the bull 'Ite vos' of Leo X instituted the Great Division between Friars Minor (Conventual) and Friars Minor of the Observance; various groups were fused in the latter body, which was given precedence over the Conventuals. The Conventuals, however, continued to hold the order's great basilicas. The same bull provided for special friaries within the Observance for those dedicated to a very strict interpretation of the Rule. Failure to implement this clause caused a splinter movement of zealot groups which finally coalesced into the Capuchins and the Reformed (canonically recognized in 1528 and 1532 respectively). The Order of Preachers (Dominicans) underwent similar if less serious crises over the issue of poverty and a body of the strict observance was established in the late 14c.; however, the Dominicans were substantially reunited under the generalate of the great Tommaso di Vio da Gaeta (1508–18). Other orders of Friars were the Minims, founded by S. Francesco da Paola in 1454 on the primitive Franciscan model, and the Servites, following the Augustinian rule.

The 16c. produced the Jesuits (founded in 1541) and several rather small congregations of clerks regular, who had many of the marks of secular clergy but who lived a common life. Generally they were devoted to pastoral and welfare work. The first, the Theatines, founded by Giampietro Caraffa (later Paul IV) and the Vicentine aristocrat S. Gaetano da Thiene, emerged from the Roman Oratory of Divine Love in 1524 (*See* CONFRATERNITIES). The Somaschi were founded at Somasca near Bergamo in 1532 by S. Gerolamo Aemiliani, a Venetian noble castellan turned evangelist; this congregation specialized in the upbringing of orphan boys. The Barnabites were founded at Milan by S. Antonio Maria Zaccaria in 1533, while the Congregation of the Oratory was founded in Rome in the 1560s by S. Filippo Neri. One of the few significant innovations among the female orders were the Ursulines, an offshoot of the Brescian Confraternity of Divine Love, founded in 1535 by S. Angela Merici. S. Angela's intention was that they should be a congregation of unenclosed women dedicated to the active life in charitable and educational work; however, the ecclesiastical authorities forced the Ursulines into the mould of an enclosed contemplative order. While the friars basically remained attached to scholastic philosophy and theology, certain sections of contemplative orders were distinguished for humanist studies and related forms of religious scholarship, most notably the Cassinese Benedictine congregation, the Lateran Canons (especially of the Badia Fiesolana) and the Camaldolese, who included Ambrogio Traversari in Florence and a group of scholars at S. Michele in Isola, Venice. OL

H. O. Evennett 'The new orders' *New Cambridge modern history* II (1958); D. Hay *The Italian church in the fifteenth century* (1977)

Renaissance A French label given to an Italian cultural movement and to its repercussions elsewhere; also, on the assumption (cf. Baroque and Enlightenment) that chronological slices of human mass experience can usefully be described in terms of a dominant intellectual and creative manner, a historical period. For Italy the period is popularly accepted as running from the second generation of the 14c. to the second or third generation of the 16c. Though there is something inherently ridiculous about describing a period of 250 years as one of rebirth, there is some justification for seeing a unity within it, if only in terms of the chronological self-awareness of contemporaries.

For Petrarch the challenge to understand and celebrate the achievements of ancient Rome led him to scorn the intervening centuries which had neglected them; he saw them as an age of intellectual sleep, of 'darkness', and his own as potentially one of light, of an energetic revival of interest in, and competition with, too long forgotten glories. Thanks to his fame not only as a scholar but also as a poet and a voluminous correspondent, this sense of living in an age of new possibilities was rapidly shared by others who worked within the intellectual framework which came to be known as HUMANISM. Perhaps the sense of living in a new mental atmosphere can be compared to the exhilaration that followed the realization that Marxist analysis could be used to look afresh at the significance of intellectual and creative, as well as political, life. The humanistic enthusiasm lasted so long, however, because its core of energy, the historical reality of antiquity, was so vast and potent, because it was uncontroversial (save when an assassin borrowed the aura of Brutus, or a paganizing faddist mocked Christianity), and because the scholarly excitement about the need to imitate the achievements of the Roman (and, increasingly, Greek) past was sustained by evidence from contemporary art and literature that it could be done. Even when the Wars of Italy had inflicted grievous humiliations on Italian pride, Vasari could still see a process of restored vigour in the arts, which had begun early in the 14c., as only coming near its close with the death of Michelangelo in 1564.

Vasari's *Lives* became a textbook of European repute. It was his contention that he was describing what followed from the *rinascita* or rebirth of the arts that launched the word on its increasingly inclusive career. For long, however, it was a 'renaissance' of this or that, of arts, of scholarship, of letters. Not until the publication in 1855 of the volume in Jules Michelet's *Histoire de France* entitled 'La Renaissance' was the label attached to a period and all that happened in it; not until the appearance of Jacob Burckhardt's still seminal *Civilization of the Renaissance in Italy* in 1860 was it ineluctably identified in particular with Italy and more generally with a phase of human development thought to be markedly different in kind from what went before and what came after.

Thereafter, 'Renaissance' became a mercurial term: not just a label for a period or a movement but a *concept*, a concept redolent (in spite of Burckhardt's precautions) of Individualism, All-Roundness, even Amoralism; man had escaped from the medieval thought-dungeon, and the world (and its expanding physical and mental horizons) was his oyster; culture was linked to personality and behaviour; the Renaissance became both the scene and the work of Renaissance Man. To a northern European world (whence the alertest scholars and popularizers came), morally confined by Protestantism and social decorum, 'Renaissance' became a symbol of ways of conduct and thought that were either to be castigated (John Ruskin, whose *The stones of Venice* of 1851–53 had anticipated the art-morality connection) or envied (John Addington Symonds's avidly nostalgic *Renaissance in Italy*, 1875–86).

A term that had become so liable to subjective interpretation was bound to attract criticism. During this century it has been challenged chiefly on the following points. (1) There is no such thing as a self-sufficient historical period. Much that was characteristic of the Middle Ages flowed into and through the Renaissance. Much that was characteristic of the Renaissance flowed on until the age of experimental science, of industrialization, mobilized nationalism, and mass media. (2) Renaissance art and literature did not develop so consistently that they can be seen in one broad Vasarian sweep. There was an early, a 'high' and a late stage (all variously dated) in terms of artistic and literary aims and style. (3) There is not a true, let alone a uniform, congruence between 'culture' and 'history' during the period; 'Renaissance' culture came late to Venice, later still to Genoa, both thriving centres of political and commercial activity. (4) To define a period in terms of a cultural élite is to divert attention unacceptably from the fortunes of the population as a whole.

Though thus challenged, mocked (the 'so-called Renaissance'), aped (the 'Carolingian' or 'Ottonian' renaissance, etc.) and genially debased ('the renaissance of the mini-skirt'), the term retains most of its glamour and much of its usefulness. It is surely not by chance that 'rebirth' rather than the 18c. and early 19c. 'revival' (of arts, letters, etc.) was the term chosen, because it applies to a society the resonance of a personal, spiritual and perhaps psychological aspiration: the new start, the previous record – with all its shabbiness – erased. It is for this additional, subjective reason a term to be used with caution. The challenges are to be accepted, however, gratefully, as having led to an enormous extension of knowledge and sensitivity. JRH

W. K. Ferguson *The Renaissance in historical thought* (1948); F. Chabod 'The concept of the Renaissance' *Machiavelli and the Renaissance* tr. D. Moore (1958); E. Panofsky *Renaissance and renascences in western art* (1960); D. Hay *et al. Il Rinascimento: interpretazioni e problemi* (1979)

René of Anjou (1409–1480) Duke of Anjou, Lorraine and Bar, Count of Provence, René inherited the Angevin claim to the Neapolitan crown on the death of his brother Louis III in

1434. From the death of Giovanna II of Naples, who had designated him as her successor, he was the captive (1431–36) of Philip the Good, Duke of Burgundy. His wife, Isabelle of Lorraine, conducted a fleet to Naples, where she defeated his rival to the throne, Alfonso V of Aragon, in the battle of Ponza (5 August 1435). But neither this success, nor his own appearance in the kingdom in 1438, could avail against Alfonso's diplomacy and he was forced to withdraw to France (1442). Other attempts to gain the kingdom, made by him personally (1433–34) or by his son John (1458–64), like his hopes for the crown of Aragon (offered by the Catalan revolutionaries in 1466), all ended in failure. His reputation as 'the good King René' must rest rather on his patronage of the arts and his own writings in French prose and verse than on his harsh rule over his French possessions. JL

Rhetoric, the studied art of using language to pleasing and persuasive effect, predated HUMANISM, but was then considered afresh, especially in terms of the genuine Ciceronian *On the orator* and the spurious Ciceronian *Rhetorica ad Herrenium*, and became both an incentive to the further study of ancient texts and the essential guide as to how the results of such study should be expressed.

In medieval Italy rhetoric was divided into the *ars dictaminis* and the *ars notaria*. The proponents of the former skill, the writing of correspondence, were professional letter-writers or, increasingly, chancery officials. The second term expressed the ability of the notary to draft legal documents, business and marriage contracts and the like, and became increasingly connected with the construction of legal arguments and forensic oratory. Humanist rhetoric from Petrarch onwards, by turning to classical orations and treatises on public speaking, fused the two into the art of stylish and effective argument, whether written or spoken. The study of rhetoric came to involve a consideration of what over-all level of style was best suited to a particular theme or audience; lengths of sentences and paragraphs and the balance and development within them of a component part of the argument; the manipulation of these parts into sections and the organization of these – as, in a simple and familiar example: introduction or exordium; the speaker's case; his arguments in favour of it; his opponent's case; his destruction of it; the summing up or peroration.

Rhetoric served the orator's desire to win approval, whether he were a lawyer in court or a politician in council or an academic speaking at the opening of a university term; rhetorical training helped him get his tone right, construct his speech and remember it. But as CICERO and QUINTILIAN taught that nothing should be argued until it was thoroughly known about, and that no sentiments could be effectively expressed unless they had been felt, their perfect orators were also perfect men, widely educated, refined in their sentiments. The rhetorical bias of humanist education thus led to the ideal of the philosopher man of affairs of multi-faceted talents. Rhetoric also sustained the writer's vision of his purpose. Though not necessarily couched in the form of an argument, his theme could, none the less, be fitted into some perfect, classically derived formulation, whether it were a history, a biography, a eulogy of an individual or a description of a city: all had fitting beginnings, middles and ends, in language to delight and impress.

Rhetoric, indeed, was a main motive for the humanist's interest in works of ancient literature: how their effects had been gained, what could be learned from them as to the use of the telling word, phrase or stylistic pitch. Not unnaturally, rhetoric also led to considerations as to whether eclecticism was better than the adoption of one man (usually Cicero) as a model; and this in turn affected discussions about the best form of Italian for a writer to use. The rhetorical dye spread, too, into the fabric of philosophical discourse; the ideal orator had to be a philosopher, and thus the philosopher had to be aware of the *ars oratoria*, or rhetoric.

Of course, in the wrong hands, the devotion to style could produce flatulence; the imitation of models, dull sycophancy; the copying of forms of argument, a niggling pedantry or a cause of confusion in the reader's mind as to which side the writer was really on. These are the qualities which have given 'rhetoric' a pejorative flavour today. Machiavelli might appear to anticipate this flavour when, in the dedication to *The prince*, he claims that what he has to offer is a plain style, not the 'long phrases or high-sounding words or any of those superficial attractions and ornaments with which many writers seek to embellish their material.' But what he was doing was implying that with severely practical matter to urge, he was correctly adopting the rhetorical level familiar as the *genus humile*, or unornamented style; in fact that he was thoroughly conscious of the rhetorical tradition within which he had learned to argue so memorably and write so well. JRH

J. E. Seigel *Rhetoric and philosophy in Renaissance humanism* (1968); H. H. Gray 'Renaissance humanism: the pursuit of eloquence' *Journal of the History of Ideas* (1963); 'Humanism and scholasticism in the Italian Renaissance' in P. O. Kristeller *Studies in Renaissance thought and letters* (1956)

Riario family In one of the rags-to-riches stories of the Renaissance the Riario became signori of Imola and Forlì solely as a consequence of papal NEPOTISM and the marriage of Paolo Riario of Savona to Bianca, sister of Sixtus IV. Sixtus was particularly fond of her 2 sons Pietro and Girolamo. Pietro (1445–74) followed his uncle into the Franciscan order and was created cardinal. He accumulated benefices on a scale remarkable even for a papal nephew, and lived a luxurious and immoral life. He was, however, a generous patron of the arts and scholarship.

After Pietro's death, Girolamo became the Pope's closest adviser and was the prime mover of the PAZZI conspiracy. In order to provide for Girolamo, Sixtus repurchased Imola from Giangaleazzo Maria Sforza of Milan in 1473, and married Girolamo to the Duke's illegitimate daughter Caterina. In 1480 the couple were also invested with Forlì. The rule of Riario cannot be accounted a success, and he proved incapable of coping either with the hostility of his own leading citizens or with the enmity of Lorenzo de' Medici. It was probably with the knowledge, if not the complicity, of Lorenzo that Girolamo was assassinated on 14 April 1488. Caterina did not panic during this crisis. She seized the fortress of Forlì, recovered the city, and governed it and Imola on behalf of her son, Ottaviano, until they were captured by Cesare Borgia in 1499–1500.

The third of Sixtus IV's nephews, Raffaello (1461–1521), was the son of Valentina Riario and Antonio Sansoni. He also was a notorious pluralist, and was created cardinal in 1477. In 1478 he nearly perished in the reaction against the Pazzi conspirators in Florence. In 1517 he was implicated in the Petrucci conspiracy against Leo X, but was pardoned after paying a heavy indemnity. The Riario family subsequently became one of the leading families of Bologna. JH

Riccio's bronze *Shouting Horseman* (London, Victoria and Albert Museum).

Ricci, Matteo (1552–1610) Jesuit missionary. He was born in Ancona and worked in China from 1582 until his death. He found ready acceptance among the mandarinate, who were impressed by the Western clocks, optical devices and cosmographical instruments which he displayed. He wrote apologetic works and mathematical treatises in Chinese. He defended the case for Chinese converts practising Confucian rites, on the grounds that these were civil not religious in character. OL

V. Cronin *The wise man from the west* (1955)

Riccio, Andrea Briosco, il (*c.*1460–1532) was a Paduan High Renaissance sculptor famed for his bronze statuettes. A pupil of Bartolomeo Bellano, who had worked for Donatello in Padua and Florence, Riccio absorbed Florentine style and amalgamated it with a vogue for statuettes in the classical manner among the humanists of the university of Padua. His training as a goldsmith led to a concentration on minute detail and subtle surface treatment, while his experience with terracotta sculpture at life size gave a monumentality to his miniature creations. His masterpiece was a Paschal Candelabrum for S. Antonio, Padua (1506–15), round which may be grouped a number of independent statuettes, most interesting of which is the *Shouting Horseman* in the Victoria and Albert Museum, London. CA

J. Pope-Hennessy *Italian Renaissance sculpture* (1958); A. F. Radcliffe 'Bronze oil lamps by Riccio' *Victoria and Albert Museum yearbook* (1972)

Rienzo *see* COLA DI RIENZO

Rimini A minor port on the Adriatic coast which had had great importance in antiquity on account of its position on the Roman road system (the Arch of Augustus, Bridge of Tiberius and Theatre remain). Though a papal possession, from the later 13c. it became the power base of the Malatesta family, who by 1334 had taken over most civic powers and regained for Rimini some political importance. The castle and so-called Temple (an unfinished reconstruction of the church of S. Francesco) for Sigismondo Malatesta are the chief remaining monuments of Malatesta rule. After a period under Cesare Borgia (1500–03), Rimini passed to Venice (1503–09); it was directly governed by the Papacy from 1527. DC

Robert of Anjou, King of Naples 1309–43 (b.1278) Dismissed as 'a miserable poltroon' by Pope John XXII, as 'the preacher king' by Dante, Robert I was also hailed by many as 'Robert the Wise'. His over-ambitious foreign policy as leader of the Italian GUELF party was accompanied by a continual struggle to maintain order within his kingdom. He gave patronage to artists (Simone Martini, Giotto, Tino di Camaino) and to early humanists (Petrarch, Dionigi di San Sepolcro). JL
R. Caggese *Roberto d'Angio e i suoi tempi* (1921–30)

Roberti, Ercole de' (active *c.*1475, d.1496) was court painter to the Este in Ferrara from 1486. Intimately related to Cossa and Tura and strongly affected by Giovanni Bellini, he achieves in his few surviving works a gaunt, mystical quality that is intensely moving. JW
M. Salmi *Ercole de' Roberti* (1960)

Romanino, Girolamo (1484/7–1559/61) presents a paradigm of the development of Brescian art during the first half of the 16c. By 1510, when he painted the *Pietà* in the Accademia, Venice, Romanino's art was already striking a balance between Lombard tradition and distinctly modern Venetian developments, which gradually came to be identified more and more with the art of Titian. In the decades following his association with the ambitious project for the redecoration of the Cremonese cathedral (1519–20), Romanino continued to vacillate between Venetian and provincial stylistic exemplars (notably Titian, Moretto and Pordenone). As in the *Coronation of the Virgin* (*c.*1535; Brescia, Pinacoteca), his art remained an ambivalent, if often forceful, provincial appropriation of early Cinquecento Venetian classicism. LP
M. Ferrari *Il Romanino* (1961); —, G. Panazza *et al. Mostra di Girolamo Romanino* (1965)

Rome Though part of the Papal State, Rome had a municipal government of its own. Its feebleness vis-à-vis the great baronial families of the surrounding countryside was revealed in the lawlessness that forced the PAPACY to establish its working headquarters elsewhere for so much of the 14c. and early 15c., and in the poverty that followed from the commune's inability to control the roads leading to the city and thus regulate its fortunes as a trading centre. For a few weeks in 1347 Roman self-government had a moment of fanfare and glory with COLA DI RIENZO, only to relapse into ineffectiveness. With the smallest merchant and professional class of any city of its size (the population was about 25,000 in 1400), without industry, international commerce or native bankers, Rome was a local market town, a livestock centre, and a slovenly host to pilgrims. In spite of the resentment it felt towards the Papacy's claim to dispose of the greater part of its revenues and the whole of its political relations with other states, Rome as a city only flourished as a parasite on the Papacy, and its fortunes only revived when, after the long interval of AVIGNON and the partially itinerant pontificates that followed, continuous papal residence in Rome became assured with the reign of Nicholas V (1447–55).

It is true that under Martin V (1417–31) a start had been made on the process that was to make Rome's fabric the rival of those of Milan, Florence and Venice. Disturbed as his pontificate was, he began repair work on St Peter's and the Vatican, restored churches and summoned artists: Masolino, Gentile da Fabriano and Masaccio (who died in Rome *c.*1428). Eugenius IV in his last years (1443–47) invited artists and sculptors. But it was with Nicholas that a firm intention to improve and embellish the streets and piazze of the city, and to rationalize their plan, was shown. The process was slow; it was, indeed, still in progress at the end of the 16c. It was sustained by individual popes, by cardinals encouraged to live magnificently by property tax concessions, and by the feeling of permanence that Rome acquired as

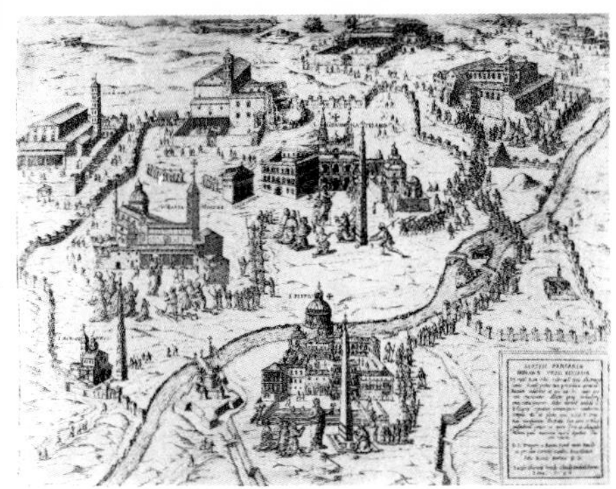

The seven chief pilgrimage churches of **Rome** in an engraving of 1590.

the papal base; partly too by the compatriots of successive popes who helped build up the population and create at last a sizeable educated and prosperous middle class.

The accusation made by Valla in 1440, that papal claims to any temporal power were based on a forged document (the Donation of Constantine), came too late to persuade Rome's civic administration to oppose an authority they so much needed on their own behalf. It was not until the 1530s, however, that, with Paul III's support and to Michelangelo's design, their seat of government, the Capitol, began to be magnificently transformed into the piazza complex of the Campidoglio.

As for the ruins of ancient Rome, though studied and surveyed, and by scholars and artists admired, they were progressively cannibalized to provide stone, marble and lime for the new Rome whose architecture owed so much to their inspiration. JRH

E. Dupré Theseider *Roma dal comune di popolo alla signoria pontificia (1252–1377)* (1952); P. Partner *Renaissance Rome* (1976); P. Pecchiai *Roma nel Cinquecento* (1948); J. Delumeau *Vie économique et sociale de Rome dans la seconde moitié du XVIe siècle* (1957–9)

Rore, Ciprien de (*c.*1516–65) Netherlands composer who studied with Willaert in Venice in the 1540s. He spent 12 years at the Este court in Ferrara from 1547, losing his job on the duke's death while Rore was in Flanders, visiting his parents. He returned to Italy after a few years abroad in the service of Margherita of Parma, Governor of the Netherlands. In 1563 he succeeded Willaert as *maestro di cappella* at St Mark's, but did not enjoy the administration the post involved and moved to Parma, where he died. A formidable composer of church music, he was one of the greatest madrigalists, showing a flair for the detailed expression of words. He was also interested (as were many Ferrarese composers) in the recreation of ancient Greek techniques, including chromaticism. DA

A. Einstein *The Italian madrigal* (1949)

Rossellino, Bernardo (1409–64) **and Antonio** (1427–79) were brothers whose marble sculpture, together with that of their close associate Desiderio da Settignano, formed the backbone of the 'sweet style' which dominated the middle years of the Quattrocento in Florence. After his masterpiece, Bruni's (d.1444) tomb in S. Croce, Bernardo devoted himself increasingly to architecture, supervising the erection (1446–51) of the Rucellai Palace in Florence, designed by Alberti, serving as papal architect in Rome (1451–53), building the new town of PIENZA in southern Tuscany for Pope Pius II, and finally being appointed architect of Florence cathedral.

Antonio's first signed work is a distinguished portrait bust of Donatello's doctor Giovanni Chellini (1456) in the Victoria and Albert Museum. Antonio collaborated with Bernardo on a number of projects, e.g. the Chapel of the Cardinal of Portugal, S. Miniato al Monte, Florence (1459–66), for which Luca della Robbia made the ceiling and the Pollaiuolo brothers painted the altarpiece. Antonio specialized in charming reliefs of the Virgin and Child and trained Benedetto da Maiano. [61] CA

A. M. Schulz *The sculpture of Bernardo Rossellino and his workshop* (1977)

Rossetti, Biagio (1447–1516) Ferrarese architect to whom Ercole I gave a unique opportunity to lay out the walls, streets and piazza of a huge extension to Ferrara, and to design a wide range of palaces and churches in both old and new city. Rossetti's churches display an interesting variety of plan and vaulting types, sparely articulated with terracotta ornament. His palaces, like the Palazzo dei Diamanti (1493f.) with its faceted rustication, are more richly decorated, while his own house is a dignified version of the local vernacular. CE

B. Zevi *Biagio Rossetti* (Ferrara 1960)

The palace façade designed by Alberti for the **Rucellai** family in Florence.

Rosso Fiorentino, Giovanni Battista di Jacopo, il (1495–1540) was a key figure in the development of Florentine Mannerism. Unusual viewpoints and close cropping by the frame, as in his *Moses and Jethro's Daughters*, the tension between form and content, the distortion of the figures and bold colour contrasts give his finest work, such as his *Deposition* in Volterra (1521), great emotional force. After periods in Florence (1513–23), Rome (1423–27) and elsewhere in Italy, he went to France and worked for Francis I at Fontainebleau. There, together with Primaticcio, he founded the style of the same name which so dramatically affected the course of French 16c. art. JW
P. Barocchi *Il Rosso Fiorentino* (1950)

Rucellai family While prominent in communal government and wealthy as cloth manufacturers from the late 13c., the Rucellai did not play a part of real importance in Florentine politics, preferring, especially in the 15c., to devote increasing time to study and the cultivated pleasures of private life. Giovanni (1403–81) built the Rucellai Palace from 1446. This was from a design by Alberti, as was another of Giovanni's commissions, the marble façade of S. Maria Novella. He was also a more perceptive patron of artists than either Cosimo or Lorenzo de' Medici. His *Zibaldone* (commonplace book) gives valuable insight into the reading and manner of life of the lettered merchants of the Quattrocento.

His son Bernardo (1448–1514), a trusted supporter of Lorenzo the Magnificent, wrote a history of Charles VIII's invasion of 1494–95, *De bello italico*, which makes precocious use of the term 'balance of power', and his grandson Giovanni (1475–1525), who entered the Church, has some reputation as a literary pioneer; he wrote free imitations of classical poems in the vernacular and one of the earliest classicizing tragedies, *Rosamunda*. It was Bernardo who laid out the gardens off the Via della Scala which became known as the Orti Oricellari (Rucellai Gardens). After his death his grandson Cosimo acted as host to discussions held there on philosophical, literary and political topics. Machiavelli took part in these and his *Discourses* were dedicated to Cosimo and to another habitué of the Orti, Zanobi Buondelmonti. Machiavelli set his dialogues in *The art of war* there, with Cosimo as one of the protagonists. JRH
Zibaldone ed. A. Perosa (1960); Felix Gilbert 'Bernardo Rucellai and the Orti Oricellari' *Journal of the Warburg and Courtauld Institutes* (1949)

Ruzante, il *See* BEOLCO, ANGELO

Sacchetti, Franco (*c.*1333–1400) Florentine bourgeois writer best known for his incomplete *Trecentonovelle* (*300 tales*); but author also of lyric poems, a short burlesque epic, and substantial vernacular commentaries on the Gospels. His novellas are both moralizing and rumbustious (but rarely bawdy), and written in a relaxed provincial language which mimics conversational and preaching styles rather than aspiring to Boccaccio's literary artistry. Modern readers can find some of them unpleasant, but they evoke contemporary scenes and attitudes very vividly. Since only one tattered manuscript survived into the 16c., it is hard to say if they were widely read. RA
Trecentonovelle ed. E. Faccioli (1970); L. Caretti *Saggio sul Sacchetti* (1951)

Sack of Rome Climax of the papal-Imperial struggle and a turning point in the history of Italy, the Sack of Rome resulted from Clement VII's adhesion to the League of COGNAC (1526). Imperial troops under the Duke of Bourbon left Milan and joined an army of mainly Lutheran *landsknechts* (January 1527). The Duke of Bourbon marched on Rome, hoping to force Clement to abandon the League and to provide money for the pay of the Imperial army. A truce made by the Pope and LANNOY failed to halt this advance, and Rome was attacked and taken on 6 May, the Duke of Bourbon being killed at the first assault. Clement escaped into Castel S. Angelo but for a week Rome itself was subjected to a sacking of a peculiarly brutal nature. Although the army was then brought back under some kind of control, it continued to occupy Rome until February 1528, when it finally left the city it had devastated, gutted, and impoverished. JH

J. Hook *The Sack of Rome* (1972); M. Lenzi *Il Sacco di Roma* (1978)

Sacra rappresentazione A dramatic form that flourished particularly in Quattrocento Tuscany, supported by lay confraternities. Written primarily in *ottava rima*, the *sacra rappresentazione* was staged in an open space with *luoghi deputati*, multiple sets used in succession. Subjects were nominally sacred, from the Old and New Testaments, pious legend and hagiography, but the injection of realistic vignette and detail from contemporary local life or of romantic elaboration was considerable. There were no limits on time; a single *rappresentazione* or *festa* could begin with the Creation and end with the Final Judgment, and available techniques of elaborate scenery made such subjects desirable. Many compositions were anonymous, but others were the work of well-known figures, among them Feo Belcari (1410–84), author of *La rappresentazione di Abram ed Isac* (1449), and Lorenzo de' Medici, whose *Rappresentazione dei SS. Giovanni e Paolo* (1491) was performed by the children of the Compagnia del Vangelista. The *rappresentazioni* were often printed in the Cinquecento and continued to be performed on municipal occasions, but eventually they became fare only for monasteries and convents. LGC

Sacre rappresentazioni del Quattrocento ed. L. Banfi (1963)

Sadoleto, Cardinal Jacopo (1477–1547) Humanist and churchman, one of the outstanding Latin stylists of his age. Born into the bureaucratic bourgeoisie of Ferrara, he sought a career in Rome, becoming secretary to Leo X and Clement VII. When Rome was under military threat in 1527 he moved to take up residence in his diocese of Carpentras, in the papal territory of the Venaissin. Here he was much frustrated by the civil authorities who represented the Papacy. He was a member of the papal commission of 1536–37 which produced the *Consilium de emendanda Ecclesia* (*Advice on Church reform*); its attack on papal absolutism must have reflected his views in particular. He was a religious moderate, sympathetic to Erasmus; while he was linked to leading Evangelicals, he was far removed from their crypto-Protestant position on grace and justification. His best-known writings are his treatise on the education of boys (*De pueris recte instituendis*, 1533) and his letter to the Genevans of 1539, an appeal for Christian unity. OL

R. M. Douglas *Jacopo Sadoleto (1477–1547) humanist and reformer* (1959)

Salt War, the Exasperated by the overriding of their privileges by papal governors, and hit by the rise in price of provisions after 2 disastrous harvests, the Perugians seized on Pope Paul III's order of 1540, that the price of salt should be increased, as an excuse to revolt. They were still seeking aid, notably from Florence and in Germany, when a papal army forced the city to surrender and swear allegiance to the legate sent to govern it. The chief focus of discontent, the area containing the houses of the old ruling family, the Bentivoglio, was buried under a new fortress, the Rocca Paolina, designed by Antonio da Sangallo the Younger. JRH

Salutati, Coluccio (1331–1406) was a humanist who established the close association between classicism and the office of Chancellor of Florence. Before gaining this position, which he held 1375–1406, he had been trained as a notary and had been Chancellor of Lucca. But he was also a devoted latinist and friend of Petrarch, whose poem *Africa* he hoped to finish. In command of diplomatic correspondence during the War of the EIGHT SAINTS (1375–78), he won renown as a powerful letter-writer. This skill was to be important again in the Florentine wars against Giangaleazzo Visconti, who is reported to have said that a letter of Salutati's was worth a troop of horse. He cultivated a Stoic gravity in private life and became a highly respected figure in Florentine society. He composed several pedantic humanist treatises: *De secolo et religione* (*On the world and the religious life*; 1381), about the arguments for the monastic life; *De fato et fortuna* (*On destiny and fortune*; c.1396), about free will; and *De laboribus Herculis* (*On the labours of Hercules*; c.1391), a long discussion of the allegorical meanings of classical legends. His main literary importance, however, was as an inspirer of other men. Throughout his Florentine career he was the centre of humanist enthusiasm and did more than anyone, except possibly Chrysoloras, whose visit he sponsored, to create the glittering humanist school of the early 15c.

Salutati's position in the history of political thought is ambiguous. His letters were powerful assertions of Florentine 'liberty' against outside enemies, but in *De tyranno* (*On tyranny*; 1400) he defended monarchy. The invention of an original republican political thought during the last duel with Giangaleazzo perhaps took place under the inspiration of his literary and political leadership, but is the work of his pupil Bruni. GH

B. L. Ullmann *The humanism of Coluccio Salutati* (1963); R. G. Witt *Coluccio Salutati and his public letters* (1976)

Salviati, Francesco (1510–63) Florentine painter and portraitist and friend of Vasari. In his frescoes in the Palazzo Sacchetti, Rome, and the Palazzo Vecchio, Florence, he epitomizes the developed Mannerist delight in wit and paradox. A *salone* with a peasant snoring over a doorway festooned with fruit and vegetables of market garden actuality next to a biblical scene of total obscurity of subject but dramatic brilliance of design; a seated hero holding a lance grasped by a cherub who is painted into a banner hanging overhead; painted 'sculptures' flying through the air; there is no end to the exuberance with which Salviati questions the rules and extends the possibilities inherent in High Renaissance art. [198, 241] JW

Salviati, Leonardo (1540–89) One of the Florentine organizers of the Accademia della Crusca (where he was known as l'Infarinato) and of its Vocabolario; he wrote 2 comedies, in part following Latin models (*Il granchio*, *La spina*), prepared an expurgated edition of Boccaccio's *Decameron* (1582), and produced, together with another Crusca academician, Bastiano dei Rossi, a critique of Tasso's *Gerusalemme liberata*. He held rigidly puristic views, supporting the linguistic primacy of Florence (in 1564 he had given a public lecture, *Orazione in lode della fiorentina favella*), but his main work, *Avvertimenti della lingua sopra'l Decamerone* (1584–86), is still important for the precision and originality of its grammatical discussions. LL

P. M. Brown *Leonardo Salviati: a critical biography* (1974)

S. Romano, battle of The 'Rout of San Romano' is best known from the 3 paintings of episodes from it by Uccello (London, National Gallery; Paris, Louvre; Florence, Uffizi); it was a minor defeat by the Florentines of the Sienese on 1 June 1432. JRH

G. Griffiths 'The political significance of Uccello's *Battle of San Romano*' *Journal of the Warburg and Courtauld Institutes* (1978)

S. Stefano, order of Knights of Founded by Cosimo I in 1562, this crusading order was based on Pisa and had its headquarters in the Palazzo dei Cavalieri, designed by Vasari. Its creation resulted from Cosimo's desire to tap the European prestige still attached to crusading values, and to provide an honour with which he could reward or placate the notables of Tuscany. Its occasional ventures, in hired galleys, were commercially successful, if piratical rather than ideological in intent. JRH

G. Guarnieri *I cavalieri di Santo Stefano nella storia della marina italiana 1562–1859* (1960)

The Battle of **San Romano** by Uccello (detail) (London, National Gallery).

Sangallo family A dynasty of Florentine carpenter-architects who came to architecture by way of modelmaking. Their surname derives from the area of Florence inhabited by the founder of the family, Francesco Giamberti, a woodworker. His sons Giuliano (*c.*1443–1516) and Antonio the Elder (*c.*1453–1534) were partners until the former's death. Giuliano's architecture combined a loyalty to Brunelleschian forms with an increasing understanding of Alberti's principles, and an intense, if non-archaeological, study of ancient architecture, recorded in surviving notebooks from 1465.

He became the favourite architect of Lorenzo the Magnificent, through whom his most important commissions of the 1480s were gained. The church of S. Maria delle Carceri in Prato (1485f.), in the plan of a Greek cross, ultimately derives from Brunelleschi, while his masterpiece, the Villa Medici at Poggio a Caiano (1485f.), was strongly influenced by Lorenzo's amateur enthusiasm for Alberti and VITRUVIUS. The first Renaissance villa to incorporate a pedimented portico and symmetrical planning around a large central hall, it foreshadows Palladian types. Giuliano designed fortresses (e.g. Sarzana, Poggio Imperiale) under Lorenzo's sponsorship, and took models of his palaces to the Neapolitan and Milanese courts. After Lorenzo's death Giuliano's architectural practice declined, although his designs influenced his friends Bramante and Michelangelo. He designed the façade of the Palazzo della Rovere at Savona for the future Julius II (1496), but lost to Bramante his architectural primacy in the Julian papacy. Ambitious but unexecuted projects were commissioned by Leo X for a Medici palace on the Piazza Navona (1513), and for the façade of S. Lorenzo in Florence. His brother Antonio the Elder developed an independent style with buildings like S. Maria presso S. Biagio at Montepulciano, synthesizing the experiences of the Prato church and of St Peter's, and with palaces both at Montepulciano and at Montesansovino, which introduced Roman High Renaissance monumentality to the provinces.

Their nephew Antonio the Younger (1483–1546) was an architect of decent professional standards, although said by Cellini to lack a certain 'noble *virtù*' because of his woodworking origins. His concern to reconcile Vitruvius with the (sometimes conflicting) remains of ancient buildings can be seen in his

Giuliano da **Sangallo**'s church of S. Maria delle Carceri in Prato.

large collection of drawings by himself, his family and his friends which forms the nucleus of the Uffizi's architectural holdings. First practising as a carpenter in the St Peter's workshop under Bramante, Antonio became an independent architect under Leo X. The Palazzo Farnese (started 1516) combined grandiose planning influenced by Vitruvian reconstructions with a sober brick façade; the Palazzo Baldassini, a reduced version, was described by Vasari as the most convenient small palace in Rome. As architect of St Peter's from 1520, Sangallo ensured the soundness of the structure, but his colossal model produced after the Sack of Rome was dismissed by Michelangelo as a badly-lit 'German' (i.e. gothic) distortion of Bramante's example. Antonio, like his uncles, was a fine military architect (see especially the Fortezza da Basso, Florence, 1534–37) and excelled in engineering (the well of S. Patrizio at Orvieto). The 'Sangallo sect', including Battista 'Il Gobbo', Bastiano called 'Aristotile' and others, tried to preserve Antonio's orthodoxy against the inroads of Michelangelo's inventive licence. [30, 73, 139] CE

G. Marchini *Giuliano da Sangallo* (1942); G. Giovannoni *Antonio da Sangallo il Giovane* (1959)

Sanmicheli, Michele (1484–1559) Veronese architect and military engineer to the Venetian Republic. Born into the building trade in Verona, Sanmicheli trained briefly as a stonemason before going to Rome, where he became a second-grade papal architect in the orbit of Antonio da Sangallo the Younger, and acquired the architectural vocabulary of Bramante and Raphael, which he was to transport to the Veneto. As architect of Orvieto cathedral he built the Petrucci Chapel (*c.*1516) and made designs for façade and campanile. In the 1520s he joined Sangallo as a FORTIFICATIONS expert in the Papal State before entering Venetian service and returning to Verona.

His three Veronese palaces, probably all constructed in the 1530s, reflect in their difference of style the competitive patronage of interlinked local families, anxious to demonstrate up-to-date architectural tastes. While the façades of the Canossa and Pompeii palaces are variations on the theme of Bramante's 'House of Raphael', the intricate bay rhythms and sophisticated ornament of the Palazzo Bevilacqua draw on Peruzzi and the local antiquities of Verona (Porta de' Borsari). Sanmicheli's religious buildings in Verona (Cappella Pellegrini at S. Bernardino; Madonna di Campagna) explore the possibilities of a Pantheon-like round plan as symbolically appropriate to a funerary chapel and a votive pilgrimage church. The city gates of Verona, the Porta Nuova (1533f.) and the Porta Palio (1555f.), demonstrate his mastery of the expressive language of the rusticated Doric order as rationalized by Serlio.

This combination of strength and precision appears too in the sadly-neglected fortress of S. Andrea on the Venetian Lido, rightly described by Vasari as one of the most stupendous in Europe. Sanmicheli's Venetian palaces (e.g. Palazzo Grimani, 1559f.) are forthright statements in a grandiose Roman language which makes little concession to the Venetian vernacular. As engineer to the Venetian Republic Sanmicheli built fortifications in Dalmatia (present-day Yugoslavia), Corfu and Cyprus. His commonsensical architecture, with its attention to fine stone detail, was a formative influence on the young Palladio. CE

L. Puppi *Michele Sanmicheli* (1971)

Sannazaro, Jacopo (1457–1530) Author of *Arcadia* and, before Tasso, Italy's most imitated pastoral poet. His other works include the *Rime* (1530), the Christian poem *De partu virginis* (*On the parturition of the Virgin*), and 5 piscatorial eclogues, a genre he invented. An extensive philological education recommended him to King Federico of Naples, whose fortunes he shared, including exile from 1501 in France. After Federico's death in 1504 he returned to Naples. *Arcadia*, a combination of verse eclogues and prose narrative, was first printed that year, although it had been composed 20 years earlier.

Initially inspired by bucolics of the Sienese school, it evolved through many phases. As a result the structure is loose and diverse, shifting unexpectedly from an idyllic opening to a tauter and more dramatic middle; and from the elegiac scene at the tomb of Massilia that ended the original version to the loftier, almost tragic last chapter and epilogue of the definitive version. Nor in the creation of setting was Sannazaro bound by his idealized Greek countryside, but blended topographical traits from all his sources. Moreover, he created an exemplary character type describing a spiritual malady, his own, that proved as contagious as the mode in which it appeared. Among notable victims are Shakespeare's Jaques. Called melancholy in the terminology of humours, it would by Baudelaire be more precisely dubbed *spleen*. LGC

F. Torraca *Gli imitatori stranieri di Sannazaro* (1892); G. Folena *La crisi linguistica del Quattrocento e l' 'Arcadia'* (1952)

Sanseverino family An ancient and illustrious Neapolitan family, the Sanseverino intermarried with all the major royal and noble families of Europe. They were frequent holders of the 7 great offices of Naples, where the head of the family was known as 'the first prince of the Kingdom', and the Sanseverino fiefs, amounting to over 300 holdings, effectively constituted a state within a state. In the 15c. the family's fortunes became intimately linked with those of the house of Aragon, since Roberto Sanseverino, Count of Caiazzo, was the main supporter of Ferrante I. Nevertheless, Roberto's son Galeazzo, who had married a daughter of Lodovico Sforza, entered French service and died fighting for Francis I at the battle of Pavia. In Naples, under Charles V, Ferrante Sanseverino, Prince of Salerno, led the opposition to a remodelled Inquisition and was the leading upholder of Neapolitan rights against Spanish innovation. JH

Sansovino, Andrea (*c*.1460–1529) Tuscan sculptor who began by modelling in terracotta and then specialized in marble carving. Andrea Contucci was in Portugal 1491–1500 as an artistic emissary of Lorenzo de' Medici. Returning to Florence, he carved 2 statues for Genoa cathedral and another 2 forming the *Baptism of Christ* for the Florentine baptistery (1502–05); these 4 statues constitute the epitome of High Renaissance sculpture, equivalent to the paintings of, for instance, Fra Bartolommeo. In 1505 he was summoned to Rome by Pope Julius II to carve a pair of marble tombs in the choir of S. Maria del Popolo, which was being redesigned by Bramante; they resemble ancient Roman triumphal arches, containing some 8 statues each. He followed this success with a group of the *Virgin and Child with St Anne* (S. Agostino, Rome), based on Leonardo's variations on the theme (e.g. the cartoon in the National Gallery, London). From 1513 until his death he was put in charge of the marble cladding of the Holy House in the Basilica of Loreto, carving 2 of the large narrative reliefs personally, and supervising an *équipe* of younger sculptors. This commission is one of the finest manifestations of High Renaissance architecture and sculpture. CA

G. Huntley *Andrea Sansovino* (1935)

Bronze statue of Mercury by **Jacopo Sansovino**, on the Loggetta di S. Marco, Venice.

Sansovino, Jacopo (1486–1570) Florentine architect and sculptor whose buildings transformed the public and private face of Venice. Jacopo Tatti adopted the surname of his master Andrea Sansovino. From the Quattrocentesque style of the latter Jacopo developed a sculptural manner which in his Roman and Florentine works (e.g. *Bacchus*, 1512; *Madonna del Parto*, 1518) is analogous to Raphael's refinement in paint of Michelangelesque forms. For the entry of Leo X into Florence in 1515, Sansovino designed a temporary façade based on a rhythm of paired columns and fictive bronze and marble sculpture suggesting triumphal arches, which contains the germ of his mature architectural solutions. It was, however, his move to Venice after the Sack of Rome (1527) that made him famous as an architect. In Venice Sansovino became part of a circle including Titian and Aretino, and his career was promoted by the enlightened doge Andrea Gritti (1523–38). He continued to work as a sculptor all his life, revitalizing the Venetian sculptural tradition with his tombs (Rangoni tomb, S. Giuliano; Venier Monument, S. Salvatore, 1555–61), reliefs (e.g. Cappella di S. Antonio, Padua) and monumental works (*Neptune* and *Mars* on the Scala dei Giganti, 1550), and founding a new school distinguished by his pupils Vittoria and Danese Cattaneo.

As *proto* (chief architect) of the Procurators of St Mark's (1529f.) Sansovino planned to reclothe the Piazza and Piazzetta with continuous 2-storey loggias. The architectural solution adopted for the Library, the first part of this plan (1537f.), derives partly from memories of Rome (Palazzo Farnese, Peruzzi's Farnesina) and partly from Serlio, then also in Venice, but also succeeds in creating an entirely Venetian High Renaissance idiom. The *loggetta* beneath the campanile, begun at the same time, is a polychrome triumphal arch in miniature, with festive composite order and sculptural programme extolling the Venetian government. Next to the Library site Sansovino rebuilt the Venetian Mint (1536f.), where the rusticated columns clasping jutting lintels deter would-be raiders with a show of architectural strength. His palaces (Dolfin, 1538; Corner at S. Maurizio, *c.*1545f.) introduced Roman scale and vocabulary to plan and elevation types essentially Venetian in character. As well as parish churches (S. Martino, S. Giuliano), Sansovino designed S. Francesco della Vigna (*c.*1534f.), drawing on Cronaca's S. Salvatore, for the Florentine branch of the same Observant order, for its plain single nave with Doric pilasters and monks' choir behind the altar.

Sansovino's early experience of designing wall tombs where sculpture and architecture played equal roles (e.g. tomb of Cardinal S. Angelo, S. Marcello, Rome, 1518) shaped his approach to architecture, which is highly plastic, concerned with effects of light and shade on a relief surface. The Venetian tradition of festive architectural display encouraged a Raphaelesque tendency towards decoration, so that in Sansovino's building the High Renaissance language of the orders is combined with a sculptural richness in tune with Venetian taste. CE

D. Howard *Jacopo Sansovino* (1975)

Santi di Tito (1536–1603), born in Borgo Sansepolcro, became the pupil of Bronzino. Known also as a portraitist, he made his most important contribution in attempting to revitalize Florentine religious painting. After working alongside Federico Zuccaro and Barocci in Rome he returned to Florence with a style containing genuine Counter-Mannerist elements (1562/3). A trip to Venice (1571–72) provided further alternatives to Florentine Mannerism. He executed 5 altarpieces for the S. Maria Novella and S. Croce cycles (1574–1602). Raffaello Borghini (*Il Riposo*, 1584) praised these and other works for their adherence to Counter-Reformation standards, but found fault with them aesthetically. Santi's efforts to establish the artistic 'reform' in Florence faltered in the late 1580s. In his last years he painted altarpieces, chiefly for provincial Tuscan churches. MH

Sanuto, Marin the Younger (1466–1536) Venetian patrician who compiled prolific diaries 1496–1533, which remain a major source of information not only concerning Venice but for the entire known world at that time. Sanuto began them as a continuation of his *Lives of the doges*, a traditional chronicle, and of his annalistic account of Charles VIII's expedition into Italy; in addition to recording private comment and local hearsay, day by day he accurately transcribed private and official correspondence, minutes of government proceedings, treaties, voting lists – all manner of documents which often survive nowhere else. This labour he intended as the basis for a comprehensive and polished history, but he was too overwhelmed by his material ever to edit it, notwithstanding his literary and humanistic pretensions (he collected an enormous library and was a friend of Aldo Manuzio and many other learned people).

None of his writings was printed in his lifetime; he failed to become official historiographer, and received no more than a small pension in 1530. Though active in political life and from 1498 recurrently elected a *savio ai ordeni*, which admitted him to the Senate, he never attained high office and only once secured a minor terraferma magistracy. It may be that his lack of wealth and some of his personal qualities, such as inquisitiveness and want of political tact (he was a vociferous constitutional purist), were to blame. He wrote at times bitterly, feeling his toil and merits to be unappreciated. DC

I Diarii ed. R. Fulin *et al.* (58 vols 1879–1902) (see biographical introduction by G. Berchet); D. S. Chambers 'Marin Sanudo, Camerlengo of Verona 1501–2' *Archivio Veneto* (1977); R. Finlay *Politics in Renaissance Venice* (1980)

Sardinia By the 13c., particularly in the coastal areas of this constantly invaded island, the influence of Pisa and Genoa predominated. Boniface VIII gave the dominion of Sardinia to James II of Aragon, although the island was not conquered by the Aragonese until 1326. The harshness of Aragonese rule provoked a number of native rebellions which were met by the imposition of a Catalan and Aragonese ruling class. This in turn provoked further rebellions and a civil war which lasted for half a century, while Sardinia also became the prey of Turkish pirates. In order to purchase the support of the aristocracy, and so counter native rebelliousness, the rulers of Aragon were forced to grant that aristocratic class a virtual autonomy. It is the local aristocracy, therefore, rather than the Spanish monarchy, that must be blamed for the economic decline of Sardinia after 1450 and for the spread of corruption and injustice throughout the island. JH

Sarpi, Fra Paolo (1552–1623) Philosopher, polemicist and historian. He was born Pietro Sarpi in Venice of plebeian parentage and became a Servite friar. He early developed mathematical and scientific interests, particularly in optics and magnetism. His wide cultural interests gained him admittance in the 1590s to circles of the patrician intelligentsia in Venice. His contacts included politicians assuming high office at the turn of the century who were pressing for a more active Venetian foreign policy and who were mistrustful of the Papacy as a political force. It was probably because of their support that the Venetian government called upon him to advise on points of dispute with the Papacy and conferred upon him in 1606 the new post of Consultant in Theology and Canon Law. During the confrontation with Paul V of 1606–07, during which the Venetian state lay under interdict, he conducted propaganda for its cause. Thereafter the state protected him against a vengeful Papacy. He continued to act as a policy adviser to the government, his forte being mastery of the historical antecedents of legal controversies involving the state interest: his cogently argued *consulti* reveal him as historian-technocrat. After the interdict, Sarpi and certain patrician associates pressed for an alliance with France and the Protestant powers against Spain and the Papacy. In pursuit of this goal, as well as of his intellectual predilections, he cultivated a European-wide circle of distinguished Protestant and Gallican correspondents and also had contacts in the English embassy in Venice.

His major work, the *History of the Council of Trent*, was intended to influence the international situation by strengthening the forces of intransigent Protestantism in northern Europe. The *History* was smuggled to England in manuscript and published there in the translation of Nathaniel Brent in 1619, under the pseudonym Pietro Soave Polano. This depicted the Council, 'the Odyssey of our age', as the culmination of a process of usurpation of authority in the Church by the Papacy, authority which properly belonged to the entire body of the clergy. The *History* is an intricate account of the machinations by which the Papacy warded off the threat posed to its own position by a Council called for the reform of the Church and achieved a denouement so favourable to itself. In the theological excursuses of the *History* Sarpi portrayed a decline of the Church from about the 4c., marked by the growth of hierarchy and of church property and by the proliferation of doctrines. Sarpi's personal religious position is ambiguous. In his letters his sympathies seem to have been for Presbyterian Protestantism, but the secret *Pensieri* suggest that he was an extreme religious radical, sceptical about much of traditional Christian doctrine. OL

Opere ed. G. and L. Cozzi (1969); G. Cozzi *Paolo Sarpi tra Venezia e l'Europa* (1979)

Sarto *see* ANDREA DEL SARTO

Sassetta, Stefano di Giovanni, il (active *c.*1423–50) Perhaps the greatest of the early 15c. Sienese painters. He mingles an innate conservatism, especially in his architectural structures, with a delight in the svelte forms of International Gothic figure design, and in the clarity and unity of Renaissance pictorial space. The essentially 14c. basis of his style, the dreamlike blending of reality and unreality, of graceful calm and visionary fervour, are all epitomized in his dismembered masterpiece, the double-sided altarpiece of 1337–44 for S. Francesco, Borgo S. Sepolcro (Louvre, Berenson Collection; London, National Gallery). JW

E. Carli *Sassetta* (1957)

Savoldo, Gian Girolamo (active 1508–48) Painter of Brescian origin, working mainly in Venice, though also traceable in Florence and Milan. Relatively few works are known, all in a distinctive and haunting style, simplified yet naturalistic, which recalls the manner of Moretto and anticipates the art of Caravaggio and his followers in the early 17c. Chiefly a painter of religious subjects, Savoldo was a pioneer of night scenes and specialized in figures in dusky Venetian landscapes, typified respectively by *St Matthew and the angel* (New York, Metropolitan Museum) and *St Jerome* (London, National Gallery). AB

D. Boschetto *Giovan Girolamo Savoldo* (1963)

Savonarola, Girolamo (1452–98) Dominican friar and 'martyr', was born in Ferrara, the son of a prominent and scholarly doctor. After a sudden conversion he entered the monastery of S. Domenico in Bologna in 1475 and acquired sufficient fame as a theologian and preacher to be transferred first during 1482–85 and again in 1490, this time at the request of

A woodcut of **Savonarola** in his cell, from his *Della semplicita della vita Christiana*, 1496.

Lorenzo de' Medici, to S. Marco in Florence, where he became prior in 1491. Prominently associated, as a preacher of ever-increasing political frankness and emotional power, with attacks on the materialism and misuse of authority by the Medici (though he had been called to Lorenzo's death-bed), his support was welcomed by the party calling for a broadly based republican constitution on Piero de' Medici's exile in 1494.

As the party's most prominent unofficial spokesman he shared the odium it incurred for its failure to recover Pisa after that city's revolt in 1495 and the alliance with France, which left the city politically and economically isolated – a predicament worsened by Savonarola's personal vendetta against Pope Alexander VI. To political opposition (further provoked by Savonarola's continuing to preach after his excommunication) was added a revulsion against the atmosphere of moral crusade which he had persuaded Florence's citizens to adopt in fulfilment of a divinely-appointed role in the purification of Italy as a whole from personal sin and clerical corruption. From being the great inspirer of Florence's self-confidence at a time of dislocating change and great danger, he became first its nagging conscience then its scapegoat. When in 1498 the government joined the Church in wishing to be rid of him, there was little difficulty in establishing (with the aid of torture) the charges of heresy which led to his being hanged and then burned.

This martyr's death, his puritanical drives against gambling and the innuendoes of carnival songs, his bonfires of vanities (already familiar symbols of public contrition), his austere attitude to the uses to which religious art should be put, the contemptuous contemporary description of his most uncritical followers as *piagnoni* (snivellers): these can obscure the extraordinary range of his following and the reasons for it. His personality had charm as well as power. His erudition, neither profound nor original, was broad enough to interest humanist scholars like Giovanni Pico della Mirandola. He was an efficient and effective prior of S. Marco and his statesmanlike dignity outside the pulpit led him to be chosen twice as ambassador to the invading Charles VIII.

Though probably always speaking with a Ferrarese accent, he wholly identified himself with the Florentines, flattering them while scolding them. He reinforced the smouldering folk-belief that they had been marked by God for a special destiny; that, while princely rule was in theory best, their intelligence required, exceptionally, a free constitution. He modified his earlier, gloomy eschatology to portray a millennium which would leave the Florentines purified, but able to pursue their familiar lives with God's blessing. His sermons, combining calls to repentance with comments on constitutional affairs, had a power to disturb and fascinate that can be vividly recaptured from those that were taken down in shorthand or published from his notes. Though the ashes of his pyre were thrown into the Arno, his ideas surfaced as one of the chief inspirations behind the Last Florentine Republic of 1527–30, when it once again declared Christ King of Florence. [39] JRH

R. Ridolfi *The life of Girolamo Savonarola* tr. Cecil Grayson (1959); D. Weinstein *Savonarola and Florence* (1970)

Savorgnan family Owners of wide tracts of land in Friuli, which they administered from their chief strongpoint, the frontier castle of Osoppo, the Savorgnan provided Venice with some of its most effective and reliable military commanders and military engineers. Prominent among them were Girolamo (1466–1529) and his son Mario (d.1574), and Giulio (1516–1595), who, as superintendent of fortifications (a position invented for him), designed defence works both on the Venetian terraferma and overseas in Corfu, Crete and Cyprus. Their fidelity to Venice was exceptional among the major feudal clans of Friuli, and the Republic also trusted them in time of war or of threatened invasion of Friuli from Austria or by the Turks with commands in the Friulian peasant militia – positions from which as a rule local magnates were barred. JRH

E. Salaris *Una famiglia di militari italiani ... I Savorgnani* (1913)

Savoy, house of Until 1945 the oldest royal family in Europe, having ruled in Savoy-Piedmont from the 11c., first as counts, then as dukes, becoming in 1720 the ruling house of the kingdom of Sardinia, and in 1861 the ruling house of Italy. From an unpromising beginning in a feudal agglomeration of estates on either side of the Alps, the house of Savoy expanded its lands through marriage, diplomacy and conquest, and consolidated them into a well-run, centralized and absolutist state which, in turn, provided the basis for the extension of the family's authority further into Italy.

Amadeus VI (1343–83), the Green Count, was the first Savoy to intervene extensively in Italian affairs. His son Amadeus VII (1383–91), the Red Count, acquired a seaport at Nice in 1388. Amadeus VIII was created first Duke of Savoy in 1416 by the Emperor Sigismund. Famed throughout Europe for his wisdom and justice, Amadeus also suffered from religious mania and agreed to accept the strange decision of the Council of Basle to elect him pope. He took the name of Felix V and abdicated as duke. His son Louis (d.1465) married Anne of Lusignan, heiress to the kingdoms of Jerusalem, Cyprus and Armenia, titles which, thereafter, were always borne by the ruling member of the house of Savoy. The lowest ebb in the family's fortunes came with a series of weak dukes in the late 15c. and early 16c. The expansion of the Swiss cantons and the Wars of Italy led to a dismemberment of the duchy at the time of Charles III (1504–53). It was not until 1559 that Savoy was restored to its ruling house in the person of EMANUEL PHILIBERT, who began the process of reconstruction which, continued by his successors, turned Savoy into a model absolutist state and a major Italian power. JH

House of Savoy

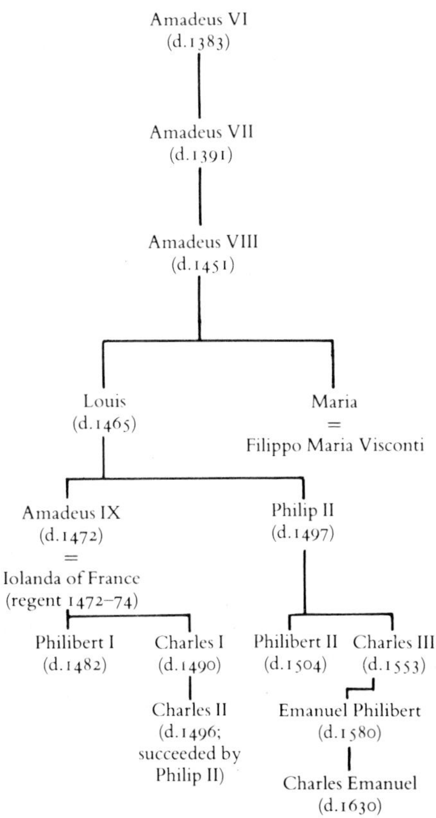

Savoy-Piedmont A mountainous and wild principality, with perpetually fluctuating borders, straddling the Alps, Savoy-Piedmont reached its greatest extent under Amadeus VI (1343–83), who annexed Geneva, Lausanne, Aosta and Turin. In 1416 it was raised from the status of a county to a duchy, but in the later 15c. and early 16c. it effectively ceased to exist; the Swiss took the lower Valais and the Vaud (1475–76), Geneva became independent (1533), and the rest of the duchy was occupied by the French (1536).

The independence of Savoy-Piedmont was restored by the Peace of CATEAU-CAMBRÉSIS (1559). France and Spain were anxious to create a buffer state between their territories. The duchy was therefore reconstituted, although without the majority of the Swiss conquests and also without the fortresses of Turin, Chieri, Pinerolo, Chivasso and Villanova d'Asti, retained by the French, or of Asti and Vercelli, retained by the Spanish. Given the condition of Savoy-Piedmont at this period, it is remarkable that the duchy should have emerged as one of the more powerful and important of Italian states in the later 16c. and 17c. It should be realized, however, that, although only a small state, it was ideally situated to take advantage of any conflict between the great powers. This is the secret of the success of Duke EMANUEL PHILIBERT, whose careful harbouring of resources meant that the duchy was placed on a sound financial footing, and who by 1575 had recovered all the fortresses originally reserved to the French and the Spanish. By the purchase of Oneglia he also extended the duchy to the south.

The personal and absolute government established by Emanuel Philibert proved very effective in moulding into one state the disparate elements of his duchy, composed of the sparsely populated and largely agricultural Savoy and the more prosperous and industrialized Piedmont. It was under Emanuel Philibert also that the capital of Savoy-Piedmont was finally settled in Turin, beginning a process by which the duchy became progressively more Italian than French. The reforms and careful management of Emanuel Philibert meant that the reconstituted duchy of Savoy-Piedmont was strong enough to withstand the excesses of his son and successor, Charles Emanuel, who, although he followed his father's Italian policy by ceding Bresse, Bugey and Gex to France in 1601 in exchange for the marquisate of Saluzzo, also squandered his resources in vain efforts to conquer Geneva and in other pointless enterprises, so that, on his death, he left his son Victor Amadeus I (1630–37) little more than a title. It was, therefore, the greatest good fortune that Victor Amadeus was married to the daughter of Henry IV of France, since it was through this alliance that he was able to recover the duchy of Savoy-Piedmont. JH

Scala, Bartolomeo (1430–97), Florentine humanist administrator, was a miller's son. He acquired a humanist and legal education in Florence and Milan (with Filelfo), then worked in the household of Pierfrancesco de' Medici and in 1459 became secretary of the Parte Guelfa. In 1465 he was appointed with Medici influence to the chancellorship of Florence, a position which he retained throughout the age of Lorenzo de' Medici, acting as an important link between the Medici and the communal administration, which he reformed. He remained in the administration under Savonarola. In addition to some conventional humanist philosophy, he composed a *History of the Florentine people* (*c.*1480–97) and a defence of the Florentine republic under Savonarola. Scala's career is an excellent example of the use of humanism by a humble man as a path to the top – he was knighted by Pope Innocent VIII – but he was not a very original thinker. GH

A. Brown *Bartolomeo Scala 1430–1497* (1979)

Scamozzi, Vincenzo (1552–1616) Vicentine architect and author of *L'Idea dell'architettura universale* (Venice 1615). Son of a minor architect, Gian Domenico Scamozzi (*c.*1526–82), Vincenzo was heavily dependent on Palladio's style, which he developed into a frigid neo-classical formula (e.g. Villa Verlato, La Verla, 1574–1615), although Palladio is almost ignored in his treatise. He designed the illusionistic street perspectives at Palladio's Teatro Olimpico, and built another classicizing theatre for the new town of Sabbioneta (1588–89). After completing the Venetian Library, the Marciana, he distorted Sansovino's plan for the Piazza by building the 3-storey Procuratie Nuove (1583f.). His masterpiece is the Rocca Pisani at Lonigo (1576), on a spectacular hilltop site, a compact, single-porticoed version of Palladio's Rotonda, which influenced Burlington's Chiswick House. Inigo Jones was also indebted to Scamozzi, whom he met in 1614, despite finding him 'secret' and 'purblind'. Scamozzi's treatise, an encyclopaedic compendium rather than a coherent synthesis, was most influential for its plates and for the book on the orders, often translated separately. CE

F. Barbieri *V. Scamozzi* (1952)

Scepticism This generic term covers several different anti-dogmatic tendencies in ancient and modern philosophy. The founder of the school is traditionally considered to be Pyrrho of Elis (*c.*360–*c.*270 BC), whose writings, along with all the other original works of the formulators of the tradition, are lost. Information about the movement is contained in later writings such as Cicero's *Academica* (*c.*45 BC), Diogenes Laertius' *Life of Pyrrho* (3c. AD), and especially the works of Sextus Empiricus (*c.* AD 160–*c.*210). The central thesis of the Sceptics is that certitude is impossible, owing to the many obstacles preventing valid empirical knowledge, in particular the absence of a criterion by which to distinguish truth from falsity. Rather than establishing a system of positive philosophy, the Sceptics emphasized the critical and negative nature of philosophy in questioning what was taken as legitimate knowledge by dogmatic schools such as Platonism and Stoicism.

Little known in the Middle Ages, the Sceptical position was revived in the Renaissance when the writings of Diogenes Laertius and Sextus Empiricus once again became available. Gianfrancesco Pico della Mirandola was the first Renaissance writer to utilize Sceptical arguments in a systematic way: his lead was followed by Francisco Sanches (1552–1623), Michel de Montaigne (1533–92), and many others. The publication of Latin (1562, 1569) and Greek (1621) editions of Sextus Empiricus was important for later diffusion. CS

R. H. Popkin *The history of Scepticism from Erasmus to Spinoza* (1980)

Schism, the Great began 20 September 1378 when a majority of the cardinals, having declared their election of the Neapolitan Bartolomeo Prignano (Urban VI) 5 months previously to be invalid because of the undue pressure exerted by the Roman mob, elected the Frenchman Robert of Geneva (Clement VII). Although the schism was caused by acute personal differences between Urban and the cardinals, most of whom, being Frenchmen, were deeply unhappy over the return of the Papacy from AVIGNON to ROME, Christendom divided along political lines once the double election had taken place, with France and her allies Aragon, Castile and Scotland supporting Clement, while England, the Emperor and most other princes remained loyal to Urban.

Most of the Italian states stood behind Urban but in Naples Queen Giovanna I of Anjou provoked a popular and baronial revolt by sheltering Clement, and for the next 20 years the kingdom was contested between, on one side, Charles III of Durazzo (d.1386) and his son Ladislas, who recognized the Roman pope, and, on the other, Louis I (d.1384) and Louis II of Anjou, who had the support of the Avignon pope. In northern Italy, the scene was dominated by the expansionist policies of Giangaleazzo Visconti of Milan until his death in 1402; from time to time both he and his opponents, the Florentines, flirted with the Avignon popes in the hope of obtaining French support, but with little effect.

Meanwhile the temporal power of the Roman popes survived despite Urban's gift for quarrelling with all his allies, and was considerably built up by his able successor Boniface IX (1389–1404). However, on his death the Roman papacy fell under the domination of King Ladislas of Naples, who drove north through Rome to threaten central Italy, causing the Florentines and most of the other Italian states to throw their weight behind a group of cardinals from both camps who met at Pisa and elected a third pope, Alexander V, in June 1409. It was the continued pressure of Ladislas that finally compelled Alexander's successor, Baldassare Cossa (John XXIII) to summon the Council of Constance (1414–18). This Council healed the Schism by deposing both John and the Avignon pope Benedict XIII and accepting the resignation of the Roman pope, thus leaving the way open for the election in 1417 of Martin V (1417–31), who set about the task of restoring the shattered power and prestige of the Holy See. The 39-year schism killed the supra-national PAPACY of the Middle Ages, for, while devout Christians agonized, practical politicians (often the same people) seized the chance to extend their jurisdiction at the Church's expense. As a result, the Renaissance popes were much more dependent on their Italian resources, and therefore far more purely Italian princes, than their medieval predecessors. *See* COUNCILS OF THE CHURCH. JKH

W. Ullmann *The origins of the Great Schism* (1948); P. Partner *The lands of St Peter* (1972)

Scholasticism The term is ambivalent. It describes the characteristic method of instruction and exposition used in medieval schools and universities: the posing of a case (*quaestio*), arguing (*disputatio*) and settling it (*sententia*). It also describes the subject matter that was particularly shaped by this method: philosophy, with its strong connection with Christian theology and its dependence on Aristotelian texts and commentaries, and theology, with its assumption that spiritual truths can be seized with the tools of formal logic. 'Scholasticism' has thus become almost synonymous with medieval thought. As such, it can appear the antithesis of Renaissance thought, especially as writers like Petrarch and Valla poured scorn on both the methods and the content of medieval scholarship.

None the less, in spite of Valla's insistence (in his *Encomion S. Thomae* of 1457) that theologians should eschew dialectic and listen anew to the sources of spiritual understanding, the gospels and the early Greek and Roman Fathers, scholastic method maintained its vitality in the areas where continuity with medieval practice was strongest, theology itself and 'Aristotelian' philosophy. Medieval scholars, moreover, notably Aquinas, were quoted with admiration even by neo-Platonic philosophers. It was because the central concerns of humanism – moral philosophy, textual scholarship, history and rhetoric – were different from those of medieval, university-based study, and were less suited to a dialectical form of exposition, that scholasticism was left, as it were, on one side. But to ignore its presence is to exaggerate the difference between the new learning and the old. JRH

P. O. Kristeller 'The scholastic background of Marsilio Ficino' and 'Humanism and scholasticism in the Italian Renaissance' *Studies in Renaissance thought and letters* (1956); S. I. Camporeale *L. Valla: umanesimo e teologia* (1972)

Science At the beginning of the 15c. almost all that we call science could have been subsumed under the twin headings of MATHEMATICS and MEDICINE. That this was no longer true by the early 17c. is a measure of the transformation effected in men's attitudes to nature by the impact of Greek science, in combination with the expanding mental horizons which were the concomitant of the expanding geographical, artistic, humanistic, philosophical and religious worlds. For all these disciplines contributed to a new understanding of the world external to man. Science, then, had its share in the concept of the 'universal man': witness both Leonardo (1452–1519) and Galileo (1564–1642). Indeed the scientific Renaissance may be taken as roughly spanning the period between the birth of Leonardo and the maturity of Galileo. Paradoxically, scientific specialization began at the same time.

Although HUMANISM was primarily concerned with problems remote from the study of nature, it made contributions to it. Many Greek texts unknown previously (PTOLEMY's *Geography*, GALEN's anatomy and physiology, much Hellenistic mathematics and physics) were discovered in the humanists' search for rare manuscripts, and Platonism challenged Aristotelianism. The Platonism of the 15c. and the worship of ARCHIMEDES in the 16c. provoked new approaches to mathematical astronomy and physics, while a later return to Aristotle helped turn what had been adjuncts of medicine into botany (Cesalpino) or zoology (Aldrovandi). Immensely stimulating was the prolonged debate over the basic metaphysical assumptions of natural philosophy which new loyalties produced, and which ultimately helped to liberate men from authority in science.

A good example occurs in astronomy. Humanism, and dissatisfaction with contemporary knowledge of planetary and calendrical computations, led first of all to the search for 'pure' texts, notably of Ptolemy's *Almagest*, which in turn led to a reappraisal and deep study of what Ptolemy had actually said. Then came attempts to 'improve' on Ptolemy by returning to his predecessors: hence Fracastoro's *Homocentrica* of 1538, and hence the view that Copernicus in his *De revolutionibus* (1543) had revived the Pythagorean hypothesis, a view to which Copernicus himself gave credence in his Preface. *De revolutionibus* lays no claim to be revolutionary, although it clearly was so in making the Earth a moving planet in an essentially sun-centred universe; indeed Copernicus followed Ptolemy so closely in the structure of the book that many who did not accept his theories could accept his tables and use them to prepare better ones. Copernicus himself had hoped to aid in the calendrical reform which had been projected under Leo X; this was finally accomplished with improved astronomical data in 1582 under Gregory XIII.

As it happens, Italian Copernicans were not many, although Galileo claimed to have known a number; one outspoken proponent was the physicist Giambattista Benedetti (1530–90), a violent anti-Aristotelian who is notable for his work on bodies in motion. Like many others, including Leonardo and Tartaglia, he tried and failed to mathematize the medieval 'impetus' theory of dynamics; more important, he broke sharply with Aristotle (even more sharply than Tartaglia) over how bodies actually fall and move as projectiles. While Tartaglia was concerned with the specific case of guns, Benedetti was interested in the general case of all falling bodies. Here, as in other branches of physics, a new admiration for Archimedes supported a growing anti-Aristotelianism. Other ancients too supported new branches of physics: for example Hero's

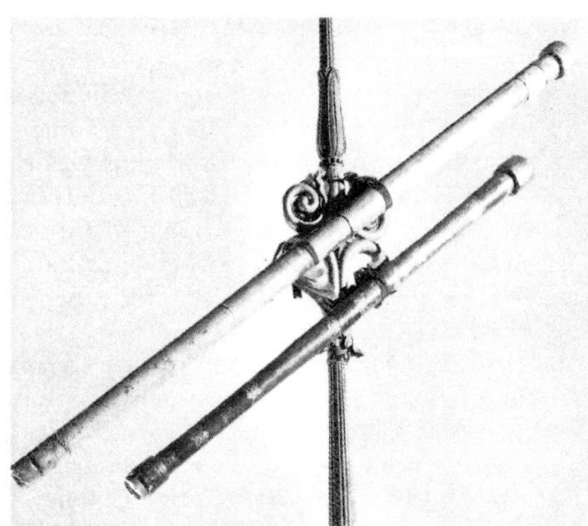

Science: Galileo's telescopes (Florence, Istituto della Scienza).

Pneumatics, unknown before the end of the 15c., encouraged work in pneumatics and hydraulics. EUCLID's *Optics* encouraged the development of mathematical work in that field (*see* MATHEMATICS), while medieval work on refraction and its application to spectacle lenses encouraged a vast expansion of practical (magnifying glasses, the telescope, the camera obscura) as well as theoretical work, all essential to the development of astronomical observation during the later 16c.

Not all science in the Renaissance followed the rational, humanist point of view. On the contrary, MAGIC, mysticism and pseudo-science flourished enormously, each branch of natural philosophy having its non-rational analogue. ASTROLOGY was still applied astronomy, as it had been for Ptolemy; now it was widely employed in medicine, and there were many medical astrologers besides Cardano. Much drug and plant lore had mystical underpinnings (e.g. the doctrine of signatures). In the physical sciences natural magic, the study of inexplicable forces like those of magnetism or refraction, was half experimental science, half pure magic (*see* DELLA PORTA, GIAMBATTISTA). Alchemy, which flourished, was unique in having no rational, theoretical counterpart, but only a technology whose proponents (like Biringuccio) despised the mystic science. In the 16c. alchemy was applied to medicine by Paracelsus (1493–1541) and his followers to produce a mystic physiology and a chemical materia medica. It was the practical pharmacy required to produce these new drugs that ultimately helped create a body of knowledge which could be combined with natural philosophy to produce chemistry. But in the 16c. alchemy alone existed, as part of the semi-illicit but wholly fascinating world of mystic, occult, Hermetic art. *See* TECHNOLOGY. MBH

Marie Boas *The scientific renaissance 1450–1630* (1962); W. P. D. Wightman *Science in a Renaissance society* (1972); *Dictionary of scientific biography* (1970–80)

Sebastiano del Piombo (1485–1547) Vasari says that Sebastiano began as a musician in Venice and then, having decided to become a painter, apprenticed himself to Giovanni Bellini and later to Giorgione. His early work from this Venetian period certainly reflects Giorgione's influence. After Giorgione's death in 1510, he went to Rome under the patronage of Chigi and helped with the decoration of his villa (today the Farnesina) by the side of Raphael and Peruzzi. The next 20 years of his life were the most prolific, as he received numerous commissions for chapels and portraits. Michelangelo befriended him and went so far as to help him with the design for the *Raising of Lazarus* (London, National Gallery) which was done in competition with Raphael's *Transfiguration*. After Raphael's death Sebastiano became the most important painter in Rome, but in spite of many commissions did not complete very much. In 1531 he was made the Keeper of the (lead – *piombo*) Seal for the Curia, for which he had to take religious orders. Blessed with a sizeable and secure income, he promptly gave up painting for the most part, and enjoyed the good life. [88] LDE

S. Freedberg *Painting in Italy 1500–1600* (1971)

Seneca, Lucius Anneus (4 BC/AD 1–AD 65) Known as 'the Younger' to distinguish him from his father, the historian and rhetorician Lucius Seneca. The younger Seneca's works were known in the Middle Ages but only became influential from the time of Petrarch onwards. They form 2 distinct groups. One comprised a series of epistles or short treatises of a philosophical nature, expressing a Stoic resignation to life's adversities. Including such works as *De ira* (on conquering the irrationality of anger), *De providentia* (on determinedly looking for the good in the apparently bad) and *De brevitate vitae* (on not wasting a moment of a life which might end at any moment), these brought Seneca into the mainstream of those

Roman moral philosophers, like Cicero, who had a strong appeal to humanists of the stamp of Bruni, Salutati, Guarino and Alberti, an appeal widened by the vigour and nimbleness of the style in which such grave sentiments were expressed. The second group comprised 9 tragedies, whose melodramatic plots, passionate speechifying, moralizing soliloquies and thin characterization had a powerful influence on the development of tragedy, especially after their translation into Italian in 1497. JRH

M. T. Griffin *Seneca, a philosopher in politics* (1976); L. Herrmann *Le théatre de Sénèque* (1924)

Serafino Aquilano (1466–1500) Serafino de' Ciminelli dall'Aquila first won a reputation as a singer, lutanist, composer and poet in the service of Cardinal Ascanio Sforza in Rome and northern Italy. There followed adulation at the courts of Milan, Mantua and Urbino. His death in Rome in the service of Cesare Borgia provoked eulogy of his talents and 28 editions of his poems by 1516. But though drawn on by Clement Marot, Sir Thomas Wyatt and Sir Philip Sydney among others, Serafino's fluent occasional verse with its popularizing conceits did not long please after the death of its charismatic originator. PH

Le rime ed. M. Menghini (1894)

Serlio, Sebastiano (1475–54) Bolognese architect whose treatises diffused the Italian Renaissance language of the orders all over Europe and produced 'more hack architects than he had hairs in his beard' (Lomazzo). Self-styled pupil of Bramante in Rome, Serlio was sufficiently close to Peruzzi to inherit and use the latter's literary estate as the basis for his own publications. Moving to Venice after the Sack of Rome, Serlio there began publication of his intended sequence of 7 architectural books. Books IV, on the orders (1537), and III, on antiquities (1540), show him shifting from a Peruzzi-inspired advocacy of variety and 'mixing' to the more orthodox stance of his later works. Invited to France by Francis I in 1541, Serlio designed the Château of Ançy Le Franc and the Grand Ferrare at Fontainebleau, where he died in 1554 after publishing 4 more books (Books I and II, on geometry and perspective, 1545; Book V, on churches, 1547; *Libro extraordinario*, on gateways, 1551. Book VII was published posthumously in 1575; 2

Serlio's enumeration of the orders in Book IV of the books on architecture.

versions of his Book VI, on domestic architecture, have been published only recently, and a work on Polybius' description of a military camp exists in manuscript in Munich). The emphasis on illustration (ultimately derived from Francesco di Giorgio) is Serlio's particular contribution to the printed architectual treatise. His combination of short text with facing woodcut plates inspired Palladio's more beautiful and graphically consistent layout in the *Quattro libri*. CE

S. Serlio *Tutte l'opere d'architettura e prospettiva* (1619; facsimile 1964); W. B. Dinsmoor 'The literary remains of Sebastiano Serlio' *Art Bulletin* (1942)

Sforza family Descendants of the Romagnol warrior Muzio Attendolo (1369–1424), whose sons assumed his nickname. Francesco rose meteorically by military opportunism and marriage to Bianca Visconti, becoming Duke of Milan (1450–66); his sons were less fortunate or skilful: Galeazzo Maria (assassinated 1476), Lodovico (deposed and imprisoned by the French 1500, d.1508), Ascanio (disappointed in hopes of becoming pope, d.1505). As dukes of Milan they promoted economic growth, monumental building and the arts but depended on professional officials, neo-feudal

Sforza

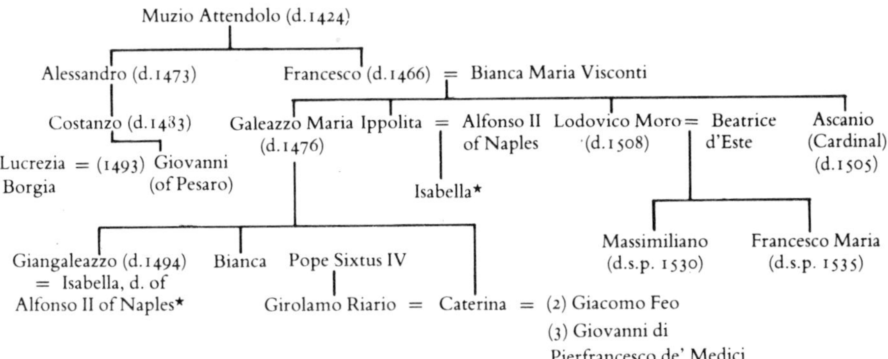

relations, military garrisons and unreasonably high taxation rather than institutionalized or informal consensus. Francesco's alliance with Medicean Florence and the Papacy helped to stabilize Italy, but Lodovico bore some responsibility for French invasions. His ineffectual sons were briefly dukes (Massimiliano 1512–15; Francesco 1521–24, 1529–35) between foreign occupations. The line of Bosio, another son of Muzio Attendolo, who married into the Roman and Tuscan aristocracy, sustained the family's eminence more permanently. DC

C. M. Ady *Milan under the Sforza* (1907)

Sforza, Caterina (*c.*1462–1509), famous for her audacity in love and war, was the natural daughter of Duke Galeazzo Maria Sforza and the wife (1477) of Girolamo Riario. They lived more in Rome than at Imola or Forlì, the possessions conferred on Girolamo by his uncle Sixtus IV, until Sixtus's death in 1484, when Caterina took Castel S. Angelo by force, hoping to intimidate the cardinals into electing a pope of their family interest. Returning to Forlì, they fell victims to a local uprising: Girolamo was assassinated (1488) and Caterina was imprisoned with their 6 children. Her escape (leaving them as hostages) into the city's fortress of Ravaldino occasioned the story – probably apocryphal – that she lifted her skirt to show the mob she could produce more children. Relieving forces dispersed the conspirators and Caterina took savage reprisals; she was equally vindictive after the death of her lover Giacomo Feo (1495).

Deprived of her lordships by Alexander VI, she was the first ruler that Cesare Borgia attacked: first Imola, then Forlì fell (November 1499–January 1500), and according to the local chronicler Cesare raped her. Caterina was taken to Rome in captivity, but after renouncing her political claims she was released (July 1501). Secretly remarried (1496) to Giovanni di Pierfrancesco de' Medici – Giovanni dalle Bande Nere was their son – she retired to Florence. Caterina was not distinguished as a patron of learning and the arts, though she did compile a book of cosmetic and medical prescriptions. DC

E. Breisach *Caterina Sforza, a Renaissance virago* (1967); P. Pasolini *Caterina Sforza* (3 vols 1893)

Sforza, Francesco (1401–66) provides the best example of an opportunist *condottiere* who became a respected prince (Duke of Milan 1450–66). When his father Muzio Attendolo was killed in battle in 1424, Francesco succeeded to his father's leadership and reputation for strict military discipline. Thereafter his principal employer was Duke Filippo Maria Visconti of Milan, whom he served in successive campaigns against Venice, and whose daughter Bianca Maria he married (1443). In the early 1430s, taking advantage of papal weakness, Francesco built up a large following and a sizeable territorial power in the Marches, with a base at Fermo, but these he sacrificed for his prospects in Lombardy. Having led Venetian forces against the short-lived AMBROSIAN REPUBLIC of Milan (1447–50), he received the city and dukedom in his own name. With the

Antonio Pollaiuolo's design for an equestrian monument to **Francesco Sforza**, 1489 (New York, Robert Lehman Collection).

friendship and financial support of Cosimo de' Medici, he imposed the Peace of LODI (1454) which was intended to curb Venetian expansion and did stabilize Italy. Though without Cosimo's learning and artistic interests, Francesco provided humanists to educate his children (one, Filelfo, wrote the *Sforziade* about Francesco's military deeds) and followed Cosimo's example as a building patron, at least in founding the Ospedale Maggiore at Milan, designed by Filarete. Though favouring the castle of Pavia as his residence, Francesco restored the much damaged Visconti fortress of Porta Giovia in Milan, a decision to be criticized by Machiavelli in *The prince* (because it was betrayed by its castellan in 1499), notwithstanding his respect for Francesco as a new prince who possessed *virtù* and succeeded in ruling a corrupted city. In government Francesco depended largely upon his secretary, Cicco Simonetta, and was less surely in control of the duchy's subject cities. In the 1470s a monumental statue of him on horseback was projected, and later Leonardo da Vinci took over the commission, but none of his ambitious designs was finally cast in bronze; a colossal clay model decomposed without leaving a trace. DC *Storia di Milano* VI Fondazione Treccani degli Alfieri (1956); C. M. Ady *Milan under the Sforza* (1907)

Sforza, Lodovico (1451–1508), the second and ablest son of Francesco Sforza, has been described as 'the perfect type of the despot' (Burckhardt), though Machiavelli had disparaged him for misjudgments which lost him the duchy of Milan. No contemporary or modern biography exists of this enigmatic figure, in spite of his major role in the calamitous French invasions of Italy, and as a patron. Known as 'il Moro', either because he was dark or because his second name was Mauro, he had a humanist education and made some attempts himself at writing (he composed lives of illustrious men, including his own father). Excluded from power after the murder of his brother Duke Galeazzo Maria (1476), Lodovico defied his sister-in-law Bona of Savoy and took over the government of her son Giangaleazzo; after the latter's death (1494) he assumed the title of Duke of Milan, relying on his good relations with the Emperor Maximilian, to whom he had married his niece Bianca Maria.

Lodovico's foreign policy just before CHARLES VIII's invasion was dominated by hostility to Naples and the influence there of Giangaleazzo's wife; in 1493 he overturned traditional Sforza diplomacy by allying with Venice and the Pope against Naples and Florence, and encouraged Charles VIII's expedition in spite of the Orléanist claim to Milan. After Charles had successfully reached Naples, however, Lodovico was a prime mover in forming the Italian League (April 1495), though he took no active part himself in the military operations which ensured Charles's evacuation of Italy. In 1496 he encouraged Maximilian's inconsequential expedition to assist Pisa against Florence, tied to its French alliance; in 1499, inadequately prepared, he

Manuscript illustration showing **Lodovico Sforza** with his nephew Giangaleazzo in the care of S. Lodovico and *Fortuna*. (Paris, Bibliothèque Nationale).

faced the attack of LOUIS XII allied with Venice. After a brief return from exile (February 1500) he was again defeated. He died, a French prisoner, at Loches, near Tours.

In his government of Milan Lodovico used trusted professionals and careerists rather than the local patriciate; though efficient, it was criticized for overtaxation. His character, descriptions suggest, was laconic and secretive. He married in 1491 Beatrice d'Este (aged 15½); if her boisterous nature appealed to him, it did not distract him altogether from his mistresses, though after her death in childbirth (January 1497) he was remorseful; his subsequent religous benefactions to ensure his own salvation were at the expense of his own best interests as ruler.

Lodovico's pleasure in the distractions of music, verbal wit and visually exciting theatrical effects probably most account for the favour he showed Leonardo da Vinci; they also had scientific interests in common. Lodovico was, however, well provided with other engineers and artists of all kinds; Leonardo received relatively few major commissions (e.g. as a painter, the *Last Supper* for Lodovico's favoured Dominicans at S. Maria delle Grazie, and some room decorations in the Castle). He was a distinguished building patron, among his main projects being the completion of the Certosa and the founding of a new cathedral at Pavia; many religious foundations benefited by new buildings, above all S. Maria delle Grazie and S. Ambrogio, where the works were designed by Bramante. Lodovico's outstanding reputation as a munificent and well-informed patron is attested by many literary courtiers (e.g. Castiglione) who bemoaned their dispersal after 1499. *See* ORLÉANS, HOUSE OF; WARS OF ITALY. DC

Storia di Milano VII Fondazione Treccani degli Alfieri (1957); F. Malaguzzi Valeri *La corte di Lodovico il Moro* (4 vols 1913–23)

Sicily The kingdom of Sicily, or 'Trinacria', founded as a result of the revolution of 1282 against Charles I of ANJOU, was ruled until 1296 by kings of ARAGON and then by a cadet branch of the Aragonese royal house (1296–1409). Economically backward, its trade largely in the hands of Catalan merchants, the kingdom was weakened in the 14c. by the frequent attempts at conquest made by the kings of NAPLES. With the death of Frederick III (1337) royal power virtually collapsed, becoming the prey of the Sicilian nobility – the 3 'semi-kings' (the lines of Ventimiglia, Chiaramonte and Passaneto), some 70 families of modest prosperity, and about 140 poor, violent and minor houses. From 1412 the crown returned to the royal line of Aragon. Under Alfonso V (1416–58) the island served as a base for his ambitions on Naples. He visited it frequently, reasserted royal power, established (1434) the university of Catania, and gave a definitive form to its parliament.

Thenceforward, despite the check which the 'Deputation of the Kingdom', the commissioners elected by its parliament, were sometimes able to exercise, Sicily was ruled by viceroys who subordinated its interests to those of Aragon. Characteristic of the hispanization of the island was the introduction of the Inquisition (1487) and the expulsion of the Jews (1492). In the 16c. frequent coastal raids by Muslim pirates of the Barbary coast emphasized Sicilian dependence upon Spanish power. Yet under alien rule only Messina, which developed a silk industry and acquired a university (1548), flourished. The island which in the 12c. and 13c. had enjoyed an important role in the story of European culture played no part in the Renaissance, and its only distinguished sons, the humanists Beccadelli and Marinaeus Siculus, and the painter Antonello da Messina, gained their fame elsewhere. *See* CHARLES V. JL

D. Mack Smith *A history of Sicily: medieval Sicily* (1968)

Siena Tuscan city-state which endured between 1355 and 1559 the two most troubled centuries in its history: a long period of economic and demographic decline, of social conflict, and of increasing instability and tension in political life. Unstable régime followed unstable régime; in one disastrous year, 1368, the city's constitution was actually changed 4 times in an attempt to accommodate its contending power groups, while, even more remarkably, the government structures of Siena were actually reformed 10 times between 1525 and 1552. Externally this was also a period of incessant, purposeless and profitless warfare, although foreign warfare was less damaging to the economy than were the numerous visitations of marauding mercenary companies throughout the 14c. and 15c. This was, in addition, a period in which the determination of the Florentines to conquer Siena became increasingly obvious. The Sienese attempted numerous solutions to their difficulties, and in 1399, despite the strength of the city's communal traditions, even resorted to the expedient of surrendering their city into the hands of Giangaleazzo Visconti of Milan. Visconti rule of the city lasted until 1404. A more positive solution was the development of the system of government by a *balia* which, in Siena, became converted into a permanent magistracy and effectively replaced the traditional communal councils.

One feature of Siena's political life at this period has always provoked comment. This was the system of *monti* or *ordini* whose very existence seemed to institutionalize civic strife. Each member of the ruling élite of Siena was a member of one of the city's 5 *monti*, and each *monte* competed with the others for a monopoly of power in Siena. Attempts were made to devise some form of power-sharing by which the *monti* could be brought to cooperate together, and these efforts were not always unsuccessful. Indeed, the periods of internal peace in Siena were ones when such coalitions worked well. This is the light in which we should see the period 1458–63, the pontificate of Pius II, when Siena effectively became a papal dependency, or the so-called *signoria* of the PETRUCCI (1487–1524), which can best be understood as the most successful power-sharing exercise of the period, in which the Petrucci acted as peculiarly effective chairmen of the various coalitions by which Siena was governed.

In the early 16c., as the economic decline of Siena accelerated, and the position of her ruling élite weakened in consequence, the successful creation of such coalitions became more difficult. Siena was constantly torn by party strife and civic turmoil and this turbulence created a kind of political vacuum in the centre of Italy from which the French hoped to profit. Charles V was forced to respond to this French threat by taking an interest in the city, and in the 2nd quarter of the century Spanish influence in Siena became increasingly obvious. After 1530 a garrison of Spanish troops looked as if it would guarantee the city's loyalty, but to make certain Charles V decreed that a fortress should be built in Siena. This action forced the Sienese into open rebellion in 1552, and the Spanish were driven from the city. With sporadic French assistance, the Sienese tried to preserve their independence for the next 3 years in what has become famous as an heroic struggle against the combined forces of Spain and Cosimo I de' Medici, but in 1555 Siena was starved into surrender, although fighting continued in the Sienese contado for another 4 years. Siena was governed directly by the Spanish until 1557, when it was sold to Cosimo, whose possession of the city was confirmed by the Peace of Cateau-Cambrésis. After 1559, therefore, the history of Siena followed that of the Grand Duchy of Tuscany. JH

J. Hook *Siena, a city and its history* (1979)

A view of the Piazza del Campo, **Siena**.

Signorelli, Luca (mentioned 1470, d.1523), an Umbrian painter, was one of the great Renaissance draughtsmen and students of the human figure and its anatomy. His masterpiece, the frescoes of the *Last Judgment* in Orvieto cathedral (1499), prefigure Michelangelo and were evidently admired by Raphael on his way from Florence to Rome to work on the Stanza della Segnatura. Signorelli was a master of foreshortening, and his geometric simplifications are particularly telling to anyone attuned to the art of Léger and of many of his modern successors. JW

Sixtus IV Pope 1471–84 (b.1414) The Ligurian Francesco della Rovere was, as a Franciscan friar, bishop and cardinal, a scholarly theologian and a model clerical administrator. As a pope his first care was to arouse European support for a crusade. In spite of almost universal indifference he did manage to assemble a fleet, which took Smyrna but then broke up in discord. He soon, however, became almost entirely immersed in the politics

Detail of the bronze effigy on the monument to **Sixtus IV** by Antonio Pollaiuolo (Rome, Museo Petriano, St Peter's).

of the peninsula. He took up the still far from completed task of re-establishing direct papal control of the Papal State, promoting relatives to high positions in the Church as his assistants in this task on an unprecedented scale. Their own ambitions complicated as much as aided his task, creating bitter rivalries within the Curia and among the Roman baronial families, and exacerbating the suspicions of neighbouring powers who had become used to a weak and unchallenging Papal State.

He was drawn into war first with Naples against Florence (1478–79), then (1482–84) with Venice (which he had promised to support in its attempt to conquer Ferrara) against Naples. From neither did the Church make any gains. Sixtus found time, however, to add greatly to the Vatican library and was the real founder of its collection of antiquities. He not only built and partly decorated the Sistine Chapel, but also established the Sistine choir, beginning the fame of Rome as a musical centre. With visitors and residents such as Leto, Argyropoulos and Filelfo, the city rivalled Florence in its attractiveness to humanist scholars. To his especial liking for Melozzo da Forlì, whom he employed to decorate the library, we owe a likeness not only of him, but also of his controversial nephews Raffaele, Giuliano (the future Julius II), Girolamo and Giovanni, together with his librarian, Platina, who points to an inscription praising Sixtus's efforts to rebuild Rome and restore its former glory. *See* ROME; PAZZI; FERRARA, WAR OF. JRH

L. Pastor *History of the popes* IV (1894); E. Rodocanachi *Histoire de Rome: une cour princière au Vatican . . .* (1925); E. Lee *Sixtus IV and men of letters* (1978)

Sixtus V Pope 1585–90 (b.1525) Felice Peretti entered the Franciscan order and won rapid fame as a preacher and theologian, becoming a cardinal in 1570. A stern reformer who had enjoyed the favour of Paul V and Pius V, he devoted his pontificate to maintaining the independence and authority of the Church. The most enduring result was a total reorganization of the Curia; the size of the Sacred COLLEGE was fixed at 70, and the 15 Congregations by which the Roman Catholic Church is governed were created. Sixtus did much to reorder the Papal State, where he waged vigorous war against bandits. He created a small fleet to curb the pirates who preyed on the coasts. At Rome he encouraged the silk and woollen industries, improved streets and fountains and, with Fontana's help, embellished the city with many new monuments. Sixtus was only able to pay for these activities by imposing new customs duties, by resorting to the sale of offices on an unprecedented scale, and by heavy borrowing. JH

Slaves as domestic servants were not uncommon. The letters of the Florentine patrician Alessandra degli Strozzi frequently complain of her problems with her disobedient slave Catherine (*la Cateruccia*). Alessandra would have preferred a Tartar, because they could endure harder work, although they were not as good-looking as the Russians. Tartars, Russians, Circassians and others were imported into Italy by Genoese and Venetian merchants, especially between *c.*1350 (when full employment after the Black Death made servants hard to find) and *c.*1450 (when Ottoman advance into the Black Sea region cut off the sources of supply). PB

I. Origo 'The domestic enemy' *Speculum* (1955)

Soderini, Piero di Tommaso (1452–1522) The most prominent member historically of an influential Florentine patrician family, Soderini was elected to the new position of gonfalonier for life in 1502. This office, which acknowledged the usefulness of the Venetian dogeship, was created to give stability and continuity to the ever-changing membership of the popular government instituted in 1494–95. As with a Venetian doge, a man with a strong character and fixed views could use the permanent chairmanship of bodies with a rotating membership to wield a measure of power. Over 10 years Soderini made many enemies, among them the overt friends of the banished Medici; those who feared the consequences of his insistence that France should remain Florence's ally; and those who had hoped to find him sympathetic to constitutional changes that would concentrate power again in an oligarchy.

Though his authority was (like a doge's) simply titular, he became increasingly identified with government and its policies. As such, he was recognized as the chief target of the papal-Spanish army that advanced on Florence in 1512 after the withdrawal of the French from Italy. In August the army took Prato and waited for Soderini's response to the demand, made by the city's leading supporters of the Medici, that he should resign. Caught between the threat of external force and a lack of internal support, he agreed and was escorted from the city to an exile that lasted until his death. JRH

S. Bertelli 'Piero Soderini "Vexilifer perpetuus reipublicae fiorentinae" 1502–12' in A. Molho and J. A. Tedeschi ed. *Renaissance: studies in honor of Hans Baron* (1971); R. S. Cooper 'Pier Soderini: aspiring prince or civic leader?' *Studies in Medieval and Renaissance History* XI (1978)

Sodoma, Giovanni Antonio Bazzi, il (1477–1549) Born in Savoy, Sodoma had moved to Siena by 1501 after training in Lombardy. Contrary to popular belief there is no evidence that he was ever a pupil of Leonardo, although his art reflects Leonardo's. Chigi brought him to Rome, where he worked in the Vatican and probably met Raphael in 1508. His work was not a success and he returned to Siena, marrying there in 1510. He made Siena his home but travelled a great deal throughout his life, working in Florence, Volterra, Pisa, and Lucca. His nickname, which Vasari claims he acquired because he 'loved little boys more than was decent', seems in fact to have appeared first in 1515 when he won a horse race in Florence and, when asked what name should be called out for the winner, answered *Sodoma*. In any case, he had 2 children and received countless commissions from religious houses and civic authorities, all of which suggests something different from what Vasari would have us believe. LDE

S. J. Freedberg *Painting in Italy 1500–1600* (1970)

Spectacles appear to have been invented in Italy at the end of the 13c. They are mentioned (as 'eyeglasses', *rodoli da ogli*) in Venetian guild regulations *c.*1300, and also in a sermon by Giordano da Pisa. Petrarch thought the invention of spectacles an argument for the dignity of man. After this date there is ample pictorial evidence for their use in close-quarters work, and, though precision lens grinding was only introduced at the end of the period, spectacles probably prolonged the scholar's and merchant's working day. PB

E. Rosen 'The invention of eye-glasses' *Journal of the History of Medicine* (1956)

Squarcialupi, Antonio (1416–80) Florentine organist and music collector who lived in Florence most of his life, and was organist at the cathedral from 1436 until his death. A minor composer, he was famous in his lifetime for his playing and in posterity for a massive and elegant manuscript in his possession (now in the Biblioteca Medicea Laurenziana, Florence) which contains a substantial part of the surviving repertoire of Italian Trecento secular vocal music. DA

Trying on **spectacles** at an optician's shop, from an engraving after Stradanus *c.*1600.

Squarcione, Francesco (*c.*1397–1468) The son of a Paduan notary, he began life as a tailor and embroiderer. There is no evidence of any formal artistic training and very little of his work survives. His claim to fame is as the teacher of Mantegna, whom he adopted as his son, but with whom he had endless legal battles. He is supposed to have studied and collected classical art and plaster casts of antiques, but there is no evidence of this in his few surviving works, and only Mantegna of all his pupils evinces any interest in antiques. LDE

Stampa, Gaspara (1523–54) The 'new Sappho' and 'honest' courtesan, celebrated in Venetian circles for her beauty, music and verse. Stampa's pose was to sing her love and betrayal by her protector Collaltino di Collalto, himself a poet. Her limpidity, simplicity and air of spontaneity were antithetical to humanist requirements of *gravitas*, and posthumous publication by her sister Cassandra (*Rime*, 1554) preserved her work without increasing its immediate fame. 'Gasparina' was rediscovered by the Romantics, persuaded wrongly of her essential affinity with themselves, and Croce lent authority to the self-created legend of passion's victim by calling her *Rime* a diary. The confessional element is, however, subordinated to obvious Petrarchistic patterns. More operatic than dramatic, more tearfully ironic than tragic, her verse calls for the musical accompaniment she was wont to supply herself. Opinion is general today that she is the most original of Renaissance women poets, certainly the best in Italy. LGC

Le rime di Gaspara Stampa e Veronica Franco ed. A. Salza (1913)

Stoicism An ancient philosophy, popular in Hellenistic times, deriving its name from the fact that its founder, Zeno of Citium (336–264 BC), was accustomed to walking up and down the Painted Colonnade (*stoa*) in Athens. The Stoics divided philosophy into logic, physics and ethics. The last, with its ideal of the unperturbable and self-sufficient sage, had a particular appeal for CICERO and SENECA, whose works continued to be handbooks of moral edification in the Renaissance. Other ancient texts of Stoic doctrine, such as Epictetus' *Manual* and Diogenes Laertius' *Lives of the philosophers*, were widely influential and frequently reprinted. Probably the most ardent revivers of Stoic thought in the Renaissance were the northerners Guillaume du Vair (1556–1621), whose *Moral philosophy of the Stoics* was widely read in both French and English, and Justus Lipsius (1547–1606), who tried to promote Stoicism as an integral philosophy to replace Platonism and Aristotelianism. More influential in popular culture than among scholarly philosophers, Stoicism nevertheless made some inroads in Italy among Aristotelians such as Pomponazzi, who endorsed the characteristic Stoic position that 'virtue is its own reward'. CS

J. Eymard d'Angers *Recherches sur le stoicisme au XVIe et XVIIe siècles* (1976)

Strabo (64/3 BC–?AD 21) Greek author whose enormous political and descriptive *Geography* was both a pioneer defence of his subject and a compilation of all that he could find out about the nature of the inhabited world as it was known in his day. He also took a scientific interest in such matters as climate, mensuration and cartography. Strabo's 'rediscovery' in the 15c. stimulated scholarly topographers and travellers (Enea Silvio Piccolomini, Biondo, Ciriaco d'Ancona, for instance) to know what to look for and how to organize their knowledge. Though less influential than Ptolemy, Strabo also helped cosmographers like Paolo Toscanelli create a mood encouraging deliberate overseas exploration. JRH

Geography tr. M. L. Jones (8 vols 1917–33); G. Aujac *Strabon et la science de son temps* (1968)

Stradiots Light cavalrymen armed with lance, scimitar and shield, raised by Venice originally from the coasts and islands of Greece in return for land grants and, when on active service, a wage. During the 15c. Albanians and Cypriots were employed and some men from southern Dalmatia, though most Dalmatian light cavalry were separately organized as *Crovati* (Croats). Stradiots were used in garrison and on coastal patrol throughout the sea empire of Venice, always posted well away from their own homes because of the police aspect of their duties which depended on their not contracting local loyalties. They were imported to Italy for Venice's wars there, gaining a reputation for fidelity, gallantry and lawlessness. They were much in demand for service in Germany and elsewhere (Henry VIII employed some in his campaign in France in 1544), and Venice was careful to foster their loyalty by allowing commands to pass from father to son and by the award of honours and pensions. From the mid-16c. companies of stradiots were employed on the Venetian mainland to combat brigandage and to make arrests – again, because they had no local ties. The derivation of the word *stradiotto* remains obscure. JRH

Straparola, Gianfrancesco (*c.*1490–1557) A writer best known for his *Le piacevole notti* (*The entertaining nights*). This was a collection of 75 stories purporting to have been told over 13 evenings during Carnival time on the Venetian island of Murano, published in 2 parts in 1550 and 1553. Its mingling of anecdotes, oriental and other folk tales and ingenious literary riddles made it extremely popular (as did a bawdiness which contributed to its being put on the Index in 1624). It contains the first known version of the story of Puss in Boots. A number of the tales were translated in William Painter's collection *The palace of pleasure* (1566), and one has been suggested as a source for Shakespeare's *Merry wives of Windsor*. JRH
Le piacevole notti ed. G. Rua (2 vols 1927); tr. W. G. Waters (2 vols 1894)

Striggio, Alessandro senior (*c.*1535–92) A fine player of viol and lute who, although he often described himself as a '*gentil'huomo mantovano*', was in fact a professional musician in the service of Cosimo de' Medici, noted for his music for *intermedii* given at royal celebrations, especially in 1566 and 1579 (the latter for the wedding of Francesco de' Medici and Bianca Capello). He wrote madrigals and some church music (including a motet for 40 voices) and was well known in other courts. DA

Striggio, Alessandro junior (1573–1630), son of the above, was secretary of state to the dukes of Mantua from 1608, after studying law. He later became court counsellor and ambassador of the Gonzagas in Milan and Spain and at the papal court, ending his life as the *Maggiordomo di Corte* and being made a marchese in 1628. He was a friend of Monteverdi, writing the libretto of his first opera, *L'Orfeo*, as well as the texts of several other works. He died in Venice of the plague. DA

Strozzi family The Strozzi clan (31 separate households in 1427) played a part in Florentine history up to the mid-16c. second only to that of the Medici. Among the earliest of Florentine bankers, they weathered the financial crisis that

The rusticated façade of the **Strozzi** Palace in Florence.

pulled down so many firms in the mid-14c. As other Strozzi had taken up permanent residence abroad in pursuit of profit, whether elsewhere in Italy or in Spain, France or the Low Countries, there were always places of refuge for those Florentine members of the clan whose prominence in domestic politics attracted that habitual penalty for backing the wrong power group: exile.

Thus Filippo (1428–91) returned to Florence in 1466, from the wave of banishments that had swept out his father on Cosimo de' Medici's return from *his* exile in 1434, as a man with foreign contacts of an importance to make him indispensable as an adviser to Lorenzo the Magnificent – and with a fortune sufficient for him to embark in 1489 upon the building of the truly palatial Strozzi Palace. Before that he had purchased the freehold of the chapel in S. Maria Novella that bears his name and commissioned Filippino Lippi to decorate it. Indeed, his 'style', culminating in the most impressive funeral of a private citizen Florence had yet witnessed, and springing from his intimacy with princely courts (especially that of Naples), may have influenced those patricians who were at last to defer to a princely government in Florence after 1530.

Even so, his son, also called Filippo (1488–1538), though he married a Medici

(Clarice, daughter of the younger Piero) and lent financial assistance to that family from 1512 to 1527, found it increasingly difficult to square his own dynastic plans with the presence of a Medici duke. He, the son of an exile, came to assume the leadership of the new wave of exiles in 1530, and after Alessandro de' Medici's assassination financed and took part in their campaign to oust Cosimo I in 1537. Filippo was captured after their defeat at MONTEMURLO and imprisoned in the Fortezza da Basso where, next year, he died – whether by suicide or assassination remains uncertain. His sons and brothers moved to France where, as businessmen, clerics, and above all as military and naval commanders, they played a prominent part during the rest of Francis I's reign and those of his successors. JRH

R. B. Goldthwaite *Private wealth in Renaissance Florence* (1968); L. Limongelli *Filippo Strozzi, primo cittadino d'Italia* (1963); E. Picot *Les italiens en France au XVIe siècle* (1902); M. M. Bullard *Filippo Strozzi and the Medici* (1980)

Subiaco is some 45 miles E of Rome. Here, at the Benedictine monastery of S. Scolastica, the first Italian printed books were produced in 1465: Cicero's *De oratore* and the *De morte persecutorum* of the 4c. 'Christian Cicero', Lactantius. An undated Donatus may have preceded them by a year. The press was installed by two German clerics, Arnold Pennartz and Conrad Schweinheim. *See* PRINTING. JRH

Sumptuary laws (from Latin *sumptuarius*, 'relating to expense') Of all governmental interferences with individual liberty, which included licences to travel or to study abroad, city gates which closed between sunset and sunrise, and so on, the sumptuary laws were in theory the most invasive before the introduction of an effective CENSORSHIP of books. Most European governments had laws regulating what men and women should wear and the levels of expenditure at which different classes might entertain. One motive was to bolster home industries (and prevent the outflow of specie) by forbidding the wearing of imported cloths. Another was to discourage sexual licence by banning fashions that emphasized the male genitals or revealed too copiously the breasts.

But the chief motive was to maintain the external signs that distinguished CLASS from class, to suppress social jealousy by restricting provocative displays of wealth. Thus the wearing of jewels and luxury materials like brocades, velvets and fur trimmings was subject to the sumptuary laws, as were the lengths of the trains and sleeves of dresses, the numbers of guests at meals, even the numbers of courses and the foodstuffs that might be served. As the occasions for jealousy were greatest in the complex social mix of commercial towns, it was particularly in Italy that these laws were elaborated – and flouted, as their repeated reenactments show and as the visual evidence of the arts confirms. *See* COSTUME. JRH

M. M. Newett 'The sumptuary laws of Venice ...' in T. R. Tout and J. Tait ed. *Historical essays* (1907)

Swiss, the At the beginning of the WARS OF ITALY the Swiss confederation included the cantons of Uri, Schwyz, Unterwalden, Zug, Glarus, Berne, Lucerne, Zürich, Fribourg and Solothurn. In 1476 their defeat of 2 invading Burgundian armies had given them a reputation as the best-disciplined and most sought-after heavy (pike-armed) infantry in Europe. With a pastoral economy that produced a low income but could survive long absences, mercenary military service had already become a tradition; this the confederation tried to maintain within a common policy, an aim encouraged by the Burgundian defeats and, still more, by the defeat of an army sent against it in 1499 by Maximilian I and his subsequent recognition of its independence. In 1501 the confederation was strengthened by the admission of the cantons of Basel and Schaffhausen.

The favoured outlet for Swiss military energy had been with the friendly power to the west, France. Both Charles VIII and Louis XII invaded Italy with Swiss contingents. But French claims to Milan, while offering employment to individuals, conflicted with the chief political aim of the confederation. This was, in conjunction with the allied region of Valais and the independent league of cantons centred on Grisons (Graubünden), to push Swiss control of the passes between Tyrol and Savoy further south. All the same, it was not until 1510 that the confederation broke its Special Relationship; in support of Pope Julius II's anti-French League, the Swiss forced Louis's troops to evacuate the Milanese in 1512 and defeated his new invading army at NOVARA in 1513. Until

1515 they remained the effective masters of the duchy of Milan, in spite of the League's reinstatement of the Sforza in the person of Massimiliano.

But the confederation's power was based on the reputation of its troops. These, in that same year, were at last defeated, by Francis I at MARIGNANO. Thereafter the Swiss played no major political role in Italian affairs and, though recruiters from the Italian states (especially Venice), as from other European powers, continued to pick up volunteers, the confederation's policy became ever more stubbornly neutral. JRH

C. Kohler *Les Suisses dans les guerres d'Italie de 1506 à 1512* (repr. 1978); V. Cérésole *La république de Venise et les Suisses* (1864)

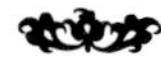

Taccola, Mariano di Jacopo (1381/2–*c.*1453) Sienese sculptor and civic administrator. His first machine sketches (of bridges and harbour works) date from 1427; in 1432 the future Emperor Sigismund became his patron and Taccola may have campaigned with him against the Turks. His *De machinis libri decem* (1449), although never printed, was very influential. It deals with all kinds of civil and military machines, many apparently original to Taccola. MBH

De machinis libri decem tr. G. Scaglia (2 vols 1971); *Liber tertius de ingeniis ac edifitiis non usitatis* facsimile and transcription by J. H. Beck (1969)

Tacitus, Cornelius (*c.*AD 55–120) was the slowest to emerge of the Roman historians. Unknown to Dante, even to Petrarch, he was found by Zanobi da Strada in one of the greatest of the neglected abbey libraries of Italy, Montecassino, between 1355 and 1357. Zanobi communicated his discovery to Boccaccio, who entered the name of Tacitus in his revision of the *Amorosa visione* and used material from Tacitus in the *De claris mulieribus* (*On famous women*). Nothing in this implies excitement in the discovery, or ideas flowing from it. And when they do flow in the civic age of Florence, with Leonardo Bruni, in the opening of his *History of the Florentine people*, or with Salutati, it is a plain recoil from the record of the Roman Emperors. The decline of Rome begins, says Bruni, with servitude to the Emperors. This stand against Tacitus is reflected in the editions, multiplied for Livy (known also in Italian, the first Decade from the 13c., Decades III and IV from Boccaccio's version), few for Tacitus, for whom Italian translations did not come till 1544 (*Histories*) and 1563 (*Annals*).

Nor must we be misled by the old prejudice, that Machiavelli's affinity was with Tacitus, his *Prince* modelled on Tiberius. This is an impossibility: the 15c. editions lacked Annals I–VI, which appear only in an edition of 1515, dedicated to Pope Leo X. And while Tacitus is absent from Machiavelli's *Prince*, most have failed to see his presence in the *Discourses on the first decade of Livy*, where, in an eloquent contrast between good and bad Emperors, Machiavelli quotes feelingly from Tacitus on the disasters that attend on the (bad) Emperors. His judgment is identical with that of Bruni and Salutati a century before, and his author, as is obvious from the title and the text of his book, is Livy. But Tacitus' time was now at hand. The addition of the missing portion excited interest, while the plunge in the fortunes of Italy in the crisis of 1527–30 ushered in the age of monarchy and saw the final eclipse of the Florentine Republic. With the edition of Beatus Rhenanus (1535) Tacitus was ready for launching on his European vogue, though it was only finally with Justus Lipsius's edition of 1575 that he became triumphant as *pater prudentiae*, his account of monarchs labelled as the *theatrum hodiernae vitae*: the setting of the modern world. For the best part of a century thereafter Tacitus swamped the European market. JHW

J. H. Whitfield 'Livy →Tacitus' in R. R. Bolgar ed. *Classical influences on European culture AD 1500–1700* (1976); K. C. Schellhase *Tacitus in Renaissance political thought* (1977)

Tansillo, Luigi (1510–68), called the leader of Neapolitan literary Mannerism, was eclectic, modelling himself (in dramatic eclogue, didactic poem, sonnet, etc.) on southern precursors (Pontano, Sannazaro), but also conflating classical and medieval sources. The idyllic and Indexed *Vendemmiatore* (*The grape gatherer*; 1552) owes something to Bembo's *Priapus*, as his short lyrics do to Petrarch. Personifications of trees, flowers, fields, insects, suggest a Romantic rather than a true pre-Baroque sensibility, the Counter-Reformationism of later years (*Le lagrime de San Pietro: The tears of St Peter*) notwithstanding. *La balia* (*The nurse*), advising mothers to nurse their children themselves, foreshadows the naturalism of a later century. LGC

B. Croce 'La lirica cinquecentesca' in *Poesia popolare e poesia d'arte* (1933)

Tapestry As historical climatologists have not shown that Renaissance Italian winters and springs were warmer than they are now, it is puzzling that Italy did not fabricate tapestries to decorate and draught-proof the stony rooms of its palaces until 1545, when Cosimo I set up a manufactory in Florence. To hardiness or stinginess (tapestry was by far the most expensive form of wall decoration) we owe the existence of such secular frescoed decorative schemes as the labours of the months in the castle at Trent (*c.*1407), the Arthurian scenes of Pisanello and the courtly ones of Mantegna in the Ducal Palace of Mantua, the delicious calendar fantasies of Cossa and others in the Palazzo Schifanoia in Ferrara – and, doubtless, many others that await liberation from white-wash or later panelling. These are all in situations where northern patrons would have used tapestries.

These were imported, chiefly from Flanders, into Italy. The influence of their hunting and ceremonial scenes in particular registered on Italian 'gothic' painting or illumination and stained glass, and in literature. But the Italians did not make them. The most famous of all 'Italian' tapestries, those for the Sistine Chapel designed by Raphael, were made in Brussels from the full-scale coloured patterns, or cartoons, now in the Victoria and Albert Museum, London. Nor is it clear whether imported tapestries were used habitually or simply to add grandeur to special occasions. Even when Cosimo's manufactory was in being, and working from designs by court artists of the calibre of Bronzino, Salviati and Allori, his own headquarters, the Palace of the Signoria (now the Palazzo Vecchio), was being decorated with frescoes. The subject is under-explored. JRH

M. Viale Ferrero *Arazzi italiani del Cinquecento* (1963)

Tapestry of *Joseph and Potiphar's Wife* designed by Bronzino, showing a tapestry hanging in the background. (Florence, Palazzo Vecchio).

Tartaglia, Niccolò (1499–1557) Born in Brescia, too poor (he said) to have been sent to school for more than a few months, never master of the classical languages, Tartaglia nevertheless became one of Italy's best respected, most controversial and most productive mathematicians, from his *Ars magna* (1545) to his vast general *Trattato di numeri et misure* (1556–60). A move to Venice brought him into touch with patricians with a strong interest in pure mathematics and also in military and naval technology. His *Nova scientia* (1537) was a pioneering work on artillery ballistics. In the *Quesiti et inventioni diverse* (1546), which he dedicated to Henry VIII at the suggestion of an English pupil, he dealt with the geometrical principles of fortifications. His *Travagliata inventione* discussed diving bells and methods of salving sunken ships. He also published a richly commented edition of the first Italian translation of EUCLID, and Latin translations of ARCHIMEDES. *See* MATHEMATICS. JRH

Storia di Brescia II Fondazione Treccani degli Alfieri (1961) Part V; P. L. Rose *The Italian renaissance of mathematics* (1975)

Tasso, Torquato (1544–95) Poet, prose writer and literary theorist. Successor to and deviator from the tradition of Boiardo and Ariosto, he gave to the court of Ferrara the third of the great *ottava rima* epic romances celebrating the Este ancestry, *Gerusalemme liberata* (1581), and the purest example of Renaissance pastoral drama, *Aminta* (1573). Even before its end, his life became a legend of poetic madness and wandering. Born in Sorrento, he shared the political exile of his father, Bernardo, and began his literary studies and his long experience of Italian courts in Urbino. He attended the universities of Padua and of

Tasso, reputed portrait by Bronzino (Modena, Galeria Mauroner).

Bologna, at 18 published *Rinaldo*, a chivalric poem in 12 cantos, and in 1565 took service with Cardinal Luigi d'Este.

Although he completed the *Liberata* in 1575, Tasso was never to be satisfied with it in relation to neo-Aristotelian canons of epic poetry or to Counter-Reformation religious orthodoxy, and restlessly he consulted scholars on one score and ecclesiastical inquisitors on the other. In 1577 he was imprisoned for a paranoid display of violence in the presence of Lucrezia d'Este. He escaped to the south but, following another outburst on his return to Ferrara in 1579, was shut up in the hospital of S. Anna, to remain there until 1586. After a pirated version called *Goffredo* appeared in 1580, the *Liberata* was published in 1581, but Tasso continued to regard the poem as unfinished while it circulated in several editions from that year on. Released from S. Anna, he went to Mantua under the protection of Duke Vincenzo Gonzaga, and thence into a ceaseless vagabondage that took him to Genoa, Rome, Naples and Florence. He received hospitality from religious orders and academies, from the Medici, from the marquis Giambattista Manso, and from Pope Clement VIII and his nephew, to whom Tasso dedicated the only authorized version of his epic, much reworked and retitled *Gerusalemme conquistata* (1593). He died in Rome in the monastery of S. Onofrio.

Tasso wrote in many genres. *Aminta* distils his reading of THEOCRITUS, VIRGIL, OVID, Sannazaro and Poliziano into a dramatization of the psychology of love which is both a neo-Platonic paradigm and a disguised reference to the Ferrarese court. His voluminous letters are literary compositions rather than personal correspondence and contain many of the themes taken up also in his 28 *Dialoghi*. His engagement in literary polemics is represented by his *Discorsi dell'arte poetica*, written for the Ferrarese academy in the 1560s and expanded into the *Discorsi del poema eroico* (1594), and by shorter disquisitions in response to critics of the *Liberata*. In 1587 he published the final version of a tragedy, *Il re Torrismondo*, a neo-Aristotelian composition of Scandinavian and chivalric content in a structure intended to imitate and surpass Sophocles' *Oedipus rex*. The *Rime* published in his later years (1591–93) include early lyrics and cover many subjects: love madrigals, sonnets and *canzoni* to Laura Peperara, Leonora Sanvitale and Laura Bendidio, religious, occasional and dedicatory poems. In 1594 he finished his theogony, *Il mondo creato*.

A consistent impulse in Tasso's troubled existence was his quest for affecting RHETORIC and for definition of its highest form. The enduring splendours of the *Liberata* are the subtlety and solemnity, the melancholy and the sensuousness achieved by eloquent device and melodic diction. His late-Cinquecento determination to bring poetry closer to Christian truth and to classical unity and grandeur without sacrifice of the charm of the chivalric romances caused him to employ the metre as well as the knight errantry, tournaments, magic and amatory adventures of the Carolingian and Arthurian poems, but to substitute a historical subject from the First Crusade, Godfrey of Boulogne's taking of Jerusalem from the Muslims in 1099, and to restrict the action to 20 cantos.

Rejecting the minstrel voice mimicked by Pulci and Boiardo and transmogrified into an ironic Ovidian instrument by Ariosto, Tasso assumes a vatic austerity like Virgil's and invokes Christian inspiration for his epic of the saintly warrior who freed Jerusalem. Into the relatively classical framework he introduces the stories of Rinaldo, supposed ancestor of the Este, lured from his duty by the pagan enchantress Armida, and of the African warrior maiden Clorinda, propelled by celestial design to semi-erotic death and baptism at the hands of the despairing Tancredi, whose unrequited love for her is paralleled by the pathetic love of Erminia for him. Supremely Counter-Reformation example of a critical movement toward the Christian epic though it be, the *Liberata* retains its hold on readers through Tasso's power to make syntax and rhetorical artifice embody the lonely travailed spirit yearning after love and certainty. *See* CRITICAL THEORY OF LITERATURE. LGC

A. Solerti *Vita di Torquato Tasso* (1895); C. P. Brand *Torquato Tasso: a study of the poet and his contribution to English literature* (1965); G. Getto *Interpretazione del Tasso* (1951)

Taxation It was the wars, rather than the public buildings, of the city-states of Renaissance Italy which made high taxation inevitable. What is remarkable about the tax systems of these states is their precocious sophistication. At a time when most European states operated with fairly crude forms of direct taxation like the poll tax and the hearth tax, the city republics of north and central Italy relied on graduated property taxes, like the Venetian *decima* (a 'tithe' of annual income from property) and the Florentine *catasto*. The advantage of this form of taxation was that people paid, or were supposed to pay, according to their means. Hence the opposition to the projected *catasto* by some rich Florentines *c.*1425–26, an opposition which Masaccio's *Tribute money* was probably intended to chide. The main disadvantage of the property tax was the time and money spent on assessment. It took 3 years for the officials administering the Florentine *catasto* of 1427 to assess the property of the 250,000-odd people under Florentine rule. Hence reassessments did not take place as often as they were supposed to. The Venetian *decima* should have been reassessed every 10 years, but in the 16c. this happened only in 1537, 1566 and 1581.

The obvious alternative or supplement to a direct tax on property was an indirect tax on consumption (a *gabella*), levied on wheat, livestock and other commodities as they entered the city, or on wine sold retail, or, most common of all, on salt, which had the advantage of being a commodity both necessary and relatively easy to control. Governments sometimes forced their subjects to buy a

A monk pays his **taxes** to the commune of Siena, on a painted book cover, *c.*1400 (New York, Metropolitan Museum).

quota of salt, thus blurring the distinction between direct and indirect taxation. Indirect taxes were commonly 'farmed'; that is, the right of collecting them was sold to private entrepreneurs at a discount. The Italian clergy were, like the clergy elsewhere, generally exempt from secular taxation, though popes sometimes authorized levies on the clergy to help pay for wars against Islam. On the other hand, the nobility, unlike their fellows elsewhere, did normally pay direct taxes. In Venice, even the doge had to file his tax return like everyone else. Whether the rich and powerful paid their fair share of taxes is another matter, on which evidence is naturally sparse. What is clear from the documents is that city-states like Florence and Venice taxed their own citizens at a lower rate than their 'subjects' living outside the walls.

Tax revenues were often insufficient to meet government needs, and the gap was bridged with loans. There were forced loans, like the Florentine *prestanze*, calculated according to what the neighbours thought a given family was worth. There was also the public debt, another financial operation in which the Italian communes were pioneers; a loan fund (*monte*) would be set up, in which interest-bearing shares (*luoghi*) could be purchased. There were 3 million florins invested in the Florentine *Monte* in 1400, and in 1425 (the time of war and financial crisis immediately preceding the *catasto*), the Florentines set up a second fund, the Monte delle Doti or 'dowry fund'. In 1526, another time of crisis, the Pope set up a loan fund, the Monte della Fede. The holders of important political offices tended to own large numbers of shares of the public debt, making the state into a kind of company in which the ruling class were the main shareholders. In the case of Genoa, much of the empire was administered by the Casa di S. Giorgio, a body founded from the amalgamation of several loan funds in 1407. PB

W. Bowsky *The finance of the commune of Siena, 1287–1355* (1970); A. Molho *Florentine public finances in the early Renaissance 1400–1433* (1971)

Technology Far more than SCIENCE, Renaissance technology advanced on the basis of medieval inventiveness. VITRUVIUS influenced architecture, and FRONTINUS the construction of aqueducts, but in the 16c. it was the discoveries of the magnetic compass, gunpowder and printing (12c., 13c. and 15c. respectively) that made the most mark. The Renaissance engineer was necessarily versatile, no distinction being made between civilian and military architects, or between architect and machine designer. Only the sea called for distinctive knowledge. Shipbuilding was a specialized craft, lacking its architects, but the Renaissance saw the development of the full-rigged ship for trade and exploration. And science (astronomy and mathematics) was now applied to permit the navigator to determine his position on the high seas. But Italians were active only in the early phases of exploration.

Canals and hydraulic technology The regulation of rivers and construction of canals has an unbroken history, for wherever society is reasonably well organized there is a need for flood control, land reclamation (which means drainage), irrigation and easier water transport. The earliest centre for such work was Milan; in the 13c. it was linked with the Ticino, while in the 15c. further canals connected the city with Lake Como and with the Po (in the latter Leonardo had some involvement). These canals soon required the development of locks more sophisticated than the medieval flash lock, and pound locks were devised in the 15c.; they are described in the 1450s by Alberti in *De re aedificatoria* (*On building; pub.* 1485) – a book which clearly demonstrates the close connection between architecture and technology in the Renaissance. Among the earliest drawings are those by Leonardo (*c.*1470), who later invented the mitre gate. One of the Milanese canals was carried on an aqueduct, a novel construction for the time.

Plans for draining the Pontine Marshes near Rome were numerous from about 1514; Leonardo's designs were well conceived, as were those of others, but little work was done until the time of Sixtus V (*c.*1586). More work there and in Tuscany was undertaken in the early 17c., involving drainage, flood control, and harbour construction (Galileo was a rather unsuccessful consultant). Rivers were also controlled to provide power. Waterwheels, for mills and general power transmission, increasingly widely used in the later Middle Ages, were now subjected to the inventive genius of the age. Francesco di Giorgio Martini, primarily an architect, was also an inventor of machines, and his designs for watermills, including a hydraulic turbine, were as original as comparable designs by Leonardo. These, and their successors, produced a host of designs for pumps, piledrivers, gearing, cranks, and governors suitable for hydraulic and other machinery, some practicable, some ingenious ideas awaiting developments in improved metallurgical and construction techniques.

Ceramics Medieval Europe lacked the sophisticated pottery techniques being developed concurrently in China and Persia, which spread to Spain to produce Hispano-Moresque ware, with copper lustre glaze over a white tin glaze. By the beginning of the 14c., Italian potters were employing tin glazes and decorating their pots with metallic salts to produce the first fine ceramic ware in Italy, rather misleadingly called maiolica (= from Majorca). Copper lustre techniques were borrowed from Spain by the 15c., and this and the next century saw the development of centres of production whose artistic achievements and styles were different and characteristic, but which all used the same techniques. These were described about 1550 by Cyprian Picolpasso (1524–79), a member of a pottery family in Castel Durante, in *Tre libri del arte vasaio* (*Three books on the potter's art*), together with full information about preparing the clay and the colours, constructing wheels, designing kilns and firing the vessels.

Glass In Italy glassmaking was particularly centred in the Venetian Republic, specifically on the island of Murano after 1291. In the 14c. coloured glass was produced there; by the mid-15c. clear glass (*cristallo*) and spectacle glass were being produced. The Italians made soda glass, using the ashes of marine plants (Northern glass necessarily used potash). The ingredients, the making of the pots in which these were melted, the construction of kilns, are all discussed in detail by Biringuccio, while the materials needed for coloured glass are described definitively by Antonio Neri in *L'arte vetraria* (Florence 1612; tr. as *The art of glass*, 1662), who also described the making of crystal glass, lead glass (highly refractive) and enamelled glass. Much of the esteem in which Venetian glass was held came from the elaborate techniques of shaping and decoration developed there, which were disseminated through Europe by glassworkers trained at Murano. It must be remembered that glass was used not only for vessels, windows and mirrors, but also for jewellery.

Mechanical arts Architects, military engineers and inventors employed a wide variety of machines, many of great antiquity (cranes), some new in the Middle Ages (windmills, sawmills, pumps and water-driven hammers), others developed in the 15c. and 16c. All are described in manuscripts of architects and engineers and then in printed 'machine books' whose lavish illustrations demonstrate the Renaissance love for mechanical ingenuity: witness the raising of the Vatican obelisk in the reign of Sixtus V, though not all devices were so practical. Much attention was paid to power transmission with elaborate gears and cranks. Machinery was applied to every aspect of life, even the library. On a more mundane level the mechanical ingenuity of craftsmen produced new methods of clothmaking (with new products such as silk damasks and figured velvets), while spinning wheels were improved.

Printing Although PRINTING from movable type was first developed in the Germanic North, the printing of playing cards was widely practised in Venice in the 15c., which no doubt explains why Venice and other Italian towns quickly took up the new technology and soon rivalled Germany in the production of printed books. The technology involved not only the use of presses (not very different from those in use for a variety of industrial and domestic purposes) and the development of viscous printing ink, but also the craft of typefounding. The oldest account is that of Biringuccio, who in 1540 described the composition (3 parts fine tin, an eighth part lead and another eighth part fused marcasite of antimony), and also the making of the mould and the matrix and the casting of individual letters in a manner essentially the same as that used for the next 3 centuries.

Pyrotechnics Properly speaking this (as in Biringuccio's book) includes all those (largely chemical) arts which involve fire, including ceramics, glass and typecasting. But it also includes mining and metallurgy, goldsmith's work, bellfounding, guncasting, the casting of bronze statues and the treatment of minerals. None of these crafts was entirely distinct: the goldsmith, the miner, the metallurgist and the assayer all needed to know how to detect and purify precious metals (gold and silver), and how to separate gold from silver. A strong ingredient of traditional usage masked a gradually increased knowledge of chemical processes. Thus, whereas in the 12c. no strong mineral acids were known, by the 14c. *aqua fortis* or parting acid (nitric acid which dissolves silver but not gold) appears; by Biringuccio's time sulphuric acid was known, as was *aqua regia* (now a mixture of nitric and hydrochloric acid, then made from a mixture of minerals); hydrochloric acid is first clearly mentioned about 1600. The making of alloys like brass and pewter and the mining of the ores of metals was widely practised; in Italy the mining of mercury (Biringuccio had been at the mines at Friuli), its use in amalgam and goldsmithing, and its poisonous effects were all familiar.

Technology: an ingenious machine to assist the scholar, from Ramelli's *Le diverse et artificiose machine*, 1588.

The smelting of ores and purification of metals involved the construction of a variety of furnaces, hearths and bellows: thus Giambattista della Porta, Cellini and Biringuccio all describe new designs of reverbatory furnaces, which were first drawn by Leonardo. The machinery associated with the arts of casting, including the boring of guns and the preparation of gunpowder, also came within the scope of pyrotechnics. Not until the very end of the 16c. were the chemical arts widely used for pharmacy, except in the case of distillation of vegetable extracts to produce alcoholic cordials and aqua vitae. *See* INDUSTRY. MBH

B. Gille *Les ingénieurs de la Renaissance* (1964), Eng. tr. *Engineers of the Renaissance* (1966); C. Singer *et al.* ed. *A history of technology* III (1957)

Terence (before 185–160 BC) Terence (Publius Terentius Afer) and Plautus took over the comedy of the Greek Menander (342–291 BC) and together transmitted it to Italy and Europe; but they are dissimilar, despite the similarity of their material (the miserly old man; the young son eager for a light of love; the mute maiden with hardly a walk-on role, who is only a slave girl in the power of a pander; the smart slave, ready to think up ways to the father's purse-strings; the parasite). Plautus was the less acceptable face of this pagan world, and as such nearly foundered, while Terence remained always available and recommended, not least for the linguistic surface of his plays.

Plautus' is a harsh world, where, for example, the slaves are always reminding us of the dangers they face (of being strung up from a beam to be lashed, or, worse, of being crucified), and where an easy and polite solution is not necessarily to be found. In Terence this subhumanity of the slave is less in evidence, and the stock situations tend to work out, with marriage to the desired girl made possible because she turns out to be a citizen, and even already in Terence one can find declarations of immutable love. From the staging of the *Menaechmi* of Plautus at the Este court in 1486, through the ensuing series of productions, in which Ariosto translated 3 plays by Terence, to Machiavelli's translation of Terence's *Andria*, Terence combines with Plautus as the basis for Italian, and European, comedy; but he supplies the gentler note, where we can see coming even the '*Amorosa invincible costanza*' ('invincible constancy of love') of Guarini's *Pastor fido*. Indeed, it is legitimate to think that Terence is the more assimilable of the two, less forceful than Plautus, but socially more comprehensible. This facility of Terence was reflected in the editions (there are twice as many incunables of Terence). And it made Terence the first author to be tackled at school, recommended as morally improving and – by Erasmus – for the purity of the language and as 'apt for the understanding of children'. JHW

An antique theatre, from a woodcut in an edition of **Terence** published in Venice in 1497.

Theocritus (*c.*300–*c.*260 BC) The pastoral verse 'idylls' of this Greek poet (born at Syracuse, Sicily), some of them in dialogue, were an important influence on all forms of Renaissance pastoral literature from his virtual rediscovery in the 1420s, through Poliziano and Sannazaro and on to Tasso. JRH

Poems ed. and tr. A. S. F. Gow (1950)

Tibaldi, Pellegrino (1527–96) Painter and architect much favoured by Carlo Borromeo, the Catholic saint and theorist of counter-reform. Tibaldi's paintings in Bologna (e.g. Sala di Ulisse, Palazzo Poggi, *c.*1554–55) demonstrate a masterly illusionism acquired in the Sala Paolina at Castel S. Angelo, Rome (1547–49). As Borromeo's architect in Milan, Tibaldi designed the Jesuit church of S. Fedele

(1569f.), which draws on Michelangelo's Christianized Baths of Diocletian for its brilliant interior system. The round, Pantheon-like church of S. Sebastiano (1576) shows that centralized churches for votive purposes were still acceptable to Borromeo. Tibaldi's last years were spent painting in the Escorial. CE

R. Haslam 'Pellegrino Tibaldi and S. Fedele' *Arte lombarda* (1975)

Time reckoning Renaissance Italians, merchants in particular, thought of time as a precious commodity which must not be wasted. They were among the first Europeans to be clock-oriented. The mechanical clock was invented in the later 13c., and from the 14c. on public clocks (some of them extremely elaborate) could be seen in the major Italian cities. Domestic spring-driven clocks go back to the 15c. and include alarm clocks (*svegliatoi*); watches appear *c.*1500. However, time was not reckoned in the modern way. Short periods were perceived in terms of the time taken to say one or two Credos or Aves. The ancient Roman system of counting the hours of the day (from sunrise) and the hours of the night (from sunset) was still in use, coexisting with the system of the 24-hour clock. 'At the second hour of the night' is a common notation, but so is 'at the 22nd hour'. In some cities, such as Rome and Ferrara, the year was considered to begin on 1 January, in others, such as Florence and Venice, at the end of March. One major change in time reckoning occurred towards the end of the period. To eliminate the discrepancies between the solar year and the ecclesiastical year, Gregory XIII issued a bull in 1582 reforming the calendar by omitting 11 days from the October of that year. PB

C. M. Cipolla *Clocks and culture* (1967)

Tinctoris, Johannes de (*c.*1436–1511) Music theorist. After studying law and theology at his native town of Nivelles (S. of Brussels) he entered the service of the King of Naples as a chaplain and singer before 1476, and was music teacher to the daughter of the house, Beatrix of Aragon. In the later years of the century he was probably in the papal choir, and he founded a music school in Naples. He wrote several influential treatises, remarkable because they codify the actual practice of his time rather than propounding abstract theories. DA

Tintoretto (1518–94) Jacopo Robusti, whose name derived from the profession of his father,

The Origin of the Milky Way by **Tintoretto**, *c.*1578 (London, National Gallery).

a dyer (*tintore*), was, with Veronese, the chief Venetian painter of the later 16c. His art derived chiefly from that of Titian, but Tintoretto was a painter of great originality, who introduced, especially into narrative subject matter, a dynamism, based upon the study of the human figure in action, rapidly sketched in chalk or paint, which deeply influenced the development of painting throughout the 17c.

A very prolific painter and draughtsman, Tintoretto worked principally for the churches and *scuole* of Venice, where his main religious cycles survive, but he was also in demand, like Titian, as a painter of mythologies, which include some of his most celebrated works (*The Origin of the Milky Way*, London, National Gallery), and for portraits, where his particular skills show to lesser advantage.

In his early biography of Tintoretto (1642), Ridolfi mentions a brief and stormy apprenticeship with Titian, and the prescription that Tintoretto wrote for his own guidance upon the wall of his room: 'The drawing of Michel Angelo and the colouring of Titian.' As well as studies from life, and from casts of classical sculpture and statues of Michelangelo, Ridolfi also describes Tintoretto's use of wax models, which he deployed in boxes with special lighting effects, a method alien to both Titian and Michelangelo, which goes far to explain Tintoretto's uninhibited approach to composition. Having worked as a decorator of furniture and on some exterior frescoes, Tintoretto first became famous in Venice with *The Miracle of the Slave* (Venice, Accademia), which he completed for the Confraternity of S. Marco in April 1548. The picture startled through the drama of its composition and the speed and fluency of its handling. It was later followed by two other stories from the legend of St Mark, commissioned in 1562, *The Finding* and *The Abduction of the Body of St Mark* (Milan, Brera, and Venice, Accademia).

In the 1550s Tintoretto started his famous canvases for the church of S. Maria dell'Orto, beginning with *The Presentation of the Virgin*, a theme that Titian had earlier treated in a famous – and more tranquil – composition. His best known series of canvases, in the Scuola di San Rocco, was initiated in 1565, with the painting of the great *Crucifixion*, some 40 feet wide. He subsequently painted histories of the life of St Roch for the sacristy of the church, and the Old Testament cycle in the large upper room of the Scuola (1575–81). The room below, decorated with scenes from the life of the Virgin, he began in 1583 and completed with studio help 4 years later. The cycle includes sombrely evocative landscapes, as in *The Flight into Egypt*, and even the most familiar subjects, like *The Annunciation*, are powerfully heightened in drama, the angel swooping towards the startled Virgin, with a host of cherubim, through a ruined doorway. Other late commissions included canvases for Palladio's church of S. Giorgio Maggiore, notably *The Last Supper* (1592–94), and those painted in the 1580s for the Ducal Palace, following the disastrous fire of 1577, when the earlier decoration, in which Titian and the Bellinis had participated, was destroyed. It was for the end wall of the Sala del Maggior Consiglio here that Tintoretto's great vision of *Paradise*, the largest of all his works, was painted in 1588. AB

Carlo Ridolfi *Le maraviglie dell'arte* (Venice 1648; life of Tintoretto also published separately 1642); H. Tietze *Tintoretto* (1948); C. Bernari and P. de Vecchi *L'opera completa del Tintoretto* (1970)

Titian (d.1576) Tiziano Vecellio, the most famous painter of 16c. Venice, was born at Pieve di Cadore, probably in the mid-1480s. For 60 years, from the second decade of the century, Titian dominated painting in Venice and northern Italy, and through his influence on such younger artists as Tintoretto and Veronese, and on the great masters of succeeding generations, like Rubens and Velasquez, he contributed essentially to the development of painting for long after his own lifetime. Equally inventive in portraiture and in religious and mythological painting, Titian attracted clients throughout Italy and Europe, working extensively for the Emperor CHARLES V, by whom he was knighted, and for his son PHILIP II. His reputation was further enhanced through the writings of his friend Aretino, who, with Titian and the sculptor Jacopo Sansovino, formed a 'triumvirate' which ruled on all artistic matters in Venice.

The young Titian was trained first in the workshop of Giovanni Bellini, but 'on seeing Giorgione's style Titian ... imitated Giorgione so well that in a short time his works were taken for Giorgione's' (Vasari). A small group of paintings, including the altarpiece of *St Mark Enthroned* (Venice, Accademia) and *The Gypsy Madonna* (Vienna; a considerably amplified variant of a late Bellini composition), form the basis for the identification of Titian's earliest works, but other masterpieces, like the *Concert Champêtre* (Paris, Louvre), are still today disputed between Titian and Giorgione.

The first documented work by Titian is the series of frescoes in the Scuola del Santo at Padua, which he completed in 1511. Here and in other paintings of the time, like *The Baptism* (Rome, Capitoline Gallery), a surprising familiarity with the work of Raphael and Michelangelo can be detected, a mastery of form added to Titian's facility in the handling of paint and colour which contributed to the huge success of his first public commission in Venice, the *Assumption of the Virgin*, forming the high altarpiece of the church of the Frari (1516–18). Altarpieces for Treviso, Brescia and Ancona followed the *Assumption*, together with a second altarpiece in the Frari, the *Pesaro Madonna* (1519–26), in which Titian transformed the character of the Venetian devotional altarpiece, formulating a diagonal composition with monumental architecture that echoes the character of the church itself.

Titian continued to develop the Giorgionesque idyll in the 1510s with *The Three Ages of Man* (Edinburgh, Sutherland loan) and *Sacred and Profane Love* (Rome, Galleria Borghese), but adopted a far more dynamic approach to mythological subject matter in 3 famous canvases, *Bacchus and Ariadne* (London, National Gallery), and *The Andrians* and *The Worship of Venus* (Madrid, Prado), which he painted for Alfonso d'Este's Camerino d'Alabastro in the castle of Ferrara (1518–23). A

Bacchus and Ariadne by **Titian** (London, National Gallery).

dynamism of the same order marked the celebrated (but destroyed) altarpiece of the *Death of St Peter Martyr*, formerly in SS. Giovanni e Paolo (1525–30). Titian's masterpieces of the 1530s are more tranquil in mood, notably the *Presentation of the Virgin* (Venice, Accademia) and the *Venus of Urbino* (Florence, Uffizi), both of which were finished in 1538. Some of the best known of the portraits were produced in these years, including those of Charles V, whom Titian met for the first time in Bologna in 1530, and Francesco della Rovere, Duke of Urbino, and his wife (Florence, Uffizi).

In 1543 Titian visited Rome, where he painted Pope Paul III and his nephews (Naples, Capodimonte) and met Michelangelo, who commended his 'lively manner' of painting but found his work deficient in drawing (Vasari). Drawing in Michelangelo's sense, however, was of less and less importance in the latest works of Titian; the brushwork is increasingly free, the colour more broken, and sombre in tone, the artist repeating many of his earlier compositions and working on each canvas over long periods of time. From the last decades date the series of mythological paintings (the *poesie*) painted for Philip II of Spain, including the *Diana and Calisto* and *Diana and Actaeon* (Edinburgh, Sutherland loan), and among altarpieces the *Martyrdom of St Lawrence* in the chapel of Philip's Palace of the Escorial. At the very last Titian left uncompleted the moving *Pietà* (Venice, Accademia), finished by Palma Giovane, and probably destined for his own tomb in the church of the Frari. [17, 164] AB

J. A. Crowe and G. B. Cavalcaselle *Titian: his life and times* (1877); H. E. Wethey *Titian* (1969–75); J. Wilde *Venetian art from Bellini to Titian* (1974)

Tolfa *see* ALUM

Torrigiano, Pietro (1472–1528) Florentine sculptor, trained in the Medici sculpture collection under Bertoldo, later specializing in modelling terracotta statues and busts. His masterpiece is the tomb in gilt bronze, marble, and touchstone of King Henry VII and his queen in Westminster Abbey (1512). He also produced the tomb of Lady Margaret Beaufort nearby (1511), a marble bust of Christ in a roundel (London, Wallace Collection), and a number of painted terracotta portrait busts: of Henry VII (London, Victoria and Albert Museum), Henry VIII and Bishop Fisher (New York, Metropolitan Museum). He later went to Spain and modelled polychrome religious statues, e.g. a Virgin and Child and *St Jerome* (Seville Museum). Evolving from the work of the della Robbia and Verrocchio, but little affected by Michelangelo, Torrigiano's sculpture is typical of the High Renaissance, of which he was the finest portrait sculptor. He played an important role in italianizing taste in Tudor England. CA

J. Pope-Hennessy *Italian Renaissance sculpture* (1971); A. Darr 'Pietro Torrigiano' *The Connoisseur* (1979)

Toscanelli, Paolo dal Pozzo (1397–82) Florentine astronomer and geographer. After attending the university of Padua he was appointed judicial astrologer by the Florentine Signoria. He constructed a gnomon on the cathedral as it was building and observed several comets. Fired by tales of medieval and contemporary travellers, he dreamed of reaching China by way of the Atlantic Ocean, whose breadth he grossly underestimated. A map illustrating this project interested many contemporaries; he perhaps sent a copy to Columbus, who certainly shared his vision, together with his rejection of ancient calculations. MBH

Town planning Regular town planning was not a Renaissance novelty. From the 13c. Italian communes reintroduced statutory building controls, laying out straight streets and piazze in their expanding cities, informed by the twin criteria of 'utility' and 'beauty'. The Renaissance brought a theoretical interest in city planning, a revised perspectival aesthetic of axial symmetry, improved surveying techniques allowing accurate city plans, and new fortifications systems which transformed city circuits.

The 'Ideal City' features little in Renaissance architectural treatises. Alberti thought that city forms should be adaptable, not only to site (VITRUVIUS), but also to differing socio-political conditions (Aristotle). The resulting bias towards pragmatic variety influences Francesco di Giorgio's multifarious illustrations of city plans. Only Filarete is Utopian, planning a star-shaped radial city, which none the less relates to medieval Milan. Architectural writers of the 16c. (except in Pietro Cattaneo's book of 1554) increasingly left whole-city planning to the military theorists, who readopted the 'ideal' radial plan, perhaps originally a misunderstanding of Vitruvius's wind diagram, as the most efficient way to service a polygonal bastionated circuit from a central arsenal. Scamozzi (1616) had to reaffirm the architect's right to plan cities against the increasing professionalism of the military engineer.

'I will not talk about designing a city *di nuovo* because it never happens' was Alvise Cornaro's counterblast (pre-1566) to the Albertian theoretical tradition. More towns were indeed built in the 13c. and 14c., when the communes established fortified markets to break the power of the feudal nobility (Scarperia, S. Giovanni Val d'Arno, etc.), than in the demographically stagnant Renaissance period. The few entirely new foundations of the Quattrocento (e.g. Cortemaggiore, 1480) usually followed a similar rectilinear gridiron plan, familiar from the Roman colonial plans which survived at the heart of many Italian towns. Ercole d'Este's *Addizione* to Ferrara (designed by Biagio Rossetti, 1492f.) adapts the layout of pre-existing country roads. The predominantly military or dynastic motives for new towns also made them vulnerable to destruction or decline: Sangallo the Younger's Castro (1534f.) for Pier Luigi Farnese, 'a new Carthage' (Annibale Caro), was razed to the ground in the mid-17c., while Vespasiano Gonzaga's new capital, Sabbioneta (1562f.), with its deliberately disrupted grid plan, was preserved by its failure to grow. The Medicean port at Livorno, enlarged by Buontalenti (1575f.) into a pentagonal city, has scarcely survived bombing in this century, but other grand-ducal foundations, like Terra del Sole (1565f.), remain intact. Palmanova (1593f.), built by the Venetians as an outpost against Austria and the Turk, is a near-perfect example of the radial military plan.

Smaller-scale interventions into existing cities are equally revealing of Renaissance ideas, alternating between Alberti's twin but conflicting recommendations: porticoed uniformity of streets and *fora*, and variety of architectural solution. Would-be uniformity appears in Nicholas V's Albertian plan for 3 porticoed streets in the Vatican Borgo, but the Borgo as actually built up after 1500 presented an assortment of strongly individualized palace façades. The desire for axial symmetry – a prerequisite of Brunelleschian perspective – influenced the repetition of Brunelleschi's Innocenti façade in the Piazza SS. Annunziata (1516f.) and Bramante's Piazza Ducale at Vigevano (1492–94), with its continuous arcades and fictive triumphal arches. The Capitoline Hill (1537f.) exemplifies Michelangelo's anthropomorphic belief in bilateral symmetry about an individuated central axis, as does Vasari's Uffizi, two ranges of repeated office units over a continuous portico, joined by a triumphal arch. But the alternative emphasis on variety had already appeared at Pius II's Pienza (1459f.), where façades of different status and treatment flank the axially-placed cathedral. Both uniformity and variety inform Sansovino's Venetian plans for a stage-set-like Piazzetta with strongly contrasted Mint, Library, loggetta and Ducal Palace leading to the Piazza San Marco, where the Library façade was to be repeated on 3 sides.

Rome's growing population and legacy of medieval neglect offered the greatest scope for radical replanning. Successive popes from Nicholas V, identifying themselves with the Emperor-builders of antiquity, created the machinery for *renovatio* by means of a strong urbanistic magistracy administering betterment taxes and compulsory purchase. Piecemeal clarifications like the Via Giulia (1508f.), the Borgo and the Tridente (1516f.) improved communications in the meandering old city, but it was not until Sixtus V (1585f.) that a veritable *piano regolatore* emerged under Fontana's direction for expansion westwards

Town planning: Michelangelo's design for the Capitoline Hill in Rome, in Duperac's engraving of 1569.

on to the hills. With Sixtus's destructive approach to pagan antiquities, the ideal of *renovatio* was replaced by that of counter-reform. *See* FORTIFICATION; ROME. CE

W. Lotz *Studies in Italian Renaissance architecture* (1977); H. de la Croix *Military considerations in city planning: fortifications* (1972); K. Forster 'From *rocca* to *civitas*: urban planning at Sabbioneta' *L'Arte* (1969); L. Salerno *et al. Via Giulia* (1973)

Tragedy Quattrocento neo-Latin forays into classical tragedy were followed by a reworking of Poliziano's *Favola di Orfeo* into a 5-act *Orphei tragoedia*, and by some rhymed verse vernacular tragedies. Trissino's *Sophonisba* (1515), called the first regular Italian tragedy, was a unified representation proceeding by an alternation of dialogue and choral ode, dramatizing an episode from Livy and establishing the unrhymed 11-syllable line as the basic metre for the genre. The Senecan element innate in all Italian neo-classical tragedy became dominant in Giraldi's influential *Orbecche* (1541), with its ghost prologue and Thyestean horrors in 5 acts punctuated by sententious choral odes. In *Altile* (*c.*1541) Giraldi introduced the *tragedia di fin lieto*, with double plot and moral happy ending.

The content of tragedy came to be drawn from increasingly varied sources: established subjects like Gothic history (Giovanni Rucellai's *Rosmunda*, 1516), Greek myth (Luigi Alamanni's *Antigone*, 1533), and Roman history (Aretino's *Orazia*, 1546) were augmented by Hebrew history (Dolce's *Marianna*, 1565), novellas (Luigi Groto's *Adriana*, 1578) and chivalric romance (Gabriele Zinano's *Almerigo*, 1590). Structure and function were debated in Aristotelian terms of peripety and catharsis, with particular intensity after Speroni's *Canace* (1541–42). Tasso's *Torrismondo* (1587) combined Scandinavian history and chivalric epic in a complex plot intended to surpass *Oedipus rex*. Aristotle's admiration for Sophocles determined many recognition scenes, as in Pomponio Torelli's *Merope* (1589). The subgenre *tragedia sacra*, in which the religious matter of the old *sacre rappresentazioni* and recent history were used in 5-act unified neoclassical structures, found its finest expression in Federico della Valle's *Reina di Scozia* (1595), a tragedy about Mary Stuart. LGC

M. Ariani *Tra classicismo e manierismo: il teatro tragico del Cinquecento* (1974); M. T. Herrick *Italian tragedy in the Renaissance* (1965)

Traversari, Ambrogio (1356–1439), one of the leading ecclesiastical humanists of the early Renaissance, was a lifelong monk of the Camaldolese order, of which he became General in 1431, at the Florentine convent of S. Maria degli Angeli. His ecclesiastical career was distinguished – he was a papal legate at the Council of Basle and one of the framers of the Decree of Union at the Council of Florence – and he contributed to the close connection between Florentine humanism and the papal court. His knowledge of Greek was based originally on the study of the New Testament and was exercised in translations of the Greek Fathers into Latin. He was also, however, an enthusiastic member of the Florentine circle, a friend of Niccoli and Cosimo de' Medici, at whose behest he translated Diogenes Laertius' *Lives of the philosophers*. He may have contributed to the programme of the Baptistery Doors. *See* COUNCILS OF THE CHURCH. GH

A. Dini-Traversari *Ambrogio Traversari e i suoi tempi* (1912)

Trent, Council of (1545–63) A General Council of the Catholic Church. From 1529 the Emperor Charles V had pressed the Papacy to call a Council, being himself faced by demands from the German princes and cities for 'a free general Christian Council in German territory'. Pope Clement VII avoided calling a Council, since those of Constance (1414–18) and Basle (1431–49) were an ugly memory for the Papacy: in these had been asserted the 'conciliar' thesis that a General Council representing the whole Church was superior to the

The Council of **Trent** in session in 1562–63.

pope. However, Paul III promised the convocation of a Council to Charles V in 1536. Charles always demanded that it should be held in Imperial territory, while the Pope wanted it in Italy. The abortive convocation in the Imperial fief of Mantua in 1537 represented one attempted compromise solution. Trent was eventually found suitable, being an Italian city ruled over by a prince-bishop but within the Holy Roman Empire. The Council had three major periods of session: December 1545–January 1548 (at Bologna from March 1547), May 1551–April 1552, January 1562–December 1563. Presided over by papal legates, it was composed primarily of bishops but also included superiors of religious orders as members with voting rights; in attendance were theological consultants drawn from the orders, while ambassadors of Catholic powers were present as onlookers.

Spanish and French bishops caused the Papacy and its legates much anxiety. They showed inclinations towards a conciliarist position. Further, the Spanish bishops, together with those from the Habsburg territories in Italy, supervised as they were by the ambassadors of the Catholic Monarch, were responsive to Charles V's policy directives. Otherwise, the Italian bishops generally followed the papal line. A major policy disagreement between Pope and Emperor dominated the Council's first period. Charles wanted the Council to confine itself to church reform, leaving aside decisions on dogma, which would only lead to a decisive rupture in Germany. Paul III wanted things the other way round, regarding disciplinary reform as a papal prerogative. The Council itself decided to deal with doctrine and reform simultaneously. However, while it quickly erected doctrinal barriers, there was no reform legislation until 1563. The Council entered a dramatic phase with the entry of the French bishops in November 1563, just at a time when key issues of reform had become enmeshed with a vexed question involving the relationship between episcopal and Papal authority: was the residence of bishops in their dioceses commanded by divine law? Behind this lurked the further question: did bishops derive their authority directly from God or mediately through the pope? This issue was eventually circumvented when the papal legate Morone succeeded in winning general assent to a hastily collated set of reform proposals emanating from the various national delegations. The Council rushed the reform legislation through in December 1563 in case its work were truncated by the death of the ailing Pope. Pius IV confirmed this legislation in January 1564.

In effect, the Council of Trent established a *modus vivendi* between episcopate and Papacy. The bishops there did not in the end press the conciliar thesis, and the Papacy's dominant position in the Church was left unchallenged. On the other hand, the powers of bishops in their own dioceses were greatly strengthened. The rather skeletal disciplinary legislation added relatively little that was new to canon law. However, the Council, as an assembly in which bishops conferred together and proclaimed their conception of their own role, helped to focus a growing sense in the middle years of the 16c. of the significance of the pastoral ministry, particularly as exercised by the bishop. In this context, the Tridentine legislation on church reform was indeed significant. *See* COUNCILS OF THE CHURCH; COUNTER-REFORMATION; REFORMATION. OL

H. Jedin *Geschichte des Konzils von Trent* (4 vols 1949–75), I and II tr. as *A history of the Council of Trent* (1957–61); —*Crisis and closure of the Council of Trent* (1967)

Trissino, Gian Giorgio (1478–1550) His creative works, more noted for classicism than for literary merit, include the first Renaissance tragedy to follow Aristotelian rules, *Sophonisba* (1515), the comedy *I simillimi* (1548), based on Plautus' *Menaechmi*, the epic *La Italia liberata da' Gotthi* (1547–48), which reveals him as a careful student (and advocate) of late Roman military practice. More significant, however, are his linguistic contributions: *Epistola* to Clement VII (1524) on orthographic reform; *Grammatichetta*; *Dubbii grammaticali*; *Il castellano* (all 1529). He rediscovered and translated (1529) Dante's *De vulgari eloquentia*, making it support his theory of an 'Italian' rather than 'Tuscan' language. His *Poetica* (1529) is important for its treatment of metre. He was Palladio's mentor and patron. LL

B. Morsolin *G. Trissino* (1894)

Triumph With growing interest from the early 14c. in the history of ancient Rome came a fascination with the city's conquests, the wars by which they were won – and the ceremony which marked their success: the victor's triumph. The knowledge that the privilege of being commemorated by one of these enormous and costly processions of warriors, loot and prisoners was given sparingly, only to the sole commander of a major victory over a foreign army of whom at least 5000 were slain, added to the glamour of the triumph. Its centrepiece was the chariot of the victor himself. Dante gave one to Beatrice in *Purgatorio* XXIX: 'Rome upon Africanus ne'er conferred / Nor on Augustus's self, a car so brave'. But it was tentatively with the relief carvings on the Triumphal Arch (1452–66) at Castelnuovo in Naples commemorating Alfonso the Magnanimous, and finally with Mantegna's superb *Triumph of Caesar* cartoons (Hampton Court), that the visual reconstruction of a Roman triumph became complete.

The **triumph** of time, from an edition of Petrarch's *Trionfi* and other works, published in 1490.

Meanwhile, in an age which did not like the idea of large numbers of victory-flushed soldiers parading through its streets, the military triumph became sublimated, as it were, into a number of less controversial forms. This was largely under the influence of Petrarch's *Trionfi* – poems describing the processions commemorating the triumphs of love, chastity, death, fame, time and eternity. Disseminated soon after his death, they soon appeared in illuminated manuscripts, and the triumph scene became a popular one for woodcuts, decorated marriage chests and other paintings, most beautifully of all on the backs of Piero della Francesca's portraits of Federigo da Montefeltro and his wife, Battista Sforza. Other 'triumphs' were invented: of the seasons, of virtues and of the arts. Nor was the theme allowed to be simply a profane one. Just before his death Savonarola published his *Triumph of the Cross*, in which the reader was invited to imagine 'a four-wheeled chariot on which is seated Christ as Conqueror.' Before it go the apostles, patriarchs and prophets, beside it the army of martyrs, behind it, after 'a countless number of virgins, of both sexes', come the prisoners: 'the serried ranks of the enemies of the Church of Christ.' This aspect of the theme was magnificently realized in Titian's great woodcut *The Triumph of the Faith*. JRH

Trivulzio family These Milanese nobles, already prominent in the 12c., came to be divided in political allegiance and to typify the aristocratic political freelance. Some members opposed the Visconti. Antonio supported the AMBROSIAN REPUBLIC (1447–50). Gian Giacomo (1441–1518) became a famous military commander in French service; previously employed by Louis XI in Brittany, in 1483 he broke with Lodovico Sforza, served Charles VIII and led Louis XII's attacks on Milan (1499–1500). He was made French Governor in Milan and led the League of Cambrai forces to victory against Venice at AGNADELLO (1509). Though defeated at NOVARA (1513) he took part in another French victory at MARIGNANO (1515). Highly educated, probably by Giorgio Valla, he commissioned in Milan (*c.*1511) an unrealized equestrian statue of himself from Leonardo da Vinci.

Teodoro, of another branch of the family, also served France, rallying its defeated forces after the battle of PAVIA (1525). Prominent churchmen of the Trivulzio family who were also French partisans included Gian Giacomo's brother Antonio (Cardinal 1500–08), Scaramuccia, Count of Melzo, a councillor of Louis XII (Cardinal 1517–27), and Agostino (Cardinal 1517–48), who served as papal legate in France and in 1527 was taken to Naples as a hostage of Charles V. DC

C. Rosmini *Dell'istoria intorno alle militari imprese e alla vita di Giangiacomo Trivulzio* (1815); *Enciclopedia Cattolica.*

Tromboncino, Bartolomeo (*c.*1470–after 1535) Composer of FROTTOLAS. The son of a Venetian wind instrumentalist, he was in the service of the Gonzaga family at Mantua for many years, and was also well known in Ferrara and Milan. He is rumoured to have murdered his wife in a fit of jealousy in 1499. Nearly 200 of his frottolas survive, showing a considerable literary taste (he was a friend of Castiglione) and a charming sense of melody. DA

A. Einstein *The Italian madrigal* (1949)

Tullia d'Aragona (*c.*1508–58) Probably the offspring of her courtesan mother's long liaison with Luigi, cardinal of Aragon, Tullia became one of the best known of cultivated courtesans. Active in Rome, Venice, Ferrara and Florence, she attached to herself a remarkable string of admirers: courtiers, bankers, clerics and princes, but above all men of letters, among them the Florentine historians Nardi and Varchi and the poet and miscellaneous writer Girolamo Muzio. Much cited in the books of others, she published poems of her own (*Rime*, 1547, dedicated to Eleanora, wife of Cosimo I), and a *Dialogo dell'infinità di amore*, dedicated to Cosimo himself. JRH

G. Biagi *Un etera romana: Tullia d'Aragona* (1886); G. Masson *Courtesans of the Italian Renaissance* (1975)

Tura, Cosmè (active *c.*1450–95) was the most craggily original and, in artistic and in spiritual terms, the most consistently intense of the school of painters centred on the d'Este court in late 15c. Ferrara. The convoluted rock forms of his draperies, at once tubular and crystalline, cut into and fault the structure of the underlying limbs that thrust against them. Flesh takes on the hardness and at times the sharpness of enamelled metal. The ruby eyes of beasts glow like precious stones; faces at rest take on a tortured quality; strange, livid pinks and reds clash with sharp greens and bright, cold blues. Virulently coloured architecture in extreme foreshortening strains and thrusts against the no less powerfully established surface; sharp foreshortenings create the substance of hard surface patterns. There is a spikiness, a sense of harshness and ferocity combined with unremitting, iron discipline, of absolute control and an unbending constancy of style, which makes his work amongst the most immediately recognizable in Renaissance art. The central panel from his monumental *Roverella* altarpiece (London, National Gallery), the *Pietà* which formed its crown (Paris, Louvre), the allegorical figure of *Summer*, the *St Jerome* (London, National Gallery), the great *Organ Shutters of St George* (Ferrara, Museo del Duomo), all speak the same language, redolent of a half-Renaissance, half-European late gothic world, in terms as strange as they are deeply moving to all those who care to understand them. JW

E. Ruhmer *Tura* (1958)

Tyrannicide Assassination of rulers (often in church, where they were most accessible, and often by cadets of their family) had long played an important part in the Italian political process. From the end of the 14c. these deeds came frequently to be gilded by biblical and classical references: to the precedents of Brutus (condemned by Dante as an arch-traitor, then raised by such republican enthusiasts as Michelangelo to heroic stature), Judith, killer of Holofernes, and David, slayer of Goliath. So the killing of

Tyrannicide: the assassination of Duke Galeazzo Maria Sforza in 1476, from a popular woodcut of 1505.

Galeazzo Maria Sforza (1476) was carried out by 3 Milanesi patricians inspired in part by the teachings of the humanist Cola Montano, while the PAZZI conspiracy in Florence was seen by Alamanno Rinuccini as an emulation of ancient glory. Intellectuals who combined a taste for violence with a classicizing republicanism featured largely too in the plots of Stefano PORCARI against Nicholas V (1453), of the Roman Academy against Paul II (1468), and of Pietro Paolo BOSCOLI against the Medici in 1513. JL

Uccello, Paolo (1397–1475) began his career as an apprentice under Lorenzo Ghiberti, working on his first bronze doors. He became famous as a perspectivist and epitomizes the type of artist whom Vasari places in his second phase of the rise of the arts from the medieval slough of barbarism. According to Vasari he learnt much and delighted in the conquest of difficulties, but as a result he tried too hard and the strain shows in his works. Uccello's reputation has never really recovered from this characterization, but his actual works are, many of them, among the most delightful to have come down from the period. His 3-part painting of the *Rout of S. Romano* (London, National Gallery; Florence, Uffizi; Paris, Louvre) (*see* S. ROMANO, BATTLE OF) carried out for a room in the Medici Palace, is, it is true, an early primer in all the possible foreshortenings of the horse. It is also a colourful pictorial equivalent of a set of medieval tapestries. The reduction of the horses in the National Gallery painting to a series of flat planes, sharply distinguished at their borders, does not reflect the severity of Uccello's style, but the severity of the overcleaning to which they were subjected at some point. What we now see is the splendid blocking in of the forms before the subsequent layers of paint provided the final, rounded transitions.

Another aspect of the development from geometrical first idea to more naturalistic final form can be seen by comparing the squared, preparatory drawing for his painted monument to Sir John HAWKWOOD with the finished fresco in the cathedral, Florence. His much ruined fresco of the Flood shows him, indeed, to be a student of Alberti, many of whose precepts are reflected in it. More than that, he is a subtle perspectivist, questioning the relationship of the new Artificial PERSPECTIVE theory to observable reality on the one hand and to its practical application in actual paintings on the other. The panel of *The Hunt* (Oxford, Ashmolean), which he probably painted in his last years, shows how far he was removed from being a dry theorist, and how superbly he was able to synthesize the demands of understanding and of art in one of the most poetic and evocative of all the products of the 15c. Florentine school of painting. [167, 178, 286] JW

J. Pope-Hennessy *Paolo Uccello* (1969); E. Flaiano *L'opera completa di Paolo Uccello* (1971)

Urbino, with its pleasant situation, was evocatively described by Castiglione at the beginning of *The courtier*, the Ducal Palace having been the setting for the fictional dialogue in 1506. Under the last MONTEFELTRO rulers Urbino enjoyed a cultural importance incongruous in relation to its size and relative poverty. Formerly notorious for their armed defiance of the Papacy, which claimed lordship over the region they controlled, the Montefeltro became loyal papal clients after Antonio returned from exile to rule Urbino (1377–1404).

The Palace is primarily the monument of Federico (Duke 1474–82; b.1444) and represents the cultural patronage which his humanist education had inspired; upon it he lavished much of the wealth he gained as a respected condottiere. Extending on to a cliff face but with access from the city's main piazza, it was demonstrably the residence of a benevolent and secure ruler, though Urbino also had a (no longer extant) defensive fortress on a facing spur of hill. The Palace incorporated some earlier buildings and passed through various distinct stages of design and construction, so that the main overseer appointed in 1468, Luciano Laurana, was clearly not its only architect (he left Urbino in 1472); Piero della Francesca, who also worked for Federico as a painter, and Francesco di Giorgio Martini were almost certainly involved, and the interior contains the work of numerous sculptors, woodworkers in intarsia, etc. Inscriptions using Federico's successive titles help to date parts of the work, but the absence of building accounts leaves much to speculation on stylistic grounds, and the grand courtyard, with its commemorative running inscription and various other

The Ducal Palace at **Urbino**.

features, was apparently completed during his successor's reign. From Urbino itself little (except, presumably, labour) seems to have been provided: although Raphael was the son of a local painter in Federico's service, and Bramante was also born there, Urbino did not have strong workshop traditions of its own, apart from the manufacture of decorated ceramic ware which was to flourish in the 16c.

Federico's sickly son Guidobaldo (1482–1508), assisted by his wife Elisabetta Gonzaga, followed his father's style of benignly accessible government and hospitality to the educated élite of Italy; their régime was interrupted by Cesare Borgia's sudden and legally unjustifiable military occupation (1502–03). In 1508 the duchy passed to Francesco Maria della Rovere (son of Guidobaldo's sister and related to Julius II), who built new town walls with angle bastions. In spite of his deposition by Leo X and his replacement, under the stringencies of war, by the Pope's nephew Lorenzo de' Medici (absentee Duke 1516–19), Francesco Maria was reinstated (1521–38). The DELLA ROVERE provide a rare case of a papal dynasty that survived its founding pope; they continued as dukes until Urbino was directly annexed to the Papal State in 1631. The capital, however, was moved to Pesaro in 1536 and Urbino reverted to its essential character as a minor mercantile centre for a region of relatively poor agriculture and pasturage. DC

G. Francheschini *I Montefeltro* (1970); J. Dennistoun *Memoirs of the dukes of Urbino* (3 vols 1851); P. Rotondi *The Ducal Palace of Urbino* (1961)

Uscoks (or Uskoks) *Uscocchi* was the name given to the amalgam of Bosnian, Croatian and Slovenian misfits and predators who had been shaken from their homelands by the Turks and, rather than move north into the fairly orderly Habsburg lands, had taken refuge at the port of Senj, south of Rijeka in the Gulf of Kvarner. By the mid-16c. the entire population, from priest to councillor, had come to rely for a living on piratical raids against shipping. Senj was the Sherwood Forest of the Adriatic, with Venice, the chief passer-by, its chosen victim. Protected by islets, shoals and an inhospitable coastline, reinforced by outlaws from other lands, and covertly supported by Austria, the Uscoks could successfully resist Venetian patrols and punitive raids until Venice went to war with Austria in the War of Gradisca (1615–17). JRH

G. R. Rothenberg 'Venice and the Uscoks of Senj, 1537–1618' *Journal of Modern History* (1961)

Valla, Lorenzo (1407–57), author of the most famous attack on the Donation of Constantine, was born and brought up at Rome in circles close to the papal court. After a humanist education he hoped for employment there, and retained a bitter resentment against the dominant Florentine writers for his failure to get it. For 3 years from 1430 he was a lecturer in rhetoric at Pavia. Here he published *De voluptate* (*On pleasure*, 1431; later called *De vero et falso bono*: *On the true and the false good*) which, in the guise of imaginary bantering discussion between the famous Florentine humanists, puts forward a serious critique of the conventional Stoic ethics derived from Cicero, as assumed by Bruni. The counter-argument is that the acceptance of virtuousness as an end in itself is both non-Christian and self-contradictory. The only acceptable ethic is EPICUREANISM, which recognizes that pleasure, however high-minded, is the utilitarian end of action or contemplation.

Valla moved to the court of King Alfonso I of Naples in 1435 and remained for over a decade. During Alfonso's struggle with Eugenius IV for recognition as king this was an anti-papal court – a background which affected Valla's writings both directly and indirectly. *De falso credita et ementita Constantini donatione* (*The Donation of Constantine*; 1440) applies new humanist standards of source criticism to the forged (8c.) document that the Papacy was using to support its claims to temporal power. Though now the most famous of Valla's works, it is less interesting than others with philosophical or religious significance. *De libero arbitrio* (*On free will*; *c.*1440) is a criticism of the treatment of this question by Boethius *c.*AD 480–524, in which he attributed foreknowledge to God and will to man. Valla said this ignored the importance of God's will, which could not be dissected by human philosophers: an argument which implied criticism of SCHOLASTICISM.

Dialecticae disputationes is a still more formidable philosophical treatise. In it Valla attacks a number of Aristotelian concepts from the dual standpoints of commonsense and philosophy, often arguing on the latter score that they had been mistranslated by Boethius and later Latin Aristotelians, and once again confronting scholasticism. Valla had always been an outstanding classicist. *Elegantiarum libri* (*On the elegancies of the Latin tongue*) is an early humanist philological treatise. In his *Annotationes in Novum Testamentum* (1444) he applied the new linguistic standards to the Latin Vulgate in comparison with the Greek New Testament. His sceptical attitude to the contemporary Papacy and contemporary Christian philosophy led to charges of heresy. In spite of this he was eventually invited to Rome (1448) to take part in Nicholas V's programme of translations from Greek, to which he contributed a Thucydides. He died there. Valla is often justly regarded as a precursor of Erasmus in his application of humanist philology to the New Testament, and in his dislike of the scholastic conflation of Christianity and Greek philosophy. GH

Opera (2 vols repr. 1962); M. Fois *Il pensiero cristiano di Lorenzo Valla* (1969); S.I. Camporeale *Lorenzo Valla, umanesimo e teologia* (1972)

Valois, house of From Hugh (d.996) to Charles IV (d.1328), kings of France had been descendants of the house of Capet. On Charles's death without an heir, the crown passed to Philip VI (d.1350), of the allied house of Valois. The last monarch in the direct Valois line was the heirless CHARLES VIII (d.1498). The crown then passed to the Valois branch known as ORLEANS, from its descent from the brother of Charles VI (d.1422), Louis, Duke of Orléans. But this was for only one reign, that of LOUIS XII (King 1498–1515). On his death without an heir the crown passed to the branch descended from the younger son of Louis, Duke of Orléans, which took its title from the county of Angoulême. From FRANCIS I to Henry III (King 1574–89) the royal house was known as Valois-Angoulême – but Valois for short, as in the so frequently cited Valois-Habsburg rivalry. The line ran out with Henry III, and his successor was Henry IV (King 1594–1610), of the more remotely allied house of Bourbon. JRH

G. Dodu *Les Valois* (1934)

Valturio, Roberto (1405–75) After working from 1438 as a papal abbreviator (drafter of briefs), Valturio returned to Rimini, his birthplace, and devoted the rest of his life to serving the MALATESTA as councillor and ambassador. So highly was he valued that his remains were placed in one of the external niches of the Tempio Malatestiana. In 1472 his *De re militari lib. XII* (*Twelve books on the art of war*; written *c.*1450) was published in Verona, dedicated to Sigismondo Malatesta. With its 82 fine woodcuts of military machines and devices (possibly by Matteo de' Pasti), it was perhaps the most beautiful illustrated book yet produced in Italy. The text, moreover, constituted the fullest discussion of military affairs that had appeared, heavily classicizing in the humanistic

A device for hoisting a man up on to fortified walls, from **Valturio**'s *De re militari*.

manner, but (in contrast to the often fantasticated woodcuts) relevant to the tactics and weapons of the day and thoroughly practical in its assessment of the qualities required in a condottiere commander. It was the only true Renaissance forbear of Machiavelli's *Art of war*. It was translated into Italian in 1483. JRH

Varchi, Benedetto (1503–65) A Florentine republican man of letters who returned from exile to enjoy the patronage of Cosimo I, Varchi used his commission to write the history of Florence from 1527 to 1538 with a combination of thorough documentation and independent political judgment that reflects creditably on both men. The *Storia fiorentina* is still a valuable source for the period. JRH

Varthema, Lodovico de (before 1470–1517) When he came to Venice in 1508 to give public lectures on his travels in Arabia, India and the East Indies Varthema was described as a Bolognese, but little is known of his life save what can be gleaned from that extraordinary chapter of autobiography, his *Itinerary*. Printed in Italian in 1511, it was translated into Latin in the same year, into German in 1515, Spanish in 1520, Flemish in 1554, English in 1577: forty 16c. editions in all. This success is understandable, for the book is the liveliest and most vividly anecdotal of Renaissance travel narratives. His background was probably that of a soldier. He disclaims, indeed mocks at, learning, as a source of pious legends. He set off in 1500 for Egypt and Syria purely in a spirit of curiosity and adventure, and with the determination of seeing new things with his own eyes. He visited Mecca and Medina, riskily disguised as a Mameluke pilgrim. At Aden he was arrested as a spy, but escaped by feigning madness and with the assistance of one of the Sultan's wives (which prompts a chapter 'Concerning the desire of the woman of Arabia Felix for White Men'). Thence he went to Persia, and from Ormuz to the Malabar coast and Ceylon, pursuing his course across the Bay of Bengal to Siam and thence to Borneo, Java and the Moluccas. He returned to Europe via the Cape of Good Hope, in a Portuguese vessel in 1508.

While he was not averse to telling a tall story (his description of unicorns is suspiciously minute), the work has the ring of truth. It gives a valuable account of the East at a time when the Portuguese were beginning to disrupt its closed world of trade. There is matter of both geographical and anthropological interest. But not the least of its merits is its reminder of the men who travelled, not with any political or economic or scientific aim, but as freelances, shrewd, tough, beguiling hitch-hikers in an age of organized discovery and colonization. JRH

P. Giudici *Itinerario di Ludovico de Varthema* (1956); Eng. tr. J. W. Jones in G. P. Badger ed. *The travels of Ludovico di Varthema* Hakluyt Society (1863); also ed. R. C. Temple (1928)

The title page of an edition of **Varthema**'s *Itinerary* published in 1517, with the author mapping out his route.

Vasari, Giorgio (1511–74) Born in the Florentine subject city of Arezzo, Giorgio was the child of a potter, and precocious enough for Cardinal Silvio Passerini, guardian of the young Ippolito and Alessandro de' Medici, to sponsor his education alongside them in Florence – presumably to act as a provincial spur to their overprivileged laggardliness. Thus began a connection with the Medici that lasted until the death of the steadiest patron of his work as a painter, architect and decorator-of-all-work, the Grand Duke Cosimo I. Thanks to a steady succession of Medicean and papal commissions (interspersed with others from individuals and religious bodies), Vasari produced an immense volume of artistic work, helped by a natural fluency and by teams of capable assistants: both were factors in his contemporary fame as an artist and his subsequent neglect – until quite recently. As a painter his quality can be gauged by the posthumous portrait of Lorenzo the Magnificent, the altarpiece of the Immaculate Conception in SS. Apostoli, the decorative schemes in the Salone dei Cinquecento and elsewhere in the Palazzo Vecchio – all in Florence; and by the Sala dei Cento Giorni (Room of the Hundred Days – the time he took to paint it) and the Sala Regia in Rome: in the Palazzo della Cancelleria and the Vatican respectively. As an architect he can be judged from the Florentine Uffizi and the Pisan Palazzo dei Cavalieri.

In spite of almost incessant artistic activity he found time to establish a more lasting and far more respected reputation as a writer. In his *Lives of the most excellent painters, sculptors and architects*, planned from 1543, published in 1550 and heavily revised in 1568, he wrote the first and still the most influential of all narrative and critical histories of art. The *Vite* drew on the same philosophical, shaping drive as distinguished the work of the great political historians of his youth, Machiavelli and Guicciardini. They embody the humanist notion that history should instruct and encourage through the record of notable careers and notable achievements: and he humanizes their humanism by infusing the biographies with the spirit of Boccaccio's novellas. Though substituting the pen for the brush, he never pretends not to be a professional artist; the *Lives* are introduced by a long technical preface on materials and procedures, and they reflect his determination to give his profession a pedigree that would enhance public respect for its practitioners. No other work of the period contains so many independent judgments. Of the facts (gleaned from tours of Italy, correspondence, reading and the questioning of artists or their surviving friends), enough are accurate to ensure the status of the *Lives* as the quarry from which all histories of Italian Renaissance art must be hewn. The judgments were based on the first developed vocabulary of critical appraisal, with such concepts as proportion, design and manner being used as a check on the success with which an artist brought his first idea to completion.

Equally revolutionary was his notion of progress in the arts. He did not attempt to press sculpture and architecture into the same pattern, but allowed for their shifting position within a route which painting had followed. When ancient Rome fell, art declined. All the Italians knew of art was the flat, lifeless style

The Uffizi, Florence, designed by **Vasari**.

derived from Byzantium. Then, around 1250, art was reborn. It grew to maturity in 3 stages. In the first (whose hero was Giotto), artists began to grope towards imitating the colours and forms of nature, the solid physical presence and the expressiveness of the living human body. In the second (whose inspiration was Masaccio), from *c.*1400 to *c.*1500, they indulged in a riot of experiment, especially in perspective and anatomy, that brought art's ability to record the real world almost to fruition, though it retained a certain harsh or rule-fettered flavour. It was in the third period, which included the careers of Leonardo, Raphael and Michelangelo, that artists not only mastered nature but triumphed over her. And when the grace and omnicompetence of a painter's hand could go, as Vasari put it, 'beyond the hand of nature', then the art of antiquity had been surpassed and the rebirth of art had led to a career for it of unparalleled achievement.

Vasari's concept of Renaissance invoked a period from the early 14c. to the 1560s when, with Michelangelo dead (in 1564), Vasari himself was left – as he fairly directly implies – to keep the momentum going on his own. It is far from a coincidence that most subsequent views of 'Renaissance' envisage the same timescale. He saw his 3 phases anthropomorphically, as representing the childhood, youth and maturity of art; the imprint of this implied critical canon has faded, but it determined the value placed upon works of art for centuries. *See* CRITICAL THEORY OF ART; RENAISSANCE.
[101] JRH

T. S. R. Boase *Giorgio Vasari, the man and the book* (1979); R. W. Carden *The life of Giorgio*

Vasari (1910); *Il Vasari storiografo e artista* Atti del congresso internazionale 1967 (1974); *Lives* ed. G. Milanesi (1875–85), being slowly replaced by ed. P. Barocchi and R. Bettarini (1966–)

Vasto, Alfonso d'Avalos del Marquis of Pescara 1525–46 (b.1502) One of the ablest of Imperial generals in Italy, Vasto served in Provence in 1524 and at PAVIA in 1525, and was captured by Doria during the siege of Naples. Subsequently he served against Florence, commanded Charles V's troops at Tunis (1535) and in Provence (1536), and became Governor of Milan in 1538 – a post in which he proved himself to be a poor administrator. He was a very cultivated man, and the author of poetry of high quality; his beautiful and talented wife was the patron of many writers and artists. JH

Vecchi, Orazio (1550–1605) Composer. Born in Modena, he became *maestro di cappella* in the cathedral after a time at Salò cathedral, and finally was appointed head of the court music of the ruling Este house, after its removal from Ferrara. A versatile composer of church music and serious madrigals, he was a genius in lighter music: his so-called madrigal comedy *L'Amfiparnaso*, for instance, though having nothing at all to do with the history of opera, told a *commedia dell'arte* story in a series of witty vignettes, ironic canzonettas or tongue-in-cheek madrigals. DA

A. Einstein *The Italian madrigal* (1949)

An illustration to **Vecchi**'s *L'Amfiparnaso*, 1597.

Vegetius Flavius Vegetius Renatus, biographical details virtually unknown, composed his Latin treatise on warfare *Epitoma rei militaris* in the last quarter of the 4c. AD. Known throughout the Middle Ages, this work, the fullest available source of technical knowledge about Roman armies, became especially influential in the 15c. and 16c. This was in part because Vegetius himself, like the humanist military reformers of the Renaissance, looked back to earlier models of military excellence, the armies of republican Rome. He provided the *locus classicus* for praise of the citizen-in-arms as against the use of mercenaries. Constantly cited was his emphasis on the need for discipline and training to support morale, on the need to prepare in peace for war. These were points that appealed as much to the moral philosopher as to the military expert; it was through Vegetius, for instance, and his emphasis on swimming, running and vaulting, that the notion of *mens sana in corpore sano* entered the mainstream of Renaissance educational theory.

But the historian and the military specialist also found much to inform and tantalize them (for Vegetius could be stimulatingly laconic) about the organization, armament and fighting methods of the legion, and the growing number of treatises on the art of war in the 16c. found the advocacy of Vegetian formations like the wedge and the saw, the 'A' and the 'L', irresistible, despite their impracticality. Though, after Machiavelli's thoroughgoing use of Vegetius in his *Arte della guerra* (*Art of war*), some Italian military writers tended to dwell on ancient Greek rather than Roman military methods (using Polybius and the purely technical author Aelianus Tacticus), Vegetius remained an important influence. No other ancient treatise covered the whole range of the subject, from the induction of troops to the use of field fortifications; and, as the role of heavy cavalry declined and formations became thinner in the face of firearms, contemporary tactics came increasingly to resemble those advocated by Vegetius. He is an outstanding example of an ancient writer drawn into the mainstream of both scholarly and popularizing humanist thought because of his relevance to Renaissance aspirations and practices. JRH

Epitoma rei militaris tr. J. Clarke (1767); ed. C. Lang (1885)

Venice Before the extension of Portugal and Spain overseas, Venice was the only European

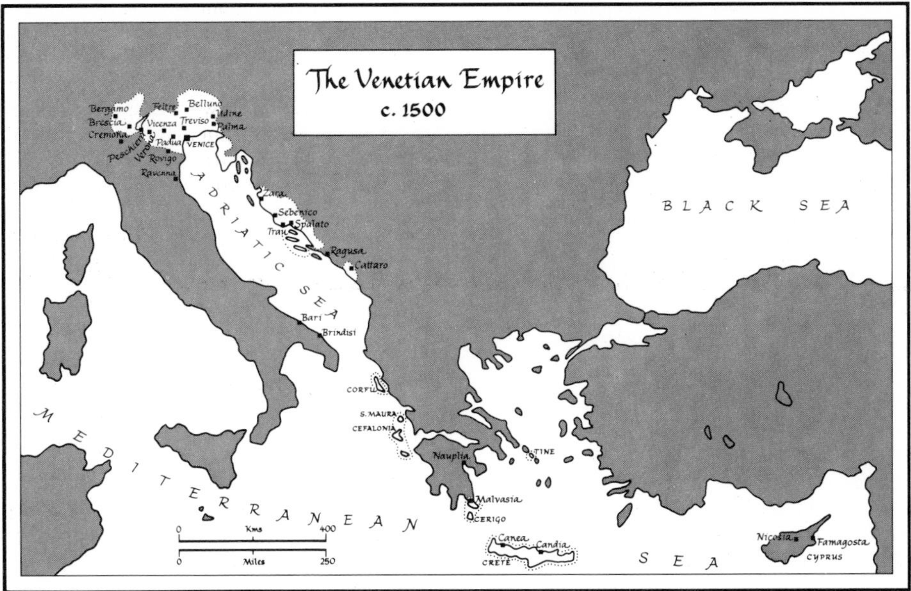

state that was also a colonial power. By 1300 Venice had successfully defended from Byzantine and Genoese attacks the string of ports and islands, reaching as far eastwards as Crete, that constituted its maritime empire. By 1340 relations with the Byzantine Emperors had been stabilized. By 1381, after a war during which the resurgent Genoese had occupied Chioggia and Malamocco and threatened the city itself across its lagoon, this rivalry too, had been settled in Venice's favour. The empire had been acquired solely for commercial reasons. Venice wanted regular and secure access by sea to the points at which Far Eastern drugs, spices and dyes and Middle Eastern cottons, silks and silverwares reached the Mediterranean: access to the Black Sea, Syria and Egypt. The need for a protected trade corridor down the Dalmatian and Albanian coasts, round southern Greece and into the Aegean was increased by the use of galleys for the carrying of these non-bulky luxury goods. The galleys provided fast and regular transport at low insurance rates, but needed regularly-spaced ports of call for the revictualling of their large crews. The system reached its furthest extent when it came to include Cyprus, ceded to Venice by its queen, Caterina Cornaro, in 1489.

Well before this it had been realized that quasi-monopolistic purchasing in the Levant required secure and toll-free access to the market points north of the Alps, once the goods had been warehoused and prepared for export from Venice. Before 1405, Venice's only foothold on the mainland had been the area bounded by Treviso (acquired 1389), Belluno and Feltre. By that year Venetian hired armies had taken Padua from its CARRARA ruler, and displaced the DELLA SCALA in Vicenza and Verona. By 1420 Friuli had been taken from Austria. By 1428 Brescia and Bergamo had been added, at the expense of the Visconti of Milan, to a land empire comprising a major part of the plains of Lombardy. These latest conquests had had to be fought for, but they were secured at the Peace of LODI (1454) and by 1500 had been extended to include Cremona and also the Polesine di Rovigo, which brought Venetian territory down to the north bank of the Po from Ferrara to the Adriatic.

Marked out by 1400 from the other Italian states by its imperial status and its exotic mingling of East with West (quite apart from the peculiarity of its site and structure), Venice by its 'theft' of its mainland empire awakened universal, if for practical reasons guarded, animosity among them. When in addition the Republic took advantage of the opening stages of the Wars of Italy to occupy useful papal (Ravenna, Faenza) and Neapolitan (Bari, Brindisi) ports, Pope Julius II's appeal to its enemies found ready support. The signatories to the Treaty of CAMBRAI represent a roll-call of all the foreign and Italian states from whom Venice had filched territories or usurped titles of suzerainty. After the traumatic defeat of Agnadello in 1509 (which made some Venetians wish they had never gone adventuring on the mainland), it took until 1517 for Venice to fight and negotiate its way back to a mainland empire which it thereafter maintained intact until the incursion of Bonaparte in 1797. All that was lost was the Romagnol ports and, by 1529, those in Apulia.

For the rest of the century Venice (with a population of *c.*115,000 in 1509, *c.*168,000 in 1563) remained a special case: independent, imperial and – at great cost in troops, fortifications and an extensive diplomatic network – impressively neutral within the antagonistic patterns of the Christian powers. While other Italian states were either the protectorates (Milan, Naples) or the edgily defiant satellites (Tuscany, the Papacy) of the Habsburg Empire, Venice, thanks to its sea empire, was treated, if impatiently, as a colleague by those who shared its vulnerability to the extension of Turkish control of the Mediterranean. In one minor (1537–40) and one major (1570–73) Turkish war Venice had Spain and the Papacy as allies. In the second Venice lost Cyprus, but its status as a European power only diminished with the slow but definite swing from the Mediterranean to the Atlantic as the source of commercial prosperity towards the end of the 16c. And for this transition Venice had prepared itself by a redeployment of capital into local industry and mainland ('terraferma') agricultural property and its improvement.

Meanwhile the Venetian constitution had remained scarcely changed since the *Serrata*, or 'closing' of the membership of the Great Council in 1297 to all but members of the 200-odd patrician clans. Henceforward they had the sole and hereditary right to belong to it and thus take a part in governing the state; from 1325 their names were inscribed in what came to be known as the *Libro d'Oro* or Golden Book. Membership of this council was automatic and for life. Too unwieldy to conduct day-to-day business, it was primarily the reservoir whence individuals were chosen to sit for short periods (to prevent their acquisition of too much power) on smaller councils. Of these the most important were the Senate, the chief policy-forming organ of government, some 200 strong; the College, which prepared the Senate's business and saw to the execution of its decisions; and the Council of Ten, responsible for state security. Chairman of all these bodies was the doge, elected through a procedure elaborately devised to protect the post from self-seeking or party-supported ambition, denied political initiative, but potentially influential because of his enduring presence in bodies whose membership was constantly changing. The unique stability of this constitution over the Renaissance centuries was a source of envy, wonder, at times imitation.

It was as a sort of malign homage to the exceptional role Venice had played in the Renaissance that Bonaparte licensed 3 phases of ideologically motivated vandalism: the hacking down of images of St Mark (emblem of domination); the removal to Paris of the horses from the Basilica (mementos of Levantine conquest – they had been looted from Constantinople in 1204); and the burning of the *bucintoro*, the ceremonial barge from which the doge, each Ascension Day, had celebrated Venice's marriage with the Adriatic and its claim to be a Mediterranean rather than a slumberously peninsular power. *See* CONSTITUTIONS; MYTH OF VENICE; COUNCIL OF TEN. JRH

R. C. Lane *Venice, a maritime republic* (1973); F. Thiriet *Histoire de Venise* (1969); R. Finlay *Politics in Renaissance Venice* (1980); D. S. Chambers *The imperial age of Venice, 1380–1580* (1970)

Venier family This Venetian patrician family produced 3 doges in the Renaissance: Antonio (Doge 1382–1400), Francesco (Doge 1554–56) and Sebastiano (Doge 1577–78). A striking example of the Venetian practice of entrusting old men with the most demanding and potentially dangerous of public duties, Sebastiano was made captain general of the sea in 1570 at the age of 74; as such he was in great measure responsible for the tactics and the morale that defeated the Turks off LEPANTO in the following year. His contention that failure thereafter to recapture Cyprus was due to the delaying tactics of Venice's allies was for years looked upon with scepticism, and his election to the dogeship at the age of 82 was possibly in part a deliberate rehabilitation. JRH

P. Molmenti *Sebastiano Veniero* (1889)

Vergerio, Pietro Paolo (1370–1444), the first major theorist of humanist EDUCATION, was born in Capodistria and studied at Padua, but came under the influence of Chrysoloras and the Florentine school during a stay at Florence in the 1390s. As the tutor of the children of Francesco Carrara at Padua he composed *De ingenuis moribus* (*Conduct worthy of free men*; *c.*1402), setting out the claims of a literary education in which, after preparatory grammar and logic, history and moral philosophy and eloquence are to take the lead in a liberal education. In 1405 he acquired a post at the papal court and joined the humanist circle there. From the Council of Constance he entered the service of King Sigismund of Hungary and disappeared into obscurity in that kingdom, where he died. GH

D. Robey 'P. P. Vergerio the Elder: republicanism and civic values in the work of an early humanist' *Past and Present* (1973)

Vergil, Polydore (1470–1555) Anglicized name of Polidoro Vergilio, who was born in Urbino. A cleric who was also a classical scholar, in 1502 Vergil accompanied the Collector of Peter's Pence, Bishop Adriano Castelli, to England as his deputy. Apart from occasional visits to Italy he spent the rest of his life there. He published in 1525 the earliest scholarly edition of a British historical source, the 6c. chronicle of Gildas, and from 1534 wrote expanding versions of the first humanistic history of Britain. This, the *Anglica historia*, retains its value as a source for the reigns of Richard III, Henry VII and Henry VIII. His earliest and most popular book, the *De inventoribus rebus* (1499), was a pioneering handbook on the origins of things as disparate as religion, gunpowder, art and prostitution. JRH

Denys Hay *Polydore Vergil* (1952)

Vermigli, Peter Martyr (Pietro Martire) (1499–1562) Protestant theologian. Born in Florence, he became an Augustinian Canon of the Lateran Congregation, and as Abbot of S. Frediano he was a leading figure in the quite significant Protestant movement in Lucca. In 1542 he fled to Switzerland and his subsequent activities were mainly in Strasbourg, Oxford and Zurich. OL

P. McNair *Peter Martyr in Italy: an anatomy of an apostasy* (1967)

Verona With its position on an important navigable river, the Adige, and at the throat of one of the most used of passes across the Alps, Verona in medieval times reflected all the Lombard conflicts resulting from the loyalties and ambitions of GUELFS AND GHIBELLINES. Controlled now by one side, now by another, and in the intervals plagued by the domestic factions commemorated in the story of Romeo and Juliet (dating from *c.*1303), by 1300 Verona had allowed the DELLA SCALA family to exchange the temporary authority of capitani for the hereditary rule of signori. After a succession of Scaligeri rulers (whose monuments are among the most powerful of the city's works of art) Verona was annexed in 1405 by Venice. Before 1797 there was only one break in Venetian rule. In 1509, after the defeat of the Republic at AGNADELLO, Verona welcomed a German occupying army. It was not until 1517 that the city was recovered – with a taint of collaboration that long made the city's loyalty a subject of concern.

The richness of the Veronese region and the commercial traffic of which Verona was the centre reconciled its citizens to the consequences of the peace derived from Venice's policy of neutrality vis-à-vis Austria to the north and Spanish Milan to the west; even the heavy burden of contributions to the massive new fortifications with which Venice surrounded the city from the 1530s was accepted, under protest, as being an inevitable component of a neutrality that, to be effective, had to be armed. The first phases of these were designed by Sanmicheli. Their much commented on innovatory quality, and the splendour of their triumphal gates (notably Porta Nuova and Porta Palio), became a source of pride. The *enceinte*, and Sanmicheli's palaces within it, constitute the chief Renaissance contribution to a city whose cultural achievements in earlier times of war and faction were not otherwise revived in times of peace. JRH

Verona e il suo territorio Istituto per gli Studi Storici Veronesi (1960–69)

Veronese (1528–88) Paolo Caliari, with Tintoretto, succeeded Titian as the chief artist of 16c. Venice. Born in Verona, as his popular name, Veronese, indicates, he was trained there by a local painter, Antonio Badile, before moving to Venice about the age of 23. The supremely visual character of Veronese's art, with its tendency towards decoration rather

The Family of Darius before Alexander (detail) by **Veronese** (London, National Gallery).

than emotional expressiveness, sets him apart from Tintoretto and partly reflects his non-Venetian origin, although his example profoundly marked the course of painting in Venice, especially during the 18c. Though alive to the most daring spatial experiments of painters like Pordenone and Tintoretto himself, Veronese was most deeply in sympathy with the decorative side of Titian's art, and, like Titian, he mastered without strain a wide range of subject matter, including portraits. The spiritual aims of the Counter-Reformation were not, however, seen to be fulfilled by his work, and in 1573 Veronese was summoned by the Inquisition and cross-examined about a *Last Supper* (now Venice, Accademia), subsequently renamed *A Feast in the House of Levi*.

Veronese's earliest commissions on reaching Venice included allegorical ceiling paintings in the Doges' Palace and the first of his works in the church of S. Sebastiano, the 3 scenes from the story of Esther which decorate the ceiling of the nave. In the *Triumph of Mordecai* the spectator, like the audience in a 'Western', sees the procession from beneath the hooves of the horses. Veronese's mastery of illusion is seen at its most brilliant in the decoration of Palladio's Villa Barbaro at Maser (1561), where the allegorical programme is ingeniously interspersed with scenes showing contemporary life in the villa, figures chasing a monkey beneath a representation of Olympus, etc. The use of architecture evocative of the simplified and harmonious style of Palladio became a feature of most of Veronese's larger compositions, whether religious or secular in theme. The huge *Marriage at Cana* of 1562–63 (Paris, Louvre), which contains a chamber orchestra before the table where Christ sits, takes place in a perspective of columned façades focused upon a church steeple, and the *Family of Darius before Alexander* (London, National Gallery), a sumptuous and moral pageant peculiarly well suited to the character of Veronese's art, is enacted within a courtyard no less lucid and gracious than the behaviour of its human occupants. Towards the end of his career pressure of commissions, including ones from the court of Prague, led to the increasing intervention in his paintings of Veronese's workshop, where his sons Gabriele and Carletto and his brother Benedetto were employed. Among the last of the works executed with the help of the studio is the splendid *Apotheosis of Venice*, which confronts the *Paradise* of Tintoretto in the Sala del Maggior Consiglio of the Ducal Palace. [82] AB

T. Pignatti *Veronese* (1976)

Verrazzano, Giovanni (d.?1528) Nothing is known for certain of the life of this explorer of the American coast from Florida to Newfoundland before he turns up in France in 1522. Perhaps he was born there, at Paris or Lyons, to a member of the Florentine merchant family of this name. In 1523 he was commissioned by King Francis I 'to explore new lands', a brief interpreted by Verrazzano as inviting him to find a route to Cathay, or eastern Asia, between the two parts of the North American coast that were already known: Florida, and Newfoundland and Labrador. It was the great merit of his voyage of 1524 that it established the continuity (which had hitherto been merely guessed at on maps) of the coast, but his report and the maps that took account of it gave long currency to a gigantic error – the idea that Tampico Sound was the narrow opening to a sea ('Verrazzano's Sea') that widened eastwards into the Pacific, thus providing the longed-for passage to Cathay. A later voyage – to Brazil – has been postulated for 1526, but remains uncertain. Nor has any clear evidence been produced for a third, in 1528, the one on which, according to Giovio (repeated by RAMUSIO) he was eaten by cannibals somewhere in the West Indies. JRH

L. C. Wroth *The voyages of Giovanni da Verrazzano 1524–28* (1970)

Verrocchio's bronze *Putto with a Fish* in the Palazzo della Signoria, Florence.

Verrocchio, Andrea del (1435–88) was trained as a goldsmith in Florence and became the greatest bronze sculptor of the late 15c., emulating Donatello. He was also a talented painter and ran a successful workshop producing many kinds of artefact for patrons such as the Medici. His major sculptural commission in Florence was the bronze group of *Christ and St Thomas* for Orsanmichele (*c*.1465–83), where his characteristic treatment of drapery, facial types, curling hair and gestures is manifest. For the Medici he produced a bronze statue of *David* – an obvious critique of Donatello's version – and the *Putto with a Fish* (Florence, Palazzo della Signoria), for a fountain at the Medicean villa at Careggi (the seat of the Platonic Academy), as well as celebrated portrait busts of Lorenzo and Giuliano de' Medici (Washington, National Gallery). His great equestrian monument to the condottiere Colleoni in Venice (1479–88) embodied a far more dynamic pose than Donatello's earlier one to Gattamelata. Verrocchio's greatest pupil was Leonardo da Vinci, while his style also greatly influenced the young Michelangelo. [208] CA

C. Avery *Florentine Renaissance sculpture* (1970); C. Seymour *The sculpture of Verrocchio* (1971); G. Passavant *Verrocchio* (1969)

Vesalius (1514–64) Andrea Vesalio, anatomist. Although not an Italian (he was born in Brabant), he was responsible for making Padua the centre for anatomy in the 16c. He studied at Louvain and Paris (where he helped to edit GALEN); he then went to Padua where he was appointed lecturer on surgery and (after a short time) anatomy, continuing to follow the newly available Galen into anatomical research. In 1538 he published 6 *Tabulae anatomiae* and a textbook, and in 1543 *De humani corporis fabrica* (*On the fabric of the human body*) with its handsome plates (plagiarized in England by Thomas Geminus in 1555) as well as its *Epitome*. He then sought and received appointment as physician and surgeon to the Imperial household, becoming physician to Philip II of Spain in 1555, in which year he also revised the *Fabrica*. This is the first large-scale, original survey of human anatomy and physiology since Galen, and is justly famous. MBH

The illustrations ed. J. M. D. Saunders and C. O'Malley (1950); *The epitome* tr. L.R. Lind (1949); C. Singer *A prelude to modern science* (the *Tabulae sex*) (1946)

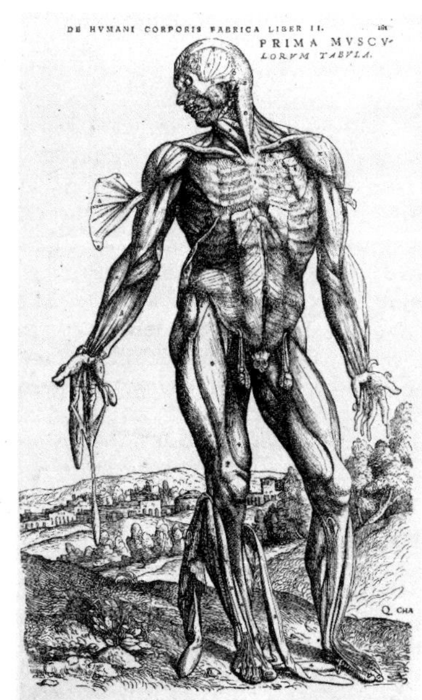

Plate from the *De humani corporis fabrica* of **Vesalius** (an edition of 1547) showing the primary muscles.

Vespasiano *See* BISTICCI, VESPASIANO DA

Vespucci, Amerigo (1454–1512) Member of an old, no longer prosperous Florentine merchant family, Vespucci joined the trading firm of Lorenzo di Pierfrancesco de' Medici and was sent to Seville in 1494 to help in their agency there, becoming its head in 1495. He was involved in the fitting-out for Spain of Columbus's third expedition and, when news arrived late in 1498 of his discovery of part of the South American coast off Trinidad, Vespucci found a place on the expedition sent under Alonso de Hojeda to explore the coast more fully. Off Trinidad Hojeda broke off to continue westwards and Vespucci turned to follow the coast to the east. He was by then pilot and effective commander.

Upon what previous experience this promotion was based is not known. Probably he was a shareholder in the expedition; this could give a presumptive right to a command. Seville, with its community of cartographers and its coming and going of oceanic vessels, was a perfect observation post for the amateur student of navigation. But given the success of this voyage of 1499, which made the first European contact with the mouth of the Amazon and Brazil, and the astonishing determination and address which took him on his second voyage of 1501 (this time for King Manuel of Portugal), from Brazil at about latitude 5 degrees south to almost as far south as the Straits of Magellan, his biographers have been tempted to postulate some previous experience at sea. This was his last known voyage. Manuel, realizing that the coast explored by Vespucci tended south-west into the zone reserved for Spain by the 1494 Treaty of Tordesillas, no longer needed his services and he returned to Spain, where in 1505 he was given the important advisory post of pilot major.

No journals survive. Three quite brief letters describing his voyage to Pierfrancesco de' Medici remained in manuscript. Garbled and misleadingly elaborated versions were, however, published in 1504 (the *New World* and *Letter of Amerigo Vespucci*). Drawing in part on these, Martin Wadseemüller showed the Americas as a separate continent in his world map of 1507, naming Vespucci in its title and adding a note suggesting that the newly established land mass should be called America after him. The success of this suggestion, which gave another man's name to a continent first explored and reported on by Columbus, has led to a vast literature of belittlement and controversy around the very few known facts of Vespucci's life. JRH

A. Magnaghi *Amerigo Vespucci: studio critico* (1926); F. J. Pohl *Amerigo Vespucci, pilot major* (1944)

Vicentino, Nicola (1511–76) One of the principal advocates of the attempt to recreate Greek music. A pupil of Willaert, he moved about 1534 to Ferrara, where he taught music to the family of Duke Ercole II d'Este. His theories involved the use of the 3 Greek *genere*, the diatonic, chromatic and enharmonic, and he was instrumental in the building of an *archicembalo* (*see* MUSIC). The most complete exposition of his views, *L'antica musica ridotta nella prattica moderna*, was published in 1555. He became *maestro di cappella* at Vicenza cathedral in 1563, but spent his last years in Milan, where he died of the plague. DA

Vida, Marco Girolamo (1485–1566) Bishop and neo-Latin poet, born in Cremona, whose epic *Christus* in Virgilian hexameters transmitted the Council in Hell motif from Boccaccio (*Filocolo*) to Tasso and thence to Milton. He also composed a defence of poetic imitation, in his *Ars poetica*, and didactic poems such as *Scacchia ludus*, which describes chess in narrating an Olympian quarrel. His conflation of the classical Golden Age with Eden in *Dialogi de dignitate reipublicae* (1556) illustrates a late Renaissance idea that permeated many works. LGC

J. Sparrow 'Latin verse of the High Renaissance' in E. F. Jacob ed. *Italian Renaissance studies* (1960)

Vignola, Giacomo Barozzi da (1507–73) Architect and author of a hugely influential codification of the orders (*Regola delle cinque ordini*, 1562), whose successful career in Bologna, Rome, and the Papal State was promoted by the Farnese family. Largely self-taught from Serlio's pattern books (*vide* Palazzo Bocchi, Bologna, 1545), Vignola developed in Rome a style in which fanciful detail was controlled within a strictly orthodox framework. In his churches he experimented with oval forms (S. Andrea in Via Flaminia, 1554; S. Anna dei Palafrenieri, 1572f.), and with the Gesù perfected the Jesuit single nave plan type with interconnecting side chapels. The Palazzo Farnese at Caprarola, where he inserted a round

Courtyard of the Palazzo Farnese at Caprarola, designed by **Vignola**.

The Florentines attacking Pistoia, from a manuscript of Villani's *Croniche* (Rome, Vatican Library).

courtyard and Bramantesque spiral staircase into Peruzzi's polygonal fortress, is the most celebrated of Vignola's fine Roman villas with elaborate terraced gardens. CE
M. W. Casotti *Il Vignola* (1960)

Vigo, Giovanni da (1450–1525) Surgeon. Born in Rapallo, he practised at Genoa, Savona and elsewhere; he was physician to Pope Julius II 1503–13. He thus had vast experience of military and civilian surgery. His two most famous works are *Practica in arte chirurgica copiosa* (*Abundant practice in surgery*; Rome 1514), in which he advocates the use of mercury in treating syphilis, perhaps for the first time (it remained in use into the 20c.); and *Practica compendiosa* (Rome and Pavia 1518; editions in French, Italian and English), which describes surgical techniques. MBH

Villani, Giovanni (*c.*1276–1348) The outstanding chronicler of medieval Florence. Although he claimed to have experienced a Gibbon-like inspiration to write while at the Roman Jubilee of 1300, the bulk of his chronicle was not put into its final form until 1333–41, continuing until just before his death from the plague of 1348. A banker who knew little Latin, Villani skilfully wove together biblical and classical strands so as to place the rise of Florence, 'the daughter of Rome', firmly in the context of world history as understood at the time. Being written in an attractive vernacular, the chronicle achieved an instant success and has influenced every writer on Florence from Dante, who knew the first 4 books, down to the present day. Modern commentators have been impressed by Villani's grasp of statistics, as shown in his description of the state of Florence in 1338, and by the tension between his detailed reporting of political and economic misfortunes and his belief in divine providence. *See* HISTORY AND CHRONICLE. JKH
Croniche fiorentine ed. I. Moutier (1823; repr. 1846 and 1857); partial tr. R. E. Selfe *Selections from the first nine books of the Croniche fiorentine* (1896)

Villani, Matteo Brother of Giovanni and continuator of his chronicle 1348–63, when he too died of plague. Matteo was a close observer of his times and deeply pessimistic; he is a more studied writer than Giovanni but his bursts of eloquence show no direct influence of classical writings. JKH
L. Green *Chronicle into history* (1972)

Villas (country estates and their buildings) The Virgilian concept of country life as a source of physical sustenance and spiritual solace, already present in Boccaccio's *Decameron*, presupposes an urbanized society nostalgic for and reliant on its rural roots. All Italian town dwellers of any means owned agricultural holdings worked by sharecroppers, visited at harvest and vintage as well as for rest and recreation at other times. Architecturally, early villas ranged from modest barn-like structures to the fortified castles still necessary in a violent countryside. While to some extent they conformed to local

The Medicean **villa** at Cafaggiolo.

traditions, and retained common functional elements like loggias for shade and storage, dovecote towers and fishponds, Renaissance architects and patrons introduced new forms, often incorporating specific references to antiquity. A distinct type, the *villa suburbana*, received the imprimatur of Alberti. Vitruvius's silence on villas, and the shortage of extant ancient examples, meant a heavy reliance on antique literary descriptions, especially the letters of Pliny the Younger (AD 61 or 62–*c.* 113) about his own villas at Tifernum and Laurentium. Gardens, an essential feature of the villa as *locus amoenus*, began in the 16c. to break out of their medieval enclosing walls, using hillside sites to generate perspectival vistas of ramped staircases, fountains, and *all'antica* statuary.

The castle/villa transition is apparent in Michelozzo's Tuscan villas for the Medici (Trebbio, Cafaggiolo, Careggi) where battlements become vestigial, and loggias begin to embrace the view. Giuliano da Sangallo's strongly Albertian villa for Lorenzo de' Medici at Poggio a Caiano introduced symmetrical planning and a pedimented loggia into an unfortified block, elevated over an arcaded podium. Built near a 4-towered dairy farm designed on rational agricultural principles new to Tuscany, Poggio was the model for 16c. grand-ducal Medici villas, built on vast concentrations of agricultural estates. The gardens at Castello and at Buontalenti's Pratolino impressed visitors like Montaigne with their fountains, grottoes and waterworks.

In Rome the High Renaissance papal court, building more for display than agricultural need, developed the suburban *vigna*, already anticipated in some respects by Michelozzo's Villa Medici in Fiesole (loggia overlooking hillside terrace) and Giuliano da Maiano's Poggio Reale at Naples (4-towered villa with *all'antica* baths and terrace over fishpond). More influential for Rome than the porticoed villa with corner towers (reflected in Innocent VIII's Belevedere and Peruzzi's Farnesina, 1505f.) was Bramante's Cortile del Belvedere, with its ascending levels, perspectival vistas, staircase ramps and niched exedra. Raphael's unfinished Villa Madama (1516f.), for the future Medici pope Clement VII, deploys a Vitruvian bath and theatre, and a range of explicitly Plinian conceits (summer and winter dining and pleasure rooms) in a plan drawing on the Imperial baths to set up a sequence of spaces of varied shape (round courtyard) and novel antique-inspired decoration (stuccoes and grotesques). Belvedere-derived garden forms were enhanced by the inventive use of water in Vignola's villas at Bagnaia and Caprarola (water stairs and water-cooled dining tables) and perfected at Ligorio's Villa d'Este at Tivoli (1560f.). The architectural themes of the Villa Madama are pursued at the Villa Giulia (1551f.), with its semi-circular court, nymphaeum and grotto, and at Ligorio's Casino of Pius IV.

With the architectural diaspora of the 1520s Roman villa ideas reached the provinces. Giulio Romano's suburban hunting lodge at Mantua, the Palazzo del Tè, grafts the Roman nature symbolism of rusticated Doric and decoration *à la* Villa Madama on to a local tradition of low courtyard villas. Giulio's triple rusticated loggias influenced the young Palladio, whose mature villa plans drew on an indigenous Veneto tradition of tripartite planning and arcaded farm buildings to incorporate barns, dovecotes and storage loggias into the hierarchical plan of the villa itself. Thus the patron's house, with grain store behind its classical temple pediment, became the centre of a working villa-farm, particularly suited to Palladio's land-based Vicentine patrons and to the Venetian nobility encouraged by law to reclaim land in the Po valley. Genoa had a tradition of towered suburban seaside villas, into which Alessi introduced Palladian rational planning in a Farnesina-like block, enriched with Roman 1530s ornament (Villa Cambiaso, 1548f.). CE

Bollettino del Centro Internazionale di Studi di Architettura Andrea Palladio (1969 vol. on villas); D. Coffin *The villa in the life of Renaissance Rome* (1979)

Virgil (70–19 BC) knows no medieval eclipse, and no decline, but he was subject to some alchemy. Before the 6c. grammarian Fulgentius made the *Aeneid* of Publius Vergilius Maro a complex allegory of human life (5c. to 6c.), already in the 4c. the prophecy of Virgil's IVth Eclogue had been transferred from an Imperial to a Christian context. Despite the growth of the legend of Virgil as magician, which spread irresistibly, a christianized Virgil meets with acceptance at the most orthodox levels. Dante is only a special case in this acceptance, for, seeing the hand of God in the rise of Rome to universal monarchy, he took Virgil to be the sacred text that celebrates this providential dispensation for the right ordering of the world. To make his allegiance complete, Dante takes the necessary step of dismissing all the nonsense of a magician-Virgil, but the context in which he does so (his reverence for a 'scriptural' Virgil) prevents us from thinking that a new criticism has been born. Nor does Dante's love for Virgil have any influence on the way (the medieval way) he writes Latin.

For Petrarch Virgil is 'splendour in speech, the second hope of the Latin tongue', and between them Virgil and Cicero are the basis for Petrarch's return to a classical purity. And since Petrarch seeks no universal formula, recognizing that the Roman Empire has long since died, there is no trace in him of the political message which was paramount for Dante. When Petrarch dismisses the magic legend of the medieval Virgil, this is the voice of reason and criticism; which also speaks when he refutes the general belief in Virgil as prophet of the birth of Christ. Virgil spoke of the highest that he knew, the Roman Empire, but, had the true light shone before his eyes, doubtless he would have turned his thoughts towards another event. Petrarch, it is true, still looks backward in one way, as he revealed in Naples in 1341, in his examination for the laureateship by King Robert. He accepted poetry as allegory, with a light in each word hidden beneath the poetic cloud. But Petrarch does not force this allegory upon us. Instead he offers Virgil, for the first time, as all his other authors from antiquity, as a cultural enrichment, to be lived with, and meditated on. This is the vital contribution of Petrarch to the understanding of Virgil, and it far outweighs the relative failure in his own reverent attempt to rival the *Aeneid* in his *Africa*, where the matter comes from the third main author

A drawing by Mantegna for a projected monument to **Virgil** (Paris, Louvre).

whom Petrarch proclaims to Europe (Livy), and the style should come – but hardly does – from Virgil. It is the communion of Petrarch with the ancient world which is the basis of Renaissance literary culture, and the manuscript of Virgil which belonged to Petrarch (now in the Ambrosiana Library in Milan) has been thought of as the main monument, the most moving document, of his personal contact with the Roman world.

From Petrarch on, the effort to purify the corrupt texts which had been handed down by scribal error was constant, but it was for long haphazard and opportunistic. With the *Plinianae castigationes* (*Emendations to Pliny*) of Ermolao Barbaro (1492) a new philology was born, based on the conspectus of the sources; and out of this there came in 1521 the *Castigationes virgilianae* of Piero Valeriano, the first *apparatus criticus* for the text. Meanwhile Virgil is the chief poet in view, superior for many to Homer, as art to untamed nature. It is only with Castelvetro that Aristotle's repudiation of didactic poetry directs a breath of criticism at the author of the *Georgics*. Sperone Speroni (1500–88) enquired why Virgil wished to destroy his *Aeneid*, and prompted the reply that it was noble in elocution, poor in invention. Even then, at the end of the Cinquecento, Bruno still defended Virgil against Castelvetro, though he was no longer put on an exclusive pedestal.

Petrarch tried to rival the *Aeneid* with his *Africa*, but he kept it to himself and it emerged too late to capture much attention, or influence others. The main effort of humanism, in the first half of the Quattrocento, was in prose, so it did not look to Virgil as a model. When Palmieri did, for his *Città di vita*, the ecclesiastical censure which his dependence on Virgil provoked ensured that it had to wait until our own time for exhumation. It was the *Eclogues*, badly translated by Bernardo Pulci in 1481, that proved the easiest to imitate, and that underlie the pastoral tradition, whether it is macaronic, as with Teofilo Folengo's *Zanitonella* (1521), or strictly regular, as with Sannazaro's eclogues, the cornerstone for the later Latin tradition and the height of Virgilian imitation. Then it was the turn of the didactic poem the *Georgics*, defended by Fracastoro in the *Naugerius* before it was labelled as an aberration from Aristotelian norms, and imitated by him in *Syphilis*, and by Sannazaro in the *De partu virginis* (*On the Virgin's giving birth*) (long forgotten, but possibly the noblest Virgilian poem of the Renaissance). But we should bear in mind that, from Poliziano's first teaching (in 1482), the young especially were encouraged to look to the lesser poets also, as easier to assimilate and imitate, and Virgil ceases to be an exclusive model. Look at the surface of Tasso's poetry, and all the ancient poets are lurking below. Nor, of course, does the Renaissance produce a poem in the purely Virgilian epic mould. This lack of response to the most massive Virgilian challenge is made more obvious by such imitations of the *Georgics* as *Le api* (*The bees*) of Giovanni Rucellai (published 1539 after his death in 1525) and *La coltivazione* of Luigi Alamanni (1546). JHW

V. Zabughin *Vergilio nel Rinascimento* (2 vols 1923); J. H. Whitfield 'Virgil into Dante' in D. R. Dudley ed. *Virgil* (1969)

Virtù The Italian word commonly means 'virtue' in the sense of Hamlet's admonition to his mother, 'Assume a virtue, if you have it not', but during the Renaissance it increasingly carried the force of Edmund Burke's 'I have in general no very exalted opinion of the virtue of paper government', in which the word signifies efficacy, actual or latent. Under the influence of the classical *virtus*, 'excellence' (with a strongly virile connotation), *virtù* could be used, as it most frequently was by Machiavelli, for example, to convey an inherently gifted activism especially in statecraft or military affairs; to possess *virtù* was a character trait distinguishing the energetic, even reckless (but not feckless) man from his conventionally virtuous counterpart, rendering him less vulnerable to the quirks of FORTUNA. JRH

J. E. Seigel 'Virtù' in P. P. Wiener ed. *Dictionary of the history of ideas* IV (1973)

Visconti family Their predominance in Milan was secured at the end of the 13c. and beginning of the 14c. by Ottone Visconti (Archbishop of Milan 1263–95) and his great-nephew, Matteo (Captain of the People 1287–1302; imperial vicar 1311–22). In 1349 the Council of the commune bestowed the *signoria* upon the heirs of Matteo in perpetuity. By this time a policy of continuous expansion had extended the family's rule to many other cities, among them Alessandria and Asti in Piedmont and Como, Novara, Vercelli, Bergamo, Brescia, Pavia, and Cremona in

An allegorical figure of Milan bearing the **Visconti** *imprese*, from a manuscript of Cicero's *De natura deorum et de divinatione* (Paris, Bibliothèque Nationale).

Visconti

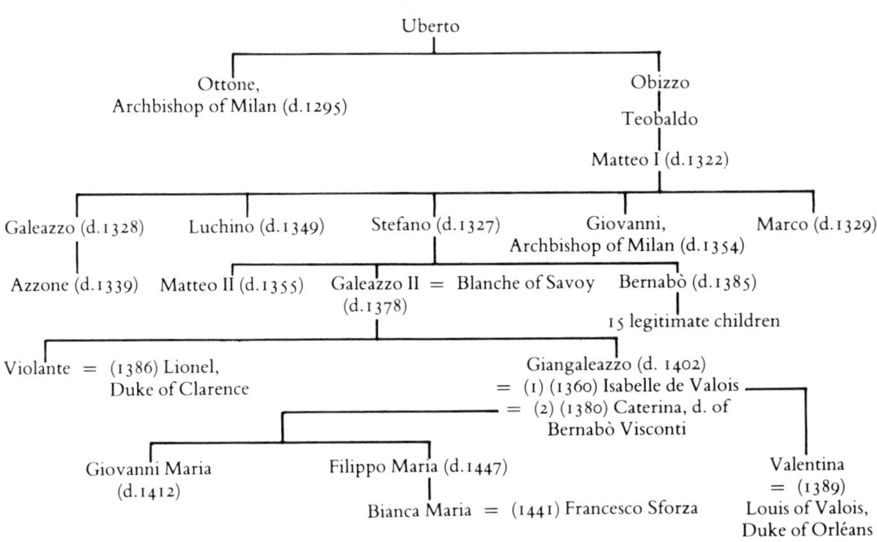

Lombardy. The Visconti never succeeded in breaking down the local particularism of the constituent parts of their dominions and forming them into a united state, but they did bring peace between hitherto rival communes; they also ensured a greater measure of internal harmony between the city oligarchies over which they ruled. Yet, even when the hostile propaganda of their enemies has been discounted, their government was accompanied by all the cruelty, violence, and aggressive will characteristic of absolute régimes.

In the 1360s marriages into the French and English royal houses confirmed the family's status as a European power and in 1395 Giangaleazzo obtained the title of duke from the Emperor Wenceslaus. Giangaleazzo's seizure of the territories of his uncle, Bernabò, in 1385 made his branch of the family the dominant power in Italy during his lifetime. His premature death in 1402 was followed by the succession of his sons, the vicious and incompetent Giovanni Maria (Duke 1402–12) and then the more able Filippo Maria (Duke 1412–47), with whom the direct male line expired. JL

Storia di Milano IV–VI Fondazione Treccani degli Alfieri (1954–55)

Visconti, Bernabò Signore of Milan 1355–85 (b.1323) Chaucer's 'God of delyt and scourge of Lumbardie', coarse-humoured, boastful of his cruelties, Bernabò was a man of strong passions. (It was estimated that on one particular occasion he was the father of 37 living children and responsible for the condition of 18 pregnant women.) In 1355 he divided with his brother Galeazzo II the territories inherited from Archbishop Giovanni Visconti. They held Milan and Genoa in common; Bernabò took as his own Bergamo, Brescia, and Como. From 1360, when Galeazzo largely withdrew from politics, Bernabò became the most powerful force in northern Italy. He resisted ALBORNOZ's attempts to restore the Papal State, lost Genoa (1358), but gained Reggio (1371). With the succession of his nephew, Giangaleazzo, to the possessions of Galeazzo (1378), Bernabò sought to exercise a virtual tutelage over him. Provoked by his menaces and contempt, however, Giangaleazzo treacherously seized him and occupied his domains (1385). Bernabò died shortly after in prison. JL

Visconti, Filippo Maria Duke of Milan 1412–47 (b.1392) Unhealthy, ugly, and obsessed by fear and suspicion, Filippo Maria

Pisanello's medal of **Filippo Maria Visconti**, 1441 (Paris, Bibliothèque Nationale).

dedicated his life to the pursuit of power ('I care less for my body than my soul, but I put my government before body or soul'). During the rule of his brother Giovanni Maria (Duke 1402–12), the Visconti territories had been largely taken over by condottieri and local factions. Filippo Maria's first act as Duke was to marry Beatrice, widow of the powerful condottiere Facino CANE, and by so doing secure his troops and the cities of Novara, Alessandria, Tortona and Pavia, which he had controlled. (Beatrice was judicially murdered on a false charge of adultery in 1418.) During the next 9 years, with the support of the condottiere CARMAGNOLA, he recovered almost all the family's Lombard possessions. He seized Genoa (1412) and acquired territories in the Val Levantina by his defeat of the Swiss in the battle of Arbédo (1422).

He could achieve further expansion only at the expense of Venice and Florence. Violation of his agreement with Florence on their respective spheres of influence led to war (1423–28), in which Venice from 1425 was persuaded to join her republican ally. Thereafter there was virtually continuous conflict among the 3 powers (1431–44). In the event it became clear that the Duke had overplayed his hand. He lost Brescia, Bergamo, Vercelli and Genoa, and was driven to still greater dependence upon powerful condottieri. Notable among these was Francesco SFORZA, to whom he gave his daughter in marriage. He died with no male heirs and – perhaps, as contemporaries alleged, because he hoped for chaos after his death – without having made any clear arrangements for his succession. JL

Storia di Milano VI Fondazione Treccani degli Alfieri (1955)

Visconti, Giangaleazzo Duke of Milan 1395–1402 (b.1351) Son of Galeazzo II Visconti and Blanche of Savoy, Giangaleazzo married in 1360 Isabelle of Valois, daughter of King John II of France, receiving as her dowry the county of Vertus in Champagne and thus the title of 'Conte di Virtù' by which he was frequently known. On the death of his father (1378) he succeeded to the lordships of Pavia, Novara, Vercelli, Tortona, Alessandria, Valenza, Casale and Asti. In the early years of his rule he appeared to follow the guidance of his uncle Bernabò, and after the death of his first wife married in 1380 Bernabò's daughter Caterina. In 1385, however, in a skilful and daring coup, Giangaleazzo seized his father-in-law, imprisoned or exiled his nephews, and reunited all the territories subject to the Visconti. The powerful position which he now occupied was emphasized when his daughter Valentina was betrothed to Louis of Orléans, brother of Charles VI of France, in 1387, and then again with the grant by the Emperor Wenceslaus of the title of Duke of Milan in 1395.

From 1385 the speed, secrecy and lack of scruple shown in his attack upon Bernabò were employed in a series of diplomatic and military campaigns which were to bring him to hegemony in Italy. In 1387, in alliance with the Carrara, he seized Verona and Vicenza from Antonio della Scala; in 1388, in alliance with the Venetians, he struck against his erstwhile Carrara friends and occupied Padua, Bassano, Feltre, and Belluno. Such triumphs inevitably roused the suspicions and hostility of other powers. In particular the rise of his diplomatic influence in the Romagna, Tuscany, and Umbria provoked the rivalry of Florence, itself seeking at this time to extend its territories. Attempts to delineate respective spheres of influence failed and were followed by 3 wars (1390–92, 1397–98, 1400–02) in which Giangaleazzo achieved an apparently overwhelming predominance. He was recognized as signore of the Lunigiana (1398), of Pisa and Siena (1399), and of Perugia, Spoleto, and Assisi (1400). In

June 1402 he took Bologna; Florence was encircled and was perhaps saved from conquest only by Giangaleazzo's death from plague.

Conforming in many ways to the conventional stereotype of the Italian Renaissance prince, Giangaleazzo combined high political skills with cold ruthlessness, reliance upon astrologers, and patronage of arts and letters. He fostered the university of Pavia, employed humanist secretaries, enjoyed the manuscript illumination of the Lombard school, and initiated the building of the Charterhouse of Pavia. It could be – as many historians claim – that his death saved the peninsula from the establishment of that 'Italian monarchy' which contemporary panegyrists and enemies alike saw as his ultimate aim. In Florence new forms of rhetorical, classicizing propaganda promoted by the civic humanists stressed emphatically Giangaleazzo's monarchical ambitions and contrasted them with the ideals of republican freedom. For this reason his premature death has been portrayed as a tragedy by nationalist historians, and as a merciful deliverance by those others who emphasize the importance of the existence of numerous independent courts and cities in the creation of Renaissance culture.

How far his ambitions were national rather than simply dynastic is not, however, clear, nor is it obvious that any national ambition he possessed could ever in fact have been achieved. Certainly his defeat of Rupert of Bavaria (battle of Brescia, October 1407), whom the Florentines had imprudently called into Lombardy against him, allowed him to pose as 'the defender of Italian liberty' against non-Italians. On the other hand, Venice showed no recognition of any threat of a national monarchy and remained neutral throughout the struggle. Above all, at his death his dominions disintegrated with such surprising speed as to suggest that his conquests were essentially ephemeral and without the potentiality of creating any lasting loyalties. JL

D. M. Bueno de Mesquita *Giangaleazzo Visconti* (1941); H. Baron *The crisis of the early Italian Renaissance* (1955)

Vitruvius M. Vitruvius Pollio, 1st century BC author of the only architectural treatise to survive from antiquity, profoundly influenced Renaissance architecture, despite the notorious obscurities of his unillustrated manuscripts. The *De architectura* was known throughout the Middle Ages in Italy (copies were owned by Petrarch and Boccaccio), but the superior manuscript found by Bracciolini coincided with increased 15c. interest in the principles of ancient architecture. The first printed edition (Rome 1486), which appeared from the circle of Leto, was followed by Fra GIOCONDO's illustrated edition (Venice 1511) and Italian translations by Cesariano (Como 1521) and Daniele BARBARO (Venice 1556; illustrations by Palladio), which catered for practising architects as well as the unlettered public.

'Utility, strength, and beauty' were for Vitruvius the 3 divisions of architecture. His idea of beauty as derived from symmetry and the modular relationship of the parts to the whole appealed to the Renaissance both for its mathematical basis, and for its recourse to anthropomorphic proportions. Vitruvius saw architecture as an imitation of nature, which must therefore follow rational principles – an idea taken up by Alberti and Palladio. His attack on the fanciful chimeras of contemporary wall paintings inspired Renaissance polemics against 'anti-classical' styles (e.g. Vasari on the gothic), but conflicted with the enthusiastic rediscovery of Grotesque decoration in Nero's Golden House.

Vitruvius's concept of *decorum* – fitting architectural solutions to the requirements of function and type – echoed Ciceronian rhetorical theory. His emphasis on site and climatic conditions was influential, and owing to his example few Renaissance theorists could ignore materials and machinery. His picture of the architect as a man of universal culture, though ridiculed by Alberti, fuelled the social aspirations of Renaissance architects. Although few ancient building types filled Renaissance needs, attempts were made to understand and revive specific Vitruvian models, like the theatre, and the Greek and Roman house. Above all, Renaissance responses to the Vitruvian orders reveal changing attitudes to his authority.

Vitruvius distinguished 3 column types, Doric (with Tuscan), Ionic and Corinthian, each with its own capital, proportions, and symbolism, derived (respectively) from a man, a matron, and a young girl. Their structural origins in primitive wooden architecture provided a rationale for their developed forms, as instanced by the Doric frieze. Alberti understood the orders, and added the ornate Composite, omitted through Vitruvius's conservatism, but did not feel constrained to stick to rigid capital forms in his own architecture. Bramante's *Tempietto* (1502) is the first Renaissance building to employ the full Vitruvian Doric, but growing irreverence in Raphael's generation is reflected in Peruzzi's belief that 'of all those beautiful [ancient] manners Vitruvius had not selected the most beautiful' (Cellini). While the programme of the Sienese humanist Claudio Tolomei for a Vitruvian academy illustrates one 16c. tendency to increased codification of the Vitruvian system, the architectural licence of Michelangelo and his followers negated the very principle of architecture as an imitation of nature. CE

M. Vitruvius Pollio *De architectura* tr. F. Granger (1931); J. Schlosser *La letteratura artistica* (1964)

Vittoria, Alessandro (1525–1608) The most distinguished sculptor of portrait busts and bronze statuettes in Venice during the last third of the 16c. Trained initially by Jacopo Sansovino, Vittoria inherited his basically Tuscan style and eventually amalgamated with it elements from the work of Sansovino's enemy, Michelangelo. Vittoria was often involved with architectural decoration, e.g. the caryatids at the entrance to the library of St Mark's (1555) and the stucco-work on the Scala d'Oro (golden staircase) of the Ducal Palace. A number of bronze statuettes of religious or mythological subjects bear his signature and his models were widely reproduced by the Venetian bronze foundries, particularly to decorate artefacts such as andirons and door-knockers. Their spiralling poses, swathed in stylized drapery, are analogous to those of Tintoretto. Vittoria's lifelike, but idealized, portrait busts of Venetian patricians are an essential ingredient of the visual image of the *Serenissima* in its heyday. CA

J. Pope-Hennessy *Italian High Renaissance and Baroque sculpture* (1963); F. Cessi *Alessandro Vittoria* (4 vols 1960–62)

Vittorino da Feltre (1378–1446) Born at Feltre, in the mountains north of Venice, the son of Ser Bruto de' Rambaldoni, he pursued university studies at Padua despite financial hardships, and had as his mentors such notable scholars as Vergerio and Guarino. Without pretending to the scholarly attainments of his teachers, he fully absorbed their ideas about EDUCATION, which stressed the stylistic and moral qualities of Greek and Roman literature, the importance of combining intellectual prowess with physical fitness and the need for a familiarity with the polite customs and graces of the time. The wealthy burghers and the cultivated courtly circles of the northern Italian city-states found this new educational ethos congenial and sought to attract the major humanist teachers to their service. Vittorino, after a brief period teaching rhetoric at Padua, accepted an invitation from Gianfrancesco Gonzaga in 1423 to establish a school at Mantua for his sons and those of his principal courtiers. Faithful to his own less privileged origins, Vittorino opened his school also to poor boys, from whom he demanded no payment. Numbers gradually grew to about 70 boys, all boarders, housed in Gianfrancesco's splendid villa *La Giocosa*.

For 22 years, Vittorino taught in and administered this school, accompanied by other scholars whom he invited from time to time. The primary discipline was grammar, and even such authors as Virgil, Cicero and Demosthenes were studied as much for their linguistic as for their intellectual content. Through patterns of instruction that may appear tedious by modern standards, Vittorino sought to instil the mastery of rhetoric and dialectic that he believed (in accordance with Ciceronian teaching) would produce eloquent and virtuous men. His school was innovatory in the breadth of its attention to the liberal arts. His pupils, having been taught languages, mathematics and philosophy, were prepared for advanced study in any field. Moreover, they had developed the self-confidence and aplomb that came with the pursuit of ancient ideals of bodily perfection through athletic competition. Although he was not a harsh disciplinarian by the standards of his time, Vittorino insisted equally on all the aspects of his régime – intellectual, physical, and moral – and reinforced the last with a strong daily diet of Christian devotional practices. Like many of his successors, he brooked no interference from parents. His school did not long survive him. WG

A. Gambaro *Vittorino da Feltre* (1946); E. Garin *L'educazione in Europa (1400–1600)* (1957); W. H. Woodward *Vittorino da Feltre and other humanist educators* (1897; repr. 1963)

Vivarini family A family of painters working in 15c. Venice, and settled at Murano. The

Part of Antonio **Vivarini**'s polyptych *Imago Pietatis and Saints* (Rome, Vatican Gallery).

paintings of Antonio, who may have been active from about 1440, mainly undertaken in collaboration with his brother-in-law, Giovanni d'Alemagna, are in the best Venetian gothic tradition, and characterized by extremely elaborate architectural detailing. Antonio's younger brother Bartolomeo (born probably about 1432) was, among Venetian artists, the one who adhered most consistently to the example of Mantegna. His nephew and pupil Alvise (the son of Antonio), who died between 1503 and 1505, shows in his last work responsiveness to the changes that were affecting the later works of Giovanni Bellini. AB

R. Pallucchini *I Vivarini* (n.d. ?1962)

Volterra, War of Volterra had been subject to Florence since 1361 but its high, isolated position and a long tradition of independence made its control a matter of great sensitiveness. In 1470 a company was formed there to develop the alum deposits that had been found nearby. Among the Florentines who assisted the Volterran partners with capital was Lorenzo the Magnificent; as his family held the concession on the only other Italian source of ALUM, at Tolfa, it was important to him that he could determine the price at which alum from this new source would be sold. Protest from Volterra against Medicean price-fixing apparently led Lorenzo the businessman to persuade the Signoria to see the controversy as a political revolt. In 1472 the Duke of Urbino, Federico da Montefeltro, was hired to attack the force hurriedly assembled by the Volterrans, and the city was sacked with appalling violence. Lorenzo's motives remain unclear, but the assumption made by his enemies and wavering supporters, that he was misusing his position in the city, clouded his reputation and possibly helped the PAZZI to believe that their plot to assassinate him would have wide support. JRH

E. Fiumi *L'impresa di Lorenzo de' Medici contro Volterra* (1948)

Warfare Apart from the lulls that followed the Peace of LODI in 1454 and the petering out of the Wars of Italy at the Treaty of CATEAU-CAMBRESIS in 1559, war was endemic in Italy. This is only surprising if Italy is thought of as a political whole. From the early 14c., with no organizing presence of the Holy Roman Empire and with thriving commercial cities reaching out for territories large enough to feed them and to keep their rivals at a distance, wars were inevitable: to make conquests, to defend them, to prevent the larger political units absorbing the smaller. And when the long period of political self-definition by arms was uneasily stilled at Lodi, foreign intervention in the peninsula from 1494 was a threat which could only be answered in kind, both as a riposte to the invasions and as a warning to domestic rivals not to take advantage of them.

The methods of warfare changed, but changed fairly evenly throughout the peninsula, so, apart from the flukes of individual military genius or luck, victory was determined more by financial staying power than by the temporary advantage of an organizational or technological breakthrough. By the early 14c. reliance on citizen armies had yielded to the employment of MERCENARIES. The former were more suited to defence than attack, were, in the factious atmosphere of the burgeoning cities, politically unhomogeneous, and – save in the still semi-feudalized kingdom of Naples – were

Warfare: a wrought iron bombardella of the late 14c. (Florence, Museo Bardini).

deficient in the shock-trooper of the age, the heavily armoured, expensively horsed man-at-arms. The conduct of war was, then, placed in the hands of professional mercenaries, CONDOTTIERI and infantry constables whose increasingly long-term contracts provided the major states with the nucleus of permanent armies: a stage reached by the mid-15c., and one as necessary for the garrisoning of frontiers as for the speedy raising of a force to repel attack in the field.

By this period infantry, in numbers, not in prestige, had become as important as cavalry (and cavalry numbers concealed men who rode towards the action but dismounted to take part in it). This change in the balance of horse and foot resulted from the enhanced use of missile troops: crossbowmen and, from towards the middle of the 15c., hand-gun men; the difficulty of storming fortifications increasingly equipped with artillery; and the similarly increasing use of field earthworks which could not be stormed by cavalry. Improved methods of fortification, both in town walls and in the field, were perhaps the major reason for the increase in the size of armies from 3000–5000 in *c.*1300 to 15,000–20,000 in *c.*1420, and, given the cost of full-time professionals, more use was made of rural subjects, both on an unpaid standby basis for local defence and on a token-paid basis for service with a field force. Both forms of service commemorated the confidence of the larger states in the permanence of their territorial gains.

With the opening of the Wars of Italy, numbers increased still further; in 1509 and again in 1529, for instance, Venice was paying nearly 30,000 men. These wars also saw the at times effective use of field artillery and of volleys of hand-held firearms (the arquebus and the musket), and confirmed the usefulness of light cavalry, notably STRADIOTS or their indigenous echoes, as foragers, skirmishers or communications cutters; and of quickly deployable horsed missile infantry. The decline in the reputation of the massive pike columns of the SWISS led to a preference for a more lightly armed infantry strengthened with a proportion of arquebusiers in each unit. Though lip service was paid to the notion that heavy cavalry were the backbone of an army, they were retained primarily as a sop to the chivalrous vanity of rural nobles and their retainers.

As the attacked, the Italian states were forced to make innovations in fortification, the organization of militias and the close integration of strategic and diplomatic aims. Otherwise the continuing use of mercenaries and of 'foreign' commanders meant that Italian military methods were, as they always had been, similar to those employed elsewhere in western Europe. It was the baffling monotony of defeat, caused chiefly by inter-state rivalry and an infirm sense of long-term shared political purpose, that made Italians the pioneers in discussing (never effectively) the reforming of armies on classical lines suggested by such authors as VEGETIUS and POLYBIUS. And it was partly the ease with which the discussion of military affairs could be switched into the long-established current of interest in the experience of antiquity that made Italy (and especially Venice) overwhelmingly the major producer of books on war throughout the 16c.

How could so much war coexist with the Renaissance: violence with culture? The dependence on mercenaries enabled artists, like other citizen-craftsmen, to get on with their work. Improved fortifications meant that devastation was in the main restricted to the countryside; only the Sack of Rome in 1527 had a checking effect on local cultural development, and even then Rome's loss was Venice's or Florence's gain: there was always a place of refuge and alternative employment for the popular artist or writer or musician. And though the costs of war soared, the low price of works of art, with the exception of elaborate architectural schemes, remained well within the budgets of the secular tax dodger or the near tax-exempt cleric. War, too, because it was intimately bound up with the process of economic and political rivalry that shaped the peninsula politically, was too much taken for granted to be seen as constituting a motive for indulging in austerity. There is no art *v.* violence conundrum here. *See* CORDOBA, GONZALO DE. JRH

M. Mallett *Mercenaries and their masters: warfare in Renaissance Italy* (1974); F. L. Taylor *The art of war in Italy 1494–1529* (1921; repr. 1973); P. Pieri *Il Rinascimento e la crisi militare italiana* (1952)

Wars of Italy In spite of the endemic warfare which characterized Italy from the 14c. to the Peace of LODI in 1454, and the occasional wars thereafter (e.g. those of VOLTERRA, 1472, of the Papacy and Naples against Florence, 1478–80, and of FERRARA, 1482–84), by general consensus the Wars of Italy are held to be those that began in 1494 with CHARLES VIII's invasion of the peninsula, came virtually to an end with the Habsburg-Valois treaties of Barcelona and Cambrai in 1529, and were finally concluded with the European settlement of CATEAU-CAMBRESIS in 1559.

The wars from 1494 do, in fact, fall into a different category from those that preceded them. Campaign followed campaign on a scale and with an unremittingness sharply different from those which had interrupted the post-Lodi peacefulness. Though foreign intervention in Italian affairs was certainly no novelty, the peninsula had never before been seen so consistently by dynastic contenders as both prize and arena. No previous series of combats had produced such lasting effects: the subjection of Milan and Naples to direct Spanish rule and the ossification of politics until the arrival in 1796 of a new Charles VIII in the person of Napoleon Bonaparte. The wars were also recognized as different in kind from their predecessors by those who lived through them: 'before 1494' and 'after 1494' became phrases charged with nostalgic regret for, and appalled recognition of, the demoted status of the previously quarrelsome but in the main independent comity of peninsular powers. And because the wars forced the rest of western Europe into new alliances and a novel diplomatic closeness, they were from the 18c. until comparatively recently seen as marking the turn from medieval to recognizably modern political times.

The wars, then, were caused by foreign intervention. In these terms they can be chronicled with some brevity. After crossing the Alps in 1494 CHARLES VIII conquered the kingdom of Naples and retired in 1495, leaving the kingdom garrisoned. The garrisons were attacked later in the same year by Spanish troops under Gonzalo de CORDOBA, sent by King FERDINAND II of Aragon (who was also King of Sicily). With this assistance Naples was restored to its native Aragonese dynasty. In 1499 the new King of France, LOUIS XII, assumed the title Duke of Milan (inherited through his grandfather's marriage to a Visconti) and occupied the duchy, taking over Genoa later in the same year. In 1501 a joint Franco-Spanish expedition reconquered the kingdom of Naples. The allies then fell out and fought one another. By January 1504 Spain controlled the whole southern kingdom, leaving France in control of Milan and Genoa in the north. A third foreign power, the German Habsburg Emperor MAXIMILIAN I, entered the arena in 1508 with an abortive invasion of the Veronese-Vicentino. He countered the rebuff by joining the allies of the anti-Venetian League of CAMBRAI: France and Aragon assisted by Pope JULIUS II and the rulers of Mantua and Ferrara. In 1509 their victory at AGNADELLO led to the occupation of the whole of the Venetian terraferma apart from Treviso.

The eastward extension of French power gained by this victory (won by a mainly French army) drove Julius and Ferdinand to turn against Louis and in 1512 the French – now also under pressure from a fourth foreign power interesting itself in Italian territory, the SWISS – were forced to evacuate their possessions in Lombardy. Louis's last invasion of the Milanese was turned back in 1513 at the battle of NOVARA and the duchy was restored to its native dynasty, the SFORZA, in the person of Massimiliano; he ruled, however, under the supervision of Milan's real masters, the Swiss. In 1515, with a new French king, FRANCIS I, came a new invasion and a successful one: the Swiss were defeated at MARIGNANO and Massimiliano ceded his title to Francis. To confirm his monopoly of foreign intervention in the north Francis persuaded Maximilian I to withdraw his garrisons from Venetian territory, thus aiding the Republic to complete the recovery of its terraferma.

With the spirit of the Swiss broken, the death of Ferdinand in 1516 and of Maximilian I in 1519 appeared to betoken an era of stability for a peninsula that on the whole took Spanish rule in the south and French in the north-west for granted. However, on Maximilian's death his grandson Charles, who had already become King of Spain in succession to Ferdinand, was elected Emperor as CHARLES V; Genoa and Milan formed an obvious land bridge between his Spanish and German lands, and a base for communications and troop movements thence to his other hereditary possessions in Burgundy and the Netherlands. Equally, it was clear to Francis I that his Italian territories were no longer a luxury, but strategically essential were his land frontier not to be encircled all the way from Provence to Artois. Spanish, German and French interests were now all centred on one area of Italy and a new phase of the wars began.

Between 1521 and 1523 the French were expelled from Genoa and the whole of the Milanese. A French counter-attack late in 1523, followed by a fresh invasion in 1524 under Francis himself, led, after many changes of fortune, to the battle of PAVIA in 1525; not only were the French defeated, but Francis himself was sent as a prisoner to Spain, and released in 1526 only on condition that he surrender all claims to Italian territory. But by now political words were the most fragile of bonds. Francis allied himself by the Treaty of COGNAC to Pope CLEMENT VII, previously a supporter of Charles but, like Julius II in 1510, dismayed by the consequences of what he had encouraged, and the Milanese once more became a theatre of war. In 1527, moreover, the contagion spread, partly by mischance – as when the main Imperial army, feebly led and underpaid, put loot above strategy and proceeded to the SACK OF ROME, and partly by design – as when, in a reversion to the policy of Charles VIII, a French army marched to Naples, having forced the Imperial garrison out of Genoa on the way and secured the city's navy, under Andrea DORIA, as an ally. In July 1528 it was Doria who broke what had become a Franco-Imperial stalemate by going over to the side of the Emperor and calling off the fleet from its blockade of Naples, thus forcing the French to withdraw from the siege of a city now open to Spanish reinforcements.

By 1529, defeated in Naples and winded in Milan, Francis at last allowed his ministers to throw in the sponge. The Treaty of Barcelona, supplemented by that of Cambrai, confirmed the Spanish title to Naples and the cessation of French pretensions to Milan, which was restored (though the Imperial leading strings were clearly visible) to the Sforza claimant, now Francesco II. Thereafter, though Charles took over the direct government of Milan through his son Philip on Francesco's death in 1535, and Francis I in revenge occupied Savoy and most of Piedmont in the following year, direct foreign intervention in Italy was limited to the localized War of SIENA. In 1552 the Sienese expelled the garrison Charles maintained there as watchdog over his communications between Naples and Milan, and called on French support. As an ally of Charles, but really on his own account, COSIMO I, Duke of Florence, took the city after a campaign that lasted from 1554 to 1555. But in the Treaty of Cateau-Cambrésis of 1559, by which France yet again, and now finally, renounced Italian interests, Cosimo was forced to grant Charles the right to maintain garrisons in Siena's strategic dependencies, Orbetello, Talamone and Porto Ercole.

The Wars of Italy, though caused by foreign interventions, involved and were shaped by the invitations, self-interested groupings and mutual treacheries of the Italian powers themselves. At the beginning, Charles VIII was encouraged by the Duke of Milan, Lodovico Sforza, jealous of the apparently expanding diplomatic influence of Naples, as well as by exiles and malcontents (including the future Julius II) who thought that a violent tap on the peninsular kaleidoscope might provide space for their own ambitions. And the 1529 Treaty of Cambrai did not put an end to the local repercussions of the Franco Imperial conflict. France's ally Venice only withdrew from the kingdom of Naples after the subsequent (December 1529) settlement negotiated at Bologna. It was not until August 1530 that the Last Florentine Republic gave in to the siege by the Imperialist army supporting the exiled Medici. The changes of heart and loyalty on the part of Julius II in 1510 and Clement VII in 1526 are but illustrations of the weaving and reweaving of alliances that determined the individual fortunes of the Italian states within the interventionist framework: no précis can combine them.

A final point may, however, be made. Whatever the economic and psychological strain produced in individual states by their involvement, and the consequential changes in their constitutions or masters, no overall correlation between the Wars and the culture of Italy can be made. The battles were fought in the countryside and peasants were the chief sufferers from the campaigns. Sieges of great cities were few, and, save in the cases of Naples in 1527–28 and Florence in 1529–30, short. No planned military occasion had so grievious effect as did the Sack of Rome, which aborted the city's cultural life for a decade. JRH

C. M. Ady 'The invasions of Italy' *New Cambridge modern history* I (1957); S. Leathes 'Habsburg and Valois' *Cambridge modern history* II (1907); L. A. Burd 'Historical abstract' in his ed. of Machiavelli *Il principe* (1891); P. Pieri *Il rinascimento e la crisi militare italiana* (1952)

Wert, Giaches de (*c.*1535–95) Flemish composer, brought to Italy at a very early age. He became *maestro di cappella* at S. Barbara in Mantua at its foundation as the chapel of the dukes, and he remained in the service of the Gonzagas for the rest of his life. He was a friend of Tasso and had an adventurous life: his wife was arrested and imprisoned for her part in a conspiracy; and he fell in love with Tarquinia Molza, a singer and noblewoman who was exiled to Modena to prevent their union. His importance as a composer lies in his fine, if eccentric, madrigals, in which he developed a kind of choral recitative technique, with words clearly enunciated almost in speech rhythms. He is thus a germinal figure in the development of monodic music, including opera. DA

A. Einstein *The Italian madrigal* (1949)

Willaert, Adrian (*c.*1490–1562) Composer and teacher of music. A Netherlander, probably born at Bruges, he studied law in Paris but soon took to music. About 1520 he went to Rome and was in the service of Alfonso I d'Este in Ferrara 1522–25. He then spent 2 years in Milan before being appointed *maestro di cappella* at St Mark's in Venice in December 1527. Apart from 2 journeys to Flanders to find singers in 1542 and 1556, he spent the rest of his life in Venice. He was a master of the Netherlandish contrapuntal style, but his importance for the Renaissance lies in 3 features of his music. His concern for the audibility of the words is borne out in the motets of his *Musica nova* (1559). His use of chromaticism according to the theories concerning Greek scales was also influential. Finally the polychoral music, or *cori spezzati* which he published was later developed by many Venetian composers. His ideas were codified by his pupil Zarlino: his practical teaching affected a whole generation of composers. DA

An etching after Parmigianino depicting a gathering of **witches**.

Witches The great witch-hunts of early modern Europe began relatively early. Inquisitors such as Bernardo da Como and Silvestro de Prierio investigated witchcraft in the Alps in the late 15c. However, in Italy witch trials remained relatively few thereafter, perhaps because of the scepticism of the intellectuals. Among these sceptics were the humanist lawyer Andrea ALCIATO, who thought that the so-called 'witches' suffered from hallucinations and needed medicine rather than punishment, and the physician Cardano, who argued that the accused confessed to whatever the interrogators suggested to them simply in order to bring their tortures to an end. In an instruction of *c.*1620, Rome itself recommended proceeding with caution in cases of witchcraft. Some well-documented examples of popular attitudes to witches come from Friuli in the late 16c., where *benandanti* ('go-gooders') claimed to fight witches 'in the spirit' 4 times a year: 'and if we win there is abundance that year, but if we lose there is famine'. Under pressure from the Inquisition, the *benandanti* eventually admitted to being witches themselves. PB

G. Bonomo *Caccia alle streghe* (1959); C. Ginzburg *I Benandanti* (1966)

Women, status of According to Burckhardt, women 'stood on a footing of perfect equality with men'. Few statements in his *Civilization of the Renaissance* are more misleading. Inequality between the sexes began at birth. The majority of the babies who were abandoned, or allowed to suffocate, or to die at wet-nurse, were female, showing that most families wanted sons not daughters. Educational opportunities for girls were extremely limited. The examples of the scholar Alessandra Scala (daughter of one humanist and wife of another) and the marchioness Isabella d'Este, who spoke Latin fluently, should not be allowed to obscure the fact that, even in towns, most girls did not go to school, and that only the well-off could afford to give their daughters a formal education at home. Respectable girls left the house only to go to church (and then veiled and under escort).

Few adult roles were open to women. They were generally expected either to marry or to become nuns or servants. The problem of girls who were forced to become nuns because their fathers could not afford to dower them was recognized as a serious one in the 15c. and 16c. Something like 12 per cent of the female population of Florence were nuns (coming especially from poor branches of prominent families). Hence the creation in 1425 of a dowry fund, the Monte delle Doti, an institution imitated elsewhere. The problem of girls who were forced to marry men they did not want was taken less seriously, though S. Bernardino of Siena declared that girls should have some say in choosing their husbands. It is not clear whether or not they could normally veto suitors they particularly disliked.

The sexual division of labour has not yet been studied in the detail it deserves, but it is clear that women undertook a variety of tasks. The wives and daughters of peasants and shopkeepers helped on the farm and in the shop. Spinning was a part-time occupation for many. Women were heavily involved in the textile industry, reeling, winding and throwing silk and weaving cloth. In the Venetian Arsenal they were employed to make sails. Some women were employed as labourers. Women also worked as laundresses and in such morally suspect occupations as fortune-teller, healer, midwife (all three associated with witchcraft), prostitute, and, at the end of the period, actress. Isabella Andreini was perhaps the most famous actress of the 16c.

The Church offered some opportunities to women of energy and determination. Women could become prioresses (like S. Caterina de' Ricci), administer hospitals (like S. Caterina of Genoa), or even found a religious order; S. Angela Merici founded the Ursulines in 1534. Vittoria COLONNA, the friend of Michelangelo and Cardinal Pole, and Giulia Gonzaga, protectress of the Neapolitan Spirituals, also found in religion some compensation for women's exclusion from full participation in social and political affairs. These last two ladies were widows, a state which afforded more freedom than that of wife or maiden, and a not uncommon one (15 per cent of Florentine households in 1427 were headed by widows). The widows of craftsmen were allowed to carry on their husband's business and to become full members of guilds. Caterina SFORZA, widow of the Count of Imola, became the ruler of Forlì. Caterina was known and respected as a virago, a kind of Bradamante.

Although armed highwaywomen dressed as men were not unknown in the 16c., this literary tradition does not seem to have made much impact on real life. It is likely that opportunities for exceptional women were greater in Renaissance Italy than in other parts of Europe, whether they wanted to be rulers, actresses (a career impossible in England, France or Spain before 1600), or writers; at least 25 women published books in Italy between 1538 and 1599. It was not unusual for Italians to argue that women were equal or even superior to men. Forty-odd treatises arguing in this way were written in Italy in the course of the 15c. and 16c. This is no doubt how Burckhardt formed his impression of the 'perfect equality' of women. It should be added that all these treatises were written by men. The first contributions by women to the debate were published in 1600, and neither suggests that the situation is satisfactory from the female point of view; *Il merito delle donne* by Modesta Pozzo, and *La nobiltà et eccellenza delle donne* by Lucrezia Marinella. *See* EDUCATION; CHILDREN; FAMILY STRUCTURE; COURTESANS; CATHERINE, ST, OF SIENA; FRANCO, VERONICA; STAMPA, GASPARA; ESTE, ISABELLA D'. PB

C. Fahy 'Three early Renaissance treatises on women' *Italian Studies* (1956); L. Martines 'A way of looking at women in Renaissance Florence' *Journal of Medieval and Renaissance Studies* (1974); I. Maclean *The Renaissance notion of women . . .* (1980)

The battle of **Zonchio**: a coloured Venetian woodcut of *c.*1500 (London, British Museum).

Zabarella, Giacomo (1533–89) Philosopher. Of a leading Paduan aristocratic family, he was professor of philosophy at Padua from 1568 until his death. Alongside other members of the Paduan Aristotelian school such as Pomponazzi, his contribution was to have overcome the conditioning influence of Scholastic commentaries and to have achieved a mastery of the Greek text of ARISTOTLE. There has been recent interest in his studies on logic and scientific methodology. OL
A. Poppi *La dottrina della scienza in Giacomo Zabarella* (1972)

Zarlino, Gioseffo (1517–90) The leading theoretician of music in the later Renaissance. Born at Chioggia, he became a Franciscan friar in 1537 before going to Venice to study music with Willaert. He published his most famous treatise, *Le istitutioni harmoniche*, in 1558, following it with various supplements which were eventually collected together in 1589. He had become *maestro di cappella* at St Mark's in Venice in 1565, and remained there until his death, resisting the invitation to become bishop of Chioggia in 1583. His humanistic theories were highly influential, largely because he was a moderate, prepared not to insist on a true revival of Greek music but to adapt the principles of a union of words and music to modern conditions. He also advocated something approaching the modern view of tuning to equal temperament. DA

Zonchio, battle of (1499) Major Venetian defeat in the Turkish War of 1499–1503 which took place off the port of Zonchio (now Navarino) in the western Morea (Greece). JRH

Zoppo, Marco (1433–78), born in Cento, was in the workshop of Francesco Squarcione in Padua in 1454, being adopted by him in 1455, and was later active in Venice and Bologna. The influence of Squarcione was superseded by that of Cosmè Tura to such an extent that the latter's and Zoppo's work have, at times, been confused. His enthroned *Madonna and Saints* in Berlin bears his signature – 'Marco Zoppo da Bologna pinsit 1471 in Vinexia'. JW

Zuccaro, Federico (1540–1609) continued the conservative reform of late 16c. Roman painting introduced by his brother Taddeo. Highly influential, he worked throughout Italy and abroad. His painting of *Barbarossa making Obeisance to the Pope* (1582; Venice, Palazzo Ducale) placed Venetian naturalism within the idiom of the late *maniera*, while his later work reveals a trend toward a stiffer academic classicism, as in the *Adoration of the Magi* (1594; Lucca, Duomo). A founder of the Roman Accademia di S. Luca, he wrote the most systematic treatise on the aesthetics and metaphysics of *maniera* painting (1607). LP
W. Korte *Der Palazzo Zuccari in Rom* (1935); D. Heikamp 'Vicende di Federico Zuccaro' *Rivista d'Arte* (1959)

Zuccaro, Taddeo (1529–66) reflected the increased pietism of the early Counter-Reformation in Rome in his development towards a post-Mannerist classicizing style. His earlier reliance on the ornamentalism of Salviati and Tibaldi is transmuted in the decoration of the Frangipani Chapel of S. Marcello al Corso (see, for example, the altarpiece of the *Conversion of S. Paul*, *c.*1563) into a clearer narrative style of counter-*maniera* which reconciles Raphael's descriptive naturalism, Mannerist surface pattern and Michelangelo's canon of form. This style is seen in a secular context in Taddeo's recondite and elaborate history paintings for Cardinal Alessandro Farnese at Caprarola (1561–66). LP
J. Gere *Taddeo Zuccaro* (1969)

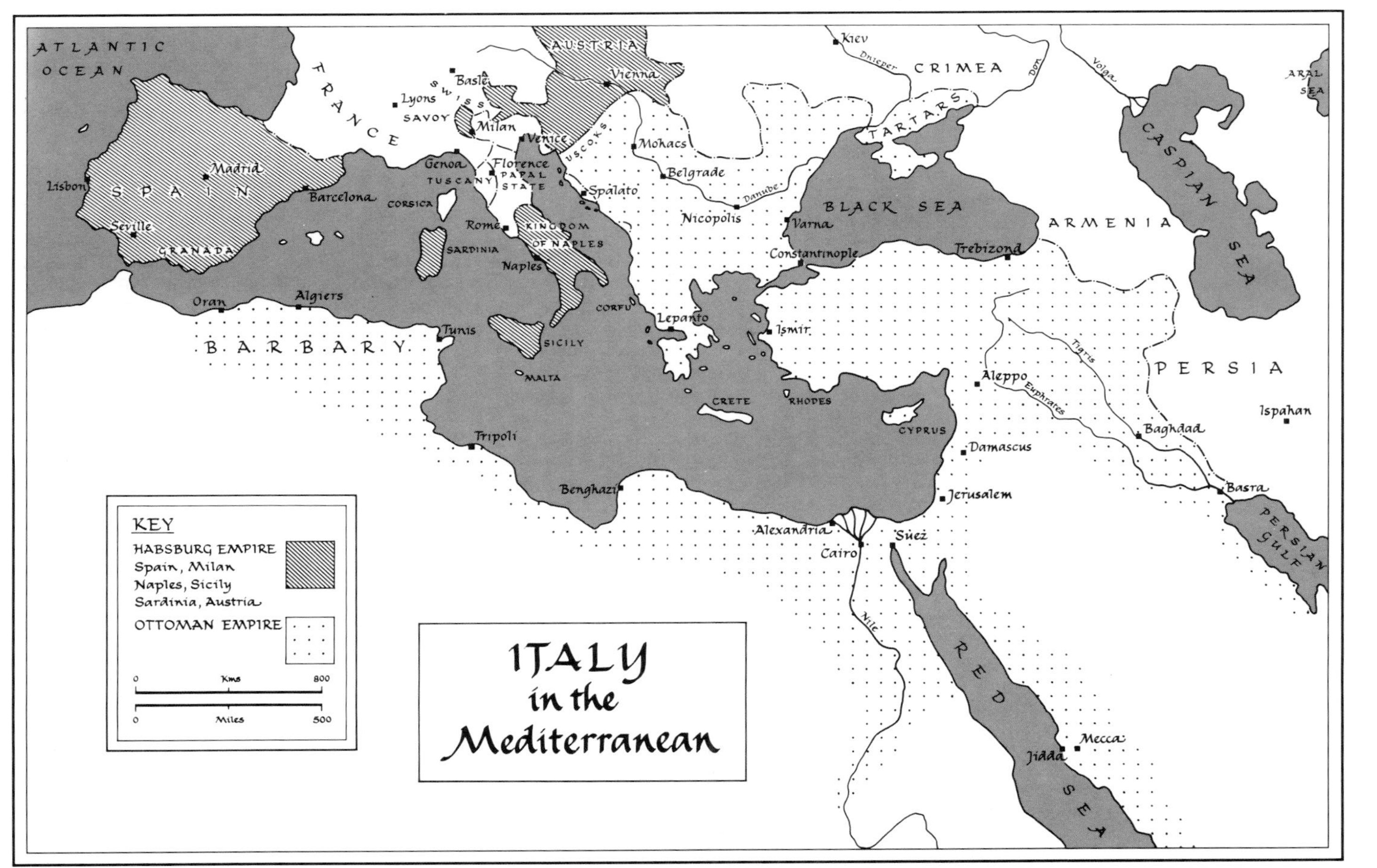
ITALY
in the
Mediterranean
KEY
HABSBURG EMPIRE
Spain, Milan
Naples, Sicily
Sardinia, Austria
OTTOMAN EMPIRE
0
Kms
800
0
Miles
500
ATLANTIC OCEAN
FRANCE
SPAIN
Lisbon
Madrid
Seville
GRANADA
Barcelona
Lyons
Basle
SWISS
SAVOY
Milan
Genoa
TUSCANY
Florence
PAPAL STATE
Venice
AUSTRIA
Vienna
USCOKS
Spalato
CORSICA
SARDINIA
Rome
KINGDOM OF NAPLES
Naples
SICILY
MALTA
CORFU
Oran
Algiers
Tunis
BARBARY
Tripoli
Benghazi
Mohacs
Belgrade
Danube
Nicopolis
Kiev
Dnieper
CRIMEA
Don
TARTARS
Volga
BLACK SEA
Varna
Constantinople
Trebizond
Lepanto
Ismir
CRETE
RHODES
CYPRUS
ARMENIA
CASPIAN SEA
ARAL SEA
PERSIA
Tigris
Euphrates
Aleppo
Damascus
Jerusalem
Baghdad
Basra
Ispahan
PERSIAN GULF
Alexandria
Cairo
Suez
Nile
RED SEA
Jidda
Mecca

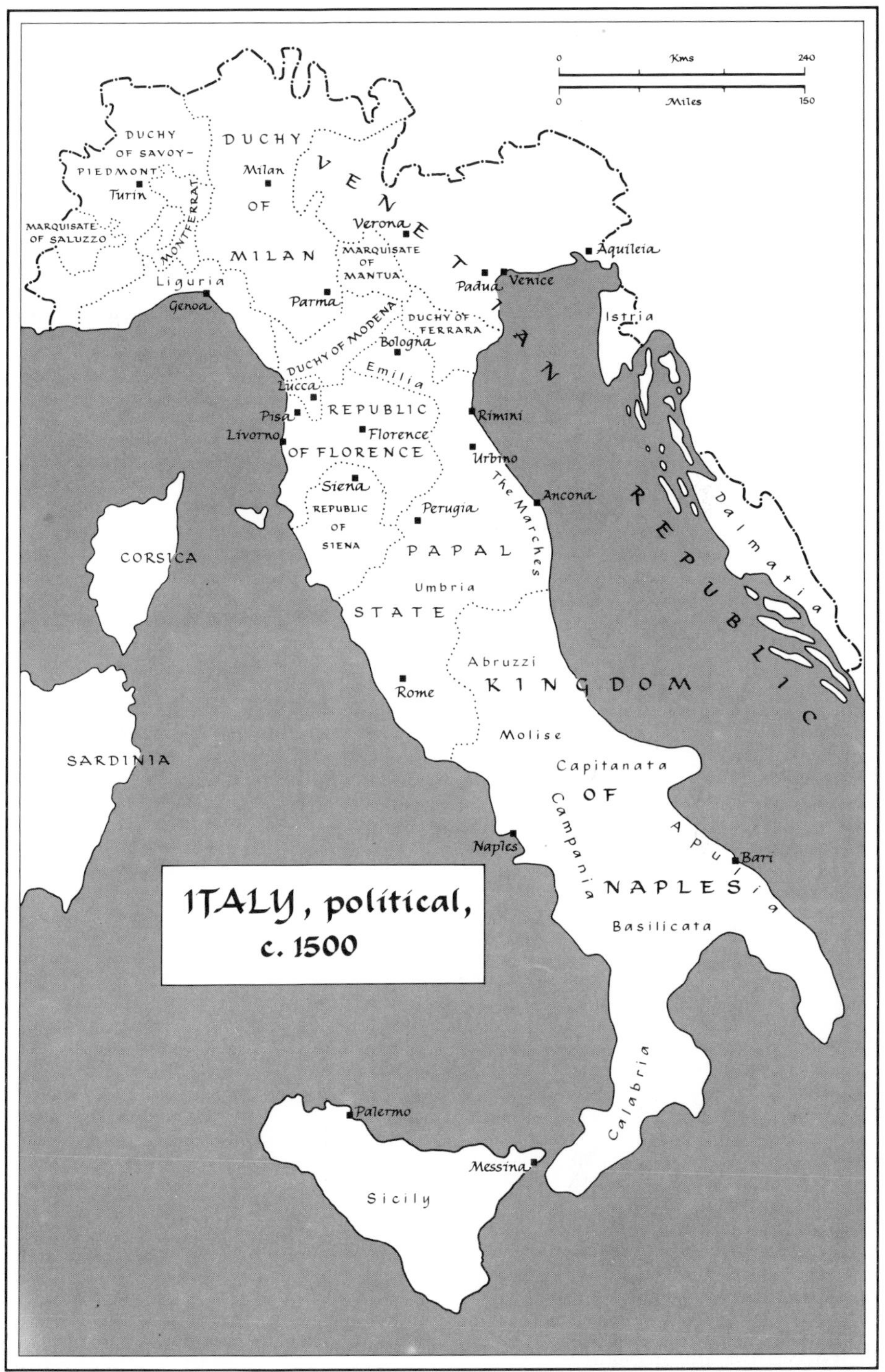

ITALY, political, c. 1500
0 Kms 240
0 Miles 150
DUCHY OF SAVOY-PIEDMONT
Turin
MARQUISATE OF SALUZZO
MONTFERRAT
DUCHY OF MILAN
Milan
Liguria
Genoa
Parma
VENETIAN REPUBLIC
Verona
MARQUISATE OF MANTUA
Padua
Venice
Aquileia
Istria
DUCHY OF FERRARA
DUCHY OF MODENA
Bologna
Emilia
Lucca
Pisa
Livorno
REPUBLIC OF FLORENCE
Florence
Siena
REPUBLIC OF SIENA
Rimini
Urbino
The Marches
Ancona
Perugia
PAPAL STATE
Umbria
Rome
Dalmatia
CORSICA
SARDINIA
Abruzzi
KINGDOM OF NAPLES
Molise
Capitanata
Campania
Apulia
Naples
Bari
Basilicata
Calabria
Palermo
Messina
Sicily

Tables of succession

	EMPERORS	FERRARA The Este (*Signori till 1393, then Marquises; Dukes from 1471*)	FLORENCE The Medici (*Dukes from 1532, Grand Dukes from 1569*)	MANTUA (*Signori till 1433, Marquises till 1530, then Dukes*)	MILAN (*Signori till 1395, then Dukes*)
1300					
1310	Henry VII of Luxemburg 1308–13				
1320					
1330	Lewis IV of Bavaria 1314–47				Azzone Visconti 1329–39
1340				Luigi I Gonzaga 1328–60	Luchino Visconti 1339–49
1350		Obizzo II 1344–52			Giovanni Visconti 1349–54
1360	Charles IV of Luxemburg 1347–78	Aldobrando III 1352–61		Guido Gonzaga 1360–69	Galeazzo II Visconti and Bernabò Visconti 1354–78
1370		Niccolò II 1361–88		Luigi II Gonzaga 1369–82	
1380					Bernabò Visconti 1378–85
1390	Wenceslas of Luxemburg 1378–1400	Alberto 1388–93		Francesco I Gonzaga 1382–1407	Giangaleazzo Visconti 1378–1402
1400	Robert of Bavaria 1400–10				Giovanni Maria Visconti 1402–12
1410		Niccolò III 1393–1441		Gianfrancesco I Gonzaga 1407–44	
1420	Sigismund of Luxemburg 1410–37				Filippo Maria Visconti 1412–47

NAPLES (*Kings*)	PARMA (*Dukes*)	POPES	URBINO (*Counts till 1443, then Dukes*)	VENICE (*Doges*)	
					1300
					1310
Robert of Anjou 1309–43		John XXII 1316–34		Giovanni Soranzo 1312–28	1320
			Nolfo di Montefeltro 1323–59		1330
		Benedict XII 1334–42		Francesco Dandolo 1329–39	
				Bartolomeo Gradenigo 1339–42	1340
Giovanna I of Anjou 1343–81		Clement VI 1342–52		Andrea Dandolo 1343–54	1350
		Innocent VI 1352–62		Marino Falier 1354–55	
				Giovanni Gradenigo 1355–56	
				Giovanni Dolfin 1356–61	1360
		Urban V 1362–70	Papal rule 1359–77	Lorenzo Celsi 1361–65	
				Marco Corner 1365–68	1370
		Gregory XI 1370–78		Andrea Contarini 1368–82	1380
Charles III of Durazzo 1381–86		*Clement VII 1378–94 / Urban VI 1378–89	Antonio di Montefeltro 1377–1404	Michele Morosini 1382	
Louis II of Anjou 1386–1400				Antonio Venier 1382–1400	1390
		*Benedict XIII 1394–1415 / Boniface IX 1389–1404			1400
Ladislas of Durazzo 1400–14		Innocent VII 1404–06	Guido Antonio di Montefeltro 1404–43	Michele Steno 1400–13	
		*Alexander V 1409–10 / Gregory XII 1406–15 / *John XXIII 1410–15			1410
Giovanna II of Anjou-Durazzo 1414–35		Martin V 1417–31		Tommaso Mocenigo 1414–23	1420

1400 · 1410 · 1420 · 1430 · 1440 · 1450 · 1460 · 1470 · 1480 · 1490 · 1500 · 1510 · 1520

EMPERORS	FERRARA The Este (*Signori till 1393, then Marquises; Dukes from 1471*)	FLORENCE The Medici (*Dukes from 1532, Grand Dukes from 1569*)	MANTUA (*Signori till 1433, Marquises till 1530, then Dukes*)	MILAN (*Signori till 1395, then Dukes*)
Robert of Bavaria 1400–10	Niccolò III 1393–1441	Cosimo *Pater Patriae* 1434–64	Francesco I Gonzaga 1382–1407	Giovanni Maria Visconti 1402–12
Sigismund of Luxemburg 1410–37	Leonello 1441–50	Piero di Cosimo 1464–69	Gianfrancesco I Gonzaga 1407–44	Filippo Maria Visconti 1412–47
Albert II of Habsburg 1438–39	Borso 1450–71	Lorenzo the Magnificent 1469–92	Luigi III Gonzaga 1444–78	Republican régime 1447–50
Frederick III of Habsburg 1440–93	Ercole I 1471–1505	Piero the Younger 1492–94	Federico I Gonzaga 1478–84	Francesco Sforza 1450–66
Maximilian I of Habsburg 1493–1519	Alfonso I 1505–34	Republican régime 1494–1512	Gianfrancesco II Gonzaga 1484–1519	Galeazzo Maria Sforza 1466–76
		Giovanni (later Leo X) 1512–13		Giangaleazzo Sforza 1476–94
		Giuliano, Duke of Nemours 1513		Lodovico (Il Moro) Sfc 1494–99
		Lorenzo, Duke of Urbino 1513–19		Louis XII of France 1499–1500
				Lodovico Sforza 150
				Louis XII of France 1500–12
				Massimiliano Sforz 1512–15
				Francis I of France 1515–21

	NAPLES (*Kings*)	PARMA (*Dukes*)	POPES	URBINO (*Counts till 1443, then Dukes*)	VENICE (*Doges*)
1400	Ladislas of Durazzo 1400–14		*Benedict XIII 1394–1415; Boniface IX 1389–1404; Innocent VII 1404–06; *Alexander V 1409–10; Gregory XII 1406–15	Antonio di Montefeltro 1377–1404; Guido Antonio di Montefeltro 1404–43	Michele Steno 1400–13
1410	Giovanna II of Anjou-Durazzo 1414–35		*John XXIII 1410–15; Martin V 1417–31		Tommaso Mocenigo 1414–23
1420	(with Louis III of Anjou 1424–34)				Francesco Foscari 1423–57
1430	René of Anjou 1435–42		Eugenius IV 1431–47		
1440	Alfonso I of Aragon 1442–58		Nicholas V 1447–55	Oddantonio di Montefeltro 1443–44; Federico II di Montefeltro 1444–82	
1450	Ferdinand I (Ferrante) 1458–94		Calixtus III 1455–58; Pius II 1458–64		Pasquale Malipiero 1457–62
1460			Paul II 1464–71		Cristoforo Moro 1462–71
1470			Sixtus IV 1471–84		Niccolò Tron 1471–73; Niccolò Marcello 1473–74; Pietro Mocenigo 1474–76; Andrea Vendramin 1476–78; Giovanni Mocenigo 1478–85
1480			Innocent VIII 1484–92	Guidobaldo I di Montefeltro 1482–1508	Marco Barbarigo 1485–86; Agostino Barbarigo 1486–1501
1490	Alfonso II 1494–95; Ferdinand II 1495; Charles VIII of France 1495; Ferdinand II 1495–96; Federico 1496–1501		Alexander VI 1492–1503		
1500	Louis XII of France 1501–03; Spanish governors thereafter		Pius III 1503; Julius II 1503–13	Cesare Borgia 1502–03; Francesco Maria I della Rovere 1508–16	Leonardo Loredan 1501–21
1510			Leo X 1513–21	Lorenzo de' Medici 1516–19; Papal rule 1519–20	
1520					

	EMPERORS	FERRARA The Este (*Signori till 1393, then Marquises; Dukes from 1471*)	FLORENCE The Medici (*Dukes from 1532, Grand Dukes from 1569*)	MANTUA (*Signori till 1433, Marquises till 1530, then Dukes*)	MILAN (*Signori till 1395, then Dukes*)
1500 1510 1520 1530 1540 1550 1560 1570 1580 1590 1600 1610 1620	Maximilian I of Habsburg 1493–1519 Charles V of Habsburg 1519–56 (abdicated) Ferdinand I of Habsburg 1556–64 Maximilian II of Habsburg 1564–76 Rudolf II of Habsburg 1576–1612	Ercole I 1471–1505 Alfonso I 1505–34 Ercole II 1534–59 Alfonso II 1559–97	Republican régime 1494–1512 Giovanni (later Leo X) 1512–13 Giuliano, Duke of Nemours 1513 Lorenzo, Duke of Urbino 1513–19 Giulio (later Clement VII) 1519–23 Ippolito and Alessandro 1523–27 Republican régime 1527–30 Alessandro 1531–37 Cosimo I 1537–74 Francesco 1574–87 Ferdinando I 1587–1609	Gianfrancesco II Gonzaga 1484–1519 Federico II Gonzaga 1519–40 Francesco III Gonzaga 1540–50 Guglielmo Gonzaga 1550–87 Vincenzo I Gonzaga 1587–1612	Lodovico Sforza 1 Louis XII of France 1500–12 Massimiliano Sforz 1512–15 Francis I of France 1515–21 Francesco II Sforz 1521–24 Francis I of France 1 Charles V of Habsburg Imperial governor thereafter

NAPLES (*Kings*)	PARMA (*Dukes*)	POPES	URBINO (*Counts till 1443, then Dukes*)	VENICE (*Doges*)	
Louis XII France 1501–03	Pier Luigi Farnese 1545–47	Alexander VI 1492–1503	Cesare Borgia 1502–03	Leonardo Loredan 1501–21	1500
panish governors thereafter	Ottavio Farnese 1547–49	Pius III 1503	Guidobaldo I di Montefeltro 1482–1508	Antonio Grimani 1521–23	1510
	Papal rule 1549–50	Julius II 1503–13	Francesco Maria I della Rovere 1508–16	Andrea Gritti 1523–38	1520
	Ottavio Farnese 1550–86	Leo X 1513–21	Lorenzo de' Medici 1516–19	Pietro Lando 1539–45	1530
	Alessandro Farnese 1586–92	Adrian VI 1522–23	Papal rule 1519–20	Francesco Donato 1545–53	1540
	Ranuccio Farnese 1592–1622	Clement VII 1523–34	Francesco Maria I della Rovere 1521–38	Antonio Trevisan 1553–54	1550
		Paul III 1534–49	Guidobaldo II della Rovere 1538–74	Francesco Venier 1554–56	1560
		Julius III 1550–55	Francesco Maria II della Rovere 1574–1621	Lorenzo Priuli 1556–59	1570
		Marcellus II 1555		Girolamo Priuli 1559–67	1580
		Paul IV 1555–59		Pietro Loredano 1567–70	1590
		Pius IV 1559–65		Alvise Mocenigo 1570–77	1600
		Pius V 1566–72		Sebastiano Venier 1577–78	1610
		Gregory XIII 1572–85		Niccolò da Ponte 1578–85	1620
		Sixtus V 1585–90		Pasquale Cicogna 1585–95	
		Urban VII 1590		Marin Grimani 1595–1605	
		Gregory XIV 1590–91		Leonardo Donato 1606–12	
		Innocent IX 1591			
		Clement VIII 1592–1605			

Glossary of Italian terms

Accoppiatore Florentine official appointed to select names of those eligible for important public offices.

Albergo Literally 'inn', the term was used in Genoa for 'clan', meaning a tight combination of related families which maintained a quasi-legal separateness *vis-à-vis* the state much later than the **consorteria** of other cities.

Arengo General assembly of adult non-clerical males with citizenship rights.

Arrabbiati 'The enraged'; the most vehement anti-Savonarolan party.

Ars nova A term taken from a French musical treatise of *c.*1320 which has come to be applied (roughly) to distinguish compositional methods used thereafter from the *ars antiqua* of the earlier period.

Arte 'Art', but more usually 'guild'; the member of a guild was an *artista*.

Bailo A key ambassador in the Levant, e.g. the Venetian *bailo* in Constantinople.

Balìa Political committee with emergency powers, e.g. to suggest and implement constitutional changes.

Banditi Men exiled for crimes.

Battuti Members of flagellant confraternities who scourged themselves (or one another) as a sign of humility and contrition.

Beffa A verbal or practical joke designed to embarrass or humiliate its victim to the delight of reader or audience.

Bigi Medicean supporters during the family's exile 1494–1512.

Bottega Shop, particularly an artists' workshop-cum-studio.

Bucintoro Venetian doge's state barge.

Candia Island of Crete, also the city of Iraklion.

Catasto A method of graduated tax assessment based on an estimate of property and income.

Comune See entry CONSTITUTIONS.

Consorteria The clan, or greatly extended family, bound to mutual support and a common policy over such matters as the defence of property and marriage alliances.

Contado The surrounding territory legally and fiscally answerable to a city.

Contrapposto A position used by painters and sculptors, especially from the 16c., whereby their figures have a twisted pose, e.g. the chest and pelvis on opposed axes.

Dolce stil nuovo 'Sweet new style': that is the style, novel and harmoniously refined in sound and sense, of the lyrical verse of Dante and some of his younger contemporaries.

Fondaco Warehouse; commercial centre of foreign merchants.

Fraticelli The Spiritual Franciscans whose resistance to the papal endorsement in 1322 of the suggestion that their order might own property led them to be tainted with heresy.

Frottola See entry.

Gonfalone Military banner; hence administrative district within a city responsible for raising a section of the civic militia. A *Gonfaloniere* was the official responsible for the district to central government; in Florence this name was also applied to the chairman of the **signoria**.

Maggior Consiglio The Great Council of Venice to which all adult male patricians belonged.

Maniera In art: personal style, increasingly (in the 20c.) with the implication that it constituted not only an individual flavour but one deliberately distinct from the reigning orthodoxy, hence Mannerism.

Maona Merchant vessel of large capacity; or a convoy of such vessels run in commercial partnership.

Mezzadria The system of agricultural tenure whereby the landlord supplied capital equipment (draught animals, ploughs, seed) in return for a proportion of the produce.

Misericordia Florentine religious confraternity dedicated to care of the sick, the dying and the (unburied) dead.

Monte Communal funded debt, paying interest to shareholders.

Ottava rima An eight-line stanza of eleven-syllable verse.

Ottimati The 'best' citizens. The inner group of citizens of greatest wealth and standing.

Parlamento The more usual equivalent of **arengo**.

Parte Guelfa The association of militant Guelfs which played a prominent role in Florentine political life in the 13c. and 14c.

Piagnoni 'Snivellers'; disparaging term applied to the devoutest supporters of Savonarola.

Podestà Official responsible for law and order; either an outsider brought into a city on a short-term contract (though this is how some became hereditary signori) or a citizen deputed to a subject town or city.

Poesia Literally a lyric poem, but also a term loosely applied to paintings of an arcadian or mythology-for-mythology's sake nature, especially those of Giorgione and Titian.

Popolo Literally 'the people', but in practice master-artisan and merchant interest groups, varying in social and economic composition from city to city and time to time, which frequently had more in common with the nobility than with the plebs, who were sometimes referred to as the *popolo minuto*.

Priore An ecclesiastical term, though more widely applicable than the English 'prior' in that it could be used of the priest of an important parish. It also was used in a secular sense e.g. of an important guild official or a member of a **signoria**.

Prov(v)editore Official in charge of grain supply, military liaison etc.

Rettore Citizen deputed to look after central government interests in a subject town or city.

Sacra conversazione Term for a religious painting in which attendant saints appear to be sharing a meditation on the significance of the central subject, usually the Virgin and Child.

Sacra rappresentazione See entry.

Scuola 'School', but also a religious confraternity and its headquarters.

Serrata In Renaissance historical jargon, the legislation of 1297 which defined membership of the Venetian Great Council and thus the nature of the hereditary patrician class.

Signore The *de facto* political chief of a city. The term is dropped when the hereditary power of his family is accepted or when he receives a title: count, marquis or duke.

Signoria The chief political council in a republican government.

Sinopia Underdrawing of a FRESCO.

Sprezzatura Controlled nonchalance of accomplishment. See entry CASTIGLIONE.

Stato The geographical area subject to single political control, but also (and almost habitually with, e.g., Machiavelli) the political régime itself in a personal sense: the ruler and his entourage.

Studio 'Study', but also 'university', as in the *studio* of Florence.

Terraferma The term usually applied to Venice's possessions on the Italian mainland.

Terza rima Hendecasyllabic lines of verse arranged in groups of three with the rhyme scheme aba, bcb, cdc, etc. to an additional closing line rhyming with the penultimate line of the last tercet.

Trecento, etc. 'The 1300s' as equivalent to our 14c.; thus also Quattrocento (15c.); Cinquecento (16c.).

Tridentine See entry COUNCIL OF TRENT; applied adjectivally to both the decrees and the ethos of that Council.

Vicar Someone standing in for the authority of a superior. In this period generally used of a local **signore** (or marquis, etc.) governing a city on behalf of the Papacy.

Virtù See entry.

Bibliographical note

The chief relevant reference works are listed below. Abbreviations employed in the bibliographies in the entries are indicated in brackets.

Enciclopedia Italiana (36 vols, Rome 1929–39)
Enciclopedia Einaudi ed. R. Romano *et al.* (8 vols, Turin 1977–). Has reached 'Memoria'. Subject-entries only.
Storia d'Italia (Einaudi) (6 vols in 10, Turin 1972–76) and *Annali* (3 vols, Turin 1978–80) (*SI*)
Dizionario biografico degli italiani (22 vols, Rome 1960–). Has reached Cavallotti. (*DBI*)
Enciclopedia universale dell'arte (15 vols, Venice-Rome 1958–67)
Dizionario enciclopedico Bolaffi dei pittori e degli incisori italiani (11 vols, Turin 1972–76)
Dizionario letterario Bompiani: opere-personaggi-indici (9 vols, Milan 1946–61); *Autori* (3 vols, Milan 1956–57)
Dizionario critico della letteratura italiana ed. V. Branca (3 vols, Turin 1974)
Storia della letteratura italiana ed. E. Cecchi and N. Sapegno (9 vols, Milan 1965–69) (*SLI*)
Enciclopedia dello spettacolo (9 vols, Rome 1954–62)

Photographic acknowledgments

in addition to sources given in captions

Alinari 26, 27 t., 39 r., 58, 60, 61, 76, 78, 80, 88, 101, 113, 114, 122, 134, 144 b., 151, 161 r., 163, 178, 187 r., 197, 198 t., 198 b., 224, 245 t., 253 t., 260, 261, 263 r., 269, 271, 327, 335 l.; Alinari-Anderson 23, 49 b., 128, 152 r., 164 r., 167 b., 186 b., 250, 254, 255, 256, 303; Alinari-Brogi 22, 31, 157, 179, 214, 284; Tim Benton, London 245 b.; Courtauld Institute of Art, University of London 38, 63 (A. Morrogh), 73 t. (By kind permission of the Earl of Leicester), 183 (Reproduced by permission of the Trustees of the Chatsworth Settlement); E.P.T., Brescia 59 t. (Novafoto); E.P.T., Ferrara 132; E.P.T., Ravenna 82; Gabinetto Fotografico della Soprintendenza alle Gallerie, Florence 66, 144 t., 253 b.; Gabinetto Fotografico Nazionale, Rome 24, 72; Giraudon 73 b., 126, 161 l., 187 l., 206 t., 221; Foto Grassi, Siena 170, 302; J.R. Hale 139, 263 l.; Reproduced by Gracious Permission of Her Majesty the Queen 27 b., 209, 265, 274; Martin Hürlimann 167 t.; By Courtesy of the Italian State Tourist Office (E.N.I.T.) 19, 25, 95, 153 b., 182 b., 186 t.r., 213, 234, 277, 287, 324, 333 t., 336; Kunsthistorisches Museum, Vienna 216 b.; Ralph Lieberman 89; Georgina Masson 306; Federico Arborio Mella, Milan 159; The Metropolitan Museum of Art, New York 75 (The Michael Friedsham Collection, 1931), 311; Museo dell'Opera del Duomo, Siena (Istituto Centrale del Restauro, Rome) 119; Reproduced by courtesy of the Trustees, The National Gallery, London 17, 59 b., 69, 100, 105, 180, 184, 191, 203 t., 230, 286, 315, 317, 332; National Gallery of Art, Washington, D.C., 161 l., 206 b., 208, 242; Perissinotto, Padua 149; Pineider, Florence 344; Royal Institute of British Architects, London 232; Guido Sansoni, Florence 135; Scala 133, 175; Soprintendenza alle Gallerie, Venice 46 t. (Cameraphoto); U.D.F.-La Photothèque 337; The Venice in Peril Fund 289 (Soprintendenza di Monumenti, Venice); Victoria and Albert Museum, Crown Copyright 281.